Criminology

A sociological introduction

Second edition

Eamonn Carrabine, Pam Cox,
Maggy Lee, Ken Plummer
and Nigel South

 Routledge
Taylor & Francis Group

LONDON AND NEW YORK

First published 2004
by Routledge
2 Park Square, Milton Park, Abingdon, Oxon OX14 4RN

Simultaneously published in the USA and Canada
by Routledge
711 Third Avenue, New York, NY 10017 (8thFloor), United States

Routledge is an imprint of the Taylor & Francis Group, an informa business

Typeset in Frutiger and Joanna by
Keystroke, 28 High Street, Tettenhall, Wolverhampton

British Library Cataloguing in Publication Data
A catalogue record for this book is available from the British Library

Library of Congress Cataloging in Publication Data
Criminology : a sociological introduction/Eamonn Carrabine . . . [et al.].
– 2nd ed.
     p. cm.
  1. Criminology. 2. Crime–Sociological aspects. I. Carrabine, Eamonn.
  HV6025.C853 2009
  364–dc22   2008025185

ISBN10: 0–415–46450–1 (hbk)
ISBN10: 0–415–46451–X (pbk)
ISBN10: 0–203–88494–9 (ebk)

ISBN13: 978–0–415–46450–5 (hbk)
ISBN13: 978–0–415–46451–2 (pbk)
ISBN13: 978–0–203–88494–2 (ebk)

Contents

List of illustrations

Plates

Figures

Tables

Boxes

Notes on the authors

All the authors work in the Department of Sociology at the University of Essex, Colchester, UK.

Eamonn Carrabine is a Senior Lecturer with research and teaching interests in the sociology of punishment, youth culture and theoretical criminology. His work has been published in leading journals including *New Formations*, *Punishment and Society*, *Sociological Review*, *Theoretical Criminology*, the *Howard Journal of Criminal Justice* and the *British Journal of Criminology*. His books include *Crime in Modern Britain* (co-authored, 2002), *Power, Discourse and Resistance: A Genealogy of the Strangeways Prison Riot* (2004) and *Crime, Culture and the Media* (2008). He was elected to the editorial board of *Sociology* (2004–6) and is currently reviews editor on *Theoretical Criminology*.

Pam Cox is a Senior Lecturer specializing in youth justice, child rights, criminal justice history, comparative criminology and gender. In 2006–7 she was Visiting Fellow at Vietnam National University and also worked as a youth justice consultant for international NGOs. Publications include: *Gender, Justice and Welfare: Bad Girls in Britain 1900–1950* (2003), *Becoming Delinquent: British and European Youth, 1650–1950* (co-edited with H. Shore, 2002) and *Crime in Modern Britain* (co-authored, 2002).

Maggy Lee is a Senior Lecturer at the University of Essex and Associate Professor at the University of Hong Kong. She previously worked as a criminal justice researcher at the Institute for the Study of Drug Dependence (now Drugscope) and as a lecturer at Birkbeck College, University of London. Her main areas of research are human trafficking and migration, policing, drugs, and juvenile delinquency. Publications include *Human Trafficking* (2007), *Crime in Modern Britain* (co-authored, 2002), *Youth, Crime and Police Work* (1998) and 'Drugs Policing' in T. Newburn (ed.) *Handbook of Policing* (2003 and 2008).

Ken Plummer is Emeritus Professor of Sociology at Essex. For many years he was a Visiting Professor of Sociology at the University of California at Santa Barbara. He has published prolifically, including *Telling Sexual Stories* (1995), *The Making of the Modern Homosexual* (1981), *Modern Homosexualities* (1992), *The Chicago School* (1997, 4 vols.), *Documents of Life – 2: An Invitation to a Critical*

Humanism (2001), *Sexualities: Critical Assessments* (2002) and *Intimate Citizenship* (2003). His textbook, *Sociology: A Global Introduction* (with John Macionis), is now in its fourth edition. His main areas of research include sexualities, humanism, human rights, health and introductory sociology.

Nigel South is a Professor whose research interests include environmental crimes and human rights; illegal and legal drug use, crime, inequalities and citizenship; theoretical and comparative criminology; and public health. He has taught at various universities in London and New York, and worked as a Research Sociologist at the Institute for the Study of Drug Dependence (now Drugscope). Recent books include: *Issues in Green Criminology: Confronting Harms against Environments, Humanity and other Animals* (co-edited with P. Beirne, 2007), *Green Criminology* (co-edited with P. Beirne, 2006) and *Drug Use in Cultural Contexts 'Beyond the West': Tradition, Change and Post-Colonialism* (co-edited with R. Coomber, 2004).

Acknowledgements

For this second edition we welcome Pam Cox back to the writing team and thank Paul Iganski (who has since moved to Lancaster University) and Ken Plummer for their excellent contributions to the first edition. Ken is now recovering well from a serious illness and hopes to work with us again on subsequent editions.

The Department of Sociology at the University of Essex continues to provide a supportive and engaging home for our collaborative criminological work. We hope that the Department's interdisciplinary spirit runs through and enlivens this book. On a personal note we thank Chris Ellis, Bill, Tess and Patrick Hayton, Alison Inman, Christine Rogers, Daniel South and Sherrie Tuckwell.

Thanks are very much due to Gerhard Boomgaarden, Harriet Brinton and Russell George at Routledge who have given expert advice and helped guide the manuscript through to publication. We also thank our anonymous reviewers who have provided very constructive feedback on both editions.

EC, PC, ML, NS
Colchester, July 2008

Permissions

Data and tables obtained from the Home Office are reproduced by permission.

Every effort has been made to contact copyright holders for their permission to reprint material in this book. The publishers would be grateful to hear from any copyright holder who is not here acknowledged and will undertake to rectify any errors or omissions in future editions of this book.

part 1 The Criminological Imagination

In this part, we outline a sociological approach to crime, consider how historians have studied crime, and raise some of the methodological issues involved in using criminological data.

Timeline

1750s and 1760s	The Classical School and Beccaria
	Fielding's London policing experiments
1780s	Bentham's panopticon
1820s	Collection of criminal statistics
1870s	The Italian or Positivist School and Lombroso
1870s–1900s	Heredity and criminal families
1910s	Intelligence theories
	Twin research, somatotypes and endocrinology
	Durkheim and functionalist criminology
	Early African-American socio-criminology
1920s	Psychoanalytic theories
1920s/1930s	Early Chicago School
	Zonal theory, life story research
1930s	Anomie theory
1930s/1940s	Differential association
1960s	Neo-Chicago School
1960s/1970s	Subcultural theory, labelling theory
	Control theory, Marxist/conflict criminologies
1970s onwards	Moral panic theory
	New criminology
	Critical criminology
	Birmingham Centre for Contemporary Cultural Studies
	The political economy of crime
	The justice model
	Administrative/actuarial criminology
	Feminist criminology
	Black and anti-racist criminology
	Foucauldian genealogies and governance
1980s	Left realism
	Resurgence of radical right
1990s	Reintegrative shaming theory
	Cultural criminology
	Postmodern criminology
	Green criminology
2000s	Globalization of crime
	Risk and actuarialism
	Criminologies of war and terrorism
	Human rights
	Public criminology

chapter 1

Introduction

Key issues

- What is criminology?
- What is sociology?
- Why a sociological introduction to criminology?
- Why are 'social divisions' important?
- How does this book work?

An introduction: the many meanings of criminology

Criminology has many meanings but at its widest and most commonly accepted it is taken to be the study of crime, criminals and criminal justice. There are many different approaches to criminology and the subject itself has been shaped by many different academic disciplines. This book focuses on sociology and criminology. It outlines the distinctiveness of a sociological approach to crime and suggests how this differs from other approaches.

What does criminology mean to you? Why have you chosen to study it? Whatever your reasons, you are not alone. Criminology is a fast-growing subject attracting thousands of students across the world. The criminal justice 'industry' is, for better or worse, expanding at a similar rate as ideas continually change about how crime should be defined, how it should be dealt with and how all this should be measured and financed. Daily life in many parts of the world is closely influenced by crime. Many newspapers, TV schedules, websites, films, books and computer games are built around crime stories of various kinds. This book offers a sociological view of these and other developments.

What counts as a criminological topic?

Criminology is relatively new as a degree subject but it began at least 250 years ago. Since then, it has been shaped by philosophers, psychologists, anthropologists, psychiatrists, medics and lawyers as well as by sociologists, social theorists, cultural analysts and historians. As Zedner (2007a) observes, one of criminology's greatest strengths is its disciplinary hybridity.

Any study of crime must involve the study of law. Criminology explores the bases and implications of criminal laws – how they emerge, how they work, how they are violated and what happens to violators. But we know that laws vary from time to time and from place to place. Laws are relative, and always historically shaped. Even something as seemingly universally condemned as killing others has moments when it is acceptable (e.g. in war). Many criminologists believe therefore that they should not be confined by the bounds of law – this would make criminology a very traditional, orthodox and even conservative discipline. Rather, criminologists should also be able and willing to take on wider matters. The most common form of crime around the world is property crime or different kinds of theft. Clearly, however, there is much more to criminology than the study of theft. As you will see, although we focus on current laws in this book, we also include an array of areas that are not quite so clearly defined by them, such as crimes against human rights, damage to the environment, hate crimes and some state crimes. To include these kinds of areas is to maintain a broad vision of forms of order and disorder and the power relations that uphold these.

It is arguably this broad vision that characterizes a more sociological approach to crime. By contrast, psycho-social and bio-medical approaches have tended to focus more closely on individual dispositions and personal motivations in relation to crime and much greater attention to physical, emotional and cognitive issues. In terms of criminal justice interventions, they have tended to be linked to evidence gathering and to the design or evaluation of strategies aiming to change criminal or chaotic behaviour. In this sense, they have viewed criminology as a more expert-based **forensic science**. This leads some to conclude that they are more grounded in the realities of crime than sociologists who work with a more 'general' approach to crime and 'less specific' notions of disorder. This book sets out what a sociologist, while respecting this view, might say in defence.

Criminological methods

In the same way that different disciplines focus on different criminological topics, they also favour different kinds of research methods. Depending on their orientation and training, a criminologist might use anything from psychological testing to global crime statistics, or from life-stories to media analysis. Chapter 2 outlines the main research methods used within sociological criminology although we aim to illustrate how these methods have been used in different studies discussed across the book. Chapter 2's website allows you to explore some of these methods for yourself and see how others have used them.

Different research methods often result directly from different approaches to knowledge. The ways in which we choose to find out about the world – which can be called our **epistemology** – are linked to our views of what we think might be relevant, what it might be linked to and why it matters. Some criminologists make very orthodox claims to be scientists: observing, testing, measuring and trying to produce law-like statements around crime. We will meet some of this work in chapters 2 and 3 where we introduce **positivism** and **experimental criminology**. However, other criminologists do not claim to be scientific in this way. For instance, in 1958, G. B. Vold published a text called *Theoretical Criminology*. Here, he was simply concerned with laying out major ways of theorizing crime rather than with testing these. Likewise, when Ian Taylor, Paul Walton and Jock Young published *The New Criminology* in 1973, their aim was not to make a scientific study but rather to make space for a new critical stance. More recently, Jack Katz (1988) and Jeff Ferrell (1998) have used **cultural criminological methods** to analyse the 'seductions' or attractions of crime, risk-taking and thrill-seeking. So, as we shall see, the study of crime takes researchers in a number of different and often conflicting directions.

Sociology and the 'sociological imagination'

Sociology can be defined as the *systematic study of human society*. But it is much more than a series of facts and theories about society. Instead it becomes a form of consciousness, a way of thinking, a critical way of seeing. As Peter Berger (1963: 34) says: 'The first wisdom of sociology is this: things are not what they seem.' By this he means that nothing is self-evident, fixed or 'obvious'.

Thus, in criminology, a sociological approach does not take for granted 'common-sense' discussions of crime – as found for example in the media. Instead, it always challenges the 'taken for granted' and asks questions about what we believe to be true about crime, why we might believe this and how crime is shaped by wider social factors.

Some sixty years ago, Charles Wright Mills claimed that developing what he called the 'sociological imagination' would help people to become more active citizens. Wright Mills (1916–62) was a US sociologist who held up sociology as an escape from the 'traps' of our lives. It can show us that society – not our own foibles or failings – can be responsible for many of our problems. In this way, Mills maintained, sociology transforms personal problems (like criminal behaviour) into public and political issues (like 'the crime problem'). For Mills 'The sociological imagination enables us to grasp history and biography and the relations between the two within society. That is its task and its promise . . .' (Mills, 1959: 4).

Sociology and the 'criminological imagination'

In this book we aim to provide a sociological introduction to criminology. From its origins in the nineteenth century, sociology has been concerned with a fundamental question: What is society? This leads us to some other basic but vital questions. What brings people into relationships with others? What holds them there? What can cause these relationships to break down? How can such breaches be repaired? If they are not repaired, what are the consequences? Sociology's focus on society as a social order means that it has always had, from its earliest days, a corresponding focus on social disorder.

As outlined in the previous sections, sociology is also about seeing the human world with a critical eye – realizing that there are general patterns of social life that shape people's life experiences, their attitudes, beliefs, behaviour and their identity. The human world in which sociologists are interested is broad and diverse in scope, ranging from day-to-day interactions between people to historical and global social phenomena. Taking a sociological perspective on that world involves trying to step outside society, becoming a stranger, so that the familiar becomes a field of adventure, not a refuge of common sense. It involves trying to look at society as a newcomer.

This way of looking at the social world involves nurturing and applying the 'sociological imagination'. In particular, it involves developing our minds to see that many personal troubles experienced by individuals – unemployment, poverty, crime victimization, to name just a few – are also public issues and that, in turn, these are interrelated with wider social forces.

In this book we aim to apply, and hopefully nurture, a 'criminological imagination'. This involves appreciating that:

- Crime is a truly sociological concept. It does not exist as some autonomous entity but is a **social construct**. While there is much agreement, what is regarded as crime varies across time, place and people.
- The criminal is also socially constructed, defined as such by the same social processes that define certain acts as crimes and others not.
- Crime control and punishment are also shaped by social influences that determine the seriousness of acts defined as criminal, and the priority with which they are to be addressed.

Sociology, social divisions and crime

The analysis of social divisions is central to the sociological enterprise. For a long time, though, sociologists focused primarily upon one major system of social division: inequalities associated with social and economic positions. Such a focus looks at how people are ranked in terms of their economic situation, their power and their prestige. It focuses especially on social class (and on caste and slavery in some kinds of societies). More recently, sociologists have recognized that other divisions are very relevant in framing all kinds of social relations, including those linked to crime and control:

- social and economic divisions: here a person's labour, wealth and income play a key role in crime;
- gender and sexuality divisions: here a person's position as a man or as a woman plays a key role in crime;
- ethnic and racialized divisions: here a person's 'race' and ethnicity play a key role in crime;
- age divisions: here a person's age plays a key role in crime.

Each of these areas of inequality and social division are addressed in this book. In particular, Chapter 5 discusses the work of criminologists who have argued that understanding of the causes and the experience of crime needs to be looked for in entrenched structural – social and economic – inequalities. Conflict analyses of crime, for instance, have drawn attention to how the crimes that poor people commit are subject to disproportionate attention by criminal justice systems.

However, it is an odd irony that conflict analyses – concerned about class and power differences – for so long neglected the importance of gender despite their focus on social inequality. If, as conflict theory suggests, economic disadvantage is a primary cause of crime, why do women (whose economic position is, on average, much worse than that of men) commit far fewer crimes than men?

Up until the 1970s, the study of crime and deviance was very much a male province. British sociologists Frances Heidensohn (1968, 1996) and Carol Smart (1976) documented the neglect of women in such study. They also showed that when women had been included, the approach had usually been highly sexist or outrightly misogynist.

The contributions of feminist scholars to the study of crime raised some fundamental questions. One relates to what Kathy Daly and Meda Chesney-Lind (1988) have called 'the generalisability problem'. This refers to whether theories generated to explain male offending can be used to explain female offending. Can women simply be inserted into theories that explain male offending, or are new theoretical developments necessary to explain female crime?

In redressing the omissions of criminology, feminist scholars saw an additional – but also an obvious – neglect of a focus upon men as men. Although crime is indeed largely – although not exclusively – committed by men, this dimension of analysis had been largely ignored: it was a key missing link. Hence, feminist criminologists began to raise the issue of masculinity and crime. They have suggested that since more men are involved in crimes, there may be a link between forms of masculinity and forms of crime. It is only relatively recently, then, that the obvious fact that crime is in some way bound up with masculinity has been taken up as in any way problematic.

We address gender, sexuality and masculinity centrally in chapters 6 and 9, but relevant issues are also raised elsewhere throughout the book. A further social division addressed in the book concerns 'race' and ethnicity. Across Western countries some minority ethnic groups, and especially black communities, are over-represented in the criminal justice process – in police stops, in appearances in court and in the prison population. Many commentators give the impression – especially in elements of the popular press – that some minority ethnic communities are somehow more criminally inclined than others. Such an impression can both reflect and reinforce racist ideologies. Various factors are at work that account for crime. Crime is not evenly distributed across the social spectrum, and age, location, gender and socio-economic position are important variables in accounting for offending and victimization.

Analysing the relationship between 'race' and crime seriously also means taking account of discrimination in the criminal justice system – a point first raised by black criminologists in the United States in the early twentieth century. In Britain, the racist murder of black teenager Stephen Lawrence by a gang of white youths at a bus stop in London in 1993 – and the inquiry into the police investigation that followed – thrust the tragedy of violent racism into the public consciousness with a potency never present before. The flawed police investigation into the murder became, for many, symbolic of the character of relations between the police and minority ethnic communities in Britain. Fundamentally, using the language of 1960s Black Power activists in the United States, the 'Macpherson Inquiry' (1999) observed that the police investigation was characterized by institutional racism. Prior to the investigation, researchers had been producing evidence of racial prejudice and discrimination among some police officers for over two decades. We focus further on issues of 'race' and criminal justice in Part 4 of this book,

'Controlling Crime'. However, the salience of focusing on 'race' and ethnicity in criminological inquiry is observed in a number of other places in the book.

To this point, we have discussed social divisions around class, gender, sexuality and 'race' as if they are discrete categories in which people live their lives. Yet in practice they are experienced 'as a totality' by individuals (Allen, 1987: 169–70). Any one person's experience at any one moment in time is a product of interacting divisions. One response to this reality, which has been put forward by Kathy Daly (1997), is the 'multiple inequalities' approach around the class–race–gender axis of investigation. She suggests that everyone is located in a matrix of multiple social relations. This means that race and gender are just as relevant to the analysis of white men as they are to that of black women.

Structure of the book

The book is organized into five parts. Following this introduction and the next two chapters on 'Histories of Crime' and 'Researching Crime', Part 2 – 'Thinking about Crime' – introduces the major movements in thought and theory, organized – to help you make sense of it all – as a chronological narrative of the key theoretical developments in historical and criminological debates. The timeline at the start of this chapter shows the major movements in criminological thinking covered by the book as a whole. The third part – 'Doing Crime' – focuses on developing an understanding of experiences and patterns of criminal activity and victimization and also considers where crime takes place. Part 4 – 'Controlling Crime' – focuses on processes, theories and problems about crime control and punishment. The fifth and final section – 'Globalizing Crime' – introduces perspectives on how global forces impact upon crime and crime control. We also look to the dynamic boundaries and likely future directions of the criminological imagination.

How to use the book

We would like you to use the book in the same way that we encourage students to use our university lectures – as a path to learning. Our lectures provide a guide to key issues – a road map of ideas, if you like – and a route through the maze of reading material. The chapters in this book serve in the same way. We try to guide you through the key topics, debates and research relevant to taking a sociological approach to criminology. However, in no way do we claim to provide the final word! Learning comes through a process of exploration, and especially through the struggle to comprehend. We would not serve you well by removing the need for that struggle. Therefore, we aim to point you in the right direction but you must take the next steps yourself. Hence, reading this book alone will not suffice. We try to guide you to the reading that we have found to be the most informative and influential for the criminological issues we deal with. However we provide only an outline. We hope that you will use our guide to select your further study and engage with it yourself. After all, in thinking critically, we are providing only our perspectives. You may develop your own. Consequently, as with all journeys there is more than one way of reaching your destination.

Special features

Chapter summaries

At the end of each chapter you will find a summary listing the key points. They are not intended to provide a full summary of the chapter, but to serve as a reminder about the key issues raised. They probably won't make much sense until you have read the whole chapter first!

Critical thinking questions

You will also find a number of 'critical thinking questions' at the end of each chapter. These are not examination questions. They are intended to get you thinking about what we see as some of the most important issues raised in the chapters. You will see that they are not questions to which you can give a 'yes' or 'no' answer. Instead, you will need to think carefully about them, revisit some of the points made in the chapter in question and in some cases consult the further reading recommended for that chapter. The book's website suggests ways of tackling these questions and also offers longer case studies and example boxes.

Suggestions for further study

At the end of each chapter you will see a section labelled 'Further study'. This section has a number of purposes. In general, it is hoped that it will serve as a resource for you for future use – something that you can return to as a guide for your reading. Under this section we list key books – and articles in some cases – that we think make the most valuable contribution to understanding the issues covered by the chapter. The reading listed ranges from books that are suitable for the new student to criminology in general, for those new to the topic of the chapter in particular, and to the student (or tutor!) wishing to develop a more in-depth understanding of the subject. Again, the book's website offers links to some full-length versions of the recommended texts.

Suggestions about more information

Finally, under the heading 'More information', we list websites that provide useful information. These, and more, appear on the book's own website which we hope will be a valuable resource for you and your studies.

Glossary

A glossary of key concepts used – highlighted in **bold** – is provided at the end of the book. Concepts – abstract representations, or mental images of things observed and experienced in the real world – provide the foundations of sociological thinking. They are therefore fundamental to a sociological approach to the study of crime, deviance and social control. 'Crime' itself is a concept. We don't necessarily witness, hear or read about 'crime' when it happens. What we do see or learn are things that we have come to think of – or conceptualize – as crime.

In the glossary we provide short definitions of key concepts used. While the glossary is intended to help you, do think about the definitions provided. Concepts don't just exist 'out there' somewhere; they are made up as abstract representations of things. In thinking about the meaning of concepts you may find it useful to consult a good encyclopedia of sociology and a good criminological dictionary where you should find the particular concept discussed in much more detail than that provided by our glossary.

chapter 2

Histories of Crime

Key issues

- What can history add to criminology?
- What have crime historians focused on and why?
- Do societies today experience more crime than in the past?
- How have views towards offenders changed over time?

Introduction

This chapter takes a step back and looks at histories of crime. It outlines key changes in the ways that historians have researched crime and criminals. Many of the other chapters include historical material on, for example, criminological theories (chapters 4 and 5), policing (Chapter 17), prisons (Chapter 18) and particular crimes (e.g. Chapter 10 on property crime, Chapter 11 on sexual crime and Chapter 14 on drug-related crime). These show how ways of dealing with and thinking about criminals have changed over time.

Many people believe that crime has got 'worse' in modern societies. By this they often mean that society has become 'more violent' and that communities have become 'less safe'. But what is this view based on? Is it accurate? What do historians and historical criminologists say on the matter? This chapter starts with an overview of recorded crime patterns, with a particular focus on violence, and then moves on to track key changes in historical studies of crime. It focuses on British examples but also uses some comparative material.

Historical patterns: declining violence

Many historians argue that past societies have been far more violent than contemporary ones. Julius Ruff's important text, *Violence in Early Modern Europe, 1500-1800* (2001), details the violence of everyday life in past societies. This violence took many forms, from military and political to community and interpersonal. Some of this violence was sanctioned by law (e.g. judicial torture) though much was not. Ruff argues that this violence reached a peak in sixteenth-century Europe but then declined over the next two centuries as European elites started to turn to other means of handling disputes and became less 'accepting' of violence.

This kind of study has been strongly influenced by German-English sociologist Norbert Elias's classic text, *The Civilising Process* (1939/1978). Elias argues that from the Middle Ages on, Europeans began to exercise new kinds of self-control over their bodies and behaviour. The emerging civilized society was marked by greater self-discipline as well as new forms of state sanctions for unruliness. Knafla (2003: xi) argues that this 'civilising process' is 'still with us today' and that it is 'bringing to an end traditional forms of social violence . . . through expanded institutions of government and police, positive law and professional courts, more rational forms of proof and a pluralistic society'.

Other comparative historical research seems to bear this out. Eisner shows that there was a 'long-term decline in homicide rates' from the sixteenth to the early twentieth century (Eisner, 2003: 83). Spierenburg (1998a) argues that codes of honour became less violent. Godfrey *et al.* (2003b: 9) suggest that there was a widespread decline in recorded violence per capita between the 1870s and the 1910s in Europe, Australia and New Zealand. Knafla finds the same for North America (Knafla, 2003). Notably, Braithwaite's comparison of 'Australian convict society' and 'American slave society' links the marked decline of Australian crime rates in the nineteenth century to the latter's long-standing use of reintegrative punishment strategies (Braithwaite, 2001).

This historical decline in violent crime arguably ended in the mid- to late twentieth century. For example, British homicide rates have increased significantly since the 1980s due mainly to a doubling in the number of murders of men aged 20 to 24 (Dorling, 2005: 29). This raises complex questions for criminologists as to the broader social shifts behind this 'return' to violence. It also raises new challenges for historians of crime who have yet to take on comparative analysis of this later period.

There have been fewer large-scale or comparative historical studies of non-violent crime. One reason for this is the difficulty of comparing the ways that different states categorize different offences and how these categorizations change over time. However, national studies show that theft and property offences were very common in the past, just as they are today. Emsley (2005) estimates that theft accounted for between a half and three-quarters of all recorded crime in England between 1750 and 1900. Petty street-based offences were also prominent, with many prosecutions for drunkenness, gambling, illegal selling and vagrancy in the same period (Gatrell, 1990). The next section suggests how and why patterns of recorded crime changed in the British case.

British prosecution patterns

British prosecutions followed the same broad pattern found in Europe and the wider English-speaking world. Recorded crime rose sharply in the early nineteenth century, then stablized until the early twentieth century, then rose again very sharply after the Second World War and particularly after the 1970s (see Figure 2.1).

Historians have explained the British pattern in different ways (see Emsley, 2005). The first sharp rise (1790s–1840s) is often linked to the modernization of society: **urbanization**, **industrialization**, migration and economic depression after the Napoleonic wars. These changes probably resulted in more people, especially younger men, committing more crime. However, historians also argue that changes in control caused an increase in prosecutions. New criminal offences were created, the courts were reorganized (which made it easier for ordinary people to initiate a case) and the new police force was set up. In addition, national criminal statistics were collected from 1805 which turned crime into a national and more easily measured phenomenon.

The long 'plateau' period where this rise flattened out (1850s–1910s) is more difficult to explain. Social changes may have meant that fewer crimes were actually committed, rather than fewer prosecutions brought. Rising living standards, lower food prices, political stability, declining interpersonal violence and adjustment to new urban industrial lifestyles, combined with the workings of a strong centralized regulatory state seem to have created – temporarily at least – more law-abiding subjects and a new public order consensus (Gatrell, 1990).

The twentieth-century rise in prosecutions is commonly explained in terms of increased opportunities to commit new kinds of crime, trends in the economic cycle, and a breakdown in the fragile public order consensus of the late Victorian period, especially in the wake of the social upheavals of the two world wars. Recorded crimes rose steeply from about half a million

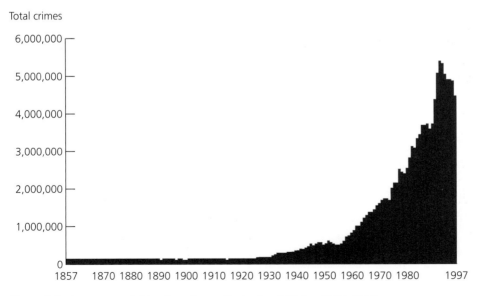

Figure 2.1 Crimes recorded by the police in England and Wales, 1857–1997.

Note: 'Crime' is used here as a shorthand for 'notifiable offences'; it excludes criminal damage of less than £20.

Source: Home Office (1999: 2).

histories of crime

13

in 1950 to 1.6 million in 1970 and then to 5.5 million in 1991 (Home Office, 1999). Post-Second World War consumer booms generated both more goods for those with disposable income as well as the desire for more goods which very likely resulted in increased property crime. In line with this, car-related offences – relatively rare in the 1950s – grew rapidly (Corbett, 2003). As discussed above, violent offences were also increasing.

So, crime patterns have clearly changed over time. Recorded crime rates have increased dramatically relative to population in the last thirty years. However, the value of historical studies here is to show that there was no 'golden-age' where crime did not occur.

BOX 2.1 How do we know about crime in the past?

Historians tend not to create 'new' data through surveys, interviews and focus groups (though some use interviews to gather memories as forms of data). Instead they use surviving records of the past – documents, images, buildings and artefacts. Histories of crime and control rely on state documents such as court, police and prison records but also church and charity papers as well as newspapers, novels, (auto)biographies, diaries and architectural sources.

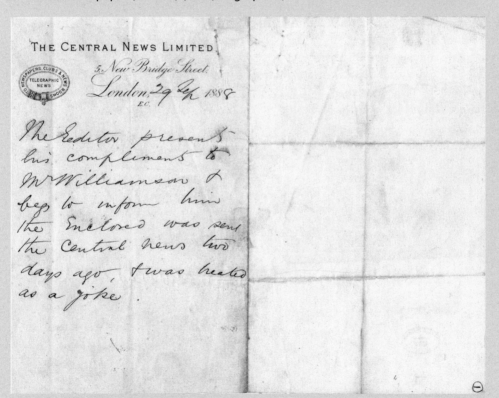

Plate 2.1a Letter from Central News enclosing a letter addressed to Central News signed 'Jack the Ripper', dated 25 Sept 1888.

Source: The National Archives/Metropolitan Police.

the criminological imagination

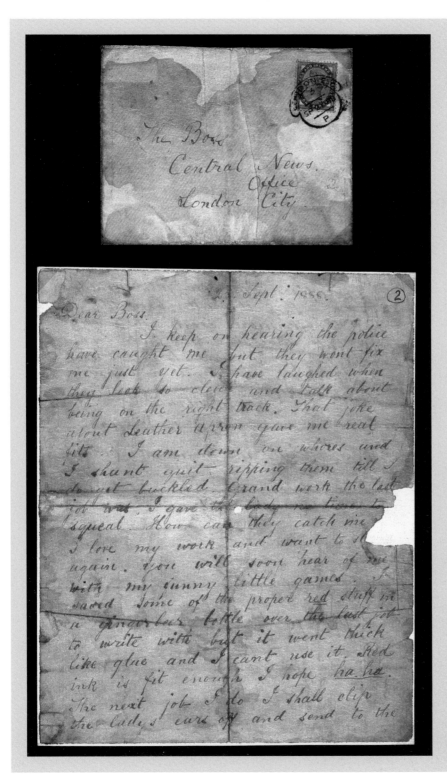

Plate 2.1b
Continued

Plate 2.1c
Continued

the criminological imagination

Trends in historical writing

Historians' views on crime have altered a lot since the 1970s, especially with the challenges of, first, 'history from below' or social history, and later, gender history and cultural history (see Godfrey *et al.*, 2003a; Emsley and Knafla, 1996; King, 1999). As this chapter shows, social historians' initial and ground-breaking concern with white male working-class criminals has given way to a broader range of studies of women, juveniles, 'race', the 'underclass' and **colonial** experiences. There is also a comprehensive body of work on the history of policing, prisons and punishment which is discussed in chapters 15, 17 and 18.

Men and crime

In the 1960s and 1970s, radical historians began to turn away from traditional areas of research (high politics, diplomacy, war, state formation, and so on) to investigate what came to be widely called 'history from below', or 'social history'. This focused on working-class lives, everyday survival and political struggles. These historians, many working within a left-wing and Marxist perspective, were interested in understanding the impact of **capitalism**, urbanization, industrialization and class formation upon people's lives.

Male workers were viewed as particular casualties of capitalism and its new levels of poverty and exploitation but were also seen as being radicalized by these. Historians like E. P. Thompson, Eric Hobsbawm, Douglas Hay and Peter Linebaugh wrote powerful studies of the many (male) agricultural labourers, (male) industrial workers and (male) unemployed who were prosecuted in their thousands for **'social crimes'** in the eighteenth and early nineteenth centuries. Many of these prosecutions resulted from the criminalization of old customs – customs which had traditionally helped ordinary people put more food on their tables. For example, with changing definitions of private property, small-scale hunting and trapping were criminalized as 'trespass' and 'poaching', and collecting (or 'gleaning') crops left over from a harvest became a form of theft. Others were prosecuted for political crimes linked to protests to protect these customary rights and also to the harsh repression of new illegal organizations (like trade unions and working men's associations) and new political activities like mass rallies calling for working men to be given the vote (Thompson, 1963, 1975 and 1991; Hobsbawm and Rudé, 1969; Archer, 1990). British social historians' work in this field influenced similar studies of 'social crime' in continental Europe (Godfrey *et al.*, 2003a: 21). Again, the aim was to examine how far the broad social and economic changes linked to modernity led to the criminalization of the poor.

According to these historians, a defining feature of 'social crime' was that most ordinary people believed these actions were justifiable. Crime was therefore interpreted as a political act, criminals as conscious or unconscious class rebels, policemen as class traitors (being of working-class origins themselves), and the courts as instruments of class oppression (Hobsbawm, 1972; Hay *et al.*, 1975; Linebaugh, 1976 and 1991). Although this broad approach attracted criticism from other historians (Blok, 1972; Langbein, 1983; Innes and Styles, 1993; Lea, 1999), it remained dominant into the late 1980s (for an overview of these debates, see Philips, 1983; Weiss, 1999: xiii–xxiv).

From the late 1980s, this view of history, class and crime began to change. Social history was critiqued from three different directions. First, studies of pre-capitalist or early modern societies

(1500–1800) showed that crime and disorder were not just by-products of 'modern' struggles (Beattie, 1986; Sharpe, 1999). Second, cultural historians argued that crime and its control held many and varied social meanings, and that these were as much bound up with issues of nation, race, sensation and science as they were with economic inequalities (Pick, 1989; Walkowitz, 1992; Kohn, 1992). Third, historians of gender and family relations highlighted many kinds of less than heroic male crimes, including domestic violence and child abuse (Behlmer, 1982; Clark, 1987; Doggett, 1992). This opened the way for new historical studies that focused on the construction of criminal masculinities.

A major claim in this work is that Western societies became increasingly intolerant of male violence. Evidence for this included harsher penalties for 'everyday' crimes such as assault. Acts of interpersonal violence which may not even have been prosecuted in the early eighteenth century were punished by large fines, imprisonment and sometimes the death penalty by the early nineteenth (Wiener, 1998). Intolerance of male violence was also expressed through the criminalization of much 'traditionally acceptable' male behaviour, from duelling to bare-knuckle boxing to wife-beating. This shift was linked to growing divisions between rough and respectable cultures, the physical withdrawal of elites from ordinary communities, the separation of public and private spaces and the introduction of the new police force in the 1830s to control unruly

Plate 2.2 Nineteenth century street fight.

Source: Coloured engraving by I. R & G. Cruikshank, in Pierce Egan's 'Life in London', 1821. Mary Evans Picture Library.

the criminological imagination

working-class communities (Wiener, 1998). Eisner similarly argues that the 'long-term decline in homicide rates' from the sixteenth to the early twentieth centuries 'seems to go along with a disproportionate decline in elite homicide and a drop in male-to-male conflicts in public space' (Eisner, 2003: 83). Feminist and gender historians have examined women and children's (predominantly girls') experiences of rape, sexual assault, incest and domestic violence (Clark, 1987; D'Cruze, 1998; Jackson, 2000) and analysed how men's intimate violence could be challenged.

Male violence may have been less tolerated but it remained embedded in everyday life as shown by apprentice riots (Griffiths, 1996), late nineteenth-century public holiday skirmishes involving 'hooligans', 'scuttlers' and other gangs (Pearson, 1983; Davies, 2000) and mid-twentieth-century clashes between different kinds of young (mostly male) **subcultures** (S. Cohen, 1972/2002; Hall and Jefferson, 1976). Spectacular outbreaks like these seem, however, to be rooted in more general cultures of 'ordinary' violence among young men in playgrounds, schools, pubs, clubs, homes and workplaces. This is not to imply that violence and crime is an unchanging or natural part of modern masculinities (see Messerschmidt, 1993; Newburn and Stanko, 1994; Collier, 1998). Definitions of 'acceptable' male violence have been contested between men themselves since at least the 1500s. The key point is that, historically, the negotiation of everyday violence has played a major role in the construction of everyday masculinities and has quite frequently resulted in informal policing directed at, or court appearances by, young men.

Women and crime

Concern about rising crime rates among women has grown in recent years. Yet historical studies show that women have a long history of offending. There is a significant pattern to this: high female prosecution rates from 1500 to 1800, falling rates from the 1800s to 1945 and higher rates from 1945 onwards. In other words, the gap between male and female prosecution rates was narrow in the first and last periods but much wider in the second.

Women in early modern Britain and Europe often appeared before courts. They were most commonly charged with property crime, slander, assault and infanticide (Walker, 2003; Arnot and Usborne, 1999a; Beattie, 1975). Slander or defamation of character was considered a much more serious offence at this time than it is today. In early modern society, to lose one's 'good name' was to lose trade, customers, trust and face. Local reputations were at the heart of local village and small town life, not least because it was difficult to make a fresh start by moving away to another community. This was to change with nineteenth-century migration and urbanization and, as a result, slander became a less important crime among ordinary people although it remained very important for elites where personal reputation still mattered greatly. In the early modern period, however, slander was a significant offence, frequently prosecuted and frequently committed by women. In continental Europe slander, gossip and rumour-spreading were often among the charges levelled at the many women accused of witchcraft (Wiesner, 2007; Roper, 1994). The same was true in Britain although there were far fewer cases (Sharpe, 2001).

Female prosecution rates were high in the early modern period for two key reasons. First, women arguably committed more offences because they were more fully engaged in public, street and neighbourhood life (Eales, 1998). Long before capitalism and industrialization they were almost all economically active (apart from a small group of elite families). Women worked in

FREE FIGHT IN A COTTON MILL.
ANNISTON, ALA., FACTORY GIRLS JOIN SIDES IN A RIOT IN WHICH MISS BROWN IS FATALLY INJURED.

Plate 2.3 Women millworkers in a free fight in a cotton mill.

Source: Unattributed nineteenth-century engraving in *Police Gazette*. Mary Evans Picture Library.

many areas, including agriculture, baking, textiles, fishing and brewing and, crucially, combined this with domestic work and childcare. Very often, children worked alongside their parents and work itself was done in or near the home. This meant that there was no clear separation of home and work as there was in the nineteenth century when capitalism transformed work. Then tasks became more specialized, workplaces were separated from homes, child labour was first intensified, then banned. Women continued to work but their lives became more closely associated with the home, childcare and domesticity (the private sphere) rather than with places outside the home (the public sphere). Some historians (Feeley, 1994) believe that early modern women's greater public presence had a clear impact on their offending behaviour in that they arguably had more opportunities to commit crime than their nineteenth-century counterparts. Others (see Arnot and Usborne, 1999a for an overview) disagree, mainly because they argue that later generations of women were not rigidly confined to the private sphere after capitalism.

The second reason why women's prosecution rates were higher in the early modern period was because of the particular nature of early modern modes of law enforcement. These were more informal and community-based than they were to become in the nineteenth century and were applied more equally to the whole community, including to women and children. As law enforcement became more professionalized, specialized and nationalized it became more masculinized. From the 1830s it could be argued that the criminal justice system revolved around entirely male police officers arresting mostly male offenders and those offenders being sent by male-dominated courts to mostly male prisons. As a result, some historians argue that women were less likely to face prosecution for serious offences in the nineteenth century than they were before because prosecution itself had become a much more serious matter (Feeley, 1994). This argument certainly works in relation to the higher courts. However, women continued to appear frequently in the lower courts (summary courts) which dealt with offences seen as less serious such as habitual drunkenness, soliciting, petty theft or child neglect. As Arnot and Usborne argue in their discussion of European trends, '[t]he lower the historian moves down the jurisdictional ladder, the larger the proportion of women' (1999b: 8).

Many thousands were also dealt with *outside* the criminal justice system for minor and moral offences such as vagrancy, alcoholism, destitution, sexual promiscuity or illegitimate pregnancy. This is an important point because it means that their experiences were not recorded in criminal statistics. Inebriates' reformatories (homes for alcoholics), religious rescue homes, hostels and, up to a point, asylums, workhouses and mental hospitals all housed large numbers of women and girls across the Western and wider English-speaking world (on the United States, see Pascoe, 1990; on Australia and Canada, see Langfield, 2004; on Britain, see Zedner, 1991b; Mahood, 1995 and Cox, 2003). Time spent in these institutions was very often much longer than an average female prison sentence. Some women and girls approached these institutions for help or shelter themselves, though the 'freedom' of such a choice was often very constrained. Many of these institutions survived well into the twentieth century but have not featured in many criminological studies (see Barton, 2005) apart from some work on the **pathologization** (or medicalization) of female crime (Dobash et al., 1986).

Twentieth-century women's experiences of crime and control have so far been studied rather less by historians, though this is beginning to change. Boritch and Hagan's (1990) study of male and female arrest rates in Toronto from the 1850s to the 1950s found that these both declined overall and showed marked similarities in relation to different kinds of offences. Most of those arrested, especially for very common public order offences, were from lower-class backgrounds. The study therefore stresses the importance of class in any study of gender and crime – a view shared by a recent survey of gender and violence in Britain over the same historical period (D'Cruze, 2000).

Histories of women's involvement in policing from the early twentieth century onwards (Brown and Heidensohn, 2000; Jackson, 2006; Schulz, 1995) also open a window on women's crime, much of which remained property- and public order-based. A high-profile minority of women were involved in more serious crimes such as murder, as detailed in two recent studies (Ballinger, 2000; D'Cruze et al., 2006). Prostitution prosecutions declined in early twentieth-century Europe (Bartley, 2000) but remained prominent at a more global level, as shown by Ringdal's (2003) ambitious 'world history' of this subject (see also Hershatter, 1997, on Shanghai).

Early feminist criminologists writing from the 1970s analysed rising female crime rates – much of what we know about late twentieth-century women's crime comes from them. Freda Adler's *Sisters in Crime* (1975), a study of US women, sparked a controversial debate still invoked today. Adler argued that a 'new female criminal' had been created by women's social liberation from the 1960s onwards. Late modern women had, first, a greater public role and therefore more opportunities to commit crime, and, second, were more likely to face prosecution as they were more likely (in contrast to their nineteenth-century counterparts) to be treated in similar ways to men.

Others rejected Adler's claims. Box and Hale (1984) argued that women might have become more socially liberated in the late twentieth century but that they also remained economically marginal (see also Smart, 1979). Structural inequalities meant that as a group they had, historically, always been poorer than men (occupying more low-paid jobs, combining periods of paid employment with periods of unpaid childcare, earning less during their working lives, therefore having fewer savings and reduced pensions, and so on). If women were committing more crime it was because of their continuing social marginality, not their greater legal equality.

Other feminist criminologists focused on the treatment of women by the police, courts and prisons. In this they have also increasingly focused on the differences *between* women, rather than the differences between women and men, and asked which kinds of women are more likely to be arrested, found guilty, imprisoned or referred for psychiatric treatment. Important as gender difference is in shaping crime patterns, it is by no means the only difference that counts. Some research has found that, on the whole, women who present themselves as more traditionally feminine, and above all as respectful and remorseful, tend to get treated more 'leniently' than other women (Carlen and Worrall, 1987; Worrall, 1990; Heidensohn, 1996). Others have shown how this construction of women can mean that some of their crimes, such as maternal child abuse, continue to remain invisible (Turton, 2007).

Youth and crime

Most prosecuted crime is committed by younger people. There are two reasons for this. This group (and young men in particular) commit more crime of a kind that people feel should be reported and younger offenders are more likely to be pursued by the criminal justice system.

Youth crime has a long and complex history. Research here focuses on two broad issues: disorderly youth cultures and youth justice procedures. From at least 1500, boys, but also girls, have been involved in riotous street cultures, gangs, property crime and violent crime, from theft, assault and vandalism to manslaughter and murder (for an overview see Cox and Shore, 2002; on girls see Davies, 1999 and Cox, 2003). From the 1800s, ways of dealing with youth crime changed significantly as this section will show.

The idea that juvenile delinquency is far from 'new' was set out most comprehensively by sociologist Geoff Pearson (1983) in his now classic text, *Hooligan*. The book charts a century of

British panics around disorderly youth starting with the Conservative government's 'short, sharp, shock' programme of the 1980s and going back to the 'hooligan' rioters of the 1890s. Pearson argued that all these were linked by a recurring and familiar set of 'respectable fears' – unruly behaviour in public space, lack of respect for traditional values, unwillingness to 'settle down'. Each adult generation experienced these as 'new' and each believed that young people's behaviour was 'worse' than it had been when they were young themselves. He explained this in terms of ongoing inter-generational tensions and the life course. The ageing process means that adults always experience the social worlds of the young as unfamiliar and as posing a threat to 'established' ways of doing things, whatever these might be. This process has been exaggerated in modern times because of the faster pace of socio-economic and technological change.

Historians support this view but take it even further by showing that youth crime and disorder has been a subject of British and European public debate since at least the 1500s. The key point here is that these debates took place long before large-scale urbanization and industrialization. Griffiths (1996, 2002) details the wide range of measures taken against unruly youths in early modern England by the church, employers, poor law authorities and the courts. European studies offer a similar picture. Parents, especially elite ones, went to great lengths to punish their young sons' immoral behaviour. Drinking, gambling, fighting and promiscuity could ruin a family's good name, with dire economic consequences. Dutch parents sent their sons away to work in the Dutch East Indies while some Spanish parents sent their sons to correctional orphanages, sometimes for several years (Roberts, 2002; Tikoff, 2002). These extreme measures show how seriously early modern youthful disorder was taken. They also highlight the overlooked fact that the sexual and moral behaviour of young men as well as young women was subject to regulation.

Industrialization and urbanization created more opportunities for youth crime and new responses to youth crime. Recorded prosecutions of children and adolescents, particularly in urban areas, rose dramatically from the late eighteenth century onwards and the new term 'juvenile delinquency' emerged soon after (see Box 2.2). This youth crime wave was linked to massive population growth and a simple increase in numbers of people under the age of 30. It was seen by authorities at the time, however, as evidence of the collapse of traditional social

BOX 2.2 Extract from 'The Report of the Committee for Investigating the Causes of the Alarming Increase of Juvenile Delinquency in the Metropolis', 1816

It was found that Juvenile Delinquency existed in the metropolis to a very alarming extent; that a system was in action, by which . . . unfortunate Lads were organised into gangs; that they resorted regularly to houses, where they planned their enterprises, and afterwards divided the produce of their plunder.

Source: 'Report of the Committee for Investigating the Causes of the Alarming Increase of Juvenile Delinquency in the Metropolis', London, 1816: 5; cited in Shore (1999: 6).

controls. Changes to the apprenticeship system were widely blamed. Young people had traditionally left home to learn a trade as apprentices or domestic servants. Apprentices had to work for a set period (often seven years) for low wages. In return, they gained a training, sometimes housing, and, crucially, longer-term job security. Young people thus swapped parental discipline for employer discipline. Further, it was expected that they would eventually marry and be 'disciplined' by their own family responsibilities. The breakdown of apprenticeship – due to demands for more flexible and mobile labour – gave young workers a new freedom (though also a new economic vulnerability) that few of their parents and grandparents had known. In some developing regions such as Southeast Asia and Africa it is possible to see similar intergenerational tensions today and comparable concerns about new levels of juvenile crime (see United Nations Asia and Far East Institute for the Prevention of Crime and the Treatment of Offenders for more on this: http://www.unafei.or.jp/english/index.htm).

Youth migration was not new but large-scale urban migration was. This shaped juvenile delinquency in two key ways: by providing more opportunities for 'dissolute' leisure activities (Springhall, 1998) and by providing more possibilities of surveillance and regulation. Towns and cities had coffee houses, gaming rooms, pubs and brothels but they also had moral vigilante groups (such as the Society for the Promotion of Christian Knowledge, or societies for the 'reformation of manners'), Christian crusaders (such as Anglican evangelists and Methodists), thief-takers, prosecution associations and later public health reformers and the police themselves. This historical period is most often read by sociologists in terms of dislocation and alienation but this overlooks the many steps taken to prevent and contain these processes. The development of new ways to deal with something now named as 'juvenile delinquency' in the early nineteenth century was part of a wider development of a new kind of state, community and control.

New ways of dealing with delinquency across the West included, from the early nineteenth century onwards, setting up juvenile reformatories, moving child cases to lower courts, abolishing child imprisonment in adult jails and creating juvenile courts. Increasing numbers of non-offending children were brought into these new juvenile justice systems through new child protection legislation (1880s onwards). Young victims of crimes such as neglect and abuse and those thought to be at risk of offending could be 'put into care' in juvenile reformatories. This kind of 'welfare policing' has been most commonly studied through the experiences of girls (Mahood, 1995; Cox, 2003) but also involved large numbers of boys.

Studies of twentieth-century juvenile delinquency are less concerned with when and why it was 'invented' and focus more on when and why formal responses to it shifted from justice (punishing deeds) to welfare (meeting needs). Historians stress that these two elements have been part of the juvenile justice system ever since it was set up. For example, in the 1940s hardliners felt that abolishing birching (corporal punishment ordered by a court) was 'too soft' on young offenders whereas 'liberals' in the same period called for careful casework by new kinds of welfare professionals such as social workers and psychologists.

That said, in Britain, the 1969 Children and Young Persons Act and its (partial) implementation by the 1970 Conservative government marked a new turn towards welfarism. Care proceedings and community-based treatment or residential care were favoured over criminal proceedings and custodial responses. The discretionary powers of social workers were enhanced and those of magistrates reduced (Pitts, 2003; Muncie, 1999). This drive to 'liberalize' had earlier historical roots but was also linked to a new post-war political consensus across social policy issues in general.

Well-known studies of twentieth-century youth subcultures such as Stan Cohen's classic *Folk Devils and Moral Panics* (1972/2002) or Hall and Jefferson's *Resistance through Rituals* (1976) describe a very different scene to that documented by juvenile justice studies. With their focus on the more spectacular world and public presence of older teenage subcultures they have more in common with early modernist studies of disorderly, but not necessarily law-breaking, youths. These studies (discussed in more detail in Chapter 6) have an important place in the development of academic criminology because they analysed the media's role in constructing 'deviant' subcultures and exaggerating (or amplifying) the destructive effects of these. Yet these more spectacular behaviours have historically only ever accounted for a small number of youth prosecutions. More mundane cases of shop-lifting, fare-dodging, theft, vandalism and car crime accounted for the vast majority of youth prosecutions in the 1970s and 1980s when these classic studies were written. Since then, the introduction of ASBOs (anti-social behaviour orders) by the 1998 Crime and Disorder Act has arguably blurred the boundary between spectacular youth cultures and actual youth crime, for example by allowing the banning of certain kinds of clothes (such as hoodies) in certain kinds of places (such as some shopping malls).

The 'dangerous class', 'underclass', race and crime

Many sociologists and criminologists argue that today's society is much more unequal than it was in the past and that social inclusion has given way to extreme social exclusion (Young, 1999a). While such inequalities are certainly deep-rooted, historical studies show that they are not new. Concerns about the 'dangerous classes' and their links to crime can be traced back in Western societies to the early nineteenth century (Morris, 1994; Crowther, 2000). They have much in common with debates around the 'underclass' in the 1990s and 'social exclusion' more recently. Broadly speaking, all these terms refer to social groups who are economically marginalized, socially stigmatized and who appear to others to live by a 'different' set of moral standards.

Definitions of 'dangerousness' were, and remain, closely linked to perceptions of class and race. In colonial contexts, native and aboriginal peoples were thought to require closer policing by white settler authorities. Special measures, such as missions and forced adoptions, were set up in the United States, Canada, Australia and New Zealand to reform these groups (Langfield, 2004; Byrne, 1993; Choo, 2001; Pascoe, 1990; see also Stoler, 2002). In societies with a history of slavery, like the United States, black people faced huge discrimination in the criminal justice system (see Chapter 5 for discussion of early black criminologists' work on this).

In Europe, the 'dangerous classes' tended to be poor, urban and white but were commonly framed as a 'race apart', as a distinctive 'breed' of person (Davis, 1989; Cox, 2002). These discourses became more pronounced with the mass migrations of people out of Ireland and southern and eastern Europe to North America, Britain and Australia. **Social Darwinist** models of the 'survival of the fittest' and racial degeneration suggested that the 'unfit' were threatening to outbreed the 'fit'. This thinking influenced criminal justice. In Britain, the 1869 Habitual Criminal Act and the 1879 Habitual Drunkards Act were designed to detect and detain 'habitual' criminals of various kinds. It also influenced criminology. American criminologist Richard Dugdale analysed 'criminal families'. His infamous 1875 study of the Jukes family – showing how murderers had married prostitutes, how mentally 'defective' women had mothered many delinquent children, and so on – inspired similar studies in Britain and Europe (Hahn Rafter, 1997; Pick, 1989). Lombroso's efforts to define 'criminal types' (through their faces, bodies, expressions and inherited characteristics, as discussed in Chapter 4) were clearly part of a much broader cultural turn towards the pathological or scientific explanations for crime (Lombroso, 1876). After 1945, the term 'problem family' was used by many social workers dealing with juvenile delinquency. At one level this was a positive development as it analysed delinquency alongside wider family relations. At another it replicated earlier characterizations of 'degenerate' families. In the 1980s and 1990s, American Charles Murray's controversial work on the 'underclass' and ethnicity continued this line of enquiry (Murray et al., 1990; see also Lister et al., 1996 for critique).

Given this context it is easy to see how racialized discourses of crime were applied to non-white immigrants. In Britain, beliefs about 'deviant foreigners' have been attached to many groups over time, from Irish, East European Jewish, Malay and Chinese migrants in the nineteenth century to West Indian migrants of the mid-twentieth to certain 'asylum seekers' of the present. Concerns about 'foreigners' of all kinds have often been accompanied by concerns about white 'underclass' behaviour. The cafés, clubs, drugs and music that grew up around historic migrant cultures in many Western cities were new cosmopolitan urban spaces which were often subject to heightened police surveillance as sites of potential 'trouble'.

Of all these groups the experiences of West Indians (mainly young men) within the criminal justice system have attracted most criminological attention in Britain. Classic studies of race and crime were closely connected to studies of class and crime. For Hall et al. (1978), historical moral panics around white underclass criminality took on new politicized forms when they settled on a new target: post-war West Indian, particularly Jamaican, migrants and their children; and the 'new' kinds of criminal behaviours they apparently brought to the deprived inner-city areas. 'Mugging' (simply a new name for the old crime of 'aggravated robbery'), 'hustling' (petty criminality involving gambling, prostitution and unlicensed gatherings) and marijuana-linked crimes (which represented a new phase of a much longer history of British drug use) were all heavily associated by the press and the public with black immigrants.

Other writers extended Hall et al.'s work, critiquing the 'over-policing' of young West Indians (notably through the use of notorious 'sus' laws – being stopped 'on suspicion' of being involved in criminal activities) and the part these played in the urban riots of the early 1980s in London, Birmingham, Manchester, Liverpool and Bristol (Holdaway, 1996; Keith, 1993).

For much of the 1980s, perceived links between class and crime were highly racialized, with urban black people viewed by liberals and hardliners alike as among the most seriously socially excluded and, by extension, among the most likely to commit crime. Of course, liberal- and left-leaning commentators, including most criminologists writing on this subject, also argued that high rates of crime and imprisonment among young blacks were also the product of the systematic racial discrimination against this group operating at all levels of the criminal justice system. As this section has suggested, this discriminatory thinking has a long history.

Summary

1   Recorded crime rose sharply in the early nineteenth century, then stabilized until the early twentieth century, then rose again very sharply after the Second World War and particularly after the 1970s. Property crime was the most common offence throughout this period.

2   Historical studies of crime have changed in focus and nature. From the 1970s, social historians interpreted crime in class terms whereas from the late 1980s onwards, this class-based view has broadened to encompass other issues like gender and age.

3   The history of crime from the nineteenth century on can be read as the history of men policing men.

4   Women and young people have long histories as offenders. Ways of dealing with both groups changed in the nineteenth century with the result that both groups were dealt with in specific parts of the criminal justice system, for example, in women's prisons and youth reformatories. Many more were dealt with at the margins of criminal justice, for example, in female rescue homes and children's homes.

5   Perceived links between social exclusion, 'race' and criminality are very long-standing. Terms for excluded groups have changed over time and have included 'the dangerous classes' and 'the underclass'. These groups have often been presented as if they were a distinct social type.

Critical thinking questions

1   **What does a historical perspective add to the study of criminology?**
2   **How would you summarize crime patterns, 1500–2000?**
3   **What factors need to be considered when trying to assess and interpret historical crime patterns?**

Further study

Cox, P. (2003) *Gender, Justice and Welfare: Bad Girls in Britain 1900–1950*, Basingstoke: Palgrave. Looks at the other side of Geoff Pearson's story by charting a history of delinquent girls.

D'Cruze, S., Walklate, S. and Pegg, S. (2006) *Murder: Social and Historical Approaches to Understanding Murder and Murderers*, Cullompton: Willan. Puts modern murder in historical perspective.

Eisner, M. (2003) 'Long-term Historical Trends in Violent Crime', *Crime and Justice: A Review of Research*, 30: 83–142. An unusual and valuable long-term and comparative look at patterns of violent crime.

Emsley, C. (2005) *Crime and Society in England, 1750–1900*, 3rd edn, London: Longman. A very comprehensive and accessible overview of the history of crime and control.

Pearson, G. (1983) *Hooligan: A History of Respectable Fears*, London: Macmillan. Classic analysis of modern historical youth cultures.

Ruff, J. R. (2001) *Violence in Early Modern Europe 1500–1800*, Cambridge: Cambridge University Press. Important study of long decline in violence.

Walker, G. (2003) *Crime, Gender and Social Order in Early Modern England*, Cambridge: Cambridge University Press. Very good overview of early modern crime, often overlooked by criminologists and sociologists!

More information

National Archives
http://www.nationalarchives.gov.uk/

Old Bailey (the Central Criminal Court in England)
http://www.oldbaileyonline.org/proceedings/publishinghistory.html

Researching Crime

Introduction

Specialist texts on research methodology and methods have proliferated in the social sciences. In both criminology and sociology, the study of 'methodology' – the theoretical principles and framework behind different ways of carrying out research – and research 'methods' – the tools or instruments used by researchers to gather their evidence – have become distinct areas within the subject.

Criminological researchers come from a variety of disciplines and draw from a range of research techniques. In recent years, criminologists along with other social scientists have become more reflective about research techniques and outcomes. This chapter explores these issues in relation to the nature of criminological data and commonly used research methods, the use of criminal statistics and **ethics**. It closes by considering a key question: whose 'side' are criminological researchers on?

Criminological research methods

Criminologists often generate their own data through their own research projects. They select their research methods according to their expertise and area of interest. Psychological profiling, genetics, urban ethnography, cultural history and social theory – and many more besides – are all currently used. As this brief list indicates, the criminological research field is very diverse (King and Wincup, 2007; Champion, 2005; Jupp *et al.*, 2000; Maxfield and Babbie, 2007; Coleman and Moynihan, 1996). Opinions are often sharply divided as to the 'best' methods to use and many researchers are unaware of work outside their own discipline.

Sociological approaches to crime research are themselves very diverse but until recently two have dominated: **qualitative**, involving methods such as interviews, **participant observation** and **ethnography** (Noaks and Wincup, 2004); and **quantitative**, using tools like surveys, statistical analysis and **prediction studies** (Bushway and Weisburd, 2005). Recently, new **mixed methods** approaches have developed across the social sciences which aim to combine these two in creative ways (Creswell, 2003). New kinds of criminological work are beginning to emerge along these lines (e.g. Schulenberg, 2007). Mixed methods are increasingly favoured among those involved in **evaluation research** and **evidence-based policy** making. Here, criminologists and other social scientists evaluate policy initiatives or generate evidence about a particular social problem with a view to designing an intervention to help to ease that problem (see website for exercises to allow you to practise your own criminological research skills).

Experimental criminology takes this further. Its defining feature is that it seeks to test out its theories in the criminal justice field and to make policy recommendations based on 'hard' evidence of what works. Sherman (2005) traces this tradition from Henry Fielding's eighteenth-century policing experiments in London (see Chapter 4), through von Liszt's offender reform programme in late nineteenth-century Marburg, through to the current randomized controlled fieldwork of the Pennsylvania-based Academy of Experimental Criminology. He argues that, this tradition notwithstanding, 'the vast majority of published criminology remains analytic and nonexperimental' (2005: 129). Sherman and his colleagues believe that criminology's future lies in a closer collaboration between analytical and the experimental approaches which will help to make the subject 'more useful'. They would like to see experimental techniques used to link criminality to the life course as well as to provide evidence to counter the United States' 'three-decade increase in prisoners'. Nevertheless, experimental criminology is problematic for many sociologists because it is based on the idea that it is possible to provide 'unbiased empirical guidance' (Sherman, 2005: 129) to shape policy debates. It favours medical-style randomized controlled experiments and tends to separate crime, criminality and control out from the wider social relations which construct them.

Social psychologists studying crime also use experimental and mixed-method approaches. **Social psychology** analyses the relationships between individuals and society. It examines how individuals relate to each other as well as to groups and institutions. Compared to straight psychology, it is less concerned with bio-medical and neurological matters and more concerned with questions of social perception. It generally seeks to explore the connections between individual perceptions, beliefs and behaviours and social structures and processes. Classic social psychological approaches to crime and deviance – such as symbolic interactionism – are discussed in Chapter 5. Social psychologists involved in crime research today are likely to use mixed methods and to focus on questions such as motivation, stigma, emotions, individual and community perceptions of crime and the receptiveness, or otherwise, of particular kinds of offenders to particular kinds of sanction (see Chapter 12). Sampson and Raudenbush's study (2004) of the grounds on which individuals form perceptions of disorder, for example, combines personal interviews, census data, police records and systematic social observations among residential groups in Chicago.

Criminological research is funded in different ways and its **outputs** can take various forms. University-based criminological research is mostly funded by academic research agencies such as the UK's Economic and Social Research Council or the Australian Research Council. These agencies allocate funds mostly derived from governments. Alternatives include research commissioned and paid for by other state bodies or by the voluntary or private sectors. Funding inevitably raises issues of ownership and the question of 'whose side' criminologists are on – an issue to be explored later in the chapter. Research findings are typically presented at academic conferences or policy consultations and published as academic journal articles or policy reports. Box 3.1 shows something of the range of outlets available and the accompanying website offers links to some of these.

BOX 3.1 Some academic criminological associations and journals

American Society of Criminology
http://www.asc41.com/
Publishes two journals: *Criminology* and *Criminology & Public Policy*

Australia and New Zealand Society of Criminology
http://www.anzsoc.org/

British Society of Criminology
http://www.britsoccrim.org/

European Society of Criminology
http://www.esc-eurocrim.org
Publishes the *European Journal of Criminology*: http://www.esc-eurocrim.org/journal.shtml

Socio-Legal Studies Association
http://www.slsa.ac.uk/

British Journal of Criminology
http://bjc.oxfordjournals.org/

Criminological data

What counts as criminological data? Many people – other than criminologists – produce information about criminals, victims, law enforcers, sanctions and rights. Criminal justice agencies themselves such as the police, courts and prisons are very important here as the main source of criminal statistics (discussed below). However, criminologists also use information that comes from outside the criminal justice system. These include:

- ■ *Mass media* contain vast amounts of crime coverage and comment. Television, film, news media and the Internet represent crime and justice in many different ways. Many students are initially attracted to criminology as a subject through these sorts of channels which are covered in detail in Chapter 20.
- ■ *Charities and voluntary organizations* have a long global history of intervening in crime and deviance and this involvement continues today. Organizations like the Howard League for Penal Reform, Women's Aid or the National Association for the Care and Resettlement of Offenders (NACRO) in the United Kingdom or Equal Justice USA in the United States play a significant role in criminal justice by providing services but also by creating criminological data and research reports. Others, like Amnesty International or Human Rights Watch, publicize state crime around the world.
- ■ *Private companies* like banks, credit suppliers and insurance agencies store and exchange huge amounts of information about their customers. A person with a criminal record or unreliable financial record can be refused some financial services. High crime rates in particular residential areas (as calculated by risk-assessors and loss-adjusters) can raise domestic and commercial insurance premiums quite dramatically.
- ■ *International bodies* are a further important source of global and comparative criminological data. Specialist agencies here include the United Nations Interregional Crime and Justice Research Institute (UNICRI), the United Nations Office on Drugs and Crime (UNODC), the European Commission's (EC) Europa – Justice and Home Affairs Unit, and the Association of Southeast Asian Nations (ASEAN) which also deals with transnational crime.

Thinking critically about statistics

Joel Best (2001) argues that people respond to statistics in three distinct ways. The 'awestruck' treat them with reverence and as if they represent the clear truth about a particular issue. The 'naïve' are more critical but also tend to accept statistics as 'hard facts'. The 'cynical' are very suspicious about statistics, believing that they are often flawed, that they can be manipulated to prove anything and, even worse, that they are deliberately used to mislead and deceive.

Best advises us, however, against being awestruck, naive or cynical. Instead, we need to be critical and to develop a questioning perspective which allows us to evaluate the merits and limitations of statistics. The critical appreciate that in summarizing complex information, statistics lose some of that complexity. Simplifications and omissions result: choices are made about how to define the problem being measured, and how to go about measuring it. In evaluating these choices, the critical make informed judgements about how to use and value statistics. The aim of this section is to encourage a critical approach to crime statistics.

Recorded crime

Criminologists generate their own statistical data in the course of their research projects. Alongside this, however, they are very likely to draw on official criminal statistics. In most countries, the main sources of formally recorded crime statistics are government departments responsible for criminal justice. In Britain, the Home Office publishes annual *Criminal Statistics*, with separate volumes for England and Wales, Scotland and Northern Ireland, on the Internet as well as in printed reports. These statistics are readily available to students, the general public, journalists and anybody else with an interest. In Canada, criminal and other social statistics are collated by federal agency Statistics Canada. It is important to note here that some governments do not routinely publish this kind of information and that some authoritarian regimes – such as China, Burma and Vietnam – actively withhold it (see UNICRI and Human Rights Watch websites for information on this kind of material).

The crimes recorded by no means reflect the full extent of unlawful activity, however. To take the case of England and Wales, the *Criminal Statistics* do not include data from police forces for which the Home Office is not responsible – for instance, the British Transport Police, Ministry of Defence Police and the UK Atomic Energy Police publish their own statistics. They also exclude

Plate 3.1 Graham cartoon from the *Manchester Evening News*.
Source: © Guardian Media Group plc.

cases of tax and benefit fraud known to agencies such as the Inland Revenue, Customs and Excise and the Department of Work and Pensions which have their own investigative functions. Even where a category of crime is included in the *Criminal Statistics*, many crimes committed do not appear in police records for a variety of reasons (see Muncie, 2001: 25–39 on these omissions).

Recorded crime statistics are not the product of a neutral fact-collecting process. The recording process itself is governed by guidelines. The appendix to the *Criminal Statistics England and Wales* states that 'the . . . process starts when someone reports to the police that an offence has been committed or when the police observe or discover an offence'. The National Crime Reporting Standard (NCRS) (introduced in the UK in 2002) requires any reported incident – whether or not it is classified as a crime – to be recorded. The police make an initial examination of the facts to determine if there is prima facie evidence that an offence has been committed; a crime report may then be made out. However, for a crime to be registered in official data, a number of things need to happen:

- recognition by a victim or possibly a witness that a potentially criminal incident has taken place
- reporting of that incident to the police
- acknowledgement by the police that a potentially criminal incident has occurred
- recording by police of the incident as an alleged crime.

There are many factors along the way which can prevent a crime being recorded. Only a proportion of possible crimes make it through what has been called 'the crime funnel' (see also Chapter 15).

It is well known, consequently, that only a small proportion of incidents that would be classified as crime are recorded by official statistics. The statistics represent only the tip of the iceberg. Early

BOX 3.2 Some sources of official statistics on the Internet

Statistics Canada:
www.statcan.ca
Key words: justice and crime

Federal Bureau of Investigation:
www.fbi.gov
Key words: Uniform Crime Reports

Australian Bureau of Statistics:
www.abs.gov.au
Key words: recorded crime

The UK Home Office:
www.homeoffice.gov.uk
Key words: criminal statistics England and Wales

Scottish Executive:
www.scotland.gov.uk
Key words: recorded crime, crime statistics

Sources: the individual government departments.

local crime surveys – discussed in a later section – revealed that many victims do not report crimes to the police. These survey findings are supported by anecdotal accounts from victims. For instance, a victim's perception about how seriously their allegation will be taken by the police will affect the reporting of crime. Once it has been reported, the police are able to exercise a certain amount of discretion in deciding what to record. Victims' complaints may be disbelieved or dismissed as too trivial. They may even be excluded to avoid work and improve the clear-up rate. Other factors affect crime records: reporting requirements for insurance claims, for instance, result in a high level of reporting of property crimes; and changing patterns of policing and targeting of crimes affect the numbers of particular crimes that come to the attention of the police (Maguire, 1997). In short, the recording of crime involves complex processes of interpretation and interaction. It is certainly not a straightforward process, hence the need to be 'critical', as Joel Best suggests.

Racist incidents: an example of thinking critically about recorded crime

Racist crime – where victims are targeted because of their 'race' or ethnicity – provides a very useful example here. Data on racist incidents for England and Wales can be found in *Statistics on Race and the Criminal Justice System*, published by the Home Office. Britain has a long history of racist crime (Bowling, 1998; Witte, 1996), but in statistical terms it simply did not exist before 1979, as it was not recorded in official statistics until then.

There has since been a huge increase in the number of recorded incidents, especially from the late 1990s (see Figure 3.1). The data seem to suggest that racist crime has escalated: certainly the 'awestruck' and the 'naive' – to use Joel Best's categories – might think so. But is this really

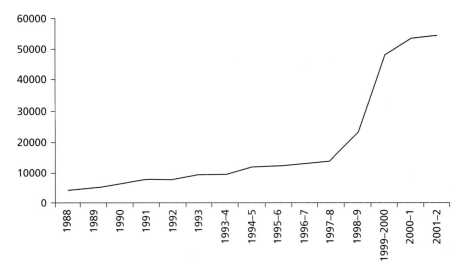

Figure 3.1 Racist incidents for all police force areas in England and Wales.

Sources: 1988 to 1996–7, *Racial Violence and Harassment: A Consultation Document*, London: Home Office (1997); 1997–8 to 1999, *Statistics on Race and the Criminal Justice System*, London: Home Office (2000); 2000–1 and 2001–2, *Statistics on Race and the Criminal Justice System*, London: Home Office (2002).

the case?

To think critically about the statistics, we would need to bear in mind the observation made above that not all crimes appear in police records. In the case of racist incidents it is clear that in the past there has been significant under-reporting by victims due – to some extent – to dissatisfaction with the police handling of reported incidents. A number of common allegations have been made by victims. Often, they have complained about considerable delays before police attend incidents (Gordon, 1990: 13). It has also been alleged that the police have frequently refused to acknowledge the racial motives behind incidents, often explaining them away as minor disputes between neighbours (Dunhill, 1989: 70). Victims of racist incidents have also complained that the police are reluctant to prosecute the perpetrators, and on occasion the victims themselves have been subject to hostile treatment from the police (Gordon, 1990: 20–1; see also Chapter 9 of this book); fear of such hostility has served as a deterrent to reporting incidents.

In taking a critical view of the number of recorded racial incidents, the apparent increase over time could quite conceivably reflect changes in police recording practices and also perhaps a greater motivation by victims to report crimes (for discussion of similar upward trends in reported sex crime, see Chapter 11). The sharp rise in the number of recorded incidents in the late 1990s following the publication of the inquiry into the racially motivated murder of teenager Stephen Lawrence (Macpherson, 1999) supports such an observation. The report not only drew widespread public attention to the problem of racist crime, but in labelling the Metropolitan Police Service as 'institutionally racist' it led to a major examination by police forces concerning how they respond to racist incidents. The definition of an incident was also broadened to include any incident which is perceived to be racist by the victim or any other person – previously, it was limited to the perception of the victim and the police. It is also likely that the establishment of racially aggravated offences for the first time in Britain under the 1998 Crime and Disorder Act made police forces more alert to such offences. The 2006 Racial and Religious Hatred Act took further action against activities which stirred up hatred against persons on racial or religious grounds.

As this example shows, a comparison of recorded crime data over time is important if hazardous. Comparison of data between countries is also problematic but raises important methodological questions for criminologists. In the United States, for example, rates of recorded race crime (e.g. those recorded by the Federal Bureau of Investigation (FBI) Uniform Crime Reports) are proportionally much lower than they are in England and Wales. One reason for this is that the criteria used for defining these crimes are far more stringent.

In 2007, disputes around the definition and policing of race crime in the United States grew into a major public issue, with many calling for a new civil rights movement as a result. Protests focused around the Jena Six – six black youths charged with the 'attempted murder' of a white co-student in Jena, Louisiana. The six and their many supporters claim that the white student had, with others, committed race crimes against black students in the school, including the hanging of a noose in the school grounds. The key point of their claim is that the white students' actions had gone unpunished whereas the actions of the six black students (which might have been charged as 'assault', for example) had been treated disproportionately. This high-profile case may yet precipitate a new approach to race crime in the United States (http://news.bbc.co.uk/1/hi/programmes/this_world/6677057.stm).

the criminological imagination

National crime victimization surveys

Since the 1970s, many countries have established official crime victimization surveys. These provide an important alternative way of generating data about crime (and especially unrecorded crime) by asking samples of people directly about their experiences of crime victimization. As Coleman and Moynihan argue, they are a key way of addressing the '**dark figure**' of unreported crime and can also be usefully compared with **self-report studies** in which different groups of people are asked, for example, to complete an 'anonymous delinquency checklist' (1996: xi–xii, 49).

In the United States, the National Crime Victimization Survey was established in 1972 and is now conducted annually. The first national crime victimization survey in Britain, the British Crime Survey (BCS), was carried out in 1982, with further surveys in 1984, 1988, 1992, 1996 and 1998. In the 2000 British Crime Survey, close to 23,000 people aged 16 and over were interviewed. From 2001 the BCS moved to an annual cycle, with 40,000 respondents interviewed per year. The BCS measures the amount of crime in England and Wales by asking people about crimes they have experienced in the past year. It asks people about their attitude to crime, whether or not they fear crime and what measures they take to avoid it. It also asks them about their attitudes to the criminal justice system, including the police and the courts. The survey findings are published in a variety of specialist reports available online on the Home Office website, and complete datasets of primary data are available for secondary analysis and can be obtained from the University of Essex Data Archive. The questions used in the BCS are also published online by the Question Bank at the University of Surrey (see the website accompanying this book for direct links and exercises on this).

National crime victimization surveys, with their focus on victims' experiences, can present a very different picture of crime than that offered by national criminal statistics, with their focus on recorded crime. A comparison of BCS data for 2002–3 with recorded crime statistics for 2002 suggests some major differences (Simmons and Dodd, 2003). According to the BCS, there were:

- three times as many offences of vandalism
- three times as many thefts from the person
- over twice as many woundings
- twice as many bicycle thefts.

In other important respects, there is less discrepancy between these two kinds of data. Statistics for vehicle theft, for example, are relatively similar across the BCS and recorded crime figures because victims more readily report such thefts to the police and to insurance companies.

As discussed in Chapter 9, crime victimization surveys have been very useful in providing insights into under-reported and under-recorded crime and to sensitize policy-makers to the range and diversity of victim experiences. However, as with all research methods, these surveys have their limitations. In almost all cases, victim surveys focus on crimes experienced by individuals or households. They do not focus on, for example, collective victims of corporate or state crime. They arguably define 'crime', 'victim' and 'criminal' in very limited terms and highlight 'conventional' crimes over others.

International, local and commercial crime victimization surveys

Large-scale international victim surveys have also been carried out enabling some international comparisons to be made here. For example, the International Crime Victim Survey (ICVS) series funded by the Ministry of Justice of the Netherlands was initiated in 1988 and has since been carried out in some fifty-five different countries. The project was set up to bridge the gap in adequate recording of offences by the police for purposes of comparing crime rates in different nations and to provide a crime index independent of police statistics as an alternative standardized measure. The ICVS is the most far-reaching programme of standardized sample surveys to look at householders' experience of crime, policing, crime prevention and feelings of insecurity in a large number of nations.

Again, as discussed in Chapter 9, there are also specific problems with using international victimization reports to measure crime. The cultural perception of crime in different countries may affect the respondents (Newman, 1999: 25). It is clear that findings from victimization surveys need to be interpreted very carefully, with the knowledge that apparent differences may reflect variations in definition as much as variations in the incidence of crime.

Local victim surveys with a narrower geographical focus have also made a significant contribution to knowledge about crime. They have highlighted the uneven distribution of risks of victimization, showing that certain age or social groups are more frequently subjected to crime than others. For example, by focusing on particular localities, local victim surveys in Britain (notably in Islington, Merseyside, Edinburgh and Rochdale) have shown the higher levels of crime prevailing in socially deprived areas and the disproportionate victimization of women, of minority ethnic groups and of the poor (Crawford et al., 1990; Kinsey, 1984; Mooney, 1993; Forrester et al., 1988). In particular, local victim surveys have revealed levels of violence and sexual crime against women higher than those revealed by mass victimization surveys, and certainly far higher than those indicated by police records (Hanmer and Saunders, 1984; Radford, 1987; Painter and Farrington, 1998). Indeed, the highest estimates of domestic violence have come from local victimization surveys, which probably reflects the problems of using narrow legal definitions in understanding sexual victimization and interviewers' insensitivity to women's personal and often painful experiences in earlier national crime surveys. For example, the first two British Crime Surveys revealed only one (unreported) case of attempted rape and seventeen and eighteen cases of sexual assault respectively in the 1983 and 1985 reports. By contrast, the first Islington Crime Survey (Jones et al., 1986) showed that one-third of the households in that area contained people who had been sexually assaulted during the previous year, and that younger women were very much more likely to be assault victims than women aged over 45.

Not all victim surveys are directed at individual victims. Commercial victimization surveys ask owners of retail and manufacturing premises about the crime they have experienced in a particular period of time. Such surveys can provide an alternative measure of crime and the extent to which particular premises are subject to repeat victimization. The Home Office carried out the first of these in Britain in 1993 and the second in 2002. The 2002 survey found that 75 per cent of retailers and 50 per cent of manufacturers experienced at least one crime in the previous year with the largest businesses (those with 50 or more employees) at greater risk (Home Office, 2005b). Overall, this kind of crime was lower in 2002 compared with 1993 which found that eight out of ten retailers and two-thirds of manufacturing premises experienced one or more of the crimes covered by the survey (Mirrlees-Black and Ross, 1995). It should be noted that some offences such as theft by staff and fraud are more difficult to detect and more likely to be under-represented.

Thinking positively about crime statistics

The critical perspective applied to crime statistics to this point perhaps suggests that the statistics provide more of an insight into official definitions of crime, crime recording and policing practice than into actual levels of unlawful activity. Thinking critically about crime statistics, though, also involves thinking about the potential they offer. For example, a major aim of the National Crime Reporting Standard introduced in 2002 has been to ensure that all incidents reported to the police are recorded – even if some are not subsequently classified as a crime and published as criminal statistics – in order to provide more accurate intelligence for local policing and for intervention by other agencies. While the statistics may not provide the reliable measures of crime that policy-makers and journalists, for instance, would wish for, they do play a central part in criminological research.

Criminologists and criminals

Generations of criminologists have tried to look beyond formal criminal statistics and to do their own research on criminal activity. In a much-quoted phrase, Robert E. Park, chair of the Department of Sociology at the University of Chicago in the 1920s, encouraged research students to 'go get the seat of your pants dirty in real research' – in short, to go and get acquainted first-hand with the social world around them.

While Western anthropologists at the time were still studying 'exotic' cultures in remote places, Park believed that anthropological methods could be used in Western urban research and that social scientists should study people in their everyday environments. He saw the city as a 'social laboratory' in which social processes and human interactions could be studied *in situ*. Park and his colleagues developed a distinctive approach to social research, social life and the study of deviance – 'the Chicago School'. Researchers in this tradition – which was extremely influential in shaping sociological criminology (as outlined in Chapter 5) – used a particular mix of mainly qualitative and ethnographic research methods. They aimed to capture the complexity of social life through interviews, the study of personal documents and, famously, observational methods. For real understanding, imaginative participation in the lives of others was required; empathy, as well as an acute eye, was the key (Bulmer, 1984).

An ethnographer participates in a given social setting, 'amid the action', for an extended period of time; makes regular observations of people and events in that setting; listens to people and engages in conversations; interviews informants about issues that cannot be observed directly by the researcher; collects documents about the group under study; and writes up a faithful representation of what they have discovered in a detailed account of their study. Major studies of crime and deviance carried out within the early Chicago School were Nels Anderson's *The Hobo: The Sociology of the Homeless Man* (1923), Frederic Thrasher's *The Gang* (1927), John Landesco's

Organized Crime in Chicago (1929), Clifford Shaw's *The Jack Roller* (1930) and Paul G. Cressey's *The Taxi-Dance Hall* (1932). Paul Cressey stated that his first objective 'was to give an unbiased and intimate picture of the social world of the typical taxi-dance hall' (a hall where customers paid to dance with young women). According to Cressey, and characteristic of an ethnographic approach:

> Observers were sent into the taxi-dance halls. They were instructed to mingle with the others and to become as much a part of this social world as ethically possible. . . . The investigators functioned as anonymous strangers and casual acquaintances . . . without encountering the inhibitions and resistance usually met in formal interviews.
>
> (Cressey, 1932: xxxiv)

In Britain, the organization Mass Observation conducted similar work and individual writers and journalists published accounts of their 'undercover' encounters. Ada Chesterton's *Women of the Underworld* (1928) and George Orwell's *Down and Out in London and Paris* (1933) are just two of many. Notably, this kind of work was not undertaken in earnest by academic sociologists or criminologists in Britain until the 1970s.

Ethnographic research in the United States lost its momentum from the 1930s with the development of more formalized sociological methodologies which tended to privilege more quantitative methods. After the Second World War, however, members of the 'Second Chicago School' such as Howard Becker and Erving Goffman (discussed below) gave it a new radical political edge which was taken further by Californian universities in the 1960s with their focus on countercultural, deviant and alternative groups. Some noted studies here include John Lofland's *Doomsday Cult* (1966), Marvin Scott's *The Racing Game* (1968), Jacqueline P. Wiseman's *Stations of the Lost* (1970), and Jack Douglas and Paul Rasmussen's *The Nude Beach* (1977). Adler and Adler (1998: xiii) summarize ethnographic research aims in this period:

> Free to go out and study those groups in close proximity, these ethnographers realized that the only sensible way to get information about hidden populations was to study them naturalistically. Disdaining the research endeavors that analyzed criminals as captured populations, these sociologists and criminologists went into bars, inside gangs, and into the inner sanctums of deviant populations to find out what constituted their realities.

Adler and Adler go on to argue that the late 1970s to the early 1990s were the 'Dark Ages' of ethnographic research. During this period, university ethics committees, cautious of the moral, ethical and legal implications of fieldwork on crime and deviance, inhibited ethnographic research.

Notably, this was much less the case in Britain where the 1970s saw a significant development of this kind of work with studies such as James Patrick's study of gang life in Glasgow (1973), Howard Parker's study of 'joy-riding' in the inner city (1974), Jason Ditton's study of fiddling and pilfering in a bakery (1977), Anne Campbell's study of violence among female gangs (1981, 1984) and Dick Hobbs's study of crime and policing in east London (1988), to name just a few.

Moral, ethical and legal issues

Ethnographic methods can sometimes (though by no means always) raise particular moral, ethical and legal difficulties. Researchers who are closely observing people involved in criminal behaviour have to decide where or whether to draw a line. Taken to its extreme, the logic of the criminological ethnography suggests that researchers should be prepared to engage in or witness criminal acts themselves. This view has been most strongly proposed by US sociological criminologists from the 1960s onwards. Ned Polsky wrote in his study of 'hustlers' that if a researcher were to

> study adult criminals in their natural settings, he must make the moral decision that in some ways he will break the law himself. He need not be a 'participant' observer and commit the criminal acts under study, yet he has to witness such acts or be taken into confidence about them and not blow the whistle.
>
> (Polsky, 1967: 133)

Soloway and Walters (1977) relate a situation in their study of heroin users in which the researcher was unwittingly involved in an armed robbery involving a car in which he was a passenger. James Inciardi inadvertently participated in a convenience store hold-up (1977).

More recently, cultural criminologist Jeff Ferrell, known for his work on US urban youth crime, has argued that 'For the dedicated field researcher who seeks to explore criminal subcultures and criminal dynamics, obeying the law may present as much of a problem as breaking it' (1998: 26). Drawing from Max Weber's notion of *verstehen*, Ferrell argues that to achieve criminological *verstehen* – that is, a deep appreciation of the lived experience of criminals and the situated meanings, emotions and logic of crime – researchers must be prepared to participate in the 'immediacy of crime' themselves.

If they are prepared to do so, however, they will need to make some ethical decisions about how far they are prepared to go, what criminal acts they are prepared to participate in and what criminal acts are inappropriate for study. They will also need to evaluate what responsibilities they might have to victims, to criminals, to those involved in crime control, to themselves and to their profession.

This kind of approach to criminological research has been critiqued from a number of quarters. Sociological researchers themselves have been divided on this issue. Lewis Yablonsky advised the 'applied sociologist' to 'proceed with caution' and to avoid 'becoming a tool' in illegal activity or 'reinforcing' criminal activity by observing rather than challenging it (1965: 71, 72). In the early 1970s, Kai Erikson attacked the covert research methods favoured by some of his colleagues as deceptive and unethical (Galliher, 1995: 175). Ferrell himself and his co-writer, Mark Hamm, warn researchers against 'thrill-seeking' for its own sake (1998: 7–8). Criminologists working on gender issues – around masculinities and femininities – have criticized this kind of work on the grounds that it can glamorize certain kinds of (male) crime and in doing so marginalize the study of other kinds of crime (see e.g. Scraton, 1990).

Codes of ethics

Most academic associations and research funding bodies have developed codes of professional ethics to promote 'good practice' in research. These, of course, apply to all kinds of research methods – not just ethnographic methods. The codes cover issues such as consent, confidentiality, access, transparency, risk assessment and data protection. Criminological associations such as the British Society for Criminology (BSC) and the International Society for Criminology (ISC) and sociological associations such as the American Sociological Association (ASA) publish these codes on their websites. Researchers at all levels – from undergraduates to professors to consultants – must now show that they have considered them in their research design.

These codes are certainly important as a way of protecting the interests of those taking part in research – those interviewed, surveyed, observed and counted – and in promoting professionalism amongst researchers. However, the problems with restrictive ethical codes highlighted by Ferrell and others in relation to ethnography are arguably relevant to many other areas of criminological and sociological research. Is a criminologist working within tight ethical codes still able to conduct effective research into 'closed' worlds of different kinds, such as the 'closed' worlds of child sexual abuse, people trafficking or corporate crime? Is it always possible or desirable for research aims to be 'transparent' and equally open to all parties? Could excessive risk assessment mean that researchers no longer take risks and, if so, what might be the effects of that? These kinds of questions are in part connected to the question of taking sides in criminological research.

Taking sides in criminological research

Becker and 'underdog sociology'

Many criminologists and sociologists have liberal leanings and a concern for inequality and injustice. Many want their research to be more than an academic exercise; they want it to contribute to social change. Debate about the sympathies of sociologists who study crime and deviance was fuelled by those working in the Chicago School of Sociology in the 1950s and 1960s – what is sometimes called the 'Second Chicago School' (discussed in Chapter 5). The School was characterized by a diverse range of perspectives, but a dominant one emerged – one that was critiqued as 'underdog sociology' (Gouldner, 1973). Prominent characters and studies here included Howard Becker's work on drug use, Erving Goffman's on asylums and Harold Finestone's on delinquency.

Howard Becker's 1966 presidential address to the Society for the Study of Social Problems, published in his famous essay 'Whose Side Are We On?' (1967), outlines their approach. Although it was published over four decades ago it is still debated in universities. As Martin Hammersley has argued, 'it continues to have relevance for us today, not least in posing fundamental questions that still need answering' (2001: 107).

Becker's point was that sociologists must take sides in their work since they cannot, by definition, be on all sides. Given this, sociologists should take the side of the subordinate party.

Since it was not possible 'to do research uncontaminated by personal and political sympathies', researchers should make these sympathies more explicit. For Becker, 'the question is not whether we should take sides, since we inevitably will, but rather whose side are we on' (1967: 239). By this he did not mean that researchers should reject impartiality, arguing that 'whatever side we are on, we must use our techniques impartially enough that a belief to which we are especially sympathetic could be proved untrue'.

Becker's position was closely connected to his wider and very influential concept of 'labelling'. Researchers should focus on the experiences of groups labelled as deviant by those in authority (who he also called 'moral entrepreneurs'). The experiences of 'deviant' groups were overshadowed because their 'right to be heard' and their 'credibility' was much weaker than that of those with the power to label, control and punish (1967: 241). It was the researcher's job to redress the balance and, in so doing, to challenge authority where necessary.

This view of criminological research has had its opponents both at the time and since. In a famous essay 'The Sociologist as Partisan' attacking Becker, Alvin Gouldner argued that

> the pull to the underdog's exotic difference takes the form of 'essays on quaintness'. The danger is, then, that such an identification with the underdog becomes the urban sociologist's equivalent of the anthropologist's (one-time) romantic appreciation of the noble savage.
>
> (1973: 37)

For Gouldner, Becker's approach 'expresses the satisfaction of the Great White Hunter who has barely risked the perils of the urban jungle to bring back an exotic specimen. It expresses the romanticism of the zoo curator who preeningly displays his rare specimens' (1973: 38). Gouldner argues that, in fact, the agenda of truly 'radical sociologists' should be to study the 'overdog', the 'power elites' who shape the legal systems, law enforcement and penal practice, rather than the underdog oppressed by them.

Ohlin and policy-forming sociology

A very different point of view emerged through the work of another scholar connected to the Chicago School, Lloyd Ohlin. Ohlin was a practitioner as well as an academic (Galliher, 1995). His work was shaped by his experiences working on parole boards and as a research sociologist in the correctional system. His methods were quite distinct from Becker's, with more of a focus on surveys than on ethnography. His analysis of deviance was also distinct (as discussed in Chapter 5). The well-known study he completed with Richard A. Cloward in 1960, *Delinquency and Opportunity*, argued that delinquency was the product of blocked opportunities connected to poverty, education and employment (and, by extension, less connected to labelling). According to this view, it was still a researcher's job to challenge authorities and policy-makers but to do so by playing an active part in the policy-making process. Researchers should use the kinds of research methods that would generate the kind of data to provide the kind of evidence that policy-makers could not ignore.

Many criminologists have adopted this stance, working with campaigners and reformers as well as policy-makers. They have been active in penal reform movements, in setting up rape crisis centres and hostels for victims of domestic violence and sexual abuse, and in challenging racism within the criminal justice system (see Knepper, 2007; Ryan and Ward, 1992; Holdaway and Rock, 1998). The emergence of **public criminology** in recent years (see Chapter 22) has given a new emphasis to this kind of public-oriented work.

These two broad concerns – to critique authorities and to work with authorities – have shaped sociological criminology from the 1960s onwards. They have helped create particular kinds of research methods – some that produce data more easily incorporated into public policy and some less so. They have also informed theoretical debates around conflict criminology, radical criminology, left idealism and cultural criminology – discussed across several chapters here. Of course, it could certainly be argued that these two broad concerns are not mutually exclusive. Nevertheless, the question 'whose side are we on' remains highly relevant.

BOX 3.3 Research design

As a student, you will probably be asked to conduct your own criminological research project of some kind at some point. Here are some factors you will need to consider in your **research design**:

Research questions

- What do you want to find out and why is it relevant?
- What are your basic theoretical questions?
- What are your corresponding empirical questions?
- How will you turn your theoretical questions into specific researchable questions?

Research methods and data analysis

- What kinds of research methods and data analysis strategies have you chosen to use and why?
- Can you use the project to develop new practical skills?
- If you're using more than one method or mixed methods how will you draw these together?

Existing research and literature review

- How has your project been shaped by your wider reading?
- How has existing research dealt with the topic you want to study?

Sampling

- How will you select your research materials or respondents?
- Do you want a random sample or a more structured/stratified sample?
- What will shape your decisions here?

Access

- How will you contact and negotiate access to the people or materials you want to research?
- Who are the **gatekeepers** in your project?
- Do you have a back-up plan if things don't work out?

Ethics

- What ethical considerations and potential risks do you need to consider?

Timeframe

- How much time have you allowed for each research task?
- How can you ensure that you will complete the project by your deadline?

See the website for practical exercises related to this box.

Summary

1. There is no distinctive methodology or set of methods used in criminological research. Criminologists' views on the purpose of crime research differ radically – both between disciplines and within disciplines (like Sociology). This is linked to the fact that the needs of offenders, victims and policy-makers are arguably different.
2. Official criminal statistics should always be treated carefully.
3. There are many sources of criminological data – students should try to look beyond their own national criminal justice system where possible.
4. Criminological researchers, like all researchers, need to have a workable research design and give careful consideration to moral, legal and ethical issues.

Critical thinking questions

1 What does it mean to 'think critically' about crime statistics?
2 Whose interests should be served by criminological research?
3 When criminological researchers 'take sides', are they 'biased' in their work?

Further study

Bushway, S. and Weisburd, D. (2005) *Quantitative Methods in Criminology*, Aldershot: Ashgate. A useful and accessible overview of quantitative approaches.

Cromwell, P. F. (ed.) (2003) *In Their Own Words: Criminals on Crime*, 3rd edn, Los Angeles, CA: Roxbury. Fieldwork accounts of crime uniquely from the prospects of offenders.

Ferrell, J. and Hamm, M. (eds) (1998) *Ethnography at the Edge: Crime, Deviance, and Field Research*, Boston, MA: Northeastern University Press. A valuable collection of essays that provides methodological, political and theoretical reflections of fieldwork on crime and deviance.

King, R. D. and Wincup, E. (eds) (2007) *Doing Research on Crime and Justice*, 2nd edn, Oxford: Oxford University Press. A comprehensive collection of essays on the practicalities and problems of doing criminological research.

More information

Statistics Canada
http://www.statcan.ca/start.html
Produces national statistics on the population, resources, economy, society and culture of Canada.

Federal Bureau of Investigation
http://www.fbi.gov/homepage.htm
The FBI is the principal investigative arm of the United States Department of Justice.

FBI: Hate Crime Data Collection Guidelines
http://www.fbi.gov/ucr/hatecrime.pdf
FBI: National Incident-Based Reporting System on Hate Crimes

Australian Bureau of Statistics
http://www.abs.gov.au/
The Australian Bureau of Statistics is Australia's official statistical organization.

The Home Office
http://www.homeoffice.gov.uk/

The Home Office is the government department responsible for internal affairs in England and Wales.

The Scottish Executive
http://www.scotland.gov.uk
The Scottish Executive is the devolved government for Scotland. It is responsible for most of the issues of day-to-day concern to the people of Scotland, including health, education, justice, rural affairs, and transport.

UK Data Archive at the University of Essex
http://www.data-archive.ac.uk/
The UKDA provides resource discovery and support for secondary use of quantitative and qualitative data in research.

The Question Bank
http://qb.soc.surrey.ac.uk/
Questions from the British Crime Survey can be read online at the Question Bank, University of Surrey.

Dmoz Open Directory Project
http://www.dmoz.org/Society/Issues/Crime_and_Justice/Prisons/Organizations/
This section of this large web directory lists some of the many voluntary organizations working in the criminal justice field.

United Nations Office on Drugs and Crime
http://www.unodc.org/unodc/index.html

United Nations Interregional Crime and Justice Research Institute
http://www.unicri.it/

EC Europa – Justice and Home Affairs
http://ec.europa.eu/justice_home/fsj/crime/fsj_crime_intro_en.htm

Association of Southeast Asian Nations
http://www.aseansec.org/

part 2

Thinking about Crime

In this part, we outline a wider range of different ways of thinking about crime – from some of the earliest 'scientific traditions' to more recent developments that link crime to conditions of late modern society. Many key terms and ideas are introduced along the way.

chapter 4

The Enlightenment and Early Traditions

Key issues

- What traditions emerged from the Enlightenment?
- What is the classical inheritance?
- What is the positivist inheritance?
- What are their key differences?

Introduction

The received history of criminology as a discipline of study often starts with influential figures and their links with landmark theoretical perspectives such as **classicism** in the eighteenth century and **positivism** in the nineteenth. Our task in this chapter is to provide an introductory account of criminology's history which begins with the writings of criminal law reformers in the eighteenth century, particularly in the work of Cesare Beccaria and Jeremy Bentham. These writers draw upon **Enlightenment** ideals and characterize the offender as a rational, free-willed actor who engages in crime in a calculated way and is responsive to the deterrent penalties that these reformers advocated. This classical school of criminology is then challenged in the late nineteenth century by writers of the positivist school, which typically includes the writings of Cesare Lombroso, Enrico Ferri and Francis Galton, who adopted a more empirical, scientific approach to the subject and investigated the criminal using the techniques of psychiatry, anthropology and other new human sciences. The positivist school claimed to have discovered the existence of 'criminal types' whose behaviour was determined rather than chosen, and for whom treatment rather than punishment was appropriate. Subsequent work has refuted many early positivist claims but the project of a 'scientific criminology' continues to this day.

A caution

One of the immediate problems with this characterization is that it implies that people only began to think about crime in a 'sensible' fashion from the middle of the eighteenth century. This is seriously misleading. As Chapter 2 showed, historians of crime have traced changing views of crime going back much further than this. Further, for sociologists, breaking social rules is an intrinsic element of social organization itself. In other words, crime is an inevitable feature of society, a point made by Durkheim in the late nineteenth century (see Chapter 5). Discourses on crime and criminals are as old as human civilization. For instance, there are various propositions about crime put forward in the writings of ancient and medieval philosophers, the theologies of Protestant and Catholic reformers and early modern legal thought. In fact, what we need to recognize is that there are a variety of ways of 'thinking about crime', and that criminology is only one version among others.

It should also be emphasized that this is not to say that criminology is our modern response to a timeless and unchanging set of questions, not least because in earlier times the mental structures and cultural sensibilities that governed thinking about the subject were very different from our own. For instance, if we take Christianity, it is clear that this system of thought did not separate out the lawbreaker as different or abnormal, but rather understood his or her behaviour as a manifestation of universal human depravity and the sinful state of all humankind. This is clearly a very different way of thinking about crime from that espoused by much criminology.

Nevertheless, traditional accounts of crime, whether these be Christian or otherwise, are not entirely remote from present thinking about the subject. For instance, if we look at the diverse literature of the early modern period, which includes criminal biographies and broadsheets, accounts of the Renaissance underworld, Tudor rogue pamphlets, Elizabethan dramas and Jacobean city comedies, we can see rudimentary versions of our present understandings of how one becomes deviant. Perhaps the most famous example is Daniel Defoe's novel *Moll Flanders*, which was published in 1722. On one level, it is a Puritan tale of sin and repentance, but it is nevertheless rich in the features with which modern criminological theories are cast. For instance, the story tells us how the offender fell in with bad company, was sorely tried by temptation, became too fond of drink, lost her reputation and was driven to crime by lust – but if we use a more neutral language to tell the tale, then we are not that far removed from contemporary criminology.

So when we think of the seventeenth- and eighteenth-century understandings of crime, what becomes clear is that crime was regarded as omnipresent temptation to which all humankind was vulnerable, but when it became a question of why some succumbed and others resisted, the explanations often trailed off into the unknowable, resorting to fate, or the will of God.

There are two points that need to be emphasized in these opening remarks. The first is that we need to be cautious of histories of criminology that begin with classicism and suggest that no one had seriously thought about crime before, even though we are going to do just that! The second is that other ways of thinking about crime did not disappear with the coming of the modern, scientific age. In fact, it is more accurate to say that criminology operates in a culture that combines many (traditional and scientific) modes of thought and action. In fact, these intuitive and instinctive understandings are often still more persuasive, for example in popular culture, than criminological research.

Enlightenment thinking about crime

It may be useful to start our understanding of recent ways of thinking about crime through a simple contrast between a public execution, staged as a spectacle, in the mid-eighteenth century and a prison timetable in the early nineteenth. The example is given in the opening pages of Michel Foucault's *Discipline and Punish: The Birth of the Prison* (1977) – a classic study to which we return later. In a long paragraph, he describes an execution in France in 1757:

> on a scaffold that will be erected [at the Place de Grève], the flesh will be torn from his breasts, arms, thighs and calves with red hot pincer, his right hand . . . burnt with sulphur, and, on those places where the flesh will be torn away, poured molten lead, boiling oil, burning resin, wax and sulphur melted together and then his body drawn and quartered by four horses and his limbs and body consumed by fire, reduced to ashes and thrown to the winds.
>
> (Foucault, 1977: 3)

This passage is followed by another long description, this time of a timetable. It is some eighty years on:

> Art. 17. The prisoners' day will begin at six in the morning in winter and at five in the summer . . . they will work for nine hours a day. . . . Art. 18. Rising. At the first drum-roll, the prisoners must rise and dress in silence . . . at the second drum-roll, they must be dressed and make their beds. At the third, they must line up and proceed to the chapel for morning prayer. . . . Art. 19. The prayers are conducted by the chaplain and followed by a moral or religious reading. This exercise must not last more than half an hour.
>
> (Foucault, 1977: 6)

The differences in systems of control are clearly illustrated. In the striking opening pages, Foucault compares the earlier forms of brutal and chaotic punishment on *the body* with the more recent forms of *surveillance and imprisonment*, which are intensely rule governed. What we are seeing here is a shift from an understanding of crime based on 'non-rational' thinking to one based upon the principles of Enlightenment thinking.

The French *philosophes* – an elite group of eighteenth-century radical thinkers – were the cornerstone of such thinking, highlighting the importance of rationality. In matters of crime, they marked a distinctive move away from systems that were capricious and 'barbaric' to systems that were to become more and more rational, predictable and disciplining (as we see in many chapters throughout this book). They were a 'solid, respectable clan of revolutionaries' (Gay, 1973: 9), and included Montesquieu, Rousseau and Voltaire. Such thinking signposted the arrival of the 'modern world'. Sociologist Peter Hamilton (1996) has suggested ten hallmarks of the Enlightenment mind:

- Reason became a key way of organizing knowledge.
- Empiricism – facts that can be apprehended through the senses.
- Science – linked especially to experimental scientific revolution.
- Universalism – especially the search for general laws.
- Progress – the idea that 'the human condition' can be improved.
- Individualism – the starting point for all knowledge.
- Toleration – the view that beliefs of other nations and groups are not inherently inferior to European Christianity.
- Freedom.
- The idea of the uniformity of human nature.
- Secularism – often opposed to the Church.

The classical tradition in criminology

Enlightenment thinking was the cornerstone of the classical approach to crime. It aimed to introduce a much more rational and fair system for organizing punishments and control. It had much less of a focus on the criminal per se and it had little concern with establishing the causes of crime. In general, its concern was to establish a more just social order.

Cesare Beccaria – 'the Rousseau of the Italians' (Beirne, 1993: 14) – is generally seen, at least symbolically, as the founder of this movement. He was born in Milan, Italy, in 1738. A humanist, he wanted more than anything to see the reform of the irrationality and unfairness of the judicial system that had existed for centuries (including the abolition of torture and capital punishment). His work draws freely from:

- Social contract theory – the theory of how imaginary individuals come together to make a society work (exemplified in the work of Jean-Jacques Rousseau).
- The view that human beings have '**free will**' – human actions are not simply determined by inside or outside 'forces' but can be seen as matters of free decisions.
- The idea of punishment as **deterrent** – rational beings will choose not to commit crimes if the punishment fits the crime.
- Utilitarianism – laws useful to the greatest number should be observed. Jeremy Bentham argued that their violation would open the door to anarchy.
- Secularism – Beccaria wanted to build a humanist theory that avoided ideas of God's law, revelation or natural justice and that focused on the living, sentient human being, subject to pains and pleasures. He wanted law to be made by human beings, and rational.

At the heart of classic thought were ideas on the nature of punishment (see the more recent development of these ideas in Chapter 15). Punishments could deter only if they were 'proportional' to the crime. Proportionality means (1) that the severity of punishments corresponds to the severity of the harm done by the crime, so that more serious crimes receive more serious punishments; and (2) that the type of punishment resembles the crime, so that others in society can best associate the punishment with the crime. Punishment must be essentially public, prompt, necessary, the least possible in the given circumstances, proportionate to the crimes and dictated by the laws.

Such ideas start to be developed in Beccaria's *Dei delitti e delle pene* (An Essay on Crimes and Punishments) of July 1764. This is one of the classics of Enlightenment thinking and early modern penology. Box 4.1 shows the range of themes he raised in this short but influential book.

BOX 4.1 Cesare Beccaria's *Essay on Crimes and Punishments*

This key text of classical thinking is a very short book devoting brief chapters to such topics as:

- Of the origins of punishments
- Of the right to punish
- Of the proportion between crimes and punishments
- Of estimating the degree of crimes
- Of the divisions of crime
- Of crimes which disturb the public tranquillity
- Of torture
- Of pecuniary punishments
- Of the advantage of immediate punishments
- Of the punishment of nobles
- Of robbery
- Of banishment
- Of the punishment of death
- Of suicide
- Of smuggling
- Of bankrupts
- Of the sciences
- Of education

Plate 4.1 Cesare Beccaria (1738–94), Italian legal theorist and political economist.

Source: Mary Evans Picture Library.

Here are some of his views for discussion:

> By justice I understand nothing more than that bond which is necessary to keep the interests of individuals united; without which, men would return to their original state of barbarity. All punishments, which exceed the necessity of preserving this bond, are in their nature unjust.

(chapter 2)

A scale of crimes may be formed of which the first degree should consist of those which immediately tend to the dissolution of society and the last of the smallest possible injustice done to a private member of that society.

(chapter 6)

A punishment may not be an act of violence, of one, or of many against a private member of society; it should be public; immediate and necessary; the least possible in the case given; proportioned to the crime; and determined by the laws.

(chapter 47)

Classical ideas may also be found in the work of the English utilitarian philosopher and penal reformer Jeremy Bentham (1748–1832). Building a moral calculus and arguing for the greatest happiness of the greatest number, he felt that punishments should be calculated to inflict pain in direct proportion to the damage done to the public interest. One of his ideas was the concept of prison design. He argued for a prison with a tower at the centre and a periphery building composed of cells from which every inmate could be observed (Plate 4.2). The cells would all have windows that would enable surveillance by prison guards. Whereas older prisons kept indiscriminate groups of people together in large, un-monitored cells, Bentham's principles were ones of visibility and inspection. Although Bentham's prison was never built, his views did encourage an increasingly rational system of penality in which prisons took on a new character (Bozovic, 1995).

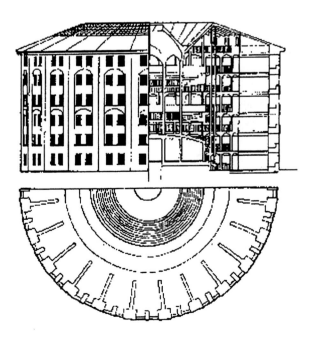

Plate 4.2 The Panopticon of Jeremy Bentham.
Source: After Barton and Barton (1993: 139).

thinking about crime

BOX 4.2 Henry Fielding: Enlightenment as experiment?

US experimental criminologist Lawrence Sherman argues (2005: 120) that 'Criminology did not begin in a Milanese salon among the group of aristocrats who helped Beccaria formulate and publish his epigrams . . . but more than a decade earlier in a London magistrate's courtroom full of gin-soaked robbery defendants.' Henry Fielding used his experiences as a magistrate at the Bow Street Court as the basis of his 1751 treatise, 'An enquiry into the causes of the late increase of robbers, etc, with some proposals for remedying this growing evil'. The treatise identified the 1750s gin craze as the cause of the crime wave and looked for alternatives to hanging as a response to this. Fielding's alternatives – a series of measures to prevent crime being committed in the first place – were arguably as dramatic as Bentham's panopticon proposal or Beccaria's proposal to calibrate punishments. These preventive measures included increasing the price of gin (through higher taxation), regulating gambling and providing low-cost housing and food for the very poor. He also began to call for a system of 'socialized' justice where a new state-funded police force, rather than crime victims, would be responsible for apprehending criminals. In 1753, Fielding was asked by the government to test out some of these measures: the result was the Bow Street Runners, forerunners of the modern police. Sherman claims this was 'a turning point in the English **paradigm** of justice' as it had demonstrated the 'failure of relying solely on the severity of punishment' to contain crime. This, we might say, was Enlightenment in practice. Fielding's **'experimental criminology'** plays as important a part in the history of the discipline as Beccaria's more well-known analytic criminology.

Plate 4.3 Henry Fielding.

Source: Mary Evans Picture Library.

Back to justice: some recent classical developments

It is important to realize that just as ideas never appear 'out of the blue' but emerge from historical change, so too do ideas rarely simply 'vanish'. They become modified, often being worked into new languages. This is very much true of classicism, which is a key to the justice system today. As we see in more detail in Chapter 15, in the latter years of the twentieth century there was a considerable revival of interest in classical thought.

In the early 1970s, the debate over what constitutes good sentencing policy was reopened. What is a just sentence? The 'Back to Justice' model suggested by Von Hirsch and his colleagues claimed that 'The severity of punishment should be commensurate with the seriousness of the wrong' (Von Hirsch, 1976: 66). They argued that:

1   The degree of likelihood that the offender might return to crime should be irrelevant to the choice of sentence. He should be sentenced on what he has done.
2   Indeterminate sentences should be abolished. Particular crimes merit particular punishments, and offenders should know what they will get.
3   Sentencing discretion should be sharply reduced. A system of standardized penalties should be introduced.
4   Imprisonment should be limited to serious offences – usually crimes leading to serious harm.
5   Milder penalties should not claim to rehabilitate, but simply be less severe punishments (Von Hirsch, 1976).

Problems with the classical model

■   The classical model presents an overly rational vision of human nature, arguing that people behave in a purely self-interested and 'free' fashion. If they can see they will be punished, they will be deterred; if they think they can get away with crime, they will. It is a model that haunts social science and it is too simple.
■   Unlike positivism, it views committing crime as making a free choice; but we may be left wondering just how really free crime is.
■   It assumes that societies work in fair and just ways, whereas often it is not possible to have justice and fairness in societies that are themselves organized in ways that are neither just nor fair. You cannot easily have 'justice in an unjust society'.

The positivist movement

The criminal type and Lombroso

Writing in the late nineteenth century, Cesare Lombroso is usually seen as the founder of modern criminology, and certainly achieved much fame or notoriety in the closing years of the twentieth century. (He is mentioned, for example, in the Sherlock Holmes and Dracula novels popular at the time.) For Lombroso, many criminals (not all) were atavistic throwbacks to an earlier form of species on the evolutionary scale. These stigmata could be found in all kinds of anomalies of the body. Many criminals, he said, may be found to have a distinctive physique: low foreheads, prominent jaws and cheekbones, protruding ears, excessive hairiness and unusually long arms that, taken together, cause them to resemble the ape-like ancestors of human beings. He is often seen as inventing the idea of the criminal body (although he was not actually the first – ideas germinate less sharply than this), which he introduced in 1876 in his book *L'uomo delinquente* (The Criminal Man), which went through five editions. (No English translation has been published, but see Lombroso-Ferrero, 1911.) In this study, he observed the physical characteristics of Italian prisoners and compared them to Italian soldiers – contrasting such items as their heads, body, arms and skin. One was the brigand Vilella, whom he studied through a post-mortem examination. In a famous passage, he remarked:

> This was not merely an idea, but a revelation. At the sight of that skull, I seemed to see all of a sudden, lighted up as a vast plain under a flaming sky, the problem of the nature of the criminal – an atavistic being who reproduces in his person the ferocious instincts of primitive humanity and the inferior animals. Thus were explained anatomically the enormous jaws, high cheek-bones, prominent superciliary arches, solitary lines in the palms, extreme size of orbits, handle-shaped or sessile ears found in criminals, savages and apes, insensibility to pain, extremely acute sight, tattooing, excessive idleness, love of orgies, and the irresistible craving for evil for its own sake, the desire not only to extinguish life in the victim, but to mutilate the corpse, tear its flesh, and drink its blood.
>
> (quoted in Wolfgang, 1960: 248)

But Lombroso's work was flawed. Had he looked beyond prison walls, he would have realized that the physical features he attributed exclusively to prisoners were actually found throughout the entire population. We now know that no physical attributes, of the kind described by Lombroso, simply distinguish criminals from non-criminals (Goring, 1913/1972). Yet although his work had many failings, he is usually credited with turning interest away from simply the *criminal law* to an understanding of the *criminal type*.

There were several others who were engaged with Lombroso in the search for the causes of crime, such as Raffaele Garofalo (1852–1934) and Enrico Ferri (1856–1928). Together they came to be identified as the Italian School. Ferri provided a view of the causes of crime under three main heads: the anthropological, telluric (physical) and social. He was against the view that any one factor could cause crime, and saw instead the need to take factors in combination. Lombroso's great contribution was to highlight the biological (or anthropological as it was often called in those days) – even though he recognized other factors. But for Ferri,

> [E]very crime from the smallest to the most atrocious, is the result of the interaction of these three causes, the anthropological condition of the criminal, the telluric [literally, 'pertaining to the earth'] environment in which he is living, and the social environment in which he is born, living and operating.
>
> (quoted in Muncie et al., 2003: 36)

The anthropological component highlighted heredity and constitution; the physical factors highlighted issues such as climate and season; and the social element stressed population, religion, education and the like. Ferri classified criminals under five basic types: criminal lunatics, the born incorrigibles, habitual criminals, occasional criminals and emotional criminals.

Researchers on crime began to examine its link with such factors as 'mental subnormality', IQ, twins, criminal families and body build. Chapter 2 discusses elements of this work in relation to histories of the criminal 'underclass'. Along the way, this meant introducing a range of 'scientific tools of measurement' – from IQ tests to criminal photography. Chapter 5 discusses how positivist approaches emphasizing the physical causes of crime influenced early twentieth-century studies of female criminality.

Statistical regularity and positivism

Another early 'scientist of crime' was Quételet (1796–1874), who was a leading statistician of the nineteenth century. Developing a theory of social mechanics, he believed that statistical research could outline the average features of a population, and that it would hence be possible to discover the underlying regularities for both normal and abnormal behaviour. In 1835 he published *Treatise on Man, and the Development of His Faculties*, in which he depicted 'average man', against which abnormal man could be measured. (He found the average man through bell-shaped curves.) Crime, then, could be studied systematically.

The publication of early criminal statistics in France (in the 1820s) meant that regularities could be spotted in such features as sex, age, climate and economic conditions. Likewise, the French sociologist Émile Durkheim (1858–1917) could study suicide rates (at that time suicide was a crime in most countries) to show that suicides also had a very definite pattern. By examining records in and around his native France, he could show that some categories of people were more likely than others to choose to take their own lives. He found, for instance, that men, Protestants, wealthy people and the unmarried each had significantly higher suicide rates than women, Roman Catholics and Jews, the poor, and married people. Durkheim deduced that these differences corresponded to people's degree of *social integration*. Low suicide rates characterized categories of people with strong social ties; high suicide rates were found among those who were more socially isolated and individualistic. In the male-dominated societies, men certainly had more autonomy than women; individualistic Protestants were more prone to suicide than Catholics and Jews, whose rituals foster stronger social ties; the wealthy clearly have much more freedom of action than the poor but, once again, at the cost of a higher suicide rate. Finally, single people, with weaker social ties than married people, are also at greater risk of suicide.

The positivist inheritance

Positivism was one of the earliest strands of criminological thinking and it is still very much alive today. A major account of positivistic criminology has been provided by the sociologist David

BOX 4.3 Cesare Lombroso (1836–1909) and his photos of criminal types

The man

Born in 1836 in Verona, perhaps more than anyone else, Cesare Lombroso is 'the founder of modern criminology'. An Italian physician who worked in prisons, he was director of a mental asylum in Pesaro, Italy, and professor of psychiatry and criminal anthropology at the University of Turin. Writing at a time when there was a widespread interest in Social Darwinism and eugenics, he drew his ideas in part from phrenology, as well as from craniology and physiognomy – which look at the structures of the brain and the mind. He was an early criminal anthropologist, founder of the positivist school of penal jurisprudence. Lombroso was a socialist, and much of his work advocated more humane treatment of criminals. He was an early advocate of the indeterminate sentence, as well as the reduction of the death penalty.

Plate 4.4 Cesare Lombroso (1836–1909), Italian physician and criminologist. Lombroso is considered the founder of modern criminology, though many dispute this.

Source: Elliot and Fry in *Nos Maîtres*, Mary Evans Picture Library.

Reading Lombroso: some extracts from his writing capture his concerns

Spot the criminal through differences

> . . . deviation in head size and shape from the type common to the race and religion from which the criminal came; asymmetry of the face; excessive dimensions of the jaw and cheek bones; eye defects and peculiarities; ears of unusual size, or occasionally very small, or standing out from the head as do those of the chimpanzee; nose twisted, upturned, or flattened in thieves, or swollen nostrils; lips fleshy, swollen, and protruding; pouches in the cheek like those of some animals; peculiarities of the palate, such as a large central ridge, a series of cavities and protuberances such as are found in some reptiles, and a cleft palate; abnormal dentition; chin receding, or excessively long or short and flat, as in apes; abundance, variety, and precocity of wrinkles, anomalies of the hair, marked by characteristics of the hair of the opposite sex; defects of the thorax, such as too many or too few ribs, or supernumerary nipples; inversion of sex characteristics in the pelvic organs; excessive length of arms; supernumerary fingers and toes; imbalance of the hemispheres of the brain (asymmetry of cranium).

(Wolfgang, 1960: 250)

Types of criminal by physical characteristics

Fig. 31. Donne omicide - Omicida.   Fig. 34. Tipo infantile (romano) - Omicida (d'anni 14).

Fig. 32. Donne omicide - Parricida.   Fig. 35. Tipo infantile (imbecille) - Assassino (d'anni 18).

Fig. 33. Donne omicide - Conjugicida.   Fig. 36. Tipo infantile (arr. di sviluppo) - Assassino (d'anni 20).

TYPES DE CRIMINELS MEURTRIERS (Voir *Explication des planches*).

Plate 4.5 Criminal types – an example from Lombroso's study that claimed to relate physiognomy to criminal nature. This plate shows young and female murderers. Lombroso's research involved the measurement and frequently the photographing of body and facial types.

Source: Reproduced in Lombroso, *L'Homme criminel*, plate lxiv, Mary Evans Picture Library.

. . . as a rule, the *thieves* have mobile hands and face; small, mobile, restless, frequently oblique eyes; thick and closely set eyebrows; flat or twisted nose; thin beard; hair frequently thin; almost receding brow. Both they and those committing *rape* frequently have ears *ad ansa*. The latter often have brilliant eyes, delicate faces, tumid lips and eyelids; as a rule they are of delicate structure and sometimes hunchbacked. . . . The *habitual homicides* have cold, glassy eyes, immobile and sometimes sanguine and inflamed; the nose, always large, is frequently aquiline or, rather, hooked; the jaws are strong, the cheekbones large, the hair curly, dark and abundant; the beard is frequently thin, the canine teeth well developed and the lips delicate; frequent nystagmus and unilateral facial contractions, with a baring of the teeth and a contraction of the jaws. . . . In general *all criminals* have ears *ad ansa*, abundant hair, thin beard, prominent fronat sinuses, protruding chin, large cheekbones, etc.

(Wolfgang, 1960: 251)

Matza (1964). In a brilliant opening chapter of his book *Delinquency and Drift*, he summarized it as having three major characteristics:

1   The criminal is a specific type of person. Thus, criminology started to draw up long classification systems of different kinds of offenders. Lombroso, for example, identified not just the born criminal, but also the emotional criminal, the morally insane criminal and the masked epileptic criminal.

2   The criminal differs from others. The focus is upon finding the different characteristics – which may range from body parts (e.g. the size and weight of skulls), body types (as in Sheldon's work) and on to personality types (as with the work of Walter Reckless). Long lists of ways in which offenders differ from non-offenders can be drawn up. This process was

advanced greatly by new technologies such as photography (which could record bodily and facial features) in the nineteenth century and fingerprint testing in the twentieth century. Most recently, chromosome typing (the XYY chromosome is said to be linked to violent offences) and DNA testing have become the focus of attention. The police now make regular use of 'criminal profiling'.

3   The criminal is 'driven' into crime through factors outside his or her control. Positivism seeks out explanations for criminal conduct as in some way out of the control of the criminal who perpetrates criminal acts. Thus, crime is caused by 'feeble-mindedness', 'atavistic regression', 'unsuccessful socialization' or 'XYY chromosomes'. Crime, says Matza, is not a free choice but is determined. Positivism is a deterministic theory.

These features can still be found in a great deal of criminological research. One major strand of such work, linked to the celebrated criminologists Sheldon and Eleanor Glueck, has been identified as the multi-factor approach. This entails sampling a large number of delinquents or criminals to see whether they present characteristics in common that are found less frequently in a general population. Often these are prospective longitudinal surveys.

The criminal career approach brings together a number of these key factors and shows how they develop over time. It looks at such issues as why people start offending (onset), why they continue (persistence), whether their behaviour becomes more serious or not (escalation) and why people stop (desistance). The major risk factors ('factors that increase the risk of occurrence of events such as the onset, frequency, persistence, duration of offending'; Farrington, 1997) include impulsivity (now often called HIA – hyperactivity impulsivity attention deficit), low intelligence, poor parental supervision, broken homes, convicted parents, socio-economic deprivation, poor schooling and 'situational factors' (Farrington, 1997). These factors are highly correlated with crime.

BOX 4.4 Summary of some biologically based theories of crime

William Sheldon's Theory of Somatotypes (based on early work of Kretschmer) links crime to body types:

- endomorph – chubby, round, not criminal
- ectomorph – skinny, frail, not criminal
- mesomorph – heavy, muscular, criminal.

Kallikak and Juke families. The descendants of Martin Kallikak's illegitimate son exhibited a remarkably high degree of criminality across several generations, and the descendants of Ada Juke included seven murderers, sixty thieves, fifty prostitutes, etc. These two cases contributed to an early view that crime and deviance were inheritable.

Twin studies compare criminality of identical twins with criminality of fraternal twins. Generally, twin studies have shown higher rate of similar criminality (concordance) (60–70 per cent) for identical twins than for fraternal twins (15–30 per cent), although some say that these percentages are exaggerated. This provides some support for the idea that genetics may play a role in criminal behaviour. Perhaps the most famous case of twin studies is to be found in the work of Karl Christiansen, who examined 3,586 sets of twins born between 1881 and 1910. In 35 per cent of the cases, both identical twins would have criminal convictions. In only 12 per cent of fraternal twins would both have criminal convictions, which provides some support for a genetic link.

XYY chromosome research. This became a particular controversy in the 1960s. 'Normal' males have an XY sex-chromosome configuration, but some males (1 in 1,000) have an extra Y chromosome, giving them an XYY configuration. Research in the 1960s found a slight suggestion of an association between XYY configuration and criminality. This led to the idea of the 'super-male criminal', full of aggression. More recent studies have refuted the idea that having the XYY configuration 'causes' men to commit crimes.

Biochemical factors. Serotonin deficiency may be related to impulsiveness, crime and violence. An imbalance involving dopamine, noradrenaline and serotonin may be conducive to deviant/criminal behaviour.

Brain dysfunction. There is some evidence that neurological defects are more common among excessively violent people than among the general population. EEG readings on some adult criminals are similar to those of normal people at younger ages (brain immaturity).

Also, old concerns like learning disabilities and new problems like attention deficit hyperactivity disorder (ADHD) may be linked to crime.

Potential criticisms

- Crime is probably the result of a combination of factors, including social, psychological, political, economic and geographic ones – rarely, if ever, biology on its own.
- Unrepresentative samples are very common in such research. Generally, such research raises severe methodological problems (how do you separate out biological from social factors?).
- Causation is often muddled with correlation: an association between bodily features and criminal behaviour does not mean that biology caused the behaviour.
- Sometimes there may be a labelling effect: society reacts to certain types, and this may generate response that are criminal.
- In general, the evidence for such research is at best limited. See Fishbein (2000).

For more on biological perspectives in criminology, see Fishbein (2000).

Problems with the positivist model

■ In contrast with the classical model, the positivist model often assumes that people are driven into crime by forces largely out of their control. It may hence argue that people are not free and not responsible for their actions. It is too prone to deny the meanings of crime in people's lives. In some ways it is a mirror image of the classical position, and what is required is a way of approaching crime which allows for both choice and **determinism**.

■ It exaggerates the differences between criminals and non-criminals. By focusing upon what makes a criminal different from the population, it tends to suggest an image of the normal and the abnormal, of them and us. In fact, many criminals overlap with the population – are indeed just like you and me; indeed are you and me.

■ It has a tendency to neglect the workings of the penal system: the law or its aspects by which crimes come to be invented and/or regulated. Crimes are assumed as givens, as unproblematic categories.

Tensions between positivism and classical thinking

Both the classical tradition and positivism come in many different varieties, and although they have their roots in the past, they are both still alive and well in the criminal justice system today. As you read this book, you may like to identify aspects of the reappearance of each. They have been extremely influential and can be seen as master moulds that organize many ways of thinking about crime. Table 4.1 suggests some of the key contrasts to be clear about.

Table 4.1 Comparison of classical and positivist schools

Issue	Classical school	Positivist school
Roots	Enlightenment	Modern science
Focus	Criminal administration	Criminal person
Approach	Philosophical – social contract theory, utilitarianism	Scientific, positivism Laws Measurements
View of human nature	Free will Hedonism Morally responsible for own behaviour	Determined by biological, psychological, and social environment Moral responsibility obscured
View of justice system	Social contract; exists to protect society; due process and concern with civil rights; restrictions on system Definite sentence	Scientific treatment system to cure pathologies and rehabilitate offenders; no concern with civil rights Indefinite sentence
Form of law	Statutory law; exact specification of illegal acts and sanctions	Social law; illegal acts defined by analogy; scientific experts determine social harm and proper form of treatment
Purpose of sentencing	Punishment for deterrence; sentences are determinate (fixed length)	Treatment and reform; sentences are indeterminate (variable length until cured)
Criminological experts	Philosophers; social reformers	Scientists; treatment experts

Summary

1   There is no straightforward history of criminology. Although it is a convention in textbooks to suggest the importance of classical theory and positivism as the founding ideas, there are many earlier ways of thinking about crime linked to demonism, religions, witchcraft and the like.
2   The classical school symbolized by Beccaria is linked to Enlightenment ideas of rationality, free will, choice and progress.
3   The positivist school symbolized by Lombroso and Ferri usually focuses on the criminal as a particular type, stresses determinism and looks at the characteristics that mark out the criminal from the 'normal'. There can be social differences as well as biological ones.
4   Classical and positivist theories suggest mutually contradictory images of crime and criminal justice. But both are alive and well today, exist in modern versions and continue to influence the workings of penal policy.

Critical thinking questions

1   **What was the Enlightenment? Consider some of the key intellectual contributions it made and then consider the different ways in which people may have thought about crime before the Enlightenment.**
2   **Consider the idea of 'a criminal type' of person. What are the most recent accounts of such a criminal?**
3   **Clarify what you understand by a just deserts model (tip: read von Hirsch, 1976, chs 27 and 28) and ponder your own penal tariff. What are the limits and difficulties of such an approach?**
4   **Look at the contradictory tensions found between positivism and classical thought. How do you see them at work in the modern criminal justice system?**

Further study

Beccaria, C. *Beccaria: On Crimes and Punishments and Other Writings*, edited by Richard Bellamy (1995), Cambridge: Cambridge University Press. A short selection of Beccaria's original writings.

Beirne, P. (1993) *Inventing Criminology: Essays on the Rise of 'Homo Criminalis'*, Albany: State University of New York Press. Looks at the intellectual history of criminology from Beccaria to Goring.

Garland, D. (2002) 'Of Crime and Criminals: The Development of Criminology in Britain', in M. Maguire, R. Morgan and R. Reiner (eds) *The Oxford Handbook of Criminology*, 3rd edn, Oxford:

Oxford University Press. An article which critically looks at the growth of criminology (mainly in the UK).

Gould, S. J. (1996) *The Mismeasure of Man*, 2nd edn, New York: W. W. Norton. A classic statement of the misuse of biological theories and measurements.

Rafter, N. H. (1997) *Creating Born Criminals*, Chicago: University of Illinois Press. A social history of biologically founded theories of crime in the United States, the study shows their influence on theories today.

Sherman, L. W. (2005) 'The Use and Usefulness of Criminology, 1751–2005: Enlightened Justice and its Failures', *Annals of the American Academy of Political and Social Science*, 600: 115–35. An article offering a critical history of theoretical criminology and arguing for wider use of experimental criminology.

von Hirsch, A. (1976) *Doing Justice: The Choice of Punishments*, New York: Hill and Wang. A clear and useful account of justifications for punishment, heavily derived from classical thinking.

More information

For more general guides to theory, see:

Burke, R. H. (2001) *An Introduction to Criminological Theory*, Cullompton: Willan. A comprehensive yet short introduction to the main criminological theories.

Cullen, F. T. and Agnew, R. (2003) *Criminological Theory: Past to Present (Essential Readings)*, 2nd edn, Los Angeles, CA: Roxbury Park. There are many Readers in criminology but this one stands out as an excellent collection of classic statements. Useful for the whole of Part 2 of this book.

Downes, D. and Rock, P. (1998) *Understanding Deviance: A Guide to the Sociology of Crime and Rule Breaking*, 3rd edn (2003, 4th edn), Oxford: Oxford University Press. For a long while this has been the most sophisticated general treatment of the full range of theories of crime discussed in this and other chapters. Regularly updated, it also provides a bibliography that signposts all the major books in the field.

Muncie, J., McLaughlin, E. and Langan, M. (eds) (2003) *Criminological Perspectives: A Reader*, 2nd edn, London: Sage/Open University. An exceptionally valuable collection of around fifty readings extracted from all the major positions and perspectives on crime ranging from Beccaria and Lombroso to Braithwaite and Smart.

Crimetheory.Com
www.crimetheory.com
A website that provides a brief introduction to a number of theories and theorists.

chapter 5

Early Sociologies of Crime

Key issues

- How did the early sociologists study crime?
- What is the functionalist approach to crime?
- What role did the Chicago School play in developing criminology?
- What are the strengths and weaknesses of each theory?

Introduction

In this chapter we turn to some of the major ways of thinking about crime introduced by sociologists, largely – but not exclusively – during the twentieth century, and with a key focus on delinquency, gangs and crime. Although much of their work has been criticized and subsequently modified, it does still provide very useful road maps into contemporary thinking about crime. We live on its shoulders.

Six major images capture the basics of these theories. These are not mutually exclusive. While they each emphasise different aspects of crime, they also share some common features. These images are as follows:

1   Crime is 'normal' in all societies – it serves certain functions and may even help keep a society orderly. It cannot, therefore, be easily eliminated. Crime may be usefully understood in mapping these functions.
2   Crime is bound up with conflict, often of a class-based nature in which crimes of the powerful are much less noticed than the crimes of the weak. Crime may be usefully understood in terms of social divisions and interests, especially economic interests.

3   Crime is bound up with tension, stresses and strains within societies. Most commonly there is a breakdown of the smooth workings of society – often called anomie (or normlessness) and sometimes referred to as social pathology or social disorganization (especially in earlier studies). Crime may usefully be understood by looking at the tensions and strains that exist within a society.

4   Crime is strongly (but far from exclusively) linked to city life. Modern cities bring with them cultural enclaves that seem more prone to generating criminal/delinquent styles of life with their own values, languages, norms, dress codes, etc. Crime may usefully be understood through mapping these 'criminal areas'.

5   Crime is learned in ordinary everyday situations. There is a process of cultural transmission, and crime may be usefully understood through looking at life histories and how people learn their everyday meanings and values.

6   Crime comes about through a lack of attachment to groups valuing law-abiding behaviour. Controls and regulations break down. Crime here may be usefully understood through the breakdown of social controls.

There are other ways of thinking about the social foundations of crime, and there have been accounts that create bridges between the positions (especially in the work of 'delinquency opportunity' theory – which attempts to synthesize positions 2, 3 and 4). In what follows, each of these ways of thinking will be briefly introduced.

The normality of crime

In his pioneering study of deviance, Émile Durkheim (1858–1917) made the curious claim that there is nothing abnormal about deviance; in fact, it is to be found in all societies and must therefore be seen as a normal part of society. He adopted a **functionalist perspective**: the theory that looks at the ways in which societies become integrated as their various parts perform various functions. Durkheim suggests that crime and deviance perform four functions essential to society:

1   Culture involves moral choices over the good and bad life. Unless our lives and societies are to dissolve into chaos, there will usually be a preference for some values and some behaviours over others. Yet the very conception of 'the good' rests upon an opposing notion of 'the bad'; you cannot have one without the other. And just as there can be no good without evil, so there can be no justice without crime. Deviance, in short, is indispensable to the process of generating and sustaining morality.

2   This also means that 'deviance' tends to clarify and mark out moral boundaries. By defining some individuals as deviant, people draw a social boundary between right and wrong. For example, a university marks the line between academic honesty and cheating by disciplining those who commit plagiarism. In all spheres of life – sexuality, religion, family life, work – people draw up codes of conduct and police 'the good'. Drawing attention to the bad may serve to highlight the good.

3   In fact, Durkheim argues that responding to deviance actually promotes social unity. People typically react to serious deviance with collective outrage. In doing so, Durkheim explained, they reaffirm the moral ties that bind them. Deviance brings people together, creating a moral

unity – often built from outrage. In the past, for instance, people would gather at executions to express their common hostility to the criminal; more recently, they often express this rage through the newspapers and the media generally.

4   On top of this, deviance may also encourage social change. Deviant people, Durkheim claimed, push a society's moral boundaries, suggesting alternatives to the status quo and encouraging change. Moreover, he declared, today's deviance sometimes becomes tomorrow's morality (1895/1988: 71). In the 1950s, for example, many people denounced rock-and-roll music as a threat to the morals of youth and an affront to traditional musical tastes. Since then, however, rock and roll has been swept up in the musical mainstream, becoming a multi-billion-dollar industry. Protest movements of one generation may be seen as deviant, but they often bring about change that becomes the norm for subsequent generations.

Functionalist theory, then, teaches us a great paradox about crime and deviance: that far from always being disruptive, it may contribute to a social system and underlie the operation of society. We will always have to live with deviance, suggests Durkheim, because it is bound up with the very conditions of social order. For as long as we want notions of the good and for as long as we want social change, deviance will be necessary.

Problems with functionalism

It is indeed likely that most societies do have crime, but we know that they differ enormously in their rates of crime. Thus, for example, the United States has extremely high crime rates – whereas some other societies, such as Japan or Iran, seem to have very low crime rates. This account does not really help us see just why these rates are so different. That said, functionalists such as Durkheim might argue that crime rates soar when societies are under stress (as we will see in the next section), and the responses of others to crime – from media reporting to public concern – serve to strengthen the society by bringing together citizens in common opposition. There is a strong connection here to contemporary moral panic theory which is discussed in Chapter 6.

But the abiding problem with functionalism is the way in which it highlights how societies are integrated, how there are shared values, how there is consensus. This may be true of relatively simple societies, but as societies become more industrialized, more fragmented, more postmodern, so it is hard to see that there is shared agreement on morality in society. Durkheim's theory may have elements of truth; but it is far from being the whole story.

The egoism of crime in capitalist society

Quite an opposite story is told within Marxist theory and conflict theory. As Box 5.1 shows, although Karl Marx (1818–83) and his collaborator Friedrich Engels (1820–95) were a long way from being criminologists, their observations about the workings of capitalism often highlighted how it was a system that generated relatively high levels of crime.

BOX 5.1 Marx and Engels on crime

Engels

Immorality is fostered in every possible way by the conditions of working-class life. The worker is poor; life has nothing to offer him; he is deprived of virtually all pleasures. Consequently, he does not fear the penalties of the law. Why should he restrain his wicked impulses? Why should he leave the rich man in undisturbed possession of his property? Why should he not take at least a part of this property for himself? What reason has the worker for *not* stealing?

. . . Distress due to poverty gives the worker only the choice of starving slowly, killing himself quickly or taking what he needs where he finds it – in plain English – stealing. And it is not surprising that the majority prefers to steal rather than starve to death or commit suicide.

. . . The clearest indication of the unbounded contempt of the workers for the existing social order is the wholesale manner in which they break its laws. If the demoralisation of the worker passes beyond a certain point then it is just as natural that he will turn into a criminal – as inevitably as water turns into steam at boiling point. Owing to the brutal and demoralising way in which he is treated by the bourgeoisie, the worker loses all will of his own and, like water, he is forced to follow blindly the laws of nature. There comes a point when the worker loses all power [to withstand temptation]. Consequently, the incidence of crime has increased with the growth of the working-class population and there is more crime in Britain than in any other country in the world. The annual statistics of crime issued by the Home Office show that there has been an extraordinarily rapid growth of crime. The number of those committed for trial on criminal charges in England and Wales alone has increased sevenfold in thirty-seven years. . . .

. . . There can be no doubt that in England the social war is already being waged. Everyone looks after his own interests and fights only for himself against all comers. Whether in doing so he injures those who are his declared enemies is simply a matter of selfish calculation as to whether such action be to his advantage or not. It no longer occurs to anybody to come to a friendly understanding with his neighbours. All differences of opinion are settled by threats, by invoking the courts, or even by taking the law into one's own hands. In short, everyone sees in his neighbour a rival to be elbowed aside, or at best a victim to be exploited for his own ends.

(Engels, 1845/1958: 130, 145–6, 149, 242, 243)

Marx

Present-day society, which breeds hostility between the individual man and everyone else, thus produces a social war of all against all which inevitably in individual cases, notably among uneducated people, assumes a brutal, barbarously violent form – that of crime. In order to protect itself against crime, against direct acts of violence, society requires an extensive, complicated system of administrative and judicial bodies which requires an immense labour force. In communist society this would likewise be vastly simplified and precisely because – strange though it may sound – the administrative body in this society would have to manage not merely individual aspects of social life, but the whole of social life, in all its various activities, in all its aspects. We eliminate the contradiction between the individual man and all others, we counter-pose social peace to social war, we put the axe to the *root* of crime – and thereby render the greatest, by far the greatest part of the present activity of the administrative and judicial bodies superfluous. Even now crimes of passion are becoming fewer and fewer in comparison with calculated crimes, crimes of interest – crimes against *persons* are declining, crimes against *property* are on the increase. Advancing civilisation moderates violent out-breaks of passion even in our present-day society, which is on a war footing; how much more will this be the case in communist, peaceful society! Crimes against property cease of their own accord where everyone receives what he needs to satisfy his natural and his spiritual urges, where social gradations and distinctions cease to exist.

(Marx and Engels, 1845/1975: 248–9)

Willem Adrian Bonger (1876–1940) was a Marxist Dutch sociologist/criminologist who committed suicide rather than submit to the Nazis, and whose PhD thesis was published in 1916 as 'Criminality and Economic Conditions'. He suggested that major shifts in crime come with the emergence of capitalism, and after an exposition of the working of capitalism, Bonger concluded that the present economic system 'weaken[s] the social feelings . . . breaks social bonds and makes social life much more egoistic'. For him, it was capitalism that generated an egoistic culture – with capitalists being greedy and workers becoming demoralized. It brutalizes many, and helps create an 'insensibility to the ills of others'. As he writes,

> Long working hours and monotonous labor brutalize those who are forced into them: bad housing conditions contribute also to debase the moral sense, as does [sic] the uncertainty of existence, and finally absolute poverty, the frequent consequence of sickness and unemployment, ignorance and lack of any training of any kind contribute their quota . . . the demoralizing of all is the status of the lower proletariat.
>
> (quoted in Muncie et al., 1996: 43)

From this he goes on to discuss four different types of crime all linked to economic conditions. These were (1) vagrancy and mendacity; (2) theft; (3) robbery and homicide for economic reasons (mainly by poor people); and (4) fraudulent bankruptcy, adulteration of food, etc. This

thinking about crime

theory can also be seen in strands of the underclass theory, and in many aspects of Marxist theory which are still alive today.

Problems with Marxism

As is well known, many of Marx's major predictions have simply not come true, and in the eyes of many, the whole theory has been discredited. All the same, Marxist criminologists do see a number of key ideas in Marx's ideas that can help in the study of crime. Those ideas have led to the broader arguments of conflict theory and new left realism, both of which will be discussed later.

Again, there is too strong a deterministic streak in the theory. It is as if being poor would necessarily drive you into crime – whereas we know that the vast majority of poor people never commit serious crimes. There is also a lurking pejorative sense that working-class life is miserable, wretched and immoral; a lot of value claims are imported into the theory, and most contemporary theories of class would find this suspect.

Cultural transmission, city life and the Chicago School

As is shown in Chapter 3, a major tradition for approaching crime and delinquency started to emerge at the University of Chicago in the first four decades of the twentieth century. Chicago was itself a leading centre for the study of sociology. It was the first major department of sociology; it produced the first major textbook; it trained a large number of graduate students; and it produced many monographs on the nature of city life at that time – including tramps, dance halls, prostitution, organized crime, mental illness, slums. Indeed, it has been said that 1920s Chicago is the most studied city of all time. Although inspired by European theorists such as Tonnies, Durkheim and Simmel, the unique contribution of the Chicago sociologists was in making the city itself a social laboratory for actual research. The study of cities and crime has remained very important for criminology.

Chicago itself was an extraordinary city: a new metropolis exploding with new populations, mass migration from all over Europe and the southern states of America, growing from a few hundred people in the mid-1880s to over 3 million in the 1930s. Its growth brought with it all the signs of modernity – from dance crazes, movies and cars to bootlegging, crime and unemployment. This was the Jazz Age.

Robert Ezra Park (1864–1944) was chair of the Department of Sociology and had a passion for walking the streets of the world's great cities, observing the full range of human turbulence and triumph. Throughout his thirty-year career at the University of Chicago, he led a group of dedicated sociologists in direct, systematic observation of urban life. In a classic line, he claimed that 'I suspect that I have actually covered more ground, tramping about in cities in different parts of the world, than any other living man' (quoted in Bulmer, 1984). At Park's urging, generations of sociologists at the University of Chicago rummaged through practically every part of their city.

From this research, Park came to understand the city as a highly ordered mosaic of distinctive regions, including industrial districts, ethnic communities and criminal/delinquent/'vice' areas. These so-called natural areas all evolved in relation to one another, forming an urban ecology.

To Park, the city operated like a living social organism. Urban variety was central: even though many people saw the city as disorganized and even dangerous, social life in the city was intoxicating. Walking the city streets, he became convinced that urban places offer a better way of life – the promise of greater human freedom and opportunity – than we can find elsewhere. But the downside may well be a growth in crime and dangerousness. These are all themes we recognize in current criminological debates, but they are far from new.

The Chicago School and crime

The Chicago sociologists borrowed from some earlier social work traditions. From the United States they were influenced by the work of Jane Addams (who ran a community project, Hull House, and also worked to map out the different parts of the city and its problems); and from the United Kingdom they had the example of the famous poverty studies of Charles Booth and others. From these opening ideas that parts of the city were perhaps more likely to harbour crime than others, the Chicago sociologists pioneered a range of approaches to the study of crime that may be briefly summarized as follows:

1   Crime may be more common in the city because the city generates a distinctive way of life. Indeed, the blasé attitude of city-dwellers and metropolitan styles – an urban way of living – bring greater tolerance for diversity and, in making the streets less communal and more anonymous, generate the possibility for a less controlling environment, but a more crimogenic one.
2   Crime can be found in 'natural habitats' or ecological zones. The city generates certain ways of life to be found in its various areas – and many of these could be linked to crime and deviance. In 1925 Ernest W. Burgess, a student and colleague of Robert Park, described land use in Chicago in terms of **concentric zones** that look rather like a bullseye. City centres, Burgess observed, are business districts bordered by a ring of factories, followed by residential rings with housing that becomes more expensive the further it stands from the noise and pollution of the city's centre.
3   Crime is basically learned in the same ways as everything else; it is normal learning. This idea of **differential association** was linked to the writings of Edwin Sutherland.
4   Crime is best studied through a range of different methodologies which when put together bring about a much richer understanding of crime than when only one single method is adopted. Thus, in his study of delinquency, Clifford Shaw gathered detailed life histories of delinquent boys, and Burgess and Shaw examined the statistical records of delinquency for different parts of the city and spot-mapped them on to the 'ecological zones' that Robert Park had helped map out. Meanwhile, Frederic Thrasher was studying 1,313 gangs in their everyday life environments – an early and important instance of participant observation. And the backgrounds to delinquency in the city come alive through studies of tramps (Anderson's *The Hobo*), dance halls (Cressey's *The Taxi-Dance Hall*), the slums (Zorbauigh) and organized crime.
5   Crime may be best dealt with through coordinated agencies: Chicago saw the start of Hull House through to the programmes of the Chicago Area Project.

The zonal theory of crime

At the heart of the Chicago theory was the idea of Park *et al.* (1925) that the urban industrial community of Chicago may be described as consisting of five successive zones (Figure 5.1):

I   The central business district tends in American cities to be at once the retail, financial, recreational, civic, and political centres. The skyscrapers and canyon-like streets of this downtown district are thronged with shoppers, clerks, and office workers. Few people live there.

II The zone in transition. This is an interstitial area where change is rapidly taking place. Here are to be found the slum or semi-slum districts.

III The zone of the workingmen's homes. This lies beyond the factory belt surrounding the central business district. It remains accessible, and is often within walking distance for the workers.

IV The better residential zone is inhabited chiefly by the families engaged in professional and clerical pursuits. They are likely to have high school if not college education. This is the home of the middle class.

V   The commuters' zone comprises the suburban districts.

Each of these zones could be studied in terms of the kinds of lifestyles that appeared there. This could be done partly through ethnographic research but also through looking at detailed

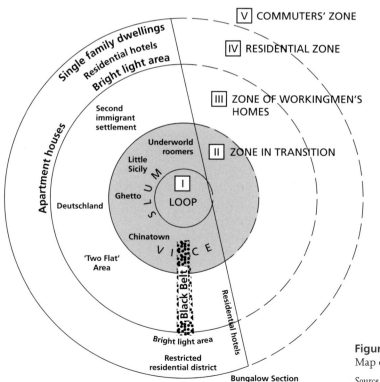

Figure 5.1

Map of the zonal theory of the city.

Source: Adapted from Park *et al.* (1925).

statistical records (see Chapter 3). Thus, parts of the city could be analysed in terms of their crime rates, or the rates of mental illness measured. Of course, as we have seen, there are serious issues in measuring crime and deviance, and figures may only be approximations. Nevertheless, what the Chicago sociologists found was that there were distinctive areas where crime rates were much higher (the zone of transition). Here ethnic cultures conflicted, housing was rundown, poverty was more widespread. *Certain parts of the city are more prone to crime.*

The work of Chicago sociologists has transformed in recent years although it retains a strong emphasis on urban culture and crime (Chapter 8 discusses its broader impact on environmental and spatial criminology). Sudhir Venkatesh (2008), in particular, has renewed Chicago's gang study tradition in his recent book, *Gang Leader for a Day: A Rogue Sociologist Takes to the Streets*.

BOX 5.2 Some classic Chicago studies

Edwin Sutherland (1883–1950): differential association theory

Edwin Sutherland has been called 'the Dean of American Criminology'. He was at Chicago only for a relatively brief time, but he wrote his study *Twenty Thousand Homeless Men* (Sutherland with Locke, 1936) and *The Professional Thief* (1937) there – the latter being a classic life story research of a thief, Chic Conwell. He moved on to Indiana University in 1936. *White Collar Crime* (1949) was published just before his death in 1950.

Frederic M. Thrasher (1892–1962): *The Gang: A Study of 1,313 Gangs in Chicago*

Thrasher's (1927) classic study took many years to complete, and concluded that there were roughly 25,000 or so members of gangs in Chicago. The gang underwent a kind of evolution from a loose grouping into a more structured form with a strong 'we' identity. It tended to emerge from play groups in the poorer part of the city. All the gangs were male; there was a general hostility towards girls and women in general because they were seen to weaken loyalty. Thrasher identified several types of gang (which we can still roughly identify today):

- the diffuse gang – never gets a proper organization;
- the solidified gang – with a high degree of morale and solidarity, and usually with a clear name;
- the conventionalized gang – the athletic club (these made up about a quarter of all the gangs he observed);
- the criminal gang – can drift into habitual crime.

Later Thrasher moved to New York University and studied the Boys' Club of New York City.

Edward Franklin Frazier (1894–1962)

A leading black sociologist who pioneered the study of black youth as well as the study of the black bourgeoisie, the black church and black families in the United States. He did his PhD at Chicago but later went on to become a leading professor in social work at Howard University.

Clifford Shaw (1895–1957) and Henry D. McKay (1899–1980)

Both were graduate students at Chicago during the 1920s and later worked as a team for the Institute for Juvenile Research near the Chicago loop for thirty years. McKay was the statistician, Shaw was the fieldworker and activist (Snodgrass, 1982). They established the Chicago Area Project in 1934 which worked with the local community in an attempt to resolve the 'delinquency problem'.

BOX 5.3 Early theories of crime and social policies

Most sociological theories of crime bring with them implications for social policy and action. Both the Chicago School and anomie theory led to some major responses to crime in the twentieth century.

Chicago sociology led in part to the setting up of the Chicago Area Project (CAP), which was inaugurated by Shaw and McKay in 1934 and is one foundation for community and neighbourhood work. Here, the focus is on community change (which can include schools, family, street) and which sees the need to integrate values and enhance the capacities of local residents. If the community supports and fosters delinquent or criminal ways of life, then the proper focus of concern is the community. These days it may also be linked to community surveillance, neighbourhood watch community crime prevention campaigns.

Mobilization for Youth (MFY) was a project that grew in part out of anomie theory. It was part of the Kennedy administration's reforms in the early 1960s and led to an expansion of opportunity in education and work for young people.

Both these projects have had limited success. Certainly some useful changes were made, and they have often served as models for other countries to follow. But because they deal with middle-range change – at the level of community – it has been argued by critics that they fail to deal with the root of such problems in the wider society. The term 'community' itself, for example, has been much criticized as being too romantic and imprecise.

Crime as learned: differential association theory

Edwin Sutherland is also identified with Chicago, and his key contribution to criminology is generally seen to be the theory of differential association, which he developed in various editions of his textbook *Principles of Criminology* (it first appeared in the 1939 edition). For Sutherland, crime was a normal learning process; we learn crime in much the same way as we learn everything else. Far from being genetic or biological, it was also not a matter of pathology or abnormal learning. Learning any social patterns – whether conventional or deviant – is a process that takes place in groups. According to Sutherland (1956), any person's tendency towards conformity or deviance depends on the relative frequency of association with others who encourage conventional behaviour or, as the case may be, norm violation.

1 Criminal behaviour is learned.
2 Criminal behaviour is learned in interaction with other persons in a process of communication.
3 The principal part of the learning of criminal behaviour occurs within intimate personal groups.
4 When criminal behaviour is learned, the learning includes (a) techniques of committing the crime, which are sometimes very complicated, sometimes very simple; and (b) the specific direction of motives, drives, rationalizations and attitudes.
5 The specific direction of motives and drives is learned from definitions of legal codes as favourable and unfavourable.
6 A person becomes delinquent because of an excess of definitions favourable to violation of law over definitions unfavourable to violation of law.
7 Differential associations may vary in frequency, duration, priority and intensity.
8 The process of learning criminal behaviour by association with criminal and anti-criminal patterns involves all the mechanisms that are involved in any other learning.
9 Though criminal behaviour is an expression of general needs and values, it is not explained by those general needs and values since non-criminal behaviour is an expression of the same needs and values.

Problems with the Chicago School

Although the Chicago School provided many of the foundational ideas of the sociology of crime, many of them are now not far short of a century old – and have been open to much refinement. Thus, although the city is still known to harbour 'natural areas' of crime, the concentric zones model is usually seen to be only one special case.

There is also a problem with what is called 'the ecological fallacy'. We cannot assume that because certain areas are more 'criminal', everybody within those areas is likely to be a criminal; this is simply not true. So the theory is not strong at explaining why some people become criminal and others do not.

Anomie and the stresses and strains of crime

Early social models of crime often assumed a certain harmony or fit between the parts of a society and its overall working. Societies functioned; and the institutions in them (from work and school to family and religion) worked to perform certain functions to keep a society balanced. How then can crime and deviance happen?

Drawing from the traditions established both by Marx and Durkheim, the US sociologist Robert K. Merton (1910–2003) saw crime and deviance emerging as an individual adaptation to pressures flowing from the social structure. In one of the most cited discussions of the twentieth century, Merton's 'Social Structure and Anomie' (1938), modern capitalist society was seen as being under pressure, and the strains and tensions within it, Merton thought, led to crime and deviance. Distinguishing between a social structure (which provided economic roots to success) and a culture (which provided norms, values and goals – the 'American Dream'), Merton argued that deviance occurred where there was an imbalance between social structure (approved social means) and culture (approved goals). The tension or norm breakdown he called **anomie**. His model was effectively what has been called a materialist one. He looked at just how important the American Dream of making it to the top through hard work and earning money was, and found that some people were so placed within society that they were unable to achieve this dream. He argued that this inability opened up a series of responses or adaptations (Table 5.1). He borrowed from Durkheim the notion of social integration and anomie.

Writing originally about North American society in the 1930s, Merton argued that the path to *conformity* was to be found in pursuing conventional goals by approved means. The true 'success story', in other words, is someone who gains wealth and prestige through talent and hard work. But not everyone who desires conventional success has the opportunity to attain it. Children raised in poverty, for example, may see little hope of becoming successful if they 'play by the rules'. As a result, they may seek wealth through one or another kind of crime – say, by dealing in cocaine. Merton called this type of deviance *innovation* – the attempt to achieve a culturally approved goal (wealth) by unconventional means (drug sales). Table 5.1 characterizes innovation as accepting the goal of success while rejecting the conventional means of becoming rich.

Table 5.1 Merton's modes of individual adaptation to anomie

	Culture Goals	Institutionalized Means
Conformity	+	+
Innovation	+	−
Ritualism	−	+
Retreatism	−	−
Rebellion	+/−	+/−

Key:

+	=	acceptance
−	=	rejection
+/−	=	reject old and substitute new

The inability to become successful by normative means may also prompt another type of deviance that Merton calls *ritualism*. Ritualists resolve the strain of limited success by abandoning cultural goals in favour of almost compulsive efforts to live 'respectably'. In essence, they embrace the rules to the point where they lose sight of their larger goals. Lower-level bureaucrats, Merton suggests, often succumb to ritualism as a way of maintaining respectability.

Merton noted other adaptations. *Retreatism* was the rejection of both cultural goals and means so that one, in effect, 'drops out': some alcoholics, drug addicts and street people are examples. *Rebellion* involves the rejection of both the cultural definition of success and the normative means of achieving it. Those who adopt this response advocate radical alternatives to the existing social order, typically calling for a political transformation of society.

What is important in this kind of explanation is that it looks at society as a whole and finds stresses and strains within the system that seem to generate 'weak spots' – crime is induced through a system that has potentials for contradiction and conflict. Merton's theory has been extremely influential in the development of 'delinquent gang theory'.

Problems with anomie theory

The problem with Merton's ideas is the presumption of goals and values. It is just possible that life was like this in 1930s America (though we doubt it), but it is certainly not like this in the early twenty-first century – which, as we see throughout this book, is often characterized as a postmodern, risk society. Societies are just too complex, have too many competing values systems and generate too much conflict for this simple unitary idea to be valid.

Nor can we assume that people are simply socialized to a common set of values: quite the contrary, much evidence points to different socialization patterns among different groups.

Further, the theory also largely seems to assume that people are driven into crime through tensions, through grim necessity. As Jack Katz and others have pointed out (see Chapter 15), we do not necessarily need to see crime as motivated by painful sources. For many crime may be fun and exciting, and it may hold its own pleasures. This is not a very fashionable theory among many criminologists, but it is one that we consider elsewhere in the book.

We do not wish to make Merton's theory sound too basic or simply wrong. Its influence lies in that it pointed sharply to the role of economic factors in shaping crime, and began to produce a genuinely social account that found the roots of crime to lie not in individual people, but in the organization and workings of the wider society. It has had many ardent followers, and it still has many adherents today.

Gangs, youth and deviant subcultures

One of these followers is Albert Cohen (1918–), who has been influenced by Merton and Sutherland, who both taught him. His *Delinquent Boys* (1955) became an influential classic. In this study, Cohen notes that delinquent boys stole for the hell of it. They engaged in short-run hedonism and in what he called a 'reaction formation' to the frustration experienced as part of a class system, especially in school. They did not steal to gain goods or property, instead, they gained status among their peers through adopting malicious, negative values – the antithesis of the middle-class values taught in middle-class educational worlds.

Cohen's study of delinquent boys pioneered the idea that boys become delinquent because of what he termed 'status frustration', the process by which people feel thwarted when they aspire to a certain status. In schools especially, Cohen noted that boys from more deprived backgrounds often found school life an alienating and frustrating experience. They were being judged by what Cohen called the 'middleclass measuring rod'. They initially wanted to be successes, but found that they had not developed the skills to do this in their family and community life. For example, reading books was alien, and being polite and well-spoken hard. Their cultural differences had poorly equipped them for school life. Cohen suggests that in their frustration they inverted the values of the school – achievement, hard work and planning for the future – and developed instead a contra culture in which values of non-achievement, playing around and not thinking of the future become deliberately – almost perversely – their goals. Activities become non-utilitarian (they steal 'for the hell of it'), negativistic (opposing the values of adult society), malicious, versatile and characterized by short-run hedonism and group autonomy.

Cohen asserted that delinquency was most pronounced among lower-class youths because it is they who contend with the least opportunity to achieve success in conventional ways. Sometimes those whom society neglects seek self-respect by building a deviant subculture that 'defines as meritorious the characteristics they do possess, the kinds of conduct of which they are capable' (1955: 66). Having a notorious street reputation, for example, may win no points with society as a whole, but it may satisfy a youth's gnawing desire to 'be somebody'. Unlike most of the Chicago sociologists, he did discuss girls – though in very stereotypical terms.

Synthesizing the theories?

The prominent work of Richard A. Cloward (1926–2001) and Lloyd E. Ohlin (1918–), *Delinquency and Opportunity* (1960), can be seen as an attempt to form a bridge between the Chicago tradition (especially Sutherland's learning theory) and the strain tradition (especially Merton's anomie theory). They suggest that the delinquent subculture has its own opportunity structures. That is, young people have access to different kinds of youthful cultures. While they may aspire to the goals set by conventional society, working-class youth – as in Merton's and Cohen's model – can easily be thwarted and cannot get ahead. But they also find that they have differential access to youth cultures too. In their own work, Cloward and Ohlin suggest that there were three major kinds of these cultures:

1   *Criminal.* The criminal youth culture is at the top of the hierarchy and means that alternative means to financial success become available. Here there are 'close bonds between different age levels of offender and between criminal and conventional elements' (Cloward and Ohlin, 1960: 171), so there is rapid integration between young and old into lives of crime.
2   *Violence/conflict.* Here there is not only little access to the legitimate opportunity structure, but also little access to the illegitimate/criminal one. Such youth may live in very unstable areas, and violence becomes the means therefore by which they seek to resolve their frustrations and problems. Violence becomes their source of status.

3   *Retreatist/drug.* Those who have neither access to the criminal culture nor the means to seek violent responses become 'double failures', and they are the most likely simply to 'drop out'. They become retreatists and turn to drink, drugs, sex and other forms of withdrawal from the wider social order.

Thus, Cloward and Ohlin maintain that criminal deviance results not simply from limited legitimate opportunity but also from available illegitimate opportunity. In short, deviance or conformity grows out of the relative opportunity structure that frames young people's lives. It was the nature of these opportunity structures and how they provide opportunities to learn deviant ways that fascinated the Chicago School. In its day – nearly fifty years ago – this was seen as a very elegant way of thinking about crime, bridging as it did the anomie tradition of Merton and the Chicago tradition of Shaw and Sutherland. To modern eyes, however, the theory looks somewhat contrived – and does not take into account a much wider range of forms of youthful culture.

There are more problems with the various Chicago theories:

■   They fall short by assuming that everyone shares the same cultural standards for judging right and wrong.
■   We must be careful not to define deviance in ways that unfairly focus attention on poor people. If crime is defined to include stock fraud as well as street theft, offenders are more likely to include affluent individuals.
■   All structural-functional theories imply that everyone who violates conventional cultural standards will be branded as deviant. Becoming deviant, however, is actually a highly complex process.

Control theories

The term 'social control', initially linked to the work of Edward Ross – who first used the term in the *American Journal of Sociology* in 1896 – is linked to the classical school of Durkheim and Mead. It started to develop as a broad theory of self-control in the 1950s. Like the other broad ideas already considered, it comes in many guises.

Neutralization theory

One of social control's earliest formulations is to be found in the work of Sykes and Matza. They argue that boys can commit delinquent acts when their commitment to the moral order is weakened, and that they can do this through what Sykes and Matza term techniques of neutralization. These techniques are stories they tell themselves which break bonds through such devices as blaming others or denying responsibility.

Sykes and Matza suggest five major techniques that enable delinquents to break 'the moral bind to law' (Matza, 1964: 181):

1   *The denial of personal responsibility.* Here the delinquent uses a kind of social word play. 'Of course I'm delinquent. Who wouldn't be, coming from my background?' He then can neutralize personal responsibility by detailing the background of a broken home, lack of love, and a host of other factors.
2   *The denial of harm to anyone.* In this pattern of neutralization, stealing a car is only borrowing it; truancy harms no one; and drug use 'doesn't hurt anyone but me'.
3   *The delinquent denies that the person injured or wronged is really a victim.* 'The [assaulted] teacher was unfair'; the victim of a mugging was 'only queer'; and the gang youth assaulted was 'out to get me'.
4   *The delinquent condemns the condemners.* 'Society is much more corrupt than I am.'
5   *Delinquent group or gang loyalties supersede loyalty to the norms of an impersonal society.* 'When I stabbed him, I was only defending my turf.' The youth places his gang or delinquent group above the law, the school and society.

Developing in close connection with this, *social bond theory* is effectively a theory of self-control. Walter Cade Reckless (1899–1988) and Simon Dinitz presented it as 'containment theory'. They looked at groups of boys to see what insulated some from crime of all kinds but not others – the techniques that neutralize 'good boys' from crime and foster 'bad boys' in it.

Social control theory

All this anticipated the general question later posed by Travis Hirschi. Most contemporary control theories effectively ask not 'Why do people become criminal and commit crime?' but the reverse and intriguing question: 'Why do most people not commit crime?'

In his earlier work, Hirschi argued that 'delinquent acts result when an individual's bond to society is weak or broken' (1969: 16). Hirschi asserts that conformity arises from four types of social controls that create a social bond (Table 5.2). The weaker they are, the more likely it is that criminal acts will happen.

1   *Attachment.* Strong social attachments encourage conformity; weak relationships in the family, peer group and school leave people freer to engage in deviance.
2   *Opportunity.* The more one perceives legitimate opportunity, the greater the advantages of conformity. A young person bound for university, one with good career prospects, has a high stake in conformity. By contrast, someone with little confidence in future success drifts more towards deviance.
3   *Involvement.* Extensive involvement in legitimate activities – such as holding a job, going to school and completing homework, or pursuing hobbies – inhibits deviance. People with few such activities – those who simply 'hang out' waiting for something to happen – have time and energy for deviant activity.
4   *Belief.* Strong beliefs in conventional morality and respect for authority figures restrain tendencies towards deviance. By contrast, people with a weak conscience are more vulnerable to temptation.

Table 5.2 Hirschi's elements of the bond

Element	Examples
Attachment	Identification with peers or parents, emotional bond between child and parent, concern and respect for parents' or peers' opinions, engaging in activities with peers, supervision by parents, intimate communications with parents, attitudes towards school, concern for teachers' opinions, general sensitivity to the opinions of others
Involvement	Time-consuming activity (work, sports, recreation, hobbies), time spent on homework, lack of boredom, amount of non-active leisure time, time spent talking with friends
Commitment	Investment in society (education, career, family), academic competence, educational aspirations and expectations, achievement orientation, expected occupation, importance of reputation
Belief	Respect for authorities, importance of and respect for law, absence of neutralizations

Later, Gottfredson and Hirschi used this question as the basis for their more general theory of crime (1990), in which one issue matters above all others: that of self-control. Individuals with high self-control 'will be substantially less likely at all periods of life to engage in criminal acts' (ibid.: 89). This changes the theory a great deal, as all the other elements now go missing. Over the years, the theory has been much tested, and some criminologists now think it has been the most influential theory of delinquency over the past thirty years.

Problems with control theory

Control theory is an odd theory of crime as it works from the assumption that most of us would commit crimes if we had the chance. It is only the social ties, bonds and attachments that prevent us from doing this. It is at least worth considering whether this is true.

This also means that it neglects offenders' motivations: the cause is apparent – a lack of control. Again, we do not need special reasons to account for crime, except to note that the bonds have broken.

More specifically, just how tight do these bonds have to be? Some argue that bonds may have to be too repressive, too overwhelming in modern societies.

Reintegrative shaming?

A theory that has developed more recently than Hirschi's and in many ways is connected is John Braithwaite's 'reintegrative shaming'. In his influential book *Crime, Shame and Reintegration* (1989), Braithwaite highlights the importance of informal, rather than formal, sanctions in checking crime. As he says, 'It would seem that sanctions imposed by relatives, friends or a personally relevant collectivity have more effect on criminal behaviour than sanctions imposed by legal authority' (quoted in Muncie, 1999: 433). Closely allied to the work on shame by Thomas Scheff (which suggests that one of the central features of life is our search for honour and the ways in which shaming plays a role in that search), the emphasis on shaming can be seen to keep us in check. Shame is linked to taking the role of 'the other' (cf. Mead, 1934), and links to pangs of conscience when confronted with the possibility of wrongdoing. We want and need the social approval of others.

thinking about crime

Shaming involves all social processes expressing disapproval that have the aim of inducing remorse in the offender. The shame that matters most is not that coming from officials such as the police or judges or courts but that from the people we care about most. It is not stigmatizing in so far as it is aimed not at the offender per se but at the act the offender commits; the ultimate aim must be reintegration. The shaming itself creates outcasts, meaning that bonds of respect with the offender are not sustained. In contrast, reintegrative shaming is disapproval dispensed in a relationship with the offender that is based on respect, with the focus on the offence, and where 'degradation ceremonies are followed by ceremonies to decertify deviance, where forgiveness, apology and repentance are culturally important' (Muncie *et al.*, 1996).

Braithwaite contends that reintegrative shaming is effective in complex urban societies as well as simpler ones. It is likely that those nations with low crime rates are those in which shaming has the greatest social power. (This is discussed further at Chapter 15.)

Written out of criminological history?

The studies featured in this chapter laid the foundations of sociological criminology but they did so in ways which prioritized the view of (mostly white) male academics who approached crime as a male phenomenon (with a focus on young white men). This closing discussion looks at the work of early black sociologists and at the few early sociological attempts to address female crime.

Early black sociologists

The study of crime in early twentieth-century America was undertaken at the same time by African-American and by white scholars: however, most works by the former remain unknown. As Young and Greene (2002: xi) write, 'the perspectives of African Americans remains on the periphery of the discipline' and 'their contributions continue to be excluded from textbooks and course material'.

Writings by African-American scholars link crime to a range of causes although their work is characterized by a focus on race and racism. 'Like other early American sociologists and criminologists, African American scholars were influenced greatly by Durkheim and the "Chicago School" and emphasise social disorganization, anomie and the ecology of crime' (Young and Greene, 2002: 5–6). W. E. B. Du Bois (1868–1963) and Monroe Work (1866–1945) used a form of social disorganization analysis to ask why blacks were so over-represented in the justice system from the nineteenth century onwards. They suggested that the ending of slavery (and the removal of a powerful form of social control) meant that freed African Americans had to adjust to new ways of living and to create new kinds of moral values, as well as having to cope with the new kinds of economic stresses of operating in a 'free market' within a society where racial prejudice continued to run high. In addition, many young southern blacks migrated to find work in northern cities – swapping the social controls of rural home for urban 'disorganization' in ways that mirrored the experiences of much more well-documented European migrants to the United States during that time.

Du Bois and Work also argued that racialized justice was quick to criminalize and then exploit black groups which meant that those groups themselves lost confidence in 'white' justice. For example, in the southern US states, a 'convict-lease system' operated in which (mostly black) prisoners were 'sold' or leased as workers to local employers – even though slavery had formally been abolished. 'The lessee then took charge of the convicts – worked them as he wished under the nominal control of the state. Thus a new slavery and slave-trade was established' (Du Bois, 1901/2002) – one in which the criminal justice system was closely implicated.

In the 1940s, other black sociologists built on this earlier tradition. E. Franklin Frazier (1949) compiled detailed surveys of work on race and crime, although he is known for his own work on black juvenile delinquency which he linked, like other Chicago scholars, to increasing social disorganization. Earl R. Moses (1947) attributed higher rates of black crime in Baltimore to racial differences in buying power, arguing that whites found it easier to get jobs and therefore easier to buy or rent property. Given the centrality of questions of race to questions of criminology, it is very important that these early studies are more fully integrated into criminological history and teaching.

Early sociological studies of women and girls

> An excursion through the twentieth century's developments in criminology is a journey through communities inhabited only by men, passing street corners and sea-fronts occupied exclusively by male youth and into soccer stadia, youth clubs and rock venues where women and their experiences fail to register even a passing comment from the researchers.
>
> (Scraton, 1990: 17)

Table 5.3 Selected African-American scholarship on crime and justice, 1900–49

Scholar	Date	Research topic
Work, M.	1900	Crime among the Negroes of Chicago
Du Bois, W. E. B.	1901	Convict-Lease system in the South
Miller, K.	1914	Negro crime
Johnson, C. S.	1922	Chicago race riot
Reid, I. de A.	1925/32	Negro prisoners
Washington, F. B.	1932–3	Care of the Negro delinquent
Moses, E. R.	1933	Delinquency in the Negro community
Diggs, M.	1940	Negro juvenile delinquency
Cox, O.	1945	Lynching
Moses, E. R.	1947	Differential crime rates between Negroes and whites
Blue, J. T.	1948	Juvenile delinquency, race and economic status
Frazier, E. F.	1949	Sociological theory, race relations and crime

Source: Adapted from Greene, H. T. and Gabbidon, S. L. (2000) *African American Criminological Thought*, Albany: State University of New York Press, Table 1, p. 5.

If much early criminology was written by college boys fascinated by street-corner boys (Heidensohn, 1996), where did this leave studies of girls? Most nineteenth- and early twentieth-century studies of female criminality were influenced by medical and psychopathological models (see discussion of positivism in Chapter 4). Women and girls' bodies, hormones and sexuality were believed to shape their behaviour as much as, if not more than, socio-economic questions about class, aspiration and anomie (Cox, 2003: 135–61; Campbell, 1981). Puberty could unsettle girls by creating adult desires in adolescent bodies. The resulting sexual tension could cause them to break moral codes or commit crime. Cyril Burt, one of the UK's first educational psychologists, calculated that 'over-potency of the sexual instinct' was linked to a significant proportion of girls' delinquency (Burt, 1925: 432). US criminologists Sheldon and Eleanor Glueck's study of 'five hundred delinquent women' in the 1930s identified a wide range of predisposing factors but still emphasized the physical. These kinds of views were long-lasting: one 1968 study of delinquent girls in London concluded that it was 'quite likely that physical defects and lack of physical attractiveness have played a part in causing delinquency' (Cowie et al., 1968: 64).

Girls and women did feature in a few early sociological studies of crime. William I. Thomas, another Chicago School scholar, edged towards a more gendered account of social dis-organization. In The Unadjusted Girl (1923) he argued that young women, especially young European migrants to the United States, were caught between old moral values and new social practices. They were more likely to be 'affected by the feeling that much, too much [was] being missed in life' because they had been 'heretofore . . . most excluded from general participation in life'. This might result in 'despair or depression' or cause a young woman to 'break all bounds' (Thomas, 1923: 72).

For many Chicago sociologists, delinquency was a solution to young people's experience of social dislocation. Alfred K. Cohen (1955) argued that girls were less likely to seek a delinquent solution because they could gain social status by forming relationships with men and, later, by becoming mothers. Boys, on the other hand, defined their success in terms of their access to money, influence and power rather than through family life. Further, girls' friendship groups were thought to be very different to those of boys which meant that they rarely joined the street gangs which so fascinated these scholars.

These kinds of views help explain why these foundational studies paid such fleeting attention to female crime – it just did not fit their moulds. It also explains why feminist sociologists and criminologists later felt compelled to challenge these and find new ways to conceptualize gender and crime (see Chapter 6).

Summary

1   The functionalist perspective on crime suggests that it is 'normal' in all societies – it serves certain functions and may even help keep a society orderly. Crime may be usefully understood in mapping these functions.

2   The Marxist theory of crime suggests that crime is bound up with conflict of a class-based nature in which crimes of the powerful are much less noticed than the crimes of the weak.

3   Anomie theory suggests crime is bound up with tension, stresses and strains within societies. Most commonly there is a breakdown of the smooth workings of society.

4   The Chicago School of sociology saw crime as being strongly linked to city life. Modern cities bring with them cultural enclaves that seem more prone to generating criminal/delinquent styles of life with their own values, languages, norms, dress codes, etc.

5   Differential association theory suggests that crime is learned in ordinary everyday situations through a process of cultural transmission.

6   Social control theory suggests that crime comes about through a lack of attachment to groups valuing law-abiding behaviour.

7   Reintegrative shaming involves all social processes expressing disapproval that have the aim of inducing remorse in the offender. The shame that matters most is not that coming from officials such as the police or judges or courts but that relating to the people we care about most.

Critical thinking questions

1   Compare the following two views – one suggests that crime is normal, the other that capitalism generates crime.

> There must be something rotten in the very core of a social system which increases its wealth without diminishing its misery, and increases in crimes even more rapidly than in numbers.
>
> (Karl Marx, 'Population, Crime and Pauperism', *New York Daily Tribune*, 16 September 1859)

> Crime is normal. . . . It is a factor in public health, an integral part of all healthy societies.
>
> (Émile Durkheim, *Rules of Sociological Method*: 76)

2   Examine the different kinds of study of crime emanating from the Chicago School. Consider how they complement each other. Do they ultimately add up to a full understanding of delinquency and crime? If not, what is missing?

3   Look at your own home city or town. Can you map out the areas of greatest crime? How would you explain this concentration?

4   Critically discuss the factors that may weaken a person's bond to society. Is such weakening likely to lead to crime and deviance?

Further study

Cloward, R. and Ohlin, L. E. (1960) *Delinquency and Opportunity: A Theory of Delinquent Gangs*, New York: Free Press.

Gabbidon, S., Greene, H. T. and Young, V. D. (2001) *African American Classics in Criminology and Criminal Justice*, Thousand Oaks, CA: Sage. Important volume examining the 'black' tradition of criminology in the United States.

Hirschi, T. (1969) *Causes of Delinquency*, Berkeley, CA: University of California Press. This is the classic statement of Hirschi's 'control theory'.

Matza, D. (1969) *Becoming Deviant*, Englewood Cliffs, NJ: Prentice Hall. Although old, this is one of the most sophisticated accounts of crime and deviance available. At its core it reviews the major traditions of anomie, cultural learning and labelling in the study of deviance; but it is highly original in its synthesis.

Merton, R. K. (1938) 'Social Structure and Anomie', *American Sociological Review*, 3 (October): 672–82. One of the most cited papers in the sociology of crime.

Reiner, R. 'Political Economy, Crime and Criminal Justice', and Rock, P. 'Sociological Theories of Crime' are both useful reviews to be found in M. Maguire, R. Morgan and R. Reiner (eds) (2007) *The Oxford Handbook of Criminology*, 4th edn, Oxford: Oxford University Press.

More information

Émile Durkheim Archive
http://durkheim.itgo.com/anomie.html
A comprehensive website on Durkheim's life and works.

University of Chicago: Department of Sociology
http://sociology.uchicago.edu/overview/history/html
Gives a brief history of the original Chicago School theorists.

The Chicago School of Pragmatism
http://www.pragmatism.org/genealogy/Chicago.htm
Provides a brief history of the foundation of the Chicago School of Pragmatism and its members.

Society for Human Ecology (SHE)
http://www.societyforhumanecology.org/
This is an international interdisciplinary professional society that promotes the use of an ecological perspective in both research and application.

Chicago Area Project
http://www.chicagoareaproject.org/
Continues to operate today.

chapter 6

Radicalizing Traditions

Key issues

- What is labelling theory?
- How did conflict theory arise and what are the questions posed by a new criminology?
- How did the Birmingham Centre for Contemporary Cultural Studies provide an advance over earlier subcultural theories?
- What is the impact of feminism on criminology?
- What has been the influence of Foucault?

Introduction

The social ways of thinking about crime discussed in Chapter 5 were very influential in shaping contemporary criminology and appeared predominantly in the first six decades of the twentieth century. In this chapter we will look at accounts of crime that came into prominence during the latter part of the twentieth century. Many of these can be seen in some way as a response to earlier theories – challenging them, debating them, extending them. Indeed, during this time there was a constant tendency to find new ways of thinking about crime – but often these new ways turned out to be little more than old ways updated, and often their newness was attacked very rapidly and they fell into decline as quickly as they appeared. But some of the theories had a more enduring impact. This chapter will briefly review these late twentieth-century theories before turning in Chapter 7 to some of the most recent trends.

The 1960s was a watershed decade. Looking back now it seemed like an era when all kinds of established authority came to be challenged; from popular culture to civil rights, revolutionary upheaval was in the air and academic disciplines too experienced some profound upheavals. In criminology, the very idea of crime and deviance is challenged. Claims from the past that we know what crimes are, we know what deviance is, that they are 'objective categories' – all these came under critical scrutiny. The thinking of the 1960s came to see such 'objective' definitions of crime and deviance as problematic. There was now a need to study the categories themselves – what they were, how they came about, and what they did to people. And much of this was political; suddenly, politics became an integral part of criminology.

This was at the time seen as quite a radical shift in emphasis and it gave rise to what was variously called the 'New Deviancy theorists', the 'Societal Reaction Perspective' or labelling theory. In the United Kingdom it generated an organization – the National Deviancy Conference – that held regular conferences and discussions at York University between 1968 and 1973 (and resulted in several books: notably *Images of Deviance* (1971) and *Politics and Deviance* (1973)) (see Box 6.1). This grouping lasted a few years. It disbanded in the late 1970s but it had effectively come to an end much earlier. After this, a new series of divisions and schisms became apparent.

BOX 6.1 From the National Deviancy Conference to the rise of the new criminologies

Background

The National Deviancy Conference (NDC) was established in 1967 as a reaction against mainstream criminology. It held conferences at the University of York between 1967 and 1976 and thereafter turned for a while into a broader European organization. Among its key founder members in the United Kingdom were Stanley Cohen, Laurie Taylor, Jock Young, Ian Taylor and Mary Macintosh.

What was the NDC responding against?

Its central position was a critique of mainstream criminology – as exemplified in work conducted at the Home Office or at the Institute for Criminology in Cambridge, which used traditional methods, lacked a firm sociological focus and was often rather conservative in outlook. Broadly, this was a time of student rebellion, growth in sociology and also a time for wider activism in various new penal reform and social change movements. These positions were brought together in a desire to radically rethink the problem of crime and deviance.

What theories did it draw from?

The NDC marked a strong concern with sociology and deviance – all its founders were sociologists, though it soon came to include radical practitioners too and members of radical change movements. It initially drew from the theories of symbolic interactionism, ethno-methodology, Marxism, appreciative ethnography, conflict theories, social movement activism, neo-functionalism, labelling theory and anarchistic criminology. Its members were writing before the arrival of a feminist criminology, though many of them were part of the newly emerging second-wave women's movement.

Examples of key texts

- Jock Young, *The Drugtakers* (1971)
- Stanley Cohen, *Folk Devils and Moral Panics* (1972/2002)
- Laurie Taylor, *Deviance and Society* (1973)
- Stanley Cohen (ed.) *Images of Deviance* (1971)
- Ian Taylor and Laurie Taylor (eds) *Politics and Deviance* (1973)

Demise and diffusion

The New Criminology (see Box 6.2) eventually critiqued much of this new radicalism and itself unfolded into a number of other positions. Some of those involved left criminology altogether and developed other fields such as cultural studies or sexuality studies. Some remained with a particular theoretical orientation and developed it further – such as those who had initially applied ethnomethodology to the study of criminal statistics (they now went on to apply ethnomethodological reasoning to other areas of social life). And others went on to develop further criminologies – left realism, discourse theory and feminist criminology – which will be discussed later in this, and the next chapter.

See Cohen (1971) and Taylor and Taylor (1973).

Plate 6.1 Stanley Cohen was one of the founders of the National Deviancy Conference. His initial work was on the mods and rockers, and he developed the idea of the moral panic. More recently he has looked at the workings of the control system and at human rights. The Downes *et al.* (2007) edited collection of essays honouring his contribution is a fitting tribute to his intellectual project. It highlights how his work over the last four decades has done much to transform the discipline from a dull social science into the site of exciting, formidable and urgent political questions, while his commitment to intellectual honesty, social justice and humanitarian practice has come to define the criminological vocation.

Source: Stanley Cohen.

thinking about crime

Briefly, the theories proposed:

- A turning away from conventional theories of crime which assumed the nature of criminal categories and control processes and asked questions about the causes of crime. Instead, it was argued that crime was a socially constructed category, that it differed throughout history and different cultures, and that there could not therefore be any 'criminal type' – since criminal types depended on who defined the laws at particular times.
- A rejection of the view that crime is caused by pathologies, disorganization, strains, stresses and leakage within a consensual society which more or less agreed on values. Instead, its focus moved to pick up on the theme of conflict: to see crime (as some earlier criminologists such as Bonger had indeed done) as a special form of conflict.
- Ways of seeing crime and deviance as ideologically driven categories that stretched the concerns of criminology away from offenders onto the role of social control.
- A re-examination of youth subcultural theories of crime, placing a much greater emphasis upon culture and cultural forms.
- A fresh concern with gender. It is striking how few theories of crime of the nineteenth and twentieth century recognized one of the most apparent facts about crime: that it is overwhelmingly committed by men. With the rise of modern (second-wave) feminism, the issue of gender was brought into criminology as a key element for thinking about crime.
- A move to see criminology as part of the very problem it tries to solve. Many interventions into the criminal sphere simply do not work in the way they are supposed to work. Instead, they tend to extend the webs of surveillance and control.

'Deviance' and labelling

For a short while during much of the late 1960s and the 1970s, labelling theory became the dominant sociological theory of crime. In one sense this was very odd, since it made few claims to try to understand what made people criminal. Quite the contrary: it tended to assume we would all be criminal if we could (in this, it had quite a lot in common with control theory, discussed in Chapter 5). Instead, it turned its focus on societal reactions to crime. Societal reactions could range from the informal responses of public opinion, families or the mass media to the more formal responses of police, courts and prisons.

Labelling theory highlights social reaction. In doing so it reworked some old ideas and put them into new contexts and shocked establishment criminology by emphasizing the contingent, constructed, fluid and symbolic dimensions of social life. The elementary understanding of the way in which criminal responses may shape crime goes back a long way: it is captured in popular phrases such as 'give a dog a bad name'. In the twentieth century the origins of the theory are usually seen to lie with Frank Tannenbaum in his classic study *Crime and the Community*. Here he argued that

> The process of making the criminal, therefore, is a process of tagging, defining, identifying, segregating, describing, emphasizing, evoking the very traits that are complained of. . . .

The person becomes the thing he is described as being. . . . The way out is a refusal to dramatize the evil.

(Tannenbaum, 1938: 19–20)

The theory has a number of roots in earlier sociological traditions, but draws heavily on the idea of W. I. Thomas that 'when people define situations as real they become real in their consequences'. This is sometimes also known as the 'self-fulfilling prophecy' (see Janowitz, 1996).

Becker, Lemert and Cohen

The key labelling theorists are usually seen to be the North American sociologists Edwin Lemert and Howard S. Becker and the South African-born but UK-based criminologist Stanley Cohen.

Edwin Lemert (1951, 1967) argued that many episodes of norm violation – from truancy to under-age drinking – often provoke little reaction from others and have little effect on a person's self-concept. Lemert calls such passing episodes **primary deviance**. He asked what happens if other people take notice of someone's deviance and make something of it. If, for example, people begin to describe a young man as a 'boozer' or a 'drunk' or even an 'alcoholic' and then push him out of their group, he may become embittered, drink even more and seek the company of others who condone his behaviour. So the response to initial deviance can set in motion **secondary deviance**, by which an individual engages in repeated norm violations and begins to take on a deviant identity. The development of secondary deviance is one application of the Thomas theorem, which states that 'Situations defined as real become real in their consequences.'

The terms 'primary' and 'secondary' deviance capture the distinction between original and effective causes of deviance: primary deviation arises from many sources but 'has only marginal implications for the status and psychic structure of the person concerned', whereas secondary deviation refers to the ways in which stigma and punishment can actually make the crimes or deviance 'become central facts of existence for those experiencing them, altering psychic structure, producing specialised organisation of social roles and self regarding attitudes' (Lemert, 1967: 40–1). Deviant ascription became a pivotal or master status. It was Lemert who argued that rather than seeing crime as leading to control, it may be more fruitful to see the process as one in which control agencies structured and even generated crime.

Howard S. Becker was a second-generation Chicago sociologist (identified with the 1950s and 1960s) whose own work focused on marijuana use and its control. Studying the ways in which cultures and careers were transformed by negative sanctions against drug use, he outlined the broad problem of labelling when he asked:

We [should] direct our attention in research and theory building to the questions: who applied the label of deviant to whom? What consequences does the application of a label have for the person so labelled? Under what circumstances is the label of a deviant successfully applied?

(Becker, 1963: 3)

thinking about crime

In what became the canonical statement of labelling theory, he announced that

> Social groups create deviance by making the rules whose infraction constitutes deviance, and by applying those rules to particular people and labelling them as outsiders. . . . Deviance is *not* a quality of the act the person commits, but rather a consequence of the application by others of rules and sanctions to an 'offender'. The deviant is one to whom that label has successfully been applied: deviant behavior is behavior that people so label.
>
> (Becker, 1963: 9)

Becker challenged standard definitions of deviant behaviour. In his research on drug users he could show how sanctions against drug use led to distinctive subcultures and careers as drug users which, he claimed, would not exist without the sanctions. Sanctions shaped the nature of drug use.

Stanley Cohen in his seminal work *Folk Devils and Moral Panics* (1972/2002) looked at one of the first major youth phenomena in the United Kingdom. This was a study of the big English youth phenomenon of the 1960s: the rise of the so-called mods and rockers (see Plate 6.2). Apart from the Teddy boys of the 1950s, these were the first major youth phenomenon of the post-war era, and sparked off a great deal of controversy. They seemed to turn the local beaches of Clacton

Plate 6.2 A youth lying on the sand at Margate, Kent, when mods and rockers clashed on the beach on 18 May 1964. The first major study of moral panics was that of this youth phenomenon of the 1960s.

Source: Associated Press.

into a battleground. Cohen had an unusual take on all this: for him, the mods and rockers came into being, at least in part, because of the very responses of the media, the police and the courts – who helped define and shape them. The term **moral panic** is introduced to capture the heightened awareness of certain problems at key moments. In his classic formulation:

> a condition, episode, person or group of persons emerges to become defined as a threat to societal values and interests: its nature is presented in a stylised and stereotypical fashion by the mass media; the moral barricades are manned by editors, bishops, politicians and other right thinking people.
>
> (Cohen, 1972: 9)

Moral panics have traditionally been short-lived and focused: a riot, a drug overdose, a violent crime, a paedophile murder. Yet, and maybe starting with AIDS, such isolated panics became almost pervasive and commonplace. As they spread out and generate higher levels of anxiety, society becomes constantly on edge about such 'problems' (McRobbie and Thornton, 1995: 560). Moral panics start to signpost persistent ideological struggles over problems constructed on an almost daily basis. There is an 'endless overhead narrative of such [a] phenomenon as one panic gives way to another, or one anxiety is displaced across different panics' (Watney, 1997: 412). Arguably, in late modern times social problems have to become more extreme – or spoken about in extreme language – if they are to be noticed. (Some of these ideas are discussed further in chapters 7, 12, 20 and 22.)

Wider contributions

Overall, labelling theory has covered a surprisingly wide range of issues and produced many classic studies. Thus, Edwin Schur's *Crimes without Victims* (1965) looked at victimless crimes and showed how the legal response to the then criminalized homosexuality, abortion and drug use generated more problems than were solved. Erving Goffman's *Asylums* (1961) and Thomas J. Scheff's *Being Mentally Ill* (1966) developed a controversial theory of mental illness based upon labelling dynamics, suggesting that there was no such simple thing as mental illness; rather, the role of the mentally ill depended upon a major identification process. And the criminologist Lesley Wilkins's *Social Policy, Action and Research* (1967) used systems theory to show how a process of deviancy amplification works: how small deviations can through a process of feedback by control agencies become major patterns of deviance.

This latter idea was subsequently used to great effect by Jock Young (1971) in his study of drug use in bohemian London, which described how the mass media transformed marijuana use into a social problem through sensationalist and lurid accounts of hippie lifestyles. As the much-cited quote from the *News of the World* (21 September 1969) on a squat in a Georgian mansion in Piccadilly makes abundantly clear:

Hippie drugs – the sordid truth
Drug-taking, couples making love while others look on, a heavy mob armed with iron-bars, filth and stench, foul language, that is the scene inside the hippies' fortress in London's

Piccadilly. These are not rumours but facts, sordid facts which will shock ordinary decent living people. Drug taking and squalor, sex . . . and they'll get no state aid.

(cited in Young, 2007b: 59)

The passage nicely captures the mix of fascination and repulsion, dread and desire that moral guardians exhibit towards the objects of their anxiety. There is a delicious irony here for the report goes on to describe how the hippies sit 'lit only by the light of their drugged cigarettes' led by the enigmatic Dr John, the pseudonym of Phil Cohen, who would subsequently become one of the leading exponents of a radicalized subcultural theory!

All in all, this was a very productive period in the study of crime and deviance. The labelling perspective brought political analysis into deviancy study. It recognized that labelling was a political act and that 'what rules are to be enforced, what behaviour regarded as deviant and which people labelled as outsiders must . . . be regarded as political questions' (Becker, 1963: 7). From this it went on to produce a series of empirical studies concerning the origins of deviancy definitions through political actions (in such areas as drug legislation, temperance legislation, delinquency definitions, homosexuality, prostitution and pornography) as well as the political bias in the apprehension and adjudication of deviants.

Labelling theory – with its rejection of so-called positivistic criminology and its deterministic understanding of human action – was closely allied to the development of the sociology of deviance. This sociology not only changed the theoretical base for the study of criminals, but also brought in its wake a dramatic restructuring of empirical concerns. Sociologists turned their interests to the world of expressive deviance: to the twilight, marginal worlds of tramps, alcoholics, strippers, dwarfs, prostitutes, drug addicts, nudists; to taxi-cab drivers, the blind, the dying, the physically ill and handicapped, and even to a motley array of problems in everyday life. It opened up the field of inquiry so that it was possible to discuss a range of areas hitherto neglected – blindness, subnormality, obesity, smoking and interpersonal relationships – thereby enabling both the foundations for a formal theory of deviance as a social property and a method for understanding the routine and the regular through the eyes of the ruptured and the irregular. Whatever these studies had in common, it was very clear by this stage that it was not conventional criminology.

Problems with labelling theory

Popular as the theory became, it was soon under attack. Among the most central criticisms made were the following:

- It is seen as a liberal theory that gives too little attention to the state, power and the economy.
- From the political right, it is seen as overly sympathetic to the criminal and deviant – a proposal for going soft on crime.
- For rigorous positivist-minded social scientists, either it is untestable or, if it is tested, is found to be severely lacking in supportive evidence.
- Criminologists were usually unhappy about its neglect of the origins of deviance. Labelling theory failed to provide any account of the initial motivations steering individuals towards deviance.

■ Closely linked to the above is the argument that labelling theorists had rescued the deviants from the deterministic constraints of biological, psychological and social forces only to enchain them again in a new determinism of societal reactions (Plummer, 1979).

Developments

Although labelling theory is always cited as one of the major sociological theories of crime and deviance, the original research and controversies that surrounded it during the 1970s have largely abated. The theory has become a quiet orthodoxy for some sociologists. Yet several of its key themes have entered criminological research under different guises. Three can be highlighted here. The first is the theory of moral panics. An idea discussed by Howard Becker over the initial concern with drugs in the United States, it was developed further in the work of Stanley Cohen in his research on the panics concerning teenage mods and rockers in beach resorts on English bank holidays in the 1960s. The focus here becomes the exaggerated responses of control agencies (largely the media) in stirring up concern and anxiety. The study of moral panics has been applied to many areas and has become a staple feature of sociological research (Thompson, 1998; Critcher, 2003; Jewkes, 2004; and see Chapter 20).

The second is the theory of social constructionism. Much recent labelling theory has moved under this different name. This is an approach in sociology which argues that 'conditions must be brought to people's notice in order to become social problems' (Best, 1990: 11). Once again closely allied to Becker's notion of moral enterprise, it looks at the ways individuals, groups and societies come to label certain phenomena as problems and how others then respond to such claims. Joel Best, for instance, has traced the 'rhetoric and concern about child victims', while Joseph Gusfield (1981) has analysed the drink-driving problem. Broadly, there is seen to be a 'social problems marketplace' in which people struggle to own social problems. This theory continues to examine the rhetorics, the claims and the power struggles behind such definitional processes.

A third area is the enhanced understanding of social control. Traditionally, many labelling theorists were concerned with the excessive encroachment of technology, bureaucracy and the state upon the personal life – often in its grossest forms such as the increasing medicalization of deviance, the bureaucratization of the control agencies and the concomitant dehumanization of the lives of their 'victims', as well as the direct application of technology in the service of control. With the political shift to the right in many Western democracies in the 1980s, such concerns were co-opted as part of a market-based laissez-faire liberalism that aimed to roll back the state and introduce privatization into social control. Despite this, labelling theorists have long been concerned with policies of decriminalization, deinstitutionalization, demedicalization, deprofessionalization and the creation of social movements concerned with such activities (Cohen, 1985).

In sum: labelling theory highlights societal reactions to crime and deviance. It has a long history but became particularly prominent in the 1960s and 1970s. Since that time, and after a number of critiques, the theory has become something of an orthodoxy. Currently, the theory of moral panics, social constructionist theories and theories of social control have become its modern-day reincarnations.

Crime as conflict

A young Karl Marx (1843/1971:137) once wrote that 'to be radical is to grasp things at root' and at the core of his political vision is class conflict, which in turn informed the radical criminology emerging in the late 1960s. A key influence here is Alvin Gouldner who launched a scathing critique of the by now dominant liberal sociology of deviance in a well-known feud with Howard Becker.

He begins by denouncing Becker's partisan sociology as 'glib' for although it might be at ease in the 'cool worlds' of drug addicts, jazz musicians and mental patients (among other outsiders) as well as taking sides with the 'underdog' against small-minded, middle-class morality, it amounted to little more than well-meaning 'zookeeping'. His complaint is that the

> pull to the underdog is sometimes part of a titillated attraction to the underdog's exotic difference . . . Becker's school of deviance is redolent of romanticism. It expresses the satisfaction of the Great White Hunter who has bravely risked the perils of the urban jungle to bring back an exotic specimen. It expresses the romanticism of the zoo curator who preeningly displays his rare specimens. And like the zookeeper, he wishes to protect his collection; he does not want spectators to throw rocks at the animals behind the bars. But neither is he eager to tear down the bars and let the animals go. The attitude of these zookeepers of deviance is to create a comfortable and humane Indian Reservation, a protected social space, within which these colourful specimens may be exhibited, unmolested and unchanged.
>
> (Gouldner, 1968/1973: 37–8)

Anticipating later developments he criticized the picture painted of the deviant as a passive victim of an intolerant society, rather than a defiant rebel against it.

As he memorably put it, the deviant was understood as 'not as man-fighting back . . . but rather, man-on-his-back' (Gouldner, 1968/1973: 39) and the focus was on the bureaucratic, caretaking institutions of society rather than the master institutions producing the suffering in the world. Others were quick to take up the challenge and take criminology in a more resolutely Marxist direction (Quinney, 1970; Liazos, 1972; Chambliss, 1976), which had been implicit in Gouldner's intervention and we will just consider one brief example here before turning to important British developments.

Jeffrey Reiman and economic conflicts

One of the most accessible statements of the conflict theory of crime is Jeffrey Reiman's (1942–) *The Rich Get Richer and the Poor Get Prison* (1979). Reiman shows how the poor are arrested and charged out of all proportion to their numbers for the kinds of crimes poor people generally commit: burglary, robbery, assault, and so forth. Yet when we look at the kinds of crimes poor people almost never have the opportunity to commit, such as antitrust violations, industrial safety violations, embezzlement and serious tax evasion, the criminal justice system shows an increasingly benign and merciful fate. The more likely it is for a particular form of crime to be committed by middle- and upper-class people, the less likely it is that it will be treated as a criminal offence (Reiman, 1979).

Ironically, for Reiman the criminal justice system is designed to fail – any success it achieves is a pyrrhic victory: it succeeds in its failures. As he says, 'On the whole, most of the system's practices make more sense if we look at them as ingredients to maintain rather than reduce crime' (Reiman, 2001: 4). It is a carnival mirror of crime: it reflects real dangers in our society, but it is a truly distorted image. We keep seeing and hearing about the wrong things in crime analysis, and the really serious crimes go missing. There are many other crimes that are far more costly and even dangerous but which never appear in the mirror. Much of his book is full of documentary evidence of the high cost of these crimes we neglect.

So, for Reiman, the goals of a policy to eliminate crime are somewhat different. Most of his criteria are linked in various ways to establishing 'a more just distribution of wealth and income and mak[ing] equal opportunities a reality' (1979: 183). His work is often not discussed seriously by either criminologists or textbooks, but his book has been through six editions, has a major website (listed at the end of this chapter), and seems to have become an idea that interests students more than it does the criminological profession. In part this may be a reflection of the fact that that very profession comes under attack in it! Nevertheless, it does provide an accessible introduction to issues that others have developed with varying degrees of theoretical sophistication and nuance.

The new criminology

Although there is a long history of conflict theories of crime (from at least Marx onwards), since the 1970s there has been a significant revitalization of interest.

A key book here was by the British sociologists of crime Ian Taylor, Paul Walton and Jock Young, called *The New Criminology* (1973; see Box 6.2). This was a substantial critique of all the theories we have so far outlined, and more besides (each chapter takes a particular theory and dissects it).

Broadly, they argued that most existing theories of crimes

- ■ had not looked at a wide enough range of questions (to take in the wider structural explanations of control as well as of crime, for instance);
- ■ had often ignored wider material conflicts at the root of much of the criminal process;
- ■ too frequently were deterministic in their assumptions and gave little role to the creative human actor willing to commit crimes;
- ■ had inadequate epistemologies (theories of how we know the truth).

They argued that limitations were not just to be found in the early theories (positivism and classicism), but equally to be found in the so-called radical or sceptical theories of the 1970s (labelling, new deviance, etc.). These failed to do many things – and the whole field had become 'exhausted, except as a form of moral gesture' (Taylor et al., 1973: 14). At the time of writing, all the authors were Marxists.

From their work, a new position started to appear that was based on the 'materiality' of crime, and was variously called critical criminology, working-class criminology or neo-Marxist

BOX 6.2 *The New Criminology: For a Social Theory of Deviance*

In this book, published in 1973, the authors, Ian Taylor, Paul Walton and Jock Young, review each of the major theories of criminology and find them lacking. They then argue that a series of key questions need to be addressed in any 'fully social theory of crime'. Their work is interesting both for its critique and for its framing of questions, and for over a decade it was one of the most influential books in British criminology. The questions it posed were:

1 The wider origins of the deviant act.
2 The immediate origins of the deviant act.
3 The actual act.
4 The immediate origins of social reaction.
5 The wider origins of deviant reaction.
6 The outcome of the social reaction on deviant's further action.
7 The nature of the deviant process as a whole.
8 The new criminology.

Plate 6.3 Cover of *The New Criminology*, published in 1973. It became a highly important watershed, taking stock of the old field of criminology and designating the requirements for a fully social theory of crime.

Source: © Routledge.

criminology. Much of it borrowed from conflict theory and Marxism. For some of these writers, the problems of the poor and the working class were not the truly serious problems of crime. On the contrary, it was the crimes of the powerful (Pearce, 1976), that deserved focus; the wrong crimes and the wrong criminals were being focused upon. This was the basis of much of the first wave of radical criminology.

Critics from all sides though were quick to highlight some of the flaws in this radical turn. Socialists worried that the 'romanticism of crime, the recognition in the criminal of a rebel "alienated" from society, is, for Marxism, a dangerous political ideology' (Hirst, 1975: 218). Stanley Cohen (1979a: 44) pointed out that socialist legality in practice means a 'model of social control in which offenders wearing sandwich-boards listing their crimes before a crowd which shouts "Down with the counter-revolutionaries!" and are then led away to be publicly shot'. As we will shortly see a wave of feminist scholarship powerfully challenged many of the assumptions on which Marxist criminology rested, while the mainstream voices from the ancient universities retorted that the radicals have ignored 'the large measure of consensus, even among the oppressed, in condemning the theft and violence that makes up the bulk of traditional crime' (Radzinowicz and King, 1979: 87). Under these kind of criticisms a bitter divide would come to split the Left during the 1980s and much of the 1990s.

Left realism

The revisionism of left realism sought to counter the resurgent right-wing criminology (see Box 6.3) through a renewed commitment to social democratic principles and a return to Merton's understanding of anomie to confront crime – where Merton's dire warning that the ceaseless striving for wealth in American society produces a fatal disjuncture between cultural goals and the legitimate ways of achieving them. Seeing crime as a serious problem, especially in inner-city areas, and one that has grown in recent years, they analyse what they call 'the square' of crime: the state, society and the public at large, offenders and victims (Figure 6.1). All four factors need to be looked at for all types of crime. Victims of crime are overwhelmingly poor, working-class people and, often, those who are margninalized and deprived because of their ethnicity. For example, unskilled workers are twice as likely to be burgled as other workers. *Much crime, then, is committed by the working class on the working class.* Jock Young (1997) argued that the causes of crime need to be looked for in deep structural inequalities. Crime is produced by **relative deprivation** – a perceived disadvantage arising from a specific comparison – and **marginalization**, where people live on the edge of society and outside of the mainstream with little stake in society overall.

All this calls for the pursuit of justice at a wide level. The left realists argue for policies involving fundamental shifts in economic situations, enlightened prison policies, environmental design and accountable police. They stress that crime needs to be taken seriously and confronted by politicians, policy-makers and academics – and the public's concerns listened to.

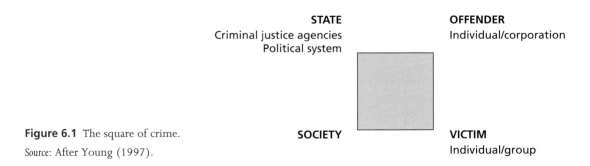

STATE
Criminal justice agencies
Political system

OFFENDER
Individual/corporation

SOCIETY

VICTIM
Individual/group

Figure 6.1 The square of crime.
Source: After Young (1997).

The stated aims of new left realists are to avoid over-general accounts of crime and to see crime in context. The specific shapes of crime, its causes and the way they are controlled change across the world as the society changes. New causes of crime and new patterns of crime appear worldwide. Ian Taylor (1999), for example, argues that the strong shift to a 'market society' since the time of Margaret Thatcher and Ronald Reagan has not just tended to promote more 'ugly' crime, but also brought more 'brutish' penal responses.

Left idealism?

With the arrival of a left realism, Jock Young (1975, 1979) and others could argue that critical criminology was fragmenting into a number of distinct strands, including what he identified as an 'idealist–realist' polarity. According to Young, the so-called left idealist position covers a range of perspectives on crime and the law – interactionism's micro-sociological approach (Downes and Rock, 1979), Marxism's macro-sociological approach (Sumner, 1976), abolitionism (Mathiesen, 1974) – and analyses of discipline and state power (Boyle et al., 1975; Fitzgerald and Sim, 1979). Arguably, what unites them is an idealization of the working-class criminal, a coercive conception of order, and an unwillingness to deal with aetiology, statistics and reform.

However, those identified as 'idealists' rejected the label and associated criticisms, and argued that their version of a 'criminology from below' against the authoritarian state and alliances with the radical penal lobby (e.g. the penal pressure group Radical Alternatives to Prison) was a response to the realities of life under Thatcherism. From their perspective there is a direct relationship between economic crises and political responses of the state and judiciary, leading to marginalization and criminalization of some groups and not others:

> [W]e are not saying that crime is not a problem for working-class people or that, contrary to the innuendo in some new realist writing, the terrible brutality suffered by many women is not a problem for them. Neither are we saying that the state cannot be reformed. . . . What we are saying is that the new realist position on law and order is theoretically flawed and, from a socialist perspective, it remains politically conservative in its conclusions about what can be done about the state.
>
> (Sim et al., 1987: 59)

Divisions remain between the different strands of critical criminology. In recent years, left realists have explored the socio-cultural context of law and order in a more reflexive fashion (Walton and Young, 1997), while others have oriented themselves towards a human rights discourse (Cohen, 2001; Scraton, 1999).

The Birmingham Centre and the new subcultural theory

Another important development that was taking place during the 1970s and early 1980s was the work based at the Birmingham Centre for Contemporary Cultural Studies (BCCCS), established in 1964 by Richard Hoggart (then a professor of English). It would be Hoggart's deputy, Stuart

BOX 6.3 Criminologies from the Right

In much of this chapter we have been describing intellectual developments from the Left, but it is also important to emphasize that over this period the Right were also energetically redefining the crime problem. Indeed, they crucially influenced the 'law and order' politics of the Conservatives under Margaret Thatcher and Ronald Reagan's Republicans in the United States. The New Right combines at least four distinct approaches. One revives nineteenth-century libertarianism and natural law philosophy to chastise the state for criminalizing 'victimless crimes' that do not 'violate anyone's rights; drunkenness, possession of drugs, prostitution, homosexuality . . . in order to police the morals of America' (Wollstein, 1967). Another vigorously emphasizes the virtues of free market economics in a fundamental critique of welfare state solutions to social problems, while the third position associated with traditionalist conservatives argues for the continuing importance of deterrence, free will and individual responsibility (van den Haag, 1975, 1985). A fourth approach is that identified with the criminology of James Q. Wilson who is variously described as a 'neo-conservative' or 'New Realist' (Tame, 1991: 140), but does differ from the libertarians, economist and traditional conservatives in important respects (as demonstrated by his numerous advisory roles during the Reagan and Bush administrations).

Wilson (1975) influentially argued that poverty does not cause crime. Despite the huge investment in welfare programmes in the 1960s and rising affluence over that decade, the crime rate soared. He took this quite startling fact as proof that sociological thinking on the causes of and solutions to crime were seriously mistaken. Instead, he claimed crime was dramatically rising on account of the collapse of the civic socialization of young people, community failure and family breakdown. With his colleague George Kelling he published one of the most influential articles in American criminology, where their 'broken windows' image is used to explain how neighbourhoods descend into crime and disorder (Wilson and Kelling, 1982). They argued that if minor incivilities – like vandalism, graffiti, begging, drunkenness – go unchecked they set in motion a cycle of decline, and this argument has achieved a certain orthodoxy amongst policy-makers in ways that have not always received the approval of Wilson and Kelling. For example, it was used to justify the tough 'zero tolerance' policing of New York in the 1990s and currently informs the anti-social behaviour agenda pursued by the Home Office through the development of new powers like Anti-Social Behaviour Orders (ASBOs) and dispersal orders. There remains though considerable disagreement over how successful aggressive policing tactics are in securing order and safety (Harcourt, 2001).

Hall, who would lead the Centre through its most influential period in the 1970s. Hall became director in 1968, before leaving in 1979 to take up the chair of Sociology at the Open University (Rojek, 2003). During his time there he encouraged many students to draw upon Marxist and critical thinking while still conducting empirical researches on crime and delinquency.

A good example of this was Phil Cohen's (1972) study of the emergence of 'mods' and 'skinheads' in the East End of London during the 1960s. Cohen, who as we have seen was involved in the radical squatter movement in London, published the seminal article 'Subcultural Conflict and Working Class Community' as one of the earliest contributions to the *Working Papers in Cultural Studies* through the Birmingham Centre. In some respects Cohen's analysis shared the Chicago School's emphasis on biography, place and change, but it also offered a distinctive class analysis of the destruction of working-class community and the erosion of its traditional culture. For Cohen (1972: 23), delinquent subcultures 'express and resolve, albeit "magically", the contradictions which remain hidden or unresolved in the parent culture'. In other words, the conflicts in adult culture are felt most acutely by the young and appear at various levels: at the ideological level, between 'traditional working class puritanism' and 'the new hedonism of consumption'; at the economic level, between a 'future as part of the socially mobile elite' or as 'part of the new lumpenproletariat' (P. Cohen, 1972: 23).

Youth style and delinquency do not solve the real crises in class relations. They are symbolic, or imaginary, attempts at resolving hidden problems, and examples of this, for Cohen, include the ways in which the original Mod style was an attempt to realize the lifestyle of the socially mobile white-collar worker, as Mods' dress and music reflected the hedonistic image of the affluent consumer. The later phenomenon of the skinhead he reads as a systematic inversion of the Mods' pursuit of the upwardly mobile option. Instead, the skinheads followed the down-wardly lumpen solution. Music and style were again the central focus of the action as they signified a reaction against the contamination of the parent culture by middle-class values, and the aggressive caricature of working-class values was regressively expressed through boots, braces and racism.

The Birmingham Centre refined this approach by explicitly drawing on Gramsci's (1971) work to locate subcultures not just in relation to parent cultures, but in a fully theorized understanding of class conflict. The conceptual framework is detailed in the chapter 'Subcultures, Cultures and Class' (Clarke *et al.*, 1976) from the collection *Resistance through Rituals* (Hall and Jefferson, 1976). Their argument is that 'cultural configurations will not only be subordinate to [the] dominant order: they will enter into struggle with it, seek to modify, resist or even overthrow its reign – its *hegemony*' (ibid.: 12; emphasis in original). The various post-war working-class youth subcultures discussed in the book are seen as movements that win back space, through issuing challenges to the status quo. However, these are not political solutions. Resistance is played out in the fields of leisure and consumption, rather than in the workplace. For Clarke *et al.* (1976), a key consequence of resistance through rituals and symbols is that it fails to challenge the broader structures of power.

One of the best examples of this approach is Paul Willis's *Learning to Labour* (1977), an ethnographic study of how school prepares young people for different positions in the labour market, as signalled very clearly in the title and the subtitle: *How Working Class Kids Get Working Class Jobs*. In his analysis of a Midlands secondary school he followed a group of working-class boys – the 'lads' – who oppose school authority and develop a subculture of nonconformity. Yet what he demonstrates is that the oppositional school culture of the lads offers only a limited resistance, and in fact prepares them for the shop-floor culture of general labouring. In other words, having a laugh, skiving, being tough, sexism and racism are all forms of preparation for coping with work and will eventually trap them in dead-end jobs. The overall point is that symbolic resistance expresses the frustrations of working-class youth but will never develop into real power. In fact, as Willis's (1977) work tragically attests, the resistance reinforces inequality.

The Centre's most substantial work is *Policing the Crisis* (Hall *et al.*, 1978), in which Stuart Hall collaborated with Chas Critcher, Tony Jefferson, John Clarke and Brian Roberts to produce the most sophisticated statement of a 'fully social theory of deviance' (Taylor *et al.*, 1973) yet achieved. The book analyses the hegemonic crisis in the United Kingdom that began in the late 1960s and anticipates the victory of Margaret Thatcher's authoritarian 'law and order' programme in the 1979 general election. The first half of the book explores the moral panic that developed in Britain in the early 1970s over the phenomenon of mugging, and the authors demonstrate how the police, media and judiciary interact to produce ideological closure around the issue. Black youth are cast as the folk devil in police and media portrayals of the archetypal mugger – a scapegoat for all social anxieties produced by the changes to an affluent, but destablized, society.

In the second half of the book they chart how the rapid deterioration of Britain's economic condition from the late 1960s meant that hegemony became increasingly difficult to sustain and the state turned from governance through consent to one based on coercion to control the crisis. The state's primary concern is to deflect the crisis away from class relations on to authority relations concerned with youth, crime and race – so that the white working class blame immigrants for the present conditions, rather than the faults contained in the capitalist system. In a discussion of the 'politics of "mugging"', Hall and his colleagues (1978) attempt to explain the rise in black criminality, which they see largely as the result of police labelling. But they do concede, within a broader consideration of black culture, consciousness and resistance, that some are forced into crime as a result of unemployment and a subcultural refusal to accept the lumpen role assigned to them under capitalism (see Chapter 20 of this book).

Some problems

Stanley Cohen (1980) (Plate 6.1) developed a forceful critique of the Birmingham Centre's work in the introduction to the second edition of his *Folk Devils and Moral Panics*, which has become highly influential as it suggests the gap that had now developed between criminology and cultural studies. He begins by explaining how the new subcultural theory of the 1970s sought to radically distance itself, in both time and place, from the American functionalism of the 1950s via 'the latest vocabulary imported from the Left Bank' (ibid.: xxviii). Yet for all the obscure Continental language, 'the new theory shares a great deal more with the old than it cared to admit' (ibid.: iv). The points of similarity are a focus on the same 'problematic':

- growing up in a class society;
- male urban working-class adolescents;
- delinquency as a collective solution to a structurally imposed problem.

Where the recent work does differ is through an 'over-facile drift to historicism' (Cohen, 1980: viii). What he means by this is that too much attention is given to contextualization and historical development within Birmingham work, which often involves a particular emphasis on 'a single and one-directional historical trend' (ibid.: viii).

Cohen also raises a number of objections against reading resistance through rituals and symbols, which can be summarized as follows:

1   It is oversimplistic to understand resistance only in terms of opposition. Some actions will
    be conservative, irrational, inconsistent and 'simply wrong' (Cohen, 1980: xi).
2   There is a tendency to read the development of youth style as internal to the group, with
    commercialization coming only later. This seriously underestimates the ways in which
    'changes in youth culture are manufactured changes, dictated by consumer culture' (Cohen,
    1980: xii).
3   Too often, subcultural activities are understood to be inherited from long traditions of
    working-class resistance which lead 'to the vexing issue of consciousness and intent' (Cohen,
    1980: xiii) and the playing down of the meaning of style and subcultures to the members
    themselves.
4   He poses the question of why we should believe the interpretations offered of these
    subcultures and to what extent there is any sociological rigour in the conclusions drawn.

This is a formidable critique, and it is important to recognize that the Marxist emphasis on class
was contested by feminists at the Centre in *Women Take Issue* (Centre for Contemporary Cultural
Studies, 1980), and the relative neglect of 'race' was highlighted in *The Empire Strikes Back* (Centre
for Contemporary Cultural Studies, 1983). Subsequent developments in cultural studies are too
diverse to document here; but as we see in Chapter 7, there have been recent moves to take cultural
criminology further.

It is also worth noting that Stuart Hall and Tony Jefferson (2006) have recently addressed the
criticisms of the *Resistance through Rituals* project in a fascinating encounter with the many
developments in subcultural theory that have happened over the last thirty years. They approvingly
cite Angela McRobbie's (one of the Centre's key members) account of the 'hoodie' phenomenon
to the *Guardian* at a time when the topic was receiving much media attention, to illustrate the
continuing salience of the approach pioneered at Birmingham:

> The point of origin is obviously Black American hip-hop culture, now thoroughly main-
> stream and a key part of the global economy of music through Eminem and others. Leisure-
> and sportswear adopted from everyday wear suggests a distance from the world of office
> [suit] or school [uniform]. Rap culture celebrates defiance, as it narrates the experience
> of social exclusion. Musically and stylistically, it projects menace and danger as well as anger
> and rage. [The hooded top] is one in a long line of garments chosen by young people,
> usually boys, and inscribed with meaning suggesting that they are 'up to no good'. In the
> past, such appropriation was usually restricted to membership of specific youth cultures
> – leather jackets, bondage trousers – but nowadays it is the norm among young people to
> flag up their music and cultural preferences in this way, hence the adoption of the hoodie
> by boys across the boundaries of age, ethnicity and class.
>   (McRobbie, 2005, cited in Hall and Jefferson, 2006: xi)

Her analysis clearly echoes the earlier tradition by situating the origins of the style in a larger
context and analyses the distinctive elements in terms of their symbolic significance (distance
from the office, projecting menace, celebrating defiance, etc.). But it also moves beyond the classic
position by suggesting how the hoodie crosses boundaries and the culture itself must be grasped
through understanding the global economy of music. This way of 'acknowledging the new

without losing what may still be serviceable in the old' is seen by them as a 'valuable motif to hang on to' as it is 'something our critics have not always managed to do' (Hall and Jefferson, 2006: xii).

Feminist criminology

Another important development within radical traditions was the arrival of feminist criminology in the mid-1970s. It is an odd irony that the conflict analyses of crime we have discussed long neglected the importance of gender – despite their focus on social inequality. If, as conflict theory suggests, economic disadvantage is a primary cause of crime, why do women (whose economic position is, in general, much worse than that of men) commit far fewer crimes than men do?

Until the 1970s, the study of crime and deviance was very much a male province. But the influential work of British sociologist Carol Smart and others changed all that. In Smart's book *Women, Crime and Criminology* (Plate 6.4), originally published in 1976, she both documented the

Plate 6.4 Cover of Carol Smart's *Women, Crime and Criminology*, published in 1976. Smart's path-breaking book brought women firmly into the sphere of criminological thinking.

Source: © Routledge.

thinking about crime

ways in which women had been neglected in the study of crime and deviance and showed that when they had been included the approach had usually been highly sexist or outright misogynist. Much later, Frances Heidensohn suggested that feminist scholarship over the past thirty years in criminology can be divided into two phases. First, there is the pioneering work that defined the agenda for the study of gender. Second, there has been consolidation, which has seen a range of studies produced in response to that agenda and debate over whether a feminist criminology is possible, or even desirable.

Broadly, we can suggest three major contributions of the feminist approach:

- as a critique of existing malestream criminology – showing how women have been neglected, how they have been misrepresented and how they may be brought back into existing theories;
- as a perspective to suggest new areas of study;
- as a way of bringing gender to the forefront and especially the role of men and masculinity in crime.

Many of these issues will feature prominently throughout the book; here though we introduce some of the initial challenges posed by feminism.

Critique of malestream criminology

In the 1970s, feminist criminology made its first contribution by making a major critique of the male bias inherent in the theories and writings of criminologists. Not only were nearly all leading theorists men, they also wrote almost exclusively about men – and when they did look at women offenders, it was usually with a set of assumptions that are at best called sexist. For instance, in one notorious case, a criminologist called Otto Pollak proposed that women are in fact more criminal than men: it is just they are also more devious and cunning and hence can 'cover up their crimes' better!

How does gender figure in some of the theories we have already examined? Robert Merton's anomie theory (see Chapter 5) defines cultural goals in terms of financial success, and this has traditionally had more to do with the lives of men, while women have been socialized to view success in terms of relationships, particularly marriage and motherhood (Leonard, 1982). A more woman-focused theory might point up the 'strain' caused by the cultural ideals of equality clashing with the reality of gender-based inequality. It could help us see that different forms of deviance may emerge for women: those that are linked to marriage and motherhood. Indeed, women who do not marry ('spinsters') and who do not have children ('childless') are often seen as 'problems'.

But feminist criminologists have gone much further than reappraising past theories and assumptions. They have opened up a whole field of new questions and issues. Among the issues have been the importance of the fear of crime in women's, and especially older women's, lives; the gendering of sexual violence, and especially the growth of awareness of domestic violence, rape and incest; and the gendering of social control.

One aspect of this has been the study of women in crime. Partly this meant the study of criminal women: girls in gangs, women prostitutes, shoplifters and other crimes with which women are more closely identified. But here we will just give two brief examples: the growing interest in the ways in which women are handled differently by the police, the courts and prisons (often through what is called a code of chivalry), and the centrality of sexual violence to much debate.

A code of chivalry?

Much work has focused around what has been called a code of chivalry involving double standards at work. Some studies have been unable to come to cut-and-dried conclusions over the issue of whether men and women are treated in different ways by the courts. In fact, one study indicated that violent women offenders received more sympathetic and individualized justice for serious crimes, while men got no comparable understanding. But the majority of the research does tend to picture courts as places that have conventional and stereotyped views of gender roles, which they then reinforce in sentencing. For example, Pat Carlen's (1983) study of Scottish courts found that distinctions were made between 'good' and 'bad' mothers, and the kind of sentence they received depended on the category into which they were perceived to fall.

What unites most authors on this topic of chivalry is that women coming before the courts experience what is known as the double bind of 'double deviance' and 'double jeopardy'. 'Double deviance', it is argued, arises primarily as a result of the fact that women's crime rates are so low. This has significant effects, because those women who do offend are seen to have transgressed not only social norms, but also gender norms. Or, to put it another way, since courts are so unused to dealing with women offenders, those who do come before them are seen as both rule-breakers and role defiant, and they may be treated accordingly. For example, in Edwards's study of female defendants before the Manchester City Magistrates' Court, she found that women were much more likely to be subject to an oppressive and paternalistic form of individualized justice. She argues that 'Female defendants are processed in accordance with the crimes which they have committed and the extent to which the commission of the act and its nature deviate from appropriate female behaviour' (1984: 213).

The argument is that double deviance leads to paternalism, protectiveness and excessive punishment for women offenders. As a result, many women offenders feel that they are placed in 'double jeopardy'. That is, they are actually punished twice. First, they face the usual sanctions of the criminal justice system, but in addition they may be more harshly treated because they are seen as deviant as women. Therefore, it is not entirely surprising to find that in most of the studies, women characterize their experience in the criminal justice system as one that is particularly unjust. It seems clear too that women also face informal systems of social control and justice.

For example, the stigma involved in the loss of reputation is particularly profound and damaging. Carlen (1983) found that a number of women offenders received beatings from their husbands, as well as the punishment meted out by the court sentence. Similarly, Frances Heidensohn argues that much of the sense of injustice felt by women who come before the courts stems from their perceptions of such agencies as male-dominated and unsympathetic to them. She puts it rather nicely: 'chivalry appears to be a medieval concept neither practised nor cherished by the courts today' (1987: 103).

Violence against women

Another major area of debate opened by feminist criminologists has been the nature of sexual violence. Domestic violence, sexual harassment, child abuse and incest, and of course rape, have all been placed formally on the agenda (they are discussed in more detail in chapters 9, 11, 15, 18 and 20). According to the United Nations, 'At least one in five of the world's female population has been physically or sexually abused by a man or men at some time in their life.' Figures vary across countries and for differing kinds of abuse; but that such abuse is both widespread and frequently condoned makes it a crucial area for understanding patriarchy.

Men, masculinity and crime

Having done this groundwork, feminists saw the obvious neglect of criminology in focusing upon men as men. Statistics repeatedly show that many more men than women commit crimes. Indeed, as Richard Collier notes, 'most crimes would remain unimaginable without the presence of men' (Collier, 1998; see also Jefferson, 2002b). This dimension had been ignored – it was a key missing link. One further contribution of feminist criminology has been to raise the issue of men, and masculinity.

If there is such a skew towards men, could this mean that the whole process of crime is connected to gender? It must be a strong probability. We are not of course saying that all men are criminal and all women are not; but we are suggesting that there is something about 'masculinity' – or at least certain forms of it – that makes it more probable that men will commit crimes. We need, for instance, to explain why it is that men commit more crimes and women fewer. And indeed, once we start to raise these issues, a whole new field of questions and problems arises.

One issue becomes the ways in which girls and women seem to be more regulated. For instance, in virtually every society in the world there would seem to be more stringent controls on women than men. Historically, our society has restricted the role of women to the home. The family is their domain. In many public spaces and bars, women remain decidedly unwelcome: these places are men's domains. And more, women on their own in public places may be looked upon with some suspicion. In some countries the normative constraints placed on women are really very great: in Saudi Arabia, women cannot vote or legally operate motor vehicles; in Iran, women who dare to expose their hair or wear make-up in public can be whipped. Women are severely restricted in their access to public spaces. In this sense, in many countries women simply have less access to the possibilities of committing crimes.

But another issue is surely the expectation in many cultures of what it means to be a man. There is now a very considerable amount of research and writing on boys and men – on 'masculinities' – in sociology. The term 'masculinities' is used to denote that there are many ways of being and doing masculinity, and these change with different kinds of social order and society. At the same time, prominent theorists such as Connell also suggest that a key feature is that of patriarchy and the ways in which men come to dominate women (in most if not all societies). These are bound up with particular times and places, and hence are far from always being the same.

Researchers such as Messerschmidt (1993, 2000), Collier (1998), Jefferson (2002b) and Mac an Ghaill (1994) have looked at boys and men in their variety to sense the processes involved in developing different kinds of masculinity. They tend to sense that there is a dominant mode of masculinity to be found in many societies (what is sometimes called hegemonic masculinity) that highlights such issues as power, dominance, aggressiveness, achievement, competition, status attainment, and the like. Masculinities are always worked at and always contested: they are never fixed and stable once and for all. And researchers also sense a variety of alternative masculinities that develop – sometimes linked to ethnicity, or being gay, or resisting common patterns (as in some versions of the men's movement). Their concerns suggest that men can be seen often as 'doing their gender' (i.e. performing as men) through various criminal activities such as football hooliganism, violence, road rage, rape and corporate crime. These crimes all have very different styles and meanings, but they can come to display men as certain kinds of men – congruently frequently with what it is expected to be in order 'to be a man'. This is an exciting new area of criminological thinking, and one in which more and more research is being conducted.

Foucault and discourse theory

One final influence on current thinking about crime and control must be mentioned here. For, in many respects, the key inspiration behind many contemporary debates within criminology has to be seen as the influential French philosopher Michel Foucault (1926–84). And yet it is vital to know that not only was he not a criminologist, he was also firmly opposed to criminology! He is a philosopher of the history of ideas, and his work looks broadly at a number of institutions each with their accompanying knowledge – criminology and the prison may be one, but he also looks at 'the birth of the clinic' as a distinctly modern way of handling health, the development of the psychiatric discourse and modern approaches to madness, and the development of our modern languages around sexuality. He even asks questions about the very idea of what it means to be an 'individual' human being in Western societies.

Plate 6.5 Michel Foucault (1926–84). Foucault was a leading critical thinker who debunked the notion of criminology as a science. His *Discipline and Punish* (1977) had a striking impact on criminological study, but in many ways, as a philosopher of the history of ideas, he was an anti-criminologist.

Source: Magnum Photos; *photo:* Martine Franck.

thinking about crime

Foucault questions the roots and patterns of ideas found in social life and how they help construct what is going on in social worlds. He holds no simple view of cause and effect or of knowledge being linear and straightforward. Instead, he sees ideas as circulating in local complexes. They are disordered, contradictory, fragmentary. For Foucault, there is no scientific hierarchy any more. Instead, he traces genealogies. In general, he has looked at a number of major changes that mark out the distinctive ways we think in 'the modern world' when compared with past ones.

We have already seen a little of his work in the opening pages of Part 2 of the book (p. 53) when he compares the transmission from forms of punishment in the *ancien régime* classical societies (which focus on the body, especially physical torture) to the micro-politics of modern, capitalist societies (which focus on surveillance, classification and normalization – especially through the medium of prisons). He is concerned with the way in which criminology as a discipline grows at the same time as a whole new apparatus of crime control is brought into being. The whole profession of criminology, he suggests, is there not really to solve the problem of crime but to extend and organize power and surveillance.

Always a radical and critical thinker, he saw dramatic ruptures with the past and suggested that these modern developments are not signs of simple 'enlightened' progress, but rather evidence of extending power and increasing surveillance. For Foucault, power is everywhere and works its way through **discourses** – bodies of ideas and language, often backed up by institutions. Thus, criminology is a discourse that invents or produces its own set of ideas and languages about the criminal as an object to be studied, backed up by many institutions such as the prison and the courts. Power works its way distinctly through this discourse to help shape the whole society's view of crime. 'Knowledge' in this view may act as a way of keeping people under control.

Many of Foucault's ideas challenge common sense. Whereas we like to see criminology as a science that studies and helps us understand crime, Foucault sees it as a discourse that extends surveillance and power relations. Whereas prisons are conventionally understood to combat crime, he sees them as mechanisms for extending crime. He is very clear what he thinks of criminology:

> Have you read any criminological texts? They are staggering. And I say this out of astonishment, not aggressiveness, because I fail to comprehend how the discourse of criminology has been able to go on at this level. One has the impression that it is of such utility, is needed so urgently and rendered so vital for the working of the system, that it does not even need to seek a theoretical justification for itself, or even simply a coherent framework. It is entirely utilitarian. I think one needs to investigate why such a 'learned' discourse became so indispensable to the functioning of the nineteenth century penal system.
>
> (Foucault, 1975/1980: 47)

As you can see, his ideas are controversial, very influential and much discussed. Some say he was one of the most brilliant figures of twentieth-century thought. Others feel that his difficult writing and complexity have detracted from engagement with what is happening in the real world (see also chapters 11, 15 and 18 for further discussion of Foucault's ideas).

radicalizing traditions

SUMMARY

1   Labelling theory focuses upon the societal reactions to crimes – the role of law, social control agencies, the media, etc., in playing their part in shaping the nature of crime. Far from crime control solving the problem of crime, control may actually serve to shape and structure it. Key theorists are Lemert, Becker and Cohen.

2   In the mid-1970s, the publication of *The New Criminology* generated a concern with a wider range of questions about crime and brought neo-Marxism and conflict theory to the fore.

3   The research of the BCCCS re-examined youth subcultural theories of crime, placing a much greater emphasis upon culture and cultural forms. It had clear links to Marxist theorizing.

4   The issue of gender was brought into criminology by feminists as a key element for thinking about crime.

5   Foucault sowed the seeds of a major 'anti-criminology' movement, arguing that criminology was a discourse through which power–knowledge relations were enacted.

Critical thinking questions

1   **Discuss the ways in which criminology has become 'radicalized' in recent years. Has this radicalization helped to provide a more satisfactory account of crime?**

2   **What are moral panics? Identify a recent one you have seen discussed in the media. Does such a panic differ very much from the ones studied by Stanley Cohen and Jock Young over thirty years ago?**

3   **Identify a contemporary youth culture. Which of the theories outlined in this chapter seem best at helping you understand it?**

4   **Trace the emergence of feminist criminology and assess its impact on redefining what criminology is.**

5   **How would you account for the fact that men seem much more likely to be criminal than women?**

6   **Given so much writing and talking about crime, why has there been so little success in its reduction?**

Further study

Becker, H. S. (1963) *Outsiders: Studies in the Sociology of Deviance*, New York: Free Press.

Lemert, E. (1967) *Human Deviance, Social Problems and Social Control*, Englewood Cliffs, NJ: Prentice Hall. Two classic studies of labelling.

Maguire, M., Morgan, R. and Reiner, R. (2007) *The Oxford Handbook of Criminology*, 4th edn, Oxford: Clarendon Press. This has become the key text: very comprehensive coverage of the whole field of crime and control by specialist writers. It is, however, expensive.

Collier, R. (1998) *Masculinities, Crime and Criminology*, London: Sage.

Messerschmidt, J. W. (1993) *Masculinities and Crime: Critique and Reconceptualization of Theory*, Lanham, MD: Rowman and Littlefield. Both are valuable introductions to the issue of gender, while N. Naffine's (1997) *Feminism and Criminology* (Cambridge: Polity) assesses the uneasy relationship between the two. Walklate, S. (2004) *Gender, Crime and Criminal Justice*, 2nd edn, Cullompton: Willan, provides a thorough overview of the field.

Taylor, I. (1999) *Crime in Context: A Critical Criminology of Market Societies*, Cambridge: Polity.

Young, J. (1999a) *The Exclusive Society: Social Exclusion, Crime and Difference in Late Modernity*, London, Sage. Two lively studies that examine the crime problem from a critical perspective.

More information

Howard S. Becker Homepage
http://home.earthlink.net/~hsbecker/.
A comprehensive site with a selection of published papers and links.

Allyn & Bacon Publishers
http://www.ablongman.com/signup
Jeffrey Reiman's book: *The Rich Get Richer and the Poor Get Prison: Ideology, Class, and Criminal Justice*, 7th edn.

chapter 7

Crime, Social Theory and Social Change

Key issues

■ What is a late modern world and how is crime changing within it?

■ What is the link between postmodernism and crime?

■ What is the globalization of crime?

■ What is the impact of the 'risk society' on crime?

Introduction

The past few chapters have suggested a number of ways of thinking about crime that have been developed by criminologists over the past century and a half. Some of the ideas are now seen as outdated, but in general they have all provoked thought and can often be seen to persist – in new forms – to this day. We are still interested in ideas of the criminal person and of justice (Chapter 4). We still look at social explanations of crime and delinquency – such as the ideas established by the Chicago School (Chapter 5). And labelling, conflict theory and feminist theory are very much alive and well (Chapter 6). In this chapter, we will consider a few of the newer social trends as a background to the rest of the book. Once again, some of the ideas will be taken up in more detail later.

At the heart of this chapter is the idea that the world we live in is undergoing significant social change and that this is having an impact not only on the ways we think about crime but on the nature of crime itself. This chapter will suggest four general trends, each of which has specific implications for criminological thinking. These are:

- the movement to a late modern society;
- the drift towards postmodernism;
- the speeding up of globalization;
- the emergence of a risk society.

While these new times call for new ways of approaching questions of crime, punishment and security, it is important to recognize that criminology is always confronted by complex social processes and it is this dynamic of continuity and change that shapes the world around us.

Crime and the movement to late modernity

Over the last couple of decades many sociologists have suggested that a somewhat different kind of society is in the making. In the past, a key distinction that drove sociological work was that between traditional and modern society (Kivisto, 1998). For Marx, it was a move towards capitalism with growing conflict and exploitation; for Durkheim, it was a shift from mechanical society to organic solidarity (from a society based on similarity to one based on differences). And for Max Weber, it was a move towards bureaucracies (a process which George Ritzer (2002) has called McDonaldization, whereby the principles of the fast food industry – efficiency, calculability, predictability and control – become increasingly applied to all of social life).

But the modern world is increasingly seen as giving way to a late modern world, or to what the sociologist Beck calls a second modernity (see also Giddens, 1990 and 1999). (Box 7.1 suggests some of the key changes here; cf. Giddens, 1990, 1999.) As Ulrich Beck has powerfully put it:

> We live in an age in which the social order of the national state, class, ethnicity and the traditional family is in decline. The ethics of individual self-fulfilment and achievement is the most powerful current in modern society. The choosing, deciding, shaping human being who aspires to be the author of his or her own life, the creator of an individual identity, is the central character of our time. It is the fundamental cause behind changes in the family and the global gender revolution in relation to work and politics. Any attempt to create a new sense of social cohesion has to start from the recognition that individualism, diversity and scepticism are written into Western culture.
>
> (2000: 165)

The criminologists David Garland and Richard Sparks (2000) have succinctly described the 'coming of late modernity' in Box 7.1. Overall these factors imply, with some force, that new ways of thinking about crime and control are now necessary.

It is against the backdrop of such major changes that contemporary crime debates emerge and we can summarize these changes briefly:

- As we enter a period of mass consumerism, so desires for commodities are increased. The need to have commodities grows, and there is an escalation in credit card use, with a potential increase in fraud.

BOX 7.1 The coming of late modernity

By 'the coming of late modernity' we mean to refer to the social, economic and cultural configuration brought into being by the confluence of a number of interlinked developments. These include:

a the transformative dynamic of capitalist production and exchange (the emergence of mass consumerism, globalization, the restructuring of the labour market, the new insecurity of employment);

b the secular changes in the structure of families and households (the movement of women into the paid labour force, the increased rate of divorce and family breakdown, the decreasing size of the family household; the coming of the teenager as a separate and often unsupervised age grade);

c changes in social ecology and demography (the stretching of time and space brought about by cars, suburbs, commuting, information technology);

d the social impact of the electronic mass media (the generalization of expectations and fears; the reduced importance of localized, corporatist cultures, changes in the conditions of political speech); and

e the democratization of social and cultural life (the 'desubordination' of lower-class and minority groups, shifts in power ratios between men and women; the questioning of authority, the rise of moral individualism).

The second great transformative force was the reorganization of class (and, in the United States, race) relations that occurred in the wake of late modernity's massive disruptions. This was made possible by the shifting economic interests of the skilled working class, the welfare state's self-destructive tendencies, and the economic recessions of the 1970s and 1980s. In the end, though, it was the political 'achievement' of leaders like Thatcher and Reagan, with their reactionary mix of free-market economics, anti-welfare social policy and cultural conservatism.

Together these dynamics changed the collective experience of crime and welfare and the political meaning of both. Late modernity brought with it new freedoms, new levels of consumption and new possibilities for individual choice. But it also brought in its wake new disorders and dislocations – above all, new levels of crime and insecurity.

Source: Garland and Sparks, 2000: 199.

- The restructuring of the labour market can lead to much more casual employment and work patterns, with more people entering the informal or underground economy. The new insecurity of employment can mean looking for alternative ways of survival, and crime may be one of these, especially in the informal economy.
- Changes in families and households have meant the growth of different kinds of household (from living alone to lone-parent households, from more and more people cohabiting to lesbian and gay partnerships) as well as growing numbers of women at work. These changes

have led some critics to suggest that as the old traditional family declines, so the older controls on behaviour become weakened (Dennis, 1993; Morgan, 1978; Phillips, 2001). Others are predicting that as the population becomes older, so there will be a growth of both crimes among the elderly and the elderly as victims of crime (at present they figure relatively low on both counts) (Rothman et al., 2000).

- As teenagers become a separate and often unsupervised age group, so their criminal activities and drug-using propensities increase.
- As girls become more equal, they may also become more prone to crime. The behaviour of teenage girls starts to change and becomes more aggressive and assertive.
- As we experience changes in social ecology, so all manner of new crimes connected to the environment come into being. Some writers have called these green crimes (they are discussed in Chapter 19).
- Shifts in demography and city life brought about by cars, suburbs, commuting – we now see the development of a 'night-time economy', and all manner of crimes that are facilitated by movement (some of these issues are addressed in Chapter 8).
- The spread of new forms of information technology brings with it new patterns of crime – from cybercrimes to mobile phone theft.
- The social impact of the mass media such as film and television can produce images of crime through which people come to live their lives (see Chapter 20).
- Since 9/11 the pursuit of security against international terrorism has posed significant threats to the very freedoms liberal principles were designed to protect.

The exclusive society and the vertigo of late modernity

An example of how crime is changing under conditions of late modernity can be found in the recent work of Jock Young. In his book The Exclusive Society (1999a) he explores three kinds of division: economic (where people are excluded from the labour market), social (where people are excluded from civil society) and the expansion of a criminal justice system (which excludes more and more people from daily life). Young suggests that whereas there used to be a more consensual world of conformity – work and family were core values, the world was 'at one with itself' (Young, 1999a: 4) – from the 1960s onwards we see a world becoming torn more and more by crisis: 'from a society whose accent was on assimilation and incorporation to one that separates and excludes' (1999a: 7). Yet pluralism also grows – what he sees as a diversification of lifestyles, the immigration of people from other societies, and the proliferating glimpses of other societies. In this sense, everyone may now become a potential deviant. We have also seen the arrival of no-go zones, curfews and gated communities, while vast numbers of people start to experience penal exclusion – approaching 1.6 million are imprisoned in the United States, with 5.1 million under correctional supervision (1999a: 18). In the new century the figure has risen to 2.2 million in prison, while 1 in 34 of the population are either in prison, on probation, or parole on any given day (Young, 2007a: 12). As we will see in Chapter 18 the United States leads the way in confining its citizens through the phenomenon of 'mass incarceration'. What is more there is a clear racial dimension to this social policy, to the extent that one in nine African-American males aged 20–29 is in prison, while a staggering one in three is either in prison, on probation or parole (Mauer, 1997).

Young sees crime as the defining feature of modern societies – it is everywhere. True, there is a central core that is ordered and embedded, becoming an almost Disney-like 'squeaky-clean' world. But a cordon sanitaire encircles it, and we find whole groups subject to the new geographies of exclusion. He suggests that in all this,

> crime has moved from the rare, the abnormal, the offence of the marginal and the stranger, to a commonplace part of the texture of everyday life: it occupies the family, heartland of liberal democratic society, as well as extending its anxiety into all areas of the city. It is revealed in the highest echelons of our economy and politics as well as in the urban impasses of the underclass.
>
> (Young, 1999a: 30)

In his *Vertigo of Late Modernity*, which he regards as a sequel to the arguments developed in the *Exclusive Society*, Young (2007a: 12–13) insists that vertigo is the 'malaise of late modernity' and it derives from two sources: 'insecurities of status and economic position'. On this reckoning 'turbo-charged capitalism' not only induces anxieties and insecurities in large swathes of the middle class, but also generates an underclass of the economically redundant and high crime rates in no-go areas of major cities. These are familiar arguments from his work, yet what is new in the book is the return to cultural criminology (through demonstrating the seductions of transgression as well as acknowledging the intense experiences of humiliation produced by exclusion) and the place of terrorism in the logics of East and West justifying violence.

Plate 7.1 Robocop – future image of crime control?

Source: © Rank Film Distributors, courtesy of the British Film Institute.

thinking about crime

Postmodernism and crime

Closely allied to the above is the arrival of ideas and practices that have been called postmodern. **Postmodernism** is a much-contested term, but in general it suggests that a much less certain and more provisional view of the world is in the making. The grand or absolute truths that were being pursued in the modern world are now challenged and in their place we find partial and limited truths. Applied to criminology, it sees the whole criminology project of modernity as misguided. It still asks the same questions and still comes up with the same answers (though in more modern forms); and still the problem of crime remains. The whole criminology project has been misconceived, and it is time to recognize that.

Postmodernism tends to focus on contexts and meanings which differ from place to place rather than on grander abstractions. It sees a world made up of many shifting differences. And this brings with it a whole series of challenges to criminology – many of which were already there in some earlier versions of labelling theory (Cohen, 1997; Young, 1999a: 33). It is perhaps too early to see whether they are going to become prominent, for in effect they would lead to the disbandment of criminology as a whole discipline as we know it now.

The basic arguments of postmodernism emphasize that the search for a cause of the criminal, the search for general theories of crime, the look for generalities are indeed searches for grand meta-narratives that have now had their day. *There is no one story to be told of crime.* Stories of crime now become fragmented, patchworked, pot-pourried. Indeed, postmodern criminology would probably not have problems with any of the ways of thinking of crime we have outlined above until they make grand claims for themselves – as being the 'truth' regarding crime.

Our view is that postmodernism suggests *a more provisional world – one that is altogether less sure of itself.* Modernity brought many changes, and the criminological challenge of the twentieth century was to sift through these changes to 'solve' the crime problem. As was hinted at in Chapter 6 through the work of Foucault, criminology did not really work very well. Indeed, the more that people studied crime, the more crime seemed to grow! Although there has been much theorizing about crime, many criminology books written and many courses taught, we seem to be no nearer to solving the problem of crime. Criminology as we once knew it may well have failed.

In the twenty-first century, this modern world is an accelerating one in which there is an increased sensitivity to diversities and differences. In this view, the world becomes less dominated by generalities and 'master narratives', and there is a turn towards 'local cultures' and their 'multiplicity of stories'. As Rob Stones suggests,

> Postmodernists argue . . . for respecting the existence of a plurality of perspectives, as against a notion that there is one single truth from a privileged perspective; local, contextual studies in place of grand narratives; an emphasis on disorder, flux and openness, as opposed to order, continuity and restraint.
>
> (1996: 22)

One study that claims to be a postmodern criminology is Stuart Henry and Dragan Milovanovic's *Constitutive Criminology: Beyond Postmodernism* (1996). It calls for 'an abandoning of the futile search for "the causes of crime"' and looks instead for 'the genealogies, drift, seductions, chaos, discourse, social constructions, structuration and structural coupling' (p. 153) as ways of thinking about crime. Constitutive criminology is based on the key assumption that human beings are responsible for actively constructing their social world primarily through language and symbolic representation, but at the same time are also shaped by the world they create. Constitutive criminologists argue that the basis of crime is the socially constructed and discursively constituted exercise of unequal power relations. For Henry and Milovanovic (1996: 116), crime is defined as 'the power to deny others their ability to make a difference'. For example, crime as 'harm' occurs when people have their property stolen from them or their dignity stripped from them, or when they are prevented from achieving a desired goal because of sexism, racism or ageism. Crime then becomes domination, whether by single individuals (e.g. robbers), collectives (e.g. organized criminals or corporations), or by state governments (as in genocide, for example). Furthermore, crime is the 'co-produced' outcome not only of humans and their environments, but also of human agents and the wider society through its excessive investment in crime – through crime prevention, criminal justice agencies, criminal lawyers, criminologists, crime news, crime shows, crime books, and so on. Indeed, criminal justice is seen as part of the problem, not the solution.

In policy terms, constitutive criminologists emphasize the need to transform the prevailing social structures and institutional systems of oppression and to change the ways we think and talk about crime (e.g. through an activist engagement with the mass media – see Barak (1994) on 'newsmaking criminology'). Although some commentators have described constitutive criminology as one of the 'new criminologies' that warrants attention (Arrigo, 1997), others are more sceptical of constitutive theory's relatively unresearched state, the complexity of its arguments, its impact on revolutionizing mainstream criminology, and its ability to offer practical strategies to reduce harm (Croall, 1996). Others worry that it still manages to assert the primacy of criminology.

A number of criminologists, for example, have more or less left the field of criminology for other priorities – priorities that no longer capture and keep them within the field of criminology. Colin Sumner (1994) famously wrote a book-length obituary for the discipline. Carol Smart, in a now classic article, sees no room for feminism within criminology – even though this was indeed her earliest claim (see Chapter 6). She now worries:

> It is a feature of post-modernism that questions posed within a modernist frame are turned about. So, for a long time, we have been asking 'what does feminism have to contribute to criminology [or sociology]?' Feminism has been knocking at the door of established disciplines hoping to be let in on equal terms. These established disciplines have largely looked down their nose (metaphorically speaking) and found feminism wanting. Feminism has been required to become more objective, more substantive, more scientific, more anything before a grudging entry could be granted. But now the established disciplines are themselves looking rather insecure and, as the door is opening, we must ask whether feminism really does want to enter?
>
> (Smart, 1990: 83)

It is an irony of the times that some criminologists have decided to leave the field altogether for other (usually political) concerns at the very time when criminology has never been more popular among students. Indeed, one of the most important developments over the last few years has been the emergence of a new cultural turn in criminology that attends to the dis-embedded, pluralistic, contested, mediated and hedonistic lifestyles encouraged by post-modernity.

Cultural criminology

The origins of cultural criminology can be traced back to the work of the Birmingham Centre and the New Criminology of the 1960s and 1970s, outlined in the previous chapter, but the 1990s also saw a resurgence of interest in the cultural (Ferrell and Sanders, 1995). In North American criminology, Jeff Ferrell (1999, 2004, 2006) has done much to emphasize the role of image, style and meaning in illicit subcultures and the mediated processes through which crime and punishment are constructed. In the British context, Mike Presdee (2000, 2004), Keith Hayward (2002, 2004) and Jock Young (2004, 2007a) provide some of the most influential accounts of the commodification of crime and the intense pleasures provoked when doing wrong. Each is influenced by Jack Katz's (1988) path-breaking book on the *Seductions of Crime* (see also Chapter 12 and Ferrell's (1992) review essay on the text). Although much cultural criminology has attracted criticism for being merely decorative or a ghetto of '70s retro chic' (Mason, 2006: 2), it does offer fresh insights into how crime and deviance are constructed, as the following examples demonstrate.

One important article charts how the decline of 'underclass' discourse in the United Kingdom and the rise of the 'chav' phenomenon are intimately related, with the 'chav' representing a popular reworking of underclass ideas (Hayward and Yar, 2006). For example, the website www.chavscum.co.uk. describes itself as 'a user's guide to Britain's peasant underclass'. However, a crucial difference pointed out by Keith Hayward and Majid Yar (2006: 10) is that the earlier commentary on the underclass relied on characterizing certain groups in the working class as suffering from a pathological relationship to *production* (the world of socially useful labour), whereas the 'chav' is in contrast defined through a pathological relationship with *consumption* – manifest in dire forms of taste poverty. As they go on to explain:

> The perceived 'problem' with this 'new underclass' is that they consume in ways deemed 'vulgar' and hence lacking in 'distinction' by superordinate classes . . . 'chavs' and 'chavish-ness' are identified on the grounds of the taste and style that inform their consumer choices. Recent popular discussions correspondingly focus upon: clothing (branded or designer 'casual wear' and 'sportswear'), jewellery ('chunky' gold rings and chains), cosmetics ('excessive' make-up, sunbed tans), accessories (mobile phones), drinks ('binge' drinking, especially 'premium lagers' such as Stella Artois), and music (R&B, hip-hop).
>
> (Hayward and Yar, 2006: 14)

Using concepts derived from the French sociologist Pierre Bourdieu they describe how this is a way of thinking that not only pathologizes but also marginalizes as the question of economic capital is divorced from cultural capital. In other words, new forms of social exclusion are constructed through consumer aesthetics that discriminate on the grounds of taste.

Bourdieu would describe this antagonistic process as a form of 'symbolic violence' whereby class inequalities are socially reproduced. Bourdieu's (1984) understanding of the sharp and often cruel class distinctions that lie behind judgements of taste has been imaginatively taken up by Angela McRobbie (2005) in an examination of the forms of female symbolic violence found in mid-evening 'make-over' television programmes. Here women of recognized taste (the experts and presenters) publicly denigrate women with little or no taste. The most famous was the BBC's *What Not To Wear* presented by the upper-class Trinny and Susannah, but there are also many newer hybrid genres that all rely on the transformation of unfortunate victims (with the help of experts) through the acquisition of status-enhancing forms of cultural capital. McRobbie (2005: 150) reveals how comments like 'she looks like a mousy librarian', 'ughh she has yellow stained teeth', and 'she looks like a German lesbian' involve a level of cruelty and viciousness that is 'reminiscent of 1950s boarding school stories where the nasty snobbish girls ridicule the poor scholarship girl for her appearance, manners, upbringing, accent and shabbily dressed parents'.

Another example is Sveinung Sandberg's (2008) account of ethnicity and violence on the streets of Oslo. Using Bourdieu's concepts of social space, capital and habitus, the article describes the hierarchies and struggles over the symbolic figure in the lives of the young at the bottom of Norwegian society. Many of these ideas on cultural criminology and street culture will be returned to in Chapter 12. The overall importance of Bourdieu's sociology is that it shows how social inequalities are culturally sustained through power relations directed towards human bodies and dispositions that reproduce structural divisions.

Comparative criminology, globalization and crime

A third trend in which contemporary criminology must be located has been the way the world has become increasingly connected. In Chapter 5 we showed how the sociologist Durkheim argued over one hundred years ago that crime was a feature of all societies. This is not to say that it is at the same level in all societies. To the contrary, there may be features of capitalism and late modern societies that bring with them the conditions for higher crime rates in some societies than in others. The rate of violent crime in the United States generally emerges as about five times greater than that of Western Europe; and the rate of property crime is twice as high. We are starting to enter here the field of criminology known as comparative or cross-cultural criminology: the branch of criminology that compares different societies and their patterns of crime and control. Nevertheless, the United Nations has conducted a number of crime surveys since 1972 and has suggested both that crime is on the increase in all parts of the world (but especially the West) and that there is an increased tendency to report crimes that occur. It was commented in 1993:

> The global picture is not an encouraging one. There has been an increase in the overall crime rate; and there is the difficult issue of the interrelationship between 'higher' and 'lower' crime rates in the context of socio-economic development. The future may be even more gloomy, as some projections seem to indicate.

> (quoted in Findlay, 1999: 22)

Globalization is a very controversial topic and it has now entered criminology. What might it mean?

- 'Globalisation has something to do with the thesis that we all now live in one world' (Giddens, 1999).

- 'The process of increasing interconnectedness between societies such that events in one part of the world more and more have effects on peoples and societies far away' (Baylis and Smith, 1997: 7).

- 'Globalisation . . . refers both to the compression of the world and the intensification of consciousness of the world as a whole. . . . [It] does not simply refer to the objectiveness of increasing interconnectedness. It also refers to cultural and subjective matter, namely the scope and depth of consciousness of the world as a single place' (Robertson, 1992: 8).

Crime has always existed across cultures – think of piracy, terrorism, espionage and arms dealing in the past, for example (Martin and Romero, 1992). What we are now seeing, however, is the multiple ways in which crime becomes not just a local phenomenon (as much of the previous discussion has depicted) but a world-linked one. Much crime flows across the globe. Hence an area of criminological thinking that is starting to develop is that of globalization and crime.

Globalization

Globalization has become a popular term over the past decade, and is used to cover a wide array of concerns. Its meaning is far from clear. To start with, and simply, we can define it as *the increasing interconnectedness of societies*. **Globalization of crime** may then be seen as *the increasing interconnectedness of crime across societies*.

Globalization refers to the various processes by which the peoples of the world are incorporated into a single world society, global society (Albrow, 1990). It suggests that 'we all now live in one world' (Giddens, 1999). More formally, David Held and his colleagues have argued that 'Globalisation is the widening, deepening and speeding up of world wide interconnectedness in all aspects of contemporary life, from the cultural to the criminal, the financial to the spiritual' (Held *et al.*, 1999).

We can get some quick idea of what is meant by globalization when we think of the imagery of worldwide multicultural companies such as Coca-Cola, McDonald's, Nike and Disneyland. These companies exist across the globe – and in a number of ways. They *produce* goods across many countries; they *market* goods across many countries; and they *present* their logos and images, which travel the globe ahead of them. Think of how McDonald's outlets can be found in many countries – even though the company had its origins in the United States. McDonald's are simultaneously loved by millions and hated by millions – as signs of convenience and the modern world, and as signs of corporation takeover and mass culture. Crime can be seen like this. It produces criminal goods, markets them and sends commodities – from arms and drugs to people and slaves – all over the globe.

But a linked concept is that of *glocalization*, meaning that each community adapts and responds to the global flow. Coca-Cola is never quite the same in each country; there are modifications made. And this is true of global crime patterns too: although drug trafficking may involve globalization – flows across the world – each culture has its distinct values and communities, which make its specific responses different.

The sociologist Manuel Castells (1998: ch. 3) has written about the 'global criminal economy' and, following the United Nations Conference on Transnational Crime in 1994, has identified at least six main forms it is taking across the world:

- *Arms and weapons trafficking.* This is a multi-billion-dollar industry whereby states or guerrilla groups are provided with weapons they should not have.
- *Trafficking in nuclear materials.* This entails the smuggling of nuclear weapon materials.
- *Smuggling of illegal immigrants.* There is now a widespread trade in people desperate to leave their home country to find security, work and a new way of life. This has been described as a modern form of international slavery, estimated to have involved around 27 million people around the world (Bales, 1999). One account estimates that Chinese criminal gangs (Triads) make some US$2.5 billion a year in trafficking migrants – often with disastrous consequences (Cohen and Kennedy, 2000: 154). For instance, in 2000 some fifty-eight Chinese people being smuggled into the United Kingdom were found dead on arrival; they had been packed into a lorry in unbearable conditions, with air vents closed. The driver was sent to prison for fourteen years.
- *Trafficking in women and children*, often linked to prostitution. Significant numbers of women and children may be moved from one country (usually the poor of Eastern Europe or the poor of Asia and Latin America) to richer countries where new sex markets are appearing (Kempadoo and Doezema, 1998).
- *Trafficking in body parts*, often called 'the new cannibalism'. Nancy Scheper-Hughes and Lois Wacquant say, 'we are now eyeing each other's bodies greedily as a potential source of detachable spare parts with which to extend our lives' (2002: 14). There is now a worldwide and thriving market in body organs from both live and dead donors. Sometimes these organs are taken from condemned or even executed prisoners (especially in China, where it is estimated that perhaps 2,000 organs are removed and sold each year (*New Internationalist*, April 1998: 15–17)). The flow is typically only one way: from the desperate poor to the needy rich (Scheper-Hughes and Wacquant, 2002).
- *Money laundering.* The increasing globalization of markets has generated multiple opportunities for criminal enterprise. The growth of **money laundering**, particularly from drug-related crime, has become a major route for the incursion of criminal activity into the legitimate economic sector. Indeed, the acceleration of free market policies, the internationalization of major speculative financial activity, the deregulation of stock exchanges since the 1980s combined with the growing bureaucratic complexity of corporate enterprises has expanded the range, scale and opportunities for all kinds of financial crime (Carrabine *et al.*, 2002: 60).

BOX 7.3 International trafficking

The illegal drug trade is found all over the world: cocaine in Colombia and the Andes, opium/heroin from the Southeast Asian Golden Triangle, all along the Mexican border, Turkey and the Balkans, or Afghanistan and Central Asia (Castells, 1998: 169). In part, the proliferation of illegal drugs in the United States and Europe stems from 'demand': there is a very profitable market for cocaine and other drugs, as well as many young people willing to risk arrest or even violent death by engaging in the lucrative drug trade. But the 'supply' side of the issue also propels drug trafficking. In the South American nation of Colombia, at least 20 per cent of the people depend on cocaine production for their livelihood. Furthermore, not only is cocaine Colombia's most profitable export, but it outsells all other exports combined (including coffee). Clearly, then, understanding crimes such as drug dealing requires the analysing of social conditions both in the country of consumption and around the world. More and more, the comprehension of crime and deviance requires moving beyond the borders of one country to look at a host of international connections (see also Chapter 14).

For Manuel Castells, the global criminal economy of trafficking (of drugs, arms, people) has expanded its realm to 'an extraordinary diversity of operations, making it an increasingly diversified, and interconnected, global industry'. Human trafficking is commonly understood to involve a variety of crimes and abuses associated with the recruitment, movement and sale of people (including body parts) into a range of exploitative conditions around the world. There is a substantial amount of literature that points to the structural and ideological conditions in a globally stratified order which are conducive to the trafficking and forced migratory movements of men and women, including economic crises, lack of sustainable livelihoods, political conflict, civil war, ethnic persecution, social inequalities, gender-blind macroeconomic policies and wider processes of global social transformation.

BOX 7.4 The globalization of social control

In addition to crime taking on increasingly international dimensions, social control has also become linked to more and more international agencies. A good example of this is the Centre for International Crime Prevention, a United Nations organization based in Vienna. Indeed, the UN has acknowledged the importance of crime prevention since 1948. At present it has three central programmes:

- The Global Programme against Corruption, which provides technical cooperation to a selection of developing and transitional countries, providing analyses of current problems and policies.
- The Global Programme against the Trafficking in Human Beings, which, as its name suggests, addresses trafficking in human beings, especially women and children. In a

selection of countries, new structures are emerging for collaboration between police, immigration authorities, victim support groups and the judiciary, both within countries and internationally (linking countries of origin to destination countries).

■ The programme for Assessing Transnational Organized Crime Groups: Dangerousness and Trends looks at organized crime groups across the world, focusing on forecasting future developments and strategies of such groups in order to facilitate the formulation of pre-emptive responses.

Rebirth of human rights theories

One of the consequences of global theories has been a major worldwide resurgence of interest in ideas concerning human rights (see Box 7.5), much of which is linked not just to rights but also to governmental mechanisms and crime. David Held and his colleagues refer to the 'human rights regime' that is spreading around the world, and cite an Argentinian human rights campaigner, Emilio Mignone, as saying, 'The defense of human dignity knows no boundaries' (Held *et al.*, 1999: 65–70). There are over 200 human rights non-governmental organizations in the United States, a similar number in the United Kingdom and the rest of Europe, and it is growing all the time. Criminology's global concerns have aroused more and more interest in such rights issues (see Chapter 21), while Lydia Morris's (2006) edited collection shows how the different traditions in sociology can contribute to the theory and practice of rights.

BOX 7.5 Some major charters of human rights

■ United Nations Charter (1945)
■ Charter of the World Health Organization (1946)
■ Universal Declaration of Human Rights (1948), which becomes the international Bill of Human Rights
■ European Convention for the Protection of Human Rights and Fundamental Freedoms, and its eight protocols (1950)
■ International Covenant on Economic, Social and Cultural Rights (1967)
■ The UN Commission on Human Rights (UNCHR)
■ The American Convention on Human Rights (1970)
■ The African Charter on Human and People's Rights (1982)
■ The Convention on the Rights of the Child
■ Specific women's rights through the Fourth World Conference of Women Declaration and Platform for Action (1995)

See Ishay (1997).

thinking about crime

The risk society: actuarial justice and contradictory criminologies

A fourth theme is that of 'risk'. 'Risk' is now a dominant theme in contemporary life, to the extent that virtually everything we do has some danger associated with it. There are two dominant explanations of our contemporary preoccupation with risk (Johnston, 2000: 23).

One originates in the sociology of modernity and is primarily concerned with the emergence of an entirely new set of 'risky' social circumstances. Anthony Giddens (1990) in his book *The Consequences of Modernity* argues that one of the defining features of late modernity is the development of a 'calculative attitude' in individuals and institutions to deal with the issues of risk, trust and security in these troubling times. He sees risk as being globalized (something that exists on a global scale rather than at a local level) yet also personalized, as it is built into people's subjective concerns about their identity.

Giddens's argument has much in common with Ulrich Beck's (1992) discussion of what he calls the 'risk society'. For Beck, the 'risk society' is a distinct stage of modernity that has replaced the 'class society' of the industrial era. He argues that politics in class society is concerned not with risk, but with the 'attainment and retention of social wealth' (I. Taylor, 1999: 207). In contrast, in the *world risk society*, new technologies are generating risks that are of a quite different order from those found throughout earlier human history. Of course, past societies were risky and dangerous places too – whole populations could be wiped out by major earthquakes, floods or plagues, for example. But Beck argues that new kinds of risks appear with the industrial world which are not 'in nature' but 'manufactured'.

These are associated with the many new technologies that generate new dangers to lives and the planet itself. These are humanly produced, may have massive unforeseen consequences, and may take many, many thousands of years to reverse. These 'manufactured risks' are taking us to the edge of catastrophe. The list of examples of new risks could be quite long: the changes in work and family patterns, fallout from the atomic bomb, the spread of networks of cars and planes throughout the planet, the arrival of AIDS as a major world pandemic, the development of genetically modified crops, the cloning of animals (and people), the deforestation of the planet, 'designer children' and 'surrogate mothering', the intensity of computer games and interaction, and so on and on. All have consequences that may be far-reaching and are at present unpredictable. Risk society, then, is a stage of development in which the pace of technological innovation generates global risks, such as nuclear war and environmental pollution.

The risk society is a society of 'fate' as class divisions have been overridden by the similarity of destinies that we all share. For Beck, those of us who live in risk societies are no longer concerned with such matters as justice and equality. Instead, we try to prevent the worst, and consequently a 'risk society is one obsessed with security' (Johnston, 2000: 24). It is important to recognize that Giddens and Beck are concerned with the sociological preconditions of risk in late modernity, and neither explicitly addresses crime or punishment – although recent discussions of moral panics have found the thesis attractive (see Chapter 20 for further commentary on the reformulation of moral panic theory in light of these developments).

The genealogy of risk

The second perspective has a rather different orientation, and has had more of an impact in criminology. This can be defined as a genealogy of risk. Broadly speaking, there are a set of authors who develop Michel Foucault's later work on governmentality (O'Malley, 1992; Garland, 1997; Rose, 1996; Smandych, 1999). In this work, risk is seen as a particular way of thinking born in the nineteenth century and is especially concerned with the historical development of the statistical and human sciences and their use of techniques to manage populations through health, welfare and social security reforms. According to this view, government during the twentieth century has become increasingly preoccupied with the management of risks through applying what are known as 'actuarial' techniques, which were developed in the insurance industries. What is important is that actuarial understandings of risk in insurance are associated with chance, probability and randomness as opposed to notions of danger and peril. It is important to keep this distinction in mind, for Beck and Giddens argue in contrast that in the risk society there has been an increase in the dangers arising from this latest phase in capitalism.

An especially influential statement of this second position is Malcolm Feeley and Jonathan Simon's (1992, 1994) discussion of what they term 'the new penology' in relation to a then largely unremarked set of transformations in criminal justice occurring in the United States. As they put it,

> the new penology is markedly less concerned with responsibility, fault, moral sensibility, diagnosis, or intervention and treatment of the individual offender. Rather it is concerned with techniques to identify, classify and manage groupings sorted by dangerousness. *The task is managerial, not transformative.*
>
> (1992: 452; emphasis added)

The new penology is based on **actuarialism**, probability calculations and statistical distributions to measure risk. Actuarialism underpins correctional policies. Feeley and Simon (1992) give the example of how at one extreme the prison provides maximum security at a high cost for those who pose the greatest risk, and at the other, probation provides low-cost surveillance for low-risk offenders. They coin the phrase 'actuarial justice' to express some of the internal tensions posed by the new penology. Jock Young (1999a: 67) develops these arguments further and explains that actuarialism is far from morally neutral as it involves the stripping of human relationships of their moral worth, 'rendering them "morally irrelevant"' (Bauman, 1995: 133, cited in Young, 1999a: 67).

The importance of Feeley and Simon's argument lies not simply in their view that the use of imprisonment, probation, parole and community punishments has in each case accelerated in recent times, but in that 'the new penology is in part the product of a societal accommodation to routinely high volumes of crime, as well as of the refinement of professional practices for monitoring, surveillance and aggregate management' (Sparks, 2000: 131). In other words, the causes of crime are no longer seen as important; instead, probabilities are central, for actuarial justice 'does not see a world free of crime but rather one where the best practices of damage limitation have been put in place' (Young, 1999b: 391).

It is clear that these authors have identified a new trend in crime control. However, one of the defining features of contemporary penal policy and practice is that they are governed by contradictory criminologies. In a series of influential publications, David Garland (1996, 2000, 2001b) signposts a set of developments associated with 'the culture of high crime societies' that are heralded in two types of contradictory criminology. One he describes as a *criminology of the self*, as it characterizes offenders as rational consumers – just like us. The second is a *criminology of the other*, which defines the offender as a threatening stranger (Garland, 1996: 446). The criminology of the self gets its support from a wide range of recent theories, which include rational choice theory, routine activity theory and situational crime prevention theory, that combine to form a criminology of everyday life (see Felson, 1998). The defining feature of these theories is that they all start from the understanding that crime is a normal, common aspect of modern living. Crime has become a risk to be calculated, by offender and potential victim, rather than a deviation from civilized conduct caused by individual pathology or faulty socialization – the hallmark of traditional criminology. Instead, the new criminologies of everyday life see crime as an outcome of normal social interaction.

What is also surprising about these new theories is the way in which policy-makers have enthusiastically taken them up. The key significance of these theories is that their programmes for action are not addressed 'to state agencies such as the police, the courts and the prisons, but *beyond* the state' (Garland, 1996: 451; emphasis in original) to the organizations, institutions and individuals of civil society. The implication, then, is that the state has a limited capacity to effect change, and instead these theories look to the world of everyday life to reduce crime. So instead of relying on prisons to deter offenders, or the ability of the police to catch criminals, the sorts of programmes advocated include things like 'replacing cash with credit cards, building locks into the steering columns of cars', using CCTV in city centres, closing discos at different times, laying on extra late-night buses and using special routes to and from football matches. The central 'message of this approach is that the state alone is not, and cannot effectively be, responsible for preventing and controlling crime' (ibid.: 453).

A central theme of neo-liberalism is being played out here, for what all these programmes are emphasizing is that citizens themselves must take some of the responsibility for controlling crime – a strategy that merges with privatization and welfare cuts that were characteristic of neo-liberal governments in the 1980s and 1990s. These are developments that have been analysed by Jonathan Simon (2007), where he argues that the United States is increasingly 'governing through crime', and Richard Ericson's (2007: 1) diagnosis of how neo-liberal politics encourages 'treating every imaginable source of harm as a crime' to be managed by the intensification of surveillance networks and the elimination of procedural safeguards in criminal law. Similarly Lucia Zedner (2005, 2007b) has emphasized how since 9/11 the pursuit of security against international terrorism has seen various provisions in the law become downgraded and even regarded as an obstacle to the fight against terror. Thus, for example, criminal prosecution is increasingly viewed as an impediment to dealing effectively with such matters as anti-social behaviour and terrorism, so that the need for new measures (like anti-social behaviour orders and control orders) that bypass the protections offered by criminal law ominously proliferate. As McRobbie (2006: 82) suggests the shoot-to-kill policy that was suddenly introduced in the aftermath of the London bombings of 7 July 2005 without 'due discussion across the departments of government, only to be seemingly re-invoked following the killing of an innocent young Brazilian man on his way to work, reflects this cavalier relation to existing law'.

However, it is also important to recognize that accompanying this administrative and largely technical, actuarial response to crime control, there has been an upsurge in the increasingly hysterical rhetoric and punitive language articulated by the political arm of the state. As Garland (1996: 460) argues, 'the punitive pronouncements of government ministers are barely considered attempts to express popular feelings of rage and frustration in the wake of particularly disturbing crimes', such as those surrounding the murders of young children that have been a deeply troubling aspect of recent times. These punitive responses are informed by a rather different criminology, which is of 'the other' and essentializes difference. As Garland (1996: 461) explains, it 'is a criminology of the alien other which represents criminals as dangerous members of distinct racial and social groups which bear little resemblance to "us"'. Consequently, offenders are defined as a different species of threatening, monstrous individuals for whom we should have no sympathy and for whom there is no effective help. The only practical and rational response is to have them taken out of circulation and incapacitated for the protection of the public, whether in long-term imprisonment or, as is the case in the United States, by judicial killing.

Indeed, Garland's (2005, 2007) more recent work has been drawn to the dynamics of capital punishment in American culture. He explains that for the most part

> American capital punishment is not about executions (which are now relatively rare – more Americans are killed each year by lightning). It is about mounting campaigns, taking polls, passing laws, bringing charges, bargaining pleas, imposing sentences, and rehearsing cases. It is about threats rather than deeds, anticipated deaths rather than actual executions. What gets performed, for the most part, is discourse and debate.
>
> (Garland, 2007: 137)

As can be seen from Figure 7.1, the number of executions peaked in the 1990s, but since then the number of death sentences has declined – reversing the longer-term trend which seemed to suggest a greater cultural acceptance of capital punishment. The reasons for this shift are open to debate, but would include the growing importance of legal clinics and innocence projects (Baumgartner et al., 2008). While the number of executions has decreased in recent years it must be remembered that more than 3,400 prisoners sit on death row with more than 12,000 death-penalty-liable homicides occurring every year (Garland, 2007: 139). Research has consistently shown that ethnicity, class and the quality of legal counsel are the main factors structuring the death penalty. The result is that poorly legally represented blacks, convicted of appalling crimes against white victims, are the groups disproportionately executed (Ogletree and Sarat, 2006).

So, to conclude, contemporary crime control is increasingly dualistic, polarized and ambivalent. As we have seen there is a *criminology of the self* that characterizes offenders as rational consumers, just like us; and there is a *criminology of the other*, which invokes images of dangerous and outcast strangers. In the former, crime is seen as a matter of routine, and the intention is to promote preventive action, whereas the latter is concerned with demonizing the criminal, while exciting popular fears and hostilities, and promoting support for state punishment. For Garland (1996: 459; emphasis in original) there is

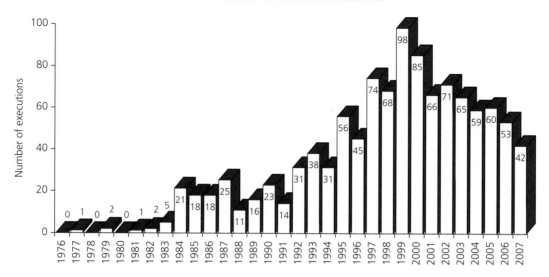

Number of executions total: 1100

Figure 7.1 Death Penalty executions in the United States.

Source: Death Penalty Information Center.

an emerging distinction between the *punishment* of crime, which remains the business of the state (and. . .becomes once again, a significant symbol of state power) and the *control* of crime, which is increasingly deemed to be 'beyond the state' in significant respects.

One sympathetic critic has argued that while Garland has grasped some of the ambivalence generated by the state in confronting its limits, his account 'achieves its effect by ignoring an array of other responses to crime which indicate quite diverse agendas and assessments of the fate of state-based crime control' (O'Malley, 1999: 181). John Braithwaite (2003: 13), however, argues that 'Garland makes a number of statements that are wrong at worst, misleading at best'. In other words, Garland is guilty of overlooking social responses to crimes of the powerful, which would reveal a rather different and more nuanced understanding of cultures of control. Jock Young (2002), in an extensive review of Garland's work, applauds the many achievements to be found in the *Culture of Control*, but finds the book guilty of a number of serious elisions (between crime and criminology, the normal and pathological and the very comparison between the United States and the UK). Further critical assessments of the work can be found in Matt Matravers's (2005) edited collection of essays that picks up on the diverse ways that crime and social order have come to structure everyday life.

Summary

1   The contemporary world may be seen through the four key ideas of late modernity, postmodernism, globalization and a risk society.

2   Late modernity brought with it new freedoms, new consumption patterns and new possibilities for individual choice, alongside new levels of crime and insecurity.

3   Postmodernism suggests that there is no longer any chance of developing one general theory of crime, one dominant narrative. Instead, the world is seen as much more eclectic and provisional.

4   As globalization speeds up and makes the world more and more 'one place', so there is also a globalization of crime – with criminal activities ranging from money laundering to the trafficking of people – spreading across national borders.

5   'Risk' is now a dominant theme in contemporary life, and flags the ways in which the pace of technological innovation generates global risks, such as nuclear war and environmental pollution.

6   There is a criminology of the self in which offenders are seen as rational consumers and crime is seen as a matter of routine; and there is a criminology of 'the other' in which offenders are seen as dangerous and outcast strangers, exciting popular fears and hostilities, and promoting support for state punishment.

Critical thinking questions

1   **Does postmodernism mean the end of modern criminology as we know it? In what ways is criminology changing?**

2   **Is it fair to say that late modernity brings with it both an increasing crime rate and different patterns of crime?**

3   **Select any two areas of crime and consider how far they have become increasingly globalized.**

4   **What is the risk society? How far does this impact on crime?**

5   **Outline some of the major social changes that sociologists have suggested are taking place in the contemporary world. What implications do these have for (a) our understanding of crime; and (b) the nature and patterns of contemporary crime?**

Further study

Altman, D. (2001) *Global Sex*, Chicago, IL: University of Chicago Press. Deals with globalization and sex, and has a considerable discussion on international prostitution.

Bauman, Z. (1998) *Globalization*, Cambridge: Polity. A useful general guide to globalization which also suggests how the processes of globalization may well be generating more social disorder and crime.

Cohen, R. and Kennedy, P. (2000) *Global Sociology*, Basingstoke: Macmillan. Excellent student text on globalization, with a key chapter on crime (chapter 9).

Ericson, R. (2007) *Crime in an Insecure World*, Cambridge: Polity. Provides a rich account of how crime has become the central dynamic organizing social relations in Western societies.

Ferrell, J., Hayward, K. and Young, J. (2008) *Cultural Criminology: An Invitation*, London: Sage. A useful introduction to the field by leading exponents of this perspective.

Findlay, M. (1999) *The Globalisation of Crime*, Cambridge: Cambridge University Press. The first major study of crime and its global features.

Henry, S. and Milovanovic, D. (1996) *Constitutive Criminology: Beyond Postmodernism*, London: Sage. This is not an easy book, but it brings together a lot of ideas already discussed. Its claim is to build a new kind of constitutive or postmodern criminology that builds upon an array of different theories and that shuns any grand theory of crime.

Loader, I. and Walker, N. (2007) *Civilizing Security*, Cambridge: Cambridge University Press. An ambitious book that seeks nothing less than to restore the question of security to the centre of democratic processes – as a public good that enriches social life.

More information

New Internationalist
This monthly magazine contains a wealth of global information.

Centre for International Crime Prevention
United Nations Office for Drug Control and Crime Prevention
PO Box 500
A-1400 Vienna
Austria

United Nations Crime and Justice Information Network
http://www.uncjin.org
Provides links and information on the United Nations organizations combating crime on an international level including the following link:

United Nations Office on Drugs and Crime
http://www.odccp.org/crime_cicp_sitemap.html
The United Nations Office on Drugs and Crime (UNODC) is a global leader in the fight against illicit drugs and international crime.

United Nations Interregional Crime and Justice Research Institute: LMS bibliographic Database
http://www.unicri.it/bibliographic_database.htm
The Library Collection includes some 6,000 authors, as well as more than 300 series and 600 publishers. Documents are classified according to the LMS bibliographic field structure and subjects that are described according to the UNCRI Thesaurus: http://www.unicri.it/unicri_thesaurus.htm

United Nations Interregional Crime and Justice Research Institute: World Directory of Criminal Resources
World Directory of Criminological Resources
www.unicri.it/html/world_directory_of_criminology.htm
This site contains more than 470 institutes covering some 70 countries. A number of countries, in particular developing ones, which do not have criminological institutes, have nevertheless requested that some of their bodies' services be included in the Directory.

http://www.culturalcriminology.org.
A website produced by criminologists based at the University of Kent, UK, that provides a resource for students interested in this growing area of criminology.

http://www.governingthroughcrime.blogspot.com
Jonathan Simon's blog that interprets current events through his own distinctive criminological analysis.

http://www.deathpenaltyinfo.org
A useful website for data on the death penalty in America.

chapter 8

Crime, Place and Space

Key issues

- Why are some places more 'crime-prone' than others?
- What are the connections between crime, control and space?
- What does it mean to think spatially about crime?

Introduction

Where does most recorded crime occur? Where do offenders and victims live and spend time? Are particular places perceived as more threatening than others, and if so, when and to whom? Is it possible to prevent crime by changing people's surroundings? How can we theorize the surroundings, environments or spaces in which we live? What does it mean to think 'spatially'? The aim of this chapter is to show how questions of **space** can enliven criminology.

Social life is conducted in social space. Consider the range of different spaces you might spend time in or pass through on a typical day: home, street, college, workplace, shop, library, bar, sports centre, cinema, friends' home. Consider by what means and at what times of day you journey between these spaces: bike, on foot, car, bus, train. Each space has its own internal rules of conduct – breaching these rules can create potential for deviance. Geographers argue that these spaces are not simply the 'backdrop' for our social interactions but that, by contrast, they help to shape the very nature of our social interactions (Gregory and Urry, 1985; Wolch and Dear, 1989). In other words, space has the power to shape social life.

What does it mean to think spatially about crime? A first stage is to ask *where* recorded crime *takes place* in addition to asking who commits crime and why. This helps to build up a profile of the places or environments where most crime and control encounters occur alongside profiles of offenders and victims. Criminologists began to focus on these issues in earnest in the 1970s, building on the earlier work of the Chicago School. Criminal justice practitioners now make routine use of crime mapping to allow them to observe spatial patterns.

A second stage is to consider *how places can be altered* in ways that might reduce crime. This can involve a number of factors, from definitions of what makes a particular location 'crime-prone' or 'safe' to the arrangement and purpose of buildings to local beliefs or memories about a place. It can also involve a number of agents, from planners, developers and politicians, who have the power to change spaces, to ordinary people who have the everyday task of negotiating existing spaces.

A third stage is to consider *how we come to know about space and crime* in the first place and what we do with that knowledge. **Mapping** statistics has been a central methodological tool in this kind of criminological research. This necessarily raises questions about the source of the statistics and the nature of mapping technology. More recently, the importance of the Internet in both areas has raised the issue of global public access to this kind of **geo-data**. This chapter looks at each of these three stages.

Offenders, offences and place

Social scientists interested in place and crime have identified themselves with different fields since the early twentieth century. Chicago School sociologists used terms such as 'urban sociology', 'human ecology' and **'ecology of crime'**. In the 1970s and 1980s, 'environmental criminology' was used until similar terms began to be more frequently used in relation to green issues (see Chapter 19). Around the same time, many criminological debates moved away from a traditional focus on the causes of crime to a 'post-welfare' focus on crime prevention and management. One of the results of this was new work on 'situational crime prevention' (SCP) and 'crime prevention through environmental design' (CPED). At present there is no single term to denote the study of crime and place. Mike Davis explores crime and control in Los Angeles as an extreme example of the 'ecology of fear' (1999). Others refer to 'socio-spatial criminology' (Bottoms, 2007) or 'crime and community' (Hughes, 2007). On the more quantitative cartographic side, 'geo-criminology' and 'crime mapping' (Vann and Garson, 2001) are more frequently used.

Park and Burgess's work in Chicago in the early twentieth century foregrounded the relationship between urban environment, actions and values. They saw social science as a form of 'human ecology' (1925). Burgess's 'zonal theory of urban development' suggested that Chicago – and other large cities – was structured around five concentric circles (see Figure 5.1). The non-residential 'central business district' was surrounded by the 'zone in transition', an area of cheap rented housing attracting different generations of migrants. Next came three residential areas of increasing affluence. Other Chicago scholars built on this model. Shaw and McKay's (1942) studies of juvenile delinquency showed that a very high proportion of young offenders had grown up in the 'zone in transition'. They explained this as an effect of the 'social disorganization' which characterized this area. A churning migrant population with shifting moral values, high levels of poverty and low levels of community cohesion produced teenagers prone to commit crime. More recent US criminological research (discussed below) linking a community's crime levels to its capacity for 'collective efficacy' has some clear links to these early Chicago studies.

If early work on crime and place focused on offenders and where they lived and socialized, later work from the 1970s onwards focused on offences and victims (Bottoms, 2007). One influential study argued that offenders tended to commit crimes in areas that were culturally familiar to them in some way but not generally their own neighbourhoods (Brantingham and Brantingham, 1991). Victim surveys (see Chapter 9) allowed '**area victimization rates**' (the level of offences against a particular group in a particular area) to be compared with '**area offence rates**' (all recorded offences in a particular area). Other studies, such as Baldwin and Bottoms's (1976) on Sheffield, questioned the link between offenders and 'zones in transition' in the UK context, stressing instead the importance of the housing market in shaping community relations.

The connections between poverty, place and crime are still much debated by criminologists. Bottoms (2007: 561–3) reviews recent studies exploring the link between deprivation and offender rates. Weatherburn and Lind (2001) find that 'economic stress' contributes to criminality because of the strains it places on parenting. Oberwittler (2005) argues that the effect of deprivation on crime is greater in the United States than in Europe because the United States, with its weak welfare system, experiences greater levels of extreme deprivation. He also stresses the importance of looking at economic disadvantage in relation to parents, friends, schools and other networks which make up a 'neighbourhood'. This emphasis on networks is echoed in the findings of Wikström and Sampson (2003). They identify two kinds of 'behaviour settings' in relation to crime: those that promote self-control and those which do not. They argue that it is not the setting (or space) alone which does this but the community connected to it. Communities with high levels of 'collective efficacy' – or high levels of cohesion and mutual trust – will be willing to intervene to challenge behaviour in a given setting and stop it from escalating. Communities with low levels of 'collective efficacy' – rather like those Burgess defined as living in the 'zone in transition' – will be less willing or able to intervene (see Bottoms, 2007 for further discussion).

Spatial distribution of crime

So, what geographic patterns do we see in current recorded crime? Recent statistics for England and Wales show a very uneven distribution (Home Office, 2007a). Some local authorities have high levels of recorded crimes across a range of crime types. These tend to be large urban areas with a mix of richer and poorer residents: London, parts of the south-east, south Wales, the north-west and parts of the north-east.

However, patterns and concentrations of crime also vary by crime type. Figures for three types of more serious recorded crime – serious wounding, domestic burglary and robbery – across 376 local authorities in England and Wales demonstrate this. Robbery and serious wounding are both concentrated in a relatively small number of areas. Eighteen local authorities have robbery rates of more than three times the average for England and Wales (average = 1.9 offences per 1,000 population). Four local authorities have serious wounding rates of more than three times the average (average = 0.3 offences per 1,000 population). There is some overlap between these two but also some significant variations: for example, urban south Wales has high rates of serious wounding but relatively low levels of robbery. Domestic burglary rates are more evenly spread across England and Wales with just one local authority with a rate of more than three times the average (average = 13.1 offences per 1,000 population). As these figures and the maps in Figure 8.1 show, crime can be highly localized.

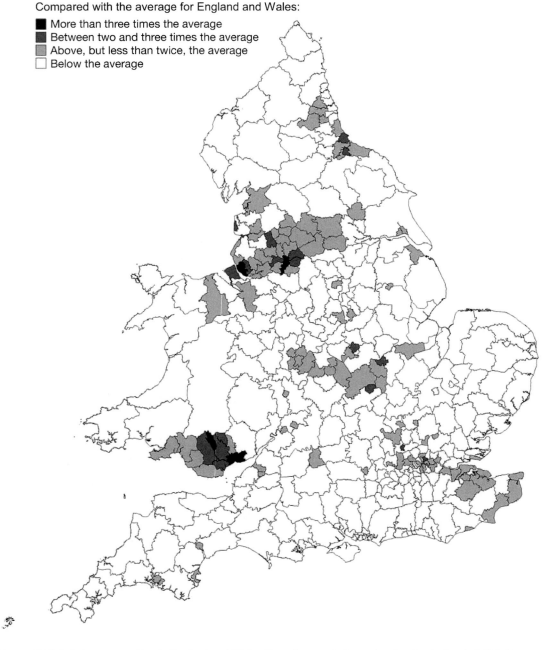

Figure 8.1(a) Serious wounding in England and Wales. Rates by population at local authority level, 2006–7.
Source: Home Office Statistical Bulletin, 2007: 115.

thinking about crime

Criminologists and policy-makers increasingly use geodemographic information systems to provide a more detailed analysis of the broad spatial patterns displayed in these types of maps. British Crime Survey data, for example, can be used in conjunction with the ACORN information system (A Classification of Residential Neighbourhoods) which categorizes UK postcodes into

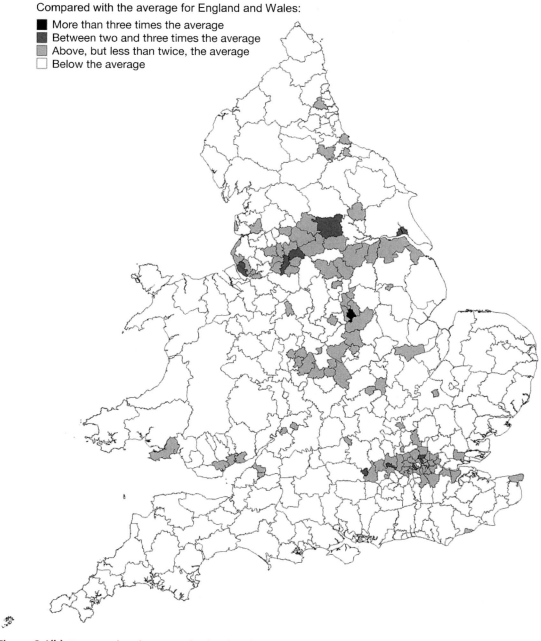

Figure 8.1(b) Domestic burglary in England and Wales. Rates by households at local authority level, 2006–7.
Source: Home Office Statistical Bulletin, 2007: 116.

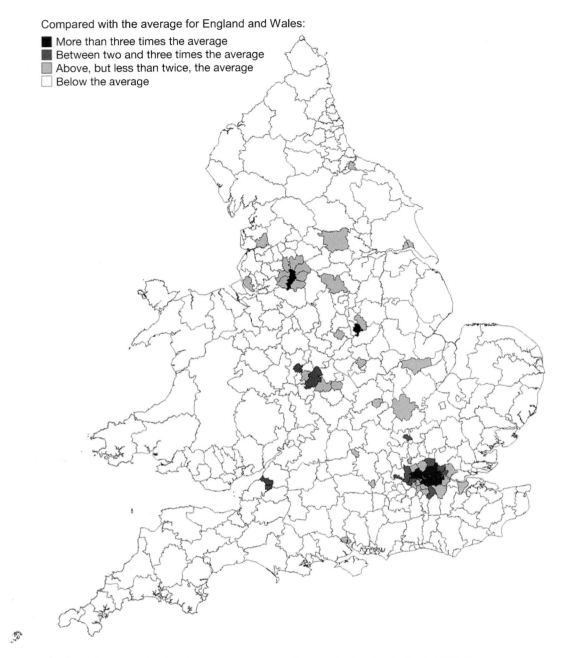

Compared with the average for England and Wales:
- ■ More than three times the average
- ■ Between two and three times the average
- ■ Above, but less than twice, the average
- □ Below the average

Figure 8.1(c) Robbery in England and Wales. Rates by population at local authority level, 2006–7.
Source: Home Office Statistical Bulletin, 2007: 117.

types based on census data, consumption profiles and lifestyle surveys. Households can then be grouped according to the demographic, employment and housing characteristics of the surrounding area. Developed by a private company, ACORN has been bought by many government agencies and local authorities as a planning tool not least because it presents household data in a more

thinking about crime

complex way than conventional classifications of class. Richer households are divided into three groups: 'wealthy achievers' (e.g. wealthy executives, affluent older people and well-off families), 'urban prosperous' (prosperous professionals, young urban professionals and students) and 'comfortably off' (e.g. young couples, secure families, older couples living in suburbs). Middling households are described as having 'moderate means' (e.g. post-industrial families, skilled manual workers, Asian communities). Poorer households are described as being 'hard-pressed' (struggling families, burdened singles, high-rise hardship) (http://www.caci.co.uk/acorn/default.asp).

Recent British Crime Surveys have analysed risk of crime by ACORN areas. The two types of household at most risk of being a victim of crime (vehicle theft, burglary and violence) were those in 'urban prosperous' and 'hard-pressed' areas. The data also showed there was some correspondence between these figures and levels of concern about crime. Compared with the average in England and Wales, levels of worry about crime and anti-social behaviour were higher in 'hard-pressed' and 'moderate means' areas and lower in 'wealthy achiever' and 'comfortably off' areas (Home Office, 2007a: 119–20). 'Urban prosperous' groups' attitudes to crime are more complex. They may be less aware of, or less concerned about, the risks they might face. In the case of students they may have much less choice about where they can afford to live than others within this group. Other researchers who have used a similar approach include Pantazis (2000) in relation to crime and social harm, Chandola (2001) on fear of crime and area differences in health and Howe (2001) on deprivation indices and violence in the community.

BOX 8.1 Case study: the night-time economy and violent disorder

In many of Britain's towns and cities the recent expansion of night-time leisure economies is seen as an important way of sustaining urban prosperity in the face of decades of industrial decline and mass unemployment. Despite the claims of some commentators it is clear that it is the mix of alcohol and profit that is the driving force behind these developments, rather than the broader cultural renaissance imagined by the more utopian planners and entrepreneurs who envisaged a flourishing of European sensibilities in this urban restructuring. Recent research has shown that urban nightlife is increasingly experiencing a form of 'McDonaldization' with big brands taking over large parts of the city (Chatterton and Hollands, 2003). While many city centres have achieved a cool status through branded and upgraded nightlife, they are also increasingly becoming more exclusive, segmented and crime-prone. Although many new opportunities have opened up, especially for young women, ethnic cultures, students and gay nightlife, this has often been sanitized and commercially incorporated into the mainstream. For instance, in Manchester's Gay Village there has been the corporate takeover of gay bars, which has not simply upgraded the premises but has made the bars increasingly look alike. The push for profit has meant that many owners have sought to open up gay venues to more mainstream and straight consumers which has led many to say that this compromises their character (Chatterton and Hollands, 2003: 173–5).

Plate 8.1 'Last arrests at the Bar please . . .' by Grizelda.

Concerns have been raised about the health- and crime-related consequences of the lifestyles revolving around weekend 'binge drinking', drug taking, risky sexual encounters, a diet of high-fat, fast food, and the threat of fights and violent assault. The booming **night-time economy** of fashionable wine bars, packed 'vertical' drinking super-pubs and carnivalesque dance music clubs are also the sites where for many an identity can be found, and friendships maintained. Yet it is important to examine the political and economic forces that create the violent disorder seen in any of Britain's city centres on most weekend nights. Much recent scholarship has attempted to situate the mass intoxication of the young in the context of post-industrial restructuring, urban regeneration and broader cultural changes. One example is Simon Winlow and Steve Hall's (2006) *Violent Night*, which despite the title offers much more than simply a description of the drinking, flirting and fighting that figures prominently in an evening out on the town. Indeed, the real strength of the text is the way it documents young people's feelings about work, relationships, education, consumption and leisure in considerable detail before analysing victims' and perpetrators' accounts of interpersonal violence. It is in this context that the weekly big night out is situated. The 'orderly disorder' of the night-time economy combines 'seductive hedonism' with unavoidable violence – although for most, it must be emphasized, being on the periphery was 'far more appealing than being actively involved in violence' (Winlow and Hall, 2006: 101).

The violence gives an edge to the night, which is heightened by excessive alcohol intake and the wild abandon which getting 'off your face' mythologizes. The violence often results from the escalation of trivial altercations, tends to be heavily ritualized, is scarcely reported and flares up in predictable 'hot spots' like taxi queues and fast-food outlets. Some perpetrators are self-anointed urban knights on quests to punish the 'arseholes', 'cunts' and 'piss-takers' who cross their path. Others take themselves less seriously and the main motivation is a general 'liking' of violence combined with the 'ability to show fortitude, conquer fear and avoid humiliation' (Winlow and Hall, 2006: 158). What unites both victims and perpetrators is a 'stoical, fatalistic and reactionary attitude to violence', which 'is a deeply entrenched and highly reproductive form of "survivalism" that infuses the localized culture and *habitus* of its male members' (Winlow and Hall, 2006: 161). As is clear from recent research the task of policing the night has fallen into the hands of private security in the bulky form of bouncers (Hobbs *et al.*, 2003) who fill the void left by the handful of public police officers delegated to maintaining public order in the area.

Crime prevention, space and communities

Crime and place, as the discussion so far has shown, are now very firmly discussed in relation to community and area dynamics. This raises the further question – is it possible to *change* these dynamics and the places in which they are played out in order to reduce crime? Put another way, can crime be cut by reshaping a space or altering community relations in a space or both? Criminological work on this first focused on changing spaces but has since moved on to focus on changing community relations.

Changing spaces: urban design and crime

US architect Oscar Newman (1972) used the concept of '**defensible space**' in the 1970s to argue that it was possible to modify the built environment to reduce the opportunity for crime and to promote community responsibility. Newman's ideas – which centred on public housing design – helped to shape new approaches within what was then still referred to as environmental criminology. 'Situational crime prevention' (SCP) and 'crime prevention through environmental design' (CPED) advocated changes in physical environments and physical objects within them. These strategies have gradually become part of everyday life in public, residential, commercial and financial urban sectors. Street fixtures – such as benches, bus shelters, playgrounds and lighting – were all increasingly designed to screen out undesirable activity. So-called 'tramp-free benches', for example, are designed to allow people to sit only for short periods and to discourage any longer-term use or 'loitering'. Surveillance equipment and CCTV is used to monitor but also to deter wrong-doing.

In addition, new rules governing behaviour in many kinds of spaces have been introduced. Most UK football grounds banned standing on the terraces in the wake of the 1989 Hillsborough disaster and introduced all-seater stadia as part of a generally successful effort to combat

Plate 8.2 Youths on a Bristol housing estate, 2007.

Source: Photo by Matt Cardy/Getty Images.

hooliganism. In 2005, one of the UK's largest shopping malls, Bluewater in Kent, banned customers wearing hoodies and baseball caps as part of a general clampdown on intimidating behaviour, swearing and shoplifting (http://news.bbc.co.uk/1/hi/england/kent/4561399.stm). In 2008, there was controversy surrounding the use of 'mosquitos' – devices that emit a high-frequency buzzing sound which cannot be heard by people over the age of 25 or so – to disperse groups of young people gathering in public spaces (http://www.liberty-human-rights.org.uk).

Urban design and surveillance were taken up by academics and planners at a time when the old focus on the causes of crime was beginning to give way to a new focus on the need to manage crime. SCP and CPED, for example, are clearly linked to Felson's 'routine activity theory'. All arguably see crime as an inevitable phenomenon that can best be managed by reducing the opportunity to commit an offence rather than by seeking to reduce individuals' desire to commit a crime in the first place.

Criminology remains divided on the implications of this shift. Some argue that it addresses the needs of, and empowers, those communities – often among the most deprived – that live with the realities of high crime rates. **Community safety** is identified as an important element in any kind of neighbourhood regeneration. Others argue that it fails to address the root causes of the poverty, deprivation and spatial exclusion which, in their view, lies behind so much recorded crime (McLaughlin and Muncie, 1999). Mike Davis (1999) offers an extreme but very interesting view here (see Box 8.2). His account of Los Angeles as an 'ecology of fear' reworks

thinking about crime

BOX 8.2 *Ecology of Fear: Los Angeles and the Imagination of Disaster*

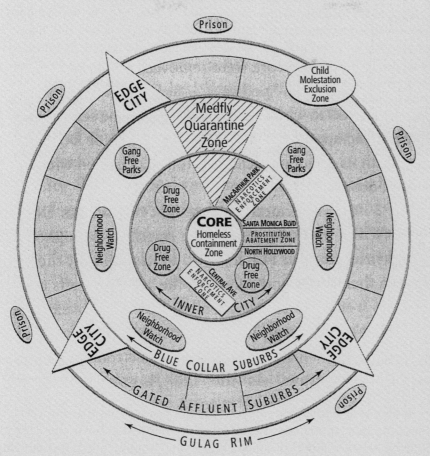

Plate 8.3 Zonal Map from the book *Ecology of Fear: Los Angeles and the Imagination of Disaster* by Mike Davis. Reprinted by permission of Henry Holt and Company, LLC.

Mike Davis charts the remodelling of Los Angeles' central downtown area in the years following the 1965 Watts Riots. Davis argues that, fearing a 'black inundation' of the old business district, leading landowners and financiers worked with the city police department, the LAPD, to design a new riot-proof financial area, Bunker Hill. The new area was put to the test in 1992 in further riots sparked by the televised beating of Rodney King, a black man, by white police officers. As Davis puts it, while other parts of the city were attacked and looted, 'Bunker Hill became a Fortress . . . Bullet-proof steel doors rolled down over street-level entrances, escalators froze and electric locks sealed off pedestrian passage ways'. The 'riot-tested success' of these defences 'stimulated demand for new and higher levels of physical security' causing a further 'erosion of the boundary between architecture and law enforcement' (Davis, 1999: 364–6).

According to Davis's zonal map, more affluent residential areas of LA and its surrounding urban areas developed 'social control districts' as a means of keeping out crime. Certain zones were designated drug-free, gun-free, graffiti-free and even child-molestation-free. This new 'disciplinary order' was created through the merging of criminal and civil codes with landuse planning into a 'new militarized landscape'. CCTV surveillance played a key role here – establishing what Davis calls 'virtual scanscapes', areas of 'protective invisibility that increasingly define where white collar workers and middle class tourists feel safe' (Davis, 1999: 366, 383). Outside these protected areas, life looked very different. Areas like MacArthur Park became 'free fire zones' where 'crack dealers and street gangs settle their scores with shotguns and uzis' and slum landlords conduct 'their own private reign of terror against dealers, petty criminals and deadbeat tenants' and schools became 'more like prisons' (Davis, 1999: 378). At the outer edge of Davis's zonal map – something which he says has 'no equivalent' in Burgess – lies the 'gulag rim' made up of the many kinds of prisons and correction units within the vast Californian penal system (Davis, 1999: 416).

Issues to consider:

- Davis's account is compelling but is it generalizable beyond Los Angeles?
- What are the social costs and benefits of neighbourhood regeneration?

original Chicago School zonal theory and argues that the linking of urban design and policing has led to a destructive militarization of urban landscapes which protects privilege and punishes poverty.

Newman's own reworking of defensible space theory (1996) stresses the need to move beyond urban design to address community relations. People should feel that they 'own' public space and share a responsibility for it – not simply that they are being monitored. This kind of thinking is evident in the more communitarian approaches to governance that emerged in the 1990s and which are also very much linked to post-welfarism. New Labour's 1998 Crime and Disorder Act has had a major impact on British approaches to crime and community. Crime was to be tackled not just by the police and the courts but by new Crime and Disorder Reduction Partnerships (CDRPs) which were set up in over 300 local authorities. The partnerships require a multi-agency approach, typically involving the police, local councils, health authorities and voluntary agencies. The emphasis is on identifying both local crime problems and 'what works' to reduce these. There are two key strategies here. First, the community is 'responsibilised' as part of a wider dispersal of power (Hughes, 2002; Crawford, 2002) and, second, these new styles of local policing encourage a new kind of attention to local trouble spots.

Increasing interest in the localized nature of crime has led to highly localized policing strategies and even localized criminal justice legislation. Dispersal orders, ASBOs, curfews and other measures are all 'tailored' to particular environments – they aim to stop certain people behaving in certain ways in certain spaces at certain times. Civil rights campaigners such as Liberty

thinking about crime

have warned that these spatial techniques represent a dangerous trend because, among other things, they sanction a move away from the principle of a common, universal criminal justice system operating equally across a state. They have launched a number of legal challenges to the government on these issues (http://www.liberty-human-rights.org.uk).

Some criminologists believe that this kind of work is valuable because it can show more precisely *where* crime problems are and *where* police should target their resources. Echoing the earlier discussion of the night-time economy, Bromley and Nelson's study of alcohol consumption and crime in a British city concludes that 'a detailed knowledge of the variety of spaces and times of alcohol-related crime and disorder is key to the development of appropriate urban design, planning and licensing policies and can be used to inform a more closely targeted policing strategy' (2002: abstract). Others are less sure. White and Sutton (1995) stress the limits of 'quick fixes' for crime, arguing against 'episodic initiatives' and technological strategies in favour of strategies 'which see crime and public safety as stemming first and foremost in the community'. Herbert and Brown (2006) argue, similarly, that the relationships between identities, values and spatial environments are complex and should not be oversimplified. Finally, this kind of analysis may work for public order offences but does not help the police to tackle other kinds of crime which take place in private as opposed to public space – white-collar crime, domestic violence, fraud and state crime, for example (for a wider discussion on policing and geography, see Evans *et al.*, 1992 and Fyfe, 1998, 2004).

Living in spaces: everyday negotiations of disorder

Community safety has become part of the UK criminal justice policy framework. But, outside the policy framework, how do communities themselves negotiate crime, risk and fear in their own neighbourhoods? Many UK households may not be aware of the policies of their particular CDRP, for example, but have nevertheless developed their own ways of dealing with crime as it affects, or seems to affect, their everyday lives.

Feminist geographers and criminologists have investigated the many ways in which women routinely adapt their use of urban space in order to guard against possible physical or sexually motivated attack – taking certain routes, avoiding certain places at night, telling others where they are going, and so on (Pain, 1991). This kind of work has since been extended to encompass other groups – such as children, teenagers and elderly people (Pain and Smith, 2008). One of the key points about such studies is that they highlight the importance of beliefs and emotions in establishing shared meanings around particular places or routes between places. A given place may have been designed as 'safe' but different groups of people may continue to experience it as risky or dangerous and act accordingly. Cultural geographers such as David Sibley (1995) have explored myth making, meaning and social exclusion in relation to 'marginal' spaces in ways which are very useful to criminology. Drawing on this, Millington's work on local reactions to asylum seekers in the south-east of England bears this out (2005). Hostile locals in Southend tended to attribute much local crime to newcomers living in 'Little Bosnia' – an area of the town which quickly acquired strong negative associations.

Modifying movements around space is one way in which people try to minimize their exposure to crime; securing their home, workplace or neighbourhood is another. A further option is to relocate altogether. Beliefs about crime and safety play a significant part in determining whether a neighbourhood gains a reputation as 'rough' or 'desirable' and therefore in shaping the workings of housing markets.

The concept of **urban flight** or 'white flight' is relevant here. Derived from the Chicago School work on patterns of ethnic segregation, it has been used in the UK to explain the movement out of the inner city by both the middle and the working classes – a movement partly driven by beliefs about crime. In the 'home counties' of south-east England urban flight is shaped by particular perceptions of ethnicity. The inner city is constructed as an epicentre of crime and disorder associated with a large black presence and the suburb as a haven of Anglo-Saxon family values and public safety (Clapson, 1998, 2003; Watt, 1998). Watt argues, for example, that white East End Londoners have moved into neighbouring Essex because of their perception that 'their' neighbourhoods have been 'taken over' – a narrative with clear racist overtones. Others suggest that this effect is particularly strong among the older generation and may be less pronounced among younger people who have grown up with multiculturalism (Back, 1996).

Mapping and the uses of geo-data

As this discussion has shown, mapping (or cartography) is a vital research tool in studies of crime and place. From Quételet and Mayhew in the nineteenth century to the first environmental criminological studies in the mid-twentieth century, maps provided visual representations of crime and a means of explaining its spatial relationships.

Satellite and Internet technology have transformed cartography, however. Geographical information systems (GISs) combine spatial analysis software, database technology and high-resolution satellite photography to create new interactive spatial visualizations of social science data. These developments are having a major impact on criminal justice practices. One site, Chicago Crime Map, offers a whole new macro- and micro-view of contemporary urban crime. It maps crime using the Chicago police department's publicly available crime reports, Google Earth software and Google Maps website. The crimes are browsable by location, time and type of crime. Chicago Crime Map is an example of a 'mashup' – a new term for a new kind of map that combines 'two or more separate data streams to create original content' (Goodman and Moed, 2007). Mashups are rapidly expanding in the commercial sector and are likely to have many civic or criminal justice applications.

Sites like this raise issues about the status of what has been termed 'personal geo-data'. Sharing such data 'outside the context of its creation' has implications for privacy, transparency and ownership (Goodman and Moed, 2007). The site vastly expands the traditional relationship between the police and the public. The police, a public body, have always produced information about private citizens in the public interest. In the past, this data has been circulated by the media and other channels but in a very selective way. The combination of Internet, browser and GIS technologies have allowed the Chicago data to be delivered in completely new ways – in a comprehensive, spatial and visual format, which can be used by individuals much more on their own terms. It remains to be seen what impact access to such information will have on 'democratizing' public experiences and perceptions of crime as well as on authorities' abilities and desire to present crime figures in particular ways. These democratizing tendencies will have

Plate 8.4 Satellite photograph from chicagocrime.org – showing detailed location of a recent crime.

to be balanced alongside serious questions of civil liberties. Does the resident whose home is identified as having been the site of crime have a right to privacy? Do his or her neighbours (or local estate agents, schools or doctors' surgeries) have a right to know what kind of crime has been reported?

Critical cartography

Maps always need to be interpreted. They are never neutral despite the fact that we often treat them as if they are. Many geographers are very critical of mapping. Even the most technologically sophisticated maps offer a representation of a given area rather than a value-free 'real' view of it (Pinder, 2003). These critics argue that whenever we look at a map we see it from the point of view or perspective of the person or object with the power to 'gaze' out over the whole territory from a position of authority. Mapping has always been a powerful tactic of governance and surveillance. Colonizers, urban reformers and police authorities have always drawn maps of 'unruly' or 'ungoverned' areas in ways which justify their efforts to 'restore' order to those areas. To give one example, Blomley and Sommers (1999) chart the efforts of a group of marginal Vancouver residents to contest the way in which their existing neighbourhood was literally erased from maps drawn up by local planners seeking to 'regenerate' it. In another example, Kurgan and Cadora's mapping of 'million dollar blocks' (see Box 8.3) uses cartography to demonstrate the extremely high cost of incarcerating large numbers of residents from 'crime-prone' zones in US cities. Here, maps are used to raise questions about crime and power not simply presented as a tool in a crime-prevention kit.

BOX 8.3 Mapping million dollar blocks

Radical mapping projects in the United States have highlighted that a disproportionate number of US prisoners come from a small number of neighbourhoods in big cities. Architect Laura Kurgan, a professor who runs Columbia University's Spatial Information Design Lab, and Eric Cadora, co-founder of the Justice Mapping Center, mapped the home addresses of inmates. They showed that while crime itself is dispersed across cities criminals living in certain areas of cities – especially those with high poverty rates and high proportions of black residents – are many more times likely to be imprisoned than those living outside these.

The high cost of imprisoning so many people from one neighbourhood or even one block led Kurgan and Cadora to coin the term 'million dollar blocks'. For example, 'the district of Brownsville's District 16 accounts for 3.5 percent of Brooklyn's population but 8.5 percent of its prison population'. Kurgan calculates that 'it cost $11 million to incarcerate people from these 11 blocks in 2003'. Her Columbia lab works with local community groups to break crime patterns through architecture and public projects and to demand a shift in state spending away from incarceration into helping people out of poverty. In Kurgan's view, 'Too much has been spent on prisons in the last 40 years and not enough on affordable housing'.

For more on this see:

- http://www.justicemapping.org/aboutus/
- http://www.newyorker.com/talk/2007/01/08/070108ta_talk_macintyre

Summary

1   Social life is lived out in social space. A spatially aware criminology considers the relationship between crime, control and place. Various terms are currently in play to describe this kind of work: socio-spatial criminology, geocriminology, crime and community are all used.

2   Early work (from the 1920s) on place and crime focused on offenders. Later work (from the 1970s onwards) focused on offences, victims and urban design. Current work could be said to fall into two groups: (i) community dynamics in a given place and (ii) high-tech monitoring of space and crime mapping.

3   Recently, criminologists have tended to focus on analysing formal policies aiming to change places and improve community dynamics. They have mixed views on the success of such policies. Cultural geographers interested in questions of crime and disorder continue to look at ordinary people's everyday understandings and negotiations of space and perceived risk.

4   Mapping is a vital if contested part of many investigations of crime and place. The transformation of the gathering, display, distribution and use of personal geo-data (which combines mapping, Internet and survey technologies) is likely to have profound implications for criminology.

Critical thinking questions

1 What do criminologists gain from looking at crime in terms of *where* it occurs?
2 Is space still neglected in much criminology?
3 Is it possible to prevent crime just by changing spaces?
4 How are communities and spaces connected?
5 What do 'mashups' offer as new forms of criminological data?

Further study

Bottoms, A. E. (2007) 'Place, Space, Crime and Disorder', in M. Maguire, R. Morgan and R. Reiner (eds) *Oxford Handbook of Criminology*, 4th edn, Oxford: Oxford University Press.

Chatterton, P. and Hollands, R. (2003) *Urban Nightscapes: Youth Cultures, Pleasure Spaces and Corporate Power*, London: Routledge.

Davis, M. (1999) *Ecology of Fear: Los Angeles and the Imagination of Disaster*, New York: Vintage Books.

Evans, D. J., Fyfe, N. R. and Herbert, D. T. (eds) (1992) *Crime, Policing and Place: Essays in Environmental Criminology*, London: Routledge.

Hughes, G. (2007) *The Politics of Crime and Community*, Basingstoke: Palgrave.

Pain, R. and Smith, S. J. (2008) *Fear: Critical Geopolitics and Everyday Life*, Aldershot: Ashgate.

Smandych, R. (ed.) (1999) *Governable Places: Readings on Governmentality and Crime Control*, Aldershot: Ashgate.

Vann, I. B. and Garson, G. D. (2001) 'Crime Mapping and Its Extension to Social Science Analysis', *Social Science Computer Review*, 19 (4): 471–9.

More information

Home Office Statistical Bulletin: Crime in England and Wales, 2006–7
http://www.homeoffice.gov.uk/rds/pdfs07/hosb1107.pdf

Chicago Crime Map
http://www.chicagocrime.org/

ACORN
http://www.caci.co.uk/acorn/default.asp

part 3 Doing Crime

In this part, we introduce a range of topical areas in the study of crime. Different crimes raise different kinds of issues and this part attends to this. We do not look at all crimes but our chosen topics include property crimes, sexual offences, professional crime, drug use and what we also introduce as 'emotional crime'. We look not just at the offenders but also at victims, which is where we start . . .

chapter 9

Victims and Victimization

Key issues

- What are the different forms of victimization? How do they relate to power differentials in society?

- How does crime impact on individuals and the wider communities?

- What kinds of offences and their victims have been subject to most political and public attention, and which overlooked?

- What is the role of victims in the criminal justice process? What is their actual experience of the justice system?

Introduction

Crime is generally understood to be behaviour that is prohibited by criminal law. In other words, no act can be considered a crime, irrespective of how immoral or damaging it may be, unless it has been made criminal by state legislation. This conceptualization appears straightforward enough. However, it tells us very little about the processes whereby certain harmful acts and victims routinely come to be identified and recognized as part of the crime problem while others remain hidden. A critical approach to the study of crime and its impact on individuals and society therefore requires us to reflect on questions such as: What is 'criminal'? How do legal conceptions of 'crime' and its victims come to be constructed?

Clearly, victims play a central role in initiating the criminal justice process. Without them, much of the work of the criminal justice process would come to a halt.

The numbers and types of cases entering the system and thereby eventually providing the workload for the courts, prison service and other conventional agencies, appear largely to be determined by the reporting behaviour of victims and witnesses, not action initiated by the police.

(Shapland, 1986: 210)

The fact that only a fraction of crime is reported to and recorded by the police, combined with low clear-up rates, means that only a small proportion of offences ever reach the court (see chapters 16 and 17). In all these cases, victim experiences can be prolonged and complex. An incident that occurred in perhaps a few minutes can become the subject of a series of inquiries that may last months or years after the event. Victims who come to court expecting that a trial will be an assertion of their wrongs can find that their probity is on trial as well.

So what do victims think of their experiences of the criminal justice system? Does the system fulfil their expectations of justice, or does the system further distress and disillusion them?

The role of victims within the criminal justice system

In contemporary Britain, the role of victims within the criminal justice process is largely confined to reporting the crime and/or providing evidence. The significance of the victim's role in these areas is compounded by the fact that the vast majority of offences come to police attention through a victim's report rather than through patrolling activities. Furthermore, most crimes are solved through information obtained from the victim or another witness rather than through 'leads' developed independently by detectives (see Reiner, 2000; see also Greenwood *et al.*, 1977, on the United States).

Historically, however, the role of the victim was very different and much more extensive. Until the establishment of the New Police in 1829, local governance was based upon the fundamental principles of deterring and solving crime through individual and community self-regulation. Most crimes were considered to be a private matter between the offender and the victim (except, for example, in cases of treason or sedition). Private thief-takers established themselves to investigate offences for victims; many thief-takers also cashed in on the rewards offered by the government for the apprehension of offenders leading to conviction. The victim, or the victim's relatives or friends, would also make the decision whether or not to prosecute an offender, pay for a variety of legal documents and other expenses of prosecution and, more importantly, take on the role of prosecutor in court. This meant in effect some victims had greater access to justice (e.g. men of property) than others (women, especially in cases of sexual offences) (Emsley, 2005; Kearon and Godfrey, 2007).

Defining crime and victimization

Not all harmful activities are seen as criminal. As Steven Box (1983) has argued, power may itself determine that the crimes of the powerful have generally been excluded from public perceptions of the crime problem and, conversely, the victimization of the powerless may be understated.

Criminal negligence leading to workplace injuries and deaths, environmental offences, the manufacture and sale of unsafe products, misconduct of corporations, abuse of power by the state, and so on, are rarely perceived as 'real' crime (see chapters 10, 13, 19 and 21). These are often offences that do not have a direct, immediate and tangible victim. They go largely unreported because of the problem of lack of victim awareness. There has been some attempt to broaden the definition of 'victims' (e.g. to include both direct and indirect victims) and to include a range of abuses and harms relating to criminal abuse of power (including impairment of victims' fundamental rights), notably through the 1985 United Nations Declaration of Basic Principles of Justice for Victims of Crime and Abuse of Power (http://www2.ohchr.org/english/law/victims. htm). Nevertheless, even when victims are prepared to take action, they and/or their families may have to embark on a long struggle to gain recognition of their victim status (e.g. through the formation of a voluntary issue-based pressure group).

Conversely, there are no clear and unequivocal criteria to determine that acts defined as 'criminal' always cause harm to society. 'Victimless crimes' such as certain sexual acts between consenting adults, prostitution, and buying and selling of some illegal drugs are often cited in this context (Schur, 1965). These are forms of behaviour that are often illegal but consensual in nature. Because no criminal victimization is occurring, the participants have no reason to complain to the police. The notion of 'victimless crime' has been used by some critics to condemn unjust laws and to further campaigns for legal reform, especially in offences against sexual morality (Jeffery-Poulter, 1991; Higgins, 1996; and see Chapter 11 of this book).

Whether or not the notion of 'victimless crime' is a valid one remains open to debate. For example, feminists are split along ideological lines on their views of prostitution as 'work', women's agency in relation to prostitution, and the distinction between 'voluntary' sex work and sexual exploitation (Murray, 1998; McLeod, 1982; Miller, 1986). Some have argued that women run the risk of physical and sexual violence at the hands of clients or being harassed by the police on the streets. Others have pointed out that society is affected because prostitution objectifies women and reinforces stereotypical notions of women. From a law and order perspective, politicians and local residents who are in favour of clampdowns have also argued that street prostitution is not victimless as it may damage the reputation and quality of life in the neighbourhood. Similar arguments and counter-arguments have been raised in relation to illegal drug use in the context of the decriminalization debate (see Chapter 14). In short, there are no clear, unequivocal definitions of 'consensus', 'harm', 'offender' and 'victim'. Such judgements are always informed by contestable, epistemological, moral and political assumptions (de Haan, 1990: 154).

The hierarchy of victimization

Clearly, some victims enjoy a higher status in the crime discourse, and their experiences of victimization are taken more seriously than others'. Many criminologists have highlighted the dangers of stigmatizing the victims and of creating victim stereotypes. Nils Christie (1986: 18) defines the status of 'ideal victim' in the following way: 'By "ideal victim" I have . . . in mind a person or a category of individuals who – when hit by crime – most readily are given the complete and legitimate status of being a victim.' Put simply, the 'ideal' victim is typified by an elderly woman or child. Such people are considered weak, vulnerable, innocent and deserving of help, care and

Plate 9.1 The father of Madeleine McCann, the 4-year-old British girl who vanished in Portugal, giving a press conference to show a missing persons poster in Arabic and French, in Rabat, 11 June 2007. The parents have launched a campaign to raise public awareness of the case in the hope that people will come forward with information that could help police find their daughter.

Source: AFP/Getty Images.

compassion. On the other hand, young men, homeless people, car owners who do not lock their cars, or a drunken victim of an assault are generally considered to be 'non-ideal victims' and less deserving of sympathy because of their characteristics (e.g. physical strength), action (e.g. their risk-taking behaviour) or inaction (they should have protected themselves).

The **hierarchy of victimization** (Box 9.1) and its impact on certain social groups may be best illustrated by the ambivalent position of women as victims of sexual and domestic violence. Historians have used a variety of sources, including court records, institutional records, newspapers and diaries, to show that in the past, only certain women and girls who presented themselves in certain ways were likely to succeed in bringing their case to public attention, or rarer still, to secure a conviction (Cox, 2003; Zedner, 1991a, b). In the contemporary context, feminist criminologists have argued that focusing on the characteristics or behaviour of individual victims as precipitating factors in crime events has a tendency to reinforce gender stereotypes in explaining cases of rape and violence against women and in distinguishing between 'innocent' and 'blameworthy' victims. Indeed, the notion of victim precipitation can easily become shorthand for 'victim blaming', as the following excerpts illustrate:

> The chronically abused wife is one who permits her husband to beat her, refuses to take punitive action afterward, and remains in the same situation so that she may be beaten

doing crime

again. . . . A wife who has been beaten for the first time may be a victim. A wife who is beaten again is a co-conspirator.

(clinical psychologist and marriage counsellor, quoted in Edwards, 1989: 165)

Women who say no do not always mean no. It is not just a question of saying no, it is a question of how she says it, how she shows and makes it clear. If she doesn't want it she only has to keep her legs shut.

(Judge Wild, 1982, quoted in Smart, 1989: 35)

It is the height of imprudence for any girl to hitch-hike at night. This is plain, it isn't really worth stating. She is in the true sense asking for it.

(Judge Bertrand Richards, 1982, quoted in Smart, 1989: 35)

As we see in what follows, such stereotyping has a serious impact on victims and the ways in which some social groups are dealt with by the criminal justice system. This in turn has led to unwillingness among some victims and witnesses to cooperate with the police and courts.

BOX 9.1 Hierarchy of victimization

The 'low-status, powerless groups' (Reiner, 2000: 93) whom the dominant majority in society see as troublesome or distasteful generally occupy the lower end of the hierarchy of victimization. Examples would be the homeless, the unemployed, those with alcohol and drug problems, prostitutes, refugees, asylum seekers, youth adopting a deviant cultural style, football fans and radical political organizations. The prime function of the police has always been to control and segregate such groups. And when members of such groups do report a crime to the police, they have to engage in a struggle to have their experiences taken seriously. This has often led to complaints from these social groups that they are being 'over-policed' as problem populations but 'under-policed' as victims. For example, the Lesbian and Gay Census 2001 in Britain found that although one in four respondents had been a victim of serious homophobic crime in the previous five years (including assault, blackmail, arson, rape, hate mail), 65 per cent of the victims did not report the crime to the police, mostly because they feared police harassment or had no confidence that the police would be sympathetic.

The hierarchy of victimization is also shaped by international politics and conditions of war. Ordinary civilians dragged into armed conflicts often suffer heightened victimization from conventional crime (e.g. theft, assault), forced displacement as well as human rights abuses including mass rape, mass killings, trafficking and torture (e.g. in the former Yugoslavia, Rwanda, Israel/Palestine). According to Human Rights Watch, some 50 million people are forcibly displaced as a result of persecution, conflict and human rights violation. Yet not all those who suffer are perceived as innocent victims worthy of our sympathy and support. For example, many refugees, asylum seekers and illegal migrants have been subject to racist attacks and exploitation at the hands of far-right groups, human traffickers, gang masters and unscrupulous employers in the European Union. Yet society's attitudes to the victimization of 'non-citizens' are shaped by stereotypes of the 'undesirable' immigrant as an 'economic scrounger', 'bogus' or 'criminal' (Goodey, 2000).

Different types of victimology

While victimologists are highly critical of the traditional offender-oriented nature of criminology and share a common interest in developing victim-centred research, they differ in their assumptions and the focus of study. Various attempts have been made to classify the different strands of victimological thought. Karmen (1990) identifies three strands within **victimology**: the conservative, the liberal and the radical-critical. Each of these strands defines the scope of the discipline differently, reflects a particular understanding of the problem of crime, and connects with different positions within the victims' movement.

The *conservative* strand within victimology defines the discipline in four ways. First, it views crime as a distinct problem with particular focus on the highly visible forms of crime victimization; second, it is concerned to render people accountable; third, it encourages self-reliance; and finally, it focuses on notions of retributive justice. This type of victimology generally aims to identify particular patterns of victimization and to examine the actions or patterns of 'lifestyle' of individual victims which may have contributed to the process of crime victimization. Indeed, many of the early victim studies within this tradition shared the assumption that victims are somehow 'different' from non-victims and that they are identifiable because they have particular, distinctive characteristics. For example, some writers set out to develop typologies of victims on the basis of psychological and social variables (von Hentig, 1948). Others, such as Mendelsohn (1956), have used the notion of culpability (from the 'completely innocent' to the 'most guilty victim') to understand the victimizing event (for some of the highly controversial studies, see Wolfgang's (1958) study of homicide and Amir's (1971) study of rape). These so-called 'proto-victimologists' typically referred to victims' conscious and unconscious role in their own victimization, and focused on individual responsibility in the escalation of a situation into a criminal incident. As Jo Goodey (2005: 11) points out, '[m]uch of this early work is now discredited for its limited and damaging interpretation of victimization minus the social context in which crime is committed'.

Although research on victimization-proneness is controversial, more recent studies from this tradition have raised some important insights into the nature of relationships between offenders and victims for policy-makers and victims' movements and organizations. In particular, the development of victim surveys has helped to place the issues of crime victimization and victimization prevention on the policy agenda (see the next section).

The *liberal* strand within victimology extends the conservative focus by including more hidden types of criminal victimization and abuses by white-collar elites, multinational corporations and businesses in their analyses. Most victims of fraud are, by definition, unaware that they have been victimized at all, or unwilling to recognize that they have been conned (Box, 1983: 17). The intense media attention paid to high-profile business fraud cases and deceptions such as those involving Barings Bank, Bank of Credit and Commercial International (BCCI) and the Maxwell pension fund has highlighted the plight of those who are their victims (including 800,000 depositors in 1.2 million bank accounts in over seventy countries in the case of the collapse of BCCI) and the devastating impact upon them (Levi and Pithouse, 1992; and see Chapter 13 of this book). The consequences of corporate crime may also extend to employees, tenants and consumers (Slapper and Tombs, 1999). This type of victimology is often concerned with making 'the victim whole again' – for example, by considering the value of restitution, mediation and reconciliation as appropriate penal strategies (Braithwaite, 2002).

The *radical-critical* strand within victimology sets out to extend the focus of the discipline even further. Its analysis extends to all forms of human suffering and is based on the recognition that poverty, malnutrition, inadequate health care and unemployment are all just as socially harmful as, if not more harmful than, most of the behaviours and incidents that currently make up the official 'crime problem'. Furthermore, it considers the criminal justice system too to be a problem contributing to victimization. Thus, 'institutional wrong-doing that violates human rights' (Karmen, 1990: 12), police rule-breaking, wrongful arrest and false imprisonment, political corruption, and deviant or injurious actions of the state that may or may not be defined as 'crimes' are treated as legitimate areas for study (see chapters 17, 19 and 21). By using broader social conceptions of victimization, this type of victimology promises to challenge dominant understandings of what constitutes the 'crime problem' and its impact on individuals and whole communities. In recent years, victimologists writing from this tradition have also turned to more structural explanations as a way of understanding the nature and process of victimization. For example, they have engaged in analysis of the wider economic and social context of victimization and structural powerlessness, and in political analysis of the rights of victims (see Mawby and Walklate, 1994).

Crime victimization surveys

A key aspect of victim-oriented research has been the development of crime victimization surveys. As Chapter 3 shows, the British Crime Survey (BCS) and other national victim surveys in the United States, Canada, Australia, the Netherlands, Switzerland have provided us with an alternative measure of crime and a more informed understanding of the impact of crime on victims, the social, economic and demographic characteristics of the victim population, and public attitudes to crime and the criminal justice system. Large-scale cross-national victim surveys such as the UN-sponsored International Crime Victimization Survey (ICVS) have also been carried out so that some international comparisons of victimization can be made (see Box 9.2). One of the key findings of the ICVS is that the experience of being criminally victimized has become a statistically normal feature of life around the world, though the type and extent of victimization vary. For all crimes the highest reporting levels are in the industrialized world. In countries of transition and developing countries, crimes were reported less frequently. The survey has also highlighted the experiences of respondents and their anxieties about crime and policing during periods of political, economic and social upheaval. For example, corruption has been identified as a main concern for survey respondents in developing countries and countries in transition. Local victim surveys in Britain with a narrower geographical focus (e.g. the Islington Crime Survey) have also made a significant contribution to our knowledge of crime. They have highlighted the uneven distribution of risks of victimization, showing that certain age or social groups are more frequently subjected to crime than others.

Although crime victimization surveys have helped to redress an imbalance in early criminological works, provide insights into the hidden figures of crime and sensitize policy-makers to the range and diversity of victim experiences with crime, they too have serious limitations. For one thing, they suffer from a general inability to tap certain forms of crime where there is no direct or clearly identifiable victim. Many crimes committed in the corporate boardroom, in the financial marketplace, on the Internet, or directed against the environment thus remain characterized by 'no knowledge, no statistics, no theory, no research, no control, no politics, and no panic' (Jupp *et al.*, 1999). Crime victimization surveys therefore carry with them limited notions about what is crime and who are the victims. They have a tendency to focus the notion of criminality on the 'conventional' crimes while other equally harmful acts (and victims) remain hidden. In particular, early surveys that examine people's 'lifestyle' (cf. Hindelang *et al.*, 1978; Gottfredson, 1984) in order to assess how patterns of leisure activities and everyday behaviour affect the risks of victimization have been criticized for ignoring the reality that lifestyles are often shaped by social forces and structural constraints.

There are also specific problems with using international victimization reports as a measure of crime. International victimization surveys that rely on standardized concepts of 'crime' tend to ignore different cultural perceptions that may affect the respondents. Indeed, respondents in different countries may have different notions of thresholds concerning what they perceive as unacceptable and harmful behaviour. All this suggests that findings from victimization surveys must be interpreted very carefully, in the knowledge that any differences may reflect definitional variations as much as variations in prevalence or incidence.

BOX 9.2 The International Crime Victimization Survey

The International Crime Victimization Survey (ICVS) conducted in 1989, 1992, 1996, 2000 and 2005 is a cross-national comparative measure of victims' experience with crime, policing and feelings of unsafety in a large number of countries. The 2000 ICVS shows that the most common reason for not reporting in all countries was that the incident was considered 'not serious enough' or there was 'no loss'. Reporting is also influenced by other factors: previous personal experiences of reporting; experience with or attitudes to the police; expectations; factors related to the particular victimization experience in hand; existence of alternative ways of dealing with this; relationship with the offender; and the 'privacy' of the issue. For all countries combined, just over 1 per cent of women reported offensive sexual behaviour. Women know the offender(s) in about half of all the sexual incidents. Victims were also asked why they did report. In general, victims of sexual incidents, assaults and threats were most concerned to stop what happened being repeated. For burglaries and thefts from cars, more than a third reported because they wanted help in getting property back, and a third did so for insurance reasons. Other victims referred to the civic obligation to notify the police. Risks for different social groups were also examined. Households with higher incomes were more at risk than those poorer ones. In poorer neighbourhoods, households in general might have higher risk, but more affluent households emerge as the most vulnerable. Younger respondents were more at risk than older ones. Men were about 20 per cent more at risk than women for robbery and assaults.

Source: Kesteren *et al.*, 2000.

Social variables in crime victimization

Individuals are differentially placed in respect of crime – differentially vulnerable to crime, and differentially affected by crime. Indeed, there is evidence to suggest that the risk of crime victimization is unevenly distributed within and between different localities and various sections of the population. Existing victim surveys in Britain and elsewhere have highlighted social class, age, gender and ethnicity as key and intertwining variables in the patterns and rates of crime victimization.

Social class

Crime victimization surveys have consistently shown that the risk from property crime is unequally distributed among the population, with the 'most marginalized social groups living in the poorest areas' generally bearing the greater burden of crime (Davies et al., 2003: 13; Nicholas et al., 2007). Similarly, Foster and Hope (1993) found in their analysis of early BCS data that pockets of high unemployment in public housing estates experienced very high rates of victimization. Indeed, many of the most deprived housing estates with drugs and/or high crime problems are found in areas evacuated by business and industry. Closure of local shops and other amenities reinforces a 'bad reputation' for the area and has adverse consequences for the availability of credit and insurance for residents (Pearson, 1987). This has produced what the Rowntree Inquiry described as 'vicious cycles of decline in particular areas and on particular estates' (Rowntree Foundation, 1995).

The significance of class in crime victimization has been a key issue for one particularly influential perspective in British criminology since the mid-1980s. As Young (1986: 21) puts it, the central tenets of 'left realism' are to recognize that crime is 'a very real source of suffering for the poor and the vulnerable' and to 'take crime seriously'. John Lea and Jock Young in their pivotal work *What Is To Be Done about Law and Order?* (1984) drew attention to the fact that most crime is intra-class and intra-racial, committed by relatively disadvantaged perpetrators on similarly relatively disadvantaged victims. Thus, working-class crime (street crime, burglary, personal violence) is seen as a problem of the first order. The task of the left, so they argue, is to accept this reality, try to understand it and do something about it, rather than deny or overdramatize it (for a critique of left realism, see Chapter 6).

Age

Contrary to popular imagination, children under the age of one are more at risk of being murdered than any other age group; many of the victims are killed by their parents or carers in Britain (Home Office, 2005a). In general, the more socially vulnerable the victim and the more private or intimate the setting of the crime's commission, the less visible the crime. In recent years there have been a growing number of revelations about the extensive abuse of children who have been in the care of local authorities.

By the late 1990s, allegations of sexual abuse and systematic violence by community and children's homes staff in Britain had surfaced in Leicestershire, Islington (London), Dumfries, Buckinghamshire, Northumbria, North Wales and Cheshire. Another example is child sexual abuse by women. Social stereotypes of femininity and motherhood mean that the criminal justice and child protection systems generally fail to identify women as perpetrators of sexual abuse, and accounts of (male and female) child victims tend to be disbelieved or minimized (Turton, 2007). Even when cases of abuse are reported and recorded, they are often considered to be 'atypical', 'one-off scandals', and something distinct from the more familiar crises of law and order.

Victim surveys have shown that young people are at least as much at risk of victimization as adults, and for some types of crime, more at risk than adults irrespective of class, gender or place. According to the 2005 *Offending, Crime and Justice Survey*, just over a quarter of young people aged from 10 to 25 had been a victim of either personal theft (e.g. mobile phones) or of assault in the previous twelve months. Significantly, those young males who had committed an offence themselves were more likely to be victims (Wilson *et al.*, 2006). Studies in Edinburgh (Anderson *et al.*, 1994), Glasgow (Hartless *et al.*, 1995) and Teesside (Brown, 1994) have produced startlingly similar results indicating routine experience by children and teenagers of different forms of abuse in the home and on the street, harassment by adults and other young people, bullying as well as other forms of serious crime (including physical assault). Few of these experiences are reported to the police, however, and youth victimization (as opposed to youth offending) remains low on the priority lists of the police and politicians. This, combined with the experience for many young people of being 'moved on', or stopped and searched, contributed to the argument that young people are over-controlled (as delinquents) but under-protected (as victims) (Loader, 1996; Anderson *et al.*, 1994). Clearly then, children and young people are affected not only by conventional crimes (e.g. theft) but also by crimes behind closed doors and crimes specific to the very young (e.g. child abuse, school bullying).

Although the elderly have lower rates of victimization from violent street crime than younger age groups, they can be subject to abuse hidden behind closed doors of private households or care homes. There are other problems with assessing the extent of elder victimization: elder abuse is not conceptualized in legal terms, is not a clearly defined offence, and has no satisfactory working definition. According to one case review of social services in England, some 5 per cent of pensioners regularly suffer victimization. This is almost certainly an underestimate. Non-reporting often results from concerns over domestic privacy, and few cases end up in official statistics, let alone in court (Brogden and Nijhar, 2000: 48–9).

Gender

Chapter 3 suggests that victim surveys and official statistics have consistently shown that men are more likely to be victims of violent attacks, particularly by strangers and by other men in public spaces, whereas women are more likely to be victimized in the home. According to the 2006/7 BCS, young men aged 16 to 24 had the highest risk of being a victim of violent crime (Nicholas *et al.*, 2007). As Dorling (2005) points out, for men aged 20 to 24 the murder rates have doubled in the last two decades. Young men in Britain are exposed to 'more fights, more brawls, more scuffles, more bottles and more knives. . . . These are the same groups of young men for whom suicide rates are rising, the same groups of which almost a million left the country in the 1990s unknown to the authorities, presumably to find somewhere better to live' (Dorling, 2005: 190). Many work-based injuries also take place, where assault and intimidation commonly occur between men – from either managers or colleagues, as a result of unsafe working practices (Stanko et al., 1998), or in the course of providing services to the public (especially in occupations such as the police and health service workers, security guards, publicans and bar staff) (Budd, 1999).

Women on the other hand are more likely to be victimized in the home. They are the main victims of reported and unreported sexual violence (Finney, 2006; Nicholas et al., 2007). This gendered pattern of violence is notable around the world, especially in Latin America and Africa (Newman, 1999). Women are more likely to have experienced persistent, unwanted attention (e.g. 'stalking') and repeat victimization (especially in domestic violence) than men (Nicholas et al., 2007; Budd and Mattinson, 2000; Finney, 2006). Such experiences of victimization are sometimes made invisible in conventional victim studies, however. Indeed, critics have argued that victim surveys that are based on measuring discrete events cannot fully comprehend the pervasive, underlying threat to security or the 'continuum of sexual violence' (Kelly, 1988) that characterizes the experiences of many women. Women routinely learn to manage their lives structured and informed by their relationships with men they know. In these relationships, many women during their lifetime learn to deal with habitual violence, bullying or prolonged abuse, in what can be described as 'climates of unsafety' (Stanko, 1990). Feminists have also pointed to the continuities of the gendered nature of violence in both war (e.g. mass rape, human trafficking) and peace ('femicide') (Jamieson, 1998; Kelly, 2005). State agents may be the violators rather than protectors of women's rights in some cases. For example, critics have pointed to evidence of international peacekeepers being involved in sex trafficking and other forms of sexual exploitation in conflict and post-conflict regions (e.g. the Balkans) and the existence of a culture of denial and impunity among the state and transnational bodies (such as the UN and NATO) (Human Rights Watch, 2002; Mendelson, 2005).

Ethnicity

Studies have found that in Britain and the rest of Europe, people belonging to ethnic minority groups are generally at greater risk of crime victimization than whites (Percy, 1998; Clancy et al., 2001; Albrecht, 2000). However, there are important variations. Smaller-scale, local area studies in Britain have revealed even more complex patterns of risk of victimization and variations within and between different groups, socio-economic factors, localities and offences (Gill, 2006; Jones et al., 1986; Crawford et al., 1990; Jefferson and Walker, 1993; Webster, 1994; Bowling and Phillips, 2002). Ethnic minority groups are also routinely subject to racial violence and harassment. Indeed, some violent offences are best seen as a 'process', as the cumulative impact of threats, domestic assaults, name calling, racial insults, abuse, graffiti and punching cannot be captured by the mere counting of each individual incident (Bowling, 1998).

Perhaps more damagingly, minority ethnic groups have pointed to persistent police failure in protecting them from racist victimization. Such criticisms have gathered momentum in the wake of the Stephen Lawrence scandal in Britain of the late 1990s in which the Macpherson

Report (1999) found 'institutional racism' to be pervasive within the Metropolitan Police (and by extension elsewhere) and that, as a result, ethnic minority groups are unjustly treated. The poor response to crime victimization of particular sections of society has serious implications, especially against a background of conflicts between the police and black communities, serious problems long associated with police use of stop and search powers and a number of successful claims against the police for civil damages (see Chapter 17). Confidence in the police and cooperation with investigations have no doubt been harmed by tensions and negative encounters between the police and those belonging to ethnic minority communities. Indeed, victimization and attitudinal surveys have provided evidence to support this. Africans and Caribbeans have generally lower levels of satisfaction with the police than do white respondents, while results are more mixed among Asian respondents (see Bowling and Phillips, 2002: 135–8).

BOX 9.3 'Honour killings'

One in ten young British Asians believes so-called honour killings can be justified, according to a poll for the BBC's Asian Network. Of 500 Hindus, Sikhs, Christians and Muslims questioned, a tenth said they would condone the murder of someone who disrespected their family's honour. Figures show thirteen people die every year in honour killings, but police and support groups believe it is many more. Religious leaders said they would hold a national conference on the issue.

Honour killing is a brutal reaction within a family – predominantly Asian and Middle Eastern – to someone perceived to have brought 'shame' upon relatives. What constitutes dishonour can range from wearing clothes thought unsuitable or choosing a career which the family disapprove of, to marrying outside of the wider community.

Family importance

One interviewee told the radio station: 'A lot of people treat their family as everything they have got. So if someone hurts their family the law might do nothing about it, you might have to deal with it.'

'Not tolerated'

Dr Aisha Gill, a lecturer in criminology at Roehampton University, told BBC Five Live that convincing the Asian community that honour killings were not acceptable was the right approach. 'I think it's absolutely essential that there is a collective responsibility, and this is not just for agencies, but for communities that are affected by it. [The government should] send out a clear message, an unambiguous message that such violence against women will not be tolerated.'

In one recent case, two men were jailed for life for murdering their relative after she fell in love with an asylum seeker. Greengrocer Azhar Nazir, 30, and his cousin Imran Mohammed, 17, stabbed Nazir's sister Samaira 18 times at the family home in Southall in April 2005. The 25-year-old recruitment consultant was killed after she asked to marry an Afghan man – instead of marrying someone in the Pakistani family circle.

Source: BBC News, 4 September 2006
http://news.bbc.co.uk/go/pr/fr/-/1/hi/uk/5311244.stm

The impact of crime

Not only are social groups and individuals differentially vulnerable to crime victimization, they are also differentially fearful about crime. Fear of crime has come to be regarded as 'a problem in its own right' (Hale, 1992), quite distinct from actual crime and victimization, and distinctive policies have been developed that aim to reduce levels of fear. British Crime Surveys now regularly investigate the levels and character of this fear, categorizing and measuring the emotional reactions prompted by crime. The BCS shows that those who are most concerned about crime tend to be women, the poor, those in unskilled occupations and those living in the inner cities, council estate areas, or areas with high levels of disorder. The young are most concerned about car-related theft. Women (especially older women) are far more likely to feel unsafe at home or out alone after dark than men. People in partly skilled or unskilled occupations are found to be more fearful than those in skilled occupations, while those who consider themselves to be in poor health or with disability also have heightened levels of concern about crime (Simmons and Dodd, 2003; Nicholas *et al.*, 2007). In another national survey of ethnic minorities, nearly one in four black and Asian respondents reported being worried about being racially harassed (Virdee, 1997). The meaning of such fears and anxieties is discussed in Chapter 12.

Victims of specific crimes may be affected by the crime itself (i.e. **primary victimization**) or the way in which others respond to them and the crimes (i.e. **secondary victimization**). A particular crime may have an effect on victims directly in a number of ways. They may be physically injured, incur financial loss or damage to property, or lose time as a result of the crime itself or of involvement in the criminal justice process. Most existing studies have concentrated on the impact of more serious personal or property crimes (as opposed to the majority of everyday crimes or other high-profile cases of business crime or criminal negligence). These studies have highlighted the acute stress, shock, sense of intrusion of privacy, and adverse physical, practical or financial effects suffered by many victims (Maguire and Corbett, 1987; Brogden and Nijhar, 2000; Lurigio *et al.*, 1990). In cases of violence, there is evidence from the British Crime Surveys to suggest that the most common emotional reaction is anger, followed by shock, fear, difficulty in sleeping, and crying. Victims of rape, sexual assault and abuse have been found to suffer persisting effects related to their physical and mental health – for example, emotional disturbance, sleeping or eating disorders, feelings of insecurity, or troubled relationships over a period of time (Maguire and Corbett, 1987; Kelly, 1988; Ruback and Thompson, 2001).

Plate 9.2 Cartoon on home security system.

Source: © Cartoon Stock, London, www.CartoonStock.com.

"George, this new home security system you bought...
how much did it cost?"

Such negative impact may be exacerbated by the reaction of criminal justice agencies and other experts (e.g. medical services) to the victim. On the basis of a series of interviews with victims of interpersonal crimes, Shapland *et al.* (1985) found that many victims in Britain were poorly informed about the criminal justice process, including the possibility of state compensation. Perhaps more significantly, the study found that victims began with very positive views of the system's response to their problems, but became increasingly critical as their cases progressed. In the initial stages, much of the sense of secondary victimization felt by victims stems from their perceptions of the police as unsympathetic. Findings that the police are insensitive to victims are common to studies across a wide range of countries in which policing structures are very different (Newman, 1999). In the later stages, victims often perceive court appearances as intimidating or bewildering.

The failings of the British criminal justice system in the treatment of female victims have been well documented (Stanko, 1994; Dobash *et al.*, 1995). In particular, there has been public concern about the police's insensitive or even hostile treatment of female victims of sexual offences – for example, in acquaintance attacks or in cases where the woman's demeanour or dress code is seen to be 'provocative' (Edwards, 1989; Hanmer *et al.*, 1989; Gregory and Lees, 1999; see also Chapter 11 of this book). The problem of secondary victimization of some victims was dramatically highlighted in 1982 by an episode of Roger Graef's ground-breaking television documentary on the Thames Valley Police which showed a very disturbing interrogation of a rape victim by two male officers. Indeed, the police response to men's violence against women is important not only for individual women's safety but also because of its social significance. The police define which types of attacks are to be taken seriously and proceeded with, and which types of attacks are to be condoned or dropped (i.e. 'no-crimed'). By making a distinction between 'innocent' and 'blameworthy' victims, the police are also making a distinction between attacks they deem to be justifiable in society and those that are not. This decision-making process demonstrates that the police do not offer unconditional protection to all victims against all forms of violence. Instead, moral judgements are constantly being made based on gendered assumptions (or stereotypical assumptions about race, age and sexuality), biases within the police occupational culture, and the associated definition of what counts as 'proper policing'. For example, calls to domestic disturbances have always been a significant part of the police workload. However, they tend to be dealt with by officers without recourse to criminal proceedings, even when evidence of assault is present. As Robert Reiner argues, '"Domestics" were seen as messy, unproductive and not "real" police work in traditional cop culture' (2000: 135). Others, however, have pointed to a 'cultural shift' in police policy and practices towards 'service provision' and some of the improvements in police responses to the problem of domestic violence in recent years (Goodey, 2005: 158).

Finally, there has been an increased recognition of the pains of indirect victimization. For example, the families of murder victims may suffer the profound trauma of bereavement, compounded by the viciousness of the attack or the senselessness of the murder (Rock, 1998). Paul Iganski (2001: 628–31) has also drawn attention to the range of harms generated by certain crimes that extend well beyond the initially targeted victim. The 'waves of harm' (see Figure 9.1) generated by hate crimes spread beyond the individual to the victim's 'group' or

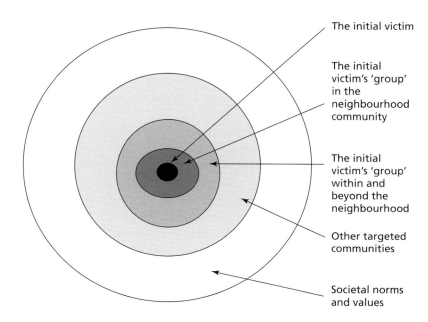

The initial victim

The initial victim's 'group' in the neighbourhood community

The initial victim's 'group' within and beyond the neighbourhood

Other targeted communities

Societal norms and values

Figure 9.1 Waves of harm and values generated by hate crimes.

community in the wider neighbourhood. As one respondent in his study explains, 'it tends to get people really anxious and excited and . . . we like to call them domestic terrorism' (Iganski, 2001: 630). Other persons who share the victim's characteristics – and come to hear of the victim's plight – may potentially be affected by a hate crime. They may respond as if they have been victimized themselves. In this sense, hate crimes constitute 'message crimes'. The wave of harm can also spread to other targeted or socially vulnerable groups within and beyond the victim's neighbourhood. Furthermore, hate crimes arguably strike at the core of societal values, offending the collective moral code (see Chapter 12).

Towards a victim-oriented criminal justice process?

It has been increasingly recognized that the victim has a key role in the criminal justice process. After all, most crime would remain hidden and unpunished without the cooperation of the victim in reporting the offence, providing evidence and acting as witness in court. The marginalization and 'silencing' of many victims in the court process has been well documented (see Chapter 16), though more recent attempts to develop a more 'victim-oriented' criminal justice system in Britain and elsewhere may have gone some way to address that (Goodey, 2005). There have been calls for increased victim participation in the criminal justice process, often in decisions as to bail, diversion from prosecution, levels of sentence and parole. A formal way of providing for victims' views to be taken into account is through what is known as a 'victim impact statement' (VIS) or 'victim statement' (VS). Such provisions are much more developed in the United States than in Britain, and have had rather mixed receptions. In Britain there is evidence to suggest that victim statements are supported by many decision-makers at the level of rhetoric (i.e. it is commonplace to endorse the idea of giving victims an opportunity to be 'heard') but not at the level of action (victim statements are sought and used only in a small minority of cases) (Morgan and Sanders, 1999). Critics have also argued that sentences should be a matter of public policy rather than dependent on the lottery of the forgiveness or anger of the victim, that the victim might feel even more frustrated and angry if the court appeared to ignore the VS/VIS, and that a more appropriate way forward might be to educate those working in the criminal justice agencies about the physical and psychological impact of victimization on individuals and families (Ashworth, 1993; for a review, see Goodey, 2005 and Walklate, 2007b).

So what are the limits and possibilities of developing a victim-oriented criminal justice system? In recent years, victim groups and voluntary or professional organizations have fought hard to raise the profile of hidden victims (e.g. trafficking victims) and to press for improved victim services and more sensitive treatment of victims by criminal justice agencies. In practice, expressions of victims' needs and interests and their recognition by the state are often mediated by power differentials and political considerations. Vocal, determined victim groups or those with most resources are generally better placed than the most vulnerable and least vocal victim groups to express their needs, lobby for change, or seek practical help or information. Furthermore, many critics have argued that the call for addressing victim needs and for orienting the criminal justice system away from the offender and towards the victim can easily become conflated with a populist 'law and order' approach to punishment.

BOX 9.4 Victim movements – some examples around the world

Victims, their families, voluntary or professional agencies and communities affected by crimes have mobilized themselves in different ways to force governments to take the problem of crime victimization seriously.

In the People's Republic of China, the Tiananmen Mothers is a group made up of the relatives of 125 victims killed during the Tiananmen Square student movement on 4 June 1989. On that day, the Chinese army, backed by tanks, stormed the square killing demonstrators. Officially, the 1989 student movement remains a 'counterrevolutionary uprising'. The government has never released any official tally of casualties, but outside groups have estimated that the number of those killed or injured runs in the thousands. The 'Tiananmen Mothers' wanted the authorities to set up an inquiry into the killings, impose punishment on the culprits, provide compensation and assistance to those who continue to suffer psychologically or financially from the crackdown, and remove the political and social stigma on victims and their families.

In the United States a more conservative rights-based victim movement has been at the forefront of campaigns for extension of their role in judicial discretion (e.g. the right to make 'victim impact statements' to inform sentencing decisions) and often for a more punitive response to offenders. For example, the national community and victim's rights organization Parents for Megan's Law was set up after a 7-year-old New Jersey girl was raped and murdered in 1994 by a paroled sex offender who had moved into her neighbourhood. The resulting legislative changes provide for stringent community notification requirements for convicted sex offenders if and when they get out of prison and, in some cases, for harsher sentences. Other victim groups have also campaigned for indefinite confinement of sex offenders or for the retention or reintroduction of the death penalty for other offenders. Civil libertarians and other critics, however, have called the Megan's Law provisions a 'badge of infamy' that is attached to certain offenders for life.

In Britain the central organ of the victim movement, Victim Support, has concentrated on lobbying for and providing services to individual victims (e.g. through the work of local volunteers), compensation, and provision for the victim in court. It has also been highly influential in shaping the government's 'Victim's Charter', which sets out the rights of victims, specifying how they are to be treated and the standards they can expect – for example, information about the progress of their case, about trial dates, and about bail and sentencing decisions. In addition, victim groups and concerned citizens have also been highly vocal in their demands for legislative changes or tougher sentencing in the aftermath of particular crimes (e.g. the murder of children, the Dunblane killings).

As Fattah (1986: 2–3) argues,

> Most victim advocates do not restrict their demands to a charter of victim rights or to a better lot for those who are victimized. These demands are usually coupled with, and in fact overshadowed by, calls for harsher penalties, stricter measures and more oppressive treatment of offenders. Getting tough with offenders is often advanced as the central or, at least, as an essential component, of society's obligation to the victims of crime. . . . In this way, the noble cause of the victims of crime is used as a pretext to unleash suppressed vindictive impulses or as an excuse to act out the inhibited aggression against the offender.

While calls for 'justice' by victim groups can become overshadowed by or equated with a 'get-tough' approach to crime and disorder, a victim-oriented criminal justice system also has the potential of paving the way for a more progressive approach to punishment. In recent years, there are signs of a growing interest around the world in communitarian ideas of reintegration and restorative justice whereby justice is primarily a process of reconciling conflicts and repairing harms or ruptures to social bonds resulting from crime (McLaughlin et al., 2003; Braithwaite, 1989; Zehr, 1990). As Chapter 15 explains, the restorative justice model, the use of reintegrative shaming techniques, mediation, and reparation aim to provide an alternative and more appropriate way of resolving disputes, confronting offenders with their wrongdoing and empowering the victims. However, one can argue that public demands for retribution as the organizing principle of justice remain as strong as ever. For criminologists, the relationships between crime victims, offenders and the community will continue to be an important and highly contentious area of study.

Summary

1   Victims play a central role in initiating the criminal justice process. In addition, there have been moves to increase victim participation at subsequent stages of the criminal justice process and to develop alternative means of resolving disputes, confronting offenders with their wrongdoing and empowering the victims.
2   Victimologists are highly critical of the traditional offender-oriented nature of criminology and share a common interest in developing victim-centred research. At the same time, they differ in their assumptions and the focus of study. There are at least three strands within victimology: the conservative, the liberal and the radical-critical.
3   Some victims enjoy a higher status in the crime discourse, and their experiences of victimization are taken more seriously than others. In this sense, 'victim' is a social construct that reflects broader power differentials and stereotypes in society.
4   The risk of crime victimization is unevenly distributed within and between different localities and various sections of the population. Victim surveys and official statistics have consistently shown that men are more likely than women to be victims of violent attacks, particularly by strangers and by other men in public spaces. Women on the other hand are more likely to be victimized in the home.

5   Victims may be affected by the crime itself or the way in which others respond to them and the crimes. There is also increasing recognition of the impact of indirect victimization on victims' families and communities.

Critical thinking questions

1   Compile a list of five local/national and five international stories about victims of different types of crime from any chosen newspaper. What do these stories tell you about the differential status of victims in media representations of crime? Is there a pattern to the types of victims who are portrayed as innocent and deserving of our help, and those who are seen as blameworthy?
2   Consider the advantages and disadvantages of increasing victim participation at different stages of the criminal justice process. What are the implications for procedural, substantive and negotiated justice (see Chapter 16)?

Further study

Goodey, J. (2005) *Victims and Victimology: Research, Policy and Practice*, Harlow: Longman. A useful text examining the key theoretical, political and policy debates in the field of victims and victimology.

Mawby, R. and Walklate, S. (1994) *Critical Victimology*, London: Sage. A critical and comparative analysis of victim services and other key issues facing crime victims within the criminal justice system.

Schur, E. M. (1965) *Crimes without Victims: Deviant Behavior and Public Policy*, Englewood Cliffs, NJ: Prentice Hall. A classic sociological text examining a range of 'victimless' crimes from the labelling perspective.

Walklate, S. (ed.) (2007b) *Handbook of Victims and Victimology*, Cullompton: Willan. An authoritative handbook on the nature, extent and impact of criminal victimization and the developments in victimology.

More information

Criminal Justice System Online: 'Victims Virtual Walkthrough'
http://www.cjsonline.gov.uk/victim/walkthrough/index.html
An interactive virtual tour that provides information about the British criminal justice process as it relates to victims of crime.

UNICRI website on ICVS

http://www.unicri.it/wwd/analysis/icvs/

Provides information on various international crime victimization surveys.

Human Rights Watch

www.hrw.org

A site dedicated to protecting the human rights of people around the world. Human Rights Watch is a non-governmental organization, funded by donations from private individuals and foundations.

United Nations Declaration of Basic Principles of Justice for Victims of Crime and Abuse of Power (1985)

http://www.unhchr.ch/htm1/menu3/b/h comp49.htm

One of the landmark documents demonstrating the global significance of victims.

chapter 10

Crime and Property

- ■ What can be identified as property crimes?
- ■ How does the pattern of property crime vary across time and place?
- ■ What are the characteristics of property crime offenders?
- ■ How is the risk of victimization socially distributed?

Introduction

Official statistics around the world suggest that by far the most frequently reported crime is property crime (Nicholas *et al.*, 2007). So what is property crime?

Broadly speaking, property crime involves stealing and dishonestly obtaining or damaging another's property, whether tangible goods or intangible property. All this may seem very straightforward. However, the distinction between what is unambiguously criminal and what is culturally tolerated behaviour is not always so clear-cut. For example, the dishonest acquisition of another's property is not always perceived as 'theft' by the offender or by the victim. Pickpocketing is seen as unacceptable and criminal, whereas hotel employees stealing food, wine or cash and hotel guests stealing linen, art or silverware from their rooms may be tolerated by the victim or justified as 'perks' or 'souvenirs' by the perpetrator. Similarly, we tend to associate 'fraud' with crime for gain or major financial scandals (see Chapter 13). Yet it is not always easy to draw a line between 'enterprise' and 'dishonesty', or between dishonest behaviour that is clearly 'illegal' and the hustles, scams and confidence tricks of 'con-merchants', false advertising of salespersons or pyramid schemes, and the behaviour of many others involved in everyday commercial exchanges.

In this chapter we look at the different forms and patterns of property crime, our attitudes towards its perpetrators, the characteristics of different types of property crime offenders, issues surrounding the risk of victimization and its distribution, and the impact of property crime on individual victims and communities. The aim is to challenge some of the popular assumptions about property crime and property crime offenders and to broaden our understanding of the crime problem and what is to be done about it.

Patterns of property crime

What we place into the category of 'property crime' makes a big difference to the range of behaviour we have to explain. Chapter 3 shows the problems of using crime and judicial statistics as a measure of actual levels of criminal activities in society. Nevertheless, crime statistics provide a useful starting point for understanding patterns of crime and the decisions of those responsible for controlling crime. From the 1830s onwards, crime has been classified into six main types:

- offences against the person;
- offences against property (with violence);
- offences against property (without violence);
- malicious offences against property;
- offences against the currency;
- and miscellaneous offences (Emsley, 2002).

The pattern that can be drawn from the statistics shows a steady increase in crime, especially property crime, in the late eighteenth century, becoming much sharper from the first decade of the nineteenth century to the close of the 1840s, and then a general decline in crime until the end of the nineteenth century, except, most noticeably, for burglary (Emsley, 2005).

Many historians have explained the changing level of property crime by referring to the combined effects of key changes in British social and economic life during this period: population growth; urbanization and the capitalization of industry; and changing levels of unemployment and economic hardship. Historians who adopted a class conflict perception of society saw property crime as an element of the developing struggle between capital and labour. They argued that new work practices brought about by industrialization, and changes in payment for labour and in notions of property ownership, meant that traditional rural popular culture and customs (e.g. gathering fallen wood for fuel, taking wild game, collecting scrap metal) were increasingly criminalized (Thompson, 1975). Seen in this light, the thefts of poor men might be understood as resistance to capitalism and new work discipline. Other historians, however, turn to social and court data that reveal a relationship between capital and labour far more complex than a simple class conflict model might suggest. They stressed the significance of changes in the administration of criminal justice (such as the establishment of the new police forces), the 'civilization' of the population, a diminishing fear about the 'dangerous classes', and a corresponding decline in the reporting and prosecuting of small-scale theft, especially in the second half of the mid-nineteenth century (see Emsley, 2005). Court records show that most thefts involved everyday objects of relatively little value and that very many of the victims were relatively poor people. In the long run, the changes in the economy meant that people had more disposable income and more movable property, and shops had more goods for consumers, which in turn prompted changes in the opportunities for and style of theft.

The dominance of property offences continued into the twentieth century. Conventional and new forms of property crime were rampant during the Second World War even though it was commonly regarded as a golden age of community spirit and national pride. The war created massive opportunities for crime for everyone – from organized gangs and professional criminals to 'ordinary' and 'respectable' people. Blackouts and bombed buildings made looting especially easy; because of rationing, many people took to fiddling and forging their food, petrol and clothes coupons; and profiteering and the black market boomed (Calder, 1991; Fraser, 1994). The steady increase of crime during the interwar and post-war periods might arguably reflect the economic difficulties generated by the Depression as well as the temptations created by the first signs of the consumer society. For certain social classes and in certain areas of Britain, consumer booms (notably of the 1930s and 1950s) generated both more goods for those with disposable income and the desire for more goods, which very likely resulted in increased property crime. The consumer booms and technological revolution of the post-war decades put into circulation a mass of portable, high-value goods such as televisions, radios and stereos that presented attractive new targets and new opportunities for crime. For example, car crime rose sharply because there were many more valuable cars available on every city street at all times and often unattended than there were before the Second World War.

The range of property crime activities has also broadened significantly and, in some cases, developed into sophisticated transnational businesses generating high profits. For example, car theft is no longer simply a domestic problem or the province of teenagers engaged in random acts of theft. 'Thefts to order' (especially of luxury cars) are now well organized and sophisticated operations – from the theft itself, the forging of plates and documentation, through to the smuggling of the cars across the US–Mexican border or to 'far-flung destinations' such as Russia and China (see Box 10.1). Developments in computing and telecommunications technology have generated greater opportunities for theft and enabled new or existing forms of deviance to be carried out more extensively, more quickly, more efficiently and with greater ease of concealment (Thomas and Loader, 2000; Jewkes, 2003a).

This argument can be extended to the emergence of 'new' everyday property crimes such as bank or credit card fraud. The expansion of automated banking and the increased use of 'plastic money' have posed a new set of risks to the banking industry and customers. The fraudulent use of stolen credit and bank cards was described as one of the fastest-growing, and most favoured, of financial crimes at local and street level in many societies in the late 1980s (Tremblay, 1986). The availability of cheap technology such as swipe machines and simple techniques such as 'skimming', which involves reading and copying secret coded details on cards, has pushed up the costs of credit card fraud even further.

Comparative experiences

With the notable exceptions of Japan and Switzerland, all the available evidence from industrialized countries points to a rapid and sustained increase in crime, especially property crime,

BOX 10.1 The globalization of car theft

In the past, stolen vehicles generally stayed inside the country within which they were stolen or, in the case of the United States, either stayed within the country or were taken across the border to Mexico, Central America and South America. Today, however, the exporting of stolen vehicles has become a global phenomenon. Cars, motorcycles, commercial trucks and vans may be stolen in the United States and Western Europe and exported to far-flung destinations such as Eastern Europe, the Middle East, parts of Africa and China. In Eastern Europe, for example, there has been a move towards capitalist economies and an increased demand for luxury cars such as BMWs and Mercedes since the fall of the Soviet Union in 1991. Given that the local supply of these vehicles is too small to meet demand, a market has been created for stolen vehicles imported from other countries.

Ron Clarke and Rick Brown (2003) suggest there are several other factors that contribute to the growing global problem of car theft. First, so many vehicles are driven across national borders each day that it becomes relatively easy to transport a stolen car across borders. Second, many used cars are routinely and legally shipped from one country to another, and some stolen car rings are able to set up their activities as legitimate enterprises of this type. Third, customs officials rarely examine every container routinely carried on cargo ships given the volume of global trade. Officials in the countries receiving stolen vehicles may also be corrupt, with customs officials and local police taking bribes to look the other way. Fourth, vehicle theft is not a high priority for law-enforcement officials in developing countries that receive stolen vehicles because they face much more serious crime problems.

Ron Clarke and Rick Brown also point out that several groups benefit from the exporting of stolen vehicles. For example, car insurance companies often raise their rates to cover the loss of the vehicles and may increase their profits as a result. The companies that ship the stolen vehicles across oceans also make a profit. Finally, car manufacturers benefit by selling new cars to the victims whose vehicles were stolen.

in the post-war period. Such increases in crime have occurred not only in periods of economic downturn and depression but also during times of full employment and exceptional living standards. The 1960s were years of affluence, yet against all conventional wisdom, crime continued to rise in cities of the United States as well as in major centres of European countries.

Criminologists are divided as to the reasons behind such increase and, by implication, what should be done about it. For example, neo-conservatives such as James Q. Wilson have singled out the immediate post-war idea of a caring welfare state, the supposed permissiveness of the 1960s and the increases in crime as proof that social democratic theorizing on the causes and solutions to crime was flawed (Wilson, 1975). The focus on the falling moral standards and weakening sources of social authority (especially in family standards) as major causes of crime had a significant influence on the law-and-order agendas on both sides of the Atlantic during the Bush, Reagan and Thatcher administrations. In contrast, writing from a left realist perspective, Jock Young has argued that even an absolute increase of prosperity at a national level tells us little about material inequality in society. According to the relative deprivation thesis, people have different expectations depending on what they feel they deserve. They may compare their economic situation with that of a reference group and feel relatively deprived when these expectations are not met. The argument is that faced with signs of evident wealth and possessions in neighbouring communities, unemployed youth could be motivated to commit street and property crimes because of emotional frustration, latent animosities and lack of opportunities (Young, 1986; Lea and Young, 1984).

However, following almost universal increases in property crime during the 1970s and 1980s, recorded property crimes in the United States, Britain and other European countries have since experienced a general decline. According to the National Crime Victimization Survey in the United States, while property crime (comprising mainly burglary, theft and car theft) makes up slightly more than three-quarters of all crime in the United States, property crime rates have continued to decline (www.ojp.usdoj.gov/bjs). In England and Wales, property crime accounted for the majority of both British Crime Survey (BCS) and police recorded crime, but generally fell during the latter part of the twentieth century (Barclay and Tavares, 2002). This trend has continued – according to the recent BCS, overall household acquisitive crime in England and Wales has fallen by more than half between 1995 and 2004/5 (Nicholas et al., 2005). Criminologists are divided as to the reasons behind such reductions in crime. While some American commentators have drawn attention to the tougher criminal justice policies and substantial increase in imprisonment rates as possible explanations, the experience of other countries provides a counter to this. Canada's record on crime, for example, mirrors that of the United States, but without an equivalent increase in prison numbers. Variations in sentencing and imprisonment across Europe also challenge the idea that harsher punishment necessarily underlies the reduction in property crime (Barclay and Tavares, 2002).

Plate 10.1 Crime prevention posters

Source: West Yorkshire Police

http://www.westyorkshire.police.uk/

The hidden figure of property crime

In 2005/6, property offences accounted for around 80 per cent of all recorded crimes in England and Wales. They include burglary, theft and criminal damage (robbery offences are officially categorized as crimes of violence). As a result, most of the activities of the police and other criminal justice agencies are geared towards preventing and controlling property crime (see chapters 16 and 17). Of course, interpreting official statistics is fraught with difficulties. Official crime statistics do not provide an objective and incontrovertible measure of criminal behaviour. Instead, they often fluctuate according to the organizational constraints and priorities of the criminal justice system. For example, changes in police practices and priorities will have a significant effect on the official crime data. High-profile planned operations against a particular type of offence (such as burglary, drugs or street robberies) will inevitably bring about an increase in arrests and the discovery and recording of many new offences in the targeted areas. Conversely, numbers may fall owing to a withdrawal of police interest in a particular type of crime.

Globally, around two in three victims of burglaries report their victimization to the police. According to the International Crime Victimization Survey (ICVS), the level of reporting is highest in New World nations (the United States, Canada, Australia, New Zealand) and Western Europe but much lower in Latin America, Asia and Africa, mainly because the incident seems too 'trivial' or the victim feels nothing can be done about it (Mayhew and Van Dijk, 1997). In some countries, notably in Latin America, fear or dislike of the police is also a factor. The extent of insurance cover is another important factor. In most African and many Asian and Latin American countries, only between 10 and 20 per cent of the victim survey respondents (as opposed to at least 70 per cent in most industrialized countries) are insured against household burglary. All this suggests that a hidden figure of property crime exists around the world.

The dominance of property crime in the official crime data reflects not only the prevalence of certain types of property crime but also their high reporting rates, especially in industrialized countries. For instance, the British Crime Surveys (BCSs) have consistently shown that thefts of cars and burglaries in which something is stolen are almost always reported to the police, partly because of the seriousness of the offence, partly because victims who are insured need to report the crime in order to make an insurance claim. On the other hand, robbery, theft from the person, and attempted burglaries where nothing is stolen have traditionally resulted in much lower reporting and recording rates (Nicholas et al., 2005).

Cross-national comparisons of victim survey data also suggest there are significant variations in the types of goods taken in burglaries, motives behind the theft and perceptions of the victims. In developing nations, stolen goods often include money, food and simple household objects such as cutlery or linen, most probably for personal use. One study in Central and Eastern Europe found that in many cases the burglars systematically stripped the home, even taking used clothes. 'In such cases the overall value of burglary might have been less, but the relative loss to the victim and the consequential impact of the crime might have been more pronounced' (quoted in Mawby, 2001: 41). Similarly, 42 per cent of the respondents in the ICVS in Africa considered the theft of a bicycle to be 'very serious'. This must be viewed within the social and economic context of the African society where less serious criminal events still pose very serious consequences in the lives of victims (Naudé et al., 2006). In the more affluent countries, where most people keep their money and jewellery in the bank or in safes, burglars generally give preference to objects that are easily resold such as electrical appliances, VCRs, hi-fi equipment, furniture and art objects.

Profile of property crime offenders

Throughout the eighteenth and nineteenth centuries, only a small number of property crimes involved large sums of money or very valuable objects, and very few cases involved violence. Perhaps unsurprisingly, most of the offenders brought before the courts in England and Wales for petty theft tended to be young, male, poorly educated (if educated at all) and poorly employed (if employed at all) in low-skilled, low-paid jobs such as labouring, domestic service and casual work. This pattern then continued into the early twenty-first century, regardless of changes in the nature of low-skilled employment. All these factors informed the overall perception of criminality and reinforced conventional understandings of 'problem populations' in society.

It is undeniable that some people commit more serious property crimes than do others, and some people are more committed to a criminal lifestyle than others. Edwin Sutherland's (1937) classic formulation of professional thieves demonstrates their characteristics as a specialist occupational group defined by a level of commitment to illegal economic activities as a means of making a living. This insight paved the way for much subsequent criminological thinking and empirical work on the 'all-purpose criminal' who makes crime a career choice and a way of life: from the 'full-time miscreants' in British towns in the early 1960s (Mack, 1964), and short-term groups drawn together for specific 'project crimes' such as the Great Train Robbery (McIntosh, 1975), to the contemporary serious crime groups (Hobbs, 1995; see also Chapter 13 of this book).

A very broad distinction can be made between professional property crime and amateur property crime. These categories reflect the different motivations, levels of temptation, degree of skill, experience and planning, and illegitimate opportunity structures. For example, Maguire (1982) has identified three types of burglar: *low level*, *middle range* and *high level*. Low-level burglars are primarily juveniles and young adults. They lack a commitment to crime and do not usually think of themselves as 'thieves'. They tend to be opportunists whose involvement in crime is usually short-lived. Middle-range burglars usually begin their criminal careers at a young age and move into and out of crime. Generally, they are older, more skilful and experienced than low-level burglars and search out targets across a wider geographic area. They also tend to have access to external sources to assist them in the sale of their stolen property. High-level burglars are well connected with sources of information about goods to steal and with 'fences' who can dispose of large quantities of stolen goods. They carefully plan their crimes and possess skills and technical expertise to overcome complex security measures.

Of course, a wide variety of offences and characteristics of offenders can be found across a spectrum of property crime. To date, research on criminal careers has tended to concentrate on (young) offenders involved in 'common' property crimes such as theft and vandalism (Farrington, 2002; Piquero *et al.*, 2007). Little research has been done on careers in other forms of property or financial crime such as consumer fraud, tax evasion, insider trading, embezzlement or money laundering. Some of these offences can be carried out only by those who hold office in a legitimate organization or occupy an advanced position in the occupational hierarchy.

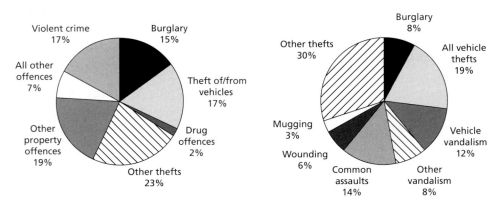

Police-recorded crime

Violent crime 17%
Burglary 15%
All other offences 7%
Theft of/from vehicles 17%
Other property offences 19%
Drug offences 2%
Other thefts 23%

British Crime Survey crime

Burglary 8%
Other thefts 30%
All vehicle thefts 19%
Mugging 3%
Vehicle vandalism 12%
Wounding 6%
Common assaults 14%
Other vandalism 8%

Figure 10.1 Police-recorded crime and British Crime Survey (BCS) crime by type of crime, 2002–3.

Source: Simmons and Dodd, 2003: 15.

Note: The BCS definition of common assault includes minor injuries. From 2002–3 the definition of recorded crime does not include minor injuries.

Offenders may also move from one form of property crime (e.g. theft) to another (e.g. robbery), or from opportunistic offences (e.g. shoplifting) to more highly planned ones (e.g. stealing of museum pieces).

Everybody does it?

We should note that in between those deeply committed to a criminal lifestyle and those who occasionally steal or defraud lie a vast range of property criminals who are 'ordinary' or socially acceptable people. Almost two-thirds of adults interviewed in a recent study in England and Wales (including those in the middle classes) admitted to committing minor fraud (e.g. having paid cash in hand to evade taxes, having lied about an insurance claim, having claimed for refunds to which they are not entitled), but rarely think their behaviour is criminal (*The Times*, 12 September 2003: 16). Similarly, studies in Canada suggest that shoplifting costs the retail trade over $1 million each day, and that between 1 in 12 and 1 in 20 customers admit to having stolen from shops (cited in Gabor, 1994: 73–4). Sykes and Matza's (1957) concept of neutralization is useful to identify the techniques that many shoplifters use to deny or deflect blame for wrong-doing away from the perpetrator (see Chapter 5). For example, shoplifters may claim that shoplifting does not really hurt the store very much (denial of the injury caused) or that a particular store deserves to be ripped off because they exploit customers (denial of the victim). Such neutralizations allow individuals to redefine shoplifting as a more acceptable form of behaviour.

Theft by employees is also extremely widespread. In Britain the British Retail Consortium calculated that staff theft during 1997 cost shops a total of £374 million – that is, more than double the losses caused by burglaries and eight times greater than the cost of robberies (Park,

doing crime

2001). The workplace has always been a key site of property crime. Indeed, Gerald Mars (1982: 1) wrote about the 'normal crimes of normal people in the normal circumstance of their work'. They include traders dealing in cash to evade VAT (value added tax), taxi drivers who fiddle their takings, warehouse employees who overload and undercharge their friends, and shop assistants and cashiers in the retail trade 'voiding' a transaction or overcharging customers and pocketing the cash.

Occupational structure is a key variable in workplace crime. Mars contends that 'fiddles' are part of the elasticity of some occupations which emphasize individual entrepreneurship, flair, adaptability and professional autonomy, and in which group control of the workforce is low. For travelling sales representatives, journalists, lawyers, health professionals, academics and other relatively independent professionals, the conditions of work may create a criminogenic environment that opens opportunities and rationalizations for rule-bending and rule-breaking. For example, store managers can 'customize' their own 'shoplifting' by recategorizing goods as old or damaged or altering stock records; journalists can fiddle their travelling expenses and slush money and rationalize these as 'perks' that come with the job. In contrast, in occupations that are highly structured and characterized by controlling rules, minimal autonomy and tight work-groups (e.g. in cargo-handling areas at airports, distribution centres and docks), fiddles often take place in the context of teamwork. Such practices are nothing new. Fiddling was common in the eighteenth century, when dockers often stole liquor, sugar or tea from cargoes as they unloaded them. Stolen items were then resold to grocers, publicans or ordinary people in the market (Emsley, 2005).

Social distribution of crime risks

Writing about the first BCS, Hough and Mayhew (1983: 15) cited the average household that could expect to be burgled 'once every 40 years'. The BCS and police recorded crime have both shown considerable falls in burglary levels since peaks in the mid-1990s. The number of domestic burglaries estimated by the BCS fell by 59 per cent from 1,770,000 in 1995 to 726,000 in 2006/7 (Nicholas et al., 2007). What these statistics fail to show is that burglary is unevenly distributed across time and space. For example, researchers from the routine activity perspective have found that the patterns of burglars are often determined by the time patterns and routine activities of their victims. Residential burglary occurs disproportionately during daytime when most households are unoccupied. Studies in the United States also show that residents of large cities, renters and households headed by African Americans, Hispanics or young people are more likely than others to be burgled (Shover, 1991).

In general, the risk of property crime victimization is unevenly distributed within and between different localities and various sections of the population.

Social class

Contrary to popular belief and anxieties about crime in rural and middle-class areas, researchers in Britain have consistently found that people living in run-down inner-city areas and areas of council accommodation are particularly vulnerable to crime problems. Successive BCSs and police statistics have shown that, in general, poorer households with few home security measures in high-crime areas and areas of deprivation are most likely to experience residential burglary (Nicholas et al., 2007). Foster and Hope (1993) found in their analysis of BCS data that households in council estates with the highest levels of council tenure and poverty face a risk of burglary around five times greater than tenants who live in areas with less concentrated levels of council tenure and where tenants are better off. These households are also more likely to suffer a repeat burglary and are most affected by the crime(s).

Repeat victimization occurs when the same location, person, household, business or vehicle suffers more than one crime event over a specified period of time (Pease, 1998; Simmons and Dodd, 2003: 17–18; for repeat victimization amongst retailers, see Taylor, 2004). According to the National Board for Crime Prevention (1994), 4 per cent of victims experience 44 per cent of all crimes in Britain. For those who are subject to repeat victimization, it may become virtually impossible to differentiate the impact of discrete crimes from the generally poor quality of life. Those living in the inner city, council estates and areas of high physical disorder are also more likely than average to experience a second burglary within the year. In response, there is evidence to suggest that uninsured small businesses and young men living in deprived, high-crime areas are more likely to have purchased stolen goods as a means of minimizing their losses (Sutton, 1998).

A similar pattern has emerged from local studies in Britain, indicating not only the problem of repeat victimization but also the 'lived reality' of people at risk. By focusing on particular localities these surveys (notably in Islington (London), Merseyside, Edinburgh and Rochdale) highlighted the higher levels of crime prevailing in socially deprived areas and the disproportionate victimization of women, of ethnic minority groups and of the poor (Crawford et al., 1990; Kinsey, 1984; Mooney, 1993; Forrester et al., 1988). Significantly, such high levels of social deprivation and crime victimization are also coterminous with higher levels of poor health.

Ethnicity

According to the BCSs, ethnic minority groups (especially Pakistanis and Bangladeshis) are generally more at risk than whites of household crimes. It is, however, extremely difficult to isolate ethnicity as a discrete variable in explaining patterns of victimization. Socio-economic factors and wider processes of racialization may be at work here, if we take into account the fact that ethnic minority households are more likely than white households to experience poverty (that is, with incomes below half the national average) and to live in socially disadvantaged areas (Modood and Berthoud, 1997). Ethnic minority groups are also routinely subject to racial violence and harassment that range from murder, damage to property (including racist graffiti), to verbal and other forms of abuse of an isolated or persistent nature (see also Chapter 9).

Age

Official statistics and self-report studies indicate the prevalence of property crime in young people's everyday life. Crime statistics have consistently found the 'typical offender' to be male (over 80 per cent of offenders known to the authorities) and young. Similarly, according to a recent survey (Wilson *et al.*, 2006), almost one in four young people in England and Wales admitted to committing at least one offence in the previous twelve months. The most commonly reported offence categories were assault and other thefts. One-fifth of 12–25-year-olds had handled (bought or sold) stolen goods. However, any focus on young people as the perpetrators of crime should not be allowed to obscure or divert our attention away from the worryingly high levels of victimization that young people suffer from their peers and adults. The BCSs have repeatedly shown that young people experience relatively more serious problems as victims of crime irrespective of class, gender or place (see Chapter 9). Few of these experiences are reported to the police, however, and youth victimization (as opposed to youth offending) remains low on the priority lists of the police and politicians.

Geography

Survey data has consistently highlighted the spatial concentration of the incidence of crime victimization – for example, in urban areas (as opposed to rural areas) and in the poorest 'striving areas' (as opposed to the wealthiest 'thriving areas').

It is not just the cities that have become synonymous with the 'crime problem'. Geographical research on crime and the use of computer-generated analyses of patterns of reported crime in different local police force areas (e.g. Crime Pattern Analysis) have pointed to particular concentrations of so-called 'hot spots' of crime. Research evidence in the United States and Britain suggests that even high-crime areas have their relatively safe micro-locations as well as their specific 'trouble-spot' areas (Sherman, 1995; Hope, 1985; Hirschfield *et al.*, 1995).

Writing from a different perspective, Ian Taylor (1997, 1999) highlights the shifting 'urban fortunes' behind the massive increase in crime in specific localities and regions in Britain from the late 1980s to early 1990s. For Taylor, the levels of crime in different localities are related to their varied capacities for responding to global economic competition, deindustrialization and post-industrial restructuring. For example, industrial areas in Northern England (such as South Yorkshire) which suffered the most recent loss of what was locally assumed to have been a secure labour market experienced the highest rates of increase in crime. On the other hand, Greater Manchester, 'the "youth capital" of the North of England with one of the largest post-Fordist labour markets in the North', had the smallest increases in property crime and crime in general (I. Taylor, 1999: 134). Yet such 'new leisure zones' and their thriving alcohol-oriented night-time economy have other well-documented problems of violence and disorder (Hobbs *et al.*, 2000; see also chapters 8 and 14).

Controlling property crime

Our ideas about property crime (what form does it take?) and property crime offenders (who are they?) have also shaped our responses to the problem. 'Common' property offences such as petty theft, burglary and forgery were among the 200 or so offences punishable by death under the 'Bloody Code' in the eighteenth century. For example, the shoplifting of goods worth five

BOX 10.2 Key developments in the law and punishment of property crime in Britain

1808	Repeal of capital punishment for pickpockets.
1820	Repeal of capital punishment for stealing in shops.
1861 and 1916	Larceny Acts cover many types of stealing and provide for greater or lesser penalties depending on the nature of the property stolen, the place, the relationship between the thief and owner.
1968 and 1978	Theft Acts codify all offences against property and create a simplified definition of theft covering all types of stealing, embezzlement and fraud. The maximum sentence for theft is 10 years' imprisonment, 14 years for burglary and life imprisonment for robbery.
1971	Criminal Damage Act – maximum punishment for damage to property is 10 years' imprisonment, life imprisonment for arson.
1981	Forgery and Counterfeiting Act.
1991	Criminal Justice Act reduces the maximum sentence for theft from 10 to 7 years' imprisonment.
1997	Crime (Sentences) Act increases prison sentences for certain categories of offenders, including a minimum of three years for a third offence of domestic burglary.
2003	Criminal Justice Act provides a wider and more varied range of short custodial sentences (e.g. 'Custody Plus', 'Intermittent Custody') for offenders (including non-violent but persistent offenders).

shillings was a capital offence, as was stealing sheep or cattle. Transportation to penal colonies and prison were also used to punish a range of offenders. Indeed, prisons of different varieties have since emerged to occupy a central role in the criminal justice system even though their precise function and effectiveness are still subject to intense political and academic debate (see Chapter 18). Then, as now, it was the 'quantity' rather than 'quality' of the offences that most concerned the public, legislators, the police and commentators on crime alike. The main exception was the periodic panic about violent street robberies (also known as 'garotting' or 'mugging' in the contemporary context) that prompted the revival of whipping for adults in the 1860s (Rawlings, 1999: 100, n. 1). Legislation and its enforcement were slow in keeping pace with the opportunities for large-scale theft, fraud and embezzlement provided by the expansion and development of the business and financial world during the nineteenth and early twentieth centuries (as they still are) (Robb, 1992; and see Chapter 13 of this book).

As Steven Box (1983) and others have indicated, there is considerable inconsistency in the way in which the criminal justice system perceives and treats 'the crimes of the powerless' as opposed to 'the crimes of the powerful' – business offenders. For example, if one measures the significance of property offences in terms of the value stolen, rather than the quantity of incidents, fraud has far greater importance than other categories. As Mike Levi (1993) points out, in April 1992 the Frauds Divisions of the Crown Prosecution Service were supervising cases involving nearly £4 billion. By contrast, the combined costs of the vast number of vehicle offences and burglaries for 1990 were estimated by the Association of British Insurers at under £1.3 billion.

Critics argue that the concentration of criminal justice responses against low-level property crime offenders has impacted most on those who are already economically and socially marginalized. For example, studies have shown that the rise in women's prosecutions in Britain from the 1980s onwards has gone hand in hand with the continuing and worsening levels of female poverty (Carlen, 1988, 1998; Pantazis, 1999; Heidensohn, 2006). Similarly, the steep increases in the numbers of women received into prisons from the 1990s in Britain have been linked to a more punitive sentencing culture, the increased numbers of women in the categories of economic and social deprivation who have been traditionally more vulnerable to imprisonment, and the increased use of custody for women convicted of theft, handling stolen goods and fraud (Carlen, 1998: 56; Player, 2005).

BOX 10.3 Looting and state negligence

When property crime takes on a more spectacular form, it forces us to reconsider our conventional assumptions about criminals, victims and the role of the state.

'One of the aftermaths of Hurricane Katrina in flood-stricken New Orleans in the USA in August 2005 is looting and lawlessness. More than a million people were evacuated from New Orleans and the surrounding areas before the hurricane struck, but Mayor Ray Nagin has estimated that up to 100,000 people decided to stay in the city. There is a feeling of foreboding as those marooned become more desperate. There is no electricity, and people who have lost everything are struggling to find food and clean water. There are reports of shootings, carjackings and thefts across the city. President Bush condemned the acts and called for "zero tolerance" against law-breakers. People have faced shoot-outs and some reports say martial law has been imposed in some areas. Armed gangs have moved into some hotels. Some have been breaking into shops, houses, hospitals and office buildings. Thieves used a forklift truck to break into a pharmacy while dozens of carjackings have been reported.

'In Mississippi, curfews are in place as the authorities try to prevent the scale of looting seen in New Orleans. In Houston, where thousands of refugees have been taken, the *Houston Chronicle* puts the blame for the disintegration of civilisation in New Orleans on inadequate protection by the government. "Looting and violence are unconscionable but were invited by the failure of federal, state and local authorities to reassert order or even provide basic sustenance for storm survivors," it says.'

Source: BBC News, August 2005
http://news.bbc.co.uk

Other forms of property crime

So far we have concentrated on the more conventional forms of crime against property in everyday life. There are of course other forms of property crime with an equally, if not more, harmful impact on individuals and communities alike.

Theft and illegal export of cultural property

The theft of cultural property is flourishing and now constitutes a major form of transnational crime. Cultural property can be defined as movable or immovable property of great importance to the cultural heritage of every people. It can include monuments such as architectural works, sculptures, paintings, manuscripts, structures of an archaeological nature, cave dwellings, and sites that are significant from the historical, aesthetic, ethnological or anthropological points of view. In Iraq, for example, priceless statues, ancient manuscripts (including one of the oldest surviving copies of the Koran) and other treasures were destroyed or stolen from the museums and libraries in a wave of looting and lawlessness following the collapse of the government of Saddam Hussein in Baghdad. Although looting of art treasures has long been a feature of warfare, illegal excavation and trade in stolen art and antiquities have been spurred by increasing pressure from the international art market. Crimes against cultural property have the potential for robbing entire cultures and nations of their cultural heritage (United Nations Educational, Scientific and Cultural Organisation, 1997). In African countries such as Mali, the purchase for illegal export of cultural objects and looting of archaeological sites have increased rapidly since the 1970s. Objects tend to acquire higher prices the further they travel from 'home'. Art treasures, human remains, religious relics and sacred objects, furniture and cultural objects in Nigeria, South Africa, Asia, Latin America, former Soviet-bloc countries and, to some extent, Western European countries such as Italy and Britain have been targeted in recent years (Box 10.4). Archaeological sites in the United States have also been looted and vandalized in the hunt for the best 'marketable' Native American artefacts.

The international trade in stolen, smuggled and looted art is estimated to be worth US$4.5–6 billion dollars per year (*New York Times*, 20 November 1995). Elaborate methods of distributing stolen art are often used to conceal the origin of the objects; as a result, it can take years to resolve disputes over the ownership of such art. For example, the Lydian Hoard, a collection of ancient treasures looted in Turkey, was purchased by New York's Metropolitan Museum of Art in the 1960s. It took the Turkish government almost twenty years to trace the whereabouts of the objects and another six years of legal action before the museum finally agreed to repatriate the objects. The illicit art market is populated by a mix of criminal organizations, individual thieves, 'fences' who act as the middle person and unscrupulous collectors as well as legitimate traders such as antique dealers and institutions, including reputable auction houses (Conklin, 1994). This is yet another example of the symbiosis between legitimate and criminal activity, just like the cross-over activities in the entertainment and gambling industries, the arms trade and many other areas (see Chapter 13).

BOX 10.4 Crime against cultural property

The British Parliamentary Report on Cultural Property: Return and Illicit Trade (2000) highlights the massive scale and impact of illicit excavations around the world. For example, the looting of the Early Bronze Age cemeteries of the Cycladic Islands in the Aegean may have resulted in the loss of 85 per cent of the relevant archaeological contents, and over 1,000 pieces of pottery worth about US$10 million are smuggled out of the Mayan region of Central America every month. Looting of sites in Italy is also a serious problem. A 1998 raid on a villa in Sicily seized some 30,000 Phoenician, Greek and Roman antiquities that were valued at US$20 million. The illegal trade, export and smuggling of Egyptian antiquities for sale abroad are known to cause substantial and irrevocable damage to Egypt's cultural heritage. The report suggests that England is one of the largest markets for illicitly traded property. Studies of antiquities from celebrated private collections in public exhibitions in Britain and North America during the 1990s, and the sale of antiquities in the London antiquities market, suggest that an alarmingly high percentage of these objects had no provenance and history.

Theft of intellectual property

Theft of intangible property, such as copyright infringement, counterfeiting of trademarks and making patented products, exists at different levels, from the individual computer owners who illegally copy video games or music at home (see Chapter 20) to the organized groups that engage in large-scale counterfeiting and smuggling.

Counterfeiting is a major activity for professional criminals in Britain, and has links globally, involving production of goods or currency and then distribution. Generally low risks and high profit margins make counterfeiting a very lucrative activity. Fake designer label clothing and other luxury items, counterfeit computer software and large-scale illegal reproduction of popular audio and video tapes are well-known examples. Some counterfeit luxury items may be produced in the same factories as legitimate goods in developing countries, which in turn raises broader questions about consumer products, value and neo-liberal capitalism. More everyday items such as soap powder, toys, shampoos, cleaning products and even tea bags have also been subject to counterfeit and have resulted in injury (Croall, 1997). Currency counterfeiting faces the problem that daily use of money makes fake versions harder to pass, but this does not mean that such counterfeit circulation is uncommon.

So who suffers and who benefits from the global trade in counterfeit goods? The answer is not always clear-cut. Manufacturers and consumers (especially the poorer consumers who buy substandard or even dangerous counterfeit goods) are generally considered to be the 'legitimate' victims (see Chapter 9). But what about those working in factories with substandard conditions and pay? According to the World Health Organization, there is widespread availability of counterfeited medicines in developing countries for the treatment of life-threatening conditions such as malaria, tuberculosis and HIV/AIDS. In Nigeria, for example, shortages of drugs and other technologies in the medical care system have led to the sale of 'counterfeit, substandard and otherwise dangerous substances', accounting for as much as 60–70 per cent of all drugs, and causing many instances of drug poisoning and death (Alubo, 1994: 97–8; and see Chapter 14 of this book). On the other hand, the counterfeiting industry arguably enables those who cannot afford the full prices to obtain similar consumer products and provides income for the unemployed, especially workers in developing nations.

Biopiracy

Finally, the question of 'who is the offender?' becomes even more contentious when applied to other non-conventional forms of property. 'Biopiracy' is a term that has been given to the practices of some companies that have asserted the right of ownership over genetic materials taken from living organisms (Manning, 2000). For instance, patent law has been extended in recent years in such a way as to allow the ownership of DNA, cell lines and other biological materials. It has become possible for transnational corporations to 'own' DNA sequences and modified genes of animals and plants and to make significant profits through royalty charges for their use. Supporters of patent law point out that weak intellectual property regimes could foreclose opportunities for biotechnology research and product development. High research costs can drive up the price of the end products, many of which are important for public health needs.

Critics, however, argue that the patenting of medicines, seeds, plants and – potentially – higher life forms by multinational corporations amounts to biopiracy and can have particularly serious consequences for the developing countries. For example, the Africa Group in the World Trade Organization has highlighted the serious implications that patents on seeds of staple food crops would have on the rights of indigenous communities to food security. It proposed that the mandated review of the Agreement on Trade-Related Aspects of Intellectual Property Rights should make clear that plants, animals and micro-organisms and their parts, and all living processes, cannot be patented. To some extent, these issues are related to the over-exploitation of the Earth and its resources especially by those in a position of power; they have prompted some criminologists to reappraise more traditional notions of crimes and injurious behaviours and to examine the role that transnational corporations and governments play in creating 'green crimes' (see Chapter 19).

New horizons in understanding property crime

There is no doubt property crime makes up an inordinate amount of reported and unreported crime. As Part 2 of this book shows, criminological explanations of why individuals commit property crime span a variety of perspectives from the dispositions of the individual offender to the social conditions associated with crime. For some offenders, survival, subsistence and drug habits may well be the primary motivations for committing property crime. Other criminologists have argued that crimes such as shoplifting have to be understood in the broader context of the creation of needs, the structuring of consumption and the commodification of desire under late capitalism. Yet these societal processes alone cannot explain the meaning or the attractions of criminality.

Cultural criminologists (see Chapter 12) argue that criminology has traditionally under-estimated the attractions in doing wrong or living 'on the edge'. The concept of 'edgework' was first put forward by the sociologist Stephen Lyng (1990; Lyng and Snow, 1986) in his analysis of voluntary risk-taking. He argues that 'edgework' can be understood as 'a type of experiential anarchy in which the individual moves beyond the realm of established social patterns to the very fringes of ordered reality' (Lyng, 1990b: 882). Edgework activities that involve an observable threat to one's physical or mental well-being can be best illustrated by dangerous sports (such as skydiving, hang-gliding and rock-climbing) or by dangerous occupations (such as fire-fighting, combat soldiering, movie stunt work). More generally, edgework can also take the form of excessive drug use (which involves negotiating the boundary between sanity and insanity) or marathon running (which tests the limits of the body). Lyng (1990a: 863) argues that volun-tary risk-taking provides 'a heightened sense of self and a feeling of omnipotence' for those who succeed in getting as close as possible to the edge without 'going over it'.

These ideas have been further developed by cultural criminologists such as Jeff Ferrell and Jack Katz. Katz (1988: 54) suggests that shoplifting can be understood as a version of a 'thrilling and sensually gratifying game'. It can be rewarding beyond the monetary gains – for example, providing the feelings of accomplishment when a theft is successful. Katz found that expressive motivations were highly prevalent in his interview data obtained from well-off college student shoplifters. Studies also found that burglars frequently cited excitement as part of their motivation, while others targeted occupied homes because such burglaries provide an 'illicit adventure' (cited in Mawby, 2001: 69).

Similarly, if we turn to the world of business, bank fraud, price-fixing or manipulating the stock market, all contain elements of the thrills and spills of risk-taking common to other aspects of social life. As Stanley Cohen (1973b: 622) reminds us, 'some of our most cherished social values – individualism, masculinity, competitiveness – are the same ones that generate crime'. Indeed, it is the excitement and a sense of machismo in beating the competition in our 'enterprise' culture that arguably induces some managers and young city professionals to perform 'dirty deeds' in covert business activities – for example, to act as spies, phone-tappers, computer hackers, safe-breakers, forgers and saboteurs (Punch, 2000).

Property crime also has to be understood within the context of the expansion of the hidden economy and increased blurring of boundaries between employment and unemployment and between legal and illegal work. Hutton's (1995) influential '40:30:30' thesis argued that in an increasingly polarized society (only 40 per cent of the population have secure employment, while the others are split between those in insecure employment and a marginalized underclass of the unemployed), the gap between benefit entitlements and realistic standards of living in a consumer-oriented society is widening. Subsequent critics have quarrelled over the exact figures (Young, 2007a: 60), but the underlying social processes continue to divide the world. In particular, commentators have argued that those young people who are without the protection of employment, family and welfare, or are trapped in the 'magic roundabout' of different training and enterprise schemes, are most likely to adopt one of the transient lifestyles or alternative 'careers' thrown up by local hidden economies, including 'fencing' stolen goods, 'hustling', unlicensed street trading, or acting as 'lookouts' or 'touts' (Carlen, 1996; Craine, 1997). Perhaps more significantly, many of these illegal activities are not considered as crime, just 'ordinary work' (Foster, 1990: 165; Taylor and Jamieson, 1997). All this points to the need to understand crime as a 'normal' rather than an 'exceptional' social phenomenon. Although property crime has been a constant focus of public and political attention, this chapter suggests that there is no singular 'crime problem' as such. Instead, there is a wide spectrum of illicit behaviour, misconduct, troubling and alarming events that are widespread and constantly occurring, and a variety of ways of conceiving of and thinking about everyday property crime.

Summary

1   Official statistics and victim surveys have consistently indicated the prevalence of various types of property crime over time, among different social groups and across societies.
2   This is evident in the vast range of illegal activities committed by the general public, the hidden and petty-criminal economies of everyday survival, the crimes committed by respectable people in the normal circumstances of their everyday jobs and by those who simply get a buzz out of leading life 'on the edge'.
3   While the risks of victimization and the impact of property crime remain highly differentiated and unevenly distributed, research studies have generally pointed to the higher levels of property crime prevailing in socially deprived areas and the disproportionate victimization of the poor, of young people and of minority ethnic groups.
4   Against a background of social change and technological advances, the range of property crime activities has broadened significantly or even developed into transnational businesses. New or existing forms of property crime can also be carried out more extensively, more quickly, more efficiently and with greater ease of concealment.
5   In addition to crimes that take place in the street or are directed at households, property crime also includes theft and illegal export of cultural property and theft of intellectual property. A critical study of these forms of crime requires reappraisal of more traditional notions of offending, harmful behaviour and property.

Critical thinking questions

1   What evidence is there to suggest that many crimes against property are committed by socially acceptable people in their everyday life?
2   What are the limitations of the official picture of property crime?
3   How might criminological research advance our understanding of previously hidden forms of property crime around the world?
4   Discuss how techniques of neutralization could be applied to the following acts: (a) theft by employees; (b) selling of DVDs that infringe copyright.

Further study

Emsley, C. (2005) *Crime and Society in England 1750–1900*, 3rd edn, London: Longman. An accessible introduction to the history of the crime problem, perceptions of criminality and changes in the courts, the police and the system of punishment.

Mawby, R. (2001) *Burglary*, Cullompton: Willan. A useful overview of the key aspects of the problem of burglary and some of the recent developments and research studies in policy responses.

Newman, G. (ed.) (1999) *Global Report on Crime and Justice*, New York: Oxford University Press. A comprehensive text from the United Nations on crime, criminal justice and international crime victim surveys.

Shover, N. (1996) *Great Pretenders: Pursuits and Games of Persistent Thieves*, Boulder, CO: Westview Press. A fascinating book on the criminal pathways and decision-making of offenders based on original studies and autobiographies of persistent thieves in the United States.

More information

The Home Office: Research Development Statistics – Publications

http://www.homeoffice.gov.uk/rds/bcs.html

The National British Crime Survey provides up-to-date annual information on different types of crime, including property crime, which may or may not be reported to and recorded by the police. Full reports and summaries of BCS findings and many other research studies funded by the Home Office can be found here.

International Crime Victimization Surveys

http://www.unicri.it/icvs/

Information, publications and statistics on international crime victimization surveys are available at this site.

chapter 11

Crime, Sexuality and Gender

Key issues

- What are the major patterns of crimes linked to sex?
- How do they link to gender?
- Why do they provoke such hysteria?
- How are sex crimes changing?
- What can be done about them?

Introduction

In the grand sweep of crime, sex offences are officially not as common as many other offences. The UK Home Office recorded 57,542 sex offences for 2006–7 – this amounts to around just 5 per cent of all violent crime. However, these crimes continue to provoke a great deal of anxiety and concern. Figures have been increasing over the last decade despite the fact that these cases remain severely under-reported. For reasons discussed in Chapter 3, being precise about criminal statistics is very difficult. There is always a large hidden figure, but in the case of sex offences such problems may be magnified because many victims do not wish to report the crimes at all – finding the glare of public recognition and scrutiny too traumatic. In some cases – often involving under-age offences – they may not even be aware that a crime has been committed. Further, even when a crime is reported, getting a conviction may be difficult: according to the Fawcett Society, a UK

BOX 11.1 Two social theories of sexuality

Gagnon and Simon's *Sexual Conduct* (1973/2005) is one of the landmark texts in the sociology of sexuality and is seen as the foundational text of what is now commonly known as the 'social constructionist' approach to sexuality. Gagnon and Simon claim that there is no one, unified pattern of sexuality; instead, there are 'many ways to become, to be, to act, to feel sexual. There is no one human sexuality, but rather a wide variety of sexualities' (Gagnon, 1973/2005, preface).

Three of their main themes will help us think about sexuality and crime:

- *Beware of the biological: it claims too much.* Sex crimes are rarely a matter of sex being a simple biological release. In contrast to classic ways of thinking about sexuality as biological, bodily and 'natural' – as *essentially* given – Gagnon and Simon aimed to show the ways in which human sexualities are always organized through economic, religious, political, familial and social conditions; any analysis that does not recognize this must be seriously flawed. Sexuality, for humans, is never just a free-floating desire. It is always grounded in wider material and cultural forces.
- *Look for the symbols and meanings.* Human sexualities are always symbolic. With sex crimes we should always be looking out for motivations that are not simply or straightforwardly sexual. Sex may be performed out of rage, as aggression, as a hunt, as a hobby, because of a scarring experience, as a mode of transgression, as a form of violence.
- *Examine sexual scripts.* Human sexualities – including sex crimes – are probably best seen as evolving through scripts that suggest – the Who? What? Where? When? and Why? of sexual conduct – as they guide our sexualities at personal, interactional and cultural-historical levels.

A second major contribution comes from the French historian of ideas Michel Foucault (introduced in Chapter 6). He argued that sexuality 'is the name given to a historical construct . . . a great surface network in which the stimulation of bodies, the intensification of pleasures, the incitement to discourse, the formation of knowledge, the strengthening of controls and resistances, are linked to one another, in accordance with a few major strategies of power' (Foucault, 1978: 106). Startlingly challenging conventional wisdom, he attacked the notion that sex had been repressed in the Victorian world, and claimed instead that sexuality in this period was a discursive fiction which had actually organized the social problems of the time. New species – like the homosexual, the pervert, the masturbating child, the Malthusian couple, the hysterical woman – had literally been invented and come into being as organizing motifs for sexual problems and the spread of surveillance and regulation. The body had become a site for disciplinary practices and new technologies.

women's rights organization, only one in twenty rapes reported to the police leads to a conviction. Often a woman's accusations in a rape case may not be taken seriously. As Sue Lees (1996a: x–xi) argued, from her extensive analysis of the police, courts and victims in London:

Table 11.1 Recorded sexual crime by number of offences 1997 to 2006/7, England and Wales

Offence	1997	1997/ 1998	1998/ 1999	1998/ 1999	1999/ 2000	2000/ 2001	2001/ 2002	2002/ 2003	2003/ 2004	2004/ 2005	2005/ 2006	2006/ 2007
Indecent assault on a male	3,503	3,885	3,672	3,683	3,530	3,611	4,132	4,110		1,003	347	76
Sexual assault on a male aged 13 and over	—	—	—	—	—	—	—	—	—	1,316	1,428	1,450
Sexual assault on a male child under 13	—	—	—	—	—	—	—	—	—	1,227	1,394	1,237
Rape of a female	6,281	6,523	7,139	7,132	7,809	7,929	9,002	11,445	12,378	693	61	25
Rape of a female aged 16 and over	—	—	—	—	—	—	—	—	—	8,192	8,725	8,228
Rape of a female child under 16	—	—	—	—	—	—	—	—	—	3,014	3,153	2,853
Rape of a female child under 13	—	—	—	—	—	—	—	—	—	970	1,388	1,524
Rape of a female	**6,281**	**6,523**	**7,139**	**7,132**	**7,809**	**7,929**	**9,002**	**11,445**	**12,378**	**12,869**	**13,327**	**12,630**
Rape of a male	347	375	502	504	600	664	732	850	894	81	22	18
Rape of a male aged 16 and over	—	—	—	—	—	—	—	—	—	444	438	413
Rape of a male child under 16	—	—	—	—	—	—	—	—	—	322	292	261
Rape of a male child under 13	—	—	—	—	—	—	—	—	—	297	364	458
Rape of a male	**347**	**375**	**502**	**504**	**600**	**664**	**732**	**850**	**894**	**1,144**	**1,116**	**1,150**
Indecent assault on a female	18,674	18,979	19,463	19,524	20,664	20,301	21,789	25,275	27,240	5,152	1,215	267
Sexual assault on a female aged 13 and over	—	—	—	—	—	—	—	—	—	15,087	17,158	16,887
Sexual assault on a female child under 13	—	—	—	—	—	—	—	—	—	4,391	4,647	4,249
Unlawful sexual intercourse with a girl under 13	148	156	153	153	181	155	169	183	212	—	—	—
Sexual activity involving child under 13	—	—	—	—	—	—	—	—	—	1,510	1,950	1,937
Unlawful sexual intercourse with a girl under 16	1,112	1,084	1,133	1,135	1,270	1,237	1,328	1,515	1,911	436	138	67
Sexual activity involving a girl under 16	—	—	—	—	—	—	—	—	—	2,546	3,283	3,210

Causing sexual activity without consent	—	—	—	—	—	—	—	—	—	239	744	224
Sexual activity etc. with a person with a mental disorder	—	—	—	—	—	—	—	—	—	104	139	163
Abuse of children through prostitution and pornography	—	—	—	—	—	—	—	—	—	99	124	101
Trafficking for sexual exploitation	—	—	—	—	—	—	—	—	—	21	33	43
Gross indecency with a child	1,269	1,314	1,271	1,293	1,365	1,336	1,654	1,917	1,987	398	120	64
Most serious sexual crime	**31,334**	**32,316**	**33,333**	**32,424**	**35,503**	**35,152**	**38,285**	**45,317**	**48,732**	**47,542**	**47,163**	**43,755**
Buggery	645	657	567	566	437	401	355	287	247	73	39	35
Gross indecency between males	520	483	353	354	286	167	163	245	260	49	20	12
Incest or familiar sexual offences	183	189	139	139	121	80	92	99	105	713	966	1,344
Exploitation of prostitution	131	142	155	215	138	129	129	127	186	117	153	190
Abduction of female	277	258	242	240	251	262	262	291	403	86	36	21
Soliciting of women by men	—	—	—	1,107	973	1,028	1,655	2,111	1,944	1,821	1,640	1,290
Abuse of position of trust of a sexual nature	—	—	—	—	—	12	417	678	792	682	463	361
Sexual grooming	—	—	—	—	—	—	—	—	—	186	237	322
Other miscellaneous sexual offences	—	—	—	10,327	9,476	8,647	8223	9,735	9,873	11,593	11,363	10,212
Other sexual offences	**1,756**	**1,729**	**1,456**	**12,948**	**11,682**	**10,726**	**11,296**	**13,573**	**13,810**	**15,320**	**14,917**	**13,787**
TOTAL SEXUAL OFFENCES	**33,090**	**34,045**	**34,789**	**46,372**	**47,185**	**45,878**	**49,581**	**58,890**	**62,542**	**62,862**	**62,080**	**57,542**

Source: http://www.homeoffice.gov.uk.rds.pdfs07/hosb1107.pdf. Home Office Statistical Bulletin, crime in England and Wales, 2006–7; adapted from Table 2.04.

It is simply inconceivable that the vast majority of women who report rape to the police are lying. Moreover, there is evidence that those women who do report are merely the tip of the iceberg, and yet this tip is further decimated as the criminal justice system runs its course.

Understanding sex offences: sex crimes, gender and violence

There are two major sets of explanations that have been used to understand an array of sex offenders. The first sets out psychological and psychiatric problems (for overview see Holmes and Holmes, 2008). With extreme cases of psychopathological sex killers, these probably have some major validity. But many sex crimes are much more common and 'everyday' than this. Their most conspicuous feature is that they are overwhelmingly committed by men. James Messerschmidt suggests that many sex offences originate with the 'ordinary' violence of boys. He suggests that

> approximately 25 percent of adult male sex offenders report that their first sexual offence occurred during adolescence. Moreover a significant proportion of all male sexual offences are committed by persons under the age of eighteen – approximately 25 percent of rapes and 50 percent of cases of child sexual abuse can be attributed to adolescent male offenders.
>
> (Messerschmidt, 2000: 3–4)

In many ways, sociologists see sex crimes as a way of 'doing gender'. Messerschmidt has powerfully merged ideas of 'structured action' and 'doing gender' to show the ways in which men can draw upon social resources in the wider culture to give different meanings to their masculinities and to make sense of various criminal actions. Certain boys use sexual and assaultive violence as what might be called a 'masculine practice'.

Feminist perspectives

This connects closely with how many feminists have understood sexual violence, which is that most sex offences, far from being pathological, are intentional behaviour chosen by men as part of their attempt to construct their masculinity as dominant and powerful. Likewise, sexual abuse is understood as an expression of masculinity, of men's desire to be in control and dominant, and it is intimately connected to normal relations within society.

Feminist sociological and socio-legal theories often link crime to masculinities (see Chapter 6). Important here are the workings of patriarchies: systems of male dominance that serve the interests of men. Power plays a key role in understanding sex offending, ranging from sexual violence to prostitution and pornography. Some US feminists such as Andrea Dworkin and Catharine MacKinnon have claimed that sexuality is organized by men for men and have denounced both 'heterosexuality' and heterosexual intercourse (for discussion, see Jackson and Scott, 1996).

The problem of violence against women includes several conceptually distinct yet overlapping concerns, which include rape, incest, battering, sexual harassment and pornography. English feminist sociologist Liz Kelly (1988) has argued that there is in fact a 'continuum of sexual violence', which ranges from the everyday abuse of women in pornographic images, sexist jokes, sexual harassment and women's engagement in compliant but unwanted marital sex, through to the 'non-routine' episodes of rape, incest, battery and sex murder. Kelly, with other feminists, suggests from research that most women have experienced some form of sexual violence. Sexual violence occurs in the context of men's power and women's resistance. Women are not passive victims. Feminist work has emphasized that they are 'survivors', with active agency, and that survival involves a rejection of self-blame, for once the abuse is made visible, it can be understood as precisely that, abuse.

Some recent feminist work departs from these kinds of studies by focusing on women's role as perpetrators of violence and child abuse. Turton (2007), for example, shows that although child abuse has been perceived as an almost exclusively male crime, a significant minority of cases involve women, typically mothers. Mothers' intimate care of young children's bodies, for example, can become abusive but such abuse is concealed through very powerful denial and harm minimization strategies. This kind of work agrees that men are responsible for the vast majority of sexual offences but examines why some women can become involved and asks why protection agencies, police and criminologists have not 'seen' these offences until recently.

Rape as social control

Until the 1970s, the dominant way of understanding the crime of rape by society, the criminal justice system and criminology was that women were to blame for their assault. In the criminology literature at the time the concept of 'victim-precipitated' rape was in full currency. It was argued that rape is most likely to occur in situations where the victim's behaviour is seen by the offender as signalling availability for sexual contact. Such situations were said to include those in which a woman agrees to sexual relations but changes her mind, fails to strongly resist sexual overtures, or accepts a drink from a stranger. Even wearing 'provocative clothing' could be taken as a sign of sexual availability. Such a way of thinking about rape was eventually seen to encourage an array of 'rape myths'. These myths are presumptions that women are tempting seductresses who invite sexual encounters, that women eventually relax and enjoy coercive sex, that men have urgent and uncontrollable sexual needs, and that the typical rapist was a stranger or black man. In fact, the typical rapist is more likely to be a man acquainted or intimate with his victim, rather than a stranger or psychopath. These myths are also reproduced in the legal system, thereby making it very difficult for women to achieve justice and to hold men responsible for the harms they have perpetrated.

For example, there are contradictory societal expectations concerning rape. One view is that if a woman is raped, she should be too upset and ashamed to report it; the other is that she should be so upset that she will report it. Both these views exist, but it is the latter that is written into the law. Any delay in reporting is used against her. Furthermore, when she is in court she is expected to appear upset as a victim, but calm and controlled as a court witness. If in court she appears lucid as a witness, she is in danger of not coming across as a victim. If she appears too upset, she runs the risk of being seen as hysterical and therefore not credible (Lees, 1996a, b). Rape was a central issue for second-wave feminists who challenged myths about its incidence, perpetrators, causes and consequences.

During the 1970s, a number of key arguments were made by feminist writers. First, Susan Griffin argued in a path-breaking article that all women inhabit a mental world where they are constantly in fear of being raped:

> I have never been free of the fear of rape. From a very early age, I, like most women, have thought of rape as part of my natural environment — something to be feared and prayed against like fire or lightning, I never asked why men raped; I simply thought of it as part of one of the many mysteries of human nature.
>
> (1971: 26)

This 'fear of rape' suggests the second argument: that men have a 'trump card' to play in keeping women in their place. Thus, Reynolds suggested that rape is a prime mode of social control:

> Rape is a punitive action directed towards females who usurp or appear to usurp the culturally defined prerogatives of the dominant role. . .[it] operates in our society to maintain the dominant position of males. It does this by restricting the mobility and freedom of movement of women by limiting their casual interaction with the opposite sex, and in particular by maintaining the male's prerogatives in the erotic sphere. When there was evidence that the victim was or gave the appearance of being out of place, she can be raped and the rapist will be supported by the cultural values, by the institutions that embody these values, and by the people shaped by these values — that is by the policy, courts, members of juries, and sometimes the victims themselves.
>
> (1974: 62–8)

Stay in your homes; stay in suitable attire; stay loyal to your husbands; stay submissive in your manner — this is the message of rape to women. Working outwards, then, from the actual impact of rape on women, the third argument starts to suggest what is happening. Susan Brownmiller, in her highly influential book *Against Our Will*, put the thesis at its most blunt: 'From prehistoric times to the present, I believe, rape has played a critical function. It is nothing more or less than a conscious process of intimidation by which *all men* keep *all women* in a state of fear' (1975: 5; emphasis in original). Such a thesis was taken up by many feminists, notably Dworkin (1981), and used as the basis for viewing male sexuality as the root of all women's oppression. Other commentators were more cautious but still emphasized rape as a form of male power over women: Clark and Lewis, for example, stated that they are not 'anti-male' but that they were opposed to 'any social system erected on the assumption of inequality between kinds of persons such that power and authority accrue only to a pre-elected subset' (1977: 166).

Feminist views here were certainly shaped and borne out by history (Bourke, 2007). Marriage laws and rape laws developed alongside each other and reflected the view that women were the 'property' of men rather than autonomous individuals with their own legal rights. In the eighteenth and nineteenth centuries, a sexual offence against a woman or girl could be viewed as the 'violation' of the 'property' of her husband or father. Rape thus became the 'theft of sexual property under the ownership of someone other than the rapist' (Clark and Lewis, 1977: 116). Women – such as those who remained unmarried or those who were economically independent – who were outside the 'ownership' or 'protection' of such men were believed to put themselves at risk of sexual offences. It was only in 1991 that rape within marriage (of a wife by a husband) was made formally illegal with the abolition of the marital rape exclusion clause – after over twenty years of feminist campaigns on the issue. Until the comprehensive UK review of sexual offences in 2003 (discussed at the end of this chapter) rape was narrowly defined as the penetration of a vagina by a penis without the woman's consent – a definition which excluded other parts of the body and male rape. Prior to the 2003 review, UK rape legislation also used a notion of consent to a sexual act that placed a very unfair burden of proof on the victim and failed to include a consideration for coerced consent or submission other than under physical duress. Box 11.2 outlines the 2003 Sexual Offences Act's definitions of rape and assault by penetration – new kinds of offences which rightly broaden the category of sexual crime.

BOX 11.2 UK Sexual Offences Act, 2003

Rape

(1) A person (A) commits an offence if –
  (a) he intentionally penetrates the vagina, anus or mouth of another person (B) with his penis,
  (b) B does not consent to the penetration, and
  (c) A does not reasonably believe that B consents.
(2) Whether a belief is reasonable is to be determined having regard to all the circumstances, including any steps A has taken to ascertain whether B consents.

Assault by penetration

(1) A person (A) commits an offence if –
  (a) he intentionally penetrates the vagina or anus of another person (B) with a part of his body or anything else,
  (b) the penetration is sexual,
  (c) B does not consent to the penetration, and
  (d) A does not reasonably believe that B consents.
(2) Whether a belief is reasonable is to be determined having regard to all the circumstances, including any steps A has taken to ascertain whether B consents.

Source: Office of Public Sector Information
http://www.opsi.gov.uk/acts/acts2003/ukpga_20030042_en_2#pt1-pb1-l1g1

Date rape

Changes to legal definitions of consent have placed a new emphasis on so-called 'date rape' or 'acquaintance rape'. Here, a sexual encounter might start out as consensual but then become coercive. Research evidence strongly suggests that many rapes occur in such settings and that most offenders and victims are acquainted in some way, however briefly. In Australia, for example, the 1996 Women's Safety Survey found that sexual assault by a boyfriend or a date accounted for 16.6 per cent of all sexual assaults which translated into around 24,000 separate incidents in the survey year (Russo, 2000). In sharp contrast to other kinds of sexual offences, victims of date rape can experience much lower levels of public support and also encounter outright media hostility for 'teasing' men, 'leading them on', being 'naive' or even for placing false accusations. The dispersal of feminist movements and the rise of so-called 'post-feminism' has meant that such hostility often goes uncountered, perhaps taking us back to old ways of 'blaming' female victims. Exceptions here might involve cases where the rape was 'drug-facilitated' with the rapist making use of drugs such as Gamma-hydroxybutyrate (GHB) and Rohypnol to incapacitate a victim. Here, intent to force sex is seen as much more clear-cut and the victim more obviously deserving of sympathy and redress.

Rape, war crime and genocide

Rape has a brutal global history bound up with conflicts, colonization and ethnic cleansing. In modern times, rape has been used as an instrument of war in the former Yugoslavia and Rwanda in the 1990s and most recently in the Sudanese province of Darfur, as documented by criminologist John Hagan (Hagan et al., 2005; see also Allen, 1996; Barstow, 2000). Feminist legal theorists, like Catharine MacKinnon who pioneered original academic studies of rape in the 1970s, are now active in this field (MacKinnon, 1998).

International criminal law has dealt with rape and sexual violence in different ways: as violation of the 1949 Geneva Conventions, the 1948 Genocide Convention, the 1984 Torture Convention, and a crime against humanity under the Nuremberg Charter. After the Second World War, the International Military Tribunal at Nuremberg declared rape to be a crime against humanity, but did not actually prosecute it. The Military Tribunal for the Far East (the Tokyo Tribunal) did convict Japanese officers of rape. Despite these legal precedents, rape has been treated by military and political leaders as a 'private crime' committed by individual errant soldiers or 'accepted' as part of war.

This changed dramatically in the 1990s. International Criminal Tribunals for the former Yugoslavia and for Rwanda both brought sexual violence charges. The Rwanda case (see Box 11.3) was a landmark judgement in that it allowed rape to be prosecuted as an act of genocide on the grounds that it could be motivated by a desire to change the genetic basis of an ethnic group by enforced impregnation. In 1998 the treaty setting up the new International Criminal Court (ICC) expressly named crimes based on sexual violence as part of the court's jurisdiction. The ICC itself began operating in 2002.

BOX 11.3 Rwanda: rape recognized as an act of genocide

In 1998 the UN International Criminal Tribunal for Rwanda (ICTR) found former mayor, Jean-Paul Akayesu, guilty of nine counts of genocide, crimes against humanity and war crimes. The verdict was the first conviction for genocide by an international court; the first time an international court had punished sexual violence in a civil war; and the first time that rape was found to be an act of genocide to destroy a group.

The Rwanda Tribunal was initially reluctant to indict Akayesu for rape. When Akayesu was first charged in 1996, the twelve counts in his indictment did not include sexual violence – despite the fact that Human Rights Watch, and other rights groups, had documented widespread rape during the genocide, particularly in his area. A lack of political will among some high-ranking tribunal officials as well as faulty investigative methodology by some investigative and prosecutorial staff of the Rwanda Tribunal accounted for this omission initially.

During the Rwandan genocide, thousands of women were targeted by Hutu militia and soldiers of the former government Armed Forces of Rwanda on their genocidal rampage. Tutsi women were individually raped, gang-raped, raped with objects such as sharp sticks or gun barrels, held in sexual slavery or sexually mutilated. These crimes were frequently part of a pattern in which Tutsi women were subjected to sexual violence after they had witnessed the torture and killings of their relatives and the looting and destruction of their homes.

During the Akayesu trial Rwandan women testified that they had been subjected to repeated collective rape by militia in and around the commune office, including in view of Akayesu. They spoke of witnessing other women being gang-raped and murdered while Akayesu stood by, reportedly saying to the rapists at one point 'don't complain to me now that you don't know what a Tutsi woman tastes like'.

Source: Human Rights Watch
http://hrw.org/english/docs/1998/09/02/rwanda1311.htm

Pornography

There is extensive debate within feminism on the issue of pornography. Some argue that pornography is central to women's oppression and must be subject to state controls (such as more intensive policing and more severe punishments for the creators, sellers and distributors). Others suggest that it is against women's interests and must be campaigned against. More recently and more controversially, pro-sex or libertarian feminists have argued that these views are outdated and that women's right to buy, view and enjoy pornography should be upheld.

Opponents of pornography argue that its connections between sex and violence reinforce masculinity and male power and depersonalize, objectify and degrade women. Their critique does not contend that there is a direct causal connection between media representations and behaviour, but rather takes issue with the fact much modern pornography celebrates violence and death as

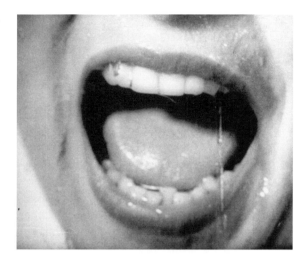

Plate 11.1 There is a long history of violence against women in films. Alfred Hitchcock's *Psycho* is considered to be a major depiction, and set into play a whole series of films in which women were brutally murdered (often in the bathroom!). This classic image features Janet Leigh in the famous scream shot.

Source: © Artificial Eye, courtesy of the British Film Institute.

well as sex. The kind of pornography that they allude to is of the highly extreme kind that involves rape, bestiality and children. Most people would wholly object to this kind of material.

However, it is not so easy to take this line on representations of women that are less obviously harmful, yet nevertheless contribute to a culturally sanctioned misogyny. One of the problems facing the feminist left is how far to take censorship while preserving democratic freedoms, since anti-pornography campaigns have attracted strong criticism from gay and lesbian groups because such legal regulation could be extended into other areas of sexual and social relations. There are also tensions between radical feminists and the perspectives of women who work as prostitutes or in the sex industry. For as Nicki Roberts, an ex-stripper, has argued,

> Feminist anti-porn campaigners or the Whitehouse brigade [Christian moral campaigners]: it makes no difference to us. Both factions clamour for more repression and censorship at the hands of the state; both divert attention away from the real issue of women's poverty in this society; and both are responsible for the increased hounding and vilification of women who work in the sex industry.
>
> (1986, cited in Edwards, 1990: 151)

The issues raised by this confront real problems in contemporary feminism, which concern the complexity of responses to justice, the law, freedom and inequality. There is no easy answer to this, but one way is to understand that not all people are controlled or oppressed with the same tenacity, tyranny or consistency.

Criminologists have linked pornography to crime in a number of different ways. These include the coercive tactics (including trafficking) that might be used to force women and children to appear in pornographic images; the extent to which pornography directly or indirectly shapes sexual violence against women and children and the illegal distribution of pornographic images (especially over the Internet).

The instrumental and symbolic role of law in sex crimes

Laws may be seen as both instrumental and symbolic. The *instrumental* role is practical: it aims to bring about some specific desired effect such as to stop rape. The *symbolic* role is one of latent concern – acting for example as a litmus for many moral panics and discourses that tap into a wide range of social anxieties. For example, it is now well documented that while, instrumentally, campaigns against commercialized prostitution in the nineteenth century certainly had real consequences in shifting public health and strengthening women's lives, they also symbolized the controversies over purity, immigration, 'dirty women', 'the age of consent'. As a cultural symbol, prostitution seems to touch all the 'evils' of the modern world and often is seen to create a contradictory tension between the exploitation of women and the lust of men. Thus, for example, nineteenth-century feminists – in the United States, Australia, Canada, Europe and the UK – led movements for moral reform, chastity and temperance which attacked prostitution, the availability of contraception and the moral debauchery of men through drink. Many of these feminists were also evangelical Christians with a highly conservative moral agenda. Indeed, the debates that we witnessed in the latter parts of the twentieth century around pornography and sexual violence were largely repeats of debates that were present at the turn of the century. Historian Judith Walkowitz comments that these historical social purity campaigns tried to 'protect' women but also 'helped to spawn a hydra-headed assault against sexual deviation of all kinds' and that 'by ferreting out new areas of illicit sexual activity and defining them into existence, a new "technology of power" was created that facilitated control over an ever-widening circle of human activity' (Walkowitz, 1984: 130–1).

Likewise, attacks on and anxieties concerning the so-called slum sex code and upon young men at taxi-dance halls in the early twentieth century were often a way of attacking lower-class men, and raised social class issues (White, 1993). 'Perverts' of all kinds seem to have stalked the nineteenth and twentieth centuries, symbolizing an anarchic, non-reproductive, 'sick' kind of sex. Race often became an issue in battles over rape and lynching. Controversies over pre- and extra-marital sex reinforced patterns of the 'normal family'. In the late twentieth century, AIDS rapidly became the symbol not only of death, but of promiscuity, permissiveness and perversions: it marked out the good and the bad. And at the start of the twenty-first century a major concern over paedophile priests in the Catholic Church energized controversies around religion, sexuality, homosexuality and child abuse (Loseke, 2003a).

Hence while, instrumentally, these campaigns try to stop a particular form of behaviour, symbolically they reassert existing moral orders. Over and over again, we find 'sexualities' being used in this way. Paraphrasing Mary Douglas's (1966) terms, we may say that sex often equals dirt and disorder, stuff out of place; and a society needs to purify itself of all this. Sexual problems emerge when there is a perceived threat to social values, be they religious, familial, feminist or medical. Behind every sexual problem there is almost certainly a perceived threat to aspects of the moral order and a group of crusaders struggling to define boundaries.

Panics around sex crimes

'Sex crimes' are a major social problem, with a history of generating anxiety and panic. Sometimes they enter public consciousness and reach levels of mass hysteria; sometimes we are hardly aware of them. And there are of course competing accounts of when and how they start to be noted and taken more seriously. Over half a century ago, the leading criminologist Edwin Sutherland summarized the passage of sex offence laws. His account still cannot be bettered:

> The diffusion of sexual psychopath laws has followed this course: a community is thrown into panic by a few serious sex crimes, which are given nation wide publicity; the community acts in an agitated manner; and all sorts of proposals are made; a committee is then appointed to study the facts and to make recommendations. The committee recommends a sexual psychopath law as the scientific procedure for the control of sex crime. The recommendation is consistent with the trend toward treatment policies in criminal justice in preference to policies of punishment.
>
> (1950: 142)

Sutherland was writing about the diffusion of such laws around 1937 in the United States. Today, much of his analysis is seen as one possible (and possibly even cyclical) response. Punitive and rehabilitative models come and go: there are periods of silence and periods when sex crime is a great issue.

The feminist writer, Jane Caputi, for example, has argued that sex crime starts to appear as a phenomenon with the famous and widely cited Jack the Ripper case in late-nineteenth century London. It not only generated huge moral anxiety in its day, but also signalled 'the age of sex crime', in which serial killers and mass murderers become more and more common – in reality and in the mythology of the times. For instance, she suggests there were 644 serial sex killings in the United States in 1966 but 4,118 by 1982 (Caputi, 1988: 1–2). She cites many examples: the 'Boston Strangler', 'Son of Sam', the 'Hillside Strangler', the 'Yorkshire Ripper', etc., as well as films that play to these fears: from the classics of M and Psycho to the more widespread teen slasher films such as the Halloween series. Her work outlines the creation of these fiends in the public minds, but at the same time shows how this is part of a wider issue of gender violence and aggression.

Taking a different view, sociologist Philip Jenkins has traced the differential responses to a hundred years of sex crimes from the late nineteenth century to current times. He suggests a different chronology:

> Originating in the Progressive era [early twentieth century], the imagery of the malignant sex fiend reached new heights in the decade after World War II, only to be succeeded by a liberal model over the next quarter of a century. More recently, the pendulum has swung back to the predator model: sex offenders are now viewed as being little removed from the worst multiple killers and torturers. And in each era, the prevailing opinion was supported by what appeared at the time to be convincing research. One reality prevailed until it was succeeded by another.
>
> (1998: 2)

He does not see these stages as evolutionary and necessarily objective: rather, they 'have ebbed and flowed – we forget as well as learn' (p. 3). 'The nature of sexual threats to children was perceived quite differently in 1915 than in 1930, and the child abuse issue was framed quite differently in 1984 than in 1994' (p. 215). At the heart of his analysis lie vigorous campaigning groups: child-savers, feminists, psychiatrists and therapists, religious and moralistic groups, and, of course, politicians.

Jenkins claims that children are at very low risk from homicide, making nonsense of the claims aired frequently in the 1980s that many thousands were killed each year by serial murders, pornographers or paedophile rings (p. 10). Looking at figures for the United States between 1980 and 1994, he concludes that despite the claims made, strangers killed about fifty-four children per year, and about five of these victims were involved as part of a sexual assault.

In summary, then, sexuality appears to be a major device used to tap into all sorts of social anxieties, to generate panic, to denote deviance and to demarcate boundaries. Studies point to many different sources of these anxieties and boundary mapping, but they include anxieties over gender roles, heterosexuality and the family; the importance of reproduction and pronatalism; concerns over the role of youth and childhood; race and racialized categories; the divisions between classes and 'class fears'; the nation-state itself; an overarching sense of moral progress and fears of decline; the very nature of ethical and religious systems; end of century/millennium fears; and even connections to the fear of death (for examples, see Bristow, 1977; Foldy, 1997; Hunt, 1998; McLaren, 1997; Showalter, 1990; Stein, 2001; Vass, 1986; Walkowitz, 1992; White, 1993).

The changing character of sex crimes

Just what can be designated a 'sex crime' changes all the time, and it will be interesting to examine a few illustrations briefly.

Homosexuality is an interesting case. For much of the nineteenth and twentieth centuries, it was against the law in most Western countries. Gradually it has become decriminalized over the past thirty years in those countries – though it does still remain illegal in some US states and in many parts of the world. Curiously, with the advance of a strong (and increasingly international) lesbian and gay movement, new issues have appeared such as universal lesbian and gay rights, including a universal age of consent and the inclusion of 'sexual orientation' in charters of human rights; and anti-discrimination laws, along with mandatory training in 'multi-culturalism' and 'gay affirmative action', have become common in many Western contexts. 'Registered partnerships' – and sometimes marriages – for lesbians and gays along with the right of lesbians and gays to adopt and have children have become key foci of a growing international lesbian, gay, bisexual and transgender movement (Adam et al., 1999). New anti-gay crimes such as 'hate crimes' have been created and turned into social problems. A major reworking of the claims being made about homosexuality has been happening over the past thirty years; it can no longer be placed easily in a Western list of 'sex offences and crimes'.

Yet while all this is going on, there continues to be massive resistance to acceptance of homosexuality in many countries. In most countries of Africa, Asia or the Middle East, same-sex relations remain taboo: largely invisible, rarely discussed, officially non-existent, and embedded in religions, laws and beliefs that are deeply inimical to homosexuality. Even today, it is illegal in approximately seventy states in the world as well as being subject to the death penalty in seven. Indeed, the partial acceptance of homosexuality in parts of the West is often used as a major example of the West's decadence (Baird, 2001: 12).

Prostitution, too, is an interesting case. It is often not against the law per se, but it is regulated because of concerns over health risks and community safety. In the UK, after the Wolfenden Report of 1957, living on immoral earnings, keeping a brothel and soliciting by a 'common prostitute' became illegal; and subsequently in 1985, 'kerb crawling' became an offence. Prostitution is not in itself illegal in England and Wales, but the selling of sexual services in a street or public place is, along with any involvement of children. In the United States, it is legal in some states, regulated in others and outlawed in still others. Research on prostitution has also gone through many phases. Recent work has put male customers rather than female clients in the spotlight. A London study (Coy et al., 2007) investigates increases in reported rates of men paying for sex in the last ten years. It links the rise to a re-sexualization of popular culture, the rise of sexual consumption as a kind of recreation and the role of the Internet in facilitating access to sexual markets. Lap-dancing, pole-dancing and soft porn are now much more visible than they were. In 2000, one in twenty-nine London men admitted buying sex in some form. More broadly, UK data on men arrested for 'kerb crawling' showed the average customer to be aged 35, in full-time work and with no criminal convictions. This raises issues about the flexible construction of masculine 'respectability' among other things.

Likewise, pornography is another form of sexual deviance that has changed over time. In the eighteenth century it was part of erotic subcultures involving men across classes (Gatrell, 2006) while in the nineteenth it became a target for social purity campaigners. Today it remains a hotly contested issue, and although there have been many versions of obscenity law, in the main these days the issue of obscenity is most closely linked to the purchasing and ownership of child pornography (new laws were introduced in the 1980s that made not just the production and selling of such porn illegal but also its purchasing and ownership). And this has now been compounded by offences linked to the Internet.

Sex crimes on the Internet

Recently, we have started to see the emergence of a new area of sex offences as more and more people come to use the Internet to make sexual contacts, buy sexual wares and view all kinds of websites that are saturated with every kind of sexual image you are ever likely to want (and not want) to see. All kinds of new potential criminal problems have emerged as a result: cyber-stalkers, cyber-rape, childhood security, paedophile abductions, camcorder sex, new forms of porn and ways of accessing it (alongside so-called cyborg sex and virtual sex). Such new forms are a largely uncharted area, and finding ways of regulating them through law and control agencies sees us with a new field of sex crimes just now in the making. In the United Kingdom, for instance, the government has created new offences in this area and set up groups such as the Task Force on Child Protection on the Internet and the Internet Watch Foundation to start tracking serious abuses on the Web (see Jewkes, 2007a).

BOX 11.4 Child pornography, globalization and the Internet

Another instance of globalization at work is the relatively recent arrival of a network of worlds linked through the Internet that caters for interests in child pornography and paedophile abuse. By most accounts, this is widespread, much condemned but hard to regulate, and has generated extensive public talk in the West.

In his study of child pornography on the Internet, Philip Jenkins shows just how difficult it is to regulate a fragmented network such as this. Although there are laws which make possession of pornographic pictures of anyone under 18 an imprisonable offence, other – often poorer – countries have much less stringent laws, and more pressures pushing children into these industries. Certainly, many of the images found on the Internet have originated in poorer, 'bandit' regions (the former communist world, parts of Asia and Latin America – and oddly, also Japan) where regulations are minimal. It may be hard to regulate in Western countries but it is even more difficult elsewhere. And as Jenkins comments, 'Lacking a global moral consensus, there will always be areas of unevenness, fault lines in moral enforcement, and the child pornographers are likely to survive in these cracks' (2001: 203).

Changes in the law concerning sexual offences in the United Kingdom

The 2003 Sexual Offences Act is seen by many as one of the most radical overhauls of sex offences legislation for over fifty years. From 1999 onwards, Tony Blair's Labour government conducted intensive reviews of existing legislation involving many organizations from lobby groups to children's charities. The reviews were set up with the following terms of reference:

- to provide coherent and clear offences which protect individuals, especially children and the more vulnerable, from abuse and exploitation;
- to enable abusers to be properly punished;
- to be fair and non-discriminatory.

The resulting 2003 Act set out to broaden traditional notions of victims in these cases and shift the historical focus from (straight) women and children to include men, gay and lesbian people and those with learning and other disabilities. In practical terms, the Act addressed this by broadening the definition of rape to include (see Box 11.2 earlier) penile penetration of the mouth and anus as well as the vagina without consent and by introducing the new offence of 'assault by penetration' with an object or a part of the body. This means, for example, that women abusers can now be charged with this kind of penetrative offence. The Act also widened definitions of 'family' in relation to familial sexual offences to include not just blood relatives but also other family members living in the same household such as foster parents, foster siblings, step-parents, step-siblings and cousins.

In addition, the 2003 Act created several other new offences with the aim of shifting the historical focus on physical, bodily assault to other less physical but equally abusive behaviours, such as sexual grooming, administering a substance with intent (to facilitate a sexual act) and encouraging children to watch sexually explicit activity on video, television, webcams or any other media. A further key change here was the redefinition of consent and new kinds of responsibilities around this crucial aspect of any sexual activity. Before 2003, a defendant who was able to prove that they honestly believed that consent had been given – however unreasonable that belief might be – was likely to be acquitted (hence the historically low numbers of convictions in these kinds of cases as discussed earlier). Since 2003, a defendant wishing to prove this has had to show that they have reasonable grounds to support their belief and must indicate what steps they took to elicit consent. The idea here is that consent must be active and not passive or assumed. An important exception here is that children under the age of 13 (and adults with certain kinds of learning difficulties in some cases) are deemed by law to be *unable* to give consent to sexual activity.

The 2003 Sexual Offences Act also changed police, court and community procedures for monitoring convicted sex offenders. The previous 1997 Sex Offenders Act had required these people's details to be recorded on sex offender registers. The new Act tightened procedures in a number of ways. Offenders must notify any change to their name or address within three days (as opposed to fourteen). If they stay at a UK address that is not their home for seven days or more, or if they spend more than three days abroad, they must notify police. These notification measures now apply to convicted foreign sex offenders visiting the UK. Certain registered offenders (suspected child sex tourists) can now be banned from travelling abroad at all if they are thought likely to endanger children as a result. A new 'risk of sexual harm order' can prevent someone from engaging in sexually explicit communication – including texting or emailing children – if they have been found to have done this at least twice before. Much of this work with sex offenders is now coordinated by Multi-Agency Public Protection Arrangments (MAPPAs) involving the police, local authorities and community organizations.

Overall, the 2003 Act aimed to create a new framework for defining and dealing with sexual crime that would reflect key shifts in late modern life, among them greater gender equality, more complex families, more emphasis on child protection and victims' rights, increased geographical mobility and huge changes in personal media technologies. Criminologists, sociologists and campaigning groups are now beginning to assess the impact of the 2003 Act. Table 11.1 shows that a significant number of offences against the new laws outlined above have been recorded – for example, incest or familial sexual offences (from 99 offences in 2002/3 to 1,344 in 2006/7), male rape (from 850 in 2002/3 to 1,150 in 2006/7) and sexual grooming (from 0 offences in 2002/3 to 322 in 2006/7). In terms of specific measures within the new legislation, Ost (2004) suggests the difficulties involved in proving ulterior motives linked to sexual grooming while Thomas (2004) and Mcalinden (2006) have both challenged the effectiveness of the sex offenders' register as a means of preventing further sexual crime, arguing that the register can infringe offenders' rights. The causes and effects of the reframing of UK sexual offences laws will prove a rich seam for criminologists in the near future.

Public reaction to the 2003 Act is difficult to gauge. Most people are probably unaware of the radical changes it made and many probably still feel that the courts are 'too soft' on sex offenders, particularly paedophiles. In the run-up to the legal review, public feelings ran high following the murder of 8-year-old Sarah Payne by Roy Whiting, a known sex offender, in southern England in 2000. A high-profile tabloid-supported campaign pushed for the introduction of 'Sarah's law' as a means to publish details held on sex offenders' registers (modelled on New Jersey's 1994 'Megan's law' enacted after a similar case). In short, many say they want to be able, as a number of US residents are, to know if they themselves are living near a paedophile. Such a measure would raise many complications, not least around the right to privacy, the high risk of vigilantism and actions based on mistaken identity. It would also, opponents argue, focus once again on 'stranger danger' rather than the very much more common dangers children face at the hands of those known to them – the very dangers which the 2003 Act attempted to address.

Public attitudes to sexuality are changing in key ways, as this chapter has indicated. These attitudes are often contradictory, however. Public feelings against paedophiles run high yet arguably children, especially young girls, are sexualized to extraordinary degrees within everyday culture. The market in 'girl goods' is highly lucrative with high-street stores selling make-up, mini-bras and thongs to the under 10s. Top Shop recently stocked a controversial badge stating 'I swallow' and Woolworths branded a girls' bed 'Lolita' though this was withdrawn after complaints. In a post-feminist culture where young female identity is seen as playful, ironic and sexually empowered it is difficult to counter this kind of hyper-sexualization (McRobbie, 2008). Yet efforts to reduce what remain the most commonly reported kinds of sexual offence – abuse, assaults and rapes against girls and women – should be seen in this contradictory context.

Sex offences in global perspective

This chapter has largely focused on UK sex offences, though there are many similarities with other Western cultures. Other societies have very different laws and hence different patterns of offence. In some strongly Muslim societies (and Iran seems a central if changing case), the degree of surveillance over the lives of children and women on a day-to-day basis makes the possibility of any norm-violations (from masturbation to homosexuality) difficult indeed. Penalties are severe and executions not uncommon for homosexuality.

In 2008, the UK Home Secretary agreed to review the case of 19-year-old gay Iranian, Mehdi Kazemi, who claimed he would be executed if his claim for asylum were to be rejected, forcing him to return to Iran. The teenager's case was taken up by gay rights activists across Europe. Kazemi moved to London in 2005 to study English but later discovered that his boyfriend had been arrested by the Iranian police, charged with sodomy and hanged. Human rights campaigners say that over 4,000 gay men and lesbians have been executed in Iran since the Islamic revolution of 1979 (BBC news website, 13 March 2008).

Honour killings take place in many Muslim communities around the world. Here, women may be punished by death (or raped) for actual (or even perceived) sexual (mis)conducts. Criminologist Aisha Gill (2006) argues that such acts use 'honour' to mask patriarchal violence.

Yet we are also now starting to sense the globalization of sexualities, in which the world becomes smaller and more interconnected: a major reordering of time and space in sexual

Plate 11.2 In the summer of 2000 in the UK there was hysteria against sex offences and paedophilia. In Paulsgrove estate, Portsmouth, people organized into Residents Against Paedophilia and went on the march.

Source: Press Association.

relations may be taking place. Talk about 'sexual problems' moves across the globe, and in the process often becomes transformed and modified by local cultures. Traditional sexual customs become subject to rapid social change. Media and digitalization generate an information age haunted by the spectres of sexuality – from cybersex to cyber-rape. Postmodern values seem on the ascendant, giving priorities to ideas of sexual differences and sexual choices. Global capital turns local sex markets into international ones. World sexual cultures become more and more interconnected. With all this, it should not be surprising to find long-standing patterns of sexualities becoming increasingly disturbed and disrupted (Altman, 2001).

doing crime

Summary

1   Reported sex crime is increasing in the UK. The reasons for this are not clear but are likely to be linked to measures to encourage victims to report, a clampdown on interpersonal violence of all kinds and the broadening of legal definitions of sexual offences.

2   Sex crimes are not as common as many other offences but they remain under-reported, despite the measures listed above. Victims of sexual offences still face considerable personal and procedural difficulties, as well as public hostility (e.g. in cases of alleged date rape), when taking action against offenders.

3   Sociologists have understood sex crimes as closely connected to the structuring of gender and the male use of power. Rape is a prime example of this.

4   Moral panics are often linked to sex crimes. At different periods in history, these panics have focused on different kinds of crimes. Public attitudes to sexuality and sex crime can be highly contradictory. Globally, sex crimes can take very different forms in different countries.

5   In 2003 a major overhaul of the sex offences legislation took place in the United Kingdom in response to broad changes in late modern life around gender, sexuality, family, child protection, media, mobility and communication technology.

Critical thinking questions

1   Why are sex crimes seriously under-reported?
2   Discuss the factors that lead some men and a minority of women to commit acts of sexual violence.
3   Consider the processes by which sex crimes become identified as social problems.
4   Discuss the various policies for managing 'sex offenders' and consider which you think are most effective.
5   Why has there been so much interest in the problem of child sexual abuse and paedophilia in recent years?
6   Critically discuss changes made by the 2003 Sexual Offences Act in the UK.

Further study

Amnesty International (2001) *Crimes of Hate: Conspiracies of Silence*, London: Amnesty International. Useful review of the ways in which homosexuality remains a crime in many parts of the world.

Foucault, M. (1978) *The History of Sexuality*, Harmondsworth: Penguin. A highly influential study of the emergence of sexual categories and knowledge in modernity.

Holmes, S. T. and Holmes, R. M. (2008) *Sex Crimes: Patterns and Behavior*, 3rd edn, Thousand Oaks, CA: Sage. A psychological approach to the profiling of sex offenders. Read for a contrast with the sociological view.

Jenkins, P. (1998) *Moral Panic: Changing Concepts of the Child Molester in Modern America*, New Haven, CT: Yale University Press, and (2001) *Beyond Tolerance: Child Pornography on the Internet*, New York: New York University Press. Two books that deal with issues of paedophilia and child abuse.

Kelly, L. (1988) *Surviving Sexual Violence*, Cambridge: Polity. One of many influential feminist texts on sexual violence.

Loseke, D. (2003b) *Thinking about Social Problems: An Introduction to Constructionist Perspectives*, 2nd edn, New York: Aldine de Gruyter. (See also Loseke, D. (2003a) 'Symposium on Paedophile Priests', *Sexualities*, 6 (1): 6–14.) Useful in laying out the constructionist position on social problems – with lots of examples.

Silverman, J. and Wilson, D. (2002) *Innocence Betrayed: Paedophilia, the Media and Society*, Cambridge: Polity. Connects moral panic theory, media and sex crimes into a very readable discussion.

Thomas, T. (2000) *Sex Crime: Sex Offending and Society*, Cullompton: Willan. A straightforward introduction to the field.

More information

Office of Public Sector Information

http://www.opsi.gov.uk/acts/acts2003/ukpga_20030042_en_2#pt1-pb1-l1g1
For information on the 2003 Sexual Offence Act

National Organisation for the Treatment of Abusers

www.nota.co.uk
NOTA is a growing group comprising practitioners, managers and policy-makers for the public, private and voluntary sectors. As a result, NOTA brings a wide variety of perspectives to interventions with sexual aggressors.

Child and Woman Abuse Unit

http://www.cwasu.org/
The Child and Woman Abuse Unit is based at London Metropolitan University and has a national and international reputation for its research, training and consultancy work. The unit exists to develop feminist research methodologies, theory and practice, especially in relation to connections between forms of sexualized violence.

The Fawcett Society

http://www.fawcettsociety.org.uk/
A UK women's rights organization which runs campaigns on sexual crime.

Date rape drugs and other date rape resources

http://news.bbc.co.uk/2/hi/uk_news/6518397.stm

chapter 12

Crime, the Emotions and Social Psychology

Key issues

- Why have the emotions been neglected in criminology?

- Is crime seductive?

- What is meant by 'fear of crime'?

- How does resentment structure 'hate' crime?

- What role does 'respect' play in violent encounters?

- Does 'shaming' restore the balance of justice between offenders, victims and the community?

Introduction

It might seem obvious that human emotions play a significant part in the commission of crime, in punishment and in social control. Indeed, the relationship between emotion and crime has fuelled the creative imagination. To take an intense emotion – passion, for instance – *la crime passionel* has inspired great works of literature, theatre, art, symphonies and the opera. It is perhaps the tragedy of crimes of passion that has inspired the artistic imagination; they are offences committed by wretched but ordinary people, not otherwise inclined to transgress. Fuelled by one or more of a myriad of emotions – the wounds of betrayal, the hurt of infidelity, broken hearts, wounded pride, spoiled virtue, jealousy, envy, and many more – they are criminalized by their acts. Passion comes to overrule reason – usually with dire consequences for the offender and the victim.

In Shakespeare's tragic tale *Othello*, the enraged Othello 'the Moor' murders his wife, Desdemona, on account of her alleged adultery, and then kills himself in deep remorse when he realizes he has been deceived into believing in her infidelity. In Bizet's *Carmen*, the smitten soldier Don José kills his love, Carmen, after she has an affair with the handsome Escamillo. In 2002, the tragic story was recast as a 'Hiphopera' by MTV and New Line Television, starring the singer Beyonce Knowles. While in the world of popular music, crimes of passion have been acted out in numerous songs. 'Delilah', the hit by Tom Jones, is a classic example of betrayal with fatal consequences and more recently Nick Cave released an entire album of 'Murder Ballads'. In this chapter we will examine how the emotions figure in criminology. We begin with describing how the emotions have been marginalized in much intellectual work, but have recently become a focal point across the humanities and social sciences.

Rediscovering the emotions

Although crimes of passion have inspired great artistic works and enthralled audiences for centuries, the subject of emotion, it has recently been argued, has been only a peripheral interest within criminological inquiry and theory. Willem de Haan and Ian Loader, for instance, suggest that

> Many established and thriving modes of criminological reflection and research continue
> to proceed in ways that ignore entirely, or at best gesture towards, the impact of human

Plate 12.1 Nick Cave's collection of murder ballads reveals the enduring popularity of blood, sex, melodrama and crime as themes in popular culture.

Source: Murder Ballads by Nick Cave and The Bad Seeds front cover image reproduced courtesy of Nick Cave & Mute Records.

doing crime

emotions on their subject matter – if you doubt this, take a quick glance at almost any criminology textbook, whether of a conventional, radical or integrating bent.

(2002: 243)

However, while the impact of human emotion on crime appears to be in the process of rediscovery in theoretical criminology, it has hardly been neglected in the past by research on crime and deviance. Many of these texts are among the foundational texts of social psychology, which can be defined as the systematic study of people's thoughts, feelings and conduct in social contexts. On this reckoning the emotions should not be reduced to psychological states, but as social and cultural practices that both come from within ourselves and from without – in larger structural processes that ritually shape how we feel and act.

Historically, indeed, a defining feature of Western thought is the way that emotion and reason have been regarded as opposing forces, with the emotional often seen as beneath the rational, as a sign of the lowly, primitive, natural and feminine. It has only been since the late 1970s that the sociology of emotions has become an established field within the discipline. Since then there appeared several major perspectives on the emotions and social life (Hochschild, 1983; Kemper, 1978; Scheff, 1979), as well as the repositioning of the emotions in classical and contemporary social theory (Barbalet, 1998; Williams, 2001; Shilling, 2002), while feminists have explained how the marginalization of emotion has worked to subordinate the feminine, the body and intimate desires (Spelman, 1989; Jaggar, 1989; Ahmed, 2004). Taken together these developments suggest that criminology has much to gain from engaging with this resurgence of interest in the emotions across the humanities and social sciences. Nor should this be a one-way conversation. Criminological work has a crucial place in revealing the importance of emotions in shaping our inner worlds as well as broader social and cultural practices.

Status, stigma and seduction

The contemporary interest in crime and the emotions can usefully be traced back to Albert Cohen's study (1955: 17) of delinquent boys, which sought to demonstrate how 'psychogenic and subcultural factors' combined to produce delinquency through the humiliating 'status frustrations' experienced by working-class boys and the alienating differences of class-based value systems. In a series of insightful pieces Erving Goffman described how all encounters are guided by certain cultural scripts that establish the ground rules for interaction. His work captures how perceptions of social worth regulate human conduct. Famously, he argued that mental patients 'suffer not from mental illness, but from contingencies' (Goffman, 1961: 135) – people who may or may not have been experiencing some degree of mental distress, but have had the misfortune to end up in an asylum and then had to adjust their self-identities in line with the 'heavy machinery of mental-hospital servicing'. In Stigma, Goffman (1963) examined how people managed 'spoiled identity', the pain and shame associated with being considered less than human. Crucially, he emphasized that we all move between normal and troubled worlds, and each of us falls short some of the time, such that embarrassment (and the anxious expectation of it) clouds every social interaction.

In important ways, Goffman exposed in Stigma the very inappropriateness of the term deviance to describe physical handicap, ethnic difference and numerous forms of social disaffiliation.

Likewise, the sharp distinction drawn between deviant and conventional values in subcultural theory was also criticized by David Matza (1964) who pointed out that juveniles intermittently drift into and out of delinquency. His focus on motivational will manages to grasp something of the immediate, intoxicating and alluring spell that delinquency casts, which he would later describe as the 'invitational edge' that deviancy offers (Matza, 1969: 111). It is this dizzying edge that Jack Katz (1988) attempts to capture in his seminal *Seductions of Crime* through concentrating on the experiential foreground of crime across a diverse range of acts that include juvenile 'sneaky thrills', armed robbery and cold-blooded, 'senseless' murder.

Each specific crime offers distinctive ways of overcoming the mundane routines of everyday life through presenting unique emotional attractions that provide 'a dialectic process through which a person empowers the world to seduce him to criminality' (Katz, 1988: 7). While Katz's work has been influential (especially in cultural criminology) it has not escaped criticism on the grounds that it

- ■ disregards the wider social context in which all action takes place (O'Malley and Mugford, 1994; Young, 2007a);
- ■ fails to secure 'serious distance' (implying that offending stories are taken at face value); and
- ■ lacks any 'systematic explanation' of the various 'motivational' accounts (I. Taylor, 1999: 224).

Yet, as Hayward (2002: 83) suggests, these objections ignore 'the failure of "background" structural theories of crime to address the fundamental question of why (under shared social conditions) one person rather than another commits crime'. It is by exploring the relationships between crime, emotion and social psychology that some of these answers are to be found.

Conceptualizing emotions

Although there are ongoing debates over how to define exactly what are emotions, what they do and how they should best be studied (Williams, 2001; Strongman, 2003), there is now much agreement that *happiness, fear, anger* and *depression* are universal to all humans and are even said to be hardwired into human neuroanatomy (Kemper, 1987). Importantly, three of the four emotions are negatively tuned (Turner and Stets, 2005: 11) and we will be exploring how these primary emotions shape and colour other emotions like hate, shame, guilt, pride, wonder, resentment, nostalgia and dread among the many feelings encountered in our daily experiences. In his influential article Theodore Kemper (1987) argues that these secondary emotions are more socially constructed and arise from specific contexts where experiences are learnt. Guilt, for example, is derived from the primary emotion of fear and the social organization of punishment, religion or nationhood inducing some experience of shame, regret and sorrow. Table 12.1 summarizes his characterization of primary and secondary emotions, which provides a useful taxonomy of the emotions. Of course, it is important to recognize that there is considerable cultural and social variation in how these emotions are experienced, expressed and practised. We now turn from these broad conceptual issues to that emotional state which has received considerable criminological attention – fear. Indeed, it has become a well-worn observation that

Table 12.1 Kemper's primary and secondary emotions

Primary emotions	Fear	Anger	Depression	Happiness
Emotions attached to primary emotions	Guilt	Shame	Ennui, sadness, resignation	Pride, loving, gratitude
Some combinations of primary emotions	Fear-anger: hate, jealousy, envy	Fear-happiness: wonder, awe, hope, shyness	Anger-happiness: vengeance, snobbery, contempt	Depression-happiness: nostalgia, yearning

Source: Adapted from Kemper, 1987; and Turner and Stets, 2005: 18.

the problems posed by the fear of crime are potentially greater than crime itself and as we will see it was this discovery that prompted the plethora of studies on the topic.

Fear of crime

Fear is a complex human emotion. While fear is ubiquitous and felt by every living creature, the actual sources of dread are socially distributed. Different societies have developed different ways of living with the dangers that haunt them. Yet contemporary terms like the 'politics of fear', 'fear of crime', 'age of anxiety', 'risk society' and most recently 'liquid fear' (Bauman, 2006; see also Box 12.1) each suggest that we are living in times of such heightened insecurity that danger lurks everywhere. A number of important social changes are said to herald this new era and break with the past – the mass media now provide us with round-the-clock news of crisis, disaster and trauma; rising social mobility brings a greater range of experiences, expectations and troubles; technological innovations have brought with them immense global dangers; and since 9/11 'new' forms of terrorism further contribute to the cultural climate of fear (Carrabine, 2008).

Although research on the fear of crime was established in the late 1960s – paralleling the growth in more general criminological interest and policy concerns over victims of crime – it had moved to the centre of intense empirical, political and theoretical disputes by the 1980s. Today, the 'fear of crime' is an area of criminological inquiry that constitutes a 'sub-discipline in itself' (Lee, 2001: 468) and 'is probably the main legacy of endless, and endlessly repeated, national crime surveys which have consistently identified it as a social problem of striking dimensions' (Ditton *et al.*, 1999: 83). Few issues trouble the public in Europe and the United States more than crime. Surveys have repeatedly shown that worries over victimization surpass losing a job, ill-health, road accidents and indebtedness as issues of major concern (Farall and Gadd, 2004: 127).

From the late 1960s, in the United States initially but later elsewhere around the world, interviewing citizens about their personal experiences of crime became commonplace. In addition to trying to obtain a more accurate view of victimization levels these national household crime surveys provide information on the public's beliefs and attitudes towards crime, policing, punishment and prevention. The British Crime Survey was first carried out in 1982 and has been

BOX 12.1 Fears in motion

The trade in safety and security is highly lucrative. To take one example, there is the quite extraordinary phenomenon of the 'Sports Utility Vehicle' (SUV) in the United States. This massive petrol-guzzling, quasi-military vehicle had at one point reached 45 per cent of all car sales in the United States and is sold as a 'defensive capsule'. It is portrayed in advertisements as offering immunity against the dangerously unpredictable urban life outside the protective armoured shell (Bauman, 2006: 143–4). According to Josh Lauer (2005) the SUV first emerged as a status symbol in the early 1980s with the introduction of the military Humvee (which stands for High Mobility Multipurpose Wheeled Vehicle) which was commissioned by the army to replace the jeep, and came to popular attention during the first Gulf War. This prompted the development of a civilian version and the continuing occupation of Iraq has only heightened their popularity.

The massive civilian Hummer was embraced as an ultra macho novelty vehicle and quickly became one of the most fashionable and popular vehicles in America, with more than a third of its sales to women drivers. Indeed, a recent television ad features a woman driving a Hummer through city streets, with the tagline, 'Slip into something more metal'. Clearly there is something more going on here than an increased fear consciousness, as the SUV is an expensive piece of 'high-end automotive jewellery' in which risk management is transformed into a symbol of conspicuous consumption (Lauer, 2005: 163–5). It is significant however that in the UK similar oversized, four-wheel-drive vehicles are frequently derided as 'Chelsea Tractors', which indicates their almost ridiculous remove from their original use among working farmers and the rural gentry (Carrabine, 2008).

Plate 12.2
Humvee
on sale.

Source:
Getty
Images.

doing crime

repeated at regular intervals since. Accompanying national surveys have been an increasing number of local crime surveys, which in the UK have been carried out in various places like Bristol, Sheffield, Merseyside, Islington and Edinburgh (Hale, 1996: 79). Typically fear of crime is often measured by responses to the question 'How safe do you feel walking alone in this area after dark?', or similar formulations, to which respondents are invited to reply by saying they feel 'very safe', 'fairly safe', 'a bit unsafe' or 'very unsafe'. The use of this question to uncover 'fear of crime' has been widely criticized, as it

■ fails to explicitly mention crime (Garafalo, 1979);
■ cannot do justice to the emotional complexity of fear (Box *et al.*, 1988);
■ ignores the fluidity of lived experiences (Goodey, 2005: 69);
■ and through questionnaires respondents are 'forced to use the same language to express very different feelings' (O'Mahony and Quinn, 1999: 232–3).

As Evi Girling and her colleagues (Girling *et al.*, 2000: 13) emphasize, these studies tend to 'discover a lack of "fit" between expert knowledge and "lay" opinion' that have come to revolve around the question of whether fear is rational or irrational in an effort to distinguish between 'warranted' estimates of risks as opposed to debilitating misperceptions of threats by particular groups of the public. Home Office research continued to find that both women and the elderly were particularly 'irrational' given the distance between their high levels of expressed fear and their low levels of actual risk. The conclusion was that women and the aged were incapable of making rational sense of the risks they faced.

Feminists quickly challenged the gendered stereotypes of women as fearful and men as fearless in much of these approaches (see, *inter alia*, Goodey, 1997; Stanko, 1997; Gilchrist *et al.*, 1998; Sutton and Farrall, 2005). Betsy Stanko (1987, 1988) was an early critic and argued that this work could not adequately grasp women's experiences and fears of sexual danger. By using alternative research methodologies (like ethnographic studies, life histories and individual interviews) significant empirical evidence was unearthed that debunked 'the myth of the safe home' (Stanko, 1988) to reveal the extent of 'ordinary violence' women regularly face and manage across public and private domains (Stanko, 1990). Such work raises 'fundamental questions of whose standards are used as markers of a reasonable or rational fear' (Walklate, 1998: 409) and suggests there are some dubious conceptual assumptions behind conventional approaches to researching fear. In any case, the debate over whether the 'fear of crime' is rational or irrational is one that can never really be resolved, as it is difficult to see what a rational fear would look like (Sparks, 1992: 10). For women fear of sexual danger is a normal condition – a 'governing of the soul' (Stanko, 1997) – such that much criminological attention has now shifted to the issue of 'ontological security' (Giddens, 1991) in an effort to grasp how inner anxieties are structured in social space.

Urbanism, anxiety and the human condition

A rich seam of work has attempted to understand the ways fears and anxieties are locally constructed. Ian Taylor (1996, 1997) has argued that the fear of crime has become a condensed metaphor, which attempts to capture broader concerns over the pace of socio-economic change.

As he explains, the rise of defensive middle-class suburban social movements organized around crime prevention

> are activated not just by immediately presenting sets of problems in the specific locality (stories of aggressive young people and actual violence on the hitherto peaceful local High Street) but by deeper fears about joblessness and house prices, and (in the case of parents with suburban children) schooling 'for success', child safety, moral socialization . . . and a host of other increasingly agitated concerns.
>
> (Taylor, 1997: 66)

On this account, worries about crime are intimately bound up with the less easily grasped or articulated troubles generated by changes in economic, moral and social life. It is a 'fear of falling' that is the defining condition of the suburban middle class in contemporary England (Taylor and Jamieson, 1998).

A point further explored by Girling *et al.* (2000) in their study of public perceptions of crime in a prosperous English market town is that

> people's responses to crime (in its association with other matters of concern to them) are both informed by, and in turn inform, their *sense of place*; their sense, that is, of both *the place* they inhabit (its histories, divisions, trajectories and so forth), and of *their place* within a wider world of hierarchies, troubles, opportunities and insecurities.
>
> (Girling *et al.*, 2000: 17; emphasis in original)

The importance of this work is that it attempts to situate people's fears in specific everyday contexts and in doing so it chimes with other recent developments that have highlighted how the individual's social location (Walklate, 1998) and inner personal senses of security (Hollway and Jefferson, 2000) shape perceptions of the wider world around them.

The introduction of psychoanalytical theory into the fear of crime debate offers much potential. Wendy Hollway and Tony Jefferson (1997, 2000) draw on the key psychoanalytical insight that anxiety is the price we pay for having a sense of self. Their work emphasizes that anxiety is a universal feature of the human condition and that dynamic 'unconscious defences against anxiety are a commonplace and constructive aspect of response to threats' (Hollway and Jefferson, 2000: 32). The specific unconscious defence mechanisms they focus on are **denial**, **splitting** and **projection** to explore how threats to the self are managed by these displacing activities. Their overall argument is that anxiety, as a pervasive yet inchoate emotion, lies behind much of the contemporary concerns over fear of crime. Drawing on their research with people living on two council estates in northern England their analysis reveals quite varied and diffuse responses to the threat of crime. The differing responses are informed by individual biography, social location and unconscious defence mechanisms. As they put it 'a rampant "fear of crime" discourse which might on the face of it be thought to exacerbate fears, could actually serve unconsciously as a relatively reassuring site for displaced anxieties which otherwise would be too threatening to cope with' (Hollway and Jefferson, 1997: 263–4).

Hollway and Jefferson (2000: 31) have introduced a notion of human subjectivity that recognizes 'the non-rational, unintentional and emotional aspects of people's actions and experience' that had largely been neglected by criminologists. Nevertheless, sympathetic critics have contended that their approach is more about 'feeling than structure' (Walklate, 1998: 411) while others argue that to 'focus only on unconscious displacement tends to ignore both the conscious strategies and various circuits of communication' (Lupton and Tulloch, 1999: 515) adopted by their respondents. But replacing the rational, unitary subject with the anxious, fragmented subject need not dispense with a socially literate understanding of subjectivity. Instead, unconscious processes combine with cognitive choices as well as social structures, like language, so that these aspects of explanation are best seen as complementary rather than alternatives (Carrabine, 2008).

Yet it would be wrong to assume that people are constantly afraid – life would be unbearable if that were so – but rather the emotional intensity varies and we find imaginative ways of ignoring or adapting to precarious environments (Tuan, 1979: 9). As Walklate (2007a: 100) has succinctly put it, fear 'is not an ever present feeling or state of mind but burns differently in different contexts'. These different contexts will include our immediate social relations, broader external forces as well as our own anxious inner worlds, such that calls for a 'psychosocial criminology' (Jefferson, 2002a; Gadd and Jefferson, 2007) will involve a greater attention to emotional life than criminologists have conventionally been prepared to pay.

Hate crime

Perhaps one of the most explicit connections drawn between crime and a specific emotion in recent years concerns the emergence of the concept of 'hate crime' in the United States. The United States Federal Bureau of Investigation (FBI) defines hate crimes as offences that are 'motivated in part or singularly by personal prejudice against others because of a diversity – race, sexual orientation, religion, ethnicity/national origin, or disability'. While the term 'hate crime' is institutionalized in law in the United States – as in the Hate Crime Statistics Act 1990 – it has gradually become a site of legal intervention in Britain:

- The Crime and Disorder Act 1998 created a number of new racially and religiously aggravated offences;
- The Criminal Justice Act 2003 introduced tougher sentences for offences motivated by hatred of the victim's sexual orientation (this must now be taken into account by the sentencing court as an aggravating factor, in addition to race or religious hate motivation);
- The Racial and Religious Hatred Act 2006 has made it a criminal offence to use threatening words or behaviour with the intention of stirring up hatred against any group of people because of their religious beliefs or their lack of religious beliefs.

The term hate crime has been adopted by the Metropolitan Police Service (MPS), and other police services, as can be seen in Plate 12.3, and the media, and has become firmly established in popular discourse. It is contestable, however, whether 'hate crime' does in fact manifest hate.

For many people, the term hate crime arguably conjures up an image of a violent crime committed by extremists, by neo-Nazis, racist skinheads and other committed bigots – in other words, hate-fuelled individuals who subscribe to racist, anti-semitic, homophobic and other bigoted ideologies. It is not surprising that many people think this way about hate crimes, because

Plate 12.3 Campaign poster to combat hate crime.

Source: West Midlands Police.

the media focus on the most extreme incidents – as is the case with crime reporting in general. The murder of Stephen Lawrence in south London in 1993, and the subsequent media coverage of the young men suspected of the murder, and the racist views they expressed, provide a prime example. Other extreme incidents in Britain that quite understandably gained notoriety include the bombing in May 1999 of the Admiral Duncan, a 'gay pub' in Soho, London (Plate 12.4), in which three died and scores were injured. The young man convicted, David Copeland, had a history of involvement with racist organizations.

In the United States the brutality of the murder of James Byrd, an African American – who was beaten unconscious, chained to the back of a pick-up truck and dragged for miles along rural roads outside the town of Jasper, Texas, in June 1998 – attracted widespread media coverage. The brutality of the murder and the fact that the two perpetrators were members of a white supremacist organization evoked painful memories of **lynching** (see Box 12.2) and historical racial violence in the United States. The callousness of the attack on the young gay man Matthew Shepard, who was pistol-whipped and left lashed to a fence in freezing conditions to die later in hospital in Wyoming in October 1998, generated considerable debate about homophobic bigotry. The incident itself and its repercussions have been portrayed in the play and film *The Laramie Project*.

Two dead and 70 injured as Soho is rocked by blast

GAY BAR NAIL BOMB HORROR

By STEPHEN WRIGHT

TWO people died and 70 were injured when a nail bomb demolished a gay pub in Central London last night.

Plate 12.4 *Daily Mail* extract, 1 May 1999.

Source: extract © Atlantic Syndication; *photo:* David Gaywood.

BOX 12.2 The politics of lynching

Lynching is a form of extrajudicial punishment involving public torture revived in the Southern United States as a response to the perceived loss of white male domination in the nineteenth century. The passage of the Thirteenth Amendment (1865) outlawed slavery and with emancipation former slaves became 'African Americans'. It has been argued that it was 'through the process of Reconstruction, the Union attempted to restore relations with the Confederate states' (Messerscmidt, 2007: 81) and it is in this context white male mob violence quickly arose as an attempt to reassert old hierarchies. For example, in May 1866, forty-six African Americans were murdered when their schools and churches were set on fire by a white male mob in Memphis. Two months later, in July, thirty-four African Americans were killed in New Orleans at the hands of a white mob (Ayers, 1984).

The lynchings were explicitly violent and looked to ancient and medieval forms of aggravated death penalty, which included burning, castration, whipping as well as hanging. Indeed, the lynch mob insisted on punishments that were barbaric, and the fact that they would outrage liberal sensibility was all part of their appeal. They were deliberately racialized and the lynch victim was often sought out as retribution for the alleged rape of a white woman by an African-American man. The public lynching has been understood as a carnival critique of official criminal justice and total rejection of the law's commitment to equality while reasserting local understandings of caste superiority. As Garland (2007: 147) explains, public torture lynching communicated 'impassioned sentiments that could no longer be expressed in the official idiom of the criminal law' and inflicted 'a level of suffering that had long since been officially disavowed'. In Chapter 15 we will examine how punishment arouses powerful emotions that can appeal to cruel tendencies in the human condition.

Paul Iganski (2006) has demonstrated how the New Labour government's specific concerns over racially aggravated offences – influenced to some extent by US legislation and debate – has led to a gradual expansion of British law in this field, from race to religion, and also sexuality and disability. His account describes the many dilemmas surrounding such legislation: from the supporting arguments that crimes motivated by hate cause damage to the victim beyond the crime itself, that this additionally infects a wider community with fear and trauma, and constitutes an assault on the dominant values of society. Opponents criticize the legislation on the grounds that

- legislating against hate is indefensible as it suggests that hurting some kinds of people isn't quite as bad as hurting others (Jacoby, 2002);
- it is a totalitarian response to prejudice as it punishes 'thought crime' in Orwellian fashion (Phillips, 2002); and
- it treats equal crimes unequally, which goes against fundamental legal principles.

The thrill of it all?

Given the range of victims of hate crimes, the variety of offenders involved and the different social situations in which hate crimes occur, there can obviously be no single explanation, and in any one incident there may be a range of explanations. However, one thing does appear to stand out: many incidents seem to be committed *for the fun of it*, for the kicks, for the excitement, as well as for other reasons. According to Jack Levin and Jack McDevitt:

> Like young men getting together on a Saturday night to play a game of cards, certain hatemongers get together and decide to go out and destroy property or bash minorities. They want to have some fun and stir up a little excitement – at someone else's expense.

The payoff in such 'thrill-seeking hate crime', as Levin and McDevitt famously called it, is psychological as well as social:

> They enjoy the exhilaration and the thrill of making someone suffer. For those with a sadistic streak, inflicting pain and suffering is its own reward. In addition, the youthful perpetrators receive a stamp of approval from their friends who regard hatred and violence as 'hot' or 'cool'.

> (Levin and McDevitt, 2002: 67)

In a 'pick and mix' of bigotry, the victims of thrill-seeking hate crimes are often interchangeable.

Excitement is not the only emotion involved in so-called hate crime. Levin and McDevitt argue that resentment – to one degree or another – can be found in the personality of most hate crime offenders, and it takes many forms. There are individuals who, perhaps because of some personal misfortune, feel rejected by, estranged from and wronged by society. They look for someone to target in venting their anger.

For others, their bitterness is fuelled by a perceived or real threat to their economic security, and some strike at those they think are to blame: newcomers, immigrants, asylum seekers. Larry

Ray and colleagues, drawing on research based in Greater Manchester, argue that much of the violence is related to the sense of shame and failure, resentment and hostility felt by young men who 'are disadvantaged and marginalised economically and culturally, and thus deprived of the material basis for enacting a traditional conception of working-class masculinity'. Such emotions, according to Ray et al., 'readily lead to violence only in the case of young men (and occasionally for young women) for whom resorting to violence is a common approach to settling arguments and conflicts' (2003: 112).

Self-esteem, shame and respect

The significance of self-esteem in violent encounters has been explored by Thomas Scheff and his colleagues. From their perspective, 'self-esteem concerns how we usually feel about ourselves. High self-esteem means that we usually feel justified pride in ourselves, low self-esteem that we often and easily feel ashamed of ourselves or try to avoid feelings of shame' (Scheff et al., 1989: 178). They propose that 'shame' is a primary emotion generated by the constant, incessant but commonly unacknowledged monitoring and negative evaluation of self in the eyes of others. Shame, however, is generally unacknowledged, and as an emotion it is seen to be socially unacceptable.

Self-esteem, in short, is a 'summary concept', representing how well a person overall manages shame. People with high self-esteem have had sufficient experience of pride to outweigh their experience of shame; they can manage shame. However, when a person has had an insufficient experience of pride, then shame becomes a calamity for them. When they experience some form of humiliation, real or imagined, rather than acknowledging it, it is masked with anger. The person is then caught in a 'shame–rage feeling trap'. According to Scheff and colleagues,

> In our theory, rage is used as a defense against threat to self, that is, feeling shame, a feeling of vulnerability of the whole self. Anger can be a protective measure to guard against shame, which is experienced as an attack on self. As humiliation increases, rage and hostility increase proportionally to defend against loss of self-esteem.

In short, violence is the consequence of trapped shame and anger. Crucially, Scheff and colleagues further argue that

> Pride and shame states almost always depend on the level of deference accorded a person: pride arises from deferential treatment by others ('respect'), and shame from lack of deference ('disrespect'). Gestures that imply respect or disrespect, together with the emotional response they generate, make up the deference/emotion system, which exerts a powerful influence on human behavior.
>
> (Scheff et al., 1989: 184–5)

These arguments have also proven especially influential on the role of shame in restorative justice practices, where it is argued that the community conferences that lie at the heart of reintegrative shaming (see Box 12.3) work not so much through the words said but on facial

BOX 12.3 Reintegrative shaming

In his classic study *Crime, Shame and Reintegration* (1989), John Braithwaite emphasized the importance of the emotions in the restoration of justice between offenders, victims and the wider community. This work provided a powerful impetus to the 'restorative justice' movement in criminology and challenge to vindictive models of retributive punishment (described in more detail in Chapter 15). The book has decisively influenced studies of conflict, reconciliation and 'peace-making' as well as enabling accounts of the place of 'emotional work' in criminal justice institutions to emerge (e.g. Karstedt, 2002). His argument is that shaming the offence, and not the offender, will reintegrate the offender back into the community while giving victims a strong role in these reconciliation processes. Crucially, though, the agents of shaming are not the victims, but the family and friends of the offender so that shame integrates rather than alienates. As he famously put it, the 'best place to see reintegrative shaming at work is in loving families' (Braithwaite, 1989: 56).

Braithwaite's arguments are closely allied to Thomas Scheff's work on shame (which suggests that one of the central features of life is our search for honour and the ways in which shaming plays a role in that search). Shame is linked to taking on the role of 'the other' (cf. Mead, 1934), and links to the pangs of conscience when confronted with the possibility of wrongdoing. We want and need the social approval of others. Shaming involves all social processes expressing disapproval that have the aim of inducing remorse in the offender. For Braithwaite, the shame that matters most is not that coming from officials such as the police, judges, courts or even victims, but that from the people we care most about. It is not stigmatizing in so far as it is aimed not at the offender per se but at the act the offender commits; the ultimate aim must be reintegration and he contends that reintegrative shaming is effective in complex societies as well as more traditional ones.

It is significant that Braithwaite developed his arguments from accounts of indigenous procedures of 'conferencing' in New Zealand and Australia, where he found that these community settings successfully combined shaming and reintegration. Critics worry whether these processes will be used against the most vulnerable groups in society or deployed only for trivial offences while conventional, custodial punishments continue to expand. It has been noted how the model of reintegrative shaming developed in Australia and currently exported around the world is one principally targeted at Aboriginal youth, intensifying police controls over this already marginalized population (Blagg, 1997). More recent Australian research has suggested that 'net-widening' may be a problem, and that more marginalized young people (including non-Aboriginal) are channelled away from youth conferencing into a youth 'justice system more punitive in its sentencing' (Cunneen and White, 2006: 107). The idealization of the family at the heart of the approach has been criticized for its reliance on defining 'others *as* others' (Ahmed, 2004: 199; emphasis in original) – those who have failed to live up to this ideal social bond – like single mothers, queer relationships, and so forth. To be fair, Braithwaite has always recognized that shaming can be used tyrannically against unpopular minorities, but it is difficult to see how the communitarian politics that informs his thinking can oppose hostile collective sentiments when that is the community's will.

expressions, gestures and physical posture (Retzinger and Scheff, 1996). We now describe how the emotions are embodied in contemporary street cultures, where crime, hustling and violence have become a defining way of life for the ghetto poor.

Stories from the street

The issue of 'respect' is a key theme explored by Elijah Anderson in his book *Code of the Streets* (1999). He argues that for many inner-city youths in his study, a street culture has evolved, what he calls a code of the streets – a set of informal rules governing public behaviour and the use of violence. It can be traced to the sense of hopelessness and to the alienation that the youths feel from mainstream society and its institutions, due to the joblessness and the pervasive racism they experience.

'Respect' is 'at the heart of the code', according to Anderson. Respect is about 'being treated "right", or granted the deference one deserves'. But gaining and maintaining respect has to be a constant endeavour:

> In the street culture, especially among young people, respect is viewed as almost an external entity that is hard-won but easily lost, and so must constantly be guarded. The rules of the code in fact provide a framework for negotiating respect. The person whose very appearance – including his clothing, demeanor, and way of moving – deters trans-gressions, feels that he possesses, and may be considered by others to possess, a measure of respect. With the right amount of respect, for instance, he can avoid 'being bothered' in public. If he is bothered, not only may he be in physical danger but he has been disgraced or 'dissed'.
>
> (Anderson, 1994: 82)

One key aspect of a person's demeanour to convey and hold respect is 'having the juice': projecting an image, a willingness to resort to violence, having the nerve to throw the first punch, to pull the trigger and, in the extreme, not being afraid to die, and not being afraid of taking another's life if needs be, if someone 'gets in their face', if disrespected.

Respect is a scarce commodity. Deprived of achieving a sense of self-esteem through participation in the jobs market, and other institutions of mainstream society, 'everyone competes', according to Anderson,

> to get what affirmation he can of the little that is available. The craving for respect that results gives people thin skins. Shows of deference by others can be highly soothing, contributing to a sense of security, comfort, self-confidence, and self-respect. Transgressions by others which go unanswered diminish these feelings and are believed to encourage further transgressions. . . . Among young people, whose sense of self-esteem is particularly vulnerable, there is an especially heightened concern with being disrespected. Many inner-city young men in particular crave respect to such a degree that they will risk their lives to attain and maintain it.
>
> (1994: 89)

Similarly, Philippe Bourgois (1995) describes in his *In Search of Respect* how the street identity cultivated by men from East Harlem, which involved limited social skills, assumed gender arrogance and intimidating physical presence, made them virtually unemployable – often appearing clumsy and illiterate before prospective female supervisors in Manhattan's booming service sector economy.

In an important critique of the underclass thesis, Carl Nightingale's (1993) ethnography of the black Philadelphian ghetto maintains that the culture of the ghetto is not only a product of alienation and isolation but rather a consequence of the desperate embrace of the American Dream:

> Already at five and six, many kids in the neighborhood can recite the whole canon of adult luxury – from Gucci, Evan Piccone, and Pierre Cardin, to Mercedes and BMW . . . from the age of ten, kids become thoroughly engrossed in Nike's and Reebok's cult of the sneaker.
> (Nightingale, 1993:153–4)

In ways that have clear echoes of Albert Cohen's earlier subcultural theory, Nightingale is arguing that structural exclusion is accompanied by an over-identification with mainstream consumer culture. As he explains:

> Inner-city kids' *inclusion* in mainstream America's mass market has been important in determining those kids' responses to the economic and racial *exclusion* they face in other parts of their lives. And, indeed, kids' experiences of exclusion and of the associated painful memories has made their participating in mass culture particularly urgent and enthusiastic, for the culture of consumption has given them a seductive means to compensate for their feelings of failure.
> (Nightingale, 1993: 135; emphasis in original)

The disturbing ambivalence at the heart of America's race relations is also captured in Naomi Klein's (2000: 76) discussion of companies like Tommy Hilfiger, whose marketing strategy is based on 'selling white youth on their fetishization of black style, and black youth on their fetishization of white wealth'. Jock Young (2007a: 51) has recently argued that these ghetto studies suggest that we need 'to return to the two stigmas which the poor confront, that of relative deprivation (poverty and exclusion from the labour markets) and misrecognition (lower status and lack of respect)'. Both of these are forms of humiliation, each generating powerful dynamics of resentment.

Humiliation, rage and edgework

At the beginning of this chapter it was observed that crimes of passion have fuelled the artistic imagination. We now turn to such crimes and draw from Jack Katz's analysis of the interrelationship of emotion and crime in his book *Seductions of Crime* (1988). In the book Katz covers a range of criminal and deviant behaviour – the ways of the 'badass', the 'hardman', the 'cold-blooded killer' and white-collar criminal – but it is instructive to focus on cases of murder that Katz analyses using a variety of documentary sources. The incidents involving what Katz calls 'Righteous Slaughter' are impassioned acts committed in moments of rage – as is the case with many murders.

In the cases that Katz analyses, the victim-to-be inflicts a humiliation upon the killer-to-be: a wife caught by her husband in *flagrante* with another man; another tortured by her husband's infidelity; a man whose virility is challenged by his partner; a neighbour offended by another neighbour parking in front of their property. In each case, humiliation arises from the violation of a respected social role, such as husband, wife, virile male, property owner. The would-be killer's reaction to the humiliation, according to Katz's analysis, is 'a last stand defence of respectability'. Their mortal act is not calculated in a premeditated sense to restore their self-worth. It is instead experienced as a compulsion, driven by rage arising from the killer's emotional comprehension of the humiliation they have suffered.

Risk, excitement and routine

Jack Katz (1988) is drawing attention to the exciting, pleasurable and transgressive dynamics that are very much at the 'foreground' of criminal activity in an effort to critique the 'sentimental materialism' (as Katz, 1988: 313–17, terms it) of much liberal and radical criminology. British criminologists have also explored these issues. Roger Matthews (2002) in his study of armed robbers, for instance, notes how during his interviews it was usually when his respondents were describing the actual robberies that the attractions of the crime would become all too apparent. Similarly, Mike Collison's (1996) research on masculinities and crimes connects these ideas to cultural consumption, risk-taking and drug use. For example, burgling a house is an activity laced with excitement but it is also riddled with risk. One of the respondents in his study described the dual-edged thrill and danger of getting caught, assault by the homeowner, or the police, or later on the street by failing in front of male friends. As one 20-year-old put it: 'I always used to leave the room they was sleeping in till last . . . they never used to hear me for some reason . . . it was scary and exciting' (Collison, 1996: 443). Few stopped to calculate the risks but rather put their faith in a mystical sense of invincibility, or hope for a run of good luck, or sometimes used drugs to ease the risk. It is useful to contrast these accounts though with Tony Kearon and Rebecca Leach's (2000) discussion of burglary where they describe the intense feelings of abjection that many victims of house theft experience.

What seems to be particularly important here, in terms of doing crime, is that this kind of 'edgework' (Lyng, 1990a, 2004) is deeply satisfying and seductive. Edgework has been described as a form of 'experiental anarchy' that is an 'experience that is much more real than the circumstances of everyday experience'. One British 19-year-old explained to Collison (1996: 435) that 'what I really want to do like to occupy my time, I'd like to jump out of planes like that, that's exciting to me, I couldn't afford things like that . . . so I just pinch cars, get chases, do burglaries and enjoy myself that way'. It is important to recognize that while this edgework is an essential part of street life for underclass male youth, it also has routine features. For what comes across in all the narratives is how surprisingly ordinary this risk-taking is. But, and this is highly significant, these activities are not thought of in this way. They would be impossible to do if they were.

The important question here is why these activities are so exciting and seductive. In answering this question the crucial factor is drugs, not just in the sense of being able to 'get off your face' through Ecstasy, amphetamines and LSD, but that they form a defining part of the irregular economy in poor communities for expendable male youth in Collison's (1996) study. For young underclass men the promised land is on the TV, and it should come as no surprise to learn that their favourite film was *New Jack City*, while real life here 'stinks'. In contrast, the drug economy provides these young men with their only realistic chance of fast living and the high life in Britain. Drug crime, like other forms of street crime, creates a space for acting out predatory forms of masculinity. Street-level drug dealing, whether this is on the corner or watched on film, and the two are frequently conflated, promises action and status success. According to Collison (1996: 441) forms of predatory street crime and excessive lifestyle among some young underclass males are not a simple response to poverty, they are attempts to 'munch' their way through consumer society and fill in the spaces of structure and identity, or in other words, to get a 'reputation as mad'.

Summary

1   Criminology has an important role to play in showing how the emotions shape our inner lives and broader social practices.
2   Fear and anxiety are central characteristics of modern living.
3   Human emotions play a central role in the criminal act.
4   The study of the emotional dynamics of crime illuminates why certain crimes occur.
5   The emotions can restore justice between offenders, victims and the wider community.

Critical thinking questions

1   Why have the emotions been marginalized in Western thought?
2   Why is 'fear of crime' an ill-defined term?
3   Why might 'hate crime' legislation be a totalitarian response to prejudice?
4   How could the arguments outlined in this chapter help us understand phenomena like 'road rage', 'lynch mobs' and 'queer bashing'?
5   What are the seductions of crime?
6   How does the 'search for respect' reproduce exclusion in North American ghettoes?

Further study

Anderson, E. (1999) *Code of the Streets: Decency, Violence and the Moral Life of the Inner City*, New York: W. W. Norton. A highly illuminating ethnographic exploration of the social and cultural dynamics of interpersonal violence in the inner city.

Bauman, Z. (2006) *Liquid Fear*, Cambridge: Polity. One of the most original sociological thinkers casts his eye over the fears and anxieties that haunt our current age.

Gadd, D. and Jefferson, T. (2007) *Psychosocial Criminology: An Introduction*, London: Sage. A lively demonstration of how a psychosocial approach sheds new light on the causes of many crimes, as well as challenging readers to rethink the similarities and differences between themselves and offenders.

Iganski, P. (2008) *'Hate Crime' and the City*, Bristol: Policy Press. A wide-ranging account analysing how we understand and ought to respond to crimes motivated by prejudice in the UK.

Katz, J. (1988) *Seductions of Crime: Moral and Sensual Attractions of Doing Evil*, New York: Basic Books. An indispensable analysis of the sensual and emotional dynamics of crime.

Levin, J. and McDevitt, J. (2002) *Hate Crimes Revisited: America's War on Those Who Are Different*, Boulder, CO: Westview. An invaluable evaluation of the social, cultural, motivational and policy context of hate and crime.

More information

American Psychological Association: 'Hate Crimes Today: An Age-Old Foe in Modern Dress'
http://www.apa.org/pubinfo/hate/homepage.html
A question-and-answer site shedding some clarification on the hate crime debate.

Hate Crime.org
http://www.hatecrime.org/
Information and links to related news articles concerning current events, political choices, and victims and further information.

National Gay and Lesbian Task Force: information on hate crime laws
http://www.nglft.org/issues/issue.cfm?issueID=12
NGLTF is the national progressive organization working for the civil rights of gay, lesbian, bisexual and transgender people.

Crime reduction
http://www.crimereduction.homeoffice.gov.uk/toolkits/fc00.htm
A typical Home Office site offering advice and information on how to tackle fear and disorder in the community.

Organizational and Professional Forms of Crime

Key issues

- How easy is it to define and understand different forms of crime concerned with the pursuit of power and profit?

- What kinds of activity have been engaged in by professional criminals in financial crime?

- In what ways do the legitimate and illegitimate worlds of enterprise overlap?

Introduction

Various chapters of this book look at forms of crime where the emphasis is largely on the individual as criminal or victim (and sometimes both) and at locations of criminality and victimization, all of which are 'everyday' and generally occurring in the home or on the street.

This chapter is concerned with forms of crime originating with or enabled by the organizational and professional frameworks and status that perpetrators can draw upon. Different areas or worlds of activity, motives and consequences are identified and discussed – although it should become apparent that there is blurring and overlap between these categories. Broadly, this chapter covers:

- crime in the world of illegal enterprise – crime as an illegal profession;
- crime in the world of lawful professions – crime as abuse of legal professional status and resources;
- crime in the world of corporate-level business and commerce – crime as subversion or inversion of good corporate behaviour, producing negligence and/or illegality.

A final note before proceeding. As with so many other topics in this book, the range of possible issues and examples that could be covered here is enormous and all that can be provided is an indicative exploration.

Thinking about organizational and professional crime

In beginning to think about these rather different forms of crime, we are now talking about offending or deviance committed by or within organized structures, groups or associations. This is not to say we are concerned here only with 'criminal organizations', for clearly, individual employees or the self-employed commit crime at work or even engage in crime as their work. Certainly it is a mistake to assume that only those stereotypically perceived as 'criminals' or officially labelled as such commit criminal offences – as Karstedt and Farrall (2007: 1–2) have found:

> There is an area of criminal activity at the very core of contemporary society . . . committed by people who think of themselves as respectable citizens and who would certainly reject the label of 'criminal' for themselves. Politicians refer to them as the 'law-abiding majority', ignoring the fact that the majority do not abide by the law, or at least are highly selective about when to and when not to comply.

Indeed, in the UK as elsewhere in the world, politicians are among those professionals, such as lawyers, health care specialists, bankers and others, who have been known to abuse their positions of trust and authority.

While bearing all this in mind, this chapter takes as the criteria for inclusion forms of crime that involve one or more of the following:

- a commitment to crime as a full-time activity – crime as a profession – working closely or loosely with others in criminal or legitimate networks;
- a benefit from and/or abuse of a professional and/or trusted position of some seniority or status – following from being an employee in an organization and/or recognition of qualifications by professional or other bodies (e.g. providing validation of specialist competence);
- a temporary or long-standing criminal association or organization for the pursuit of profit and/or power;
- a business or corporation that in part or whole 'goes wrong' and engages in crime or has actually been established as a legal organizational 'front' for criminal activity.

The case of 'everyday crime' at work, such as pilferage and fiddles, sometimes referred to as 'hidden economy' or 'blue-collar crime', is discussed elsewhere (see Chapter 10; Mars, 2006).

Self-evidently, certain forms of crime depend on features of an organization – for example, planning, coordination, concealment, group membership and hierarchy. This applies to diverse examples of crime: for example, a 'project crime' (McIntosh, 1975) such as the raid on the Securitas cash depot in Kent in February 2006 when criminals posing as police officers kidnapped the depot manager and his family, tied up fifteen staff members and made off with up to £50 million in cash; or the coordinated concealment of financial mismanagement, misappropriation and fraud, as in the case of the international energy giant Enron and the subsequent wave of financial scandals, to be dealt with later in this chapter. Other crimes may seem to be tied to individual activity – for example, the fraudulent lawyer or doctor – but when examined can be seen to rely on factors such as: the exploitation of systems, organizations and professional standing that all insulate the individual from suspicion or scrupulous investigation; abuse of trust and qualifications bestowed and supposedly guaranteed by professional associations; and victimization of clients and customers of services that are being offered.

Numerous studies have highlighted characteristics common to both illegitimate and legitimate profit-oriented organizations. These include:

- entrepreneurialism
- risk-taking
- rule-breaking
- specialist division of labour
- investment strategies
- managing evasion of unwelcome regulation
- avoidance of harmful scrutiny or control
- manipulation of financial systems and loopholes to avoid tax liabilities.

It can help to clarify what this chapter is focusing on if we note briefly what is excluded here. For example, youth crime may involve gangs and other more or less 'organized' groups (Wright, 2006; Hobbs, 1997; Newburn, 2002a; South, 1999a). However, the nature of organization in such cases is, in Britain at least, generally of a short-lived, immature and non-elaborated form. Where more complex structures do emerge, these may provide socialization into more established crime groups. These are readily seen as professional crime associations involved in control of territory for power and profit, and in illegal activity such as drug importation and dealing. In cases such as these, at least some of the characteristics listed above will apply, and indeed the tradition of study of youth gangs from Thrasher (1927) onwards has been partly typified by the search for the forms of structure and value systems that sustain involvement of certain youth in gangs, delinquency and crime (see Chapter 5) leading to criminal careers (Foster, 1990: 165; South, 1999a). On the other side of the criminal justice fence, the incidence of crime and deviance in organizational contexts such as the police and prisons is important to note here, but it has simply made sense to refer to such crime – for example, corruption – in the chapters on these particular topics.

Crime in the world of illegal enterprise

Professional crime was seen by Sutherland (1937: 197) as based upon a craft that had been learned, and it was this achievement that defined the 'professional' thief (or safecracker or forger or whatever) as someone who had learned their trade and, like 'physicians, lawyers or bricklayers' (ibid.), developed a variety of abilities and skills. (Here we can see elements of learning theory and Sutherland's idea of differential association; see p. 78.) Of course, as many critics have pointed out, this is simply too neat and offers a rather romanticized notion of a career in crime, which in fact may provide little or no opportunity to learn skills or develop any expertise in a particular field of crime (Hobbs, 1994: 441; Ruggiero and South, 1995: 129–32). Nonetheless, the important point in Sutherland's work on 'the professional thief 'was to draw attention to the idea of 'full-time crime'.

As Hobbs (1994: 444) notes, 'the practice of crime as a full time occupation can be traced to the decline of the feudal system in England, and to the need for those leaving the land to develop alternative forms of economic subsistence within the context of urbanization and the emergence of capitalism' (Roebuck and Windham, 1983). Full-time miscreants (Mack, 1964) were established in major metropolitan areas by the eighteenth century as the areas of the rich and the poor grew, and did so in ever-sharpening contrast. The business of the fence – a buyer and seller of stolen goods – was then, as now, a staple of the irregular and illegal economy of the city (Klockars, 1975; Sutton, 1998). Other forms of 'crime as business' were carried out by individualist criminal entrepreneurs or criminal 'firms' (Hobbs, 1988) – frauds, counterfeiting, robbery – but there are no signs in the history of British crime of large-scale organization and the comments by Low (1982: 195; Hobbs, 1994) concerning the underworld of Regency England are still largely applicable today: '[T]here were some big criminal entrepreneurs, but on the whole the criminal underworld was not organized, or even much influenced by its leading citizens: fortunately for the rest of society it remained essentially a community of small operators.'

In Britain today, criminal 'organizations' are probably more accurately described as semi-formal or informal associations of professional criminals (relatively small gangs, groups and networks) that remain small to medium-scale in the size and scope of their operations. They have been and remain subject to considerable flux and change in terms of membership and goals (Hobbs, 1995, 1997; Dorn et al., 1992; Campbell, 1991). Nonetheless, it is, of course, the distinction of exhibiting some form of organizational capacity and modus operandi that means they are being discussed here and are the target of increasingly well-resourced and strategically directed policing agencies that are investing in better intelligence and smarter thinking to match the characteristics of modern organized crime.

> Criminal networks are becoming more fluid, extended and flexible, in part due to the use of specialist 'service providers' to assist with money laundering, logistics, documents, and other enablers. Meanwhile, the increased availability of information technology has both facilitated various crimes and spawned new forms of criminal activity.
>
> (SOCA, 2006/7)

Naturally, this complexity extends to the ways in which organized forms of crime have developed and operate in other countries and it would be foolish to believe that there is any kind of universal model. Indeed, a study of forty criminal groups in sixteen nations carried out by the United Nations Centre for International Crime Prevention (2000) found very different phenomena, quite different to the popular images of structured hierarchies and more in line with SOCA's view, exhibiting relatively loose structures based on dynamic and flexible networks.

Professional organized crime in Britain, 1930s–2000

The roots of modern professional organized crime in Britain lie in the 'hard man' gang culture of major cities such as Glasgow, Liverpool, Leeds, Birmingham and Newcastle (Freeman, 1996–7), the resilience of the illegal economies that prospered within but also assisted communities of poverty and marginality, and the enduring structure of the 'traditional neighbourhood family firm' (Hobbs, 2001; Samuel, 1981; Foster, 1990; Lea, 2002). In addition, social and population changes during and after the First World War were important: the dislocation of war in Europe brought refugees to Britain, some of whom settled into the criminal economies of survival and illegal opportunity; the old system of social class status, difference and deference was being eroded; and new opportunities for crime were emerging. Kohn (1992) explores these themes in relation to the emergence of subcultures of drugs and crime in the early twentieth century. However, as was the case with alcohol **Prohibition** in the United States from 1920 to 1933 and with the market for illegal drugs later in the century (see Chapter 14), where there is a prohibition of a commodity or service for which there is a demand, then an illegal supply, or the scope for corruption, will emerge (Nadelman, 1990). In Britain in the 1920s and 1930s, it was not the prohibition of alcohol sales but the illegality of street gambling, with resulting high profits for the bookmakers who could legally take bets at racecourses, that drew the attention of criminal groups (Campbell, 1994: 22). As Hobbs describes, 'These gangs operated several forms of protection racket. The gangs controlled the pitches, renting them at extortionate prices to the on-course bookmakers. . . . Fights were deliberately started if payment was slow and non-repayable loans were demanded. Profits were enormous' (Hobbs, 1994: 450).

The Second World War created the conditions for further social change but also reinforced the national experience and defining mentality of 'the British Isles' as something to be preserved against evil from elsewhere – a characteristic contributing to popular perceptions of organized crime. Specifically in relation to crime in this period, while community spirit and patriotism are seen as having helped Britain through 'the dark days of the Blitz' and the threat of invasion, a contrasting spirit of opportunism and profiteering was also evident, and illegal markets grew up around minor fiddling of ration allowances and a significant trade in 'state-controlled goods or commodities that were in short supply' (Hobbs, 1994: 450). With the extension of rationing into the 1950s, 'competent criminals . . . found that the post-war market hardly differed from its wartime equivalent' (ibid.).

However, it was London in the late 1950s and the 1960s that became the location and period most associated with a high-profile 'gangland' in Britain, epitomized by the operations of the Kray brothers in the East End of London and the Richardson gang south of the river Thames (Pearson, 1973; Morton, 1992). The Krays cultivated celebrity and were photographed with show-business and sporting friends at charity events and at clubs in which they had an interest; the Richardsons had legitimate business dealings in scrap metal and illegitimate expertise in long firm fraud (Levi, 1981; and see Box 13.1), and were spreading their business interests beyond London before their arrest. But even so, at the end of the day, none of this was 'organized crime' on a grand scale.

Plate 13.1 The hearse containing the body of the infamous gangster Reggie Kray arrives at Chingford cemetery, having travelled some 12 miles through London's East End past crowds of well-wishers, 11 October 2000. Kray was buried alongside his brother Ronnie to bring to a close a final chapter in the history of the London hardmen who were both imprisoned for murder in 1968.

Source: © Reuters 2000; *photo:* Jonathan Evans.

BOX 13.1 Long firm fraud

In a long firm fraud, the fraudsman simply sets up in business as a wholesaler, and places orders with suppliers with the intention of evading payment.

Initially payment is prompt in order to establish creditworthiness. Then larger orders are placed. When delivered, the goods are promptly sold for what they will fetch.

Primary objectives of a long firm fraud

- To establish credibility with manufacturers and suppliers.
- To obtain as many goods as possible over a credit period extended as long as possible.
- To make little or no payment to suppliers and creditors.
- To dispose of goods obtained with the minimum of delay.
- Abscond with the proceeds.
- Avoid identification and prosecution.

Source: Merseyside Police, Crime Prevention: Business Advice
http://www.merseyside.police.uk/html/crimeprevention/business/fraud/long-firm.htm

In the 1960s and 1970s, affluence, consumerism, changing morality and new technologies expanded opportunities for criminal development and exploitation of various markets. Pornography, the counterfeiting of goods and VAT fraud were attractive and carried fewer risks than crimes such as armed robbery (Campbell, 1991). But the age of the criminal entrepreneur really arrived with the 1980s and the political promotion of a 'culture of enterprise' by the Conservative government of Margaret Thatcher (Hobbs, 1991). This is not to say that the market ideology of the new brand of conservatism 'caused' criminal enterprise, but many commentators agree that this was a period of significance in the reorientation of national values and the promotion of materialism. Suddenly, the wheeling and dealing culture of young men 'on the make' was a popular value system to aspire to, and markets – both legal and illegal – received a boost, domestically and internationally. Although women were also high achievers in this culture of aspiration, the impact in relation to crime was largely (though not exclusively – see the example below) a masculine matter (Newburn and Stanko, 1994; Messerschmidt, 1993; and see Chapter 14). While it was the so-called Big Bang of government-imposed deregulation in the financial operations of the City of London that changed the environment for business crime (see Carrabine *et al.*, 2002: 97; I. Taylor, 1999), the big bang that fuelled the new crime economy was undoubtedly the drugs 'explosion' of the 1980s (Dorn and South, 1987; and see Chapter 14). The central commodities here were heroin and cannabis, then later cocaine, Ecstasy, LSD and amphetamines. In turn, the drugs economy has had its own influence on the global legal economy and its institutions (Castells, 1998; and see Chapter 7).

Writing at the end of the 1980s, the crime reporter Duncan Campbell (1991: 8) suggested that

> In a way, what has happened to British crime parallels what has happened to British industry. The old family firms . . . have been replaced by multinationals of uncertain ownership, branches throughout the world, profits dispersed through myriad outlets. . . . The 1990s [was] seen as a boom time for them, with the exploitation of a recreational western culture that wants its luxuries and its drugs. The legitimate businesses will run alongside the illegitimate ones.

Arguably this picture still holds. Some of the reminiscences of criminals such as safebreakers and thieves, recounted by Hobbs (1995), illustrate a world based on 'traditional' criminal crafts and skills that largely disappeared alongside a world in which manufacturing thrived and people worked in the same trades from generation to generation. The sharp contrast of the old with the new breed of criminal specialists is nicely relayed by the case of the 'female drug dealer who dresses smartly, uses a mobile phone and would not look out of place in a merchant bank or city finance house. Looking smart is part of her business method and she uses her gender to "fool" clients and police officers, who assume that as an attractive woman she is less competent' (Croall, 1998: 240; Hobbs, 1995: 25).

Ethnicity, outsiders and the organization of crime

The study of organized crime as a business pursuing profit and power has been largely dominated by US research. Until as late as the 1980s this was greatly preoccupied with the operations and threat of the US Mafia or Sicilian Cosa Nostra and with themes such as the dangers of conspiracy and subversion from within US society with links to external 'alien' roots. Prior to the fall of the Soviet Union, the twin threats of communism and organized crime obviously shared a high profile, although interestingly, throughout the period of the Cold War, J. Edgar Hoover, Director of the FBI, felt the former to be the greater threat. The classic, highly influential work on the Mafia as a highly organized and stratified empire of crime, spanning the United States from coast to coast, was Donald Cressey's (1969) *Theft of the Nation*. However, this portrayal has been seriously questioned and the evidence upon which Cressey drew is now seen as discredited, as it relied heavily on the testimony of one key source whose reliability is doubted. This image of a Mafia empire dominated by the dons of major crime families was frequently depicted by the image (still used in newspaper graphics today) of an 'octopus of crime' with a controlling head and tentacles spreading out and embracing the nation (or the globe). In fact, much subsequent criminological research and law-enforcement intelligence have demonstrated the mythical nature of this creature and instead emphasized the diversity of cooperating and competing criminal organizations – sometimes referred to as 'disorganized crime' (Reuter, 1984). This reconceptualization does not suggest that such criminal groups do not exist or that they are incompetent or lacking in organizational skills or structures. Rather, it simply emphasizes a more realistic picture of the mixed and fragmentary character of the criminal economy than is provided by images of monolithic and monopolistic criminal conspiracies.

Since the 1960s and accelerating since the 1980s, other criminal networks and associations have been identified as operating on their own home territory and globally. So the picture of **global** organized crime groups now includes not only the well-known Mafia but also Colombian and Mexican cartels, Nigerian criminal networks, Japanese Yakuza, Chinese Triads, Russian Mafiyas, Jamaican Posses, and others (Castells, 1998: ch. 3; Southwell, 2002; Paoli, 2003; Galeotti, 2003; Hill, 2003; Booth, 2001). Importantly, whatever form it takes, 'organized crime' is therefore easily seen as a threat from beyond national borders, and reactions can be strongly fuelled by national anxieties and prejudices. For Britain this point is worth further consideration.

Historically, although some crime groups such as the Sabini family were successful in the racetrack and then the greyhound, drinking and gambling businesses during the years from 1910 to the Second World War (Hobbs, 1994: 450), in general there has been little sign of 'alien threat'. Maltese gangsters attracted some police and newspaper notoriety in the 1950s, and attempts by figures with American Mafia connections to move into the legalized gambling industry in Britain in the 1960s were effectively stamped on by the police and Home Office. Indeed, part of the celebrity of the Krays and the Great Train Robbers of 1963 was that in the 'swinging sixties', when English culture was seen as exciting and breaking the mould, here were distinctive examples of a 'home-grown' 'underworld' taking on 'the establishment' on their own terms. All this struck a popular chord (Campbell, 1994: 134; Carrabine *et al.*, 2002: 87–8).

Since the 1970s and 1980s, however, multi-ethnic Britain has produced criminal groups based on its own diverse ethnic communities, although, as Ruggiero (2000) and others have shown, 'contrary to alien conspiracy theories the "outsiders" do not change the society. Rather the society and its existing structures provide the opportunities for crime and deviance, as well as the accompanying motivations and rationalizations' (Carrabine *et al.*, 2002: 90). The extent to which ties into ethnic communities translate into international criminal operations or conspiracies is complex and debatable. On the one hand, Stelfox (1998: 400), a detective superintendent in the Greater Manchester Police, notes:

> Evidence given to the Home Affairs Committee on Organized Crime (1994) suggests that locally based criminals in the UK are unlikely to be members of any international organized crime group. At most some gangs from ethnic communities will belong to local variations of traditional crime groups from their country of origin. . . . They may acquire the name of a traditional crime group through a process of labelling by the community, the media or the police, or they may adopt it themselves as a way of enhancing their status in the community. But the use of a name such as Triad, does not necessarily imply an operational connection with an organized crime group.

And in relation to one of the most notorious but probably most misused labels for black criminal groups – the Yardies – Stelfox (1998: 400) remarks that this term

> is often used as though it was the name of an organized crime group such as the Mafia or the Cosa Nostra. However it originated as the name given to criminals in Jamaica. Latterly it has come to be used as a description for any Afro-Caribbean criminal involved in drugs distribution but does not refer to any single group which could be considered as an organized crime group.

As Stelfox notes, to be identified by law enforcers as a dangerous force may serve the interests of a criminal group. At the same time this can also serve the interests of resource-hungry law-enforcement agencies keen to draw attention to the seriousness of the challenges they face.

Organized crime as local and global

As Hobbs (1998) indicates, it is increasingly the case that even the most localized crime group can connect to the global stage (whether dealing in commodities from elsewhere or seeking to move profits out of the country), while 'current research indicates that even the classic "international" criminal organizations function as interdependent *local* units' (ibid.: 419; emphasis added). Hence, today we must consider at least some, though not all, forms of organized crime activity in terms of both local dimensions (e.g. 'doing the job', distributing 'the goods') and international connections and resources (e.g. overseas demand for stolen works of art, for drugs such as Ecstasy produced in the UK, for wildlife items – rare animals, birds, eggs; or overseas banks, lawyers, accountants and others that can help to launder profits or disguise the provenance of stolen goods). While a 'local' criminal project such as a raid on a warehouse or a lorry hijacking can still be seen as a familiar kind of venture, we also begin to see the complexity of the late modern criminal economy. We can give some sense of this 'big picture' in the following way.

Following the organized terrorism attack on the World Trade Center in 2001, President Bush announced (on 24 September 2001) the intention of the United States to 'choke off' the sources of funding for terrorist groups by seizing or freezing their assets. This was a strong and easy political soundbite to make. However, if such a strategy is to be effective beyond the governmental borders of the United States, then it has to involve the banking systems of other countries because these are twenty-four-hour, globally interlocking and mutually interdependent structures. This point may seem to take us into the territory of political crime and the financial criminals who help hide funds and indeed it does. But it is also a further reminder of the idea of 'glocalization'. Put simply, this is the proposition that the local matters to the global and vice versa. Leaving aside the specific nature of terrorist groups (we could talk instead of the assets of illegal arms traders, pornography distributors, drug traffickers, etc.) we need to recognize the enormous scale of the movement of murky money at the global level. The question that follows is, where do these criminal profits come from? The following passage is taken from a report on money laundering prepared for the United Nations. It illustrates the interlocking global complexity and 'glocalized' nature of late modern criminal economies as well as the kinds of links and chains that transform illicit cash from the street into digital transactions on the legal, electronic financial markets:

> Sweatshops in big cities in the industrialized countries hire illegal aliens who are brought in by smuggling groups that may also deal in banned or restricted commodities, are financed by loan sharks who may be recycling drug money and make cartel agreements with trucking companies run by organized crime families, all in order to sell their goods cheaply to prestigious and eminently respectable retail outlets that serve the general public. The masses of street peddlers in the big urban centres of developing countries sell goods that might be smuggled, produced in underground factories using fake brand-name labels or stolen from legitimate enterprises, thereby violating customs, intellectual property and larceny laws. They pay no sales or income taxes but make protection payments to drug gangs that control the streets where they operate. The drug gangs might then use the protection money as operating capital to finance whole-scale purchases of drugs or arms.
>
> (Blum et al., 1998)

While financial crime and money laundering have continued regardless of new efforts aimed at control, there has probably been some stimulation of other forms of criminal enterprise as a result. According to one analyst of the growing shadow economy of counterfeit goods,

> The counterfeiting trade exploded in 2001 due to the terrorist attacks. Tightened banking regulations meant it was harder for criminals to store cash, so reinvesting it in a cash-generative business like counterfeiting makes sense. The War on Terror changed priorities in law enforcement, diverting attention away from 'harmless' crimes like counterfeiting and focusing Customs inspectors' attention on other threats.
>
> (Phillips, 2005, 2006)

Fake fashion is a good example of how the apparently innocuous – a nice but cheap piece of designer-label clothing from a market or temporary shop – connects to the local and global illegal and exploitative transactions underpinning the criminal economies described by Blum et al.

BOX 13.2 Counterfeit crime and the fake fashion economy

■ Counterfeiting is a huge business – possibly 7 per cent or more of world trade according to Phillips (2006) and other sources (e.g. OSCE – the Organisation for Security and Cooperation in Europe) – with transnational movement of illegal goods and cash, involving China, Taiwan, countries around the Mediterranean, all the way to sweatshops and factories doing 'work on the side' in many parts of the UK.

■ It can involve exploited slave labour or high-tech pattern theft and copying.

■ It has consequences for the legal workforce, undercutting prices and leading to loss of jobs (the majority being women in the clothing and fashion accessory industries), affects the profits of producers and investors which can damage confidence in the economy – knock-offs have knock-on effects.

■ It is hard to detect – many people like to have a 'designer label' item even though they know it is a fake, others who have been fooled are reluctant to acknowledge this and complain.

■ It is hard to prosecute – intellectual property rights are often at the core of the problem of what – if anything – has been stolen; the rights to designs and patterns, etc., have to be established and proven to be the subject of 'theft'.

Crime in the world of lawful professions

The American criminologist Edwin Sutherland was notable not only for his work on the idea of the professional criminal, but even more so for his elaboration of the idea of 'white-collar crime'. Sutherland first drew attention to this important concept in his address to the American Sociological Society in 1939, published the following year (Weisburd *et al.*, 2001: 1–26). It is widely acknowledged that this was a major insight both theoretically and politically, and indeed it was once even suggested that were a Nobel Prize awarded for criminology, Sutherland would have been a worthy recipient for this contribution (Nelken, 1994a: 361). However, dispute around definitions arose almost straightaway. For a start, Tappan (1947) criticized Sutherland for attaching the term 'crime' to a variety of activities that did not necessarily break any criminal laws. To some extent this was, of course, Sutherland's point: the criminal law focuses downward on the poor, marginal and powerless, not upward on the affluent, mainstream and powerful. Yet the respectable middle and upper classes can engage in business and professional activities that can be far more financially or physically injurious to others, and with wider repercussions, than the offences for which working-class criminals are prosecuted and convicted. Furthermore, a factor of even greater importance for Sutherland (1949: 13) was that the crimes of respectable professionals violate the trust that society places in them: 'The financial loss from white-collar crime, great as it is, is less important than the damage to social relations. White-collar crimes violate trust and therefore create distrust: this lowers morale and produces social disorganization.'

Defining and identifying 'crimes' of the powerful

The application of the term 'crime' here is a signal about what may indeed not be legally 'criminal' but arguably should be, given its far-reaching seriousness. This is a tradition that has continued in critical criminology and does not mean that writers are ignorant of the law when they refer to, for example, the 'crimes' of the powerful (Pearce, 1976; Tombs and Whyte, 2003; and see Chapter 6) but rather that they are drawing attention to biases in the law-making and criminal justice systems (Reiman, 2001). Such biases, and the incidence of hidden crimes of the powerful they disguise, remain highly controversial within criminology and related policy debates. Some writers have called for local and national crime surveys to include coverage of business crimes, consumer victimization and similar experiences (Tombs, 2000) and argued that methodological problems can be addressed. However, as others, such as Spalek (2007: 7), have pointed out:

> there is little political incentive to include white collar offences in the British Crime Survey as their inclusion would mean an increase in the overall level of 'crime' and vicitimisation recorded. This would place pressure on politicians to tackle this large area of social injustice, an area that . . . has traditionally attracted minimal state regulation since this has been viewed as imposing too many costs on business.
>
> (Snider, 2000)

One of the purposes of accruing power is to gain the privileges that it brings when used. In the case of crime and criminal justice, the use of power can redraw the line of legality and acceptability in the interests of some but not others and privilege their position so they stand above investigation and prosecution.

Definitions and breadth

A further definitional problem arises in relation to what Sutherland was actually including in his idea of 'white-collar crime'. As Nelken (1994a: 362) has pointed out, Sutherland's original concept

> is built on the *overlap* of (at least) three different types of misbehaviour (crimes). The first refers to any crime committed by a person of high status (whether or not in the course of their occupation); the second to crimes committed on behalf of organizations (by people of any status); and the third to crimes committed against organizations (whether or not these are carried out by people working in the same organization, another organization, or no organization at all). Sutherland focuses on that *area of overlap in which people of high status use organizations to commit crimes for their organizations* – against workers, consumers, or other organizations including competitors and the government. [emphasis added]

In general, this area of 'overlap' (italicized in the preceding quotation) is useful as a guide to the discussion in this and the next section, but here we also focus on crimes committed by 'high-status' criminals on their own behalf. It is clearly wise to bear in mind the difficulty criminologists have had in providing hard-and-fast distinctions between white-collar and corporate criminality. It is also not entirely clear where all these definitional problems place those working within the public sector, for example, civil servants and politicians within the offices of national and local government. Here, too, professionals qualified as specialists in law, management, medicine, accountancy, and so on, work with autonomy and discretion, and with similar opportunities to their commercial-sector counterparts to connive at corrupt practices and derive benefits from fraud, bribery, theft and malpractice. Furthermore, in the world of 'politics as a profession', Cohen (1996b: 11) reminds us that the one thing as old as political power is political corruption:

> [T]he post-Watergate era has seen a quite unprecedented and uninterrupted series of public scandals about corrupt government in Western democracries. . . . In some cases, criminal activities (bribery, corruption, embezzlement, theft) were used for personal greed, in others for party political gain, in yet others to subvert basic and constitutional rules.

One Secretary-General of Interpol, Cohen notes, has remarked that 'it is becoming difficult to draw a clear line between what he called "normal" political business corruption and hard core, organized crime activity' (ibid.).

Of course, just because the criminological debate about the concept of white-collar crime is generally dated back to Sutherland's work does not mean that such crime was previously unknown! The business boom of Victorian England produced early versions of the banking frauds and stock swindles that became familiar in the 1980s (Robb, 1992). Further, from the nineteenth century onwards, the growth of commerce, of bureaucratic methods of organization and administration, of offices and their practices and technologies of accounting and filing, and of divisions of labour, all produced the infrastructure and conditions for the successful running of capitalism but also for the increasing diversity of criminal opportunity (Karstedt et al., 2006).

Crime and the professions

We expect to be able to trust professionals, and this is the basis on which we 'entrust' them with our finances, our health, our security and personal information, or give permission to them to act upon our behalf in all manner of intimate ways and relationships. As mentioned, Sutherland noted the damaging consequences of the abuse of trust as a key feature of white-collar crime and it is worth considering how these and other effects follow from examples of such crime.

The following discussion of some areas of professional practice illustrates both common themes within, and specific examples of, the criminality of trusted professionals. We can do no more than be indicative here and readers should remember two important points about what follows. First, we are not arguing that crime in the professions is so prolific that 'you can't trust anybody these days' (although this is a fairly common saying!). Second, however, we do emphasize that we are not just talking about 'a few bad apples', and the cases cited here should not be assumed to be extreme scenarios. As with the long history of police misconduct and corruption, we are talking about crimes and deviance that are largely hidden but quite widespread and deeply damaging.

Bankers as criminals

As Rawlinson (1998: 356) puts it,

> when money becomes a commodity in itself, subject to the vagaries of the market, banks find themselves caught up in the same competitive battles as other enterprises. Attracting customers becomes crucial, provoking banks into a less discerning concern over the quality of clients during straitened times.

The classic case of an outwardly legitimate and successful large-scale enterprise that actually harboured a wide range of illicit activity is that of the international but partly London-based Bank of Credit and Commerce International (BCCI) (Passas, 1995; Croall, 1998: 282–3; Punch, 1996). To operate as a criminal organization required the knowing involvement of many banking personnel, and the Governor of the Bank of England subsequently described BCCI as dominated by a 'criminal culture', although, as Spalek (2001) points out, the victims of the conspiracy also included numerous employees. Those who were part of the conspiracy reaped high profits, with the losers being ordinary savers and some commercial and public body investors who lost the funds of shareholders and taxpayers. Croall (1998: 282) notes that

> at his trial, one of the participants, Abbas Ghokal, was said to have run up a £795 million debt to the bank and to have been involved with a series of swindles, false documents, and a sham financial structure which funded his lavish lifestyle.

But BCCI is perhaps only the most prominent example of banking crime, and notable of course because its activities were exposed. Other financial institutions, such as those operating in tax havens like the Channel Islands, the Cayman Islands, Lichtenstein and elsewhere, offer services to those who wish to remove their funds from the attention of tax and other authorities and may make few enquiries and little distinction between 'clean' and 'dirty' money.

The case of Nick Leeson is probably at the other end of the scale of criminal ambition, for it was not Leeson's intention to criminally bankrupt Barings Bank, but this is what he managed to do by his uncontrolled dealing on the Singapore stock market and the consequences that emerged in 1995. Leeson's criminality lay in his concealment of enormous mounting losses and, as with a gambler believing their luck will change, his continued use of yet more of the bank's money in attempts to recoup his losses (Punch, 1999). But if Leeson was criminal in his actions, it could also be said that his managers back in London were guilty of incompetent oversight and rule-breaking themselves, 'sending sums of money to Leeson in Singapore for amounts that in some instances exceeded both the bank's assets as well as limits set by the Bank of England' (Gobert and Punch, 2003: 19).

Following this case and the huge publicity it generated (including a 1999 film of the story called *Rogue Trader*, starring Ewan McGregor), it might have been assumed that a system failure of such proportions would be unlikely to occur again within a major bank. However, in 2008, 31-year-old Jerome Kervial, cost French bank Société Générale €4.9bn (£3.7bn) in a fraud involving four times as much money and probably the largest in financial history. This scandal hit France's second-largest bank, wiped out profits for 2007 and damaged European markets already fragile due to a credit crisis. Three main criminal charges followed – fraudulent falsification of banking records, use of such records and computer fraud. Like Leeson, Kervial confessed to acting well beyond his 'limited authority' throughout 2007 and 2008, indicating that checks were inefficient or non-existent. According to the bank he was 'Aided by his in-depth knowledge of the control procedures resulting from his former employment in the middle-office, [and] managed to conceal these positions through a scheme of elaborate fictitious transactions'. While Kervial was swiftly dismissed from his job, the offer of resignation by chief executive Daniel Bouton was rejected and instead he and the senior management were given a vote of confidence by the board of the bank. According to the *Guardian* newspaper, 'Roger Steare, professor of organizational ethics at Cass Business School in London, said the SocGen scandal was further evidence of a "systemic deficit in ethical values" in the banking industry', adding that

> This latest rogue trader scandal is yet more evidence that while rules-based regulation and controls work for kids in the playground, it won't stop adults doing the wrong thing. The banking industry used to have a reputation for honesty, trust and prudence. This latest scandal, on top of the massive losses in credit markets, and the ongoing incidence of mis-selling to retail customers, indicates that there is a systemic deficit in ethical values within the banking industry.
>
> (Fiona Walsh and David Gow, 2008
> http://www.guardian.co.uk/business/2008/jan/24/creditcrunch.banking)

Health professionals as criminals

Medical practitioners have expertise and autonomy and can engage in the frauds and fiddles of white-collar criminality. In the United States a huge number of fraudulent claims are made to insurance companies for treatment that has not actually been carried out and, on a smaller scale, there have been a number of cases in the United Kingdom in recent years in which doctors and dentists have claimed payments from the National Health Service for visits to patients or for treatments that have not occurred. The same insulation from close scrutiny and the deep trust that society places in doctors can also be abused in the most extreme way, as was demonstrated in the case of Harold Shipman, a British GP working in Todmorden, Yorkshire, then later in Hyde in Greater Manchester. Over the course of twenty-three years, Shipman is believed to have murdered at least 215 of his patients. He had previously been convicted in 1976 of obtaining pethidine (a strong opiate-type drug) by forgery and deception, and later that year, in the name of a dying patient, he obtained enough morphine to kill 360 people. Nonetheless, he was simply given a stiff warning from the General Medical Council and allowed to continue to practise as a GP. Shipman was convicted in January 2000 and given fifteen life sentences but committed suicide in 2004.

Since this case, it has been proposed that all NHS trusts and the police should have investigation teams to check on doctors and nurses suspected of abuse and malpractice. The inclusion of nurses partly follows from the case of Beverley Allitt. Allitt was a British nurse who received thirteen life sentences in May 1993 on being convicted of murdering four children and attacking nine others while working on a children's ward between February and April 1991. The subsequent Clothier Inquiry report noted that vital clues about what was happening were missed during the time she was employed at the hospital. But Allitt will not have been the first such case and has not been the last. In 2006, Benjamin Geen, a casualty nurse working in Oxfordshire, England, was convicted of two murders and grievous bodily harm to patients whom he caused to collapse with respiratory arrest and then helped to resuscitate because he enjoyed the excitement of the crisis and response. Part of Geen's modus operandi was to inject dangerous drugs he had stockpiled – something that was supposed to be far more difficult to do under measures introduced in the aftermath of the Shipman affair. Hesketh (2003) has referred to this kind of offending as 'medico-crime' and suggested it is time for a police and health professions protocol and the establishment of regional groups of specially trained police officers who would be better placed to carry out investigations in medical contexts. As Hesketh points out, just like any other member of the general public, health professionals can commit a huge variety of everyday crimes but there are also those that are particularly facilitated by their relationship with patients.

Health and pharmacy professionals deal on a daily basis with medicines that are themselves very valuable commodities and targets for theft. Historically and today, some professionals abuse their positions and divert medicines for personal use (usually stimulant or sedative drugs for recreation or for an addiction) (Strang et al., 1998). Of course, such drugs are also stolen in small-scale burglaries and larger-scale warehouse raids or lorry hijackings. Medicines may be stolen or diverted because they have great value in the illegal trade in drugs or may be profitably sold for their original medical use in Third World regions where they are scarce. The latter practice might actually occur because a Western government has declared a product unsafe for domestic consumption but is willing to allow or overlook the sale of the same product to other parts of the world (Dowie, 1979) – a phenomenon based on hypocrisy and creative interpretations of the law that extends to a range of hazardous goods (Harland, 1985). Braithwaite's (1984) and Abraham's (1995) studies of the pharmaceutical industry illustrate how the promotion of a benign image masks

- price-fixing
- improper influence on regulatory systems
- industrial espionage
- knowing distribution of unsafe drugs
- the 'dumping' of drugs that are not approved by Western countries in developing states desperate for medicines and with laxer regulations.

Medical and pharmaceutical deviance and malpractice come to light via public complaints, professional bodies and the courts but, as Jesilow et al. (1985) remarked over twenty years ago, this remains an understudied area – a fact that is all the more surprising given the importance of health care for everyone.

Lawyers and accountants as criminals

Like health professionals, lawyers and accountants are generally 'safe hands' and trustworthy, but occupy positions in which it is easy to act in unscrupulous fashion and abuse trust. Both types of professional can be employed by criminal organizations or themselves operate corruptly by, for example, inflating fees, forgery, pocketing money that should be passed on to clients, and engaging or colluding in frauds or even blackmail. The specialist expertise of accountants and lawyers and the high regard in which they are held as professions leave many opportunities for abuse of their position. For example, asylum seekers needing advice and support concerning residence in the UK should use only services licensed by the Office of the Immigration Services Commissioner (OISC, established in 1999 under the Immigration and Asylum Act). However, as the National Criminal Intelligence Service reported in its 2003 Threat Assessment of Serious and Organised Crime, 'a small number of corrupt solicitors and immigration advisors support the facilitation process by fraudulently completing asylum or work-permit applications for clients'. The OISC also noted that 'many are also involved in illegal activities such as document forgery and people trafficking' (McVeigh, 2003).

Accountants from the local high street to big names like KPMG have been scrutinized by accountancy academics like Sikka (2008; Association for Accountancy and Business Affairs) and found wanting in their conduct. KPMG, for example, has admitted in the United States to 'criminal wrongdoing' and paid a $456m fine in a major tax fraud case, while a UK tax tribunal found a tax-avoidance scheme designed by the highly respected firm of Ernst and Young to be unacceptable. The scheme was described by a Treasury spokesperson as 'one of the most blatantly abusive avoidance scams of recent years' and could have cost the taxpayer over £300m per year but no prosecutions or inquiries have followed (Sikka, 2008).

The theme of connections between the local and the global is made by some of these examples. However, the examples of BCCI and the pharmaceutical industry also confirm the difficulty of establishing precise definitions of white-collar and corporate crime. BCCI was a case involving corrupt individuals within a corrupt organization that nonetheless somehow managed to operate as a legal, respectable and apparently competent institution for many years. Pharmaceutical companies have been the subject of various criminological studies and journalistic investigations exposing corporate criminality, but the question of the responsibility that the decision-makers within a company actually bear has proved to be far less straightforward than we might think (see Box 13.3).

Crime in the world of corporate-level business and commerce

Crimes of the powerful

Pearce's book *Crimes of the Powerful* (1976) was a Marxist critique of the bias of law, capitalism and control systems in favour of a ruling class and at the expense of the working class (see also Chapter 6). He used case studies from the United States to show how corporate interests had at times struck alliances with and made use of organized crime to suppress the labour unions, and how the law had been used to control the powerless through the criminalization of troublesome activity. In the same critical tradition within criminology, probably the most sustained and continually updated catalogue of examples of crimes of the powerful is the US overview by Jeffrey Reiman, nicely (and accurately) called *The Rich Get Richer and the Poor Get Prison* (2005, 7th edn; also discussed in Chapter 6). In a supplementary essay to the book, Reiman and Leighton (2003) focus on what they call 'the big crime story of 2002', which, for a change, was not 'the usual tale of murder and mayhem among the poor' but 'a long and complicated saga of corporate financial shenanigans that caused a significant drop in stock market prices'. The energy stocks corporation Enron, along with its compliant auditors Arthur Andersen (another example of accountants acting unprofessionally), were at the heart of scandalous revelations about unscrupulous and illegal business practices, but the case was soon followed by similar exposures at major companies such as Tyco, Xerox, AOL-TimeWarner, and by problems at some major US banks such as Citigroup.

While Enron boasted a remarkable record of growth and was symbolized by an impressive headquarters with a statue of the Enron symbol proudly displayed outside, in fact the enterprise was something of a house of cards and on 2 December 2001 was declared bankrupt – one of the largest bankruptcies ever, with debts of over $31 billion. As Reiman and Leighton (2003) explain,

> Enron was subsequently accused of having perpetrated a massive 'disinformation' campaign, hiding the degree of its indebtedness from investors by treating loans as revenue, hiding company losses by creating new firms with company capital and then attributing losses to them and not to Enron, and encouraging company employees to buy and hold Enron stock while its executives apparently knew of its shaky condition and were busy selling off their own shares.

The culture of corrupt practice at Enron was not limited to US operations however. In 2007 three UK bank employees were convicted in the United States for wire fraud and received sentences of 37 months each in prison. The so-called 'NatWest Three', Giles Darby, David Bermingham and Gary Mulgrew, employees of a subsidiary of the UK NatWest bank, conspired with the Chief Finance Officer of Enron, Andrew Fastow, to defraud Greenwich NatWest of the true value of its holdings in a Cayman Islands investment company. The three bankers apparently made a profit of £1.1m each while Fastow and another Enron employee made even more.

While fraud and financial malpractice are one key area of corporate criminality, they are not necessarily the most injurious. Corporate negligence and management failing have also been held to be responsible for a variety of events in which great loss of life has occurred. In the UK, key

Plate 13.2 Night view of the Enron sign at the company headquarters in Houston. Enron employees leave the building in downtown Houston, Texas, late on 7 February 2002. Under harsh questioning before Congress, former Enron corporation Chief Executive Jeffrey Skilling shouldered no blame for the bankrupt energy trader's collapse and said he had no reason to believe it was in financial trouble when he left in August 2001.

Source: © Reuters; *photo:* STR.

cases from the late 1980s to today include the sinking of the *Herald of Free Enterprise* ferry; the King's Cross fire; and rail crashes at Clapham, Paddington, Southall, Ladbroke Grove, Hatfield, Potters Bar and Cumbria. Although public inquiries and academic studies can point to failings within the actions or inaction of organizations and individuals, the law in the UK has only recently introduced provision for the prosecution of a crime of corporate homicide or corporate manslaughter. After much promising and then stalling by the Labour government, legislation in this area finally came into force on 6 April 2008 as the Corporate Manslaughter and Corporate Homicide Act 2007 (see Box 13.3).

BOX 13.3 Timeline for legislation on corporate manslaughter and homicide

- Under the Conservative government, in 1996 the Law Commission produced a report, *Legislating the Criminal Code: Involuntary Manslaughter* that highlighted the ineffectiveness of the law in this area and published a draft bill that recommended the creation of an offence of 'corporate killing'.
- In 1997 the Labour Party manifesto promised to legislate on corporate manslaughter.
- After Labour's 1997 election victory the then Home Secretary, Jack Straw, said that 'the new government believed those whose criminal negligence caused the deaths of innocent people should not escape punishment' (Bright, 2002: 6).
- The Confederation of British Industry has vigorously opposed plans for new legislation, arguing that it would be unworkable (Hodge, 2003: 3).
- But under current legislation, the Crown Prosecution Service is reluctant to bring corporate manslaughter cases because they are notoriously difficult to prove and win. 'There have only ever been five successful prosecutions and these have all been against small companies' (King, 2003: 10).
- Labour failed to follow up its manifesto commitment to legislate, but in 2000 did commence a wide consultation exercise about the proposed new offence. Not all those in the business world oppose action, and Ruth Lea of the Institute of Directors said in 2002, 'For business to look as if it is getting away with murder is extraordinary. It's common justice that if someone is killed through gross negligence that someone should be held responsible' (Bright, 2002: 6).
- In May 2003 the then Home Secretary, David Blunkett, announced the intention to publish a draft bill on reform of the law, but critics say this will concentrate 'virtually all the punishment on companies, rather than their managers and directors'.
- The history of demands for laws on corporate killing go back to at least 1965 when the bridge that Glanville Evans was working on collapsed and he fell into the River Wye. A prosecution failed, and since then, 'more than 31,000 people have been killed at work or through commercially related disasters such as train crashes. Safety reports have shown that management failures are responsible in most cases' (Hodge, 2003: 3).

doing crime

- Gary Slapper, writing in the Times Online (18 July 2007: 1), welcomed the new Act noting that 'Globally, more people are killed each year at work than are killed in wars' and that this legislation makes prosecution and conviction an easier prospect than previously. This is not to say that the 'threshold of guilt' has been lowered – the Act

   criminalizes only an organization whose gross negligence has resulted in death. . . . The new law will apply not just to the UK's 2.3 million companies but to partnerships, other employers like trade unions, and to some non-commercial organizations. After much debate in Parliament, the new law will now also be applicable if the death of someone in custody resulted from gross negligence in the prison service or from those controlling police cells.

Transnational corporate crimes

With regard to business crime in a transnational context, Michalowski and Kramer (1987: 34) suggest that

> The increasing global reach of modern transnational corporations [TNCs] aggravates the difficulties of arriving at a satisfactory conception of corporate crime. TNCs at times engage in practices which, while they would be illegal in their home nations, are legal in a number of host nations.

Whether originating from legal or illegal sources, such crimes may have consequences related to social, health and economic as well as law-enforcement issues in Britain or other countries.

The relocation by Western TNCs of high-pollution industries in less developed countries is notable here (Michalowski and Kramer, 1987: 37), resulting in the costs of crimes and offences against the environment and wildlife, and related damage to human health now and for future generations (Beirne and South, 2007; Croall, 1998: 280; and see Chapter 19).

Another example would be the enormous international catalogue of health and safety offences and breaches of regulations that have led to deaths and injuries as a result of what some have termed 'corporate violence' (Croall, 1992; Wells, 1993; Slapper and Tombs, 1999) and the crimes of toxic capitalism (Pearce and Tombs, 1998). As Pearce and Tombs (1998: ix) note, 'If the chemical industry has provided enormous material benefits, equally the costs have been enormous, even catastrophic', yet 'the destructive nature of the industry – the death, injury, ill-health, and environmental devastation which it causes – remains particularly poorly recognized and challenged.'

This latter idea raises an important question about the context of crimes of large-scale organizations, for despite the phrase coined by these authors, capitalism does not have a monopoly on such offending. The common characteristics of cost-cutting, negligence and under-investment in health and safety have featured as readily within the bureaucratic cultures of enterprises of communist and totalitarian states as they have in capitalist ones. In this respect, and in conclusion, when looking at large-scale, 'corporate' organizational crime, we can bring together the themes of:

- businesses operating to subvert or invert good corporate practice (see Gobert and Punch, 2003);
- the significance of transnationalization and globalization in respect of where crimes are committed and in terms of their effects;
- and the irony that we live in a world much improved by advances in science, industry and technology yet which now also suffers the multiple, unintended (though not always unforeseen) consequences, generating a constant awareness of the dangers of life in a 'risk society' (see Chapter 7).

Summary

1 Professional crime is changing, and while robbery and burglary will always be with us, new generations of career criminals seek to keep themselves at the cutting edge of developments. In the commercial, electronic and financial sectors, criminal entrepreneurs seek profitable loopholes and niches to exploit. At the same time an enormous amount of business is transacted involving prohibited goods and services (pornography, drugs and people smuggling).
2 Law-enforcement agencies can respond only if they too keep at this cutting edge as indicated by investments in intelligence and specialist staffing to match the characteristics of modern organized crime.
3 Criminologists actually know relatively little about the workings of white-collar and corporate crime, and this has changed little since the early 1990s when Nelken (1994a: 367) noted that 'far more is needed on the modus operandi – the "how" of white collar crime (motivation, meaning, actions, decisions, alliances, escape routes, "techniques of neutralization" etc)'.
4 It remains as plain as ever that there is enormous disparity in the way that different crimes are treated and that a fair justice system would seek to rectify this through more effective investigation and prosecution of the crimes of the powerful.
5 Transnational crime is now a major challenge (Jamieson et al., 1998; Gros, 2003).

Critical thinking questions

1 **Professional criminals and organized crime groups are among the most popular subjects of novels, television programmes and films. Review a small sample and identify the key characteristics of the criminal careers and/or organizations featured.**

2 Is 'greed' the explanation for both professional and corporate crime? If not, what else do we have to consider?

3 Draw or describe a hypothetical 'chain' that could link a crime (you choose) committed in Edinburgh to a contact in Rotterdam and an air ticket to the Cayman Islands.

4 If we accept the benefits of a more globalized society, do we have to accept the accompanying risks of globalized crime?

5 Check news reports and the websites of professional associations such as the British Medical Association or Solicitors Complaints Bureau for evidence about the misconduct or criminality of professionals.

Further study

Croall, H. (2001) *Understanding White Collar Crime*, Buckingham: Open University Press. A key text reviewing studies and theories concerning white-collar and corporate crime.

Friman, H. R. and Andreas, P. (1999) *The Illicit Global Economy and State Power*, Oxford: Rowman and Littlefield. Contributors cover crime networks, links with states, the trades in drugs and in hazardous waste, and the wider global context.

Hobbs, D., Hadfield, P., Lister, S. and Winlow, S. (2003) *Bouncers: Violence and Governance in the Night-time Economy*, Oxford: Oxford University Press. Ethnography and analysis of licit and illicit aspects of the growing night-time economy, also discussing regeneration schemes, use of private security, and drug and alcohol problems in pub- and club-land.

Weisburd, D., Waring, E. and Chayel, E. (2001) *White Collar Crime and Criminal Careers*, Cambridge: Cambridge University Press. Longitudinal, quantitative study of the backgrounds and criminal careers of white-collar criminals, challenging some taken-for-granted assumptions.

Winlow, S. (2001) *Badfellas: Crime, Tradition and New Masculinities*, Oxford: Berg. A study of crime, culture, masculinity and community based on insightful ethnography and fieldwork.

More information

Web of Justice
http://www.co.pinellas.fl.us/bcc/juscoord/eorganized.htm
This site provides numerous links to other websites concerned with crime, corruption and power.

United Nations
http://www.unodc.org/unodc/organized_crime.html
This site on organized crime provides a source about global developments in crime and control and links to national sites.

Nathanson Centre

http://www.yorku.ca/nathanson/search.htm

This site provides a searchable bibliographic database to help locate other relevant studies.

Criminal Justice Resources

http://www.lib.msu.edu/harris23/crimjust/orgcrime.htm

This site provides links to other sites both official – such as the FBI and the Royal Canadian Mounted Police – and unofficial – such as journalist and community sites – concerned with various forms of crime.

Association for Accountancy and Business Affairs

http://www.aabaglobal.org/

Paul's Justice Page

http://www.paulsjusticepage.com/

This site provides useful links and material concerning corporate crime and crimes of the powerful.

Drugs, Alcohol, Health and Crime

Introduction

> There are signs that the 'pot culture' may, after all, be just a passing fad. The police are one factor; but the rival attractions of drink are another.
>
> (Auld, 1973: 568)

That was the headline to an article appearing in *New Society* magazine in 1973 yet, just over thirty years later, in 2007, an article in the news journal *The Week* reported on 'The cannabis boom' and noted that nearly 60 per cent of the drug sold in the UK today is now 'home grown' compared to only 10 per cent ten years ago. So, what has happened? Some things have stayed the same. The police have continued to enforce laws against drug cultivation and supply but there have always been questions about how effective such policing can be. The attractions of alcohol can sometimes be forgotten when social concern about illegal drugs seizes media attention, but as Auld said in 1973 – and is just as true today – 'alcohol remains the dominant social drug in our society'.

Some things have changed and, as discussed in Chapter 13, of particular relevance here is the entry of serious organized crime into the illegal drugs market since the late 1960s and early 1970s, and the term 'home grown' is a reference to the fact that supply to the UK market no longer comes mainly via import but from domestic production on cannabis 'farms' run by Vietnamese and other criminal gangs using illegally trafficked labour and sophisticated equipment in converted houses and buildings (Daly, 2007). Globalization, migration, consumer choices and public opinion are all elements of the changes affecting availability and patterns of use of illegal drugs and alcohol over the past thirty to forty years.

What perhaps remains unchanging is that the 'drugs problem' is one of the main headline crime stories of our times. As such, it can often seem a relatively simple issue of drug supply, user demand and associated crime. In fact, it is a highly complex subject in which problems of international politics, the legacy of history and the subcultures of use, as well as the economics of drug markets, law enforcement and provision of treatment services all interact. By contrast, alcohol and its association with crime has been relatively neglected, although in fact it is probably of more real influence as a factor in crimes of violence and crimes on the road. Importantly, drugs and alcohol are also health issues yet criminology largely overlooks the significance of health as affecting and reflecting the lives and behaviours of people (see Box 14.1). This chapter therefore adopts an innovative approach to these subjects and takes a holistic approach to the study of illegal and legal drugs in society.

BOX 14.1 Thinking about links between illegal drugs, alcohol, crime and health

Consider, for example:

- the link between intravenous drug use and AIDS/HIV or hepatitis C;
- the contribution of alcohol to crimes of violence – a problem not just for the police but also, in the United Kingdom, for the National Health Service;
- the fact that manslaughter deaths on the road caused by intoxication are recorded not just in the crime statistics but also in the mortality statistics;
- that offenders with mental health problems face additional difficulties and the courts and services face additional considerations in dealing with them;
- that alcohol may be a legal 'drug' but supplying alcohol to minors is illegal, and over-indulgence by young people can lead to health hazards and hospitalization;
- that medicine and, in particular, psychiatry are powerful systems of social regulation or social control.

doing crime

Controlling illicit drugs and alcohol

Drugs and alcohol have been the subjects of varying forms of control. Their histories diverge from the early twentieth century, with alcohol remaining legal while drugs such as cannabis and opium became illegal.

In the eighteenth and nineteenth centuries it was largely the 'demon drink' that was seen as a problem for society, a threat to the health and morals of the individual and his or her family, and subversive of the good habits and social order of a civilized society.

BOX 14.2 Binge drinking and moral panics: historical parallels?

In the journal *History and Policy*, the historian Peter Borsay provides a thought-provoking comparison of concerns about the consumption of gin in an earlier period and about binge drinking today. The parallels provide material for discussion but there is also a debate to be had about how different life and society is today compared to then and what this means for patterns of consumption and intoxication. Borsay points out that patterns of consumption were affected by the differing levels of taxation on different kinds of alcoholic drink. One question to consider is whether this is still the case today: From the 1690s taxation changes favoured the distilling industry, thereby encouraging consumption of a great deal of gin with some claiming that 'each inhabitant of the city was consuming roughly a pint of the substance a week'. This produced social or domestic problems and by 1751 changes in the economy, drinking behaviours and legislation meant consumption was falling. Hogarth's famous picture of this same year reflects concerns of the time.

So what parallels might be drawn between the concerns about binge drinking today and the alarm about the 'Gin Craze' of the eighteenth century?

> Firstly, the media play a critical role. The police and health professionals clearly have direct and regular contact with the phenomenon, but most older citizens make their acquaintance with binge-drinking primarily through the media, especially TV and the newspapers. Certainly it is the media who control how we see it; it is they who create the visual and written images and texts that determine perceptions of the phenomenon. Moreover, though we might like to think that the newspaper photographer or TV cameraman just point their lenses in a random way at the goings on, common-sense suggests that there is a good deal of calculation behind the production of the images.
>
> Secondly, my impression from these images is that though young men are undoubtedly present it is young women that are the media's focus – scantily clad, sometimes roaming around in groups linked together by arms, other times staggering helplessly on their own, occasionally collapsed in the gutter vomiting.

Plate 14.1 'Gin Lane' (1751) by William Hogarth.

Source: Trustees of the British Museum.

doing crime

Thirdly, where men are shown it is usually engaged in acts of bravado, damage to property, and inter-personal violence.

Fourthly, the setting is invariably urban rather than rural, city centre rather than suburban, and outdoors rather than indoors. Binge drinking is thus portrayed as a public and urban phenomenon.

Fifthly, pervading many reports is a sense of governmental inaction and complacency. The world is falling into chaos, but the state is doing little to address the problem. Indeed, where the government does act, it is to introduce measures such as allowing twenty-four-hour drinking that, from a commonsense point of view, seem likely to inflame rather than relieve the problem.

Sixthly, one of the reasons given to justify the de-regulation of licensing hours is the example of Europe, where it is argued that permitting an all-day drinking culture encourages a more mature and civilized approach to alcohol consumption. However, such a line of argument simply fuels a xenophobic response in the media, where de-regulation is portrayed as yet another example of loss of autonomy and cultural identity as Britain is Europeanized.

Finally, though the media may project the crisis, behind it are a series of organizations, professional bodies and pressure groups drip-feeding information and statistics, and pursuing agendas which inevitably reflect their own take on politics and society.

Source: *History and Policy*, September 2007
http://www.historyandpolicy.org/papers/policy-paper-62.html

Drug politics and policy in the United Kingdom

Concerns about respectability and restraint were paramount for the new middle class; an emerging medical profession had ambitions to expand its influence and provide expert opinion; and the women's movement, religious groups and elements of working-class socialism all embraced a commitment to **temperance**. The agenda for *control* of intoxication had emerged. New, scientific specialisms produced theories of 'disease' to explain a variety of conditions such as alcoholism and addiction but also, for example, homosexuality, insanity and criminality (see Chapter 4). New clinical terms such as 'narcomania' and 'morphinism' (see Berridge, 1999) reflected new approaches to knowledge, power, control of the body and the triumph of rationality over unreasonable desire (Turner, 1996). So we see medical treatment directed at the moral and mental health of individuals; the popularization of images of the drunkard or opium smoker as a broken body, degraded and enslaved; and the celebration of the moral values of abstinence and hard work.

In the early twentieth century, the agenda for drug control was partly shaped by a continuing commitment to controls by the law and the police (Lee and South, 2008). Some of the laws that came into force were the result of domestic concerns (Kohn, 1992) but from around 1912 to the 1920s the drug issue also became internationalized, with treaties and agreements being produced to define and categorize drugs and establish what was prohibited and what was permissible in legal trade for medical and research purposes (McAllister, 2000). Effectively, this is an early example of 'globalization' – a theme referred to in several chapters. In Britain – but not, for example, the United States – a different form of control was also exercised through the medical profession. Following the Rolleston Committee report of 1926, doctors had won the right to prescribe drugs such as heroin and morphine to dependent users or 'addicts' and thereby 'maintain' them in a way that was aimed at enabling them to live as a useful citizen and keeping them from the criminal market for drugs. While on the one hand this was an early example of the medicalization of a social problem (Zola, 1972; Conrad and Schneider, 1992), it was also an important early precedent for the practice that in the 1980s became known as harm reduction.

The late 1960s and early 1970s saw increasing criminalization of drug dealers and drug users caught by the police in possession of prohibited drugs. At the same time, users seeking or directed to treatment services (the new Drug Dependency Units established from 1967) faced a tougher and more abstinence-oriented regime. This further medicalization of the problem developed under the direction of psychiatrists, emphasizing how drugs have become associated with mental health. (This link is returned to later.) From the 1980s to today, in the face of increased use of heroin, cocaine and crack and public health concerns about AIDS/HIV and Hepatitis C, practice-based responses have increasingly reflected harm-reduction principles (Strang and Gossop, 2004, 2005).

Recent trends have seen efforts made to increase the availability and take-up of treatment alongside increase in powers to impose penalties for refusing or breaking treatment orders and repeated offending. The rationale for this was provided by the chief executive of the National Treatment Agency (NTA) on its launch in 2001, that 'It is sound criminal justice policy to invest in drug treatment. At the same time, we have to look at the drugs strategy as a whole. It is just as important that putting more money into treatment will provide better health care for the user and address the public health agenda by continuing to support harm minimisation' (Hayes, 2001). However, just as the idea of harm reduction proved controversial, this justification for treatment as a means to achieve crime reduction has also attracted criticism. On 30 October 2007, a BBC report questioned the apparently low rate of success in treatment measured as 'getting people off drugs' (i.e. becoming abstinent). After some statistical claims and counter-claims the outcome seemed to be a poor rate of success for the NTA with acknowledgement that at the end of 2006/7 only 3 per cent of people in treatment for drug problems had completed and become 'drug free'. Of course, as ever, the issue is not really that simple. In some cases, treatment as a 'cure' or 'solution' is possible and achieved but in many cases treatment and forms of long-term support and intervention, whether by counselling or maintenance with drugs such as methadone, are required and effective (Bean and Nemitz, 2004).

As this suggests, the law-enforcement agenda has remained at the centre stage of policy since the 1980s and been strengthened, focusing on national and international large-scale traffickers (Dorn et al., 1992) and on links between drug trafficking and professional organized crime groups (see pp. 276–7 and Chapter 13). Money-laundering of the profits derived from drugs is a large-scale and complex business in itself, and since 11 September 2001 has become an even higher enforcement priority, owing to concerns among intelligence agencies that such funds help to support terrorist groups (Levi and van Duyne, 2005).

Prohibition and control remain the dominant message yet there is still considerable energy and effort expended on debates about the best way to 'deal' with 'the drugs problem'. For some, it is not self-evident that prohibition of drugs is necessary, and far from evident that it is a successful policy. So various positions compete: proposals for legalization or decriminalization (see Box 14.3), **harm reduction**, stepping up the eradication of drug crop cultivation and anti-smuggling efforts, zero tolerance approaches to use, more effective treatment, and so on. Thus, in the early twenty-first century we can see increased *contestation* about drugs. This is easy to see in the disagreements that emerge around government proposals for a Drug Strategy. As the latest version of an approach first introduced in the mid-1980s, the government has published a ten-year drug strategy for 2008–18. This followed a consultation exercise during 2007, but not the right kind of consultation according to some critics, with the *Observer* (21 October 2007: 26) reporting that this was a 'sham' 'according to one of Britain's leading think-tanks on narcotics, which warns that the current policy is fuelling a crime epidemic'. A report from the Transform Drug Policy Foundation called 'After the War on Drugs: Tools for the Debate' argued that 'It is clear our drug policy cannot continue down the same failed path forever. . . . Prohibition's failure is now widely understood and acknowledged among key stakeholders in the debate' (Doward, 2007: 26). This actually serves quite well as an illustration of the situation noted in another response to the consultation by a different independent body, the UK Drug Policy Commission, which suggested that 'The drug policy debate has for some time been dogged by polarised perspectives. In particular, public debate in the media tends to revolve around being either "soft" or "tough" on drugs issues with no real effort to explore and promote, in a meaningful way, what works' (UKDPC, Response to Consultation Paper, 2007).

BOX 14.3 Legalization/decriminalization: pros and cons

The debate about the 'decriminalization' or 'legalization' of drugs is both old and new. It is old in the sense that drugs that were once legally available have come to be controlled, but at the beginning of the twentieth century there were debates about whether this was best done by the methods of policing or those of medicine (Lee and South, 2008; Berridge, 1984). In the United States, after the 1914 Harrison Act, law enforcement became the dominant approach, while in the United Kingdom, after acceptance of the Rolleston Committee report published in 1926, medical management was allowed but within the framework of legal control.

In terms of the recent debate (Inciardi, 1999), the supporting argument for the legalization option is that presently illegal drugs cause less harm than legal drugs: it is their illegality that is responsible for related harm (e.g. through adulteration; through the committing of crime to obtain drugs; and because of the profitability of illegal supply, hence the growth of major crime groups and the incentive to commit violence or murder to protect profits). A counter-argument is that legal drugs are widely available, illegal drugs are not: the health, social and crime-related consequences of the widespread legal availability of drugs are therefore unknown. The decriminalization/legalization arguments are unlikely to gain government support in the foreseeable future because of the powerful influence of international pro-hibitionist agreements and assumptions that this would be politically unpopular with the voting public. However, recent research and independent inquiries (Runciman, 2000; RSA, 2007) have suggested that in fact there is room for greater flexibility in the interpretation of these treaties than governments have generally acknowledged, and so a careful yet more imaginative 'middle way' may be possible. In preparing their report on drug policy matters, published as 'Drugs – facing facts' (RSA, 2007: 295), the Royal Society of Arts working party commissioned a survey – one of the largest so far undertaken – from YouGov and found that 'a clear majority of people indicated that they would be happy to see the personal use of "soft" drugs such as cannabis either made legal or the penalties for their possession lowered'. The authors qualify this by noting that such results need to be treated cautiously but this does suggest that public opinion is not as hardline and fixed as politicians seem to assume.

The anomaly of alcohol control

Among the concerns of social reformers in the nineteenth century, the abuse of alcohol loomed large. It is therefore intriguing that the control of alcohol went in the opposite direction to that of other drugs. During the First World War, regulations under the Defence of the Realm Act introduced both the first legal controls over cocaine and opium and also the alcohol licensing laws, which restricted the opening times of public houses and considerably tightened up the regulations relating to the sale, purchase and consumption of alcohol. However, thereafter drugs became subject to ever-increasing and widening controls but alcohol availability was liberalized. War-time restrictions were barely enforced, and while the Licensing Act 1921 signalled that alcohol was an intoxicant that needed some regulation, throughout the twentieth century it became, as the Royal College of Psychiatrists (1986) put it, 'our favourite drug'. Outlets multiplied, from beyond the pub to the corner shop and now the supermarket and cross-Channel hypermarkets, and drinking patterns changed, with women greatly increasing their consumption since the 1980s (Alcohol Concern, 2000). For all this, the legal status of alcohol does not mean it has no connections with crime. Entirely to the contrary: for example, because there is value in avoiding the higher taxation on alcohol imposed in Britain, smuggling from across the Channel is profitable; and alcohol is a serious intoxicant associated with crime in various ways. This is returned to below.

However, it is drugs that have had the higher profile in relation to crime and social problems. Therefore, the following questions arise:

- Where do drugs come from? Is this a local, national or global issue?
- How much of a problem do drugs pose? How many people take drugs and who says it's 'a problem' at all?
- What are the connections between drugs and crime?

Drugs as a global issue

The opium trade in the nineteenth century

The original international opium traffickers were the great colonial traders such as Britain and the Netherlands (McAllister, 2000: 9–39). In the nineteenth century, Britain invested heavily in

BOX 14.4 What is heroin?

Heroin (medical name diamorphine) is one of a group of drugs called 'opiates' which are derived from the opium poppy (*papaver somniferum*).

Opium is the dried milk of the opium poppy. It contains morphine and codeine, both effective painkillers. Heroin is made from morphine and in its pure form is a white powder.

The main source of street heroin in the UK is the Golden Crescent countries of South West Asia, mainly Afghanistan, Iran and Pakistan.

Today street heroin usually comes as an off-white or brown powder. For medical use heroin usually comes as tablets or injectable liquid. A number of synthetic opiates (called opioids) are also manufactured for medical use and have similar effects to heroin (e.g methadone, a drug which is often prescribed as a substitute drug in the treatment of heroin addiction).

Source: Edited from: Drugscope, the UK library and information resource on drugs
http://www.drugscope.org.uk/resources/drugsearch/drugsearchpages/heroin.htm

the export of opium from India to China, and although opium became a profitable commodity for China itself (Berridge, 1999: xxvi), originally the country was a victim of market exploitation by the British Empire. Britain wanted certain luxury goods that China produced but needed to balance the trade and did so via the export of opium. When China sought to close its ports to this importation, Britain went to war against China on two occasions (1839–42 and 1856–8) to secure the future of its profits. This history partly explains why domestic control over opiate use in Britain was so limited at this time.

The drugs trade in the late twentieth and early twenty-first centuries

Since the end of the 1970s and the early 1980s, changes relating to the geopolitics of opium production and to international trafficking routes have been significant. The British opiate market of the 1960s was primarily fed by a combination of leakage of pharmaceutically produced drugs from the legal prescribing system and then by 'street heroin' produced and distributed from the Golden Triangle region of Southeast Asia (Ruggiero and South, 1995). However, by around 1980 what became known as the Golden Crescent area (including Afghanistan and Pakistan) was producing most of the heroin reaching Britain.

Today, post-Taliban Afghanistan has not seen the reduction in opium production that was supposed to follow from military action but instead a massive increase. According to the 2007 Annual Report of the United Nations Office on Drugs and Crime (UNODC), Afghan opium production accounts for 92 per cent of total world supply and had reached a record level of 6,100 tonnes: 'With 165,000 hectares under opium cultivation in 2006, up almost 60% from 2005, the harvest out-stripped global consumption by 30%. Poppy cultivation in Helmand province alone rose by 162% compared with 2005.' Corruption, crime and political opportunism all combine to consolidate and protect the bases of the 'narco-economy'. In response to this problem it has sometimes been suggested that opium production in Afghanistan could be licensed and the drug be produced for the medical market. However, as others point out,

- there is currently no shortage of opium legally produced for medical purposes and indeed there has been overproduction since 2000;
- there is a real difference between the conditions of stability and security in places like Tasmania and Turkey where the licit cultivation takes place and the conditions of failed infrastructure and lawlessness in Afghanistan (Rolles, 2007);
- furthermore, even if some or all of the opium grown could be diverted to legitimate use, this would do little or nothing to diminish the demand for illegal opium-based products and the incentives to farmers and traffickers to engage with the criminal market would remain.

Alongside increasing availability, the fact that heroin produced from these sources can be smoked and does not need to be prepared for injection has been a contributory factor in the widespread upsurge in heroin use from the 1980s onward. In retrospect, the 1980s was a watershed decade (Dorn and South, 1987). The explosion of the international heroin trade was quickly followed by the growth of the cocaine market, with Colombian crime groups initially aiming production at demand in the United States but by the end of the 1980s also targeting Europe (Streatfeild, 2002; Ruggiero and South, 1995; see also Chapter 7). Money laundering, corruption of police and customs officials, the stimulation of local drugs micro-economies based on drug supply and demand, and the profits from acquisitive crime generated to pay for drugs all followed (Lee and South, 2008) while the price of drugs has largely proved to be inflation-resistant. In the words of a report produced in 2003 by the Prime Minister's Strategy Unit, 'over the past 10–15 years, despite interventions at every point in the supply chain, cocaine and heroin consumption has been rising, prices falling and drugs have continued to reach users. Government interventions against the drug business are a cost of business rather than a substantive threat to the industry's viability' (p. 94).

Plate 14.2 Pod-picker working in opium poppy field in Jalalbad, Afghanistan.

Source: Time & Life Pictures/ Getty Images.

doing crime

Upper-level drug trafficking is truly global and can be found to involve organizations in most nations and with varying degrees of size and complexity. Flexibility and in many cases the small size of the core of key personnel, with expendable contacts and networks at the periphery and extending outward, make these illegal businesses particularly hard for law-enforcement agencies to effectively penetrate and close down (Dorn *et al.*, 2005).

A cross-cultural view

There is, however, another way of looking at global drug use. This is to acknowledge that if we jettison Western preconceptions and adopt a more cross-cultural perspective, we will find that in some countries or cultures, drugs are not a 'problem' but can be:

- a long-established socio-cultural asset
- a form of support
- the basis for socialization
- and for belief systems.

In some other contexts where drugs *have* become a destructive force this may have followed from Western influences (e.g. the intrusion and activities of organized crime groups). Drug use *per se* is far from predictive of problematic behaviour or problematic social outcomes and various forms of 'traditional' drug use have their roots in practices that are hundreds, if not thousands, of years old, for example, the use of opium by rural dwellers in India or coca chewers in Bolivia and Peru. In many such examples the substances involved are sacred to those who practise them and international conventions aiming to prevent their use could be argued to be unreasonably ethnocentric (Coomber and South, 2004).

Global trafficking origins, routes and destinations today are shown in Figure 14.1.

Are drugs 'a problem'?

Certainly governments, the media and the public see drugs as a major threat to society. Even the strongest supporters of liberalization or legalization would acknowledge that drugs cause harm to individuals, families and the wider community, although their argument is that these harms and problems follow from the criminalization of drugs and drug users, and the inadequacy of support services

Of course, the 'problem' status of drugs can also be seen in terms of the labelling or social constructionist position (see Chapter 6) that this is a result of the application of labels and processes of stigmatization representing the agenda of moral entrepreneurs and agents of control rather than a rational policy. The effect of stigmatization may also be to enable or cause drug users to affirm their identities as deviant, rebellious and members of subcultures differing from 'straight' society (Young, 1971). On the other hand, there are arguments that the moral and cultural landscape has changed and that drugs have come out of the subcultures and on to the dance-floor. In fact, we are probably talking about two different landscapes. For the homeless heroin user, stigmatization and their distance from mainstream society remain highly important in influencing their sense of identity, lifestyle and opportunities (Green *et al.*, 2005). For today's

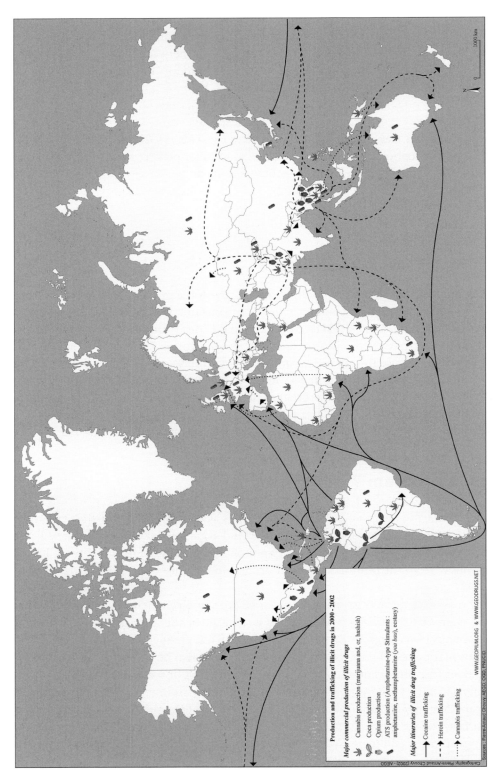

Figure 14.1 Map of production and trafficking of illicit drugs, 2000–2.

Source: Pierre-Arnaud Chouvy, AEGD, OGD, PNUCID. Published in *Geopolitical Drug Newsletter*, 11 September 2002: 4–5.

recreational drug users, official definitions and prohibitions seem to be increasingly ignored or subverted, and new scripts and meanings about the place of drugs in everyday life are being created, incorporating cannabis, Ecstasy, amphetamine and cocaine (South, 2004).

According to one argument, use of at least some kinds of drugs has now become *normalized* for many young people (Parker *et al.*, 1998). But is this true? And, if so, what does this mean? One position is that although '**normalization**' does not mean that everyone is now a drug user, nonetheless, it is now non-acquaintance with drugs or drug users that has become 'the deviation from the norm'. The idea of 'social supply' is not new – users of drugs sharing or selling drugs at non-profit rates with other users known to them is an obvious way of reducing costs and increasing the sociable element of drug experiences. However, it may be becoming an even more common pattern, especially in relation to drugs like cannabis or Ecstasy (Coomber and Turnbull, 2007; South, 2004).

The opposing argument is that drug use has not become a 'normal' activity for the majority of young people: prohibitions, peer-group resistance, parental attachment and preference for alternative expressive activities remain central to their lives. Both arguments (Parker *et al.*, 1998; Shiner and Newburn, 1999; South, 1999b) would seem to have some validity across late modern societies, and MacDonald and Marsh (2002) usefully suggest that a process of 'differentiated normalisation' may be occurring, with some young people remaining anti-drug abstainers, some being frequent recreational users, and some serious, problematic drug users.

Whatever the composition of the market, the spending power involved is enormous for what is still a supposedly illegal and hard-to-access market – 'Home Office estimates of the scale of the drug trade, between £4bn and £6.6 bn in 2003–04, suggested the amount spent on drugs each year was equal to 33% of the tobacco market and 41% of that for alcohol' (Travis, 2007; Matrix Knowledge Group, 2007).

While some studies suggest that drug use has been in decline or has stabilized, others suggest that at least some forms of drug use are increasing.

BOX 14.5 Statistics on young people and drug misuse: England, 2006

Key facts

- In 2005, 11 per cent of secondary school children in England reported using drugs in the month prior to interview while 19 per cent reported using drugs in the year prior to interview.
- Among 11 year olds, 4 per cent had sniffed volatile substances in the last year while 1 per cent had taken cannabis. Among 15 year olds, 7 per cent reported using volatile substances compared to 27 per cent who used cannabis.
- Among secondary school children who had taken drugs in the year prior to interview in 2003, 43 per cent reported wanting to give up immediately, but 13 per cent said they did not want to stop.

- In 2003, 17 per cent of secondary school children thought it was acceptable to try cannabis, 10 per cent thought it acceptable to try sniffing glue and 4 per cent believed it OK to try cocaine.
- Of young adults aged 16–24, 26.3 per cent reported using drugs in the year prior to interview in England and Wales in 2004/05; 16.3 per cent had used drugs in the month prior to interview. Almost half (45.8 per cent) reported that they had ever used drugs.
- More young men than young women reported using drugs in the year prior to interview (32.9 per cent compared with 20.8 per cent).
- Among young people aged between 10 and 25 living in England and Wales in 2004 who had ever used drugs, almost half (48 per cent) reported first using a drug between the ages of 10 and 15.
- Deaths related to drug misuse fell between 2000 and 2004. Among young people under the age of 30, deaths fell from 583 to 401.

Source: The Information Centre, NHS Knowledge for health and social care
http://www.ic.nhs.uk/statistics-and-data-collections/health-and-lifestyles/drug-misuse/statistics-on-young-people-and-drug-misuse:-england-2006

Apart from surveys, we can also look at law-enforcement statistics about drugs and crime but must also recognize that these are limited in what they can tell us. Realistically, such statistics can reflect only what is known, that is drug offences and related crimes that have been detected, seizures made and convictions secured in the courts – although some extrapolations can be made from current trends. Drug offences are not reported in the same way that robberies or burglaries are (see chapters 9 and 10) – the participants in a drug sale will not report their transaction and are unlike, for example, the victim of a robbery who will probably be quick to involve the police and their insurance company. Statistics suggesting seizures of large amounts of drugs may be seen as an indicator of enforcement success. Alternatively, they could be interpreted as evidence of the success of traffickers because it takes only a few large seizures to inflate law-enforcement 'performance indicator' figures yet a drop in seizure statistics does not necessarily mean there has been a drop in importation and dealing. In most countries, police and customs agencies generally feel unable to realistically claim much more than a 10 per cent interception rate. In the UK, seizures of heroin, cocaine and cannabis seem to have been increasing in recent years.

Drugs are used by many different people and in many situations. Here are typical findings from national and local surveys carried out in the UK:

In general
- Drug use has increased significantly in recent years. This includes increases in use of medicines and an increase in cigarette smoking, alcohol consumption and illegal and other socially unacceptable drugs, especially among young people.
- Illegal drug use is only an occasional activity for most people.
- Most illegal drug use is experimental or on a relatively controlled, recreational basis.
- Most people who use drugs – be it legal or illegal substances – do not come to serious harm.

BOX 14.6 Seizures of drugs in England and Wales, 2005

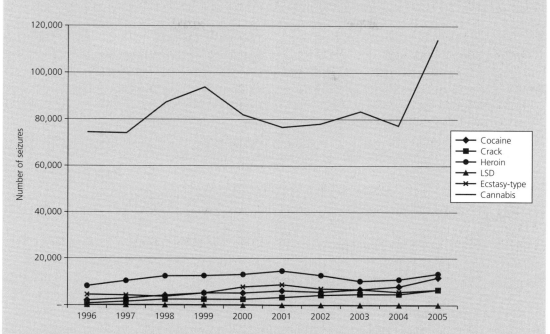

Figure 14.2 The number of seizures for main drug types, England and Wales, 1996 to 2005.

There were 161,113 drug seizures by police and HM Revenue and Customs in England and Wales in 2005 – 50 per cent up on the previous year. This increase is largely accounted for by an increase in cannabis seizures with 114,202 seizures involving cannabis in 2005, an increase of 47 per cent compared to 2004. This increase is thought to be associated with the introduction of cannabis warnings from 1 April 2004.

■ In 2005 there were 38,605 seizures of class A drugs (up 31 per cent since 2004); 6,807 seizures involving class B drugs (up 7 per cent since 2004); and 117,297 seizures involving class C drugs (up 54 per cent since 2004).

■ Heroin and cocaine were the most commonly seized class A drugs in 2005; there were 13,331 seizures of heroin (up 20 per cent since 2004) and 11,913 seizures of cocaine (up 51 per cent since 2004).

Source: Home Office Statistical Bulletin 17/07, 25 October 2007, Emma Reed.

■ Recent trends mean that soon the majority of parents of school-aged children in many areas will have tried illegal drugs when they were young.

Age of use
■ Use of drugs (other than medicines) tends to become significant by the age of 14 for many young people, and both numbers using and quantities consumed increase throughout the remaining teenage years.
■ Most young people moderate their use of, or completely stop using, illegal drugs and moderate their alcohol use by their mid- to late twenties when they 'settle down' and take on adult responsibilities.
■ A small, but significant, number of people continue to use illegal drugs, and particularly cannabis, into their thirties. Many of these people are parents.

Drugs and crime

The most evident examples of drugs and crime activity can be distinguished at two levels:

■ street-level drugs offenders, including the activities of users sufficiently dependent that they become involved in crime to generate funds, or those already engaged in criminality who are then initiated into drug use;
■ the activities of professional crime groups involved in organizing drugs distribution.

There is a small industry producing research on the drugs–crime connection but for all this – or perhaps because of the variety of studies and different kinds of evidence – there is no single conclusion about the nature of this relationship. Of course, there is no dispute about the fact of an association between drugs and crime but there is disagreement about how direct or mediated the link may be. It is obviously clear that the very illegality of drugs will make their possession and supply an offence but thereafter matters are less straightforward. Put simply: does drug use lead to crime or does involvement in a criminal lifestyle lead to drug use?

Heroin and crack users with a serious addiction may be committing a considerable amount of acquisitive crime to fund their habit (Bennett *et al.*, 2001) but, at the same time, as Seddon (2002) argues, a link between drugs and crime is in fact only found among a minority of drug users – the 3 per cent or so of illicit drug users who are termed 'problem' users. Within this group, the association is primarily between use of heroin and/or crack cocaine and commission of certain economic/property offences (especially drug selling, shoplifting, burglary and other theft). For others, the course to drug use may be through involvement in an array of routes into delinquent and criminal lifestyles (Auld *et al.*, 1986; Hammersley *et al.*, 1989; Pudney, 2002), and drugs are just one commodity bought and sold in the pleasure markets of the late modern illicit economy (South, 2004; Hobbs *et al.*, 2003).

BOX 14.7 Key points from statistics on drug offences and offenders in England and Wales, 2003

This is an extract from *Findings 256* published by the Research, Development and Statistics Directorate of the Home Office. The brief report shows data on known drug offences and offenders in England and Wales in 2003. These statistics report on police cautions, court proceedings and HM Customs and Excise compounding for drug offences ('compounding' is where payment is made of a compound settlement in lieu of prosecution for minor cannabis possession offences).

Key points

■ In 2003 the total number of drug offences in England and Wales rose 5 per cent from the 2002 level to 133,970.
■ Class A offence numbers rose 6 per cent to 35,610, Class B rose 5 per cent to 94,520 while Class C offences decreased 2 per cent to 1660.
■ In total, 110,640 people were found guilty or were cautioned for drug offences in 2003.

Among this group of known drug offenders:

■ 90 per cent were known to have committed possession offences.
■ 70 per cent of all drug offenders in 2003 had committed cannabis possession offences; 7 per cent heroin possession; and 5 per cent cocaine possession.

The most common disposals used for known possession offenders (i.e. possession only and not possession with intent to supply) in 2003 were:

■ cautions (45 per cent),
■ fines (26 per cent), and
■ absolute or conditional discharges (11 per cent).

About 10 per cent of all drug offenders in 2003 had committed dealing offences. Cannabis and heroin dealing each accounted for 3 per cent of all drug offenders, cocaine dealing accounted for 2 per cent of all drug offenders.

The most common disposals used for known dealing offenders in 2003 were immediate custody (60 per cent), and Combination, Community Rehabilitation or Community Punishment Orders (19 per cent).

■ Fewer women than men were cautioned or found guilty for drug offences.
■ Among those found guilty or cautioned for drug offences, possession offences tend to be committed by younger people (63 per cent committed by those under the age of 25);

Criminal groups and the drug market

A 2007 Home Office report on organized crime and its profits and costs to society observed:

> That the UK illicit drugs market is dominated by organised criminal groups is well known. The industry is typically characterised by a vertically disintegrated supply chain: drugs are imported in bulk to the UK, sold onto different middle market groups (where numerous transactions may occur), before being sold to dealers and then the final user. The source country varies depending on the drug in question. For heroin the largest supplier is Afghanistan, and for cocaine it is Colombia. The researchers assume that the entire market is organised. Although there are some exceptions – for example some cannabis is grown and consumed by the same person – these instances make little difference to the total organised crime market size.

There is, by now, a very extensive international literature on drug trafficking and related serious, organized crime. Hobbs (1998: 415) has summarized trends in the operation of British professional crime groups (see Chapter 13; and see also Dorn and South, 1990; I. Taylor, 1999) and the ways in which the drugs market has attracted increased involvement from professional criminals since the 1980s.

> The flexibility that is apparent within the contemporary serious crime 'community' assures . . . considerable scope for innovative engagement with the market. These engagements create disintegrated criminal firms . . . operating within multiple, interwoven networks of legitimate and illegitimate opportunity. . . . Within the drug market . . . trade is carried out between networks of these small flexible firms, for disorganized crime mirrors disorganized capitalism.

In other words, the drugs market provides opportunities for entrepreneurial criminals to trade in a highly profitable commodity. In many ways, such illegal enterprise will have characteristics not dissimilar to those of legal businesses, albeit that while disagreements and contract disputes in the legal market may be resolved via the courts, increasingly the illegal drugs market uses violence and even murder as a form of dispute resolution and contractual enforcement.

When Hobbs refers to such business as 'disorganized', he does not mean those involved are incompetent; rather, he is pointing to the fragmented and fluid nature of the market (Reuter et al., 1990; Bean, 2002: 97–119). This understanding of the entrepreneurial mix in the market is important and has replaced the once prevalent and more limited notion of a simple 'pyramid' model of the market, familiar in police intelligence at one point (Broome Report, 1985). This model assumed the dominance of drugs trafficking organizations by a 'Mr Big' or several such hidden hands and was shaped less by evidence of market structure and more by an expectation that the hierarchical organization of police detective work reflected a hierarchy of criminal organization. In other words, at divisional level, local police countered local dealers and related crime; force-wide drug squads were more intelligence led and pursued middle-level dealers; while regional crime squads and their 'drugs wings' targeted drug crime operating nationally and internationally (Bean, 2002: 123). The idea of the mixed, fluid and relatively open market is more useful, and even where major cartels can be pointed to – such as that led by Pablo Escobar in Colombia in the 1980s – these are operating in competitive markets, accompanied by significant levels of corruption and violence. Indeed, some recent research suggests that the fragmentary, flexible, temporary and ad hoc nature of some forms of transnational crime, such as heroin and cocaine trafficking and smuggling of humans, means that 'traditional' crime organizations such as Triads and La Cosa Nostra are of declining significance (Zhang and Chin, 2003). The example of the involvement of Vietnamese gangs in the UK cannabis trade with which this chapter opened shows how relatively easy it is for new entrants to flourish in a flexible trade and market.

Controlling drugs

Efforts to exercise control have been reflected in a long series of legislative Acts (see Box 14.8) and through an increasing emphasis on drugs as a problem for everybody: a community issue requiring action from within the school curriculum, from housing associations and local government housing departments, and from health services (Lupton et al., 2002). This agenda was a key element of the Crime and Disorder Act 1998, which established local partnerships led by police and local councils to develop integrated strategies for the reduction of drug misuse and dealing. The response and organization of law-enforcement agencies has become increasingly specialized and sophisticated through the decades, from local drugs squads (Collison, 1995) to national agencies such as the Serious Organised Crime Agency for the United Kingdom (SOCA), launched in April 2006. The Annual Planning document for SOCA for the year 2006/7 acknowledged that its remit meant countering 'the damage caused to people and communities by serious organized crime' but that in practice operations would be guided by the view that drug trafficking, particularly where Class A drugs such as heroin and cocaine are involved, is the single, greatest organized criminal threat to the UK (see also Chapter 13; and Lee and South, 2008).

BOX 14.8 Timeline: UK legislation and influences on the control of drugs

1908 The Poisons and Pharmacy Act regulates sale of cocaine.

1912 The Hague Convention (International Opium Convention) requires signatory nations to limit opiate use, manufacture and trade to medical purposes; close opium dens; and implement laws against unauthorized possession and/or sale.

1916 The Defence of the Realm Act, Regulation 40B controls the possession of cocaine.

1920 The Dangerous Drugs Act implements the Hague Convention; this is mainly concerned with opium but also introduces some controls on cannabis.

1925 The Dangerous Drugs Act amends the 1920 Act and restricts the import and export of coca leaf and cannabis.

1926 The Rolleston Committee Report (Interdepartmental Committee on Morphine and Heroin Addiction) recommends that the prescribing of morphine and heroin be allowed where it is part of a therapeutic programme of maintenance for the incurably addicted or of gradual withdrawal.

1951 The Dangerous Drugs Act consolidates previous Acts.

1961 The First Brain Committee Report (Interdepartmental Committee on Drug Addiction) fails to detect signs of change and feels that new controls on heroin and cocaine are unnecessary.

1965 The Second Brain Committee Report discusses a significant increase in drug use and recommends that doctors 'notify' the Home Office about addicts in treatment, and restrictions on the availability of heroin and cocaine prescriptions.

1967 The Dangerous Drugs Act implements the Brain recommendations and introduces police powers to stop and search individuals and vehicles for drugs.

1968 The Medicines Act regulates the production and distribution of medicines, e.g. whether they are available only on prescription, or without a prescription but only from a pharmacist, or generally available from any shop.

1971 The Misuse of Drugs Act – still the main legislation (with subsequent amendments) covering controlled drugs, divided into three classes:
Class A, e.g. heroin, cocaine, LSD, opium;
Class B, e.g. amphetamines, barbiturates and, previously, cannabis, which has (from 2004) moved to –
Class C, also including, for example, steroids, various tranquillizers and stimulants.
(For more on the cannabis classification debate see Box 14.9.)

1979 The Customs and Excise Management Act – which complements the 1971 Act, penalizing trafficking in controlled drugs.

1986 The Drug Trafficking Offences Act introduces provisions for seizure of the assets of traffickers unless they can be proved to have no connection with the profits of drug crime (importantly, the burden of proof was moved from the prosecution to the defendant); it also made the sale or supply of certain drugs paraphernalia illegal (e.g. cannabis pipes).

1988   The Road Traffic Act makes it an offence to drive if unfit owing to drink or drugs. The police can stop those they suspect of being under such influence and request saliva, urine or blood samples to test.

1994   The Drug Trafficking Act updates the 1986 Act.

1997   The Crime (Sentences) Act introduces minimum sentences of seven years for those convicted of a Class A drug trafficking offence for the third time.

1998   The Crime and Disorder Act introduces a new Drug Treatment and Testing Order (DTTO).

2000   The Criminal Justice and Courts Act introduces a new sentence of Drug Abstinence Order.

2005   Drugs Act introduces new powers relating to intention to supply a controlled drug, drug offences searches, and detention of suspected drug offenders; includes mushrooms containing psilocin, etc., as Class A drugs.

Sources: originally adapted from the Runciman Report (2000), J. Cohen (2002) and updated for this edition.

BOX 14.9 *The cannabis classification debate, Philip Johnston (9 January 2008)*

Question: When is a Government review not a government review?
Answer: When Ministers have already made up their minds in advance.

Should cannabis remain a Class C drug?

In summer 2007, shortly after he became prime minister, Gordon Brown announced a review of the decision to reclassify cannabis from a Class B drug to a Class C substance. This reclassification was carried out when David Blunkett was Home Secretary. In 2001, he said he was 'minded' to make the move but had asked the Government's Advisory Council on the Misuse of Drugs (ACMD) to look at the issue. This group, made of up senior scientists and experts in the drugs field, duly obliged, recommended a lower classification and cannabis became a Class C substance in 2004. There were many critics of this decision; and with an election looming in 2005, Charles Clarke, by then Home Secretary, decided the best way of ensuring it did not become a major issue in the campaign was to announce another review by the very same ACMD. It went away and thought about it and came back a few months after the election with the recommendation that it should remain a Class C drug. The committee conceded that regular cannabis use can have 'real and significant' mental health effects. The modern form of the drug is far more potent than that used in the 1960s because of the high content of THC, the ingredient that provides the 'buzz'. But the advisers concluded that it was unlikely to cause schizophrenia. The council said that while cannabis could produce harmful effects, these were 'not of the same order as those of substances within Class B'. Mr Clarke decided that the confusion which would be caused by another change in the law would outweigh the advantages of tightening it up again.

What could possibly have changed in the past 18 months since the same committee reached this conclusion? When Jacqui Smith, the latest Home Secretary, wrote to Professor Sir Michael Rawlins, the chairman of the council, requesting a further review of evidence, she conceded that 'cannabis use has fallen significantly'. But she added: 'There is really public concern about the potential mental health effects of cannabis use, in particular the use of stronger forms of the drug, commonly known as skunk.'

However, this was precisely the point the ACMD looked at last time and concluded there should not be a change. If it now comes up with a different view, it will call into question the judgment of the advisory body.

If it comes up with the same conclusion it is, of course, then open to ministers to overrule it since it is, as its name suggests, only 'advisory'. But in that case, and if that is what they wanted all along, why did they not just get on with it months ago?

Source: http://blogs.telegraph.co.uk/politics/
threelinewhip/jan08/cannabis_classification.htm

Alcohol and crime

The principal focus of concern about alcohol and crime is the contribution it makes to levels of violence in society – whether hidden in the household or highly visible on the streets. In 2005 a report from the Faculty of Public Health of the Royal Colleges of Physicians in the UK pointed out that

> In England and Wales, alcohol is thought to play a part in approximately 1.2 million violent incidents – almost half of all violent crimes, with devastating health consequences for victims, their family, friends and the wider community. While health, police and other public services deal with the consequences of alcohol-related violence, such staff are also victims, for example, 116,000 NHS staff are assaulted each year, primarily by patients and relatives.
>
> (http://www.fphm.org.uk/resources/AtoZ/bs_alcohol_violence.pdf)

Raistrick *et al.* (1999: 55) have summarized a wide body of research and noted several other connections between alcohol and crime:

- Intoxication may tip the balance between contemplating crime and committing it.
- Alcohol use may be a financial motive for crime.
- Alcohol problems can produce a home environment in which antisocial and abusive behaviour occurs, such as domestic violence, child abuse and cruelty towards animals.

doing crime

As we saw earlier, there is a long history of public anxiety about binge drinking, alarm about rowdy and violent behaviour on the streets, and desire to prohibit drink because of its effect on morals or its encouragement of socializing with 'bad company'. According to the early criminologist Cesare Lombroso (see also Chapter 4),

> Alcohol . . . is a cause of crime, first because many commit crime in order to obtain drinks; further, because men sometimes seek in drink the courage necessary to commit crime, or an excuse for their misdeeds; again, because it is by the aid of drink that young men are drawn into crime; and because the drink shop is the place for meeting of accomplices, where they not only plan their crimes but squander their gains . . . it appears that alcoholism occurred oftenest in the case of those charged with assaults, sexual offences, and insurrections. Next came assassinations and homicide; and in the last rank those imprisoned for arson and theft, that is to say, crime against property.
>
> (Lombroso, 1911/1968: 95–6)

However, it is not as clear, as Lombroso implies, that alcohol 'causes' crime; rather, it appears to have an effect in relation to crime (Alcohol Concern, 2001; All Party Group on Alcohol Misuse, 1995; The Lancet, 1999; Man et al., 2002; McMurran and Hollin, 1989: 386; Raistrick et al., 1999; Dingwall, 2005):

- ■ Data from the British Crime Surveys and other sources consistently show that heavy drinking and drunkenness are linked with aggression and violence.
- ■ Facial injuries and wounds to the victim are associated with heavy drinking by the assailant (although the victim may also have been drinking).
- ■ Drinking and driving is the leading cause of death among young people aged 15–24.
- ■ The British Medical Association suggests that the offender or victim had been drinking in 65 per cent of murders, 75 per cent of stabbings, 70 per cent of beatings and 50 per cent of fights or domestic assaults.
- ■ One-third of people are intoxicated when they are arrested.
- ■ Heavier users of alcohol are more likely to have criminal records and to admit to criminal acts than those who are moderate drinkers or non-drinkers.
- ■ Even when alcohol and committing crime can be shown to be related it is difficult to point to a causal direction, i.e. which came first – the drinking or the crime?

Alcohol consumption obviously has an effect on the drinker, but it is easily understood that social contexts and psychological factors influence how these effects are experienced and manifested. Similarly, understanding the role of alcohol (or indeed other drugs) in relation to the committing of crimes needs sensitivity not just to the interaction between pharmacology and physiology, but also to immediate social context and wider cultural norms. As with the idea that users 'learn' how to interpret and 'enjoy' drug effects (Becker, 1963), so it is the case that belief about how alcohol is 'supposed' to affect behaviour, alongside the influences of context and culture, is as important in shaping behaviour as the amount of alcohol consumed (Borrill and Stevens, 1993; Pearson, 1992; Deehan, 1999).

Images of alcohol use on television, in films and in advertising promote an association with desirable lifestyles, fun, sex and success, with obvious connections to the culture of the

Plate 14.3 Young people drinking in Newcastle city centre – part of a thriving night-time economy.

Source: © North News and Pictures.

carnivalesque and seductions of crime (Presdee, 2000; Katz, 1988) that have been discussed in relation to youth offending, hedonism and substance use (Collison, 1996). Such advertising is designed to appeal to both young men and young women. Use by the latter has been increasing steadily since the 1980s. Nonetheless, it is particularly in relation to masculinity that the association between alcohol consumption and offending, including violence, has been seen as a serious problem (Tomsen, 1997; Graham and Wells, 2003).

The economic boom of the night-time economy (Hobbs *et al.*, 2003) has assisted the regeneration of some inner-city areas and has created opportunities for employment and leisure in the 24/7 city but has also led to developments of criminological interest: a new arena for masculine play and power, to be enjoyed but also fought over; the proliferation of venues legally selling alcohol and where drugs are illegally easily available; development of protection rackets and turf wars between criminal entrepreneurs; increases in alcohol-related injuries requiring medical attention; and in relation to control, the growth of the use of bouncers and private security as the feudal forms of regulation of the night-time life of the city (see also Chapter 18).

Whether alcohol use is related to disorder and violence in the community or in the home, there are many avenues to explore for explanations of links. The complexity of this task is indicated by the intertwining of alcohol dependence, offending and imprisonment, and indications of mental illness and social exclusion (see Box 14.10).

BOX 14.10 Offenders, alcohol and mental health

■ One study revealed that 63 per cent of men and 39 per cent of women serving prison sentences had been hazardous or harmful drinkers in the year prior to incarceration (Singleton *et al.*, 1997).

■ As many as 90 per cent of prisoners have a mental illness and/or substance misuse (including alcohol) problem (Department of Health, 2001).

■ People who are dependent on alcohol are more likely to be homeless on release from prison than those who are not (Revolving Doors Agency, 2002).

Source: Alcohol Concern website.

Drugs, alcohol, crime and community: a public health issue

Drug users have a likelihood of facing more health problems than the general population (Neale, 2004), some of which follow from methods of use (e.g infections, tetanus, hepatitis) and some from the problematic past histories and current lifestyles commonly found among heavy drug users. The National Association for the Care and Resettlement of Offenders (NACRO, 2001: 15) has suggested that 'background research into the relationship between health and youth crime is far from extensive', but 'That which exists . . . suggests a high correlation between substance misuse, adverse mental health and a range of other health-related problems on the one hand, and offending by children and young people on the other.' While this correlation is worrying by itself, it becomes doubly so when the problems of rehabilitation and reoffending are considered. As the government's Social Exclusion Unit noted in 2004, 'Physical and mental health can be a key determinant as to whether someone offends' (http://archive.cabinetoffice.gov.uk/seu/page3887.html) and the fact that the 'physical and mental health of prisoners is generally much worse than that of the general population' is a strong indicator that many ex-prisoners will reoffend.

Connecting crime and health issues

In a broader sense, while the impact of crime on the psychological and social health of victims of crime has been acknowledged (see Chapter 9), it has probably not been well understood. Research by the Public Health Alliance (McCabe and Raine, 1997) found that

> The effects of the fear of crime, rather than crime itself, on the health of individuals and communities has been largely underestimated. In particular, the impact of 'incivilities' on well being is not well recognized . . . both victims of crime and non-victims identified a deterioration in their quality of life and adopted a range of coping mechanisms likely to be detrimental to health, in particular increased use of alcohol, smoking and use of both licit and illicit drugs.

Contemporary criminology has largely overlooked health as a variable of relevance but, at the same time, public health has also tended to neglect violence and assault as relevant. As Shepherd and Farrington (1993: 89–90) observe: 'Until recently, assault has not been treated as a public health problem, despite the fact that it is a major threat to health and a major cause of disparities in health between richer and poorer segments of the community.' Shepherd and Lisles (1998: 355) found that overall, and consistent with the findings of the British Crime Survey, 'about four times more incidents [involving violence and assault] come to the attention of [Accident and Emergency Departments] than are recorded by the police'. Such data are a potentially important source of information about violent crime (Hobbs *et al.*, 2002: 354) that goes unreported in criminal justice statistics.

In a valuable review of the literature, Robinson *et al.* (1998) have identified several categories of connections between health and crime, including:

- the impacts of crime and fear of crime on physical and psychological health;
- the health needs of victims;
- costs to the health services.

Crime-related injury and victimization lead to health problems and the need for services. However, costs to the health services (and hence wider society) do not solely result from care of the injured. In recent years, violence against health service staff in Britain has increased significantly, and so worrying is this trend that the National Health Service (NHS) has made a key policy commitment to reduce violence against its employees. Further, as is familiar to any viewers of prime-time hospital and police drama series, the emergency services are repeatedly exposed to events such as major accidents or to physical and emotional damage to victims, which in turn contribute to mental ill health and post-traumatic stress for emergency service staff (Brayley, 2001). Hence, the costs of crime and violence to society are felt directly and indirectly in personnel and financial costs to health and related services.

Crime, public health and social inequalities

With reference to violent crime and health inequalities, a study by Shepherd (1990: 293–4) shows that the assault rate was higher the greater the ranking of the area of residence in terms of social and material deprivation. More recently, Hope (2001) has investigated the positive correlation between social deprivation and crime victimization. On a national scale, data from the British Crime Survey for 2000 reflect higher 'concern' about crime among deprived groups – the poor, those in unskilled occupations, residents in inner-city and council estate areas – and also reports that those who considered themselves to be in poor health or who had a limiting illness or disability had heightened levels of concern about crime (Kershaw et al., 2000: 47–9, table A7.9).

The importance of public health and its relevance for crime and victimization issues was given serious emphasis by the Acheson Report (1998: 53) on health inequalities. This report observed that both fear of crime and violence and victimization can have damaging consequences for health. It noted the simple but significant (yet frequently neglected) point that increased risk of ill health *and* of crime victimization are highest among those already most disadvantaged. Furthermore:

> Although the evidence is incomplete, the link between income inequality, social cohesion and crime has important policy implications. It suggests that crime prevention strategies which only target the perpetrators and victims of crime and the high crime areas in which both groups live, will not achieve a significant reduction in crime unless they are accompanied by measures to reduce income inequality and promote social cohesion.
>
> (Acheson, 1998: 54)

Hence, public health is sometimes described as 'social medicine', and its aims can be seen to coincide with much work in criminology concerned with the effects of social exclusion – for example, strategies for health improvement that require reductions of inequalities and of poverty, of pollution, of sources of ill health and transmittable disease in the community, and of crime and victimization.

Public health as social policing

Public health can be seen as a benign system of inspection, information gathering, regulation and intervention but also, precisely because of these characteristics, can be understood in the sense developed by Foucault (1975/1980) as part of the dispersal of disciplinary power throughout the major institutions of modern society. Public health therefore has a role in the 'policing' of our health and of services and businesses that have an impact on our health, deploying various professionals such as health visitors, nutritionists and environmental health officers (who focus on pollution, food purity, hygiene in food stores and so forth; on 'food crime' see Croall, 2007). Public health is also about preventing disease and illness and promoting reduction of harm. So, to return to drug misuse and AIDS/HIV, the public health approach adopted in the United Kingdom has been far more effective than the US emphasis on a response by the criminal justice system (Stimson, 1995). It is also important to see that in the contemporary context of public policy, multi-agency strategies and initiatives have come to occupy a central place. As noted earlier, following the Crime and Disorder Act 1998, health authorities have been required participants in the development of crime and community safety partnerships and strategies, while the Drug Treatment and Testing Orders, introduced under the same Act, require the court, probation and statutory and voluntary sector drugs agencies to work together.

The idea of recognizing physical and mental health as relevant to understanding crime is receiving interest in various ways. But of course this is not a new development. As earlier chapters indicate, it can be 'functional' to society to identify, blame and stigmatize those who are 'tainted' or 'misfits': the vagrant, the imbecile, the pariah marked by disease, from the leper of the Middle Ages to the AIDS victim today. Religious, moral and medical judgements have long created categories of risk and danger and techniques for redemption, rehabilitation or treatment (Cohen, 1985). Since the nineteenth century, the medical profession – in particular, psychiatry – has come to be the secular successor to religion as the arbitrator of status as 'healthy' or 'sick', and has acquired the power to exercise forms of authority that can be hard to challenge. Some writers, both sociologists of health and medicine (Zola, 1972; Conrad and Schneider, 1992) and criminologists (Cohen, 1985; Sim, 1990), have drawn attention to the power of medicine as a form of social control.

Medicine as a form of social control

Medical and psychiatric interventions as social control

Antidepressant drugs such as tranquillizers have been seen by some as a pharmaceutical tool that society uses to pacify women discontented with the drudgery and limitations of domestic life. The medicalization of female deviance, the drive to normalize women's behaviour according to particular ideals of femininity and the tendency of medical professionals to over-prescribe mood-altering drugs for women, are common practices (Ettore, 1992). In the United States, significantly more women than men receive prescriptions for antidepressants, tranquillizers and sedatives. Within prisons (see following section), the use of psychotropic drugs on male inmates is often justified with reference to 'problems of institutional control', while female inmates tend to be drugged in the name of 'treatment' in an attempt to correct their deviant behaviour in a psychological–social–physiological manner. Such drugs in prison have been described as a 'liquid cosh', their use being a soft technique of control and prison management (Sim, 1990).

Proposals to 'modernize' mental health legislation have been subject to recurrent debate about how to balance protection of the rights of the mentally ill individual versus the public who may possibly be 'at risk'. This is not a subject where the science is infallible, the risk easy to determine or the principles involved clear-cut. For example, the idea that someone may be examined and then placed in some form of incarceration based on 'the opinions of others regarding the likelihood that they would behave dangerously at some point in the future' (Farnham and James, 2001: 1926) obviously lends itself to controversy and dispute. How reliable can prediction of future behaviour be? There is an important debate here. Society rightly expects government to act to minimize harm to citizens and provide protection from dangerous people but some may see such proposals as a 'conscious deception', employing diagnoses with little credibility (ibid.). Others – politicians, members of the general public, pressure groups representing victims of violent, disordered offenders – might argue that public safety is always the overriding priority.

Medicalization of control in prisons

The use of psychotropic drugs to control inmates in institutions is far from new. In the nineteenth and early twentieth centuries, those committed to prisons or asylums might be given 'sleeping draughts' to 'modify' their behaviour. Following the Second World War, the emergence of the multinational drug industry produced large-scale manufacture and availability of powerful new drugs with sedative or other behaviour-modification properties (McAllister, 2000). Particularly from the 1970s, as prisons experienced crises of disorder and protest, the demand for enhanced security meant that medical management of prisoners took on new significance. In the United States there is similar evidence of use of psychotropic drugs in prisons since at least the 1970s. These offer a 'quick, cheap and effective' aid to the warehousing of increasing numbers of inmates in cramped conditions.

Diagnosis and medication may vary in relation to gender and ethnicity, and in one UK study, Genders and Player (1987) found that large doses of antidepressants, sedatives and tranquillizers were prescribed to women in prison, who received proportionately five times more medication as men. Around ten years later, a 1998 parliamentary debate gave rise to concerns that strong tranquillizing drugs are routinely prescribed to young women prisoners who mutilate themselves, and are also used as pacifiers and substitutes for illegal drugs despite the side effects of their own addictive potential (Hansard, 22 October 1998: col. 1400).

Critics also argue that psychiatric medicine and the criminal justice system operate with ethnocentric assumptions or racist stereotypes that are introduced into medical or legal judgements. Hence, African and Caribbean psychiatric in-patients are more likely than whites to be defined as 'aggressive', placed in secure units and subjected to invasive forms of treatment such as intramuscular medication and electroconvulsive therapy. During the 1980s a number of cases involving black prisoners in Britain raised concerns about the nature of their psychiatric assessments, the inappropriate and/or inadequate medical treatment they received, the question of force-feeding, the use of drugs as a technique for control, and their certification as mentally ill, leading to transfer to a mental hospital, thereby influencing the criteria for eligibility for release.

However, yet again there are two sides to the issue, for one very important criticism of the prison system is that far too many people with mental health problems and other illnesses are held in totally inappropriate prison conditions when they should be in hospital settings.

Medicine and the criminal justice system

The medical and allied health professions have come to play an increasingly central role in the criminal justice system:

- Medical experts are called to give evidence at criminal trials, though not without controversy: psychiatric diagnoses once credible may now be criticized, for example the idea of homosexuality as a dangerous perversion. Since 2003, medical evidence about the statistical improbability of more than one infant death occurring in a family has been seriously questioned, leading to several convictions for murder being overturned, prosecution cases failing, and since 2004, steps have been taken to reopen a number of past cases.
- The courts may receive psychiatric reports on offenders to help determine their fitness to stand trial and their comprehension of their actions and the consequences.
- Secure hospitals run as psychiatric and therapeutic institutions are the 'prisons' for those who cannot, for various reasons, be sent to traditional jails, but these institutions also perform valuable therapeutic functions.
- The police employ 'police surgeons' – that is, medically qualified staff (usually contracted local GPs) – to provide health assessments and care for those held in custody.
- Prisons have medical wings with their own health care staff (although the system is now being incorporated into the NHS).
- Psychiatric nurses in secure institutions need to employ therapeutic techniques but also are effectively jailers and may need to use techniques of restraint and coercion. The majority will work to high standards, but, as with prison officers, there are cases of serious abuse of power and patients.
- In relation to drug offenders, as already indicated, the criminal justice and health systems are increasingly linked, with the latter seen as offering those willing to take the opportunity, a diversionary route away from crime and from punishment by the criminal justice system.

The report from NACRO (2001) referred to earlier suggested that 'current developments in social policy present real opportunities for broadening the debate and incorporating the results into a humane and constructive approach to reducing youth crime', and made the case for 'joined-up' thinking and for multi-agency approaches to community problems that cross crime prevention and public health. As others have suggested, in some cases this might usefully and sensibly involve redefining some crime matters as public health matters. The policing and regulation of drug misusers is an obvious candidate, as proposed by Maher and Dixon (1999) and, rather notably, in 2002, by the Drugs Subcommittee of the Association of Chief Police Officers (NACRO, 2002: 14).

Alcohol services have frequently and justifiably complained that when compared to the priority and funding attached to dealing with illegal drug problems, they have been the neglected Cinderella services. Yet as we have seen, alcohol is as relevant to a strategy for reducing crime and victimization as illegal drugs. Of particular note here is the increasing significance of the night-time economy, fuelled by the economics of the successful leisure industry and welcomed by local and national government as a contributor to urban regeneration. This high-profit industry also produces high profits for the Treasury as highly taxed alcohol sales boom. Yet there is a clear tension between this development and certain concerns on the crime reduction and policing agendas, as late-night 'binge' drinking is associated with public disorder and violence, local residents' fear of crime and victimization is increased, and the new leisure landscape is increasingly 'policed' not by public police but by private security and bouncers (Hobbs *et al.*, 2003).

Summary

1   In this chapter we have described the history of controls and policy concerning alcohol and illegal drugs. We have discussed the complex relationships between alcohol, drugs and crime, and also examined the widening availability of drugs and alcohol.
2   The idea that drug use is becoming 'normalized' can be seen as an important but debatable proposition. Certainly, though, for some intoxicant consumers, a mix of alcohol and illegal drugs has become a regular menu of choice. This has important implications for education about 'drugs' but also for health.
3   The chapter has adopted a holistic approach and addressed not only crime and control matters but also the health implications of rising alcohol and drug use, broadening out to also consider other dimensions of the link between health and crime, such as mental health problems and social deprivation.
4   The introduction of health issues into criminological consideration is overdue and also draws attention to the role of health professionals as gatekeepers and controllers. The specialism of public health can be seen as social medicine but also as a form of surveillance and control. This function is explored in relation to debates about the role of psychiatrists.
5   Health services and therapeutic/control interventions also extend into the prison system and are part of new forms of diversion into treatment for drug-using offenders appearing before the courts.

Critical thinking questions

1   Consider the debates about decriminalization versus the prohibition of drugs. What is the evidence on both sides?

2   Can you provide examples of how 'good intentions' in the criminal justice and health systems have produced 'bad outcomes'?

3   Consider the growth of the night-time economy and its implications for crime and disorder.

4   Read this chapter alongside Chapter 13 and review the links between drugs and major crime from the local to the global.

Further study

Bean, P. (2002) *Drugs and Crime*, Cullompton: Willan. A review of the literature on drugs and crime with particular focus on criminal justice responses.

Berridge, V. (1999) *Opium and the People*, revised edn, London: Free Association Books. The 'classic' social history of the place of opium in English life in the nineteenth century, its legality and the development of moves towards control.

Roberts, M. (2003) *Drugs and Crime: From Warfare to Welfare*, London: NACRO. A thorough and lively overview of the criminological and policy literature concerning drugs, criminal justice, treatment and prospects for policy change.

South, N. (ed.) (1995) *Drugs, Crime and Criminal Justice*, 2 vols, Aldershot: Dartmouth.

South, N. (2002) 'Drugs, Alcohol and Crime', in M. Maguire, R. Morgan and R. Reiner (eds) *The Oxford Handbook of Criminology*, 3rd edn, Oxford: Oxford University Press. These volumes reprint various classic and more recent studies covering drug use, cultures, crime and criminal justice.

More information

Drugscope
http://www.drugscope.org.uk/
An invaluable site with access to an online encyclopaedia about drugs and to Drugscope's library.

Alcohol Concern
http://www.alcoholconcern.org.uk/
This site provides links to many other useful sites.

part 4

Controlling Crime

In this part, we look at the workings of the social control process – at the philosophies behind it, and how it may be changing shape in the twenty-first century. We focus on the police, the courts, prisons and their alternatives.

Thinking about Punishment

Introduction

This chapter provides an overview of criminological thinking on punishment, which can be simply defined as 'a legally approved method designed to facilitate the task of crime control' (Garland, 1990: 18). However, the fact that punishment causes pain, suffering and harm, raises important ethical dilemmas. Consequently the punishment of offenders requires moral justification, for, as Nicola Lacey (1988: 14) points out, the power to punish derives from the legal authority of the state to do things that would otherwise be 'prima facie morally wrongful' (see also Box 15.1). Moral philosophy is the contemporary branch of thinking that concerns itself with distinguishing between the age-old questions of identifying what is 'right' and 'wrong' and establishing 'good' and 'evil' through defining what ought to be the proper goals of punishment. Such questions are explicitly normative in that they ask what aims and values a system of punishment must fulfil if it is to be morally acceptable.

BOX 15.1 Why punish?

The following passage from the Russian novel *Resurrection* by Leo Tolstoy originally published in 1899 is widely quoted by philosophers:

> He asked a very simple question: 'Why, and by what right, do some people lock up, torment, exile, flog, and kill others, while they are themselves just like those they torment, flog, and kill?' And in answer he got deliberations as to whether human beings had free will or not; whether or not signs of criminality could be detected by measuring the skull; what part heredity played in crime; whether immorality could be inherited; and what madness is, what degeneration is, and what temperament is; how climate, food, ignorance, imitatitveness, hypnotism, or passion affect crime; what society is, what its duties are – and so on . . . but there was no answer on the chief point: 'By what right do some people punish others?'
>
> (Tolstoy, cited in Matravers, 2000: 1)

Tolstoy's question asks what justifies the deliberate infliction of suffering on those who do wrong? As we will see modern philosophical thinking treats punishment as a crucial element in the classic liberal problem of how the individual should relate to the state. Ultimately, liberal theories are concerned with individual rights and freedoms. On this basis punishment is justified 'in so far as it protects the freedom of individual citizens to go about their lives safe from the threat of crime' (Duff and Garland, 1994: 3), while individual rights are advocated as essential defences against the abuse of power by the state.

Of course, most judges or magistrates passing a sentence do not justify their decisions in the language of moral philosophy and if pushed they would tend to do so quite simply through recourse to 'what the law prescribes, what the Court of Appeal or the Magistrates' Association recommends, or what the local bench has agreed upon' (Walker, 1991: 6). Yet this can only, at best, amount to a principle of ensuring consistency – it does not explain why it is 'right' to punish in any meaningful sense or what greater 'good' might be achieved through inflicting more harm. Consequently, justifications of punishment are firmly rooted in broader moral and political philosophies that often conflict.

A second distinctive perspective can be regarded as a sociology of control for while it does attend to the uses of punishment it does so through considering the wider aspects of social control to reveal the 'deeper structures' of penal systems (Cohen, 1984). Although there is a tendency to evade complex normative issues this approach nevertheless does 'raise basic questions about the ways in which society organizes and deploys its power to punish' (Duff and Garland, 1994: 22). The difference can be put simply through using Barbara Hudson's (1996: 10/2003: 10) distinction which maintains that the philosophy of punishment deliberates on how things *ought* to be whereas the sociology of control tells it like it really is through explaining why particular societies adopt specific modes of punishment.

Although the principles of each philosophical justification will be emphasized it is important to recognize that the different rationalities coexist in uneasy hybrid combinations. As Nigel Walker (1991: 8) puts it, in 'practice Anglo-American sentencers tend to be eclectic, reasoning sometimes as utilitarians but sometimes, when they are outraged by a crime, as retributivists'. Similarly while there are competing forms of sociological explanation, which often fundamentally differ over how the same issues should be interpreted, the overall argument is that punishment, as a social institution, is an inherently complex business that needs to be approached from a range of theoretical perspectives, as no single interpretation will grasp the diverse meanings generated by punishment. Indeed, the problem of punishment is also one of the most enduring in political theory and has developed into an established subdiscipline of moral philosophy.

Philosophical justifications

Every time a court imposes a sentence it emphatically declares, in both a physical and symbolic sense, the sovereignty of the political power to which it owes judicial authority. Most criminologists would argue that as a consequence of this

> close proximity between the power to punish and the wider power to *rule*, it has become an axiom of political theory that the act of judicial sentencing requires to be justified by reference to some greater moral or ethical principle than merely the will of either the sentencer or the *de facto* law-giver.
>
> (Brownlee, 1998: 34; emphasis in original)

There are a number of competing justifications, which are rooted in opposing ideas over what the purpose of punishment should be. They fall into two distinctive groups. Those which see the aim of punishment as the prevention of future crimes are generally referred to as **reductivist**, and those which look to the past to punish crimes already committed are typically known as **retributivist**. In practice, however, most criminal justice systems fashion quite contradictory justifications so that the different rationalities often uncomfortably coexist and tensions between the two perennially arise. For instance, in criminal justice it is recognized that the pursuit of crime prevention (as a general good) must be subject to the specific constraints of procedural justice so that the innocent are not deliberately punished nor the guilty excessively punished (Duff, 1996: 3). These perennial tensions between the crime control and due process orientations of criminal justice are often compared to pendulum shifts between two competing values, with neither quite extinguishing the other, but a changing balance between them.

Reductivist principles

Reductivism justifies punishment on the grounds of its alleged future consequences. These arguments are supported by the form of moral reasoning known as utilitarianism. Although the origins of utilitarian thinking can be found in the fifth century BC in Plato's dialogues with Protagoras, a Thracian philosopher (Walker, 1991: 142), this moral theory was most famously advanced by Jeremy Bentham (1748–1832) as he argued that moral actions are those which produce 'the greatest happiness of the greatest number' of people. For punishment to reduce future crimes the pain and unhappiness caused to the offender must be 'outweighed by the avoidance of unpleasantness to other people in the future – thus making punishment morally right from a utilitarian point of view' (Cavadino and Dignan, 2002: 34). By pointing to a future or greater 'good' reductivist principles focus on the instrumental 'ends' of punishment. In doing so, utilitarian justifications of punishment make two further important appeals: 'that human well-being matters and that moral rules ought to be evaluated in light of their effect on human well-being' (Matravers, 2000: 5).

Utilitarian philosophy establishes what is good to do on the grounds of social usefulness and it judges actions by their consequences. It stipulates that 'the good' is human happiness, not some abstract metaphysical property, like the idea of 'natural rights', which Bentham famously dismissed as 'nonsense on stilts' or an empirically unknowable object, as in the will of God. Bentham's intention was to establish the law on a rational basis, which for him meant the facts of pleasure and pain rather than the vague fictions of natural rights – ideas driving much social reform in the nineteenth century (Carrabine, 2006: 192–3). The utilitarian justification of punishment is that the wrong experienced by the offender is outweighed by the compensating good effects for overall human well-being. The avoidance of further crime can be achieved through a number of strategies, such as:

- deterring potential criminals;
- reforming actual criminals; or by
- keeping actual or potential offenders out of circulation.

Deterrence

Deterrence is based on the idea that crime can be discouraged through the public's fear of the punishment they may receive if they break the law. For Bentham and contemporary thinkers a distinction is drawn between *individual* and *general* deterrence. Individual deterrence is said to occur when someone finds the experience of punishment so unpleasant that they never wish to repeat the infraction for fear of the consequences.

There is a long history of governments introducing severe punishments through claims that harsher penalties will produce special deterrence effects. The results, however, are modest at best. For instance, the introduction of 'short, sharp, shock' regimes into detention centres for young offenders in England and Wales by the Conservative government in the early 1980s 'proved to have no better post-release reconviction scores than centres operating the normal regime' and likewise, the popular American 'boot camps' of the 1990s, based on the aggressive training regimes of US marines, 'have not been shown to be at all effective in discouraging reoffending' (Dunbar and Langdon, 1998: 10).

In addition to these empirical doubts over the effectiveness of such strategies there are also more general moral objections raised against individual deterrence as it can

- be used to justify punishing the innocent as what matters is the communication of the penalty (Duff, 1996: 3);
- allow for punishment in excess of that deserved by the offence; and

■ is primarily concerned with offences that might be committed in the future, rather than the offences that have actually been committed (Hudson, 1996: 27/2003: 25).

Individual deterrence then is of little value as a moral justification for penal policy. On the other hand, general deterrence seems to offer a more plausible justification. This is the idea that offenders are punished, not to deter the offenders themselves, but to discourage other potential offenders. There can be little doubt that the existence of a system of punishment has some general deterrent, but it is important to recognize that the effects are easily overestimated. In recognition of these difficulties reductivists can also justify punishment on the basis of reform or rehabilitation.

Reform and rehabilitation

The term 'reform' is generally used to refer to the nineteenth-century development of prison regimes that sought to change the offender through a combination of hard labour and religious instruction, whereas 'rehabilitation' describes the more individualized treatment programmes introduced in the twentieth century in conjunction with the emergence of the welfare state (Garland, 1985). Both are based on the idea that punishment can reduce crime if it takes a form that will improve the individual's character so that they are less likely to reoffend in the future.

When the 'rehabilitative ideal' was at its height in the 1950s and 1960s it was strongly informed by positivist criminology, which viewed criminal behaviour not as freely willed action but as a symptom of some kind of mental illness which should be 'treated' like an illness. From around the mid-1970s it became widely assumed that whatever reform measures were chosen the research showed that 'nothing works' (Martinson, 1974). This message became accepted, less because of its validity, and more because it suited the mood of the times, in which there was a general move to the political right on both sides of the Atlantic and a widespread backlash against any form of welfarist solutions to social problems.

However, there are indications that rehabilitation is undergoing something of a revival as there have been recent attempts to find 'what works' (McGuire, 1995; Hollin, 1999; Crow, 2001). Few now maintain the appropriateness of 'medical' models of punishment, or claim that science can provide a cure for all criminality (though see Plate 15.1 and Box 15.2 for the turn to cognitive behavioural therapy (CBT) in recent probationary practice). Rehabilitation programmes are now seen as measures that might 'facilitate change' rather than 'coerce a cure' (Cavadino and Dignan, 2002: 38). Aside from the question mark over the effectiveness of rehabilitation programmes there are important moral objections raised by the very assumption that criminals need reform – a view criticized in Aldous Huxley's *Brave New World* (1994, first published in 1932) and Anthony Burgess's (1962) *Clockwork Orange* – and, as is seen later in this chapter, by the criminologist Stanley Cohen (1985) who offers a dystopian vision of an oppressive control net that intrudes into practically every aspect of our lives (see also Box 15.4).

Incapacitation

The idea that an offender's ability to commit further crimes should be removed, either physically or geographically (through locking them up, removing offending limbs or killing them), is generally referred to as incapacitation. In contrast to other justifications of punishment the logic of incapacitation appeals to neither changing the offender's behaviour nor searching for the causes of the offending. Instead it advocates the protection of potential victims as the essence of

BOX 15.2 A short history of probation

The search to find alternatives to imprisonment has taken many twists and turns over the last century. From the introduction of probation in the late nineteenth century, through to an increasing use of fines, to the more recent expansion of community penalties in the 1960s and 1970s there has been a quest to find less expensive, but still demanding, forms of non-custodial sentence (Worrall and Hoy, 2005). The origins of probation, which remains the main form of supervising offenders in the community, lay in religious missionary work and humanitarian concerns over the plight of the poor. For example, the Church of England Temperance Society played an active role in the courts by promoting the moral reform of offenders through abstinence from alcohol in the late Victorian era. Religious sensibilities played a prominent role in the campaign for a probation law in Britain, which came to fruition in the 1907 Probation of Offenders Act. This legislation allowed for the informal supervision of offenders in the community, in place of other punishment, if they seemed likely to reform.

It was not until the 1950s that probation services everywhere in Britain were provided by salaried, trained specialists rather than by a mixture of professional social workers and well-meaning amateurs. Throughout its history probation has been marked by a diverse mix of justifications and has encompassed a range of concerns: a way of reducing rising prison populations; a method of reducing crime or drunkenness; a means of saving souls from damnation by divine grace; and/or a way of easing personal and social problems experienced by offenders (Vanstone, 2007: 19). Especially important to the emerging professionalization of the probation service were the influence of psychological ideas and the facilitation of change through therapeutic work. This new approach adopted the old term 'casework' (which in its original use by the Charity Organization Society meant simply 'work on cases') to denote a process of one-to-one work in which the offender's needs and motivations were char-acteristically hidden behind a 'presenting problem', which could be revealed through a process of insight that involved working back to childhood to understand problematic behaviour (Whitehead and Statham, 2006: 56).

Most probation officers were trained as social workers and for much of the mid-twentieth century probation officers worked according to a 'treatment model' where probation was seen as a social service designed to prevent further crime by changing the offender's conduct. The demise of the 'rehabilitative ideal' in the 1960s and 1970s undermined the 'treatment model' on which probation in the post-war era had come to rest and gave rise to the pessimism of 'Nothing Works'. Critics from across the political spectrum were uniform in discrediting probation. Marxist criminologists argued that the treatment model of probation was paternalistic and coercive; pragmatists argued that it simply did not work; conservatives insisted that it was too soft and should be replaced by tougher sentences.

Over the last decade or so there has been something of a renaissance in probation under the 'What Works?' agenda where cognitive behavioural programmes have been optimistically embraced (see Plate 15.1). These programmes are based on the assumption that offenders commit crimes because of misperceptions and cognitive behavioural therapy targets specific unacceptable behaviours and seeks to modify these by correcting distortions in the way offenders think about their crime. The programmes cover a range of specific problem behaviours like anger management, drink driving and sex offending. Critics though have argued that enthusiasm for the cognitive behavioural approach should not result in the neglect of providing basic literacy and social skills, nor should the wider social problems leading people into crime be ignored (Worrall and Hoy, 2005).

The history of probation is one characterized by a diverse mix of political, religious and social concerns, but for many commentators the setting up of the National Offenders Management Service (NOMS) in 2004 has effectively ended the existence of an 'autonomous probation service with a distinctive ethos and primary task to work, in the main, with offenders in the community' (Whitehead and Statham, 2006: 3). The complaint is that NOMS brings probation into much closer alliance with the prison system and this fatally compromises the traditional identity and role of the probation service. It was not just this merging of these two agencies with very different cultures and ways of dealing with offenders that was controversial but the principle that 'all the functions of the Probation Service in a given geographical area could be transferred to a private or voluntary sector bidder' (Raynor, 2007: 1087). For critics this is yet further evidence of New Labour's unstinting faith in the ability of the private sector to reform public services and fundamental rejection of welfare policies.

punishment, as opposed to the rights of offenders. Many contemporary criminal justice strategies currently subscribe to the doctrine of incapacitation. In part, this is because it fills the void created by the collapse of rehabilitation and the associated argument that 'nothing works' in the 1970s, but also because it claims to offer a means of social defence through removing offenders from society and thereby eliminating their capacity to commit further crimes.

Examples of current criminal justice sentencing policy that are informed by the logic of incapacitation include the 'three strikes and you're out' penalty and selective incapacitation, both of which usually involve long periods of incarceration. More generally, incapacitation has become the main philosophical justification for imprisonment in countries that subscribe to the notion that 'prison works' as it takes many persistent and serious offenders off the streets and thereby, it is claimed, reduces the crime rate (Murray, 1997).

The model for this approach is what is known as the American 'prison experiment', because in the United States there has been a dramatic growth in the prison population over the last thirty years (Mauer, 2001). For instance, in 1970 there were 196,000 prisoners in state and federal prisons in the United States, but by the turn of the new century the figure exceeded 2 million and it has been estimated that if current US trends continue, '30 per cent of all black males born today will spend some of their lives in prison' (Garland, 2001a: 6). Critics argue that the 'experiment' has been funded by the diversion of public expenditure from welfare to the prison, while the level of violence, particularly among the young and disadvantaged, continues to devastate life in many North American cities (Currie, 1996); others point to the alarming racial dimension to this strategy of containment (Wacquant, 2001). Over a decade ago it was revealed that one in nine African-American males aged 20–29 is in prison at any one time, and that a staggering one in three is either in prison, on probation or parole (Mauer, 1997).

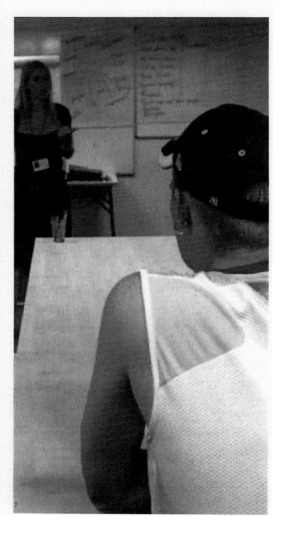

In Essex this year, we more than met all performance measures for accredited programmes.

People completing their programme requirement amounted to 126% of target.

Changing the habits of a lifetime...

IT IS ALWAYS POSSIBLE for skilled staff to prepare a detailed analysis of what has led someone to commit crime. The resulting document can often chart a life of misery, penury, sometimes abuse, often neglect, possibly mixed with plain bad luck, and plain bad management.

Diagnosis is only the beginning, however. Afterwards comes the hard stuff.

The individual needs to take on the responsibility for what they've done. They have to want to stop doing it. They must believe that it is possible. Then they need to find a way to change what is often solidly entrenched behaviour.

Anyone who has tried to kick a smoking habit will know of the denial, the resistance, the procrastination, and then the massive effort it takes to make the changes necessary for cutting it out altogether.

Looking at the distorted attitudes and thinking, learned over a lifetime, that must start changing before any serious move away from crime can occur, it is easy to appreciate that ours is a more complex task.

Programmes have been crafted to tackle the ingrained thinking, and achieve under-standing of what are complicated issues for anyone. Cognitive Behavioural techniques, combined with good groupwork skills, are important in achieving gradual change that will stick. Internalising the issues is vital.

When people understand their own motives, their own trigger points, and then learn the practical skills for changing their responses, success is possible.

Plate 15.1 This image is taken from a typical Probation Service report and highlights the current faith in cognitive behavioural techniques. Note the emphasis on individual responsibility, distorted thinking and internalized issues in an effort to define crime as a symptom of entrenched unacceptable behaviour.

Source: Essex Probation Service Annual Report 2005–6.

The question of why the United States has embarked on such a divisive social policy of mass incarceration has received considerable attention. It is clear that the prison explosion has impacted disproportionately on young, less educated African-American men and has deepened already entrenched inequalities. Many are critical of the idea that the cause is simply due to an increase in crime committed by that particular population. Bruce Western's (2006) analysis of national data sets reveals that despite the huge increase in the incarceration rate of black men in the last quarter of the twentieth century, they were less involved in crime in 2000 than in 1980. Moreover, the data suggest that the racial disparities in imprisonment for drug offenders (the 'War on Drugs' is often said to be the key driving force fuelling penal expansion) are not primarily due to race differences in offending. Indeed, the actual evidence suggests that the current prison boom is not a simple and straightforward response to crime, given that crime rates were *declining* before the massive prison expansion even began (Gilmore, 2007). It is thus to broader cultural, institutional, political and structural forces that recent scholarship has turned in an effort to grasp the factors that shape criminal justice policy (see Gottschalk, 2006; and Bosworth and Flavin's 2007 edited collection of essays on these issues).

Retributivist principles

In its simplest form, retributivism is the view that wrongdoers should be punished because they deserve it, irrespective of any future beneficial consequences. This principle dates from antiquity. For instance, the Code of Hammurabi is among the first written legal codes and enshrined the phrase 'an eye for an eye' in 1750 BC in Babylon, which is based on the concept of lex *talionis* – the 'law of retaliation'. This principle was developed by the Enlightenment philosopher Immanuel Kant (1724–1804) into a highly influential critique of utilitarian justifications of punishment, which use offenders 'merely as means' rather than fully recognizing their humanity so that even the innocent can be deliberately punished if it is expedient to do so. For Kant the duty to punish was a **categorical imperative** that restored the moral equilibrium – a view that led him famously to declare that even on the dissolution of society 'the last murderer remaining in prison must first be executed' (cited in Walker, 1991: 77).

Kant introduced a crucial distinction between what it would be *good* to do on the grounds of utility and what we have a *right* to do (Murphy, 1994: 49). Missing this important distinction between desire and duty reveals the illiberal consequences that can flow from utilitarian reasoning as there will be times when the individual is sacrificed for the general welfare of the many, with torture being perhaps the most controversial example (see Box 15.3). In Kantian terms justice is an issue of doing right rather than what would be good to do. Nevertheless, it was the increasing attraction of utilitarian justifications in the nineteenth and twentieth centuries that led to retributivism falling from favour as it appealed to archaic and reactionary feelings of revenge; yet one of the more striking developments of the last thirty years has been the revival of retributivist ideas under the guise of 'just deserts'.

Just deserts

During the 1950s and 1960s the penal system was generally understood to be an important element in the welfare state's programme of social engineering that would prevent crime through deterring potential offenders and incapacitating actual offenders, and it was hoped that treatment programmes would rehabilitate offenders. As we have seen by the mid-1970s the institutions of the welfare state were under serious attack from all shades of the political spectrum not simply because of their perceived failure but also because of their moral costs. In addition to neo-

BOX 15.3 The torture debate

The debate on torture has gathered force in the wake of the 'War on Terror'. The treatment of 'unlawful combatants' at Guantànamo Bay and the humiliating practices experienced by Iraqi prisoners at Abu Ghraib each have revealed the extent to which torture has become commonplace in the post 9/11 climate, and Britain's denial that its territories have been used for 'extraordinary rendition' (where suspects are moved to 'interrogation centres' in third-party countries where they are held outside the law) has also been challenged by human rights investigators (Doward, 2008: 3). Nevertheless, much of the emphasis is now on what has been termed 'preventive investigational torture', that is where torture is used to obtain information to thwart terrorist attacks; several justifications have been advanced to support this position (Dershowitz, 2002; Bagaric and Clarke, 2005; Greenberg, 2006). In one way or another each draws on Bentham's utilitarian reasoning and his justifications were invoked by the police and other security agencies around the world long before the 9/11 attacks (see Morgan, 2000; for an account of the origins of modern torture, see Welch, 2007).

Bentham, however, seemed to be aware of the dangers of torture – even if there are short-term advantages (such as extracting information that saves hundreds of lives); in the long run torture fatally undermines the principles and legitimacy of liberal democracy itself. Much of the current debate though rests on what has been described as the 'ticking-bomb' scenario. This is used to show how torture can be morally justified:

> Apart from a few orthodox Kantians, there is hardly a soul who would not have to concede that in an extreme enough situation, in which hundreds of lives could be saved by using force to extricate the information needed to find and defuse a ticking bomb from the person responsible for placing it, if no other means were available, severe force could, and possibly even should, be used to extract the information.
>
> (Kretsmer, 2007: 123)

As Slavoj Žižek (2002: 5–6) wrote in response to these recent ideas that torture can be justified by keeping within 'reasonable' bounds, this is the worst kind of 'liberal illusion', not least since the ticking-bomb scenario is deceptive: in the vast majority of cases torture is not carried out to find ticking bombs, but for quite different reasons (to punish enemies, or to psychologically break prisoners, or to terrorize an entire population, etc). As he explains, a 'consistent ethical stance has to reject such pragmatic-utilitarian reasoning'. Others have maintained that an absolute prohibition on torture has to be made. Any relaxation on prohibition will, it is argued, inevitably lead to the use of torture in wide-ranging situations that are completely removed from these 'ticking-bomb' scenarios (Kretsmer, 2007: 124).

conservative critics (Wilson, 1975) liberal thinkers also began to reassert the importance of justice over utility and of individual rights against the claims of the state (Rawls, 1972; Dworkin, 1978). One important 'manifestation of this moral shift was that theorists began to focus on the rights of the guilty as well as those of the innocent' (Duff and Garland, 1994: 10). This gave birth to a prisoners' rights movement that chimed with broader conceptions of civil rights so that the need to protect prisoners and others from the arbitrary and discretionary powers of state bureaucracies became paramount (Fogel, 1975).

It is in this context that the 'new retributivist' arguments emerged and formulated the principle of 'just deserts', which insists that offenders should only be punished as severely as they deserve, in reaction against the unfair excesses of rehabilitation and the 'get tough' incapacitative drive from conservatives. The leading advocate of this movement, Andrew von Hirsch (1976), proposed that greater consistency and certainty should lie at the centre of the criminal justice system with punishment fitting the crime rather than the person. Key elements here are *proportionality* – the offender should be sentenced according to what the act deserves; and *denunciation* – condemnation of the offence through restoring the moral equilibrium while expressing social disapproval.

These principles, in certain important respects, recall the classical criminologist Cesare Beccaria's (1738–94) arguments for due process in the criminal justice system and are based on a similar understanding of the social contract, which is supposed to apply equally and fairly to everyone. Retributive punishment is thereby seen as ensuring that offenders do not profit from their wrongdoing. Yet, as critics have argued, the fundamental flaw in this line of thinking is that it is only applicable if social relations are just and equal, otherwise there is no equilibrium to restore. It is the case, however, that offenders tend to be already socially disadvantaged so that punishment actually increases inequality rather than reducing it (Cavadino and Dignan, 2002: 42).

Hybrid compromises

So far we have been setting out the fundamental philosophical justifications and discussing their respective limitations, yet it is important to emphasize that in practice most criminal justice systems combine these differing rationales in uneasy combinations. For instance, it is generally acknowledged that the 'just deserts' approach to criminal justice proposed by liberals critical of rehabilitation in the 1970s had by the 1980s become co-opted by the political right (Hudson, 1987). The clearest indication of this is the strategy pursued by the Conservative government which culminated in the Criminal Justice Act 1991. This piece of legislation repeatedly emphasized the principle of 'just deserts' as the aim of criminal justice with a greater stress on proportionality in sentencing, yet at the same time the Act designated community penalties (discussed in more detail below) as 'punishment in the community' in an effort to reinforce the tough 'law and order' image of the government.

Shortly after the legislation was introduced, the Conservatives appeared to abandon 'just deserts' in an effort to further strengthen their punitive credentials in favour of another hybrid combination of incapacitation and deterrence – famously declared by the then Home Secretary, Michael Howard, in his insistence that 'prison works'. For some critics the 'populist punitiveness' of John Major's Conservative government has continued under New Labour (Carrabine et al., 2000: 194–6). One indication of this is the insistence that imprisonment should not be reserved only for serious offenders but is also suitable for persistent petty offenders. This directly contradicts the principle that punishment should fit the crime, and it has been reported that when Jack Straw was Home Secretary he explicitly stated that he wanted to end the 'just deserts' philosophy through arguing that 'it is time to make the sentence fit the offender rather than the offence' (Cavadino and Dignan, 2002: 53). Others have argued that 'penal populism' has enabled various governments to rely less on the experience of civil servants and academics in the formulation of criminal justice policy and instead politicians seek to tap into what they believe to be the general public's appetite for tough punishment (Pratt, 2007).

Clearly the fundamental justifications can exist in different combinations but to explain why these uneasy compromises might be more than simply passing fashions it is to sociological forms of explanation that we need to turn.

BOX 15.4 Restorative justice: a new justification for punishment?

Some criminologists are now arguing that restorative justice brings fresh and more just relationships between offenders and victims. The arguments are based partly on the principle of reparation in that those who offend should do something to repair the wrong they have done, and in so doing acknowledge the harm they have caused. Although reparation can take many forms and has a long history (see Box 15.2), such as paying a fine (through the courts) to compensate a victim or carrying out unpaid work that will benefit the community, there is an important sense in which there is a recognition of the rights of victims to have redress for the harm they have suffered. It is partly as a result of these developments that restorative justice has gained momentum as an alternative to modern Western systems of punishment.

Over the past fifteen years the principles of restorative justice have moved from the margins of criminology to the centre of lively debates not only in the discipline but also in criminal justice policy. The origins of restorative justice are diverse and yet all arise from disillusionment with modern systems of criminal justice. Its supporters include penal abolitionists, social theologians, postcolonial critics and the victims movement who are united in their efforts to redefine justice as a process of shoring up rifts in communities through helping the victim and offender overcome their trauma through forms of 'reintegrative shaming' (Braithwaite, 1989). Scandinavian penal abolitionists (Christie, 1977) have been arguing since the 1970s that state punishment is oppressively authoritarian and ought to be based on an alternative conceptualization of 'redress' that disperses decision-making among a much more heterogeneous community (de Haan, 1990). Another important set of developments have been the 'rediscovery' of distinctive indigenous systems of justice. For instance, 'family group conferences' arose through Maori criticism of the dominant Western juvenile justice system that had stripped the community of responsibility for dealing with its young, whereas 'sentencing circles' were revived in the Yukon Territory, Canada, and are 'an updated version of the traditional sanctioning and healing practices of Canadian Aboriginal peoples' (Bazemore and Taylor-Griffiths, 2003: 78).

Although there have been scattered mediation schemes in England and Wales since the 1970s, the Crime and Disorder Act 1998 and the Youth Justice and Criminal Evidence Act 1999 have formally introduced elements of restorative justice as a mainstream response to youth offending in a number of different ways, including family group conferences based on the New Zealand model, reparation orders for offenders aged 10 and older, and consultation with victims before any reparative intervention is organized (Gelsthorpe and Morris, 2002: 246). Restorative justice is not without its critics who point out that there are few safeguards to protect the most vulnerable groups from the pious moralizing of reintegrative shaming.

Making offenders face up to their wrongdoing can lead to some serious abuses of power, as critics suggest:

> The potential for coercion and even bullying of young people, outnumbered and outwitted by a 'room full of adults', none of which has direct responsibility to safeguard and promote the best interests of the child and, moreover, where there may be a collusion of interests on the side of the victim, must be recognized and must be actively prevented by the 'good practice' of participants (as there are few built-in legal or procedural safeguards).
>
> (Haines and O'Mahony, 2006: 119)

This absence of accountability compounds the lack of protection for the offender in terms of appeals to legal process and due rights (Ashworth, 2003); while a former supporter has become highly sceptical of the claims made by the more evangelical advocates (Daly, 2002). Others argue that only human rights can guarantee fair treatment in restorative justice approaches (Hudson, 2005: 66). Fundamental issues remain over whether restorative justice challenges or casts the net of social control deeper into the community.

Sociological explanations

Instead of asking questions over punishment's effectiveness or justification, sociologists 'attend to the ways in which penal policy is determined by political forces and the struggle of contending interests, rather than by normative argument or relevant empirical evidence' (Duff and Garland, 1994: 32). In exploring the deeper role punishment plays in society a number of competing perspectives can be identified. Each is informed by a social theory that can be traced back to the 'founding fathers' of sociology as authors tend to adopt a Durkheimian approach or a Marxist position and then critically disregard other ways of thinking. What this chapter will now do is set out the main sociological explanations of punishment that are derived from the work of Durkheim, Marx and Foucault before discussing feminist critiques of these 'malestream' perspectives.

Although these diverse approaches cannot simply be bolted together to form the definitive sociological statement on punishment, as there are fundamental differences of interpretation, there is an important sense in which sociology reveals the complex and multifaceted dimensions of punishment as a social institution that otherwise remain hidden. Nevertheless, the overall argument follows David Garland's (1990: 2) insistence that criminologists must develop 'a more pluralistic approach' to capture the 'richness of meaning' generated by punishment.

Durkheim and social solidarity

The distinctive contribution of Émile Durkheim (1858–1917) lies in the way he examined the relationships between crime, law and punishment to reveal the mechanisms that create and sustain social solidarity. This sociological approach is often referred to as functionalism, as he argued that whatever aspect of social life is being studied it must be approached from the perspective of discovering what role it performs in preserving social stability and promoting moral consensus. Although his ideas have been dismissed for their inherent conservatism, there is an important sense in which he draws attention to the functions punishment plays in maintaining social order in the face of rapid economic change and political upheaval.

Durkheim's theory of punishment is initially advanced in his most famous book *The Division of Labour in Modern Society* (1893/1960) and is then extended in the article 'Two Laws of Penal Evolution' (1901/1984) to give a more nuanced understanding of historical change. In *The Division of Labour* he develops his classic theory on the emergence of specialized work in modern societies through distinguishing between simple, pre-industrial societies in which there is little division of labour and more advanced societies, where people perform complex, specialized tasks.

At the core of his work is a concern with social solidarity, by which he means the shared conventions, meanings and moralities that hold societies together. In each type of society he saw punishment playing an important role in the creation of solidarity and he goes so far as to say that 'passion is the soul of punishment' as it arouses furious moral indignation and a ritualized expression of social values against those who had violated the sacred moral order. Even though modern 'penal systems may try to achieve utilitarian objectives, and to conduct themselves rationally and unemotively', the strength of Durkheim's account is how it reveals that 'at an underlying level there is still a vengeful, motivating passion which guides punishment and supplies its force' (Garland, 1990: 31).

Punitive passions and degradation rituals

There is an important sense in which Durkheim draws attention to the expressive qualities of punishment, how 'all healthy consciences' come together to reaffirm shared beliefs through dutiful outrage that constructs a 'public wrath' (cited in Giddens, 1972: 127). In the controversial work of the German philosopher Friedrich Nietzsche (1844–1900), an altogether more sinister account of punitive sentiments is offered in his *Genealogy of Morals*, where he argues that punishment gratifies sadistic and cruel tendencies in the human condition. He explains that to 'witness suffering does one good, to inflict it even more so – that is a harsh proposition, but a fundamental one, an old, powerful, human all-too-human proposition . . . in punishment there is so much that is *festive!*' (Nietzsche, 1887/1996: 50; emphasis in original). In his history of ethics Nietzsche (ibid.: 46–7) sought to expose how the Judaeo-Christian and liberal traditions of compassion, equality and justice are products of brutal and cruel processes – how they 'have long been steeped in blood' and 'not even with old Kant: the categorical imperative gives off a whiff of cruelty'. Of course, modern penal systems refute any association with cruelty, humiliation, malice and sadism, but Nietzsche insists that these passions continue to exist even though we are now in what the psychoanalyst Sigmund Freud (1856–1939) would call **denial** as 'the pleasure in cruelty' barely troubles 'even the most delicate hypocritical conscience' (ibid.: 49).

A less disturbing account of punitive passions is outlined by the Chicagoan social psychologist George Herbert Mead (1863–1931). Mead followed Durkheim by maintaining that there was a close relationship between punishment and social solidarity, but his account differs in that he argued that the collective hostility towards a criminal had the effect of 'uniting members of the community in the emotional solidarity of aggression' (Mead, 1918: 591). Mead did not regard this intense emotion as healthy but that it promoted a number of harmful consequences. As Claire Valier (2002a: 31) puts it, 'the spirals of rage emanating outwards from a heinous crime were traumatising rather than healing'.

The Durkheimian tradition has continued to provide insightful analyses of how penal rituals provoke symbolic and emotive effects. For instance, the Danish sociologist Svend Ranulf argued that criminal law developed as a consequence of middle-class moral indignation (Barbalet, 2002), while Harold Garfinkel (1956a: 420–4) insisted that the rituals of the courtroom should be understood as a 'degradation ceremony' as 'moral indignation serves to effect the ritual destruction of the person denounced' by defining the accused as an enemy of all that is good and decent in society – a view subsequently developed by Pat Carlen (1976) in her analysis of *Magistrates' Justice* (see also Chapter 16).

Plate 15.2(a) Two women shout abuse at a police van carrying Maxine Carr from Peterborough on 18 September 2002. Carr was arrested and charged with attempting to pervert the course of justice over a police investigation into the murder of two young girls in Soham, Cambridgeshire.

Source: © Reuters; *photo:* Ian Waldie.

(b) A boy stands next to a banner as he awaits the departure of Ian Huntley from Peterborough Magistrates' Court on 10 September 2002. Police mounted a heavy security operation outside the court after hundreds of protestors turned up the previous month when Maxine Carr, Huntley's girlfriend, was charged with perverting the course of justice.

Source: © Reuters; *photo:* Darren Staples.

thinking about punishment

The legacy of the Durkheimian tradition has been summarized by drawing attention to the fact that in modern penal systems there is a crucial division

> between the *declaration* of punishment, which continues to take the form of a public ritual and which is continually the focus of public and media attention, and the *delivery* of punishment that now characteristically occurs behind closed doors and has a much lower level of visibility.
>
> (Garland, 1991: 125; emphasis in original)

So while Durkheim and his contemporaries identify the *function* of modern punishment in reassuring public sentiment, they have rather less to say about the *form* it takes – issues that are addressed in the following perspectives.

Marx and political economy

Marxist analyses of punishment not only address a whole range of themes ignored by Durkheim, but also reinterpret many of those that Durkheim does consider. Karl Marx's (1818–83) legacy to sociology was to insist that societies must be understood in terms of how economic structures condition social practices. Consequently, Marxists tend to consider punishment in relation to economic structures and examine the class interests served by penal practices. In marked contrast to Durkheim, they argue that punishing offenders for breaking laws maintains and reinforces the position of the ruling class, rather than benefiting society as a whole, and that punishment as a social institution plays an important political role as a repressive state apparatus.

One of the earliest Marxist analyses of punishment was carried out by the German Marxist scholar Georg Rusche. It was later written up with the assistance of Otto Kirchheimer and published in 1939 through the exiled Frankfurt School of Social Research in New York, as *Punishment and Social Structure*. It is a work that charts the changing deployment of penal methods from the Middle Ages up to the early decades of the twentieth century. Rusche and Kirchheimer's analysis highlights the relationships between the form that punishments take and the economic requirements of particular modes of production. They argued in a much-quoted passage that

> Every system of production tends to discover punishments which correspond to its productive relationships . . . it is self-evident that enslavement as a form of punishment is impossible without a slave economy; that prison labour is impossible without manufacture or industry, that monetary fines for all classes of society are impossible without a monetary economy.
>
> (Rusche and Kirchheimer, 1939/1968: 5–6)

These arguments have subsequently been criticized on the grounds of what is known as economic determinism, as they excessively (and eventually incoherently) rely on the concept of 'labour market' to explain forms of punishment.

Nevertheless, they emphasize what other commentators have called the principle of **less eligibility** as vital to the management of inequality in capitalist societies, by which they refer to 'the standard of living within prisons (as well as for those dependent on the welfare apparatuses) must be lower than that of the lowest stratum of the working class' (Rusche and Kirchheimer, 1939/1968: 108). Their basic thesis has been developed by Dario Melossi and Massimo Pavarini (1978) who argue that the reason why the prison has developed as the response to crime in capitalist societies is because of the development of wage labour, which crucially has put a price on time. An important consequence of which is that it now seems natural that criminals should pay for their crimes by doing time, since workers are rewarded for their labour by the hour. Although this argument does rightly emphasize the importance of economic relations on penal practices, it does so in a way that minimizes the significance of other crucial factors. This political economy approach has been revived in Alessandro de Giorgi's (2006) ambitious attempt to provide a materialist explanation for the development of new technologies of control since the 1970s up to the present day.

Punishment, ideology and class control

In contrast, other Marxists have stressed the role of punishment in ideological class struggles and the maintenance of state power rather than labour market conditions and systems of economic production. The elements of such an interpretation are present in the work of the Russian legal theorist E. B. Pashukanis (1924/1978) as he argues that the penal sanctions of capitalist societies articulate bourgeois mentalities and ideological conceptions relating to the commodity form: an exchange transaction, in which the offender pays a debt and concludes the contractual obligation through serving a prison sentence (a clear influence on Melossi and Pavarini, 1978). In this manner the ideological content of capitalist societies and bourgeois values (like fair trading and liberty) are reaffirmed in spite of the harsh realities that exist in such societies (such as inequality and impoverishment).

As Garland (1990: 118) argues, this account is developed by the social historian Douglas Hay (1975) in his analysis of eighteenth-century criminal law, drawing attention to its dual functions of ideological legitimation and class coercion. In particular, he regards the expansion of capital punishment as a 'rule of terror' on the part of the landed aristocracy over thousands of landless poor, with the exercise of clemency (where the lord of the manor speaks to fellow gentry on behalf of a tenant at risk of severe punishment) regarded by Hay as a central factor contributing to the culture of deference still in evidence today among rural peasantry. Writing from within a humanistic tradition of Marxism, E. P. Thompson contends that the law can function ideologically to legitimate the existing order, but that

> people are not as stupid as some structural philosophers suppose them to be. They will not be mystified by the first man who puts on a wig. . . . If the law is evidently partial and unjust, then it will mask nothing, legitimize nothing, contribute nothing to any class's hegemony.
> (Thompson, 1975: 262–3)

The clear implication is that the law is an 'arena for class struggle' rather than the exclusive possession of a ruling class (Thompson, 1975: 288). However, critics of this form of Marxist analysis point out that the criminal law and penal sanctions command a wide degree of support from the subordinate classes (the very population said to be controlled and regulated by such mechanisms of class rule) and that such practices afford a degree of protection previously unrealized (Fine, 1985). Nevertheless, one of the strengths of Marxist analysis is that it invites us to think of punishment not as a simple response to crime but as an important element in 'managing the rabble' (Irwin, 1990: 2) – matters that are now considered in the work of Michel Foucault who, for some, marks a decisive break with Marxism.

Foucault and disciplinary power

Over the past thirty years or so the French philosopher Michel Foucault (1926–84) has cast an enormous influence over criminology – even though he was rather scathing of the discipline. His work can be located in a tradition begun by Nietzsche, who was highly sceptical of Western rationality, and continues in the disenchanted sociology of Max Weber (1864–1920), who wrote pessimistically of an 'iron cage' of rationality and bureaucracy that will ultimately imprison us all. Foucault's (1977) *Discipline and Punish* is not simply a detailed analysis of the emergence of the prison in the nineteenth century (see Chapter 18) but is also an account of how power operates in the modern era. The book opens with a striking juxtaposition of two entirely different styles of punishment that illustrate the fundamental transformations that had taken place in penal practices, namely the disappearance of the public spectacle of violence and the installation of a different form of punishment by the early nineteenth century, which is captured in a bland listing of the rules from an institutional timetable used in a Paris reformatory (see p. 53).

On a broader scale, these developments are illustrative of how power operates in modern society and he sets himself the ambitious task of 'writing the history of the present' (Foucault, 1977: 31). One influential commentator has summarized Foucault's argument in the following way:

> the 'Great Incarcerations' of the nineteenth century – thieves into prisons, lunatics into asylums, conscripts into barracks, workers into factories, children into school – are to be seen as part of a grand design. Property had to be protected, production had to be standardised by regulations, the young segregated and inculcated with the ideology of thrift and success, the deviant subjected to discipline and surveillance.
>
> (Cohen, 1985: 25)

The new disciplinary mode of power which the prison was to represent belonged to an economy of power quite different from that of the direct, arbitrary and violent rule of the sovereign. Power in capitalist society had to be exercised at the lowest possible cost, both economically and politically, while its effects had to be intensified and extended throughout the social apparatus. Although Foucault's work continues to be influential, as we will see in the next section, it has been criticized for

■ its 'appalling' historical inaccuracies (Braithwaite, 2003: 8);
■ its 'impoverished' understating of subjectivity (McNay, 1994: 22);
■ its preference for 'ascetic description' over normative analysis (Habermas, 1987: 275); and for
■ not being able to tell the difference between prison and life outside.

The punitive city and surveillance society

It is more than a little ironic that at the very moment when Foucault's (1977) analysis of the 'Great Incarcerations' was published, many Western societies seemed to be radically reversing the institutional response to deviance through processes of **decarceration** and the use of alternative sanctions in the community. Community corrections came to be regarded as a more humane and less stigmatizing means of responding to offenders, while treating mental illness in the community was generally seen as preferable to the asylum. However, a number of authors were sceptical and argued that treatment in the community amounted to malign neglect, with the mentally ill left to fend for themselves in uncaring environments (Scull, 1977). In criminology, Stanley Cohen (1979b, 1985) has maintained that the development of community corrections marks both a continuation and an intensification of the social control patterns identified by Foucault (1977). This 'dispersal of discipline' thesis insists that there is now a blurring of where the prison ends and the community begins (see Box 15.5) with an accompanying increase in the total number of offenders brought into the system.

BOX 15.5 A vision of social control

Stanley Cohen wrote this over twenty years ago – does it still sound like the future?

Mr and Mrs Citizen, their son Joe and daughter Linda, leave their suburban home after breakfast, saying goodbye to Ron, a 15-year-old pre-delinquent who is living with them under the LAK (Look After A Kid) scheme. Ron will later take a bus downtown to the Community Correctional Centre, where he is to be given two hours of Vocational Guidance and later tested on the Interpersonal Maturity Level Scale. Mr C. drops Joe off at the School Problems Evaluation Centre from where Joe will walk to school. In his class are five children who are bussed from a local Community Home, four from a Pre-Release Facility and three who, like Ron, live with families in the neighbourhood. Linda gets off next – at the GUIDE Centre (Girls Unit for Intensive Daytime Education) where she works as a Behavioural Contract Mediator. They drive past a Threequarter-way House, a Rape-Crisis Centre and then a Drug-Addict Cottage, where Mrs C. waves to a group of boys working in the garden. She knows them from some work she does in RODEO (Reduction of Delinquency Through Expansion of Opportunities). She gets off at a building which houses the Special Parole Unit, where she is in charge of a 5-year evaluation research project on the use of the HIM (Hill Interaction Matrix) in matching group treatment to client. Mr C. finally arrives at work, but will spend his lunch hour driving around the car again as this is his duty week on patrol with TIPS (Turn In a Pusher). On the way he picks up some camping equipment for the ACTION weekend hike (Accepting Challenge Through Interaction with Others and Nature) on which he is going with Ron, Linda and five other PINS (Persons In Need of Supervision).

(Cohen, 1985: 224–5)

While Cohen (1985) chronicled the recruitment of friends, relatives and neighbours into the web of surveillance through curfews, tracking and tagging that now pervades the 'punitive city' (Cohen, 1979b), a debate ensued over the applicability of Foucault's ideas to contemporary patterns of punishment (Bottoms, 1983; Nelken, 1989; I. Taylor, 1999). Other developments since the 1990s include the rapid expansion of electronic, information and visual technologies, all of which greatly enhance the surveillance capacities of the state (see Chapter 20 on crime and the media). Today, surveillance operates in so many spheres of daily life that it is impossible to avoid (see Plate 15.3). A situation well described in the following passage:

> Most of our social encounters and almost all our economic transactions are subject to electronic recording, checking and authorization. From the Electronic Funds Transfer at Point of Sale (EFTPOS) machine for paying the supermarket bill or the request to show a barcoded driver's license, to the cellphone call or the Internet search, numerous everyday tasks trigger some surveillance device.
>
> (Lyon, 2001: 146)

Likewise urban fortress living has quickly moved from a dystopian vision (Cohen, 1985) to become a reality, particularly in Los Angeles (Davis, 1992, 1999) so that contemporary surveillance is both inclusionary – offering a sense of safety, security and order for some city dwellers – and exclusionary for others – prohibiting certain teenagers from entering panoptic shopping centres while planners develop sadistic street environments to displace the homeless from particular localities. John Fiske (1998) has further analysed the video surveillance of the American city to reveal how it is a rapidly developing control strategy focused on the young black male and is a disturbing instance of the totalitarian undercurrents in late modern democracies. Whereas Ray Coleman and Joe Sim (2000: 636) have argued that the deployment of CCTV in city centres is not simply a crime-prevention technology but is a troubling response to 'gaps left by a series of legitimation deficits around policing and in urban governance generally' (see the recent edited collections by Haggerty and Ericson, 2006; and Lyon, 2006, for further commentary on surveillance in these times of 'post-privacy').

Plate 15.3 Banksy's 'What are you looking at?', Marble Arch, London.

Feminist challenges

It will be clear that these main philosophical and sociological traditions have largely ignored the punishment of women and it is only in the past thirty years or so that studies of the control of women have appeared. Nevertheless, it is important to emphasize that the study of gender continues to be marginalized and, as Ngaire Naffine (1997: 5) has argued, criminology remains a male-dominated discipline consisting largely of academic men studying criminal men. Naffine maintains that the 'costs to criminology of its failure to deal with feminist scholarship are perhaps more severe than they would be in any other discipline'. A clear instance of this is the widespread finding that when women are punished, this is as much about upholding conventional gender stereotypes as penalizing criminality (Carlen, 1983; Edwards, 1984; Howe, 1994).

Moreover the control of women indicates processes of **transcarceration**, which is defined as the movement of offenders between different institutional sites (Lowman *et al.*, 1987). Feminist studies have shown how there is a continuum of regulation in women's lives that encompasses the penal system, mental health and social welfare systems through to informal social (and antisocial) controls (Cain, 1989; Smart, 1995). The overall picture that emerges from this work is a more nuanced understanding of disciplinary control once the variable application to women and men is considered. For instance, it is clear that women are much more likely to be controlled by psychiatry and social work while men are more readily incarcerated. It would seem that gender divisions are as fundamental to structuring punishment as those of class and race.

Feminist jurisprudence

In recent years there have been a growing number of proposals for a 'feminist jurisprudence' (Carlen, 1990; Daly, 1989; Naffine, 1990) based on two main premises. The first is that legal categories which are supposedly gender-neutral are in fact a reflection of male dominance (MacKinnon, 1987); the second, and much more controversial among feminists, is that there is a kind of reasoning, characteristic to women, that is excluded from criminal justice decision-making (Hudson, 2003: 180). While feminist scholars continue to emphasize the need to bring women's experiences and voices into criminological and legal theorizing, there is widespread dispute over whether there is a universal 'female voice'.

The idea that women have a distinctive form of moral reasoning that is more concerned with finding solutions to specific and concrete problems than men, who are more preoccupied with the application of general abstract rules, is primarily associated with the work of Carol Gilligan (1982) in her book In a Different Voice. She termed the female moral style 'the ethic of care', in contrast to the male 'logic of justice', and argued that both voices should have equal weight in moral reasoning; in practice, 'women's voices were misheard or judged as morally inferior to men's' (Daly, 2002: 65). Consequently, feminist criminologists have called for legal processes to admit expert witnesses with specific feminist viewpoints to qualify masculine constructions of crime and punishment (O'Donovan, 1993; Valverde, 1996).

This concept of feminist moral reasoning is controversial. Carol Smart (1989) has argued that it advances a view of men and masculinity as beyond culture and history, which serves to distort women's experiences. At the same time the work appears to want to replace one unitary view of the world, the male view, with another unitary and, ultimately, distorting, female view. Sandra

Walklate (2001: 167) further explains that this 'desire to replace one world view with another fails to remove feminism from the traps of both essentialism (men and women are naturally and fundamentally different) and determinism (people, men nor women, have no choice)'. Overall, Smart's work is sceptical as to whether it is possible or even desirable to strive for a way of thinking through the law that represents all women's (or even all men's) experiences. Nevertheless, these debates effectively demonstrate that criminologists need to examine crime and punishment from a gendered perspective.

Summary

1   The power to punish derives from the legal authority of the state to do things that would otherwise be prima facie morally wrongful. Consequently, the pain, suffering and cruelty caused by punishment require some form of moral justification.
2   This chapter has reviewed a number of competing philosophical positions that seek to legitimate the harm (e.g. deterrence, retribution, rehabilitation, etc.) through to forms of moral reasoning that define what ought to be the proper goals of punishment.
3   In contrast sociological approaches to punishment have tended to consider the wider aspects of social control. Here the deeper structures of penal systems are excavated to show how penal policy is determined by political forces rather than by abstract philosophical argument or relevant empirical evidence.
4   The chapter has also described how the punishment of women challenges conventional thinking and reviewed the arguments surrounding feminist moral reasoning.

Critical thinking questions

1   Compare the differences between reductivists and retributivists over how punishment should be justified and how much punishment ought to be inflicted.
2   In what ways, if any, is the current American 'prison experiment' a 'totalitarian solution without a totalitarian state' (Bauman, 1995: 206)?
3   Why might punishment provoke solidarity and hostility among the public?
4   How does the principle of 'less eligibility' continue to inform contemporary practices of punishment?
5   In a pamphlet for a prisoners' rights campaign, Michel Foucault (quoted in Eribon, 1992) once remarked that '[T]hey tell us that the prisons are overcrowded, but what if the entire population is over imprisoned?' What do you take to be the implications of this assertion?
6   Can you make a case for feminist jurisprudence?

Further study

Bosworth, M. and Flavin, J. (eds) (2007) *Race, Gender and Punishment: From Colonialism to the War on Terror*, New Brunswick, NJ: Rutgers University Press. An important collection of essays demonstrating how white American anxieties over race and ethnic minorities continue to shape penal practices.

Cavadino, M. and Dignan, J. (2007) *The Penal System: An Introduction*, 4th edn, London: Sage. An indispensable guide, which provides an accessible overview of the field.

Garland, D. (1990) *Punishment and Modern Society: A Study in Social Theory*, Oxford: Clarendon Press. This is an authoritative discussion of sociological explanation, save for feminist challenges to the discipline.

Hudson, B. (2003) *Understanding Justice*, 2nd edn, London: Sage. A wide-ranging and accessible guide.

Scott, D. (2008) *Penology*, London: Sage. A concise and imaginative introduction to the field.

Smart, C. (1995) *Law, Crime and Sexuality*, London: Sage. A book giving insight into feminist analysis in this area.

Walker, N. (1991) *Why Punish?*, Oxford: Oxford University Press. A lively introduction to philosophical positions.

More information

The Home Office: Publications: A Guide to the Criminal Justice System in England and Wales

http://www.homeoffice.gov.uk/rds/cjspub1.html

Publication available online, on the criminal justice process in England and Wales.

Criminal Justice System

http://www.cjsonline.org/home.html

This is another site that has useful information on the criminal justice process in England and Wales.

Crown Office and Procurator Fiscal Service

http://www.crownoffice.gov.uk/

This site has information on the Scottish criminal justice system plus a selection of other links for reference.

Criminal Justice System Northern Ireland

http://www.cjsni.gov.uk/

A site on the criminal justice process in Northern Ireland.

Proceedings of the Old Bailey

http://www.oldbaileyonline.org/

A fully searchable online edition of the largest body of texts detailing the lives of non-elite people ever published, containing accounts of over 100,000 criminal trials held at London's central criminal court.

Restorative Justice Online
www.restorativejustice.org
Excellent resource providing access to thousands of publications on restorative justice.

chapter 16

The Criminal Justice Process

Key issues

- What are the key stages of the criminal justice process?
- What happens when the process goes wrong?
- What do we mean by 'justice'?
- How do different social groups experience the criminal justice process?

Introduction

Questions of crime and questions of the control of crime are not easily separated. Patterns of recorded crime are, after all, to a very large extent determined by efforts made by various kinds of gatekeepers to report, detect, judge and punish criminal activities. This chapter provides an overview of the key stages of the criminal justice process in the United Kingdom and the key institutions involved: the police, the Crown Prosecution Service, the Probation Service and the judiciary. It looks at some of the main gatekeeping decisions that underpin the working of each area, the principles and realities of justice, and the main sociological approaches to the everyday activities of the courts.

Historical context

Historians and sociologists have looked at how and why criminal justice processes and allied forms of and ideas about deviancy control underwent significant changes at particular points in time (see, for example, Ignatieff, 1978; Rothman, 1971; Foucault, 1977). In his book *Visions of Social Control*, Stanley Cohen (1985: 13–14) wrote of the transformations in the master patterns and strategies for controlling crime, delinquency and other types of socially problematic behaviour from the pre-modern to the modern period in Western industrial societies. As Chapter 15 shows, many of these key transformations are reflected in the changing principles and practices of punishment. There have been other major shifts: for example, the increasing involvement of the state, the development of a centralized, rationalized and bureaucratic apparatus in deviancy control, and the increasing professionalization and expansion of accredited experts. These were evident in the developments of criminal justice in Britain in the nineteenth century, notably the central elements of the adversarial trial (e.g. legal representation, and the ability to call and examine your own witnesses, to cross-examine the prosecution witnesses, to address the jury) and the emergence of a full-time, trained police force and other professionals such as lawyers and medical experts (Emsley, 1996; Rawlings, 1995). Gradually, policing, prosecution and other activities within the courtroom came to be seen as skilled work and the preserve of specialized formal agencies and professional agents.

Another key aspect of the modern criminal justice process is that criminal cases are no longer regarded as a private affair between the victim and the perpetrator of crime. In general, once a crime has been reported to the police, most victims are unaware of the processes involved in detection and in deciding whether or not to prosecute. Instead, decisions on how to deal with crimes are regarded as the concern of the state, its prerogative and duty, and trials become a contest between the state (as prosecutor) and the offender (as defendant). As Nils Christie (1977, 2000) has argued, the growth of the modern 'crime control industry' means that crime or 'conflicts' have become the official 'property' of the state. As we shall see, the organizational framework of the courts underlines this point. The opposing parties, the judge, the structural position of the experts, the construction of a case and conduct of trial based on formal criminal procedures and rules of legal relevance – all this underlines that the court system is a social organization for the handling of conflicts. Both victims and offenders become marginalized in this situation. They face the problem of entering the courts as non-professional outsiders and passive spectators where they lack knowledge of the courtroom as a process (for more recent debates about victim participation in the criminal justice process, see Chapter 9).

Overview of criminal justice institutions

Elements of the formal legal–correctional apparatus for the control of crime and delinquency such as the police, courts and prisons are found in virtually all countries, albeit with different names and involving different criminal justice procedures. There are also significant variations in the legal system within the United Kingdom. For example, the age of criminal responsibility is 8 in Scotland and 10 in England and Wales, and Northern Ireland. Young offenders are generally dealt with in specialist forums, notably the Scottish Children's Hearings System, in which lay panel members consider and make decisions on the supervision and welfare needs of the child. The public prosecution services also have different roles and responsibilities. Unlike its counterpart in England and Wales (see the subsection on the Crown Prosecution Service below), the Procurator Fiscal Service in Scotland has a wider responsibility for directing the investigation and prosecution of crime and diverting offenders from court by issuing a warning. Once the case comes to court, the 'not proven' verdict is a unique feature of the Scottish legal system. The political processes of devolution have also brought about a number of key changes as well as continuities to the criminal justice system and practices in the Scottish context (McAra, 2005). Finally, criminal justice institutions are sometimes subject to intense political scrutiny. In Northern Ireland the Criminal Justice Review Group was set up in 1998 under the Good Friday Agreement to undertake a wide-ranging review of criminal justice, and made 294 recommendations for change in areas as diverse as the prosecution service, courts, the judiciary, youth conferencing, community safety, victims and witnesses, law reform and international co-operation.

In England and Wales the criminal justice institutions have undergone much scrutiny and reform in recent years, partly as a result of new problems such as terrorism, partly as a result of the shifting political environment (e.g. politicians' desire to display their 'toughness on crime', EU harmonization), and partly because of an ongoing drive towards modernization and efficiency in the public sector. The law and order budget has grown to a total cost of around £13 billion per year and constitutes the fourth largest component of total public expenditure (after social security, health and personal social services, and education). Within central government, the Home Office, the newly created Ministry of Justice (MoJ) and the Attorney General's Office are the main departments with overall responsibility for the criminal justice system and its agencies in England and Wales.

- The Home Office is responsible for crime and crime reduction, policing, security and counter-terrorism, borders and immigration, passports and identity.
- The Ministry of Justice (from May 2007) has responsibilities for criminal law and sentencing, reducing reoffending, and prisons and probation. The MoJ also encompasses the responsibilities of the former Department for Constitutional Affairs (DCA), overseeing Magistrates' Courts, the Crown Court, the Appeals Courts and the Legal Services Commission.
- The Attorney General's Office oversees the Crown Prosecution Service (CPS), which is responsible for the independent prosecution of nearly all criminal cases instituted by the police, the Serious Fraud Office and the Revenue and Customs Prosecutions Office.

Under the current Labour government the purpose of the criminal justice system is

> to deliver justice for all, by convicting and punishing the guilty and helping them to stop offending, while protecting the innocent. It is responsible for detecting crime and bringing it to justice; and carrying out the orders of court, such as collecting fines, and supervising community and custodial punishment. . . . The key goals for the Criminal Justice System are to help reduce crime by bringing more offences to justice, and to raise public confidence that the system is fair and will deliver for the law-abiding citizens.
>
> (http://www.cjsonline.gov.uk)

While politicians tend to suggest that these goals are all equally achievable, the reality is that choices have to be made over which are to be prioritized. As we see throughout this chapter and others, the criminal justice process involves many conflicting values, aims and interests,

BOX 16.1 Adversarial versus inquisitorial approaches to criminal justice

The system of justice in England and Wales is sometimes referred to as an 'adversarial system' of justice. This is different from an 'inquisitorial system' of justice, as found in some other countries. In the adversarial system the magistrate(s) or jury decide on a verdict, having heard two opposing presentations of the case. The prosecution and defence parties present their case as they see fit and tactically cross-examine witnesses. Not guilty pleas result in a contest (hence the term 'adversarial') between the two parties arguing over the facts of a case. This might be contrasted to the inquisitorial approach adopted in many continental European countries, where there is a continuing judicial supervision of the process from the beginning of the investigation to the decisions in sentencing. In an inquisitorial system a judge is involved in the preparation of evidence by the police and in how the various parties are to present their case at the trial. The judge questions witnesses while prosecution and defence parties can ask supplementary questions. The influence of the judge in the trial process tends to reduce the level of contest between the two parties. In contrast, the English judge will usually have little knowledge about the case before the trial; he or she will not have been engaged in supervising any investigation, taking statements from witnesses or the accused, or making bail decisions. Nor, except in rare circumstances, would he or she be consulted over decisions to release from prison (Home Office, 2000a: ch. 4; Uglow, 2002).

such as convicting the guilty versus protecting the innocent from wrongful conviction; ensuring just processes versus achieving just outcomes; protecting the rights of defendants versus meeting the needs of victims (see Chapter 9); enforcing the law versus maintaining order (see Chapter 17); and delivering punishment (see Chapter 15) without imposing disproportionate cost, with consequent harm to other public services.

Key stages of the criminal justice process

There are several key stages of the criminal justice process (Figure 16.1). Chapter 3 explains that official statistics on reported and recorded crime indicate not 'real' amounts of crime but how events are defined and processed by social control agents. Official offenders are not representative of all those who break the criminal law; instead, they should be seen as those who have survived the **process of attrition**. A proportion of convicted offenders who reoffend may subsequently re-enter the criminal justice process and go through the key stages again. Others are, in effect, 'filtered out' of the criminal justice process between the commission of a deviant act, its discovery by the victim, its reporting to and recording by the police, then during charge, prosecution, conviction and at the point of sentence. In other words, attrition rates provide a measure of the proportion of cases that are filtered out of the criminal justice process. So how do decisions taken at each stage affect the wider processes of assessing, managing and punishing offenders?

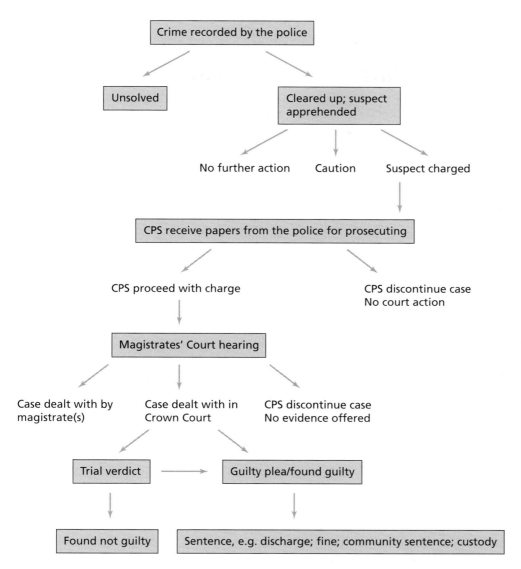

Figure 16.1 The criminal justice process.

We can identify a number of institutions and decision-makers involved in the key stages within the criminal justice process in England and Wales.

The police

The police are by far the most researched group in the criminal justice system (Brown, 1996). They are also, perhaps, the most significant, because of their gatekeeping function in the system. The police operate as an important initial filter on public reports. Although the police have a

BOX 16.2 Attrition rates around the world

One way of measuring the effectiveness of criminal justice systems is to examine the attrition rates of selected types of crime as they proceed through the system. In effect, this measure reflects which proportion of cases entering the system are resolved, closed or dispensed with by criminal justice agencies. Levels of attrition can be measured at a number of points within the criminal justice process – for example, the number of police-recorded cases that are actually prosecuted, the number of recorded or prosecuted cases resulting in a conviction.

According to the United Nations Survey of Crime Trends, and for the period 1980–2000, a conviction was likely to be achieved in one out of every four cases of homicide and one out of every eight cases of robbery. There are, however, considerable regional differences. In sub-Saharan Africa, for example, a conviction is obtained in only one of every eighteen cases recorded by the police. In Latin America, where fewer prosecutions are initiated, the ones that do occur are more likely to result in a conviction (about one in seven cases). In the European Union, a conviction is obtained in every two recorded cases. The attrition rates for robbery show a slightly different picture. On average, only one in every forty cases of reported robbery in Africa resulted in a prosecution for the period 1990–2000. In Latin America and the Caribbean, one conviction is recorded for approximately every fifteen reported cases. Both North America and the European Union show one conviction for every nine cases of reported cases of robbery, just above the global average.

Source: http://www.unodc.org/pdf/crime/forum

statutory responsibility to record crimes, they retain much discretion about whether and how to deal with possible offences that come to their attention. Reports from the public may be disbelieved, or considered trivial, or deemed not to concern a criminal offence. According to British Crime Survey figures, only 32 per cent of all offences are reported and recorded by the police. Put another way, this means that roughly a third of crimes against individuals and their households end up in the recorded crime count. Notwithstanding the adoption of the National Crime Recording Standard (NCRS) by all police forces in England and Wales in 2002, there remains considerable variation in the police recording rates between different force areas and offence types: from thefts of vehicles (92 per cent) to thefts from the person (63 per cent) and robbery (53 per cent) (Nicholas et al., 2005). The number of offences 'discovered' by the police themselves are also subject to changes in law-enforcement priorities and activities. More proactive policing and high-profile planned operations against a particular type of offence (e.g. drugs or burglary) will inevitably bring about an increase in arrests and the discovery and recording of many new offences in the targeted areas. Conversely, numbers may fall if there is a withdrawal of police interest in a particular type of area.

Even if a suspect is detected and charged, police still retain significant discretion over the processing of cases. Police arrest does not always lead to prosecution. In general, around one in four suspects are released from pre-charge detention with no further action (NFA), and many suspects (especially young people) are dealt with outside the court system through the use of police cautioning. Although there are national standards that set out the formal criteria for prosecution and caution (e.g. evidential sufficiency or public interest), police working rules have continued to shape the exercise of police discretion and case outcomes (Lee, 1998; McConville *et al.*, 1991; and see Chapter 17 of this book). The influence of the initial decisions taken and the way in which information is gathered, sifted through and put together to become a case by the police also endures through later decisions, such as bail, mode of trial and plea.

The Crown Prosecution Service

Once the police have begun proceedings, the case is passed to the Crown Prosecution Service (CPS). Created under the Prosecution of Offenders Act 1985 as part of wider criminal justice reform in England and Wales, the CPS consists of salaried lawyers whose task is to review cases to decide whether prosecution commenced by the police should continue, to consider the appropriateness of charges and to conduct prosecutions in courts. The police were seen as too close to the case and inclined to proceed under a crime-control model even when there is insufficient evidence against the suspect or to ignore vital clues considered irrelevant to the case for prosecution. The argument was that a new prosecuting agency would encourage greater impartiality, efficiency and consistency in the approach to prosecution. As well as the CPS, other bodies such as Customs and Excise, HM Revenue & Customs, the Serious Fraud Office and the Department of Trade and Industry also bring prosecutions.

In principle, the CPS as a public prosecution service exists to provide effective scrutiny of cases, to secure consistency in decision-making and to filter out weak prosecution cases from the criminal justice process. Their decision on whether to prosecute an offender is guided by the Code for Crown Prosecutors (2004), which sets out the two crucial tests involved: evidential sufficiency and public interest. First, the CPS must be satisfied that there is a 'realistic prospect of conviction' (i.e. the magistrates or jury are more likely than not to convict) on the available evidence. Second, Crown prosecutors must consider whether it is in the public interest for a prosecution to be brought. The main public interest factors considered to mitigate against prosecution include:

- The likelihood of a small or nominal penalty
- The offence was committed as a result of a genuine mistake
- The loss or harm was minor
- There has been a long delay since the offence
- A prosecution will adversely affect the victim's physical or mental health
- The defendant is elderly or at the time of the offence suffering from significant mental or physical illness.

Other public interest factors considered to favour prosecution include:

- The likelihood of a significant sentence
- Use of a weapon or violence threatened
- Premeditated or group offence
- Victim particularly vulnerable, put in fear, or suffered personal attack, damage or disturbance

- Offence motivated by racial, sexual, religious, disability or political discrimination
- Likelihood of repetition.

To many observers, the independence of Crown prosecutors is the key to effective control of police discretion. In practice, typically fewer than one in ten cases sent to the CPS are discontinued (Home Office, 2002a: table 6.2). The low discontinuance rate could be due to the strength of the cases. But commentators have pointed out that working relationships and shared assumptions between the CPS and the police may also be relevant factors here. As Doreen McBarnet (1981: 100) argues in her seminal study in the Scottish context, cases for prosecution and convictions in court are socially constructed in nature:

> [S]trong and weak cases do not miraculously appear after an incident ready formed like tablets of stone on Mount Sinai. They are the product of a process of construction in which both the technical skills of lawyers and the structural opportunities and limitations offered by the legal system play their part in shaping what facts get into the courts and just how strong or weak a case can be *independent* of the incident in question. [emphasis in original]

In the process of case construction, the 'independence' of the CPS is limited because of its reliance on the police for information (Crown prosecutors cannot realistically go through all paperwork or listen to all taped interviews), its organizational position (they are on the same side of the adversarial system) and its operational philosophy (to ensure that the prosecution policy is carried out efficiently) (McConville *et al.*, 1991). Clearly, prosecution decisions are taken in a working context that brings the CPS into contact not just with the local police but also with victims and magistrates. Any attempt to understand practical decision-making must, therefore, take into account the organizational and operational contexts in which the decisions are made.

The judiciary

In a liberal democracy, the doctrine of the separation of powers dictates that there has to be a degree of separation of functions between the three essential bodies of the state: the legislature, the executive and the judiciary. For example, the judiciary, which adjudicates upon conflicts between state institutions, between state and individual, and between individuals, is independent of political influence in its members' interpretation of the law and their judgements in a particular case. In practice, the separation of powers has never been absolute, and the imprecision of the doctrine has sometimes led to different interpretations of the meaning of, or even acrimonious debates about, 'judicial independence' (e.g. over sentencing policies and practices).

Three sets of decision-makers have evolved in the judiciary through the past ten centuries in England and Wales: magistrates, judges and jury. Criminal cases are dealt with in either the magistrates' court or the Crown Court (usually involving the more serious cases or when the defendant elects for a Crown Court trial). When defendants are aged under 18, their cases are generally dealt with in the specialist youth court.

There are about 30,000 lay magistrates and about 140 district judges (formerly known as stipendiary magistrates) (Ministry of Justice, 2007). In contrast to district judges, who are full-time legally trained professionals and normally sit alone in larger urban courts, lay magistrates (also known as Justices of the Peace) are chosen from a cross-section of the community. They are unpaid, sit part-time on local benches and represent an important lay element in the process whereby the public play a part in the administration of justice and sentencing. In practice, the composition of the lay magistracy is unbalanced, less in terms of gender than of age, race and class (Morgan and Russell, 2000). How this affects the quality of justice is subject to debate, but there is evidence to suggest that some defendants (especially those from an African or Caribbean background) consider magistrates' courts to be biased towards the prosecution, are more likely to opt for trial by jury, and believe that the Crown Court offers a fairer and fuller hearing with a higher chance of acquittal (Hedderman and Moxon, 1992; Fitzgerald, 1993). More recently, there has been much resistance to government's attempts to restrict the right to trial by jury. According to a public survey conducted on behalf of the Bar Council and the Law Society in 2002, most of those surveyed believe a jury of twelve individuals is most likely to reflect their own and society's views and values, and that they get a fairer trial from a jury than from a judge (www.dca.gov.uk/criminal/auldcom). Indeed, much of the criticism of judges is based on the perception that they are out of touch with 'what ordinary people believe'. This is often shorthand for the view that judges impose excessively lenient sentences, even though the actual sentencing patterns and high imprisonment rates in Britain reflect a rather different reality (see Chapter 18).

The vast majority (around 95 per cent) of criminal cases are dealt with entirely in magistrates' courts. The remaining cases are heard before a judge (who decides on the sentence) and jury (who decide on guilt). The Crown Court, which usually deals with more serious and complex cases, is presided over by a full-time judge. It also hears appeals against conviction in a magistrates' court, or decides on sentences in the more serious cases referred from magistrates' courts. The jury system has been hailed as a symbol of participatory democracy. The involvement of the public in the criminal justice process arguably gives people confidence in its fairness, ensures that unpopular or unjust laws cannot be enforced and operates as a defence against the oppressive use of state power. The right to be tried by twelve of one's peers has also been described by many as a fundamental right (Darbyshire, 1991), even though it is hard to draw any meaningful conclusions about the democratic credentials of a country by the presence or absence of a jury system. For example, Germany and the Netherlands do not have a jury system in criminal cases, while Belgium and France use it only in serious cases. Critics of the jury system suggest that jury trials are costly and time-consuming. There are many trials in which juries fail to prevent wrongful convictions – from the high-profile cases of miscarriage of justice (see Box 16.2) to the more routine successful appeals against convictions. Critics also argue that juries may not be representative of society, and that trials for some crimes (such as major frauds) may be too complex for juries to follow (see Findlay and Duff, 1988).

The Probation Service

The Probation Service (now part of the National Offender Management Service alongside the Prison Service) plays a key role in the criminal justice process at the sentencing stage in the United Kingdom. It assists magistrates and judges in their sentencing decisions through the provision of pre-sentence reports and bail information reports. It is also responsible for supervision of offenders in the community. In the area of youth justice, the Crime and Disorder Act 1998 established Youth Offending Teams (involving, for example, the police, social services, education, probation and health services) to assess young offenders, to reduce youth offending within a context of wider problems (from poor parental supervision and domestic violence or abuse, to truancy, school exclusion, substance misuse or mental health problems) and to enforce community sentences for young offenders.

Probation, or the practice of releasing offenders from court with some kind of condition that they behave themselves in future, has of course been central to the history of community sentences (Raynor and Vanstone, 2002; May, 1991). Originally set up as a community response to offending in the nineteenth century (as 'police court missionaries'), the Probation Service became a formalized agency of full-time professionals under the Probation Offenders Act 1907. Against a background of emerging psychological and environmental explanations of crime and human behaviour (see Chapter 4), the original role of probation practitioners was to 'advise, assist and befriend' the offender (e.g. through one-to-one supervision and practical help). However, as the rehabilitative ideals increasingly came under attack and the debate over 'toughened-up' community-based penalties (e.g. intensive probation, inclusion of more demanding conditions, curfew) intensified in the latter half of the twentieth century, the role of the Probation Service in delivering public protection, risk management and 'proper punishment' in the community remains highly contentious (see Chapter 15). David Smith (2005), for example, argues that under

Plate 16.1 The Birmingham Six with Chris Mullen, MP, outside the Old Bailey in London after their convictions were quashed, 14 March 1991. Left to right: John Walker, Paddy Hill, Hugh Callaghan, Chris Mullen, MP, Richard McIlkenny, Gerry Hunter, William Power.

Source: © PA Photos 2003; *photo:* Sean Dempsey.

controlling crime

the new slogan of 'Enforcement, Rehabilitation and Protection' the work of the Probation Service has been rebranded in ways that have distanced it from social work in terms of its purposes and values.

Taken together, these institutions have the main responsibility of administering justice and managing and controlling the official criminal population up to the point of sentencing. Their decisions and activities at any one point in the criminal justice process have a cumulative effect at a later stage of the process. Of course, crime and its control have never been the concern of criminal justice professionals alone. Statutory organizations working in the areas of public health, education and housing at central and local government level have developed their services and multi-agency partnerships around particular notions of 'antisocial behaviour', crime prevention and community safety (Newburn, 2002b; McLaughlin and Muncie, 2000). Penal establishments have been built with private money and run by the private sector (Matthews, 1989). Charities and voluntary groups have also been very much involved with crime- and treatment-related work since at least the nineteenth century (Cox, 2003). Prostitutes, abused children, child abusers, vagrants, drug and alcohol users, mentally disordered offenders, battered women, ex-prisoners and many other groups have all been the subject of specific charitable campaigns by organizations ranging from the Female Mission to the Fallen to Women's Aid, from the Temperance Movement to Alcoholics Anonymous, from the Howard League for Penal Reform to the National Association for the Care and Resettlement of Offenders (NACRO). All this suggests that different elements of civil society, broadly defined, play a major part in the definition, detection, and reform of criminals.

The nature of criminal justice

So what kind of justice does the British criminal process deliver? There are at least three approaches to understanding the nature of criminal justice: by examining respectively the procedural safeguards (i.e. **procedural justice**), the substantive outcomes (i.e. **substantive justice**), and the negotiations and social interactions involved in the routine production of justice (i.e. **negotiated justice**).

Procedural justice

The criminal justice process is the most explicit coercive apparatus of the state. It is therefore crucial in a liberal democracy that police and courts can interfere with the liberties of citizens only within the constraints of law, not by the arbitrary exercise of power. This in essence is the rule of law — that is, the sovereignty or supremacy of law above every individual. For those caught up within the criminal justice process, principles of legality and equality before the law demand that a person's legal rights are protected, that there are checks and balances upon judicial power, and that justice is administered according to standards that are publicly known, fair and seen to be just. Formal independence of the courts from the state is an essential check on the power of executive government. Independence from the other criminal justice agencies also makes the courts a neutral forum, which is a key part of due process. The concept has been brought to bear in a number of stages of the criminal justice process. For example, arrested persons must be informed as to what the charges are and be given the opportunity to defend themselves. Evidence gathered by the police should be reliable and acquired by lawful means. Proceedings should normally be conducted in open court so that justice is seen to be done. There should be clear standards of proof and strict rules and formal procedures of evidence to ensure that evidence admitted into court is of an admissible nature and fairly presented (see Ashworth, 1998; Sanders and Young, 2007).

When legal rules and procedures are ignored or not impartially applied, injustice in the form of abuse of power or wrongful conviction can occur. Wrongful convictions can result through police malpractice, because the prosecution withholds evidence, because the trial judge is biased or from faulty forensic evidence (Greer, 1994). The cases of the Birmingham Six, the Guildford Four and the Maguire Seven are among the most publicized examples of miscarriages of justice. In each of these cases, the defendants were wrongfully convicted and served long prison sentences for alleged Irish Republican Army (IRA) terrorist acts. Their convictions were eventually quashed by the Court of Appeal following years of campaigning by relatives, friends and public figures for a review of their cases (Rozenberg, 1993). Andrew Ashworth (1998: 14) sums up the abuse of power by the police and other deficiencies within the criminal justice process that were exposed by these cases: the concoction or falsification of evidence by police officers; oppressive

BOX 16.3 Miscarriages of justice

The most high-profile 'miscarriages of justice' in Britain concerned alleged Irish Republican Army (IRA) terrorist suspects who were imprisoned for up to sixteen years on false confessions and dubious evidence in the early 1970s before being released. The wrongful convictions focused on the cases of the 'Birmingham Six' (for two explosions in Birmingham which resulted in 21 deaths); the 'Guildford Four' (for explosions in Guildford and Woolwich); and Judith Ward (for several explosions, including one on an army bus). After years of campaigning, all their cases went to successful appeals, and ten of the eleven people concerned in these cases were released in 1991–2 and given compensation (the eleventh had already died in prison). It was subsequently revealed that the suspects had been assaulted by the police, intimidated with further threats of severe violence, deprived of sleep, and relentlessly questioned. Some 'confessed' or signed confessions that were fabricated by the investigating officers. The police were also found to have withheld vital information from the courts.

Another notorious case is that of the 'Cardiff Three', convicted in 1990 of the murder of a Cardiff prostitute. Their convictions were also overturned by the Court of Appeal (in 1992) on the grounds that the interrogations amounted to bullying and oppression by the police and a 'travesty', and that the interviews should have been excluded from evidence. This case is particularly significant because it occurred some years after the implementation of the Police and Criminal Evidence Act 1984 (PACE), which put in place regulation of pre-trial investigation and routine tape-recording of police interviews. This perhaps suggests that the officers did not think that their approach was unacceptable. (For information concerning PACE, see Box 17.4.)

questioning and violence by the police; non-disclosure of vital evidence by forensic scientists and/or by the prosecution to the defence; slow and cumbersome appeal procedures; and a general reluctance to accept that the police had not told the truth.

By the early 1990s, public confidence in the police and the justice system had eroded to such an extent that a royal commission was appointed (Royal Commission on Criminal Justice, 1993). Attempts have since been made to introduce stronger legal safeguards for defendants, and the Criminal Cases Review Commission was created under the Criminal Appeal Act 1995 to investigate miscarriages of justice and to refer cases back to the Court of Appeal. The Human Rights Act 1998 also incorporates rights protected under the European Convention on Human Rights into domestic law and has since been used to mount a number of challenges to the criminal justice system (concerning, for example, the right not to incriminate oneself, and the rights of prisoners). Critics, however, have pointed to other recent legislative developments that give extensive powers to the state in the aftermath of the terrorist attacks on the United States on 11 September 2001 (e.g. on detention, disclosure of information and use of wiretaps under the Anti-terrorism, Crime and Security Act 2001 and the Prevention of Terrorism Act 2005 in the UK, the PATRIOT Act in the United States). For example, the Prevention of Terrorism Act 2005 in the UK has been criticized by the Human Rights Watch for empowering the state to impose restrictions on terrorism suspects (including indefinite 'house arrest') on the basis of a 'reasonable suspicion' and subject only to delayed and narrow judicial review. 'The lack of procedural safeguards seriously undermines the right to a fair trial, the presumption of innocence and the right to an effective defence' (http://hrw.org/backgrounder/eca/uk). The current 'war on terror' may provide justifications for further expansion of policing and emergency powers and a concomitant erosion of procedural safeguards for individuals. More generally, the point remains that criminal justice professionals work in a social context with built-in assumptions about how cases are constructed and how critical questions that may embarrass other actors in the system are to be filtered out. As Maurice Punch points out in relation to the systemic failures of criminal justice:

> What raised the miscarriages of justice to the system level was the collusion of other actors in the system – supervisory officers who did not intervene when violence occurred, senior officers who signed 'dodgy' statements, forensic specialists who went to work uncritically (and even unprofessionally), prosecutors who did not probe sensitive areas in the material given to them, judges who turned a blind eye to discrepancies in evidence and the Home Office which forestalled an appeal for so long.
>
> (2003: 188)

Seen in this light, miscarriages of justice are neither rare nor exceptional instances of wrongful imprisonment. Instead, error is the norm and a mundane feature that is an inbuilt feature of the criminal justice system; this is why the many attempts to reform the system have ended in failure (Naughton, 2007).

So far, we have concentrated on unsafe convictions and miscarriages of justice where the innocent are imprisoned as clear examples of where the criminal justice process 'goes wrong'. Critics would argue that the process also fails to deliver justice where it fails to prosecute and/ or convict many who should be prosecuted and convicted. For example, the extremely low convictions for rape, as a percentage of recorded complaints (falling from around 32 per cent in 1977 to 5.6 per cent in 2002), have been identified as a 'justice gap' by many feminists and criminal reform groups (Kelly *et al.*, 2005). Victims may feel let down or angry as a result; however, there is evidence to suggest that their treatment by criminal justice agencies and the court experience itself can also produce a sense of unfairness, bewilderment or pain (see Chapter 9).

Substantive justice

'Unjust' or ineffective outcomes may arise even when legal rules are formally adhered to and supposedly 'neutral' criteria in criminal justice decision-making (for example, in cautioning, bail decisions, sentencing) are applied. A classic example is the differential impact of a fine on offenders with and without financial means. Furthermore, concerns have been raised, both from within criminology and from within social movements (such as the feminist movement and anti-racist activist groups), that existing criminal justice policies and procedures may have the effect of punishing a higher proportion of one social group than another.

Gender

The question of whether male and female offenders are treated differently in the criminal justice system has been subject to much criminological debate. The so-called chivalry hypothesis – that is, that the police, courts and other agencies extend greater leniency towards all women – has been disputed by most empirical studies (Eaton, 1986; Carlen, 1983; Daly and Bordt, 1995; Player, 1989; and see Chapter 6 of this book). Instead, there is evidence to suggest that the opposite is true: that some female offenders and delinquents may be 'doubly punished' for transgressing their gender roles (more 'troubled' than men) and are more likely to be disciplined in a penal–welfare complex (Gelsthorpe, 1989; Cain, 1989; Allen, 1987; Steward, 2006; but see Hedderman and Hough, 1994).

Other feminists have also argued that equality of treatment in effect means treating women 'the same as men' and questioned whether this is always appropriate to the circumstances surrounding women's offending and the resources and treatment they may need to help them reintegrate into society or avoid reoffending (Hudson, 1993; Naffine, 1995). As Mary Eaton (1986: 97) concludes in her seminal research study,

> Hillbury Court treats men and women equally, i.e. they receive similar sentences when they appear in similar circumstances. However, men and women rarely appear in similar circumstances – the differences in their recorded criminal involvements are as marked as the differences between the sexes in other areas of life. Formal equality within the strictly defined area of the court does not affect the substantial inequality of women and men who appear before the court.

Indeed, structural inequalities meant that as a group, women had, historically, always been poorer than men (occupying more menial jobs, combining periods of paid employment with periods of unpaid childcare, earning less during their working lives, therefore having fewer savings and reduced pensions, and so on). Studies have suggested that the rise in women's prosecutions and imprisonment rates in Britain and elsewhere can be explained by a rise in specific crimes, almost all related to continuing and worsening levels of female poverty: benefit fraud, prostitution, irregular migration and drug-related offences (Carlen, 1998; Pantazis, 1999; Hedderman, 2004; Lee, 2007a). Some men and women – for example, young black men, minority ethnic women, gays and lesbians, and those belonging to minority faith groups – are also more likely to experience multiple forms of marginalization than others. Adopting legal safeguards and giving equal treatment to the few men and women who appear before the court in similar circumstances may satisfy the court's procedural criteria of justice, but this does not in itself achieve 'just' and effective outcomes.

Ethnicity

The majority of studies have consistently shown that black people (especially young black males) are over-represented throughout the criminal justice process, with proportionately more being stopped and searched (Norris *et al.*, 1992; Home Office, 2000b; Jefferson and Walker, 1992; Clancy *et al.*, 2001), arrested by the police (Bucke, 1997; Home Office, 2005c), being prosecuted in court (Home Office, 2005c; Phillips and Brown, 1998) and being sentenced to prison once in Crown courts (Hood, 1992). Whether these variations are due to any direct discrimination against minority groups in the criminal justice process (as Hood's sentencing study has shown) or a combination of other factors (e.g. patterns of offending, suspects entering not guilty pleas, not showing appropriate signs of 'remorse') has been subject to intense debates. Quantitative research methods are typically used to assess whether race has a separate or independent effect on decision-making over and above any other factors such as age, class or area of residence (see, for example, Hudson's (1989) survey of sentencing decisions and finding of 'residual discrimination' against African and Caribbean males in more mundane offences). There are, however, particular problems in attempting to isolate the variable of 'race' and measure the possible extent of racial discrimination at particular stages of the criminal justice process (see Reiner, 1993).

While adopting legal safeguards and ensuring procedural justice may have some impact on the worst excesses of 'institutional racism' within the criminal justice system (Macpherson, 1999; and see Chapter 17 of this book), this does not address the underlying racist constructions of criminality or other 'antisocial' behaviour, the patterned social and economic inequalities, and the associated exclusionary and monitoring processes of ethnic minorities as a social group (Bowling and Phillips, 2002; Bosworth *et al.*, 2008).

Negotiated justice

The third approach to understanding the nature of criminal justice is to consider the negotiations and social interaction involved in the routine production of justice. In principle, the trial is the focal point of the ideology of democratic justice. The trial is generally portrayed as rational decision-making within the overall values of the rule of law. It is where the process of legal battle is not only carried out but put on public display. But we should be cautious in accepting trial outcomes in these terms – there are elements in the management of the courts and trials that directly contradict and undermine this. As Uglow (2002) has argued,

Offenders are processed and disposed of as efficiently as possible in terms of time and resources. Key performance indicators relate to such issues as cost per case, the time taken between first appearance in magistrates' court and committal or between committal and trial or the backlog of cases for a particular court. . . .This leads to pressure to speed up cases and to the negotiation of outcome. The defendant's role can be reduced to passivity especially where there are on-going professional relationships between the defence and prosecution lawyers, the police, probation services, court administrators and judges. Thus there is a divergence between the official and articulated ideals of the courtroom and the organizational reality that exists behind them.

In practice, the vast majority of cases processed through the criminal justice system are routinely resolved through a guilty plea. In the magistrates' courts, over 90 per cent of defendants on summary trial plead guilty. Most of these cases involve relatively minor matters that almost always end in a fine. A contested trial in a magistrates' court is therefore very rare. It is not surprising that the nature of most courtroom appearances has been described as 'routine, boring, ritual, unproblematic processing of cases' (Carlen, 1976). Even in the Crown Court, the rate of guilty pleas is around 60 per cent.

A number of classic sociological studies in the 1960s and 1970s in Britain and the United States have examined the interactional, informal and bureaucratic aspects of the routine production of a guilty plea (Bottoms and McClean, 1976; Skolnick, 1966; Baldwin and McConville, 1977; Carlen, 1976). A particularly contentious issue is the use of plea bargaining between prosecution and defence. In the US context, the widespread use of explicit negotiations over charge and sentence is seen to facilitate smooth functioning of the justice system; it is seen as beneficial, as there is no risk of complete loss at trial for either side in the courtroom drama. However, such bargaining has been criticized for the pressure it places on innocents to plead guilty and the fact that it penalizes those who exercise their constitutional right to trial. From a different perspective, some critics have also argued that plea bargaining allows offenders to escape appropriate punishment for their crimes. Although explicit plea bargaining over sentence with the judge is not permitted in England and Wales, some form of 'sentencing discount' does exist for early guilty plea, and plea sometimes determines not just the length but also the type of sentence (Sanders and Young, 2007). In the context of negotiated justice, it is perhaps inevitable that some innocent people plead guilty. According to a research study commissioned by the Royal Commission on Criminal Justice, over 10 per cent of those who plead guilty in the Crown Court claim to be innocent (Zander and Henderson, 1993).

Even when a case goes to trial, we might also think about the trial as storytelling. Often it is the side that puts together the most credible narrative that wins. Studies conducted from a micro-sociological perspective have highlighted how justice is negotiated and judicial order is maintained through control of the formal rules and symbolic boundaries of courtroom interaction. The use of a high level of ritual in the formal procedures, and complex legal language and gestures by court professionals to 'cool out' defendants and to systematically deny them a speaking part, has been well documented (Cicourel, 1968; Parker et al., 1989; Dell, 1971). For example, Pat Carlen (1976) has shown how control in court is achieved through 'situational rules'. The court team – magistrates, judge, clerk of court, police, lawyers, probation officers – manages to make the defendant a 'dummy player' by ruling any challenge he or she poses to the ritual,

BOX 16.4 Cost-effectiveness model of case management in criminal justice

A series of reforms have been implemented in England and Wales since the 1990s to improve efficiency and case progression and to reduce delay and costs in the criminal justice system. Fundamental changes about case management procedures, the allocation of work and performance targets have been introduced in the magistrates' and Crown courts, including fast-track hearings for cases that are likely to be guilty pleas, pre-trial reviews, and plea and directions hearings in order to improve communications, ensure the smooth progression of cases during a full trial or hearing, and to save costly court and lawyers' time.

According to the Department for Constitutional Affairs Annual Report 2006/7, the vision is to deliver a CJS that is:

Simple: dealing with some cases by way of warning, caution or some other effective remedy to prevent re-offending without the court process.

Speedy: those cases that need the court process will be dealt with fairly, but as quickly as possible.

Summary: a much more proportionate approach still involving due process – for example dealing with appropriate cases the day after charge or during the same week.

In addition, the government promises to 'get a grip on "Very High Cost Cases"' (defined as those cases lasting 41 days or more at trial). The proposals centre around establishing a panel of quality assured defence providers competing on the hourly rate in return for access to an increased volume of such cases.

Source: http://www.dca.gov.uk/dept/report2007

administration or legitimacy of the law as being 'out of place, out of time, out of mind, or out of order'. All this reflects the imbalance between the power and resources available to the prosecutor/state as opposed to the individual accused. The geography of the court carries this on: the elevated bench, private access to judge's chambers, the judge's throne-like chair, the defendant in the dock, the public at the back of the court so that we are allowed to observe but not to participate. Carlen suggests that the organization of space is such as to impede communication, especially for those who are not part of the routine cast (including both the victim and the accused). Distances are much greater than one would normally use for disclosure of private or traumatic incidents, or indeed for effective intervention. Communication is conducted and carefully managed through the lawyers. Indeed, the mode of discourse in the courtroom involves either interrogation or monologue, both of which are extraordinary or even resented when they occur in day-to-day conversation.

Of course, sociologists have long been interested in the actual 'drama of interaction' and the use and avoidance of the rules of interaction. Erving Goffman (1959) wrote of 'the presentation of self 'and an individual's efforts to create specific impressions in the minds of others, especially through the use of distinctive elements such as 'performances' (props, costume, rituals). In the courtroom setting, the dramatic elements of the spatial, presentational and linguistic conventions all help to create the court as a sharp rite of transition. The high level of ritual contributes to the sense of the authority of the court and towards establishing the authoritative version of the events and interpreting and explaining those events not merely in the courtroom but also for the outside world.

The ceremonial stripping of an individual of their dignity as a prelude to judicial punishment has also been thoroughly explicated and analysed by Harold Garfinkel (1956a, b). He wrote of the 'degradation ceremonies' through which an entire community formally stigmatizes an individual and destroys their total identity: 'Any communicative work between persons, whereby the public identity of an actor is transformed into something looked on as lower in the local scheme of social types, will be called a "status degradation ceremony".' The ceremonial order of the court proceedings represents one particular form of 'status degradation ceremony' in the modern context. There are various conditions of a successful degradation ceremony:

- The denunciation must be public.
- The denouncer must be invested with the right to speak in the name of wider ultimate values of the community.
- The denounced person and event must be defined as instances of a uniformity, not as unique, an accident or a coincidence.
- The characteristics of the typed person and event should be contrasted with a counter-conception (e.g. the features and habits of a mass murderer versus the features and habits of a peaceful citizen).
- The denounced person must be ritually separated from a place in the legitimate order (i.e. made to stand out/made 'strange').

As Garfinkel (1956a, b) suggested, the trial is a process of recasting the defendant away from their own identity and into a stereotyped social role (mugger, hooligan, drunk, vagrant). The trial becomes a degradation ceremony that reduces the defendant to a lower status. Through this process, broader patterns of social authority and of social power are once again demonstrated.

Criminal justice in crisis?

Critics have argued that by the end of the twentieth century, it was the criminal justice system itself that was put on trial. Although the criminal justice agencies in the United Kingdom enjoyed an unprecedented period of growth in overall resources and powers, the official crime rate escalated to unparalleled levels.

> The sheer number of individuals entering and re-entering the system was threatening to paralyse the functioning of the courts. . . . Spiralling rates of reoffending were increasing levels of victimization and the public's fear of crime and growing intolerance generated demands for more police officers, tougher policing strategies and harsher sentences, which

in turn thrust even more people into the system. . . . To cap it all, a series of high profile miscarriages of justice undermined public confidence in the ability of the criminal justice system to identify the guilty and protect the rights of the innocent.

(McLaughlin and Muncie, 2000: 170)

Against this background of 'failure to deliver', some Home Office statements even conceded, in classic Durkheimian fashion, that a certain level of crime is normal and inevitable and that it is unrealistic to expect any set of policies to drastically reduce the crime rate (Young, 1992: 104). Global processes present another set of challenges to criminal justice. Criminal justice systems around the world may be becoming more globalized or converging through the impact of neo-liberal economics, cultural interdependency, policy and technology transfer, and international human rights conventions. But as Janet Chan (2005: 342) has argued, the convergence of criminal justice policy (e.g. zero-tolerance policing, the privatization of prisons) is not always seen as a positive development: 'For example, the "exporting" of inappropriate criminal justice policy from powerful nations to others is a controversial area.' At the same time, criminal justice systems remain highly sensitive to distinctive national cultures and politics of reform and subject to localized difference, negotiation and resistance. There is no doubt that contradictions and tensions in the criminal justice system in terms of values, interests, stated aims and actual practices will continue to exist.

Summary

1   Official statistics on crime do not indicate 'real' amounts of crime but how events are defined and processed by social-control agents. The key stages of the criminal justice process include discovery of the offence by the victim, reporting to and recording by the police, charge, prosecution, conviction and sentence.
2   A number of institutions and decision-makers are involved in the key stages within the criminal justice process up to the point of sentencing in England and Wales: the police, the Crown Prosecution Service, the judiciary and the Probation Service. Their decisions and activities at any one point in the criminal justice process have a cumulative effect at a later stage of the process.
3   Unsafe convictions and miscarriages of justice whereby the innocent are imprisoned are clear examples of cases in which the criminal justice process has gone wrong. Victims may also feel let down by the criminal justice process when it fails to prosecute and/or convict many who should be prosecuted and convicted.
4   There are at least three approaches to understanding the nature of criminal justice: by examining the procedural safeguards (procedural justice), the substantive outcomes (substantive justice), and the negotiations and social interactions involved in the routine production of justice (negotiated justice).

Critical thinking questions

1   Consider the key stages of the criminal justice process and identify the factors that could affect whether a case proceeds to the next stage or is filtered out of the criminal justice process. How can we ensure that the decisions taken are always fair and just?

2   Look at 'The Proceedings of the Old Bailey' website (see under 'More information'). In what ways would the props, rituals and status degradation ceremonies in twenty-first-century courtrooms differ from those in the eighteenth century?

3   Find out about the gender, age and ethnic composition of the lay magistracy in your local area (the Magistrates' Association website is a useful starting point). How does it compare with the national picture? And do you think that a more balanced lay magistracy would necessarily deliver better justice?

Further study

Davies, M., Croall, H. and Tyrer, J. (2005) *Criminal Justice: An Introduction to the Criminal Justice System in England and Wales*, 3rd edn, Harlow: Longman. A very useful introductory text on the key components, policy and practice issues in the criminal justice system in England and Wales.

Duff, P. and Hutton, N. (eds) (1999) *Criminal Justice in Scotland*, Aldershot: Ashgate. A socio-legal account of the Scottish criminal justice process and its constituent institutions.

McBarnet, D. (1981) *Conviction: Law, the State and the Construction of Justice*, London: Macmillan. A pioneering socio-legal study of the routine construction of justice in court.

McConville, M. and Wilson, G. (2002) *The Handbook of the Criminal Justice Process*, Oxford: Oxford University Press.

Sanders, A. and Young, R. (2007) *Criminal Justice*, 3rd edn, Oxford: Oxford University Press. Two accessible and very useful texts which synthesize and review the key concepts, debtates and controversies in criminal justice.

More information

Home Office
http://www.homeoffice.gov.uk

Ministry of Justice
http://www.justice.gov.uk

Crown Prosecution Service

http://www.cps.gov.uk

World Factbook of Criminal Systems

http://www.ojp.gov/bjs/abstract/wfcj.htm

This factbook provides narrative descriptions of the criminal justice systems of 45 countries around the world.

Criminal Justice System

http://www.cjsonline.org

This is another site that has useful information on the criminal justice process in England and Wales.

Crown Office and Procurator Fiscal Service

http://www.crownoffice.gov.uk/

This site has information on the Scottish criminal justice system plus a selection of other links for reference.

Criminal Justice System Northern Ireland

http://www.cjsni.gov.uk/

A site on the criminal justice process in Northern Ireland.

Proceedings of the Old Bailey

http://www.oldbaileyonline.org/

A fully searchable online edition of the largest body of texts detailing the lives on non-elite people ever published, containing accounts of over 100,000 criminal trials held at London's central criminal court.

chapter 17

Police and Policing

Key issues

■ What is the difference between 'the police' and 'policing'?

■ What are the key characteristics of police work?

■ Why do we need effective systems of police accountability?

■ What is the future for policing?

Introduction

In a book entitled *The Future of Policing*, the authors Rod Morgan and Tim Newburn (1997: 10) argue: 'We must establish what the fundamental role and function of the police are to be. But we must also decide how and by whom these responsibilities are to be defined.' Clearly, these authors are talking about how police work may change in the future. But given that the modern English police were established in 1829, it might seem strange that it is still necessary to be asking questions about 'what the **police** do' and 'to whom are they accountable'. Yet these remain important questions now and for the future.

In this chapter we address these questions, outline the history of the police, review some of the key debates surrounding the police institution, police powers and accountability, and consider the diversity of **policing**. As Robert Reiner (2000: 1–2) has argued: '"police" refers to a particular kind of social institution, while "policing" implies a set of processes with specific social functions. . . . A state-organized specialist "police" organization of the modern kind is only one example of policing.' Given that police work is about the exercise of authority and the regulation of conflicts in society, it is inherently controversial and inevitably contested. The police must be seen in terms of 'what they do' and 'how they do it' but also be discussed critically, so we also look at 'what they do but shouldn't do'.

Historical origins and continuities

Originally, the idea of 'police' had its roots in the idea of the good order or administration of the city-state (Emsley, 1996). In modern democracies, police rely upon consensus, legitimacy and legal authority, although there are also many examples from the twentieth century and today of states that are more authoritarian and employ police in explicitly political ways to support their regime. The police states of Nazi Germany and the Soviet Union were extreme examples.

In Britain, the full-time, professional police we are familiar with today developed from a patchwork of policing of a highly variable pattern. Towns and country parishes generally relied on community-based systems of the 'watch', local constables and private 'thief-takers', but there was little uniformity and, according to many historians, considerable inefficiency (Emsley, 1996; Rawlings, 2002). In cases of riot and disorder, a military solution was an option, employing local militia or the army. Nonetheless, even in the late eighteenth and early nineteenth centuries, the national mood was suspicious of a 'standing police force', not least because of fears of Continental systems of police spies. Influential political objections and the reluctance of the wealthy classes to support an initiative likely to lead to an increase in taxation defeated several attempts to introduce a Police Bill, and parliamentary committees considered and rejected the idea of a police force for the capital five times! However, the Home Secretary in Wellington's government, Sir Robert Peel, was a committed advocate of the benefits of a public force and persisted with the idea, eventually gaining the support of Parliament for the 1829 Metropolitan Police Act. This covered Greater London but not the City of London (an anomaly that continues, with the latter still having its own small police force). The new police and their commissioner were made responsible to the Home Secretary. Under the Municipal Corporations Act of 1835, major boroughs throughout England were obliged to establish forces answerable to the local watch committee, with the process being completed for other areas of the country from 1856.

Importantly, some of the issues facing the new police of the nineteenth century are still raising questions today. First, the police personify the coercive power of the state, and from the start played a pivotal role in regulating people's everyday activities through their patrol practices. The principal arguments put forward in Parliament for the creation of the Metropolitan Police were that it would be valuable in helping to prevent crime. But with increased anxieties about fast-growing cities and slums full of poor, anonymous and potentially 'dangerous classes', there was a gradual extension of the powers of the new police to regulate city life (Emsley, 1983; Petrow, 1994).

Not every section of society was affected in the same way. The police were often called upon to enforce a law that favoured one social group over another – for example, evicting tenants, enforcing the masters' terms of employment, and maintaining order at workers' demonstrations. A variety of new legislative powers, by-laws and regulations designed mainly to cope with the problems generated by industrialization and urbanization tended to direct police attention to particular social groups such as the homeless, loitering youths, beggars, Gypsies, travelling hawkers and prostitutes (Emsley, 2005). In effect, enforcing the new statutes (e.g. over vagrancy or street trading) meant that police work increasingly impinged upon the lives of what Vic Gatrell *et al.* (1980: 335) described as 'the 30 per cent or more at the base of the social pyramid'.

The new police also performed the important symbolic and legitimating function of representing and enforcing the values of dominant authority. They were (and still are) often represented as 'the thin blue line' that divides order from chaos. The introduction of street patrolling led to an increase in the number of arrests for misdemeanours, especially drunkenness and disorderly behaviour by men. Again, it was in those poor working-class districts that men were to be found indulging in the boisterous customs, recreations and pastimes such as Sunday drinking, cock-fighting and street gambling which offended Victorian perceptions of public morality and which the new police were directed to control as 'domestic missionaries' (Storch, 1976).

Second, the new police did not receive an easy welcome from the public and had to gain acceptance over time. The relationship between the police and the policed was particularly fraught in some communities. According to some historians, working-class hostility to the police continued well into the second half of the nineteenth century, as evidenced in the numbers of assaults on the police (Storch, 1975; Weinberger, 1981). Other accounts of policing in some working-class neighbourhoods related to the feud-like relationship between the police and young people in the interwar years (Cohen, 1979b; Pearson, 1983). As Eugene McLaughlin (2007: 4) points out, a great deal of cultural and political work had to take place in order for 'this most "un-English" of institutions to be first of all sheltered from popular resentment and gradually transformed into one which could be celebrated as "a very *English* institution . . . a reassuring symbol of all being well and tranquil in the world"'.

The post-war period was the high point of public support for, and belief in, public policing in Britain. The cosy image of the helpful and much admired English bobby, with its heyday in the 1950s and early 1960s, was idealized in the BBC television series *Dixon of Dock Green* from this period. The 'Dixonian policing model' is still routinely evoked as a form of shorthand to define the traditional values of English policing, national unity, cultural cohesion, neighbourliness and law and order. Nevertheless, distrust of the police, allegations of abuse of discretionary police powers and the over-policing of particular social groups at the neighbourhood or street level remain. Indeed, police use of force, mass 'stop and search' operations, excessive surveillance and unnecessary armed raids, especially in the centres of African, Caribbean and Asian communities, have continued to be controversial (see Bowling and Phillips, 2002; Keith, 1993; Cashmore and McLaughlin, 1991). Take police use of 'stop and search' powers as an example. According to Home Office statistics, black people were recorded as being eight times more likely to be stopped and searched than white people (Home Office, 2002c: 5). Indeed, insensitive policing was seen to have played a pivotal role in triggering the urban riots that occurred in Britain in the early and mid-1980s (Scarman, 1981). The over-policing of particular sections of society has serious implications, especially against a background of the continuing revelations about police misconduct and miscarriages of justice (see Box 16.3).

Third, in the nineteenth century, police clashed with protestors and rioters in conflicts over strikes, rights, poverty, and in opposition to the police themselves (Emsley, 2005). Given that protestors and rioters often appealed to 'the common good' (e.g. defending communities or challenging unjust laws), the policing of public order was – and still is – morally ambiguous. In the United States too, the early 1960s saw major political concern and debate about civil rights and law and order. As Waddington (1996: 116) has argued,

Few would now suggest that those who rioted periodically throughout the nineteenth century in pursuit of the franchise or trade union rights were morally wrong, although illegal violence was certainly used in doing so. Those who opposed Moseley's Fascists in the 1930s are rarely considered in hindsight to have been a riotous mob, but are credited as defending higher political ideals. . . . Black civil rights activists who systematically defied racist laws are sanctified and their leader – Martin Luther King – has acquired the status of a secular saint. . . . The verdict of history is that the 'bad guys' in these, and many other confrontations, between states and their respective citizens are the forces of repression – principally the police.

In the late twentieth century and early twenty-first century, police have been involved in confrontations with trade union and social movements concerned with national strikes (the miner pickets), protests against the building of new motorways (New Age travellers) and export of live animals, and one-day global demonstrations against multinational capitalism and world poverty. Indeed, there are many examples of police in both authoritarian states and democracies using tear gas, pepper sprays, water cannon, plastic bullets and baton charges to disperse illegal assemblies and riotous crowds, with a view to restoring a particular form of 'order'. Since the 9/11 terrorist attacks in the United States, there has been a renewed emphasis on strengthening security involving a more visible presence of paramilitary units in a number of countries. All

Plate 17.1(a) Seattle police block the street during a protest march against the World Trade Organization (WTO), in front of the Washington State Convention Centre in downtown Seattle, 3 December 1999.

Source: © Reuters 1999; *photo:* STR.

Plate 17.1(b) A demonstration by hunger marchers is broken up by mounted London police, 13 November 1932.

Source: © Mary Evans Picture Library; *photo:* Achille Beltrame in *La Domenica del Corriere*.

BOX 17.1 Policing public protests

The 2001 G8 summit in Genoa will be remembered for the massive police security operation and violent clashes between protesters and police. The city had undergone a $1m facelift in the months leading up to the summit. But almost a week before the summit had even started local citizens had seen their city fill up with police, military and special forces, and they watched a four-metre-high fence go up around the red zone. One said the riot and wrecking of their town was not a surprise to anybody:

'It didn't surprise me at all, you could see it coming and I think both the police and the anarchists got what they had come here for.'

The controversial operation by Italian police against the headquarters of the anti-globalisation protests at the G8 summit was a joint operation between the state police and the military police, the *carabinieri*. The *carabinieri*, the military police, in particular have a fearsome reputation. Football supporters in Italy have long complained about the heavy-handed approach of the *carabinieri* to crowd control. Much of the coverage of the raid on the Genoa demonstrators' base has focused on the relish with which both police forces are alleged to have attacked the campaigners and the tradition they have of suppressing left-wing protests. In all 230 demonstrators were injured in two days of violence at the summit, and one was killed by police. Many of the *carabinieri* deployed in Genoa were young men serving their year of compulsory military service. Much of the alleged brutality at Genoa and the killing of one Italian protester have been attributed to the inexperience of the conscripts.

Source: BBC News Online, 27 July 2001.

this highlights the important fact that public order policing is 'irreducibly political'; it is 'a highly visible representation of the relationship between state and citizen' (Waddington, 1996: 129), and raises the question of whose order police have to maintain (see also Jefferson, 1990; McLaughlin, 2007).

Police roles and functions

Most Western, continental European countries have several police organizations, whereas the United Kingdom has only one (albeit with different jurisdictions in Scotland and Northern Ireland). For example, in France the military-style police *Gendarmerie* operate alongside a patchwork of local forces; similarly, in Belgium the national police force, the *Rijkswacht*, operates alongside some 589 municipal police forces (Mawby, 1999).

The primary forms of police in England and Wales are the forty-three statutory metropolitan and regional forces. The police are distinguished from other public services by their specific capacity to exercise legitimate coercive force (Bittner, 1974). Indeed, the authority that the police exercise in compelling the compliance of other citizens is underwritten by the fact that police officers are 'monopolists of force in civil society' (ibid.). There are also a number of 'specialist' forces operating with the authority of the state but within particular 'private' spaces, for example the British Transport Police, the Ministry of Defence Police, the Royal Parks Police and the UK Atomic Energy Authority Police. In addition, there is a new national 'FBI-style' law-enforcement agency, the Serious Organized Crime Agency (SOCA), which brings together the National Crime Squad, National Criminal Intelligence Service, part of Customs and Excise, and Immigration dealing with organized immigration crime into a hybrid policing and intelligence body in the UK (from 2006) (Bowling and Ross, 2008).

Historically and in the contemporary context, the image of public police has been predominantly one of crime-fighter. On this view, the primary police roles involve:

- the prevention of crime
- the detection of criminals
- the preservation of order.

The question of whether the police actually have an effect on crime is a central one – though not easily answered. First, there are major problems of interpreting the rise and fall of recorded crime rates (see chapters 3 and 16). Second, there is little evidence to suggest that any police strategy alone can reduce crime (Audit Commission, 1993; Eck and Maguire, 2000). Increasing police patrols is a measure that would seem to be popular with the public, but unless this increase were to a level of saturation that many might begin to find uncomfortable – more of an intrusion than a guarantee of security – then the chances of the police being 'in the right place at the right time' would be somewhat slim. Indeed, one study estimated that a patrolling officer in London was likely to pass within 100 yards of a burglary in progress once every eight years, and even then might not know that the offence was taking place or be able to catch the perpetrator (Clarke and Hough, 1984: 6–7).

An alternative strategy is 'hot-spot' policing whereby patrolling officers focus on a single problem (e.g. drug dealing) in a single location. Although there is evidence that this may reduce crime in the area, there is lingering concern that such intensive police efforts may merely work to displace crime to other locales. For example, targeted police operations appear to have limited long-term impact on drug-dealing activities and drug availability, and some local drugs economies continue to flourish (Lupton et al., 2002; Edmunds et al., 1996; Jacobson, 1999). In addition, such concentrated police efforts cannot occur in all locations at all times, so their use will necessarily be limited. The most prominent example of intensive 'hot-spot' policing in action is the so-called zero tolerance strategy in New York City from the mid-1990s (see Box 17.2). The strategy is based on the principle that by clamping down on minor street offences and incivilities, more serious offences will be curtailed. This often translates into more intensive policing or specific operations against under-age smoking or drinking, obstruction by street traders, public urination, graffiti writing, and the arrest or moving on of beggars, prostitutes, pickpockets, fare dodgers, 'squeegee merchants', abusive drunks, litter louts, and so on (Burke, 1998; Silverman, 1999). Many politicians and senior police officers have argued that the approach is a success, reducing rates of robbery and murder. Critics, however, question the precise reasons for any decline in crime rates and the efficacy of the zero tolerance strategy overall. Indeed, there are question marks over the social costs involved and whether it is ever possible to disentangle the effect of good police work from broader changes in the economic and social context (Bowling, 1999; Greene, 1999).

BOX 17.2 Zero tolerance policing in New York

The NYPD approach incorporated some of the ideas derived from Wilson and Kelling's 'Broken windows' theory, but it became associated with the term 'zero tolerance'. In popular discourse, zero tolerance policing (ZTP) conveyed a policy of tough enforcement on the street, constant police pressure with high visibility, vigorously tackling 'disorder' and focusing on minor offences (e.g. fare dodging, begging, urinating in public places, graffiti), 'crime mapping' and targeting of 'hot spots' as well as hounding frequent offenders. Zero tolerance policing has been credited for reducing crime in New York, including serious and violent crime, improving quality of life and 'reclaiming' parts of the city (subway stations, parks and areas around public buildings). However, critics have argued that crime was already falling in New York before the introduction of ZTP and that this phenomenon could also be witnessed in cities that did not propagate ZTP. In San Diego, using largely a community-oriented approach that was the antipathy of ZTP, crime also dropped. Zero tolerance and the notion of 'fixing broken windows' could easily lead to intolerance, exclusion and demonization of out-groups. It was argued by critics that the assertiveness of ZTP could turn into aggression, and there were examples of excess violence by the police. There was also a steep rise in citizen complaints about abuse of authority, discourtesy, use of obscene language, and other infractions that indicate a brazen force.

Source: Punch, 2007: 17–20.

The detection or 'clear-up' rate (i.e. the proportion of cases in which a suspect was identified and charged) has been used by many as the standard indicator of police effectiveness in crime-fighting. In Britain, detection rates have been generally falling across almost all crime types, albeit at different rates, at a time of unprecedentedly increased resources. Only a small proportion of cases (about one in four recorded cases) are ever 'cleared up' by the police. Police efficiency also varies significantly according to the types of offences. Those types of offence where there is a high likelihood of the victim being able to identify the offender (e.g. violence against the person), or because knowledge of the offence directly identifies the offender (e.g. possession of drugs), will inevitably have a higher detection rate than others (e.g. burglary). In 2002–3 the detection rates varied from 12 per cent for burglaries, 16 per cent for theft and handling stolen goods, 50 per cent for violent crimes, to 93 per cent for drug offences (Simmons and Dodd, 2003).

In practice, a great deal of police work is mundane and not directly crime related. Research studies have consistently shown that a high proportion of police time is actually spent carrying out tasks that do not involve crime control – for example, calming disturbances, negotiating conflicts and responding to a wide range of emergencies (see Audit Commission, 1993; Shapland and Hobbs, 1989). Indeed, many classic studies of the police role in the 1960s and 1970s in the United States (Bittner, 1967; Cumming et al., 1965) and in Britain (Banton, 1964; Cain, 1973) point to the service elements in police work and the role of the police as a twenty-four-hour 'social service' (Punch and Naylor, 1973).

In the contemporary context, the balance between the crime-fighting and the service roles of the police remains a 'highly contentious issue' and subject to intense policy debate. The important point is that the police officer is not, and never has been, simply a law-enforcement officer. As the first major study of police in Britain, that by Michael Banton (1964), suggests, the police often resolve problems or disputes by forms of 'peacekeeping' intervention that do not rely on law enforcement: 'the most striking thing about patrol work is the high proportion of cases in which policemen [sic] do not enforce the law' (1964: 127).

In recent years the police have increasingly been expected to achieve performance indicator targets and to reorientate the culture of policing around an explicit mission of service delivery and ethos of consumerism. For some criminologists, this is an indication of the way police work has become part of a managerialist approach to crime control (see following section). Others have emphasized that we now live in a society concerned with the calculation and removal of risk (Feeley and Simon, 1994), and that the police have become a key element in the risk-reduction matrix of control. In the Canadian context, Ericson and Haggerty (1997) argue that the police have now become 'knowledge brokers' in a risk society. In this context, one of the main functions of the police is to process information into a number of systems for a range of commercial and government agencies or community organizations (health, insurance, public welfare, financial matters, education) and their risk-management needs, rather than for criminal prosecution and punishment. Computer and information technology has therefore become central to policing. This emphasis on police knowledge work is also evident in the development of transnational policing in Europe, as the main tasks of Europol include collecting and analysing intelligence, preparing situation reports and crime analyses, and maintaining a central database for various crime categories (Sheptycki, 1998).

Police culture

Police organizations are known to be characterized by features of the police occupational culture. As Robert Reiner suggests,

> An understanding of how police officers see the social world and their role in it – 'cop culture' – is crucial to an analysis of what they do, and their broad political function. This is not to suggest a one-to-one correspondence between attitudes and behaviour . . . many observational studies of police work have shown that officers regularly fail to enact in practice the attitudes they have articulated in the canteen or in interviews. . . . An important distinction can indeed be made between 'cop culture' – the orientations implied and expressed by officers in the course of their work – and 'canteen culture' – the values and beliefs exhibited in off-duty socializing.
>
> (2000: 85)

It should be emphasized that the police culture is neither monolithic nor unchanging. It varies according to the views of police elites, department styles, the power structure of a community, different patterns and problems of the policing environments, and specific situations. Some elements of the police occupational culture are shared by front-line officers and managers alike, although there is evidence that points to the internal differences and tensions between 'street cops' (with their sense of professionalism based on experience and grounded knowledge) and 'management cops' (with a more bureaucratic and education-based notion of police professionalism) (Ianni and Ianni, 1983; Holdaway, 1983).

Nevertheless, there are some general characteristics of the occupational culture that are common to police forces in modern liberal democracies. In summarizing existing knowledge of police culture, Reiner (2000: 89–101) wrote that police culture emphasizes the following core features:

- a sense of mission
- action orientation
- cynicism
- suspicion
- isolation and solidarity
- conservatism
- racial prejudice
- machismo
- pragmatism

Taken together, these core features of police culture reflect a fundamental police world view of 'them and us'/'insider versus outsider'. They are also linked to the perception of the police officer as a 'craftsman' whose skills are essentially honed through practice at the 'sharp end' out on the streets (see Manning (1979) on the need to become a 'good practical copper'). These values, norms and craft rules are important because they shape the **working rules** that police officers internalize, which in turn become the effective principles that guide their decision-making and use of discretion (Skolnick, 1966; Policy Studies Institute, 1983; McConville et al., 1991).

Police discretion is inevitable and sometimes desirable, given the nature and circumstances of everyday police work: the need to make choices at every level about priorities, the need to interpret general legal rules in specific enforcement situations, the need to resolve the conflict between demands for high productivity and due process, and the low visibility of street-level policing from the point of view of managerial scrutiny. The problem is that police discretion is often exercised in discriminatory ways. The social functions and focus of police work remain remarkably stable over time, as some social groups were and still are more likely to be subject to police attention than others (for a discussion of 'police property', see Lee, 1981; see also Chapter 9 for a discussion of 'hierarchy of victimization'). A series of biases involving not only police stereotypes shaped by the occupational culture but also elements of the law, organizational deployment and police practices, cumulatively produce patterns of bias on lines of class, gender and ethnicity (Brogden et al., 1988: 146–50). Critics argue that the stereotypes used by the occupational culture have also resulted in discrimination against black police officers (Holdaway, 1996; Holdaway and Barron, 1997), female officers (Halford, 1993; Anderson et al., 1993; Martin, 1996) and gay or lesbian officers (Burke, 1993). The extent to which police culture and practices can be altered is debatable, as attempts at reform have led to rather mixed results in Britain and elsewhere (Foster, 1989; Skolnick and Bayley, 1986; Chan, 1997; Crank, 2004). Others have highlighted the need to consider the changing dynamics of occupational socialization and the ways in which 'each generation of officers both re-enacts police culture and renews it at the same time' (McLaughlin, 2007: 57).

BOX 17.3 The Stephen Lawrence murder and the Macpherson Inquiry in Britain

On 22 April 1993, Stephen Lawrence, a young black teenager, was murdered in an unprovoked attack carried out by white assailants. The police investigation into his death was grossly inadequate and the racist nature of the attack given little attention. A long campaign by Stephen's family and supporters called for an official inquiry into the police handling of the case, failure to follow up important information available at the start of the investigation, and lack of success in providing evidence that could lead to the prosecution of identified suspects. The call for an inquiry was resisted by the Metropolitan Police and rejected by Conservative Home Secretaries. In 1998 the new Home Secretary, Jack Straw, asked Sir William Macpherson, a former High Court judge, to chair an official inquiry into the case. Sir William examined three specific allegations against the police: that they were incompetent, racist and corrupt. Macpherson (1999) did not find evidence of corruption but firmly concluded that the police investigation had been 'marred by a combination of professional incompetence, institutional racism, and a failure of leadership by senior officers'. Individuals had failed, but so had the system; and the micro-processes of conduct in the Lawrence case exposed the institutionalized shortcomings of the Metropolitan Police.

Naturally, comparison was made with the report prepared by Lord Scarman into the riots in 1981, which had found evidence of racism within the police and made important recommendations concerning police–community relations and the need for racism awareness training for the police. Macpherson's reminder of the intervening lack of progress in improving police recruitment of minorities and changing police culture has been disturbing. Perhaps more significantly, he went further than Scarman and argued that racism was a problem that could be viewed as pervasive throughout the Metropolitan Police (and, by implication, throughout the police service nationally). The report referred to the idea of institutional racism to describe this state of affairs, defining it in the following way:

> The collective failure of an organization to provide an appropriate and professional service to people because of their colour, culture or ethnic origin. It can be seen or detected in processes, attitudes and behaviour which amount to discrimination through unwitting prejudice, ignorance, thoughtlessness and racist stereotyping which disadvantage minority ethnic people. ... Often this arises out of uncritical self-understanding born out of an inflexible police ethos of the 'traditional' way of doing things. Furthermore such attributes can thrive in a tightly knit community, so that there can be a collective failure to detect and to outlaw this breed of racism.
>
> (Macpherson Report, 1999: para. 6.34)

Police accountability

So what can we do to ensure that the police do the job required of them? This in essence is the meaning of **police accountability**. To whom are the police accountable, and do mechanisms set up to control police actions actually work? There are three models of rendering police accountable for their actions: legal accountability, political accountability and managerial accountability.

Legal accountability

Under the model of legal accountability of police work, the law provides control over police actions by laying down particular limits to police powers and how they can be exercised. For example, in Britain the Police and Criminal Evidence Act 1984 (PACE) gave new powers to the police but at the same time incorporated more controls over their use. These include requirements to tell suspects why they are being arrested or stopped and searched, and to record the incident (see Box 17.4 on PACE). However, critics argue that such rules require police to offer legally acceptable justifications for their decisions and operations after they have been undertaken, and that this form of retrospective accountability is indirect and limited (Lustgarten, 1986; Brogden et al., 1988; McLaughlin, 1994; Macpherson, 1999; Scarman, 1981). Indeed, the continuing police misconduct and the miscarriages of justice that took place since the implementation of PACE (see Chapter 16) provide a clear reminder of the limited effectiveness of legal control of police actions.

BOX 17.4 The 1984 Police and Criminal Evidence Act (PACE)

The 1984 Police and Criminal Evidence Act (PACE) sets out the powers of the police and the procedures they must follow in relation to investigation of offences, arrest and detention.

- It aims to regulate police practices by balancing police powers with safeguards for suspects.
- It originates in the report of the 1981 Royal Commission on Criminal Procedure, which formalized various existing powers as a general power 'to stop and search people or vehicles' where an officer has reasonable grounds for suspecting possession of stolen or prohibited items.
- It introduces new safeguards regarding the questioning of suspects: the requirement to tape-record the interview and to have a complete account of the entire interview.
- It allows the suspect the right to have a solicitor present and to say nothing to the police. This measure helps protect against self-incrimination and, coupled with audio (and possibly in the future video) recording, safeguards against the police seeking false confessions.

Political accountability

Given the selective nature of police work (i.e. responding to a near-infinite amount of crime with finite resources), critics argue that police choices about which laws to uphold, against whom, and by what means are inevitably political decisions (Brogden et al., 1988: 161). Under the model of political accountability, control over police operations is to be taken by political institutions in a democracy 'on behalf of the people'. The Police Act 1964 established a 'tripartite' structure of control in England and Wales (with the exception of London, where the Metropolitan Police Authority was not established until 1999), comprising the chief constable, the Home Office and the Police Authority (made up of locally elected councillors, magistrates and, under the Police and Magistrates' Courts Act 1994, 'independent' members). The precise relationship between police authority, chief constable and the Home Office has been subject to considerable debate (Jefferson and Grimshaw, 1984; Reiner and Spencer, 1993; Jones and Newburn, 1996). Local police authorities had a responsibility to secure and maintain an adequate and efficient force for the area, had the powers to appoint chief constables and could require their retirement on efficiency grounds, and shared police costs with central government. In practice, most police authorities were less than equal partners with their chief constables and were unable to exert effective control over policing policies, actions and priorities, though a small number of police authorities were very active and high-profile opponents of their local chief constables and police policies in the 1980s, notably in Merseyside and Manchester in northern England (see McLaughlin, 1994).

Managerial accountability

Finally, the government has been at the forefront in pressing for a fundamental shake-up of the managerial structures and processes, personnel policies, and working practices of the police organization in order to promote sound management and cost-effectiveness. More specifically, these changes have involved the government setting national policing objectives and quantifiable performance indicators covering key operational functions to facilitate inter-force comparisons, explicit costing of all activities, adaptation to a competitive environment characterized by market relations, service contracts and agency status, as well as standardizing recruitment, equipment and training (Savage et al., 2000: 26–30; McLaughlin and Muncie, 2000). Such changes have to be understood against wider managerialist reforms introduced by successive British governments from the 1980s to extract administrative efficiency, effectiveness and 'value for money' from their substantial financial investment in criminal justice agencies. The police have been subject to increasing inspection and regulation via a revamped HM Inspectorate of Constabulary (HMIC), periodic reviews by the Audit Commission, a 'Best Value' rolling audit that applies to all public services, the National Policing Plan, the National Intelligence Model, and the National Policing Improvement Agency. The police are now compelled to rationalize the purpose and scope of their activities, to provide detailed information about the costs, resource use and evidence of police effectiveness, and to be responsive to market conditions. Although performance targets, league tables and charters for 'consumers' of police services may be crude (and easily manipulated) indicators of police performance, they have placed police work under the spotlight as never before. Indeed, local police forces and police authorities may be compelled to account publicly for differences in effectiveness in detection, efficiency, resourcing and people's levels of satisfaction with the police.

Taken together, these formal mechanisms are designed to ensure that the police do the job required of them. There are also special mechanisms set up to deal with police abuse of power, such as the complaints and discipline procedure. The Police Complaints Authority (PCA), which was set up in Britain in 1985, involved a degree of external involvement in the handling of police complaints but was seen by many complainants as an ineffective and compromised body (Maguire and Corbett, 1991). As Sanders and Young (2002: 1065) argued, many people with grievances were deterred from activating the formal complaints procedure and instead prosecute or sue the police. In particular, civil claims increased in number throughout the 1980s and 1990s, involving the awarding of significant punitive damages against the police in some cases. The PCA gave way to an Independent Police Complaints Commission (IPCC) under the Police Reform Act 2002. Although most complaints continue to be dealt with by the police, the IPCC staffed by civilians has the power directly to investigate or supervise complaints which are more serious or are considered to involve issues of public confidence (e.g. deaths in police custody, serious corruption, miscarriages of justice, racist conduct) (McLaughlin, 2007: 175–9). Whether or not the IPCC can live up to its promise of building a police complaints system that enjoys the confidence of all sections of the community and the police service remains to be seen.

Police deviance and criminality

There is a long history of police deviance and malpractice in Britain and elsewhere (Mollen Commission, 1994; Sherman, 1974; Punch, 1985). As Maurice Punch (2003: 171–2) argues, many of the cases that have been exposed impinge on fundamental abuses of the rule of law, due process and human rights:

> In Spain there was a secret unit (GAL) that carried out the murders of ETA members (i.e., Basque separatists) associated with terrorism. The former Minister of the Interior and a number of police officers have been jailed in relation to this clandestine policy. . . . In South Africa testimony before the 'Truth Commission' revealed close cooperation between the police and the underworld in attacks on ANC (African National Congress) members during the period of the apartheid regime (Truth and Reconciliation Committee 1999). . . . In New York the Mollen Commission (1994) revealed that corruption and violence seemed to go together. Suspects were 'tuned up' (severely beaten) by officers. Some police officers were closely involved with drug dealers, had themselves become drug users and were prepared to do dirty work for the dealers (including 'riding shotgun' for them and even committing murders).

In Britain, in recent years the problem of police misconduct and rule-bending has attracted a great deal of public and official attention. Indeed, research and official inquiries have found evidence of a range of corrupt activities in police work, including: opportunistic theft; acceptance of bribes to lie on oath; providing tip-offs to criminal associates; destroying evidence; planting of drugs or stolen property on individuals; illegal searches; involvement in violence; participation by police officers in drug dealing; and protection of major drug operations (see Newburn, 1999). Most officers facing criminal or disciplinary procedures are from the lower ranks but there have also been cases involving some senior officers (Her Majesty's Inspectorate of Constabulary, 1999).

In 1998 the then Commissioner of the London Metropolitan Police, Sir Paul Condon, acknowledged that there may have been up to 250 corrupt police officers serving in his force at this time, which suggests that the pursuit of an unknown number of criminal investigations may have been seriously compromised. In response, a special squad of anti-corruption investigators, including accountants and private surveillance experts, was established to target officers believed to be implicated not only in accepting bribes but also in offences that included planning and carrying out armed robberies, large-scale drug dealing and violence against the public. Such a high-profile response to police corruption is reminiscent of the campaign of Sir Robert Mark, the reforming chief of the Metropolitan Police in the 1970s, who was charged by government with rooting out corruption, particularly in specialized units such as the Obscene Publications Squad and the Drugs Squad.

Why does police misconduct matter? Police deviance often arouses in the public a sense of disillusionment and betrayal. After all, citizens expect public officials to be impartial, trustworthy and dependable. This is particularly true of the police, who enforce many of the laws at their discretion, who have the power to deprive someone of their freedom and to use legitimate force, and who can carry out or refrain from an investigation into the conduct of individuals or groups that could lead to severe sanctioning. Police deviance is therefore generally assumed to undermine public confidence in the police. In some cases, police misconduct has also led to the imprisonment of innocent people while the guilty remain unpunished. Indeed, public confidence in the police has been damaged by continuing revelations about their involvement in the suppression of evidence, leading to wrongful convictions and gross miscarriages of justice, as well as involvement of some officers – occasionally on a very wide scale – in routine rule-bending in order to secure convictions. For example, in the 1980s, the now-disbanded entire Regional Crime Squad of the West Midlands Police in Britain was found to have fabricated evidence, physically and psychologically abused suspects, and written false criminal confessions (Walker and Starmer, 1999; and see Chapter 16).

The suspicion that a large number of convictions may be unsafe has not abated, and the Home Office has even had to establish a special Criminal Appeals Unit to examine a long history of cases in which confidence about the actions of the police and/or reliability of the evidence can

Plate 17.2 CCTV video camera in front of the French National Assembly in Paris (13 October 2005).

Source: AFP/Getty Images.

be seen as in doubt. Part of the problem is that association with lawbreakers (e.g. informants) and contact with sources of temptation (such as large sums of money, especially in drug cases) are in fact intrinsic to the job of policing. Indeed, police rule-bending and rule-breaking can be seen not only as a problem of the deviant cop slipping into bad ways (i.e. the 'rotten apple' metaphor), but as an indication of systemic failures (the alternative metaphor of 'rotten orchards') (Punch, 2003). Such failures are inextricably related to the nature of police organizations (e.g. the low visibility of police work), the character of occupational culture (internal solidarity, 'cutting corners'), and the particular opportunities and pressure for results presented by the environment that is policed.

Privatization, pluralization and transnationalization in policing

The history of policing demonstrates the recent nature of the idea that the 'public police' are the natural and only holders of certain powers and responsibilities relating to crime. In fact, the notion of a 'public monopoly' over policing is and always has been a fiction (Garland, 1996; Jones and Newburn, 2002: 133). The public 'police' should not be assumed to be the providers of everything that might be described as 'policing'. Certainly, since the 1960s and 1970s there has been a growing division of policing labour in society owing much to the expansion of the private security sector (South, 1988). The history of private provision is, of course, much longer, going back to private associations and patrols in the nineteenth century, and continuing through the establishment of private guard companies before the Second World War. According to Jones and Newburn (2002: 134), 'in Britain, the 1951 census of population estimates about 66,000 private security employees compared with approximately 85,000 police officers', indicating that the plurality of policing was well established if not well recognized even then. One reason for the relative invisibility of this sizeable number is that many such employees would have been 'in-house' watchmen and guards. In more recent decades, business models have encouraged the use of the service sector and the 'downsizing' of non-essential staff, which would mean the replacement of such in-house staff by contracted security.

The contract sector has also been able to provide services that replace those previously provided by state bodies, on the grounds either that public service resources are then 'freed up' or that they are a cheaper but also more efficient provider. So, patrols of public space and the use of security companies to escort and guard prisoners replace jobs previously undertaken by police or prison officers. The policing of public but privately owned space – the 'mass private property' of shopping malls (Shearing and Stenning, 1987) – has arguably changed the street-level face of policing. To some commentators, this 'rebirth of private policing', where order maintenance functions shift from state agencies to the free market supplied by security firms, has fundamentally changed our conceptions of policing as a state-centred activity (Sheptycki, 1995). The role in prisoner supervision also reflects the fact that private companies now run some prisons. All this has become a transnational industry of significance, with private companies bidding for contracts across national jurisdictions. As Button (2002: 25) notes, there is now a large global security market containing some very sizeable companies that operate on an international basis (for example Group 4 Falck, Securitas, Securicor and Wackenhut). Group 4 Falck, for instance, operates in fifty countries, has a £1.6 million turnover, employs 125,000 staff worldwide and provides services from guarding and the management of prisons to the provision of ambulance and fire-fighting.

As the public police are placed under increasing pressure to mimic the private sector, a modern slimmed-down 'entrepreneurial police' may have to take on

> the role of (a) accrediting and managing a consumer-driven 'mixed economy' of security and policing services; (b) developing specialist 'products' to 'trade' on the national and international security market; (c) professionalizing core competencies in criminal investigation, prosecution; and forensics and/or (d) co-ordinating confidential information flows between a range of private and public institutions.
>
> (McLaughlin, 2007: 97)

It is obviously important to understand contemporary policing in terms of this plurality. Loader (2000; and see Button, 2002: 15) has offered a classification of policing organizations along the following lines:

- policing by government – Home Office police forces and agencies such as the National Crime Squad;
- policing through government – services supplied by contractors (private security) but on behalf of government;
- policing above government – international developments at levels of cooperation, intelligence-sharing, strategy, etc., such as Europol and Interpol;
- policing below government – officially endorsed activities such as Neighbourhood Watch, as well as officially discouraged vigilantes and other extra-legal 'popular justice' groups.

To some critics, the proliferation of policing institutions and processes indicates that security itself has become increasingly commodified and Spitzer (1987) argues that nowadays security is bought and sold in the marketplace like any other commodity. But the problem is that the consumption of that commodity (e.g. in the form of bolts, alarms, CCTV surveillance, street patrols) may not produce a corresponding feeling of security. Instead, the opposite may happen: 'the more we enter into relationships to obtain the security commodity, the more insecure we feel' (Spitzer, 1987: 50). Furthermore, there is the problem of a highly inequitable system of policing in which the rich can buy protection from private police and retreat behind 'gated' enclaves (see Davis, 1992, on Los Angeles), coupled with 'a poor police policing the poor' (Bayley, 1994: 144). The expanding surveillance capacity of the transnational policing enterprise in the name of a global 'war' on drugs and terrorism is also a concern. However the futures for policing in the twenty-first century map out, the issue of police powers, the impact of policing, and the control of public police and alternative forms of policing will remain high on the criminological agenda.

Summary

1   The police are distinguished from other public services by their specific capacity to exercise legitimate coercive force. Notwithstanding the popular image of the police as crime-fighters and their role in preventing crime, detecting criminals and maintaining order, a great deal of everyday police work is not crime related.
2   Historically and in the contemporary context, a series of biases involving the social functions of police, elements of the law, police occupational culture and organizational deployment have produced patterns of bias in police work on lines of class, gender and ethnicity.
3   Police accountability matters, because police work is about the exercise of authority and the regulation of conflicts in society, which is highly controversial and contested. There are three models of rendering police accountable for their actions: legal accountability, political accountability and managerial accountability.
4   Police rule-bending and rule-breaking can be seen not only as a problem of individual deviance but also as an indication of systemic failures. Systemic failures are related to the nature of police organizations, the character of occupational culture, and the particular opportunities and pressures presented by the environment that is policed.
5   Contemporary policing is also carried out by a variety of individuals, groups and techniques.

Critical thinking questions

1   The 'Robocop' scenario of 'the future of law enforcement' is of privatized, heavily armed police officers. Debate what policing in Britain might look like in twenty years' time.
2   According to the ideas of Max Weber, organizations like the police should enjoy considerable support and be able to exert authority: 'dominant groups are able to issue commands and orders that the subordinate actors accept as the basis for their own behaviour. . . . Domination takes this form of authority when it is based on a claim to the legitimacy of the commands' (Scott, 1996: 23). Do the police today actually have this kind of authority and legitimacy?
3   'Bad apples' or 'rotten barrels'? Discuss in relation to police deviance.

Further study

Banton, M. (1964) *The Policeman in the Community*, London: Tavistock. A pioneering sociological study of the police based on an analysis of field diaries of a sample of Scottish police officers, observation, and interviews (both in Britain and in the United States).

Emsley, C. (1996) *The English Police: A Political and Social History*, 2nd edn, Harlow: Longman. An accessible introduction to the history of the 'new police' and the changing social and political contexts in England from the nineteenth to mid-twentieth centuries.

Johnston, L. (2000) *Policing Britain: Risk, Security and Governance*, Harlow: Longman. A useful overview of the key issues in the study of police, public and commercial policing and risk management in the UK.

McLaughlin, E. (2007) *The New Policing*, London: Sage. The most up-to-date and stimulating text on the contemporary developments and key debates in policing, security and crime control in the UK and the United States.

Newburn, T. (ed.) (2003/2008) *Handbook of Policing*, Cullompton: Willan; and Newburn, T. (ed.) (2005) *Policing: Key Readings*, Cullompton: Willan. Two comprehensive collections of readings that examine the issues, debates and recent transformations in many key areas of the police and policing.

Reiner, R. (2000) *The Politics of the Police*, 3rd edn, Oxford: Oxford University Press. An excellent text covering the history of the police, the sociology of policing, and the law and politics of the police in the UK.

More information

UK Police Service

http://www.homeoffice.gov.uk/police/
This site provides links to official police forces – both regional and non-regional – and related organizations.

Police Complaints Authority

http://www.pca.gov.uk/
The PCA is an independent body set up by the government to oversee public complaints against police officers in England and Wales, plus the National Crime Squad, National Criminal Intelligence Service, British Transport, Ministry of Defence, Port of Liverpool, Port of Tilbury, Royal Parks and UKAEA police.

Association of Police Authorities

http://www.apa.police.uk/apa/
The national voice for police authorities in England, Wales and Northern Ireland. Includes publications and links to other useful sites.

State Watch

http://www.statewatch.org/
State Watch is a non-profit-making voluntary group founded in 1991. This site provides useful police policy documentation and investigative case studies in Europe.

chapter 18

Prisons and Imprisonment

Key issues

- What are the international differences in imprisonment?
- Why has incarceration become the dominant response to crime?
- How is the prison system in crisis?
- What are the causes of prison unrest?

Introduction

Imprisonment provokes profound questions of justice to the extent that the use of penal institutions provides a stark barometer of the condition of democracy in any society. This point has long been recognized; as de Tocqueville observed in the 1830s, while 'the United States gives the example of the most extended liberty, the prisons of that same country offer the spectacle of the most complete despotism' (Garland, 1990: 11). Prisons continue to be the most controversial institutions in modern penal systems and occupy a central place in popular sentiment and political rhetoric on punishment, even though in no jurisdiction are the majority of convicted offenders actually sent to prison (Sparks, 2002: 202). The task of this chapter is to examine imprisonment as a social practice that generates deep-seated disputes, while introducing the key themes that define contemporary prisons in Western societies, not least since there is considerable consensus that the penal system in England and Wales has been in a state of ever-deepening crisis since the 1960s.

While few informed commentators would deny that the penal system has serious, if not irreversible, problems, perhaps the key question is: How is it able to maintain a semblance of order for most of the time in the face of grave and often intractable difficulties? Moreover, the term 'crisis' implies a critical point in time, usually short-lived, when a situation either ends in catastrophe or the danger is averted. Yet the penal system has not yet totally collapsed (though it came close to it in April 1990) nor has it, or various governments of the day, begun genuinely to address the structural properties that give rise to the periodic symptoms of malaise (such as overcrowding, brutality, riots, strikes, and so forth) to anything like the extent necessary to proclaim a dramatic improvement in the condition of the system. Instead it makes more sense to view the penal 'crisis' as an enduring feature of the past few decades, which is composed of several interweaving components that compromise not only the ability of the state to maintain order but also challenge moral sensibilities on what the purposes of imprisonment might, or ought to, be. In other words, the severe problems in prisons that are the subject of this chapter are as much moral and philosophical matters as practical and material ones.

Comparing penal systems

The penal crisis, at a very basic level, can be regarded as simply too many offenders and too few prison places, which has given rise to overcrowding, understaffing, decrepit conditions and poor security; and a prison sentence continues to be the harshest penalty available to the courts of England and Wales. Currently around 120,000 people are annually received into 139 institutions, at a cost to the taxpayer of £26,412 per prisoner per annum, and providing employment for over 48,000 staff to keep them there (Prison Service, 2005). All of this stands in stark contrast to the situation just over fifty years ago, for in 1946 there were about forty prisons, approximately 15,000 prisoners and around 2,000 staff (Morgan, 2002: 1117).

The reasons for this striking increase are complex and even though conclusions drawn from international comparisons should always be treated with caution, it is clear that England and Wales consistently use imprisonment to a greater extent than practically every country in Western Europe. For instance, in 2006, 148 persons were incarcerated per 100,000 population in England and Wales, compared to 95 in Germany, 90 in Greece, and 66 in Norway (Walmsley, 2006: 5). Such crude comparisons also indicate that England and Wales lie some way behind the global leaders in imprisonment – Russia, the United States, China and South Africa – as well as most of the countries in Eastern Europe (see South and Weiss, 1998, and Cavadino and Dignan, 2005, for further comparative analyses of penal systems).

There are more than 9.25 million people held in prisons throughout the world. Yet almost half are found in just three countries – the United States (2.19 million), China (1.55 million plus an unknown number of pre-trial detainees and prisoners in 'administrative detention') and Russia (0.87 million) – from data collated from 214 independent countries and dependent territories across all five continents (Walmsley, 2006: 1). As commentators have noted, it is truly striking how three countries at the extreme ends of cold-war politics, with 'such dramatically different histories, cultures and patterns of crime, should hold, as it were, gold, silver and bronze positions in the world league table of numbers of prisoners' (King, 2007: 98).

In this chapter we will be primarily concerned with documenting the problems to be found in the English and Welsh prison system. While Scotland and Northern Ireland each have their own separate systems, much of what we discuss extends beyond national boundaries. In order to

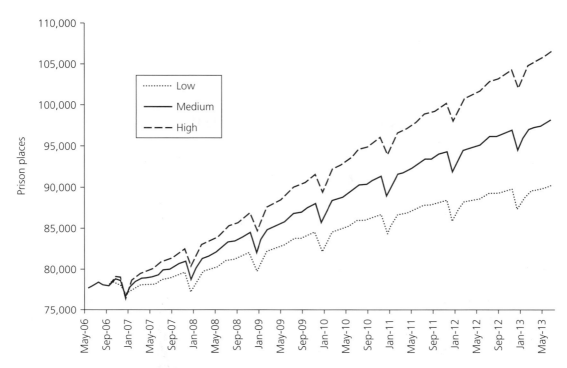

Figure 18.1 Alternative scenarios for prison population, 2006–13.

appreciate the problems of the present, it is vital that the concerns of the past are first outlined, as these issues continue to shape contemporary penal systems.

Origins of imprisonment

Before the eighteenth century, imprisonment was only one, and by no means the most important, element in systems of punishment. Throughout pre-industrial Europe, courts drew upon a much wider range of sentences than is possible today. The range of penal measures included aggravated forms of the death penalty, such as breaking on the wheel (with bodies left to rot on the device as warnings to the living), through to minor sanctions such as warnings not to repeat the offence. In between lay a diverse variety of more and less serious forms of corporal punishment (such as mutilation, branding and whipping), forms of public shaming (such as the pillory), forms of bondage (such as galley servitude, transportation and the workhouse), banishment, fines, and a host of other minor prohibitions (Spierenburg, 2005).

The historian Ralph Pugh (1968) has described how in medieval England imprisonment came to serve three main uses:

■   custodial (detaining those awaiting trial or sentence);
■   coercive (forcing fine defaulters and debtors into making good their misfortune); and
■   punitive (as punishment in its own right).

prisons and imprisonment

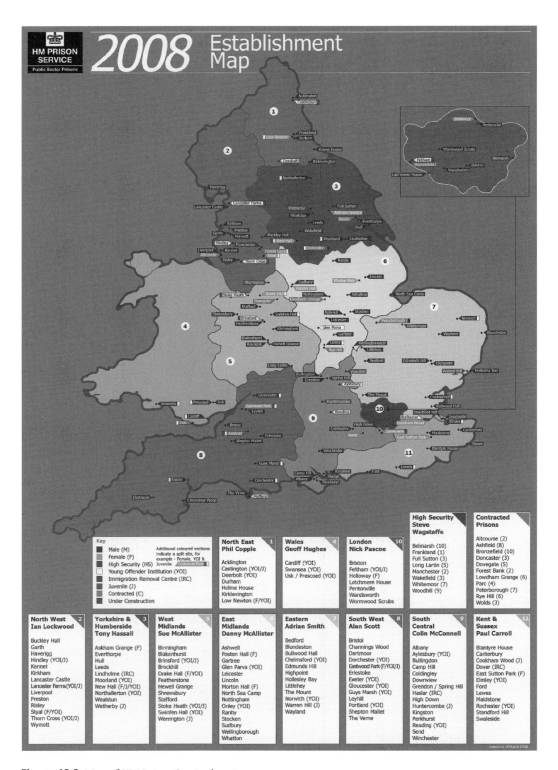

Figure 18.2 Map of HM Prison Service locations.

controlling crime

These legal distinctions continue to be significant, yet it is important to recognize that the main purposes of the medieval prison were custodial and coercive, with the sentences likely to have been corporal or capital, and it was not uncommon 'for a person to be sentenced and hanged or flogged on the same day' (McConville, 1998: 118).

However, as feudal systems began to break down, with the advent of mercantile capitalism, large numbers of people migrated from rural areas to burgeoning towns and cities. This new population was viewed as being composed of vagrants, beggars, robbers and the unemployed, so that during the sixteenth and seventeenth centuries there began to emerge a range of secular institutions (that are the precursors of modern imprisonment) across Europe, which sought to confine the growing numbers of poor, homeless and dispossessed citizens. From the 1500s, bridewells, workhouses and transportation to colonies came to complement conventional forms of corporal and capital punishment, as a means of distinguishing the 'deserving' from the 'undeserving' poor and fuelling colonial expansion (see the timeline in Box 18.1 for historical details of the developments discussed in this chapter).

BOX 18.1 Timeline: key developments that created the modern penal system

1166 The Assize of Clarendon, legislation by Henry II that sought to establish a gaol in every English county, a task completed by the thirteenth century.

1556 The first bridewell is converted from a little-used royal palace in London (known as Saint Bridget's well) into the earliest recorded 'house of correction'.

1717 The Transportation Act provides for the considerable expansion of transportation to the colonies (which had begun over a century earlier).

1779 Hulks are introduced: broken-down transportation ships (also referred to as 'floating hells') moored on river banks that act as penal warehouses in the wake of losing the American War of Independence.

1779 The Penitentiary Act includes proposals for improved diet, paid labour in prisons and the building of two 'ideal penitentiary houses'.

1823 The Gaol Act imposes a new classification system involving the separation of men and women.

1838 A separate juvenile prison is established at Parkhurst.

1852 Transportation is abandoned and government introduces the Australian 'ticket of leave' scheme, the precursor of parole.

1865 The Prison Act formally amalgamates the gaol and house of correction.

1868 Public ceremonies of execution end.

1877 Prison Act brings control of local prisons under central government and a Prison Commission is established under the charge of the Home Secretary.

1895 The Gladstone Committee on Prison reports and recommends rehabilitation and treatment as priorities for the prison system rather than simply punishing offenders.

Nevertheless, it was eighteenth-century Enlightenment critics who promoted the prison as the generalized response to crime, as opposed to the public spectacles of suffering that were losing their legitimacy in England as well as in other parts of Europe (Spierenburg, 1984, 1998b). While there are competing explanations as to why the prison came to be the dominant response to crime from the end of the eighteenth century, which are discussed below, it is important to emphasize that for much of the eighteenth century the bridewells, workhouses and local gaols were characterized by disorder and neglect. It was this widespread squalor, disease and corruption that a number of penal reformers, including John Howard and Elizabeth Fry, campaigned to end. They were opposed to the indiscriminate mixing of men and women, the lack of segregation between the tried and the untried, the open sale of alcohol, the gambling and the generally filthy conditions, with diseases such as typhus being rife. Many of the institutions were also run as private enterprises for profit – there is evidence that many bridewells had become lucrative brothels (Zedner, 1995).

Influenced by religious piety and Enlightenment reason, the reformers advocated the benefits of classification, isolation and sanitation. Howard's widely publicized description of the abuses and distress encountered in these institutions and his comprehensive proposals for change, combined with the effects of the American War of Independence of 1776, which left the government with nowhere to send those sentenced to transportation, lay behind the 1779 Penitentiary Act. These two developments led central government to build new prisons known as 'penitentiaries' in an effort to reform the convicted and deter any others (Harding et al., 1985). The Act promoted a new vision of imprisonment that would unite the punitive and reformative through hard labour and religious instruction in a system where prisoners were classified into groups, while profits from their labour paid prison staff.

During the nineteenth century it was increasingly assumed that only the state could be entrusted with preventing neglect and creating reformatory systems of prison discipline through solitary confinement, surveillance and the daily grind of the treadmill. This assumption led to the 1863 Penal Servitude Act and the 1865 Prison Act (which abolished the distinction between gaols and houses of correction to create a 'new' institution known as 'prison') and culminated in the nationalization of the prison system in 1877 which brought prisons under centralized state control.

Why prison?

The question that needs to be answered is why the prison became the dominant response to crime across Europe and North America from the end of the eighteenth century. Until the 1970s the explanation would have been that imprisonment represents an enlightened, humanitarian, progressive response over the barbarism of earlier epochs. This Whig view of history emphasized how early forms of punishment, based on vengeance, irrationality and cruelty, had been replaced by informed, professional and expert intervention, and would celebrate the zeal of benevolent reformers in explaining why contemporary penal systems exist. However, this interpretation has been widely challenged by a range of 'revisionist' histories of the 'Great Incarcerations' (Cohen, 1985).

The earliest work that looked behind the rhetoric of reformers and asked why particular punishments gain prominence during certain historical periods is provided by George Rusche and Otto Kirchheimer (1939/1968). As Chapter 15 shows, their argument is informed by a Marxist understanding of social relations and highlights the relationships between the form of punishment and the economic requirements of particular modes of production. For instance, they argue that the prison emerged with the advent of industrial capitalism as a means of creating a submissive and regulated workforce.

Their account has been criticized for the way in which it provides a one-dimensional explanation of penal relations that prioritizes the significance of the labour market at the expense of other factors. A more sophisticated account is Michael Ignatieff's (1978) analysis of the birth of imprisonment. He rejects economic functionalism and argues that incarceration was a response to the crisis in class relations wrought by the Industrial Revolution as it served to establish the legitimacy of the law, and was understood as an element of a larger vision of securing popular consent in an increasingly unequal, class-divided society.

However, the most influential 'revisionist' history of imprisonment is Michel Foucault's *Discipline and Punish* (1977), which argues that the emergence of the prison does not mark a more humanitarian form of punishment. Instead it represents an attempt to punish more efficiently and extensively to create a disciplined society, through the techniques of surveillance, classification and examination perfected in the new institutional spaces (e.g. Bentham's Panopticon). The originality of Foucault's argument lies in the importance he attaches to the relationship between power and forms of knowledge.

The emergence of the prison is just one instance of the dispersal of new forms of knowledge and his project is to examine how domination is achieved and how individual subjectivity is socially constructed. The prison has always been a failure, as it does not reduce crime, yet the reason why it persists is because it stands at one end of a continuum in which surveillance and regulation have become normalized throughout society. Foucault coins the phrase 'carceral archipelago' to describe the chain of people-processing institutions (e.g. asylums, barracks, factories and schools) that stretch out from the prison to imply that Western liberal democracies are intimately bound up with forms of oppression.

Although 'revisionist' histories continue to be influential, a number of critics have found fault with the way in which:

- all social relations have been described in the language of domination;
- complex processes are oversimplified;
- the instrumental aspects of punishment are exaggerated; and
- the wide social support for punishment is ignored (Garland, 1990).

Moreover, there is a failure to consider the punishment of women, which problematizes thinking on the role and development of incarceration. For instance, why women are more likely to be treated as 'mad' rather than 'bad' poses questions that conventional and revisionist historians are unable to answer.

In addition, feminist historians and criminologists have demonstrated how the ideological practice of institutional confinement began much earlier for women than for men. Mary Bosworth's (2000) analysis of the Hôpital de la Salpêtrière – the main hospital–prison complex for women in Paris from 1656 up to 1916 – indicates that many of the practices commonly held to originate in nineteenth-century penitentiaries in fact emerged far earlier in the seventeenth and eighteenth centuries. Likewise, Sherrill Cohen (1992) emphasizes how the existence of separate institutions for women across Europe from the sixteenth century onward, such as Magdalene houses for 'repentant' prostitutes, combined penitence, religious instruction and reformative labour in ways that anticipate developments in the nineteenth century.

It was also the case that women made up a considerable percentage of the population of bridewells. It has even been estimated that for much of the seventeenth and eighteenth centuries in London the number of women confined in bridewells was often greater than the number of men (Matthews, 1999: 14), while Victorian responses frequently 'drew attention to "crimes of morality" committed by women, such as prostitution or public drunkenness' (Zedner, 1991a: 309). Clearly the lessons to be learnt from 'herstory' are not only that the confinement of women in the early modern period challenges conventional and revisionist chronologies, but also that women were central to the burgeoning practices of institutional exclusion, segregation and control. As Bosworth (2000: 277) puts it, 'considering the gendered nature of the history of imprisonment broadens the focus and understanding of the criminologist about the meaning of confinement'.

The modern prison estate

Imprisonment in England and Wales continues to be dominated by this Victorian legacy. Nevertheless, it is important to recognize that there are now a range of institutions that can be grouped under two main types. First, there are local prisons and remand centres whose primary task is to receive and deliver prisoners to the courts, and to allocate those serving sufficiently long enough sentences to the second set of institutions. These are young offender institutions and adult training prisons, which are further subdivided into closed and open institutions for men and women. This subdivision reflects a prisoner security classification and the level of security that institutions provide. All prisoners are classified A, B, C or D according to a scheme devised in 1966 by Lord Mountbatten (Home Office, 1966) following a series of notorious prison escapes that pushed the issue of security to the top of the political agenda.

Mountbatten's recommendations have done much to shape the penal system of today. Category A prisoners are those 'whose escape would be highly dangerous to the public or police or to the security of the state' and while Mountbatten thought that such prisoners would probably be no more than 120, a more recent estimate puts the figure at some 700 (Morgan, 2002: 1143). Category D prisoners are those 'who could be trusted under open conditions' (Home Office, 1966). Category B and C prisoners are those held in closed conditions providing more or less security. Trial and remand prisoners are, with the exceptions of those provisionally categorized as A, all assumed to be Category B.

The allocation of sentenced Category A prisoners has been the subject of a long-running controversy. Mountbatten called for the concentration of all Category A prisoners into one single-purpose maximum-security fortress that would not only ensure that high-risk prisoners were to be kept in secure surroundings but that security could be relaxed in other regimes. This proposal was quickly rejected on the basis that concentrating all high-risk prisoners within a single fortress would mean that maintaining order and providing a constructive regime would be near impossible in a prison composed of 'no-hopers'. Instead a policy of 'dispersal' was adopted, in that maximum-security prisoners should be spread around among a few high-security prisons. There are currently five 'dispersal' prisons plus a further five that have high-security arrangements, and it is becoming increasingly common for institutions to have multiple functions.

It is fair to say that while the **dispersal policy** might have solved the problem of perimeter security, it has intensified the problems of internal control. For within the prison system the presence of a small number of maximum-security prisoners affects the vast majority of other prisoners who are subjected to much more custodial regimes. It is also important to recognize that the system of classification maintains a sharp differentiation between dispersal prisons, training prisons and local prisons, to the extent that the latter have come to bear the brunt of the chronic overcrowding, squalid conditions and understaffing that characterize some of the dimensions of the prison crisis, while the dispersal and training prisons have to a large extent been protected. The crisis is composed of the following sets of interrelated issues:

- an expanding prison population;
- overcrowded and decrepit conditions;
- authority and legitimacy deficits; and
- severe social consequences.

Contemporary crises

The expanding prison population

In order to make sense of the increases in the prison population it is instructive to consider longer-term trends. It is clear that since the 1950s the growth in the prison population has consistently kept ahead of available space in penal institutions. This is in marked contrast to the interwar era, when prisons were routinely half full. For instance, in 1928 there were only just over 11,000 prisoners in a system that could offer 20,000 cells. By 1938 the number of prisoners remained around the 11,000 mark, but many prisons had been closed on the grounds that they were no longer required (Stern, 1993: 24).

This is a striking difference to the post-war era, in which there was a fivefold increase in recorded crime (from 280,000 in 1938 to 1,334,000 in 1965). During this period the courts' proportionate use of imprisonment actually decreased (with the fine replacing probation as the main form of sentence), yet the prison population tripled – from 11,100 in 1938 to 32,500 in 1968 (Bottoms, 1987: 181). Even though the prison population rose modestly during the 1980s, and reached a peak at around 50,000 in 1988–9, it then declined in the early 1990s to around 45,000. Between 1993 and 1998 it increased rapidly by some 47 per cent to reach 65,300 and then declined slightly only to increase from January 2001 to reach a new peak of 71,220 in June 2002 (Home Office, 2002a). In March 2006 the prison population in England and Wales stood at 77,004, a rise of 2,603 on the year before (Prison Reform Trust, 2006: 4). In February 2008 the prison population reached a record of 81,681 and the Prison Service declared the system 'full' for the second time in eight months with court cells used to confine the overflow (Ford, 2008: 1). The soaring rise in the prison population is all the more remarkable as it has taken place against a backdrop of steadily declining crime rates, however measured, since the mid-1990s (Simmons *et al.*, 2002). At a basic level the increase is due to the courts sending more people to prison and imposing longer custodial sentences when passing judgement. Andrew Millie and his colleagues (2005: 108) have argued that prison growth is a combination of factors, including:

- a more punitive climate of opinion;
- a more punitive legislative framework;
- sentencing guidelines that counteract leniency;
- some changes in patterns of offending; and
- sentencers' perceptions of changes in patterns of offending.

Nevertheless, it is important to recall that there has been a policy of **bifurcation** operating across criminal justice policy since at least the mid-1970s (Bottoms, 1977), which enables governments to pursue both 'soft' and 'tough' sentencing options simultaneously. For instance, in the mid-1980s, 22 per cent of prisoners were serving sentences of over four years, but by the mid-2000s this figure stood at 46 per cent of adult male prisoners (Home Office, 2001: 76). These changes are partly explained by the introduction of parole in 1967 and subsequent developments in its use (see Morgan, 2002: 1130–2), but the important point to note is that long-term prisoners dominate life in most training prisons and consequently preoccupy prison administrators, with important consequences for the remaining prisoners.

Overcrowding and conditions

Prison overcrowding is predominantly a post-war phenomenon and even though there have been episodic attempts to expand the prison estate, for the most part these efforts have been insufficient to stave off serious overcrowding in the system. The problem is partly explained by the inflexibility of prison space, but there have been, and remain, clear policy preferences to concentrate overcrowding in local prisons and remand centres so that resources can be used to optimize the regime in training prisons and make best use of the facilities available there. The rationale behind this policy is the assumption that for prisoners serving short sentences there is too little time to achieve results. For example, at the end of the last century 'roughly 80 per cent of local prisons and around one-third of all prisons were overcrowded by more than 20 per cent (with the worst handful being of the order of 70 per cent overcrowded)' (Sparks, 2001: 213–14). Prison reform groups have pointed out that since the Labour government came to power in 1997 the number of prisoners sharing cells designed for one offender has risen from 9,500 to 18,000 – a practice known as 'doubling up' (Doward, 2007b: 19).

The effects of overcrowding contribute to a sense of crisis in many ways. Most obviously the problem of numbers has a deleterious impact on conditions, and it is beyond doubt that prisoners who begin their carceral career, and most do, in a local prison will typically find themselves in the midst of the worst conditions that the penal system can inflict; overcrowding has been a daily feature of life within many of these institutions for over three decades. The problem of numbers has to be located in the context of dilapidated physical conditions in which prisoners are contained, combined with poor sanitation, scarcely edible food, decaying cramped cells, clothing shortages and brief, inadequate family visits. Compounding this wretchedness is the severely restricted and oppressive regimes that are imposed since there is neither the space, facilities nor resources to provide prisoners with a range of training, work and educational opportunities when there are too many prisoners to cope with. Such abject conditions have been condemned by the European Committee for the Prevention of Torture (1991), which concluded that the overcrowding, insanitary facilities and impoverished regimes found at three Victorian local prisons (Brixton, Wandsworth and Leeds) amounted to inhuman and degrading treatment. Currently there are extraordinary plans to convert sea containers imported from China into temporary jails in an effort to ease the overcrowding crisis (Doward, 2007a: 18) – which recall the eighteenth-century floating hulks (see Box 18.1).

Authority and managerialism

The crisis of authority (Cavadino and Dignan, 2002: 200–5) refers not only to the long and bitter industrial relations between prison staff and management, but also to major changes in the philosophy and organizational form of prison administration. In the post-war era there has been a shift in the source of authority in prisons from a highly personalized form of charismatic power to systems based on bureaucratic rules and procedures. Further organizational changes have also meant that the Prison Service, formerly a Department of State within the Home Office, became a semi-autonomous executive agency in 1993 and privatization (the contracting out of public services to the private sector) is now an important and controversial feature of the penal landscape. Indeed, since the early 1990s many of the newly built and privately managed prisons have been local prisons, which tend to have better regimes and facilities than the 'traditional locals' – suggesting that there is now a two-tier local prison system with the old prisons bearing 'the brunt of overcrowding and reduced regimes' (Morgan and Liebling, 2007: 1118).

It is highly debatable, however, whether these organizational changes have been able to tackle the continuing crisis of authority, as there are clearly deep and long-standing legitimacy problems in the Prison Service, caused in some respects by the demise of rehabilitation in the 1970s as the guiding purpose of penal practice. The subsequent turn to managerialist issues in the 1980s and 1990s only served to undermine a sense of mission within the service, save for meeting narrow management objectives and performance indicators. It is also highly significant that the definitive statement on the causes of prison riots in the English context emphasized the importance of **legitimacy** in securing the acquiescence of the confined (Woolf and Tumim, 1991). In particular, the implication is that there are variable conditions which render it more or less likely that prisoners will accept, however conditionally, the authority of their custodians.

Social consequences

Youth custody

It is no coincidence that the modern youth justice system emerged in the middle of the nineteenth century, at the same time as 'adolescence' and 'juvenile delinquency' were 'discovered'. The deep ambivalence of the Victorians towards children were played out in the various discourses surrounding childhood – children were simultaneously idealized, worshipped and protected as well as being feared, exploited and regulated (Hendrick, 1990). During this period many social reformers and philanthropists directed their energies towards 'saving' and 'protecting', demanding that young people should be removed from the 'adult' prison population and placed in separate institutions. The Youthful Offenders Act 1854 provided the basis of the reformatories for the 'dangerous classes', and legislation three years later established 'industrial schools' for the 'perishing classes' (Hebdige, 1988: 21).

The Children Act 1908 was a major piece of legislation that created juvenile courts, barred under-14s from prison and created 'borstals' to cater for 16- to 21-year-olds (a 'juvenile-adult' category) based on welfare principles. The Children and Young Persons Act 1933 further under-lined the move towards welfare through prohibiting capital punishment for those under 18, and reorganized the reformatory and industrial schools into 'approved schools' which provided young offenders with education and training, while remand homes kept juveniles apart from adults. In the post-war period the dramatic rise in crime and prison overcrowding contributed to continuing changes in penal policy. Legislation introduced the detention centre in the 1950s, which was intended to provide a brief, unpleasant custodial experience for young offenders; although their development was slow they would return under the guise of a 'short, sharp shock' in the 1980s.

The Children and Young Persons Act 1969 proved to be a high-water mark in the welfare era and introduced the principle of diversion. The general aim was to keep young offenders out of the youth justice system or, only where it was absolutely necessary, to send them to juvenile court for 'care', and to 'treat' young offenders rather than punish them. These developments have pro-voked considerable debate among criminologists over their 'net-widening' effects and intensifi-cation of disciplinary power (Cohen, 1985). The Act also abolished the system of approved schools and remand homes and replaced them with 'community homes', and it was intended that detention centres and borstals should be phased out and replaced by 'intermediate treatment'.

However, in 1970 a Conservative government replaced a Labour administration and refused to fully implement the Act; it became blamed for failing to deal with rising juvenile crime, while the emphasis increasingly switched from a 'welfare' approach to one of 'justice' on all sides in the debate. As the 1970s progressed it became obvious that a process of bifurcation, or a 'twin-track approach' (Bottoms, 1977), was occurring with custodial sentences increasing for serious juvenile offenders while the use of cautions was adopted for less serious offenders.

The election of a Conservative government in 1979 that took a pledge to 'stand firm against crime' saw the return of traditional criminal justice values in the Criminal Justice Act 1982, but also saw borstals and indeterminate sentences replaced by 'youth custody' – with the institutions becoming known as Youth Custody Institutions. As Lorraine Gelsthorpe and Allison Morris (2002: 240) argue, the 1980s witnessed 'a period of "law and order" and "crime control", with policies which were designed to reassert the virtue and necessity of authority, order and discipline'. Widespread concerns over increases in juvenile crime in the 1990s, fuelled by joyriding in deprived council estates, widespread publicity over persistent young offenders and the murder of James Bulger by two 10-year-old boys, forced the main political parties into rethinking their positions on crime and punishment into what has become known as 'populist punitiveness' (Bottoms, 1995).

One of the consequences was a fierce controversy over whether the principle of *doli incapax* should be upheld. This refers to the age of criminal responsibility; in England and Wales it is 10 years, and children under that age cannot be found guilty of a criminal offence. Children between 10 and 13 were presumed to be *doli incapax* (incapabale of criminal intent) and despite vehement opposition from the Home Secretary the principle was 'upheld on the grounds that there is wisdom in protecting young children against the full rigour of the criminal law' (Gelsthorpe and Morris, 2002: 241). Nevertheless, the age of criminal responsibility is unusually low in comparison with most of the rest of Western Europe, where offenders under the age of fourteen are dealt with by civil proceedings.

The principle that children and young people under a certain age are *doli incapax* (incapable of evil) has come under sustained critique since the mid-1990s from both major political parties. It is a common law presumption, which has been enshrined in law since the fourteenth century, and was crucial to New Labour's efforts to reform and 'remoralize' (by focusing on individual responsibility) criminal justice. The Home Secretary announced that the principle would be abolished in the Crime and Disorder Act 1998, so as to 'help convict young offenders who are ruining the lives of many communities' on the basis that 'children aged between 10 and 13 were plainly capable of differentiating between right and wrong' (cited in Muncie, 2004: 251–2). The measure has drawn much criticism when first suggested and, more recently, by, among others, the Council of Europe Commissioner for Human Rights, who described it as an 'excessive leap' and even recommended that the age of criminal responsibility be raised 'in line with norms prevailing across Europe' (cited in Morgan, 2007: 218).

There is considerable debate over whether the New Labour government elected in 1997 has ushered in a 'new youth justice' (Goldson, 2000). Certainly there have been many new proposals and activities under the Crime and Disorder Act 1998 and the Youth Justice and Criminal Evidence Act 1999. These are too numerous to detail here (see Goldson and Muncie, 2006, for an overview), but significantly include the setting up of the Youth Justice Board, the creation of Youth Offending Teams and the restructuring of the non-custodial penalties available to the youth court (including elements of restorative justice – see Chapter 15). Some critics have argued that New Labour virtually 'invented' the concept of 'antisocial behaviour' and have shown it is intimately bound up with the government's politics of crime and disorder (Tonry, 2004).

Antisocial behaviour orders (ASBOs) were introduced under the Crime and Disorder Act 1998 (and subsequently amended in the Police Reform Act 2002 and the Anti-Social Behaviour Act 2003), but what might constitute antisocial behaviour is notoriously difficult to define and legally imprecise (Hughes and Follett, 2006). Andrew Ashworth (2004: 288) argues that ASBOs are 'incoherent' and questions whether the conversion of a civil order by 'sleight-of-hand' into a criminal penalty has led to 'a subversion of fundamental legal values'. Jill Peay (2007) has raised a number of concerns over the inappropriate application of ASBOs to those with mental and behavioural disorders. She notes how one survey revealed that of the ASBOs imposed on those under the age of 17 from April 2004, 35 per cent of the children were diagnosed with a mental health disorder or a learning difficulty. The following two examples from the survey conducted by the British Institute for Brain-Injured Children (BIBIC, 2005) sadly demonstrate her concerns:

> First, the case of a 14-year-old child with the cognitive ability of a 7-year-old, learning difficulties, a language impairment and suspected attention deficit hyperactivity disorder.

He had a nine o'clock curfew imposed on him, yet he could not tell the time. Not surprisingly, he repeatedly breached the curfew and had spent 13 of the previous 24 months in custody for breach. Yet, during this period, he committed no other criminal offence. Secondly, the case of another young man with learning difficulties whose ASBO banned him from a particular street: on questioning, he said it was ok if he ran down the street because he was not stopping. Whether this is the interpretation of a budding lawyer, or a simple misunderstanding, the potential for breach is obvious.

(Peay, 2007: 231–2)

Critics of New Labour's youth justice policy are especially concerned with the government's continuing reliance on custodial sentences for young offenders. Campaigners argue 'that the Government's "obsession" with teenagers on street corners had contributed to the sharp rise in the number of young people in prison', in particular there has been 'a ninefold rise in the number of children under 15 being sentenced to custody' (Bright, 2003: 9). It has been estimated that 40 per cent of young people in prison have been in local authority care while a staggering 90 per cent have mental health or substance-abuse problems. Nearly a quarter have literacy and numeracy skills below those of an average 7-year-old, and a significant proportion have suffered physical and sexual abuse (Kennedy, 2004: 292). Some of the tragic consequences of youth custody are detailed in Box 18.4.

BOX 18.2 Alternatives to prison

Some alternatives to prison have quite considerable histories, while others have been introduced only relatively recently. Anne Worrall (1997) identifies three distinctive groupings. 'Self-regulatory' penalties involve some form of public shaming that is assumed to be sufficient to deter offenders from further lawbreaking. 'Financial' penalties generally tend to be paid to the central administration of a criminal justice system, though it is possible, and some would argue desirable, for some form of compensation to be paid to the victim. 'Supervisory' sentences have increased in number since the 1970s and involve elements of rehabilitation (through education and welfare programmes), reparation (through unpaid work in the community) and incapacitation (through curfews and electronic tagging).

The use of alternatives to prison gathered force as part of a **decarceration** movement (see also Chapter 15) in the 1970s when various non-custodial sentences came to be regarded as a more humane and less stigmatizing means of treating offenders. Equally importantly, many governments were keen to find less expensive, but equally demanding, alternatives to imprisonment in the face of growing economic problems facing welfare states. Many proponents have since argued for displacing the use of specific parts of the prison system (e.g. juvenile detention), while others have concentrated on advocating alternative community-based sanctions. The overall pattern has been one of expansion, with such penalties accompanying rather than being an alternative to an increasing prison population.

BOX 18.3 Timeline: key dates in youth custody

1838 The first separate juvenile prison is established at Parkhurst.

1901 A penal reformatory to house young offenders opens at Borstal, Kent, a name that in time would come to be applied to all institutions for young offenders.

1908 The Children's Act creates a separate system of juvenile justice.

1948 Criminal Justice Act promotes wider use of borstals, though more punitive detention centres would come to prominence in the 1950s.

1969 The Children and Young Persons Act 1969 introduces the principle of diversion based on the ethics of 'care' and 'treatment'.

1982 Borstal training replaced by youth custody and the ideological reintroduction of the 'short, sharp shock' in detention centres.

1999 The Youth Justice and Criminal Evidence Act is a key element in New Labour's restructuring of juvenile justice.

2003 The Anti-Social Behaviour Act and Criminal Justice Act introduce a whole raft of provisions extending legislation over young offenders.

BOX 18.4 Child deaths in custody

In August 2004, 14-year-old Adam Rickwood became the youngest child to die in penal custody in recent memory. Between 1990 and 2005 twenty-nine children died in penal custody, all but two of the deaths were apparently self-inflicted. The extent to which imprisonment is a psychologically damaging experience is revealed, for example, by the fact that between 1998 and 2002 there were 1,659 reported incidents of self-injury or attempted suicide by child prisoners in England and Wales (Goldson, 2006: 148).

There has also been considerable media attention and outrage over the routine use of physical restraint in penal custody:

> Restraint techniques vary according to the type of institution. They include inserting a prison officer's knuckles into a child's back to exert pressure on their lower ribs and using the back of an officer's hand in an upward motion on the child's nose. Such techniques can legally be applied for up to half an hour.
>
> (Doward, 2007c: 13)

Hundreds of children are still subject to these restraints, despite the death of 15-year-old Gareth Myatt, who died in a Home Office approved restraint technique called a 'double-seated embrace'. Seven-stone Gareth choked to death on his own vomit as two male members of staff and a female colleague held him down on his bed at Rainsbrook Secure Training Centre in Northamptonshire in April 2004. The subsequent inquest recorded a verdict of accidental death, but was critical of the Youth Justice Board (YJB) and the private company that runs Rainsbrook. A report by the YJB offered to the inquest as evidence estimated that as many as '30 per cent' of restraint techniques were used to counter 'non-compliance, specifically resistance to going to bed or moving from one location to another' (cited in Doward, 2007d: 6).

Penal reformers have argued that little has changed since the publication of an independent inquiry into the treatment of young offenders in custody by Lord Carlile in 2006, which not only criticized the routine use of physical restraint, but also condemned the forcible strip-searching and solitary confinement that have been used to manage the behaviour of children in prison. In January 2005, Gareth Price, a 16-year-old, died while being isolated in the segregation unit at Lancaster Farms young offenders' institution in Blackburn. At Stoke Heath in Shropshire, for example, the Carlile inquiry found that between April and September 2005, children were placed in solitary confinement for up to seven days on 73 occasions. Eighteen of these were held for between seven and 28 days and, quite incredibly, four for more than 28 days.

Gendered prisons

It has been estimated that women, on average, make up about 4 per cent of the total prison population (Walklate, 2001: 169). Since imprisonment is largely experienced by young adult men, most criminologists argue that the organization and culture of the prison system reflects this dominance to the extent that there are very different regimes for male and female prisoners. For instance, the tendency has been to define women prisoners as mad or sad rather than bad, and the regimes have reinforced traditional stereotypes of motherhood and domesticity (Carlen, 1983; Bosworth, 1999).

The fact that there are far fewer women in prison poses serious consequences: there are only seventeen or so geographically disparate institutions, which both makes it extremely difficult for female prisoners to sustain relationships with friends and family and compounds the marginalization of women in the system. However, this has begun to change, as the drastic increases in the female prison population over the past decade and a series of scandals have pushed the issue of women's imprisonment to the forefront of policy debates.

For instance, the dramatic rise in the numbers of women in prison can be seen in the increase from an average of 1,560 in 1993 to 4,248 in 2006, with an all-time high of 4,672 reached in May 2004 (Prison Service, 2008: 1). Most of the rise is due to the significant increase in the severity of sentences. For example, in the Crown Court in 1991 only 8 per cent of women convicted of motoring offences went to prison, by 2001 that figure had increased to 42 per cent. Similarly, women convicted of theft or handling at the Crown Court are now twice as likely to go to prison as in 1991, while in the magistrates' courts the chances of a woman receiving a custodial sentence has risen sevenfold (Prison Reform Trust, 2006: 14).

The sense of crisis in women's prisons extends far beyond numbers. Since the mid-1990s the media have widely reported on the shocking practices of manacling mothers in labour, and the degrading methods of drug testing; Holloway prison, the largest prison for women, was deemed too filthy to inspect by the Chief Prisons Inspector; and in 2002 more women killed themselves in prison than ever before. Some of these issues are highlighted in Box 18.5, which graphically illustrates the point that prisons, 'even the most reformed ones, produce damage and diseases, in varied forms and intensity they produce damaged and ill people' (Gallo and Ruggiero, 1991: 278). Although women make up only 6 per cent of the prison population, 20 per cent of prison suicides from January to August 2004 were women, with nearly half of all self-harm incidents involving women (Scraton and Moore, 2004: 35–6).

BOX 18.5 The pains of imprisonment

A young woman hanged herself in prison last Wednesday morning. She was 29, awaiting trial for petty theft – that is, she had not been found guilty of any crime – and had been in jail for less than 26 days.

Her death has not yet been announced and her name will remain a secret until later this week, when her family has been informed. Once it is made public, however, the Government will be forced to make another stark admission: that her death has made 2002 the year more women killed themselves in prison than ever before.

Britain's prison population is soaring. Last week the Government admitted that the number of prisoners would increase by almost 40 per cent over the next decade, taking it to more than 100,000 for the first time.

The figures conceal a more desperate story: that of a female prison population out of control and increasing at three times the rate of its male counterpart. It is a population in which over 90 per cent of its members have severe mental health problems, 63 per cent attempt suicide and almost 95 per cent harm themselves in some way during their sentence.

Stephanie Langley, sentenced at the age of 25 to 14 years for drug smuggling, reduced to 11 years on appeal, believes prisons have become a dumping ground for mentally unstable women. 'I saw people come in to prison totally sane and normal and, six months later, be zooming about the exercise yard in a totally mad way pretending to be an aeroplane,' she said. 'I watched people scar themselves with glass, razors, scouring pads, cleaning equipment, burn themselves and dig holes in themselves. It wasn't attention seeking – it was pure desperation. My best friend committed suicide because she, like almost every other woman there, had had a very traumatic life and just couldn't cope with prison,' she added.

Britain imprisons a greater percentage of its female population than any other country in the European Union, except Portugal and Spain, and the number continues to soar; around 11,000 women have been imprisoned so far this year – about 20 per cent of whom are on remand.

In the past year alone, there has been a 23 per cent increase in the size of the female population and a 180 per cent rise in the past decade . . .

Langley made around seven serious attempts to commit suicide during her sentence. She also regularly cut her wrists and ankles with razors, hoarded sedatives to take them all at once and developed a range of eating disorders and psychological problems.

'I had been a deeply troubled girl before I went to jail, but this was slowly killing me. There was no one to help me, no one I trusted. In a man's prison, there's a solidarity, but in a woman's prison there's nothing but madness, aggression and pain.'

Langley was raped when she was a teenager and exposed to a range of sexual abuse during her childhood. Yet in Durham Prison she was forced to work alongside Rosemary West.

Source: Hill (2002:10) *The Observer*, News Section, 1 December 2002.

Half of all women in prison are on prescribed medication, such as antidepressants or anti-psychotics, with two-thirds having children under the age of 16, which has been estimated at some 24,000 children (Kennedy, 2004: 285). One in four women in prison have spent time in local authority care as a child, while over half have suffered domestic violence, and one in three has experienced sexual abuse (Prison Reform Trust, 2006: 15). The government's own *Strategy for Women Offenders*, published in 2000, recognizes that the 'current system does impact differently on women and men' (cited in Scraton and Moore, 2004: 36). For instance, Pat Carlen (1998: 10) has argued that women's imprisonment 'incorporates and amplifies all the anti-social modes of control that oppress women outside the prison' and that the very rationales for reducing the imprisonment of women have been subverted and are now used to lock up more women through processes of 'carceral clawback' (Carlen, 2002).

Ethnicity, nationality and racism

The picture presented by the statistics is that prisoners in England and Wales are dis-proportionately young, poor, members of ethnic minorities, with few occupational skills, or academic qualifications, and are likely to be suffering from psychiatric distress (Sparks, 2001: 215–16). Recent figures indicate that at the end of 2005, one in four of the prison population, 19,549 prisoners, was from a minority ethnic group, which compares to one in eleven of the general population (Prison Reform Trust, 2006: 22). There are a number of reasons for this over-representation. One key factor is nationality, and it has been noted that 12 per cent of the prison population comprises foreign nationals (a growing trend observed across Europe), while another is that the relative youthfulness of ethnic minorities compared to the white population means that over-representation is all the more likely to occur (Morgan and Liebling, 2007: 1121). Foreign national prisoners come from 168 countries, but over half are from just six countries (Jamaica, the Irish Republic, Nigeria, Pakistan, Turkey and India), and a quarter are Jamaicans, which is the largest single group by far (Prison Reform Trust, 2006: 23).

Coretta Phillips and Ben Bowling (2007: 445) have argued that the historical context for understanding 'race relations' in prisons must acknowledge the strong support for the National Front among many prison officers in the 1970s, combined with much evidence of brutality and harassment (Gordon, 1983), that led to the introduction of policies to combat racism in the early 1980s. Elaine Genders and Elaine Player (1989) have provided substantial evidence of racial discrimination within prisons. For example, they found that the best jobs were regularly allocated to white prisoners, as prison officers believed that Afro-Caribbean prisoners were arrogant, lazy

controlling crime

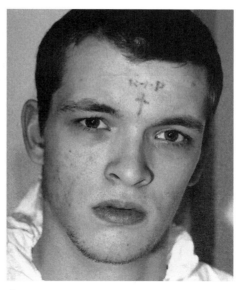

Plate 18.1 Zahid Mubarek was killed by Robert Stewart in March 2000 in a racist attack in Cell 38, which they shared at Feltham Young Offenders' Institute. Official reports have since found evidence of a persistent culture of racism not only at Feltham, but also similar patterns of racial prejudice throughout the prison system.

Source: Photonews Service Ltd Image Library.

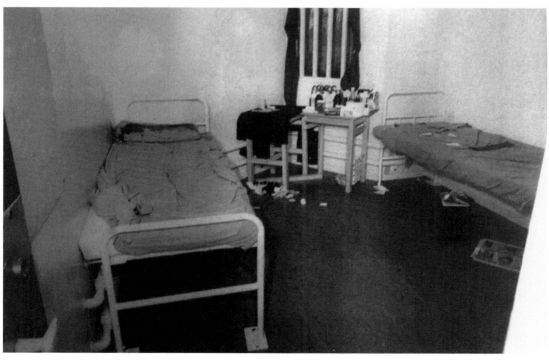

prisons and imprisonment

and anti-authority. More recently, the official inquiry into the racist murder of Zahid Mubarek in March 2000 by his white racist cellmate in Feltham Young Offenders' Institution found that institutional racism pervaded Feltham, which led to the Prison Service inviting the Commission for Racial Equality to carry out a formal inquiry into racism in prisons. The report identified twenty 'systemic failures' by the Prison Service to prevent the murder (Commission for Racial Equality, 2003).

The government resisted the demand by Mubarek's family for a full public inquiry, and an independent public investigation into Zahid's murder was set up only after the House of Lords ruled that human rights law justified their campaign for such a report. The three-volume report

BOX 18.6 Prisoners and rights

The modern prison was born in the late eighteenth century, and since then it has been justified according to the utilitarian aims of deterrence, incapacitation and rehabilitation, or the retributive principles of just deserts, hard labour and less eligibility. Each of these often conflicting goals has come to dominance at some point over the past two hundred years, and have been combined in uneasy compromises ever since. Throughout Europe, up until the eighteenth century, trials were usually held in secret, with the accused often unaware of the specific details of the case against them, and torture was routinely used to extract confessions. As Foucault (1977) emphasized, this intense secrecy stood in stark contrast to the sheer visibility of punishment as a public spectacle. Although the legal rights of the accused (rights to a fair trial, innocent until proven guilty, due process constraints, and so forth) have since become regarded as essential defences against arbitrary and oppressive practices, the convicted are still tainted by the feudal doctrine of 'civil death', which was based on the assumption that the proven criminal was an 'outlaw' without any legal rights (Tappan, 1954: 99).

Many critics have argued that prisons have remained 'lawless agencies' (Greenberg and Stender, 1972) and that in 'Britain . . . the law for most purposes tends to stop at the prison gates, leaving the prisoner to the almost exclusive control of the prison authorities' (Zellick, 1974: 331). The continuing irony is that while there is a complex web of rules and regulations surrounding a prisoner's daily life, the institution itself possesses enormous discretion with the rule of law practically non-existent. The authorities enjoy considerable power over the confined as the rules themselves are not only extensive and vague but prisoners are often unaware of their specific content. Indeed, they are frequently denied access to the mass of standing orders, circular instructions and service standards that supplement the statutory rules. The formal rules do not, in any case, provide a code of legally enforceable rights for prisoners, and the courts have generally been reluctant to intervene in prison life even when prisoners have had solid grounds for challenging decisions.

Such factors reveal the continuing legacy of 'civil death' and compound the arbitrary character of prison regimes because legal authority offers no defence against the highly discretionary power of the custodians. Lord Denning's (1972) ruling in *Becker* v. *Home Office* that the Prison Act did not give 'any colour of right' to a prisoner confirmed the long-standing judicial view that prison managers should be left to manage and that prisoners are unreliable troublemakers. Hence his comment that if 'the courts were to entertain actions by disgruntled prisoners, the governor's life would be made intolerable' as the 'discipline of the prison would be undermined' (cited in Schone, 2001: 72). However, the past thirty years have seen some important developments in prison law and the emergence of some judicial recognition of prisoners' rights (detailed in Carrabine, 2006, and van Zyl Smit, 2007).

It is important to put this judicial activism into sociological perspective. Although many of these cases have been hard won, their actual impact on prisoners' lives has been very selective, and this highlights the difficulties of relying on the legal establishment to defend and define rights (Carrabine, 2006: 202–3). The successes have been restricted to residual individual liberties such as correspondence with lawyers, access to courts, disciplinary hearings and release procedures – all matters which the judiciary are confident in dealing with. In contrast, the courts have not intervened in controversial administrative issues, such as transfers, segregation and living conditions which have a debilitating effect on prisoners. The fact that the courts have had such a negligible impact on most areas of prison life is partly explained by the long-standing scepticism towards natural rights in English political life, while the continuing deference to parliamentary sovereignty ensures that 'the statutory regime governing prisons in England is concerned, not with the definition of the prisoners' legal status or the creation of legally enforceable rights, but with clarifying lines of political control and accountability' (Lazarus, 2004: 251).

Of course, prisoners do not attract much public sympathy nor is there any political capital to be gained in the cause of prisoners' rights. But it is precisely because of their marginalization and vulnerability that the confined need protection. As the Chief Inspector of Prisons, Anne Owers, has explained:

> It is particularly the marginalized who need the protection of human rights: by definition, they may not be able to look for that protection to the democratic process, or the common consensus. And most of those in our prisons were on the margins long before they reached prison (look at the high levels of school exclusion, illiteracy, mental disorder, substance and other abuse); and may be even more so afterwards (with difficulty in securing jobs, homes, continued treatment, and even more fractured and community ties). Prisons exclude literally: but they hold those who already were and will be excluded in practice.
>
> (Owers, 2003: 1–2)

It is significant that she goes on to document, among other things, the human rights abuses that routinely occur to children in English prisons (such as strip-searching, segregation and intimidation) while highlighting the systemic failures that lead to deaths in custody and recognizing 'that much of what I am describing would not found a successful human rights challenge in the courts' (Owers, 2003: 4). Her implicit argument is that human rights are not simply legal entitlements, but are moral obligations that 'ought to condition social relations in and beyond prison walls' (Carrabine, 2006: 204).

(available at www.zahidmubarekinquiry.org.uk) heard evidence of a persistent culture of racism not only at Feltham, but of similar patterns of racial prejudice throughout the prison system. It heard, for instance, reports of 'gladiator games' where officers were accused of putting white and black prisoners in a shared cell and then placing bets on how long it would take before violence would break out between them (Temko, 2006: 5). It has also been argued that the brutal deaths of individuals from ethnic minorities while in prison custody is similar to the deaths of African/Caribbeans in police custody, as there is 'a tendency for prison staff to overreact to disruptive behaviour by African/Caribbean prisoners, whereby the stereotype of "Big, Black and Dangerous" seems to predominate in determining their response' (Bowling and Phillips, 2002: 208). It is beyond doubt that racism and racial discrimination structure daily life in prison.

Prison sociology

Prisoner subcultures and 'mind games'

Much of the classic literature in sociology (e.g. Clemmer, 1958; Sykes, 1958; Goffman, 1961; Mathiesen, 1965; Cohen and Taylor, 1972/1981) arises from monograph research on life in prisons. These studies have illuminated the day-to-day routines and struggles within institutions. Although this early work was preoccupied with prisoner subcultures and how they mitigated against the pains of imprisonment, especially in American penitentiaries, more recent British sociological writing tends to emphasize the complexity of responses to confinement. This varies a great deal according to the category of prison, the quality of its regime, and the shifting patterns of stratification.

For example, Richard Sparks and his colleagues (1996: 176–81) have indicated in their study of two long-term dispersal prisons (where one might expect the presence of well-developed subcultures) that simple analogies based on class structures, with 'gangsters' portrayed as the 'ruling class' and 'nonces' as a 'lumpenproletariat', are seriously misleading. Instead, a rather more fluid pattern of competing groups (based on ethnic or regional affinities as much as on 'business' interests) were more in evidence than the rigid separation of roles and group solidarity that was a defining characteristic of the classic subculture research.

As Rock (1996: 40) puts it, with reference to a woman's prison, there is not one prisoner world but several. This point is developed by Carrabine (2004) in his discussion of the culture of a local prison, whose captive membership is constantly in flux as new prisoners arrive to be allocated elsewhere, others are returning from dispersal prisons under 'transfers', yet more will be seeing out short-term sentences, while there will always be those deemed as 'unsuitable' for training prisons – the 'old lags' who have been imprisoned on many previous occasions. His argument is not only that antagonisms, friendships and influence constantly have to be renegotiated amid the frantic pace of daily change and upheaval on the wings and landings of local prisons, but that it is the staff occupational culture that plays a pivotal role in shaping institutional interactions, not least because prison officers spend a far greater proportion of their working lives in the same place than either the prisoners or their managers.

Another illustration of sociological analysis is provided in Kathleen McDermott and Roy King's (1988) discussion of the 'mind games' played on the wings and landings of five English prisons. They provide a number of game metaphors to illustrate the various degrees of conflict between prisoners and staff. For example, one of the most basic prison rituals is going to the lavatory, and this is one of the many routine degradation rituals faced in prisons as the toilet was then a bucket in the cell (the practice of 'slopping out' was said to have officially ended in April 1996, although there continues to be evidence that prisoners do not have adequate access to toilets).

Consequently, one way of making do is through what McDermott and King (1988: 360) call *pass the parcel*, which refers to the way in which excrement is wrapped up in parcels and thrown out of a window. It is partly functional as it relieves prisoners from spending time with the stench; yet it is also a gesture of anger, as it has to be cleared up by someone else and using prison clothing as the wrapper brings the issue back to the authorities, where it belongs. However, the game is not played by the staff, as they do not clear up the mess, they organize prisoners to do this and ultimately the prisoners also suffer through clothing shortages.

Survival games continue when prisoners are permitted outside their cells, as their encounters with staff, prisoners and arbitrary rules that govern their lives increase. For staff to survive they have to develop skills both to avoid an assault in the heat of the moment and, in the longer term, to avoid reprisals in a future riot. Prison staff are often in the situation where they have to bear the brunt of prisoners' frustrations but are powerless to relieve them, and they tend to play the *sloping shoulders game*: this is where an officer passes on a prisoner's request to a superior, invariably away from the landing, so that the officer is not immediately turning down the request. Meanwhile, prisoners are involved in *charades*. This is usually played by sex offenders who are anxious to avoid the label 'nonce'. For example, one prisoner was called this by another prisoner in their study, and though the sex offender knew he would lose, he challenged the prisoner to a fight. This earned him respect and an avoidance of the more severe beating he would have later received from a group of prisoners in his cell or in the recess.

Prison riots and the problem of order

Few would deny that prisons are dangerous places, and while violence is often described in terms of the characteristics of individual prisoners, such an understanding leaves much unexplained (Edgar *et al.*, 2003). The level of violent incidents in prisons indicates that intimidation, assaults and abuse form part of the everyday routine, whereas riots and disturbances are much rarer and pose a '*special problem* of the occasional complete or near-complete breakdown of order' (Sparks *et al.*, 1996: 2; emphasis in original).

Riots and disturbances can be further distinguished in the sense that a riot involves the authorities losing 'control of a significant number of prisoners, in a significant area of the prison, for a significant amount of time' (Useem and Kimball, 1989: 4), whereas a disturbance is a step down from a riot, as there are fewer prisoners involved and the administrators do not lose control of any part of the institution, but can still involve collective protest over conditions, through refusing to eat or stopping work for example. While these definitions can be criticized for their vagueness, they do have the advantage of highlighting the ways in which the problem of order is a daily feature of institutional life; even though major riots are rare events they do not abruptly occur in an otherwise tranquil vacuum and have multifaceted causes.

Moreover, the term 'riot' is a pejorative one summoning images of frenzied mob violence. Historians have indicated how the label has been used by ruling elites to discredit the revolutionary crowd in European history (Rudé, 1964). Prison riots are disturbing, complex and diverse events that raise profound questions over human action, social structure, historical context and political reasoning. In Bert Useem and Peter Kimball's (1989) examination of nine prison riots in the United States, they provide a fresh understanding of prison disorder because it introduces the issue of legitimacy as crucial to structuring institutional stability. Their argument is that well-managed prisons instigate conformity, whereas breakdowns in administrative control render imprisonment illegitimate in the eyes of the confined.

This study anticipates Lord Woolf's conclusion that the 25-day occupation of Strangeways prison in Manchester, England, during April 1990, was due to widely shared feelings of injustice, and the explicit argument is that there are variable conditions under which the confined accept or reject custodial authority (Woolf and Tumim, 1991). It is difficult to underestimate the significance of Woolf's report as it not only marks a decisive break with previous government understandings of prison unrest but is universally regarded as the most important examination of the prison system in the past hundred years. The recipe of reform he advocated is widely understood as one which will take the prison system out of the nineteenth century and into the twenty-first.

The concept of legitimacy locates the study of prison riots in the broader problem of order familiar to social and political theorists. By doing so, it establishes that there are no simple answers to the question of why prisoners rebel in the ways that they do (Carrabine, 2004, 2005). In fact, it raises the pressing issue of how such matters as age, class, gender, race, religion and sexuality challenge a universalizing notion like legitimacy. Perhaps the unsettling conclusion to be drawn from this case study on prison riots is that they ought to happen more often. Explaining why they do not involves recognizing that prisons typically generate diverse forms of social order in spite of frequently illegitimate distributions of institutional power and severe crises outlined earlier in this chapter. Ben Crewe (2007: 143) has argued that in the UK prisoners are increasingly encouraged to self-govern and 'assume responsibility for the terms of their own incarceration, in a way that represents neither direct coercion nor autonomous consent'. As Richard Sparks and his colleagues (1996) pointed out over a decade ago, there is some quite considerable variation in the ways that prisons achieve a semblance of order and that these matters are sociologically complex.

Summary

1   Prisons are the most controversial institutions in modern penal systems and occupy a central place in popular sentiment and political rhetoric on punishment.
2   The chapter has reviewed a number of competing explanations of the historical reasons why the prison became the dominant response to crime across Europe and North America from the end of the eighteenth century.
3   The account of the modern prison estate that followed demonstrated how there are a range of interrelated issues that contribute to a sense of crisis in the system, with grave social consequences.

4   The chapter has also included illustrations of sociological analyses of prison life in relation to 'mind games' and the problem of order.

Critical thinking questions

1   In what ways does gender challenge historical and contemporary accounts of imprisonment?
2   What are the key components of the prison crisis?
3   Why does youth custody involve elements of rescue, rehabilitation and repression?
4   Can you explain why the prison system is orderly most of the time?

Further study

Cavadino, M. and Dignan, J. (2007) *The Penal System: An Introduction*, 4th edn, London: Sage. The best criminological introduction to imprisonment, which covers the central issues in a broad and lively fashion.

Jewkes, Y. (ed.) (2007b) *Handbook on Prisons*, Cullompton: Willan. Is an excellent edited collection of essays written by many of the leading academics in the field as well as professionals who have worked in and around prisons.

Matthews, R. (1999) *Doing Time: An Introduction to the Sociology of Imprisonment*, Basingstoke: Macmillan. This is a more detailed sociological account of imprisonment.

Stern, V. (1993) *Bricks of Shame*, London: Penguin. This is a compassionate and thought-provoking examination of the institution.

More information

The Home Office
http://www.homeoffice.gov.uk
Provides access to a wide range of information on the CJS generally.

The Home Office: Publications
http://www.homeoffice.gov.uk/rds/pubsintro1.html
Provides access to a wide range of publications.

HM Prison Service
http://www.hmprisonservice.gov.uk/
Contains news, reports, statistics and prison rules for prisons in England and Wales.

Scottish Prison Service

http://www.sps.gov.uk

Contains news, reports, statistics and prison rules for prisons in Scotland.

Prisons and Probation Ombudsman

http://www.ppo.gov.uk/

The Prisons and Probation Ombudsman provides access to annual reports and publications.

Report of Her Majesty's Chief Inspector of Prisons

http://www.homeoffice.gov.uk/justice/prisons/index.html

A link to a report by the Inspector of Prisons can be found here along with further information on the Inspectorate.

Howard League for Penal Reform

http://www.howardleague.org/

Information, links and publications on penal reform.

National Association for the Care and Rehabilitation of the Offender (NACRO)

http://www.nacro.org.uk/

This site has information on penal reform and lists relevant publications.

Prison Reform Trust

http://www.prisonreformtrust.org.uk/

Information on the Prison Reform Trust, which aims at creating a just, humane and effective penal system.

Youth Justice Board for England and Wales

www.youth-justice-board.gov.uk.

Contains information on policies, news, press releases and details of youth offending teams.

The Guardian: Prisons

http://www.guardian.co.uk/prisons

The *Guardian*'s coverage of prison issues is an excellent resource.

The Observer: Special Reports

http://www.observer.guardian.co.uk/crimedebate

This offers further critical commentary on prison issues.

The Zahid Mubarek Inquiry

www.zahidmubarekinquiry.org.uk

This site is a link to the final report.

part 5

Globalizing Crime

In this part, we examine some of the newer issues that are now on criminologists' agenda. These include such matters as 'green crime', the importance of the media, human rights and globalization. A concluding chapter considers the future of crime control and criminology in the twenty-first century.

chapter 19

Green Criminology

Key issues

- What is a 'green criminology' and what can be identified as 'green crimes'?
- How are green crimes identified and 'criminalized'?
- What are the social costs of 'green crimes'?
- How do social movements shape 'green crimes'?

Introduction

Criminology is seeing the development of critical thinking around green issues, producing case studies and theory that meet and interweave with aspects of philosophy, political science, sociology, economics and the environmental sciences. This is reflected in the growing body of published work on green criminology that has emerged in recent years (e.g. Lynch, 1990; Edwards *et al.*, 1996; Clifford, 1998; Boyd *et al.*, 2002; White, 2005; Beirne and South, 2007; South and Beirne, 1998, 2006; Sollund, 2008).

Although the context – the environmental challenges now facing us all – will be familiar, it may be less immediately obvious how this relates to criminology. So, as a starting point, take the issue of climate change and the wide-ranging socio-political implications of this and other environmental risks. It may not yet be easy to fully comprehend these consequences but Abbott (2008), for example, shows that increasing temperatures, rising sea levels and weather volatility could, by 2050, have led to

- resource wars over food and water;
- the plight of up to 200 million 'environmental refugees' fleeing devastation;

- an inflation of ethnic tensions and conflicts;
- the prospect of the police and border services of countries closing down rather than opening up borders;
- violent protests against polluters.

Previously only foreseen in the realms of science fiction, these are new scenarios of harm, crime and conflict for our future reality and old responses are unlikely to be effective.

The plundering of the Earth's resources has only recently been thought of as a crime. Yet, as is now well known, the Earth and its resources are being wasted and overexploited. Through this, numerous crimes, violations, deviations and irregularities are perpetrated against the environment. These *green crimes*, then, may initially simply be defined as *crimes against the environment* (South, 1998a, b).

Globalization and the risk society

Environmental degradation is nothing new, but it was really only in the latter years of the twentieth century – as pollution accelerated – that global awareness of the problems grew. It is now apparent that any understanding of the natural environment and its problems must also be global in scope. Regardless of divisions into nation-states, the planet constitutes a single **ecosystem**, defined as *the system composed of the interaction of all living organisms and their natural environment*. This must mean that responses to this global problem cannot be the task of one country alone; the problem is part of the process of globalization that we have discussed throughout this book (see especially Chapter 7).

We may also see this problem as part of what the German sociologist Ulrich Beck (1992) has called 'the **risk society**', whereby *modern industrial societies create many new risks – largely manufactured through modern technologies – that were unknown in earlier days*. The new technologies are generating risks that are of a quite different order from those found throughout earlier human history. Of course, past societies were risky and dangerous places too: whole populations could be wiped out by major earthquakes, floods or plagues, for example. But Beck argues that new kinds of risks appear with the development of the industrial world that are not 'in nature' but are 'manufactured'. These are associated with the many new technologies that generate new dangers to lives and to the planet itself. These dangers are humanly produced, may have massively unforeseen consequences, and may take many, many thousands of years to reverse. For Beck and like-minded commentators, these 'manufactured risks' are taking us to the edge of catastrophe, posing 'threats to all forms of life on this planet' and presenting us with an 'exponential growth of risks and the impossibility of escaping them'.

Risk is associated with a society that tries to break away from tradition and the past, and where change and the future become more valued. All these changes – from the railway to the computer, from genetic engineering to nuclear weapons – have consequences that we cannot easily predict. The emergence of '**green crimes**' is part of these new risks, bringing new patterns of crime which could not have been easily foretold a century or so ago.

BOX 19.1 A brief history of environmental degradation

Pre-1500	Global extinctions of whole species – up to 90 per cent were lost at the end of the Permian and Cretaceous periods; many large mammals lost; some species through overhunting. Microbe movements leading to epidemics; long-term natural climate changes.
1500–1760	European ecological expansion and capitalist growth starts to lead to rising resource shortage and land degradation; demographic movements and ecological transformation of the Americas.
Modern: 1760–1945	Capitalist industrialization, urbanization, concentration, ecological expansion and colonialization . . . local resource exhaustion, urban air, soil and water pollution, change in rural environments and forest loss, some global extinction of species and some contribution to global warming.
Contemporary	Global warming, marine depletion, water in short supply, deforestation, desertification, soil exhaustion, overspills, hazardous waste, acid deposition, nuclear risks, decline of the global ecosystem comes with Western growth and consumption. Socialist industrialization, industrialization of the South, new risks from technology and warfare.

Sources: Harrison and Pearce, 2000; Held *et al*, 1999: 391.

Green criminology

Green criminology takes 'harm' as a central concept and addresses violations of what have been variously termed 'environmental morality', 'environmental ethics' and 'animal rights' (Beirne and South, 2007: xiii). In so doing, it aims to uncover sources and forms of harm caused by the unjust exercise of power and the persistence of social inequality. Of particular interest is how certain forms of harm are denied, overlooked, excused, or constructed as 'crimes' but only within the boundaries of certain acceptable understandings (see Cohen, 2001, for insights into these processes). This kind of perspective is similar to the social harm approach described by Hillyard *et al.* (2004: 1) and involves 'a focus on all the different types of harms which people experience from the cradle to the grave'. A green criminology counts among its avenues of investigation the 'why, how and when' of the generation and control of such harms and related exploitation, abuse, loss and suffering. Gender inequalities, racism, speciesism and classism are all key categories for such an approach. Walters (2007: 199) puts this well when he argues that

> green criminology must not be reduced to green party politics [but] must be a position premised on the principles of environmentalism and broader issues of environmental justice. Such an approach recognizes that environmental victimology is as much about issues of race, class, poverty, trade and economics as it is about the environment. Moreover,

a green criminology must harness discourses in both risk and rights. It must be a 'global criminology', one that examines notions of transnational justice within expanding global economies. This is a high-wire act omitted from the criminological repertoire but essential within changing international economic and political landscapes where crime respects no sovereign domains and where crime control must be dynamic.

Harms, connections and consequences

An important aspect of green criminology is the way that it directs attention to causes of harms, crimes and conflicts, and related connections and consequences, usually overlooked or neglected in criminology. Consider, for example, discussions about policy in the Middle East: these now recognize that conflict management is also a matter of resource management, where access to water is open to contestation (Namrouqa, 2007). This is, of course, not a source of difficulty limited only to this region but given the absolute importance of water, has been, and will increasingly be, reproduced around the globe. As climate change makes new, devastating contributions to the incidence and scale of 'disasters', these occur alongside continuing inequalities that mean the impacts of such disasters have unequal and differentially distributed results. At the end of 2007 the annual 'World Disasters Report' produced by the International Federation of Red Cross and Red Crescent (IFRC) Societies noted that during the past decade the number of 'disasters' had increased by 60 per cent with the number of deaths doubling from 600,000 to 1.2 million. Although the statistics include plane and train crashes, the impact of these will generally be relatively small compared to the loss of life and damage resulting from floods, earthquakes and other weather-related events (Campbell, 2007: 15). Frequently overlooked, however, is the extent to which people in disaster zones face discrimination. The Disasters Report 'raised questions about how aid agencies respond to certain groups during crises – including the disabled, those whose access to education has been restricted and women', suggesting that, as with the distribution of resources generally, there is inequality in the way aid efforts are directed (ibid.). For example, as the 2003 IFRC Disasters Report noted:

> There is an inequality in the way aid efforts are distributed across the globe . . . [with] a focus on aid efforts in high profile conflicts at the expense of long term suffering in chronic emergencies. Countries targeted in the 'War on Terror' such as Iraq and Afghanistan have received a lot of media attention and also a lot of humanitarian and reconstruction aid, but other countries away from media and political attention, such as Angola, Somalia and the Democratic Republic of Congo, although as deserving, received less aid.

Squires and Hartman (2006) pursue a similar line of enquiry but focusing on the catastrophe of Hurricane Katrina and its devastating impact on New Orleans. While evidence about the impact of climate change on phenomena such as hurricanes remains disputed, it is far less easy to reject the televised and other well-documented evidence of the uneven social impact of the hurricane and how race and class divisions were deeply implicated in this. Examining this end of the chain of connections and consequences, Wachholz (2007: 161) has explored the bearing of climate change on women's vulnerability to male violence and has shown how

The asymmetries in social, political and economic power that exist both between and within countries are influencing how individuals experience, respond to, and recover from the environmental hazards and the natural disasters that climate change brings in tow. . . . In this sense . . . climate change must also be understood as a social process that is situated within the context of unequal distributions of power and privilege.

Harms to the planet and its inhabitants: a typology

The case for a reappraisal of traditional notions of harms and crimes, offences and injurious behaviours has been made well by many scholars. We must re-examine the role that societies (including corporations and governments) play in damaging our shared environment. In a very simple fashion we can identify four clusters of harms and crimes causing and/or resulting from the destruction and degradation of the Earth's resources: air pollution; deforestation; species decline and animal abuse; and water pollution and resource depletion. Significantly, most (if not all) of these have been the subject of legislative efforts (if not necessarily legislative success) in recent years.

Harms and crimes of air pollution

Fossil-fuel burning releases about 6 billion tons of carbon into the air each year, adding about 3 billion tons annually to the 170 billion tons that have settled since the Industrial Revolution. The rate of growth in carbon emissions is around 2 per cent per year. Harms and crimes here result from pollution of the air by cars and planes, as a result of wars, burning of corporate waste and those responsible are governments, big business and ordinary consumers.

In the UK, the government Environment Agency notes that 'Emissions from major sources of pollution, such as transport, are tackled through various measures at European, national and local level. Local authorities control air pollution from smaller industrial processes.' However, there have always been problems of inadequacy of resources for enforcement of such rules and laws (Hutter, 1986; du Rees, 2001). At the same time, support for sanctions can wax and wane, illustrating how vulnerable to political values and the social construction of public agendas environmental law actually is. This is notably so in the United States and is well illustrated by just one example produced in the transition from the Clinton to Bush administrations. The former had supported the Environmental Protection Agency in mounting legal action against more than fifty power plants for offences such as attempting to avoid requirements to install emission-reducing equipment and seeking to exploit loopholes in the 1990 Clean Air Act. However,

BOX 19.2 Further information

There are numerous sources for information and statistics about environmental change. A key source used here is the World Resources Institute, a non-profit, independent organization. Their website is at: http://www.wri.org/

following assumption of office by President Bush in January 2001, the new administration suspended or diluted legal enforcement and various lawsuits in progress at the time (Borger, 2001: 12).

Harms and crimes of deforestation

The world is losing 7 million hectares of fertile land a year due to soil degradation, and about 10 million hectares of forest land a year. Although there is less land, more food is needed. The world has lost half its forests over the past 8,000 years, and just in the latter part of the twentieth century, between 1960 and 1990, about 20 per cent of the world's tropical forest was lost. Between 70 and 95 per cent of the Earth's species live in the world's disappearing tropical forest. The world is becoming increasingly urbanized: 37 per cent in 1970, the figure is projected to be 61 per cent by 2030.

In response to some of this, one fashionable idea has been to promote schemes to buy tropical rainforest to preserve it and reduce destructive development. However, 'research by Brazilian and US scientists shows that the most effective way to stop logging in the Amazon is to protect Indian lands, which occupy one fifth of the Brazilian Amazon. But the lands of many tribes remain unprotected' (Brazzilmag.com, 17 October 2007). Backed by Survival International, representatives of the Yanomami tribe of the Amazon rainforest have argued that this trend to take over their land 'is linked to a health and social crisis among indigenous people, including sickness, depression, suicide, obesity and drug addiction' (Jowit, 2007: 43). As has happened to displaced native peoples elsewhere (see e.g. Samson, 2003), it is argued that separation from traditional lands is related to '"the physical and mental breakdown" of indigenous communities, whose lifestyle and culture is already under threat from mining, logging and resettlement' (Jowit, 2007: 43). Davi Kopenawa, a shaman from the tribe, described these implications in the following way:

> You *napepe* [whites] talk about what you call development and tell us to become the same as you. But we know that this brings only disease and death. Now you want to buy pieces of rainforest, or to plant biofuels. These are useless. The forest cannot be bought; it is our life and we have always protected it. Without the forest, there is only sickness.

Here harms and crimes are caused by those involved in the destruction and misuse of such environments and traditional lands; those who exploit natural resources without regard to questions of justice about ownership and rights; and those supplying illegal markets that are based upon the sale of valuable but controlled and sometimes irreplaceable natural commodities. The expanding and controversial area of bio-prospecting, bio-patenting and **biopiracy** is relevant (see also discussion in Chapter 10), representing a global market for the products of ancient and tropical forests or other remote regions as well as the commercial appropriation and reinterpretation of indigenous knowledge previously preserved by passage from generation to generation (South, 2007). Bio-patenting or biopiracy yields enormous profits for Western corporations yet little or no return for the inhabitants of the source sites. Depletion of sources could have consequences of immediate and long-term effect for global health as experts note that

Medicines for HIV and cancer could be lost because plants used in their preparation are facing extinction. . . . Deforestation and over-collection now threaten the survival of up to 400 key plant species, according to a survey by Botanic Gardens Conservation International. The at-risk plants include yew trees whose bark is used in cancer drug Paclitaxel and autumn crocus which helps to fight leukaemia. . . . More than 50 per cent of drugs prescribed by doctors are derived from chemicals first identified in plants.

(Powell, 2008: 12)

Harms and crimes of species decline and animal abuse

The planet is losing fifty species a day; 46 per cent of mammals and 11 per cent of birds are said to be at risk. By 2020, 10 million species are likely to become extinct. And yet there are major traffics in both animals and animal parts across the world – mirroring global markets for human slaves and for human body parts (Lee, 2007b). In these trades, bodies and body parts of numerous species have become simply commodities.

The UK Environment Agency website (January 2008) draws public attention to the global trade in endangered species; this shows how what was once seen as a marginal or slightly eccentric concern has become a key message from central government agencies:

> The illegal trade in endangered species is big business, estimated to be worth about £3.5 billion a year world-wide. Levels of illegal trade in some animals are bringing them close to extinction. Tourists play a part, by buying gifts on holiday made from skins or ivories of protected animals.

National and international laws exist to protect animal and plant species but apart from the under-resourcing of enforcement noted above there are other reasons why such laws can be ineffective. Among these can be genuine ignorance of restrictions, or historical and culturally grounded motives for denial, as well as rejection of any reasons why such restrictions should apply or be necessary:

> Many native UK species are endangered, and we have legislation designed to protect them. Many people do not realise that some plants, for example many types of orchid, are protected. It is illegal to pick any wild flowers or plants without the permission of the landowner/occupier.

(UK Environment Agency website, January 2008)

BOX 19.3 Further information

For more information on species extinction and related issues see the website of the World Conservation Union and the fact-file at: http://cmsdata.iucn.org/downloads/species_extinction_05_2007.pdf

Criminology should be taking seriously old crimes and new violations that arise in relation to land animal and aquatic life. For example, the resurgence of dog fights, badger baiting and other 'animal spectacles' for entertainment purposes, reported by official agencies and the media in both the UK and North America. In a court case in Birmingham, England, in September 2007, ten men were sentenced for organizing and attending a dog fight. As the fight had been filmed the court could see and hear 'Barks of pain and phrases such as "shake him" and "come on boy" . . . as the dogs bit each other so badly that one was covered in blood, with barely any hair left on its face' (Campbell, 2007: 33). In an age of late modernity, civilized behaviour and universal education, it should be more surprising than it is to find that practices and attitudes more in keeping with life in earlier centuries persist. Yet messages to the public are clear. In the UK, the Environment Agency reports that

> Cruelty to wildlife includes illegal snaring, poaching, poisoning and hunting. Landowners, gamekeepers or other individuals carry out these activities where they see certain animals as pests. . . . Badger baiting is now outlawed, however other species are still persecuted. Birds of prey continue to suffer poisoning, trapping and shooting, despite having been fully protected for decades. This crime is particularly associated with shooting estates, where the birds are perceived to be game predators.

Harms and crimes of water pollution and resource depletion

As we move into the twenty-first century, it is estimated that around one billion people around the world, mainly in developing countries, lack safe drinking water and this may reach 2.5 billion by 2025. Freshwater ecosystems are in decline everywhere. On a daily basis, almost 40,000 men, women and children die from diseases directly related to drinking polluted water (http://www.globalwater.org/). Some 58 per cent of the world's reefs and 34 per cent of all fish may be at risk.

In 2003, the journal *New Scientist* (11 January, p. 6) reported on the use of the technique known as 'blast-fishing' (using dynamite or other explosives to stun or kill fish, making them easier to catch) and how this is leading to the destruction of many coral reefs throughout Southeast Asia and along Africa's east coast. Yet 'the scale of the problem is often not appreciated as most blasts go undetected'. In the UK, importers of illegal stocks of live fish

> can make large profits from buying fish cheaply from non-approved sites abroad and selling them on to fisheries in the UK. Illegally introduced fish may bring parasites and disease, alter natural habitats, compete with native fish for food, and cause genetic alteration through breeding.
>
> (UK Environment Agency website, January 2008)

Poaching remains a problem, as it has for centuries, but not merely in the sense of being an offence against property owners. Poaching can also represent inequalities of resource distribution, employ methods that are damaging or highly destructive to stocks and other species, and even have links to more serious forms of organized crime because of the high end-price of particular delicacies, and the exploitation of impoverished gatherer-poachers by paying pittance wages or rewarding labour with addictive drugs (see Box 19.4).

BOX 19.4 The shellfish connection

The large mollusc called abalone is a prized delicacy in the Far East and elsewhere. Commonly gathered from the sea coast around South Africa, this green, rubbery shellfish has a surprising connection to organized crime as the following two case studies describe.

Fishing for abalone in South Africa can be used as an example that highlights important concerns regarding approaches to compliance in fishery industries. Identified by the media from 1995 as the 'abalone war', due to the eruption of violent conflict, the government responded with armoured vehicles, helicopters and the army and navy to quell violence in coastal communities and to send a tough message to poachers.

However, following the democratic elections of 1994, the country was immersed in policy transformation and reform of laws and access to fisheries – in order to reallocate fishing rights in a way that would reflect the national population ratio of 80% black and 20% white. This had significant implications and potential opportunities for small-scale fishers who were significantly margninalised during apartheid. As a result, at the same time as there were violent confrontations with the authorities, abalone poachers were lobbying government for legal access to resources.

Although there have subsequently been significant changes to the industry, broadening and redistributing access to the resource, the most concentrated government effort has been on policing and law enforcement. Despite this focus, the past decade has seen international organised crime syndicates becoming firmly entrenched in the abalone trade as the demand for this lucrative product in the Far East outweighs supply. In addition, the resource has been severely degraded, the commercial industry is likely to collapse in the next five years and coastal communities have been infiltrated by gangs and affected by social upheaval. The immediate response of government to the 'abalone war' was to respond to conflicts, without embracing a long-term approach that would impact on the fundamental triggers to the problem. Thus, the collapse of the fishery, the impact on the marine ecosystem and the socio-economic repercussions to fishers and coastal communities, are now almost inevitable.

(edited from Hauck, 2007: 277, 280)

As green rubbery sea creatures are emptied from a bin liner into a sink in the police interview room at Muizenberg, Cape Town, a shabby white man looks on guiltily. He is the first link in an international multi-million-pound illegal trade that has brought Triad gangs and drugs to South Africa and is tearing the Cape region apart. . . .

The stolen abalone, an endangered and protected species, would have been eventually sold to predominantly Chinese buyers for around £225 a kilo. And that's the problem: the enormous value of the delicacy has brought the Chinese Triad gangs to South Africa. In a cash-free transaction, the Triads swap the abalone for the ingredients to make methamphetamine or 'tik'. Hundreds of tonnes of abalone is smuggled out of the Cape every year, to be exported through Hong Kong, according to Wildlife Department officials who say that the local abalone is on the brink of extinction.

(from Kiley, 2007: 41)

Secondary or symbiotic green crimes

Aside from direct (primary) damage and destruction caused to environment and species, we can also refer to symbiotic (secondary) green crime as growing out of illegal or negligent government or corporate activity, which can even include the flouting of rules set by such bodies themselves to regulate environmentally sensitive activities.

State violence against oppositional groups

States condemn 'terrorism' but are perfectly capable of resorting to terrorist-type methods when in conflict with oppositional groups. A notorious example is the 1985 sinking of the Greenpeace flagship *Rainbow Warrior* in Auckland harbour, New Zealand (Plate 19.1). This was a crime of terrorist violence carried out by commandos from the French secret service. In this operation, sanctioned at cabinet level within the French government, 22 kilos of explosive was used to blow up the Greenpeace ship as an expression of French anger over its use in protest activities against French nuclear tests in the Pacific. Miraculously, of the thirteen crew on board, only one was killed in the blast (Day, 1991: 281–4).

In his book *The Eco-wars*, Day (1991) charts a variety of similar state-sponsored acts of violence and intimidation against environmental activists or groups. His comments on these and the *Rainbow Warrior* affair are highly relevant to the idea of a criminology that takes environmental issues and politics seriously:

> The most unusual aspect of the *Rainbow Warrior* affair was that, to some degree at least, the murder mystery was solved. Although justice was not done, the truth came out. There

Plate 19.1 The *Rainbow Warrior* lying in Auckland harbour, New Zealand, on 10 July 1985, after being sunk by French agents just before it was due to sail to Mururoa Atoll in the South Pacific to protest against French nuclear testing in the area.

Source: © Associated Press;
photo: *New Zealand Herald*.

have been many other acts of state terrorism linked with the anti-nuclear war but it is seldom possible to prove that they are linked directly to government officials. Indeed, if the agents had not been caught red-handed, there is no doubt that Greenpeace activists would have been scoffed at for pointing the finger at the French government. Their accusation would have been dismissed as just one more lunatic fringe conspiracy theory. Why, after all, would the French government worry about the activities of a small-scale anti-nuclear protest group? Surely only a total paranoid would believe that violent action was necessary to stop such a group. The answer is that when it comes to nuclear issues the French – and the governments of *all* nuclear powers – *are* paranoid. In every case where a government has committed itself to nuclear weapons or nuclear power, all those who oppose this policy are treated in some degree as enemies of the State.

(Day, 1991)

The crimes and harms that lie at the door of the nuclear state are numerous though many more will remain unknown due to the secrecy surrounding the industry. The use of nuclear weapons, the use of extraordinary powers by police and security services to guard nuclear secrets, and recent proposals to build new nuclear power plants have all, rightly, produced much debate. Walters (2007: 188 and *passim*) has provided a thorough analysis of the links between eco-crime and radioactive waste and nuclear industry activities:

The range of risks associated with commercial enterprises in research, power production, telecommunications, medicine and pharmaceuticals as well as state activities in military defence and war, all utilise varying degrees of radioactive substances that produce waste.

The dumping of toxic radioactive waste at sea has been widely documented (Ringius, 2001; Parmentier; 1999) and as Walters also notes, 'the transportation and illegal trafficking of toxic waste in Italy is so widely acknowledged that an Italian dictionary has an entry for "*ecomafia*" to describe organised criminal networks that profit from dumping or illegally disposing of commercial, industrial and radioactive waste (Legambiente, 2003)'.

Hazardous waste and organized crime

The limited or ineffective regulation of waste dumping, especially in advanced Western industrial nations, has created a highly profitable domestic and international trade in illegal disposal and dumping of hazardous toxic waste. Both weak and serious regulation can lead to illegal and dangerous disposal of waste – the former because rules are easily flouted and the latter because the costs of legitimate disposal can encourage illicit practices and services to deal with difficult waste. This has manifested itself in new forms of corporate organized crime, sometimes – perhaps even frequently – with tacit state acknowledgement (Szasz, 1986; Scarpitti and Block, 1987; Van Duyne, 1993; Ruggiero, 1996). Toxic and general waste dumping is an increasingly significant crime. Ruggiero (1996: 139–40) cites cases involving criminal groups from Germany transporting hazardous waste into France, and an entrepreneur in northern England who ran a legal waste-disposal firm and alongside this a service providing illegal dumping of 'hard to dispose of' waste. As noted above by Walters and reported by Ruggiero (ibid.), Italy has offered some particularly striking examples of this new area of criminal entrepreneurship:

> In Italy, traditional organized crime based in the south has often offered waste-disposal services to entrepreneurs operating in the north. Among the firms serviced in 1990 was ACNA, which produced dioxane and operates in Lombardy. In describing this activity of organized crime in Naples, the Commissione Antimafia. . .commented: 'The seawater of large parts of Naples province is polluted mainly because of illegal waste dumping, authorized dumping constitutes only 10 per cent of the total waste actually disposed of in the bay of Naples.'

In 2008, the public health concerns about waste disposal in Naples drew international media attention with news stories of steady contamination of parts of the city and its hinterland by decades of illegal waste dumping and burning (Reuters, 17 January 2008, 'Naples waste linked to death and disease').The causes are seen to be 'political ineptitude, corruption and crime' which have prevented the establishment of an up-to-date and safe disposal system but maintained reliance on poorly managed landfill sites that have then been corruptly used for tipping of hazardous materials.'An even bigger source of pollution', reports Reuters (ibid.), 'is the Camorra, the Naples mafia which runs a lucrative line in dumping and burning rubbish illegally. More than domestic trash, the Camorra focuses on disposal of industrial waste which it brings to Campania from Italy's rich north – one of a string of crimes against the environment earning the mafia an estimated 6 billion euros a year.'

More broadly, Ruggiero (ibid.) comments that

> The illegal disposal of hazardous waste has been thoroughly studied in the USA, where in some cases the involvement of organized crime reaches all aspects of the business, from the control of which companies are officially licensed to dispose of waste to those which earn contracts with public or private organizations and to the payment of bribes to dump-site owners, or the possession of such sites. . . . Paradoxically, the development of this illegal service runs parallel with an increase in environmental awareness, the latter forcing governments to raise costs for industrial dumping, which indirectly encourages industrialists to opt for cheaper solutions.

The criminalization of environmental offences

There are many legal and policy issues raised by green crimes. Various populations may be exposed to hazardous waste and emissions, but cases attempting to establish liability and responsibility for this have often proved unresolvable in courts of law.

Consider how we should respond to green crimes. The use of criminal and civil law, and of effective enforcement strategies, leads to a debate about criminalization as an effective tool for regulation. Although there are now many international laws in place, the case against this approach alone is that (1) there are frequently legal problems in getting to the stage of bringing a prosecution, and (2) if this does happen, pollution cases are notoriously difficult to prove in terms of culpability and 'knowing intent'; (3) even if a prosecution is brought and is successful, penalties are usually modest relative to the damage done: if the corporation is fined, it will absorb such costs and/or simply pass them on to consumers. Attempts to identify and sanction key responsible individuals have had only rare success (Geis and Dimento, 1995; Ridley and Dunford, 1994).

Potentially more effective is Braithwaite's (1989) notion of 'shaming' (see also Chapter 9). Adapted for present purposes, this is an argument based on the proposition that corporate image is a more vulnerable target for censure and sanctions than corporate assets. Bad publicity and the projection of a negative image about offending businesses can hurt public relations, profits and share prices. The argument would be that being a bad corporate citizen is bad news for a company; it hurts community relations and finds disfavour with government, and with other businesses in the same sector that desire a clean image. In some respects this view carries a degree of realism and sophistication in its strategy that are lacking in the 'get tough' enforcement, and 'let's cooperate' compliance models. However, this is also an argument with its own limitations, not least in that it may be naive about the extent to which corporate business really cares about 'image', or conversely it may well underestimate how hard business will fight to undermine critics (Rowell, 1996). It is also a view that may overestimate the extent to which the general public actually care about what corporations do, especially if their offences are committed in another country, and particularly if this is in the developing world.

The making of green crimes: criminalizing environmental issues

A major part of criminology is concerned with the study of law-making – criminalization. Although environmental crimes highlight a new field of criminalization in the making, its roots lie in the recent past. In most industrialized countries, health statutes and criminal laws usually date from the late nineteenth and early twentieth centuries.

Early legislation

Think of Western Europe in the 1940s and 1950s. Each nation was committed to a programme of reconstruction and reindustrialization. The aim was to build a better post-war world, and indicators of economic growth suggested that this was a possibility, not a dream. However, in major cities across Europe, centres of growing populations, expanding transport systems and new enterprises, as well as in regions of high industrial concentration, a new social problem was being produced. In itself, of course, this 'new' problem – pollution – was hardly unfamiliar to these cities and regions. The industries of the nineteenth century – mining, smelting, refining, and so on – all changed the landscape and affected air quality, with health consequences for local populations. It was the scale and severity of pollution that were new. For example, in London in 1952 the number of deaths caused by the 'killer smog' (which sounds like a science-fiction fantasy but was actually dense atmospheric pollution) caused public alarm and calls for action, leading to the Clean Air Act 1956. With the opening up of Eastern Europe it slowly became apparent that such problems were even greater in some areas there (Carter and Turnock, 1993).

Growth of environmental legislation

Legislation in various forms has gained pace internationally since the mid-twentieth century, and the 1972 United Nations Conference on the Human Environment is generally credited with giving rise to further enhanced awareness of the need for environmental regulations. It led to a Declaration and an Action Plan with 109 recommendations in six broad areas (including human settlements, natural resource management, pollution, educational and social aspects of the environment, development, and international organizations) and to a programme to manage the 'global commons', and established a UN environment programme. Subsequent world conferences include the Earth Summit held at Rio in 1992 and Earth Summit 2 in New York in 1997. Most recently the Bali Climate Change Conference in December 2007 produced a new 'action plan', though with fairly predictable claims and counter-claims about whether this amounted to a real 'breakthrough' or still left too much room for both industrial and rapidly industrializing nations to do too little until it is too late.

Green crimes, social costs and social exclusion

An important aspect of green crimes – as with so many crimes – is their link to inequalities. Indeed, we can speak of *environmental racism* as the pattern by which environmental hazards are perceived to be greatest in proximity to poor people, and especially those belonging to minorities. Historically, factories that spew pollutants have been built in and near districts inhabited by the poor, who often work there. As a result of their low incomes, many could afford housing only in undesirable localities, sometimes in the very shadow of the plants and mills. Although workers in many manufacturing industries have organized in opposition to environmental hazards, they have done so with limited success, largely because the people facing the most serious environmental threats have the least social power to begin with. As with many crimes, then, there are identifiable victims, who are often from less advantaged groups. We can see this as happening both locally and globally.

Developing nations as 'dump sites'

Since the mid-1970s, most Western countries have toughened up anti-dumping and pollution laws and regulations. It would be naive, however, to suppose that such problems have been mitigated, let alone eradicated, by tougher laws. What the regulations in advanced Western nations have done is to create an international trade in dumping. Toxic waste defined as unsuitable for landfill burial in the West may be shipped to developing countries that do not have similar regulatory laws, or lack enforcement resources, or that welcome such waste because its disposal yields profit, paid for in needed foreign currency. This whole combination of factors is conducive to corruption. In many cases, the export of such waste would not normally be granted export licences by North American or West European regulatory agencies, and the proper procedure should be for such waste to be reprocessed to reduce its toxicity before disposal. This is, however, potentially very expensive, and hence the waste may be moved illegally. Toxic waste does not seem to be a problem so long as we can find somewhere else to dump it other than our own back yard.

Local communities as dump sites

Environmental discrimination is a fact of life for many poor communities. Restrictions on housing opportunities (often through discriminatory practices) have led to all manner of environmental hazards. Thus, black communities often find their housing situated right next to 'garbage dumps, hazardous-waste landfills, incinerators, smelter operations, paper mills, chemical plants, and a host of other polluting industries' (Bullard, 1990: xiv); 'industries often follow the simplest opportunities and dump their stuff in economically poor and politically powerless black communities'. Developments in southern California – what has been called the Toxic Rim – present a picture of an unfolding ecological nightmare in which victims simply do not count. As Davis (1994: 19) reported (see also Davis, 1993, on the legacy of military and nuclear arms testing):

> choking on its own wastes, with its landfills overflowing and its coastal waters polluted, Los Angeles is preparing to export its garbage and hazardous land-uses to the eastern Mojave and to Baja California. Instead of reducing its production of dangerous wastes, the city is simply planning to 'regionalise' their disposal. In sum, the formation of this waste-belt will accelerate the environmental degradation of the entire American West (and part of Mexico). Today, a third of the trees in southern California's mountains have already been suffocated by smog, and animal species are rapidly dying off throughout the polluted Mojave Desert. Tomorrow, Los Angeles' radioactive and carcinogenic wastes may be killing life as far away as Utah or Sonora. The Toxic Rim will be a zone of extinction.

In this scenario, US domestic pollution problems are displaced to a toxic rim inhabited only by those who 'don't count'.

Moreover, as already stated, the disposal of waste generally, and toxic waste in particular, as well as the siting of controversial high-pollution industries, are also displaced or 'regionalised' in another way: by exporting them to the developing world. Here the environmental victims may still remain largely hidden or forgotten, at least until catastrophe occurs.

In response, environmental activism has emerged in the affected (often black) communities, and is often linked to national groups. The call for social and environmental justice has been taken up within a wide network of activists engaged in 'toxic struggles' (Hofrichter, 1993), who employ strategies similar to those of the the civil rights, anti-war and anti-nuclear movements. As Hofrichter (ibid.: 4) defines the idea, environmental justice

> is about social transformation directed toward meeting human need and enhancing quality of life – economic equality, health care, shelter, human rights, species preservation and democracy – using resources sustainably. . . . Environmental problems . . . remain inseparable from other social injustices such as poverty, racism, sexism, unemployment, urban deterioration, and the diminishing quality of life resulting from corporate activity.

BOX 19.5 Green crimes affecting local communities

Love Canal is an area near Niagara Falls, USA. In 1978 and over the next two years, the story of past dumping of hazardous toxic waste in the area emerged. This was a very serious story because of what had been built on the land after the dumping. In the 1940s, Love Canal was an abandoned navigation channel, and for years a company called Hooker Chemical had simply disposed of thousands of drums of toxic chemical waste directly into the canal (Szasz, 1994: 42).

In 1952 the canal was covered up. A year later, the Hooker company sold the land to the Niagara Falls Board of Education. A school was built. Developers built homes and 'unsuspecting families' moved in. In the 1970s, after heavy rains, chemical wastes began to seep to the surface, both on the school grounds and into people's yards and basements. Federal and state officials confirmed the presence of eighty-eight chemicals, some in concentrations 250 to 5,000 times higher than acceptable safety levels. Eleven of these chemicals were suspected or known carcinogens; others were said to cause liver and kidney ailments (ibid.).

The Love Canal case received massive media attention and for a while highlighted the fact that damaging the environment with no regard for future generations was not illegal or a crime. New US laws had already been drafted, though, and in 1979 stricter federal regulations were introduced (though many were then reversed by the Reagan administration; see Snyder, 1991: 226–7; Vogel, 1986). At the time, the US Environmental Protection Agency estimated that 80 per cent of waste was being disposed of 'improperly, inadequately or illegally' (Szasz, 1994: 44).

This emergent and strengthening environmental justice movement has provided the 'conceptual starting point' for the exploration of ideas such as environmental racism and victimization, and the need for an environmental victimology (Williams, 1996).

Fighting back: green movements of resistance and change

Globally, there are numerous political and pressure groups working around environmental issues, albeit in both positive and negative ways. Pro-environment groups range from the extreme (those that embrace terrorism), and the controversial (a philosophy that places animal life as equal in importance to human life, e.g. various animal rights campaigns), to the more local forms of NIMBYism (Not In My Back Yard!) through the 'new social movements' of New Age travellers and ecofeminism, to middle-range versions of the political left, centre and right (Paehlke, 1995), as well as local, specific-interest groups ('save our wildlife' or NIMBY protesters; Szasz (1994)). The importance of the feminist critique of masculine violence against the environment (Collard with Contrucci, 1988), and, in the United States, the emergence of networks of black activists working against environmental damage to their communities (Bullard, 1990), are expressions of protest that a forward-looking criminology should take note of.

However, broader political critiques of the state and capitalism have also been directed towards environmental crimes which may symbolically be held to stand for much more. One of the most famous examples in Europe, described by Day (1991: 219–20) as being the 'first ecologically motivated assassination', was the 1980 murder of Enrico Paoletti by the far-left group Front Line. Paoletti was industrial director of a subsidiary of the Swiss Hoffman La Roche corporation, which operated a chemical plant in Seveso, northern Italy. In 1976, an explosion at the plant resulted in the release of a dioxin cloud that killed virtually all the town's domestic animals and caused severe skin disease problems for many adults and children. The explosion was shown to be the result of negligence, and Paoletti and several other executives were arrested. However, defence lawyers produced various legal obstructions, causing delay, and all were released on bail. Paoletti's subsequent 'execution' was justified by Front Line as the exercise of punishment that the formal system of prosecution was unable to deliver.

We should also note the incorporation of green issues into mainstream political party agendas, into the work of the important bureaucracies charged with overseeing environmental issues, and into popular (largely, but not exclusively) middle-class, eco-conscious frameworks: for example, in Britain, as membership of trade unions has declined, membership of green and animal welfare organizations has risen dramatically.

On the other hand, the significance of a 'backlash' against green concerns should not be underestimated. Rowell (1996) identifies the main source of such a movement as arising from corporate and political power in the United States. While we must acknowledge that such power is globalized, nonetheless it would be foolish to underestimate the specificities of European political and policy processes. Pressure groups and politicians concerned about pollution, the rights of communities, evasions of environmental law, and so on, already work very successfully within the world of European Union (EU) lobbying and legislation at Brussels, and in other parts of Europe. In many ways, the ground on which to build policy-oriented criminological work is fertile rather than barren – not least because the environment is treated as a pan-national responsibility, a 'public good' for which the EU may be more concerned than the individual member governments, which will often prioritize domestic interests (although they too must recognize that it is not in national interests to have a population suffering the consequences of a deteriorating environment). Hence, despite the complicity of the state in some cases of environmental damage and the power of corporate offenders, there is no desire here to present a 'conspiratorial' view or to assert or imply that 'nothing can be done'.

The development of public health improvements, the massive proliferation of environmental legislation, and the resources put into regulation, inspection and prosecution all demonstrate social commitment to environmental protection. From the local activism of community groups through issue-prioritizing bureaucracies to the breadth of international law, there are powerful pressures at work, and tools available, for environmental action. How long this may be the case is, however, a different question.

A green backlash?

A criminology concerned about social justice on an equitable planet should take advantage of such current opportunities, for there are also less promising assessments of how environmental issues will fare in the future. Rowell (1996: 372) considers the future of the global backlash against environmental concern and suggests that this will start to get worse. As disputes over resources intensify in the coming decades, so we may well have overt conflicts around 'water, wood, whales, metals, minerals, energy, cars and even consumerism'. Rowell has documented how state and corporate power has been mobilized against such new 'enemies':

> [W]ith the collapse of communism, environmentalists are now increasingly being identified as a global scapegoat for threatening the vested interest of power: the triple engines of unrestricted corporate capitalism, right-wing political ideology and the nation state's protection of the *status quo*. . . . The green backlash, born out of both the success of the environmental movement and its failure, is still to run its course. Many more activists will be intimidated, beaten up, vilified and killed for working on ecological issues.
>
> (ibid.: 372)

In his book *Green Political Thought* (1990: 158), Dobson argues that in many respects, green strategies for change 'respond to post-modern celebrations of difference, diversity, unfoundedness and humility'. To pursue this view, it might be argued that modernity celebrates economic development and that its cost–benefit calculations regarding the environment rest largely on whether environmental resources can reproduce themselves or more can be found. Only when this modus operandi is endangered does conservation become an issue for the corporate and political agendas.

On the other hand, a *postmodern* view of global resources would celebrate their diversity, the amazing fecundity of the natural world, and the opportunities for experiential and aesthetic pleasure that are offered. Hence, conservation *per se* might not be a postmodern virtue, but the need to ensure the continuation of diversity is a postmodern necessity. This proposition raises the challenge of what a postmodern form of 'regulation' might involve.

Ways ahead in a risk society

Why is there so little effective protest about environmental damage? Why is it so difficult to engage mass support for environmental concerns? (Beck, 1995). These questions find one answer in the perspective put forward by Beck in his celebrated book *Risk Society* (1992). For Beck, the limited project outlined here – to suggest some foundations for a green criminology – would be just one aspect of the need to reformulate scientific and social thought generally in the direction of 'thinking green'. Beck argues that how pollution and other threats are interpreted is frequently limited and constrained by a hegemonic clutch of narrow ideas and viewpoints: environmental issues are 'generally viewed as matters of nature and technology, or of economics and medicine' (ibid.: 25; emphasis in original):

> [W]hat is astonishing . . . is that the industrial pollution of the environment and the destruction of nature, with their multifarious effects on the health and social life of people, which only arise in highly developed societies, are characterised by a *loss of social thinking*. This loss becomes caricature – this absence seems to strike no one, not even sociologists themselves.

The argument here is that criminology similarly needs to be reminded of this absence of 'social thinking about the environment'. To add a green perspective to criminology is neither a threat nor an irrelevance; rather, it offers another possibility for enrichment of the field, as well as reflecting an awareness about vital twenty-first-century issues.

From the policing of motorway protests, through international Customs efforts to curb trade in endangered species and toxic waste, to future crimes that are on the horizon – for example, trafficking in the products of genetic engineering of animal, plant and human life – a whole new future for criminological research is opening up. Far more than many subjects of traditional criminological concern, green issues connect with changes in the world we live in now and, perhaps even more importantly, the world the next generation will inherit.

The green criminology agenda

Green criminology has the potential to provide not only a different way of examining and making sense of various forms of harm and crime, responses and controls (some well known, others less so) but can also make explicable much wider connections that are not generally well understood. The field of environmental law is now well established and although the laws themselves are by no means secure or implemented consistently (O'Hear, 2004), the practical problems that such law turns upon are criminological matters such as offences and law enforcement. International treaties depend on compliance and regulation; conflicts will increasingly be fought over environmental resources. The environment is subject to theft and exploitation, in need of protection and – just as in the fight against other forms of crime – will require specialist policing and intelligence services and the enforcement of agreements and rules.

In a world of talk about global security and human rights we should reflect that such goals will never be fully realized unless we can preserve the planet and also care about environmental rights.

Summary

1   As part of the many ways in which criminology is developing, diversifying and maturing in the twenty-first century, there has recently been the growth of a green criminology that focuses upon crimes against the environment.

2   These crimes may come about simply because of the violation of international agreements and laws about the environment; or they may come about through various forms of exploitation, corruption and associated state or corporate crimes which find ways of avoiding or abusing such legislation.

3   Green crimes are a feature of a global risk society and need to be located in such a framework.

4   At this early stage in its development, a green criminology has four main tasks:

    (a) to document the existence of green crimes in all their forms and to evolve basic typologies and distinctions such as that between primary and secondary green crimes;

    (b) to chart the ways in which the laws have been developed around this area, and to assess the complications and political issues generated;

(c) to connect green crimes to social inequalities;

(d) to assess the role of green social movements (and their counter-movements involved in a backlash) in bringing about such change.

Critical thinking questions

1   Do we really need a 'green criminology'? Is it just another field of study that is really part of white-collar and organizational crime – another instance of the crimes of the powerful that does not really need its own special 'field' of study?

2   Look up green social movements, such as Greenpeace, on the Web, and explore some of the latest campaigns and issues. (See the 'More Information section' at the end of the chapter.) In the light of what you have read in this chapter, can you see where there is a potential for both primary and secondary green crimes?

3   What do you understand by the 'risk society'? How might criminology use such an idea?

Further study

Adam, B., Beck, U. and Van Loon, J. (eds) (2000) *The Risk Society and Beyond*, London: Sage.

Beck, U. (1992) *Risk Society*, London: Sage. The now classic and key statement of the emergence of a risk society, though it is far from being an 'easy read'.

Beck, U. (2000) *World Risk Society*, Cambridge: Polity Press.

Bierne, P. and South, N. (2007) *Issues in Green Criminology*, Cullompton: Willan.

Brown, Lester R. *et al*. (eds) (2004) *The State of the World: 2004. A Worldwatch Institute Report on Progress toward a Sustainable Society*, London: Earthscan. Published annually, this collection of essays focuses on a range of environmental dangers in global perspective. Chapter 9 of this edition discussed 'Controlling international environmental crime'.

Carson, R. (1962) *Silent Spring*, Boston, MA: Houghton Mifflin. This book about the dangers of chemical pollution helped launch the environmental movement in the United States and elsewhere.

Edwards, S., Edwards, T. and Fields, C. (eds) (1996) *Environmental Crime and Criminality: Theoretical and Practical Issues*, New York: Garland. A very welcome collection of essays on the subject of 'environmental crime and criminality'.

Garner, R. (2001) *Environmental Politics*, 2nd edn, London: Prentice Hall. Provides a succinct summary of the main issues, splits and groupings around 'environmentalism'.

The journal *Social Justice* brought out a special issue, 'Environmental Victims', and the editor, Christopher Williams, proposes the development of an 'environmental victimology' (Williams, 1996: 6).

More information

One of many mappings of the environmental crisis can be found in the *AAAS Atlas of Population and Environment* (Berkeley: University of California Press, 2000) edited by Paul Harrison and Fred Pearce. Probably the prime resource for up-to-date information and discussion on ecosystems and the environment is the World Resources Institute (http://www.wri.org/wri/).

The online environmental community
http://www.envirolink.org/
A major resource for websites connected to the environment.

Europe and Environmental Crime
http://europa.eu.int/comm/environment/crime/
The pages of the European online site that deals with the environment and crime.

Earthscan
http://www.earthscan.co.uk/
Provides resources and books giving information about the state of the environment.

Friends of the Earth
http://www.foe.org/
Major activist website.

Greenpeace
http://www.greenpeace.org/international_en/
Major activist website.

chapter 20

Crime and the Media

Introduction

The relationships between crime and the media have long been the subject of intense debate. In particular, a preoccupation with the supposed harmful effects of popular culture on public morality has been a recurring theme in social commentary since at least the sixteenth century – when it was argued that popular songs were especially dangerous as they all too often presented criminals as heroes (Barker and Petley, 1997: 7). For instance, in 1751 the famous author and then magistrate Henry Fielding wrote, in response to a widely reported crime wave, his *Enquiry into the Causes of the Late Increase in Robbers*. In this work he complained that the 'too frequent and expensive Diversions among the lower kinds of People . . . hath almost totally changed the Manners, Customs and Habits of the People, more especially of the lower sort' (cited in Pearson, 1983: 186–7). As Hal Gladfelder (2001: 163) explains, the problem for Fielding was that the 'reckless and levelling pursuit of pleasure is dangerous not just because it leads the poor into robbery and theft when they run out of money; rather, pleasure for the "lower Orders" is already criminal itself'. Fielding is clearly characterizing the urban poor as a dangerous class apart from respectable society – an alien and disruptive race resisting 'the hierarchical authority embodied in the law' (Gladfelder, 2001: 14). As we will see, debates over the harmful effects of the media continue to be driven by this same powerful combination of class antagonism, generational fear, social change, symbolic decline and technological development.

Yet at the same time, the media, and popular culture more generally, are fascinated with crime. Whether this be as diverse forms of 'entertainment' in such staples as cop shows, crime novels, comics and films or as 'news' in television documentaries, newspaper articles and broadcast bulletins. To the extent that maintaining a distinction between 'fact' and 'fiction' is becoming increasingly difficult. This is partly a consequence of the rapid growth in 'reality' TV that blurs the 'boundaries between fact, fiction, and entertainment' (Carrabine *et al.*, 2002: 129) in such programmes as *Crimewatch, Police Camera Action, Car Wars* and, more recently, *Street Wars*. In addition, the live broadcasting of spectacular events on rolling news programmes has become common, such as the O. J. Simpson car chase and subsequent trial, while the enormity of the destruction of the World Trade Center on 11 September 2001 owed much to the fact that the graphic images were televised around the world so that initial reactions were formed 'within established media interpretative frames (including the plots and images of countless Hollywood movies)' (Stevenson, 2003: 1).

Blurring boundaries

Nevertheless, it is important to emphasize that the popular fascination with crime has a long history and that the boundaries between fact and fiction have always been fairly fluid. For instance, much of the recent scholarship on crime writing in the seventeenth and eighteenth centuries (Davis, 1983; Gatrell, 1994; Rawlings, 1992) examines how the flourishing commercial trade in crime and execution reports (in such genres as criminal biographies, gallows speeches and trial reports) vicariously mapped for readers a transgressive underworld, with their popularity owing as much to the development of new printing technologies and improved means of book distribution, as a lens 'that brought into focus much of what was most disturbing, and most exciting, about contemporary experience' (Gladfelder, 2001: 5). It is this complex dynamic between the popular fascination with and the heightened anxieties of crime portrayed through the media that is one of the issues explored in this chapter.

The transformations in media technology wrought by print, telegraph and wireless communication that gave birth to the electronic age from the mid-twentieth century have been described by some commentators as a phenomenon of **mediatization**. This is defined as a powerful force eroding divisions between 'fact and fiction, nature and culture, global and local, science and art, technology and humanity' to the extent that 'the media in the twenty-first century have so undermined the ability to construct an *apparent* distinction between reality and representation that the modernist episteme has begun to seem somewhat shaky' (Brown, 2003: 22; emphasis in original). In other words, the advent of postmodernity has meant that it is becoming increasingly impossible to distinguish between media image and social reality (Osborne, 1995: 28). These are provocative arguments that have profound consequences for how criminologists should understand the relationships between crime and the media.

In criminology three distinctive approaches can be identified. The first assesses whether the media 'through depictions of crime, violence, death and aggression' can be said to 'cause' criminal conduct (Kidd-Hewitt, 1995: 1), in what has been called the 'ill effects' debate (Barker and Petley,

1997). The second examines how crime news unjustly stereotypes groups (Cohen, 1972) in the orchestration of moral panics (Hall et al., 1978) and thereby heightens public fear of crime. The third and more recent development attends to a broader consideration of how crime and punishment have been consumed (Carrabine et al., 2002), imagined (Young, 1996) and represented (Sparks, 1992) in popular culture, which begins from the basis that there is a diverse range of media forms to excavate, as opposed to the singular preoccupation with news content found in earlier critical media studies (Cohen and Young, 1973). This chapter begins by reviewing these three approaches and concludes with a discussion of crime in cyberspace. The Internet provides an especially challenging site for criminologists to investigate as it is 'frequently depicted as a dark virtual domain inhabited by a mixture of dissenting computer hackers, organized criminals, extremist political groups and purveyors of pornographic images' (Thomas and Loader, 2000: 1).

Media effects, popular anxieties and violent representations

The question of whether media representations of violence have damaging effects upon audiences is one of the most researched issues in the social sciences, and despite the amount of time and money spent on the topic no clear evidence for or against such behavioural claims has yet been produced (Livingstone, 1996). Given that several thousand studies have failed to reach convincing conclusions, it is not only reasonable to suppose that 'the wrong question is being asked' (Brown, 2003: 108) but that the agnostic verdicts also expose the limits of 'empirical social science' (Reiner, 2002: 396).

Most of the **'effects' studies** are based on banal and outmoded understandings of science whereby a group of subjects typically undergo various forms of exposure to a media stimulus (such as a film, programme, or video extract) in an approximation of laboratory conditions and some aspect of their behaviour is measured in relation to attitudes before and after the experiment. Critics argue that:

- the artificiality of such experiments fatally compromises them (Surette, 1998: 122–3);
- they fail to 'place "effects" in their social contexts' (Murdock, 1997: 69);
- there is a spurious 'psycho-logic' in the studies as they rely on 'mechanistic fairy-tales about how audiences process messages' (Vine, 1997: 125).

None of these critics denies that the media have 'effects', as the point of the media is to communicate, but the problem is assuming that the relationship is simple and straightforward while misunderstanding the ways in which media socially construct reality.

Nevertheless, in public opinion the overwhelming view is that there is a direct causal link between media violence and real violence, and it is this 'common-sense' assumption that drives the dominant research tradition rather than challenging the question itself. In doing so it is important to recognize that the 'effects' debate is as old as popular culture, with the most recent controversies surrounding 'video nasties', computer games and the Internet. As Sheila Brown (2003: 27) argues, the 'debate gathered force through high profile cases exemplified in the UK by the murder of Liverpool toddler James Bulger (Smith, 1994) by two young boys who were famously alleged to have viewed video nasties'. In trying to explain the appalling murder, police speculated that the boys had copied scenes from *Child's Play 3* (1991), a film rented by the father of one of the boys a month before the murder. The judge thought that 'violent video films may in part be an explanation' (cited in Schubart, 1995: 222) and the *Sun* newspaper launched a campaign to burn all copies of the film – even though it was never actually proved that either child had ever seen the video. Clearly, it is the appeal of such simple and convenient mythologies that demands explanation.

One way of approaching the issue is to consider who is supposed to be at risk from the supposed harmful effects of the media. As Martin Barker and Julian Petley (1997: 5) argue, it is not 'the "educated" and "cultured" middle classes, who either don't watch such rubbish, or else are fully able to deal with it if they do so', instead 'those who are most "affected" are the young, especially the working-class young'. They go on to explain how in the nineteenth century the music hall and lurid stories in 'penny dreadfuls' were blamed for inciting hooliganism, while almost since its inception the cinema has been accused of encouraging 'copycat' crime. From the 1930s, when Hollywood was blamed for the growth of 'motor bandits', up to *Natural Born Killers* in the 1990s, there has been a constant claim that violence in the media is imitated by young viewers.

Likewise Graham Murdock (1997: 68) points out that the 'simple image of direct effects draws its power from a deep reservoir of social fear and dogma which first formed in the mid-nineteenth century as commentators begin to link the social costs of modernity with the proliferation of new forms of popular entertainment'. These arguments correspond with Pearson's (1983) 'history of respectable fears', which demonstrates how popular anxieties in the present often rely on idealized images of the past and are driven as much by generational fear as class antagonism in the creation of moral panics over social problems.

It is important to emphasize that in refusing to ask different questions the complex issues of how the media represent violence have yet to be adequately addressed in criminology and it is on such matters that future research should be directed. For instance, one question might be how the 'eroticisation of violence and the spread of pornography as an industry' have altered the 'newsworthiness of sex crimes' and redefined 'acceptable behaviour' (Osborne, 1995: 43), while the press coverage of rape trials continues to distort and demean victims (Lees, 1996b; Meyers, 1997). As Brown (2003: 114–15) suggests, criminologists need to appreciate 'the many faceted ways in which violence is inscribed within media representations'. A focus on the diverse meanings generated by violence might also explain 'why the audience of a splatter movie react with laughter instead of fear when faced with violence, blood, mutilations and killings' (Schubart, 1995: 218).

Meanings of violence

Zygmunt Bauman's (1995) argument that the global reach of media technology has brought a new barbarism into the fabric of our everyday lives is especially important in developing a more nuanced understanding of mediated violence. Global news stories involving war, terrorism, hatred, killing and starvation have meant that now ordinary interactions take place amidst this backcloth of cruelty. Bauman claims that the sheer volume of these images has a desensitizing effect on viewers and produces a mass indifference to the spectacle of cruelty. To put this point in global perspective, it has been estimated that only a seventh of the world's population live in relatively secure democratic zones of peace. The rest live in zones where warlords, random acts of violence, civil and international wars are commonplace (Keane, 1996).

Michael Ignatieff's (1994) political journalism in *Blood and Belonging* has also described this descent into barbarism. For instance, Ignatieff explains that large parts of the former Yugoslavia are now ruled by figures that have not been seen in Europe since late medieval times – the warlord. He describes the warlords of Serbia and Croatia as 'bandits', 'criminals' and 'serial killers', wandering around a feudal landscape with their postmodern apparatus of mobile phones, faxes and state of the art weaponry. Away from the roadblocks, banditry and visible warfare of the Balkans, similar processes are at work in Ignatieff's account. Germany, for example, is struggling to contain ethnic nationalism in its modern Western European form – the white racist youth gang. For Stanley Cohen (1996b) the atrocities that have become a daily part of life in so many parts of the world are a consequence of the collapse of distinctions between political dispute and criminal violence.

Nick Stevenson (1999: 132) has suggested that this spectacle of cruelty underlines the stark contrast 'between viewers whose main experience of violence is mediated and those who are living within the orbit of the constant threat of its eruption'. A point that he further develops through a discussion of the study by Phillip Schlesinger and his colleagues (1992) of women viewers of violent films, which revealed that even 'the most sympathetic portrayal of women who were subject to violence was viewed by women who had similar experiences with extreme forms of ambivalence' (Stevenson, 1999: 132). The overall concern, especially with regard to acts of sexual violence, even if they were negatively represented, was that they could be watched in a pleasurable way and thus legitimate violence against women in real life.

It is also important to acknowledge the place of violent representations in broader cultural context. Indeed, so ingrained are disturbing images (incest, rape, cannibalism, torture, murder, and so on) in the masterpieces of Western literature and art that literary critics have suggested that these great works have endured precisely because they enable readers to indulge in the most taboo of fantasies from safe distances (Fielder, 1982; Schechter, 2005; Trend, 2007). Grotesque violence is deeply embedded in human storytelling:

> Shakespeare and Marlowe understood that violence and horror were crowd-pleasers, as did Robert Louis Stevenson and Charles Dickens (whose *Uncommercial Traveller* includes a story about a man who makes his wives into meat pies). Even so rarefied a writer as Henry James appreciated the appeal of the sensational, framing his own most popular story – the supernatural chiller 'The Turn of the Screw' – with a scene in which a group of friends are swapping spook-stories by the fireplace. When one of the party announces that he knows a tale that can top all the others for sheer 'ugliness and horror and pain,' his listeners can't wait to hear it. 'Oh, how delicious!' cries one of the ladies, nicely summing up the titillating pleasure afforded by such nasty diversions.
>
> (Schechter, 2005: 8–9)

More unsettling is Stephen Eisenman's (2007) argument that there is a powerful cultural force, which he calls the 'pathos formula', that is central to Western culture and aesthetics. Here victims of cruelty are shown to actively participate and even take pleasure from their own destruction (his examples range from the dreaming eyes of saints in Renaissance paintings, as they await death by torture, to the way that the Abu Ghraib prison torture scenes were explicitly sexualized and organized to be photographed). Such arguments suggest that the desire for disturbing imagery and horrific stories is not a pathological departure from social norms. Rather, it is *the* norm (Trend, 2007: 12). Confronting why this is so is the crucial criminological question here.

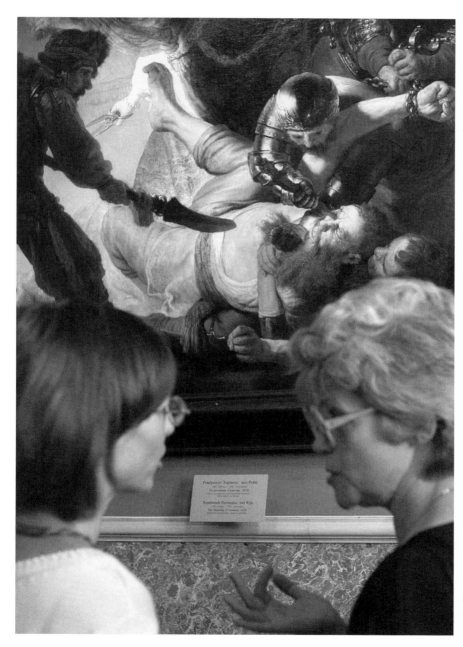

Plate 20.1
Visitors viewing Rembrandt's 'The Blinding of Samson'.

Source: Alexander Drozdov/AFP/ Getty Images.

Dramatizing crime, manufacturing consent and news production

Investigating the ways in which the press and broadcast news report crime is now an established field in criminology, and owes much to the pioneering work of critical scholars in the 1960s and 1970s who sought to unmask the ideological role of the media. The central issue is not whether the media cause troubling 'copycat' behaviour by young people, but rather how the media promote damaging stereotypes of social groups, especially the young, to uphold the status quo. As Chapter 6 shows, Stanley Cohen's (1972) formulation of moral panic has proved to be highly influential, with the argument is that demonizing deviants serves to reinforce boundaries of normality and order (see Box 20.1). In fact, there is evidence to suggest he initially intended the term to be 'a modest and descriptive one' (Sparks, 1992: 65) as he subsequently cautioned against being 'obsessed with debunking' (Cohen, 1985: 156) and in his more recent work is concerned with explaining the apparent public indifference to media images of distant suffering through forms of **denial** (Cohen, 2001). Nevertheless, it is important to recognize that in his and Jock Young's (1971) early studies there was a strong Durkheimian emphasis on how societies are able to cohere through uniting in moral indignation against deviant groups.

In this regard both Cohen and Young saw the media's need to maintain circulation in competitive markets through the 'ethos of "give the public what it wants" involves a constant play on the normative worries of large segments of the population; it utilizes outgroups as living Rorschach blots on to which collective fears and doubts are projected' (Young, 1973: 316). Moreover this process was only possible through 'exaggerating grossly the seriousness of events' (Cohen, 1973a: 228). As Young (1974: 241) then explained, 'newspapers select events which are *atypical*, present them in a *stereotypical* fashion and contrast them against a backcloth of normality which is *overtypical*' (Young, 1974: 241).

The emphasis on how the media distort reality was subsequently developed through a neo-Marxist understanding of ideology by Stuart Hall and his colleagues at the Birmingham Centre for Contemporary Cultural Studies in their (1978) *Policing the Crisis: Mugging, the State, and Law and Order*. In this book the somewhat vague Durkheimian notion of social control is replaced by a more rigorous concern with state power. Hall *et al.* (1978) introduced Gramsci's (1971) concept of hegemony to understand the timing of the moral panic that emerged in the early 1970s around mugging as an important element in securing consent at a time of political crisis. These have proved to be controversial arguments, and their analysis has been criticized for claiming that the criminality crisis over mugging was contrived by ruling elites to deflect attention away from the economic crisis facing the British state, while others accuse the authors of ignoring the impact of crime on the working class (Young, 1987).

Nevertheless, the overall legacy of this approach is that it is a sustained attempt to analyse the 'social production of news' to reveal the ways that the media 'inculcate and defend the economic, social, and political agenda of privileged groups' (Herman and Chomsky, 1988: 302). More recent studies have qualified the conspiratorial determinism of these earlier accounts, but crucially they do not reject the view that political forces and economic constraints 'limit access to the production, distribution and consumption of information' (Schlesinger and Tumber, 1994: 8). Robert Reiner (2002: 404–6) defines this work as 'cultural conflict', as it highlights the struggles that take place on newsroom floors between journalists, editors, owners and sources.

BOX 20.1 Classic moral panic theory

Developments in the American sociology of deviance (which are discussed in chapters 5 and 6), combined with the British statistician Lesley Wilkins's (1964) understanding of 'deviancy amplification', laid the groundwork for analysing mediated moral panics. In both Stanley Cohen's (1972/2002) and Jock Young's (1971) pioneering work, there was an emphasis on the much publicized conflicts between youth subcultures and establishment forces in the 1960s. Cohen's study uses the notion of deviancy amplification to explain how the petty delinquencies of rival groups of mods and rockers at seaside resorts were blown up into serious threats to law and order. Identifying a number of stages in the social reaction, he divides the media inventory of the initial skirmishes into three phases: exaggeration, prediction and symbolization.

First, the media exaggerated the numbers involved, the extent of the violence and the damage caused. The seriousness of the events was further distorted by the use of sensational headlines, melodramatic reporting and unconfirmed rumours presented as objective fact. Second, predictions in the inventory period implicitly assumed that what had happened would inevitably happen again with even more devastating consequences. Third, the media coverage involved a form of symbolization where key symbols acquire semiotic power: 'a word (Mod) becomes symbolic of a certain status (delinquent or deviant); objects (hairstyle, clothing) symbolize the word; the objects themselves become symbolic of the status (and the emotions attached to the status)' (Cohen, 1972/2002: 40). One of the consequences of symbolization is that it leads to sensitization. Here, otherwise unconnected events are linked into a pattern by various moral entrepreneurs (judges, the police, politicians, and so forth) and understood as symptomatic of the same underlying menace. Calls for action are stepped up, which leads to further marginalization and stigmatization in a deviancy amplification spiral, punitive legislation is rushed through Parliament and new control measures proliferate.

Cohen goes to some length to situate the moral panic over mods and rockers in social context. In particular, the hostile reaction revealed much about how post-war social change was being experienced – the new affluence and sexual freedom of teenage youth cultures in the 1960s fuelled jealousy and resentment among a parental generation who had lived through hungry depression, world war and subsequent austerity. Although there is an implicit social psychology here that recognizes there are real problems at stake, the actual object of anxiety is displaced by a more diffuse fear or a mystification of the dangers posed. Thus he insists that moral panics are a product of 'boundary crises' (the term is Ericson's, 1966). They occur when a society has some uncertainty about itself. This ambiguity is resolved through ritualistic confrontations between the deviant group and the community's official agents, whose duty it is to define where the boundaries lie and how much diversity can be tolerated. In effect they clarify the normative contours at times when the boundaries are blurred. In this way moral panics tend to occur when society is undergoing rapid change, when the need to define boundaries is particularly acute.

Yet while these accounts might portray a more fluid and contingent picture of news production, they do not fundamentally change the role of crime news. It has been argued that in the final instance the 'news media are as much an agency of *policing* as the law-enforcement agencies whose activities and classifications are reported on' (Ericson *et al.*, 1991: 74; emphasis in original). In other words, they 'reproduce order in the process of representing it' (Reiner, 2002: 406). In addition, journalists are 'better seen as bureaucrats than as buccaneers, [and] begin their work from a stock of plausible, well-defined, and largely unconscious assumptions' (Curran and Seaton, 1994: 265). Such studies continue to argue that the organizational requirements of news production reinforces a tendency towards the standardized and ideological nature of news content so that the state is able to secure consent for its actions.

Current debates

However, some have come to argue that in today's news environment of digital, satellite and cable technologies, with news coming in many different forms, including 'serious', 'soft', 'hard' and 'popular', delivered online as well as in traditional print and global broadcasting, and with the increasing concentration of media ownership, new approaches to 'the complex and more differentiated field of news production' (Cottle, 2003: 16) will need to be developed. One example is the growth in 'alternative media' exemplified in the network of Independent Media Centres or *IndyMedia* (http://www.indymedia.org) that came to prominence during the demonstrations in Seattle against the World Trade Organization summit meeting there on 30 November 1999 to provide an outlet for the anti-capitalist movement. It has since expanded into 'the most thorough working-out on the Internet of the conditions and processes of alternative media projects' (Atton, 2003: 53). Other news sites featuring what has been described as 'participatory journalism' include *OhmyNews* and *Wikinews* in further efforts to democratize the media landscape. Stuart Allan (2006) has shown how the emergence of blogging alongside the rise of the 'citizen journalist' reporting on events such as the South Asian tsunami, London bombings and Hurricane Katrina (often involving new technologies like digital cameras and mobile phones) are shaping journalistic practice in some quite surprising and profound ways.

Other critics have become wary of using the notion of moral panic, as it is often used indiscriminately and 'applied to anything from single mothers to working mothers, from guns to Ecstasy, and from pornography on the Internet to the dangers of state censorship' (Miller and Kitzinger, 1998: 221), and have insisted that the concept is 'deeply in need of revisiting and revamping' (McRobbie, 1994: 198). For instance, it has been suggested that the 1990s witnessed a 'total panic' around young people from Alcopops through to the film *Trainspotting*, via riots on peripheral council estates to children murdering children (Brown, 1998: 46–52).

In order to 'revamp' moral panic theory, a number of authors (Carrabine, 2008; Critcher, 2003; Jewkes, 1999; Reiner *et al.*, 2001; Thompson, 1998; Ungar, 2001) have turned to the concept of 'risk society', as formulated by the theorist Ulrich Beck (1992), to understand contemporary anxieties and insecurities. For instance, it has been argued that the increased frequency of dramatic moral narratives in the mass media in the 1990s is partly a response to the increased pressures of market competition, but is also a key means by which the at-risk character of modern society is magnified and is particularly inclined to take the form of moral panics in modern Britain due to factors such as the loss of authority of traditional elites, anxieties about national identity in the face of increasing external influences and internal diversity.

(Thompson, 1998: 141)

Chas Critcher (2003: 164), one of the co-authors of *Policing the Crisis*, has conceded that it may well 'be useful to rethink moral panics as discourses about risk' in his overview of the topic.

Malcolm Feeley and Jonathan Simon (2007) have argued that in the United States moral panics have now become an institutionalized part of social life and are a routine part of governing through crime. One of the examples they give is the AMBER alert system that was initially developed by the Dallas Police Department and Texas area broadcasters following the abduction and murder of 9-year-old Amber Hagerman in 1996. Once the police become aware of a child abduction in progress, broadcasters provide an early warning system alerting the general public to the fact and provide details useful in identifying the child or the abductors. In 2002, Congress enacted the AMBER alert system and implemented it nationally. Gerry and Kate McCann began campaigning in March 2008 for the introduction of a similar European-wide system after the disappearance of their daughter, Madeleine, from Portugal the year before. As it now operates

Plate 20.2 The AMBER alert system in action.

Source: Getty Images.

in the United States, the system automatically notifies broadcasters, special announcements interrupt regular radio and television programming, text messages are sent to mobile phones, notices are flashed on highway bulletin boards as well as distributed across the Internet and messages are instantly printed on lottery tickets. Feeley and Simon's overall conclusion is that at some point this case stopped being a moral panic and instead became institutionalized – a background norm for understanding concerns over safety and security while at the same time encouraging a new kind of political subjectivity that sees danger and menace everywhere.

Nevertheless, one of the main problems with the classic formulations and the recent attempts to refine the concept of moral panics is captured in Richard Sparks's (2001: 199) telling criticism that these authors remain committed to a

> style of analysis which treats the detailing of media 'contents' or 'mythologies' (depending on methodological preference) as a largely self-sufficient activity, and which tends to enter grand and mostly unsustainable generalizations about their hold on public opinion or their ideological predominance.

Of course, this is not to suggest that investigating media representation is unimportant but to caution against assuming a straightforward relationship between state power, media content and public opinion. It is also important to emphasize that the news is only one source of information about crime and that there is a 'complex intertextuality of media forms' (Brown, 2003: 24) that include film, drama, documentary, radio, fiction, 'true crime' and 'reality TV' that media audiences commute between in their daily lives. It is to this diversity that we now turn.

Imagining transgression, representing detection and consuming crime

There is a sense in which stories of transgression are central to every culture's imagining of its origins, while the process of discovery is often said to be a universal function of all narrative fiction. For instance, 'detective fiction has been compared with the myth of original sin, the first loss of innocence in the Garden of Eden, and the myth of Oedipus, whose discovery of his origins is also a discovery of his crimes' (McCracken, 1998: 51). In Gladfelder's (2001: 7) discussion of literary scholarship on the rise of the novel from the mid-seventeenth century, he explains how commentators were

> unsettled from the outset by the genre's concentration on the experience of a range of socially disruptive figures familiar from the network of criminal narrative: socially climbing servants (as in *Pamela*), illegitimate and outcast children (as in *Tom Jones*), runaway and fortune-hunting adventurers (as in *Robinson Crusoe*).

Yet it is the pleasures and dangers posed by transgression and 'Otherness' that make such narratives so seductive for readers. We will return to the ambiguity provoked by criminal texts below, for it is important to begin by offering a glimpse of the diversity of crime narratives that can be encountered through television viewing, cinema-going and reading popular fiction.

To take popular fiction, the detective story is one of the most studied **genres**, as its origins are usually traced from Edgar Allan Poe's 1841 short story 'The Murders in the Rue Morgue'. Here the narrative is organized around the intellectual genius of a detective hero, Auguste Dupin, who reconstructs the scene of a crime and catches the guilty party through the clues and traces left behind. It was this innovation that Conan Doyle was to translate into a commercially successful formula in his Sherlock Holmes stories, the first of which appeared in 1887 (Bennett, 1990: 212). However, in accounting for the development of detective fiction we need to recognize its rich social meanings, rather than simply celebrate the individual genius of a particular author. In exploring these developments, Carrabine *et al.* (2002: 120–31) draw on the work of the literary critic Walter Benjamin (1892–1940) to examine how the 'private eye' of detective fiction complements the 'panoptic eye' of disciplinary power, through rendering social relations totally legible to the gaze of power, as it has been argued that the classical detective story embodies the totalitarian aspiration of a transparent society rendered visible through the exercise of power and the registration of knowledge (Moretti, 1990: 240).

Yet, one of the central themes that begins to emerge in the early twentieth century, and continues up to contemporary representations of crime on television, at the cinema and in literature, concerns the 'ambivalent but central place of the city in modern sensibility and the place of the individual moral agent in the face of social organizations too extensive to direct or comprehend' (Sparks, 1992: 36). In other words, a far more ambiguous and complex set of relationships obtain between the city, crime and detection. A sense of the range of narratives is given in Table 20.1, which is taken from Reiner's (2000) discussion of media representations of policing and will allow the reader to compare and contrast the ways in which class, power and place structure the various stories.

In his discussion of the concepts of narrative and genre, Nick Lacey (2000: 229) argues that the 'TV cop programme is one of the most interesting genres broadcast on television' as it 'is a genre that is continually being "reinvented" as new variations are tried in an attempt to replace tiring cornerstones of the schedules'. Moreover, there is an important sense in which 'detective fictions might be considered to be phenomena which bear the imprint of their times' (Sparks, 1993: 99). This position is developed by Charlotte Brundson (1998: 225) when she argues that the genre 'in its many variants, works over and worries at the anxieties and exclusions of being British and living here, now'. An indication of her style of analysis is given in Box 20.2 where she discusses the popular detective series *Inspector Morse* in the context of a broader discussion of 'heritage television' that offers 'a certain image of England, partly through its dominant structure of feeling, an elegiac nostalgia, and partly through its production values and export destiny, which offer the (tasteful) pleasures of money on the screen' (Brundson, 1998: 230).

More recently there has been a move towards the 'medicalization of crime' in the genre with the focus shifting away from the police as the solvers of mysteries on to forensic pathologists and criminal psychologists (Brundson, 1998: 242). Examples of this genre hybridity include *Cracker* (1993–), *Dangerfield* (1995–9), *Silent Witness* (1996–), *Waking the Dead* (2000–) and *Wire in the Blood* (2002–), which are part of a broader diversification of the police procedural formula in an effort to increase and keep audiences in an increasingly competitive television market. This influence can be seen in how the American producer of *CSI: Crime Scene Investigation* (2000–) 'had demanded a show so stylistically different that a channel-surfing audience would be forced to stop and view the unusual looking images' (cited in Lury, 2005: 38). Competition for TV

Table 20.1 Law enforcement stories

TYPE	HERO	CRIME	VILLAIN	VICTIM	SETTING	POLICE ORGANIZATION	PLOT STRUCTURE
Classic sleuth	Grey-celled wizard (usually amateur)	Murder by person(s)/method unknown	Personal motive – outwardly respectable	Exceptionally murderable	Respectable upper-class, often rural	Honest, well-meaning, rule-bound plods	Order – crime – red herrings – deduction – order restored
Private eye	Self-employed. Motive: honour. Skill: dedication, moral intuition	Greed and/or passion murder. Mystery not crucial	Apparently respectable and/or professionals. Several cross-plotting	Not always clear. Client (i.e. apparent victim) often morally dubious	Respectable upper-class façade masking corruption, and underworld links	Brutal, corrupt, but may be tough and efficient	Moral disorder – private eye hired – blows, brawls, bullets, broads and booze – use of moral sense – 'solution' – moral disorder continues normally
Police procedural	Routine cops, using footwear, fingerprints and forensic labs	Murder, usually for gain. Whodunnit less important than how apprehended	Usually professional and not sympathetic	Ordinary, respectable folk. Weak, guileless innocents	Cross-section of urban life, including cops' home	Team of dedicated professionals. Hierarchical but organic division of labour restored	Order – crime(s) – one damn thing after another – use of police procedures – order
Vigilante	Lone-wolf cop or amateur	Bestial behaviour by habitual, not necessarily economic, criminal	Psychopathic. Unsympathetic even if 'analysed'	Tortured innocents, though gullible	Urban jungle, ruled by naive, incompetent elite	Rule-bound bureaucrats v. wise street cops	Rampage in urban jungle – ruthless chase – elites try to restrain vigilante – defiance – 'normal' jungle life restored
Civil rights	Professional, dedicated, legalistic cop	Mystery to allow hero to exhibit professionalism	Usually personal motive, with modicum of sympathy to justify concern for rights	Respectable/ influential: strong pressure for 'results'	Unequal society. Money and status 'talk'	Servants of power	Unfair order – crime – innocent accused – professionalism – solution – fairer order

Undercover cop	Skill is courage + symbiosis with underworld: ability to 'pass'	Organized racket	Professional organized structure. Leader unknown (or proof required)	Ordinary citizens	Underworld	Team of professionals to give hero back-up	Order – crime – infiltration – hero's rise in racket – solution – combat – order
Police deviance	Honest 'loner' cop	Police brutality or corruption	Other law-breaking cops	Suspects or ordinary citizens	Police station + underworld	Rotten basket, or bad apples	Police deviance – investigation – control of deviance or of investigator
Deviant police	Rogue cop or Freudian fuzz	Police protagonist's brutality or corruption	Professional crooks who 'invite' his brutality or corruption	Suspects, processed by protagonist, or general public	Police station + underworld	Generally honest but bad apple(s)	Temptation – fall of protagonist – chance of redemption – redemption/death
Let 'em have it	Elite gangbusters	Organized racket	Known gang (maybe unknown leader)	Ordinary folk	Underworld v. overworld	Tough combat unit	Order – rackets – battle – victory – order
Fort Apache	Team of routine cops	'Raids', skirmishes with ethnic minority enemy	Ghetto toughs, and renegade or foolish whites	Ordinary folk	Police outpost in hostile enemy territory	Beleaguered minority. Camaraderie broken by discipline and deviants	Cold war – incident – threat of all-out war – troublemakers neutralized – cold war
Police community	Routine patrol cops: very human	Many petty misdemeanours. Tempt cop to cynicism	No specific person. Real villain is despairing cynicism	Ordinary citizens. Many are unsavoury 'assholes'	Police station/car, contrasted with city jungle and domestic tensions	Brotherhood, 'family' of disparate types	Picaresque. Will cop save or lose his soul?
Community police	Routine patrol bobby: very human	Petty, if any	Prodigal son, if any	Ordinary folk. Salt-of-the-earth types	Organic integrated community	Microcosm of larger community. Non-divisive hierarchy and specialization	Order – everyday human problem – police use moral wisdom + social bonds – order restored

Source: R. Reiner (2000) *The Politics of the Police*, 3rd edn, Oxford: Oxford University Press, pp. 150–2.

Plate 20.3 The BBC's highly successful police drama *Life on Mars*, centred on a modern, forensically minded detective transported 'back to the nick in time'. Here he is confronted with the unreconstructed alpha-male policing methods of 1970s cop shows in the iconic, camel-coated shape of Chief Inspector Gene Hunt, who 'never fitted up anyone who didn't deserve it' and his fellow hard-drinking, rule-bending Manchester police officers. The series had great fun playing with the contrasts between then and now, but was no simple exercise in nostalgia as it maintains an ambivalence towards the past.

Source: Kudos Film and Television.

BOX 20.2 *Inspector Morse*

Inspector Morse (Zenith for Central Television, 1987–93, with subsequent single films) was the most popular television crime series of the late 1980s, regularly attracting audiences of around fifteen million. Set in contemporary Oxford, the twenty-eight broadcast films were based on the novels of Colin Dexter, with additional scripts by, among others, Juliet Mitchell, Alma Cullen, Daniel Boyle and Peter Buckman, and starred John Thaw (Inspector Morse) and Kevin Whately (Sergeant Lewis). . . . For our purposes, the other interesting quality of *Inspector Morse* is the way in which, although it is clearly and firmly located in a present in which there are heroin addicts ('The Dead of Jericho', 1987), American tourists ('The Wolvercote Tongue', 1988), female pathologists (third season, 1989) and too much fizzy beer, it also seems to be set in the past. On the one hand, the high production values and the focus on the single investigator (with sidekick) link the series with other 'retro-crime' series such as *The Adventures of Sherlock Holmes* (Granada TV, 1984–5), *Agatha Christie's Poirot* (LWT-Carnival Films, 1989–), *Campion* (BBC1, 1989) and *Miss Marple* (BBC1/A&E/Network 7, 1984–92), many of which were also extremely successful, particularly in terms of overseas sales. This is the terrain of the private investigator and the English country-house murder. *Morse* is the only one of these series set in the present, but it shares some of the iconographic elements of an England of village greens, country pubs and yokel locals. However – and this contributes a pleasing tension to the series – the casting of John Thaw as Morse repeatedly returns us to the history of the police series on television, for Thaw's previous success as Inspector Regan of *The Sweeney* (1975–8) underlies his stardom as Morse, providing, for the viewer familiar with this history, a *frisson* at every burst of bad temper and the memory of another type of crime story. Indeed, the very first *Morse*, 'The Dead of Jericho', appears to offer a self-conscious recognition of John Thaw's generic history, opening and closing with Morse's maroon classic Jaguar smashed up in two different, unavoidable (and successful) bids to stop escape attempts by villains. It is as if we are being forcibly reminded that in the 1970s we watched a different kind of police series. Regan would not have given a second thought to the crashing of his car; Morse's pain is palpable, but the uncomfortable integrity of the two men is very similar. Jack Regan, dismissing the attractions of promotion in 1975, observed that there was 'nothing up there except ulcers and disappointment' ('Jackpot', tx 9 January 1975). Morse too is shown not to get promotion. The inference in each case is that it is their responsibility toward a higher morality rather than to their superiors, which prevents their elevation. While *The Sweeney* was aggressively contemporary in a way which contrasts strongly with *Morse*, the two share the invocation of what is presented as an old-fashioned integrity. The morality in both series suggests that individuals are responsible for their wrong-doing, even if only Jack Regan and Morse have the unerring gaze with which to detect this responsibility.

Source: Brundson, 1998: 228–9.

audiences in an era of hundreds of cable and satellite channels has meant that prime-time programming has had to develop distinctive visual styles and elaborate story arcs to seduce viewers (Carrabine, 2008). The CSI franchise has received much recent attention amongst criminologists as it seeks to assert the reliability of scientific expertise and forensic technology in detection (Leishman and Mason, 2004; Gever, 2005; Cavender and Deutsch, 2007).

Addressing audiences

So far we have been primarily concerned with the representation of crime but it is important to emphasize that particular cultural technologies, like cinema, television, fiction and news publishing, each have distinct properties and histories that regulate not only the conditions of their production, but also the manner of their consumption. For instance, television viewing takes place typically in a *private* domestic context and has a characteristically conversational mode of address, whereas cinema-going is primarily a *public* event and its typical mode of presentation is the single, complete performance (see Abercrombie, 1996: 10–12 who identifies at least seven key differences). In other words, while film and television might appear to be ostensibly similar media – they combine sound and image, are used primarily for entertainment and information, and use the conventions of narrative fiction – we need to be alert to the distinctiveness of cultural technologies and be aware that readers and viewers deploy specific interpretative frameworks in positioning themselves between the world and the **text**.

An example of this is the distinction between 'quality' newspaper titles – the 'un-popular press' as they are dubbed by some 'lowbrow' editors (Allan, 1999: 112) – and the 'tabloid' news. Regarding the former, John Fiske (1992: 49) argues that a 'believing subject' is constructed as someone who generally accepts the claims made as true, for the 'social reality it produces is the habitat of the masculine, educated middle class, the habitat that is congenial to the various alliances formed by the power-bloc in white patriarchal capitalist societies'. In contrast, he argues that

> The last thing that tabloid journalism produces is a believing subject. One of its most characteristic tones of voice is that of sceptical laughter which offers the pleasures of disbelief, the pleasures of not being taken in. The popular pleasure of 'seeing through' them . . . is the historical result of centuries of subordination which the people have not allowed to develop into subjection.
>
> (Fiske, 1992: 49)

While Fiske (1992) can be criticized for romantically privileging resistance, many readers will have experienced their own 'sceptical laughter' at some tabloid stories and his emphasis on the pleasure of the text is one that has a considerable legacy in cultural and literary theory (Barthes, 1973). As Carrabine et al. (2002: 131–4) have argued, there are a range of psychoanalytical and sociological approaches to media audiences that criminologists need to engage with in order to understand the pleasures of crime.

One approach is to draw on Sigmund Freud's (1958) essay on 'The Uncanny' – a term covering the unfamiliar, weird, creepy and dismal experiences provoked by reading horror stories. It has been argued that an important 'feature of the uncanny is the ambiguity of the known/unknown which makes our reaction ambivalent; we are curious and repelled, we feel both pleasure and fear when facing the uncanny in fiction' (Schubart, 1995: 227). This feeling of ambivalence is central and arises 'not when we face the unknown, but when we face the previously known and now forgotten' (Schubart, 1995: 226) and horror is at its most effective when it is left to the readers' imagination to conjure up the monstrous. As Scott McCracken (1998: 50) argues in relation to detective fiction, 'we read for the uncertainties provoked by the mystery rather than the security given by the solution'. As has been recognized in the fear of crime debate (discussed in Chapter 12), the psychoanalytical preoccupation with subjectivity can open up new avenues for criminologists to travel (Hollway and Jefferson, 2000), while others have begun to unravel the ways in which anxieties around crime are intimately bound up with feelings towards place and changing fortunes in the face of globalization and free market processes (Taylor, 1997; Girling et al., 2000).

Crime in cyberspace

We now turn to a key media technology that has so far been discussed only briefly, as the Internet is part of an information revolution that has crucial implications for representations of crime as well as offering opportunities for committing and being a victim of crime. The Internet is a global network of interconnected computers, and while rumours that

> it started life as a sinister US military experiment may be somewhat exaggerated . . . a computer network called ARPANET run by the US Defense Department from 1969 was a primary component of the super-network which would eventually become the internet, and the US Government was definitely interested in a network that could withstand nuclear attack.

> (Gauntlett, 2000: 4)

For some commentators 'the criminal reality of the Internet is not the all engulfing "cyber-tsunami", but, like the terrestrial world, a large range of frequently occurring small-impact crimes' (Wall, 2001: xi). The types of activity that might be regarded as criminal include:

- accessing, creating and distributing child pornography;
- websites espousing misogynist, homophobic or racist hate;
- copyright violations of intellectual property rights through 'digital piracy';
- electronic harassment (including spamming, stalking and extortion);
- hacking (encompassing simple mischief through to political protest).

However, Douglas Thomas and Brian Loader (2000: 2) have encouraged us to regard 'cybercrime as a significantly new phenomenon', the processes of economic globalization, which are being facilitated by the Internet and web-based information and communication technologies (ICTs), not only provide the conditions for the lucrative expansion of international information markets but also raise, as Manuel Castells (1996, 1998) argues, the prospect of globally organized criminal networks.

The new ICTs not only make it much easier for criminals to bypass national boundaries but also offer 'more sophisticated techniques to support and develop networks for drugs trafficking, money laundering, illegal arms trafficking, smuggling and the like' (Thomas and Loader, 2000: 3). Yvonne Jewkes (2003b: 20–1) suggests that cybercrimes can be classified into two categories: 'new crimes using new tools', which are crimes like hacking and sabotage through viruses, and 'conventional crimes' using ICTs, which include fraud, stalking and identity theft. She acknowledges that there are a number of additional activities that are not strictly illegal but would be considered harmful to some users, including certain forms of pornography and unsolicited email in the form of 'spam'. Her discussion provides a useful characterization of some of the most serious crimes and harms posed by ICTs, which we now briefly outline.

Types of cybercrime

As we will see in more detail below, most public concern over the Internet centres on *child pornography* and the dual problems of illegal pornography of minors, and children accessing sites with pornographic content (Chatterjee, 2001). However, it has been argued that, ironically, it was online pornography that fuelled the rapid growth of the Internet and illustrated its commercial promise (Di Filipo, 2000; Wall, 2001), while demands for tougher sanctions have provoked fierce debate about censorship and, it is argued, reveal 'much about the fear of technological advancement and about authorities' inclination to police *people* under the guise of policing crime' (Jewkes, 2003b: 22; emphasis in original).

The use of the Internet to perpetuate *hate crime* especially from groups on the political far right – including neo-Nazi, White Aryan Resistance, Ku Klux Klan and anti-gay groups – remains largely unregulated with several thousands of sites preaching violence and intolerance. As Brown (2003: 164) suggests, this 'immediately deflates the claims of those who see in the cyber a global community, for the "community", as in the real world, is itself the focus of political and pathological hatred'.

A major consequence of the information and communications revolutions is that they have significantly undermined *intellectual property rights*. The most well-known case is that of Napster, the free music download service that was forced to suspend operating in 2001 when the Record Industry Association of America took it to court for copyright infringement. The numerous peer-to-peer file-swapping services that have since emerged suggest that 'digital piracy' will continue to undermine record company profits – it has even been estimated that 'something like 4 million people are online at any moment down-loading and sharing music tracks from which the companies derive no royalties whatsoever' (McNaughton, 2003: 6).

There are a number of forms of *electronic harassment*, which range from 'spamming' (unsolicited commercial email) to online personal defamation, stalking, extortion and identity theft. It has been 'estimated that up to 750,000 US citizens will have their identities stolen in 2002 for the purposes of accessing credit card accounts, securing loans and cashing cheques' (Jewkes, 2003b: 26). *Hacking* is an activity that involves breaking into computer systems and networks to 'embrace so many different virtual acts of sabotage, intrusion, infiltration, and "theft", or "fraud" that a unifying definition is not immediately apparent' (Brown, 2003: 157–8). In working towards a definition, it is important to recognize that the more criminally oriented 'are normally defined as "crackers"' (Cere, 2003: 152), while Paul Taylor's (1999, 2000, 2003) work rejects the dominant, contrasting images of hackers as either rebellious cyberpunks or microserf geeks trying to bring down governments and intelligence agencies, and instead repositions them in a male-dominated world acting out psycho-sexual fantasies.

Rinella Cere (2003) has examined the role of 'hacktivism' in circulating information and gathering support for radical politics and the anti-capitalist movement. She considers the uprising of the indigenous people, the Zapatistas, against occupation by a tyrannical government in Chiapas, Mexico, which began on 1 January 1994, as the first political struggle to become a 'cyberwar' and contends that 'despite the difficulties of access and attempts at sabotage by the Mexican state, the Internet has succeeded in the promotion of passionate discussion not just about the struggle in Chiapas, but more widely about the failures of global capitalism and market-driven neoliberalism around the world' (Cere, 2003: 155).

Meanwhile the issue of *state surveillance* of citizens has been a rather under-reported aspect of ICTs, but one which was brought into sharp focus by the events of 11 September 2001 and, in particular, use of the 'Echelon network', a US intelligence search system that is, it is claimed,

> used to monitor communications traffic (especially Internet and mobile phone com-munications) of European citizens, politicians and military personnel; a sophisticated

'eavesdropping' device that is justified on grounds of terrorism and crime, but has been found routinely to intercept valuable private commercial data (Hamelink, 2000). In addition, listening devices called 'carnivores' have been installed at several ISPs [Internet Service Providers] to monitor email traffic.

(Jewkes, 2003b: 30–1)

The implications of these monitoring activities have been understood as 'one element of the creeping normalisation of surveillance that embraces CCTV cameras, electronic databases, "smart" identity cards, digital fingerprinting and all manner of other innovations presented in the name of technological progress' (Jewkes, 2003b: 34). For instance, the *commercial surveillance* of consumers on the Internet is an additional and rapidly growing phenomenon, ranging from the so-called cookies (client-side persistent information), which give extensive tracking capacities to companies eager to exploit data on individuals, to the data-processing company Internet Profiles (I/PRO) which provides information on how well and by whom sites are used. I/PRO's clients are said to include Yahoo!, Compuserve and Netscape amongst others (Lyon, 2001: 102).

David Lyon's (2003) work assesses the consequences of increased surveillance in the aftermath of 9/11 – where consumer data has merged with that collected by policing and security forces. As with other developments, 9/11 did not prompt the introduction of communications interceptions, as it is after all one of the oldest methods of surveillance used by military intelligence agencies, but 'not long after 9/11 it became clear that forms of business analysis were being retooled for anti-terrorist purposes' (Lyon, 2003: 119).

The links between military power and surveillance technologies are also developed by Stephen Graham (2006: 266) in what he describes as the US 'Revolution in Military Affairs' in the urban battlespaces of the Middle East and other areas of the global South that 'embed stark biopolitical judgements about the varying worth of human subjects'. Drawing on the category of *homo sacer* (see Box 20.2, which has the philosopher Slavoj Žižek's classic account of the term) denoting 'bare life' he explains how

those deemed to be 'abnormal' within surveilled and simulated urban space-times and ecologies in global south cities will, as examples of what Agamben (1998) has called 'bare life', be exposed to increasingly autonomous surveillance systems designed to sustain continuous, automated and cyborganized state violence.

(Graham, 2006: 266)

Taken together these activities strongly suggest that criminologists need to be at the forefront of debates questioning what constitutes cybercrime and recommending suitable responses to the harm generated in cyberspace.

Child pornography

Much public concern is focused on the Internet where the problems of children viewing obscene imagery and the harms posed by child pornography itself dominate attention. Criminologists

BOX 20.3 Bare life and sovereign power

When Donald Rumsfeld designated the imprisoned Taliban fighters 'unlawful combatants' (as opposed to 'regular' prisoners of war), he did not simply mean that their criminal terrorist activity placed them outside the law: when an American citizen commits a crime, even one as serious as murder, he remains a 'lawful criminal'. The distinction between criminals and non-criminals has no relation to that between 'lawful' citizens and the people referred to in France as the 'Sans Papiers'. Perhaps the category of *homo sacer*, brought back into use by Giorgio Agamben in *Homo Sacer: Sovereign Power and Bare Life* (1998), is more useful here. It designated in Roman law, someone who could be killed with impunity and whose death had, for the same reason, no sacrificial value. Today, as a term denoting exclusion, it can be seen to apply not only to terrorists, but also to those on the receiving end of humanitarian aid (Rwandans, Bosnians, Afghans), as well as the Sans Papiers in France and the inhabitants of the favelas in Brazil or the African American ghettoes in the US.

Concentration camps and humanitarian refugee camps are, paradoxically, the two faces, 'inhuman' and 'human', of one sociological matrix. Asked about the German concentration camps in occupied Poland, 'Concentration Camp' Erhardt (in Lubitsch's *To Be or Not To Be*) snaps back: 'We do the concentrating, and the Poles do the camping'. . . . The logic of *homo sacer* is clearly discernible in the way the Western media report from the occupied West Bank: when the Israeli Army, in what Israel describes as a 'war' operation, attacks the Palestinian police and sets about systematically destroying the Palestinian infrastructure, Palestinian resistance is cited as proof that we are dealing with terrorists. This paradox is inscribed in the very notion of a 'war on terror' – a strange war in which the enemy is criminalised if he defends himself and returns fire with fire. Which brings me back to the 'unlawful combatant', who is neither enemy soldier nor common criminal. The al-Qaida terrorists are not enemy soldiers, nor are they simple criminals – the US rejected out of hand any notion that the WTC attacks should be treated as apolitical criminal acts. In short, what is emerging in the guise of the Terrorist on whom war is declared is the unlawful combatant, the political Enemy excluded from the political arena.

This is another aspect of the new global order: we no longer have wars in the old sense of a conflict between sovereign states in which certain rules apply (to do with the treatment of prisoners, the prohibition of certain weapons etc). Two types of conflict remain: struggles between groups of *homo sacer* – 'ethnic-religious conflicts' which violate the rules of universal human rights, do not count as wars proper, and call for a 'humanitarian pacifist' intervention on the part of Western powers – and direct attacks on the US or other representatives of the new global order, in which case, again, we do not have wars proper, but merely 'unlawful combatants' resisting the forces of universal order.

Source: Žižek, 2002: 1–3.

recognize that there are many difficult moral questions surrounding pornography, but would emphasize that there are different kinds of content found on websites and its varying legal status:

> The majority of internet based pornography is adult consensual pornography, whether it is soft-core sexual imagery or even hard-core imagery depicting penetration and other sexual acts. Although subject to moral strictures, its consensual nature leaves it largely non-contentious within most western jurisdictions, and with some caveats, within the boundaries of law. Even 'extreme' pornographic materials depicting acts on the borders of consensuality are unlikely to be prosecuted so long as the acts are consensual. . . . It is only where there is clear evidence of violence against one or more parties by the other that an investigation may take place, and then usually only after a formal complaint has been made to the police.
>
> (Wall, 2007: 107–8)

However, it is the fear that children will be unwittingly exposed to such material that exercises much alarm and has led to the growth of Internet filtering software that is at best only partially effective in blocking access to explicit content – suggesting that there are no easy technological or legislative remedies here given the supply and demand for illicit material.

The difficulties faced by the police in their attempts to tackle the trade in abusive images of children have been well described (Jewkes and Andrews, 2005), as has the phenomenon of online 'grooming' (O'Connell et al., 2004), whereby adults deceive children into sexual conversation and interaction. When considering the problems posed by online child pornography it is important to recognize, however, that although the abuse is not new, and there is a long history of commercial production (O'Toole, 1998), the Internet has transformed the ways in which it is produced, distributed and consumed (O'Donnell and Milner, 2007). It also forces criminologists to rethink the ways social problems are constructed, as the following admission from one of the leading studies on the subject makes clear:

> Despite activists' claims to the contrary, child porn is extremely difficult to obtain through non-electronic means and has been so for twenty years, so I believed it was equally rare on the Web. I was wrong. It is a substantial presence, and much of the material out there is worse than most of us can imagine, in terms of the types of activity depicted and the ages of the children portrayed. This is not just a case of soft-core pictures of precociously seductive fifteen-year-olds. Having spent a decade arguing that various social menaces were vastly overblown – that serial killers and molesters did not lurk behind every tree, nor pedophile priests in every rectory – I now found myself in the disconcerting position of seeking to *raise* public concern about a quite authentic problem that has been neglected.
>
> (Jenkins, 2001: 9; emphasis in original)

Philip Jenkins's overall position has been one that draws attention to the socially constructed nature of reality – how problems become defined and created by assorted claims makers (victims, politicians, professionals, social movements and the media) each attempting to develop frames of understanding that categorize troubling events. As he explains, there are many versions of social constructionism. The 'strict' constructionist is not especially interested in the truth or accuracy of a problem, but instead concentrates on the collective work involved in claims making (with sociology being one further voice pressing definitional claims on the world). In contrast, the 'contextual' constructionist adopts a more moderate line and is not simply concerned with debunking but recognizes that there is a real, plausible problem out there. The questions then are: Why do some issues become perceived as social problems in certain times and places (but not others)? and What methods are used to establish claims? (Jenkins, 1998: 5). Examining the changing frames in which a problem is understood can capture how issues are stirred up through the mass media as well as showing why some issues are not taken seriously enough.

Summary

1   The popular fascination with crime has a long history and the supposed harmful effects of the media on morality have been a recurring theme in social commentary.
2   This chapter has assessed whether the media cause violence through representations of violence and concluded that such arguments rest on idealized images of the past and are driven by a combination of generational fear and class antagonism.
3   In addition we have outlined the extent to which the news media produce negative stereotypes of social groups and discussed the arguments around the concept of moral panic.
4   Much criminological attention has focused on the news media. In this chapter we have also examined a broader range of narratives about criminality found in popular culture and considered how stories of transgression are central to story telling.
5   The chapter has also addressed the diverse forms of criminal conduct found on the Internet and concluded with a discussion of the recent merging of state and commercial surveillance activity.

Critical thinking questions

1   What do you understand by the term mediatization?
2   Why do present-day anxieties rely on idealized images of the past?
3   Do you think that the concept of moral panic has outlived its usefulness?
4   Are you a 'believing subject' of broadsheet newspapers?
5   In what ways, if any, does cybercrime challenge conventional thinking about crime?

Further study

Carrabine, E. (2008) *Crime, Culture and the Media*, Cambridge: Polity. Develops many of the ideas presented here as well as covering some of the latest developments in the field.

Greer, C. (2008) *Crime and Media: A Reader*, London: Routledge. Is an edited collection that gathers together an impressive range of classic and key readings.

Jewkes, Y. (2004) *Media and Crime*, London: Sage. Provides a lively and accessible introduction to the material.

Sparks, R. (1992) *Television and the Drama of Crime*, Milton Keynes: Open University Press. An influential examination of 'cop shows' that draws on social theory, media studies and criminology in an innovative fashion.

More information

Independent Media Centre
www.indymedia.org
Daily articles produced by a collective of independent media organizations and journalists.

Media Studies.Com
http://www.newmediastudies.com
A website for the study of new media, with articles, reviews, guides and other resources.

'Moral Panics' podcast
http://britac.studyserve.com/home/lecture.asp?ContentContainerID=124
A discussion on 'Moral Panics: Then and Now' by Stan Cohen, Stuart Hall and David Garland at the British Academy in March 2007.

Terrorism, State Crime and Human Rights

Introduction

In the decades spanning the twentieth and twenty-first centuries, international concern with human **rights** has gained increasing prominence. The criminologist and social commentator Stanley Cohen has remarked that 'with the so-called death of the old meta-narratives of Marxism, liberalism and the Cold War, human rights will become the normative political language of the future' (1993/1996a: 491). It does indeed seem the case that the discourse of human rights has become one of the dominant paradigms through which transnational crimes such as human trafficking and international and domestic conflicts are now viewed. This development has been mirrored in recent years by concerns about terrorism and anxieties about security following the attacks of 11 September 2001 on the World Trade Center and the Pentagon in the United States and the London bombings of 7 July 2005. A so-called 'war against terrorism' has followed and underpinned war in Afghanistan and invasion in Iraq, a non-accountable prison regime holding Al-Qaeda suspects at Guantánamo Bay, and the erosion of legality and ethics in the name of national security and the fear of 'credible threats'. Ironically, at the very same time that the importance of human rights has been recognized on a larger scale than ever before, states are demanding ever-greater powers to carry out surveillance and detention – with bigger budgets, more sophisticated technologies and fewer restrictions on their scope. The use of the strategy of 'extraordinary rendition' of terrorist suspects by US intelligence agencies is a prime example (see Box 21.1). As Cohen also argued, in many countries around the world, state agents are the normal violators rather than guarantors of legally protected rights for citizens (1993/1996a). Few criminologists though, have explored the relationship between human rights, state crimes and terrorism and few textbooks explore the connections. This chapter seeks to discuss the links that have been made and suggest some additional directions.

BOX 21.1 'Extraordinary rendition'

CIA flying suspects to torture?

Scott Pelley reports on the CIA's rendition program

You may not have heard the term 'rendition,' at least not the way the Central Intelligence Agency uses it. But renditions have become one of the most important secret weapons in the war on terror.

In recent years, well over 100 people have disappeared or been 'rendered' all around the world. Witnesses tell the same story: masked men in an unmarked jet seize their target, cut off his clothes, put him in a blindfold and jumpsuit, tranquilize him and fly him away.

They're describing U.S. agents collaring terrorism suspects. Some notorious terrorists such as Khalid Sheikh Mohammad, the mastermind of 9/11, were rendered this way.

But as Correspondent Scott Pelley reports, it's happening to many others. Some are taken to prisons infamous for torture. And a few may have been rendered by mistake.

"The option of not doing something is extraordinarily dangerous to the American. Scheuer created the CIA's Osama bin Laden unit and helped set up the rendition program during the Clinton administration.

"Basically, the National Security Council gave us the mission, take down these cells, dismantle them and take people off the streets so they can't kill Americans," says Michael Scheuer (a former senior CIA official). "They just didn't give us anywhere to take the people after we captured." So the CIA started taking suspects to Egypt and Jordan. Scheuer says renditions were authorized by Clinton's National Security Council and officials in Congress – and all understood what it meant to send suspects to those countries. "They don't have the same legal system we have. But we know that going into it," says Scheuer. "And so the idea that we're gonna suddenly throw our hands up like Claude Raines in 'Casablanca' and say, 'I'm shocked that justice in Egypt isn't like it is in Milwaukee,' there's a certain disingenuousness to that."

CBS reporter Scott Pelley then observes: "And one of the things that you know about justice in Egypt is that people get tortured," to which Scheuer replies: "Well, it can be rough. I have to assume that that's the case." . . .

But doesn't that make the United States complicit in the torture?

"You'll have to ask the lawyers," says Scheuer.

Is it convenient?

"It's convenient in the sense that it allows American policy makers and American politicians to avoid making hard decisions," says Scheuer. "Yes. It's very convenient. It's finding someone else to do your dirty work."

Source: Abridged from CBS '60 Minutes' report, 6 March 2005
http://www.cbsnews.com/stories/2005/03/04/60minutes/main678155.shtml

The emergence and institutionalization of the human rights paradigm

The development and value of human rights has been eloquently examined in different ways by many eminent authors (see e.g. G. Robertson, 1999; S. Cohen, 2001). For present purposes some key features of the history and principles of human rights will be outlined here to set the context for the discussion that follows.

There are perhaps two key periods in history that marked the emergence of the notion that individuals, irrespective of the state in which they are citizens, have some fundamental and inviolable rights. The first period was an age of revolutions during the latter half of the eighteenth century when America struggled for independence from Britain and France sought the overthrow of a system of monarchy that abused its power. The idea of the 'liberty of the individual' as a precondition for, and a restriction on, the power of the state was a key political principle for which these revolutions were fought. They laid down a legacy of 'rights' that were the precursors of contemporary human rights as institutionalized in human rights legislation. Both the Declaration of the Rights of Man and the Citizen following the 1789 French Revolution and the incorporation of the 1791 Bill of Rights into the US Constitution left enormously important and influential models for the future of human rights in Western societies. However, given the connections made in this chapter, it is important to note that during the French Revolution several of the most fervent and radical leaders of this search for a new world subsequently oversaw the period known as the Reign of Terror (5 September 1793 to 28 July 1794). This Reign of Terror was characterized by mass executions by guillotine and justified by one of the most famous leaders of the Revolution, Maximilien Robespierre, in a view that combines terror and justice in a way worth noting: 'Terror is nothing other than prompt, severe, inflexible justice.'

The second historical period of significance in the creation of a universal system of human rights lay in the ashes of the Second World War and the Holocaust. The United Nations Universal Declaration of Human Rights in 1948 was framed in response to the horror of Nazi genocidal policy, the inhumanity of the concentration camps and the abomination of the gas chambers and other extermination projects of the Nazis that have come to be called the Holocaust, and the terror of the Japanese military occupation of Asia (Robertson, 1999). The trials at Nuremberg of individual Nazis prosecuted for their crimes following the end of the war, laid down a legal legacy that led to the UN Declaration. Charges were framed in a new terminology as 'crimes against humanity'. The logic of this charge was that future state agents who authorized torture or genocide against their own populations could be held criminally responsible in international law and might be punished in any court capable of capturing them. For the first time it could be said that individuals had a right to be treated with a minimum of civility by their own governments.

With the Universal Declaration, the idea of human rights triumphed in principle; in practice these rights were not always observed. The Charter's pledges on human rights were severely restricted, in that the duty was to promote human rights not to guarantee them as a matter of law for all citizens. Over the next half-century the UN Declaration would be flouted again and again by criminal organizations (and, as we will see, by the state), sometimes in ways amounting to gross violations.

Human trafficking

Many transnational crimes involve serious violations of human rights of the victims. One example is the trafficking of men, women and children for sexual and labour exploitation. Described by the Council of Europe as a threat to 'the human rights and the fundamental values of democratic societies', human trafficking is a violation of basic human rights of a person under the UN Universal Declaration of Human Rights, including the right to be free from slavery or servitude; right to freedom of movement; right to life, liberty and security; right to health; and right to free choice of employment. Yet human trafficking is not a new problem. Instead, it has historical parallels with the traffic in and exploitation of black Africans in previous centuries, when the colonial slave trade was considered not only a lawful but desirable branch of commerce by European empires. According to Kevin Bales (2005), human trafficking as a contemporary form of slavery is marked not by legal ownership of one human being by another or long-term enslavement but by temporary ownership, debt bondage, forced labour and hyper-exploitative contractual arrangements in the global economy. Trafficking in persons is, therefore, best understood as a phenomenon that has retained some of the core aspects of previous forms of servitude and human trade while also adapting to meet changing economic, cultural and political realities.

Then, as now, the role of the state in human trade has been far from straightforward. Initially through mercantilist policies and subsequently through the benefits of colonial economies and trade, European states had a vested interest in maintaining chattel slavery and the trade in slaves; the trade was taxed and regulated much like other forms of commerce. The eventual British-led campaign to outlaw slavery and the traffic in slaves within the empire and beyond has been described as one of the first global prohibition regimes directed at activities which were seen as threats to the safety, welfare and moral sensibilities of international society. Yet even in the face of such prohibition, states either retained or allowed some elements of the trade and of servitude to continue in order to advance their colonial interests. In the contemporary context, while there is obvious concern to protect victims and to prevent a range of trafficking harms, states have also been criticized for conflating 'a war against trafficking' with immigration and asylum controls. Taking a longer and wider view of human trafficking, and states' own actions in creating and controlling it, therefore helps to illuminate the ways in which present experiences of trafficking are invariably connected to those of the past (Lee, 2007b).

Susanne Miers (2003) has identified the main forms of human trade that have persisted or emerged in the twentieth century: bonded labour systems and forced labour in sweatshops, private households and on farms in South Asia, Western Europe and the United States; exploitation of child labour in cottage industries or quarries on the Indian subcontinent, as camel jockeys in the Gulf States or as soldiers in Africa; and servile marriage in South Asia and Muslim societies. Some scholars have highlighted the role of transnational organized criminal groups in human trafficking and suggested that their penetration of the political sphere (especially in Latin America and the former Soviet states) has led to criminal corruption of the political process (Shelley, 1999). Others, however, have highlighted the involvement of state agents (e.g. military and international peacekeeping and reconstruction personnel) in facilitating the forced sex trade in conflict and post-conflict regions such as the Balkans. This has brought human trafficking for sexual exploitation onto political and human rights agendas and placed the role of the state in the continuation and expansion of traffic in women under the spotlight (Mendelson, 2005).

Criminology, human rights and crimes of the state

In an essay that was somewhat ahead of its time, written under the banner of the emergent 'critical criminology' of the late 1960s and early 1970s (see Chapter 6), Herman and Julia Schwendinger (1970/1975) argued that criminologists should not confine their attention to crime as defined by the criminal law enacted by nation-states. Instead, they should apply a humanistic alternative to traditional legalistic notions of crime: fundamentally, they should become the defenders of human rights rather than guardians of social control imposed by the criminal law. Criminology was to become a political activity as well as an academic enterprise. Herman and Julia Schwendinger's argument served as a critique of the neglect of human rights by academic criminology. Part of the explanation for the omission arguably lies in what David Matza suggested was the success of positivist criminology. In his book *Becoming Deviant* (1969), Matza argued that 'among their most notable achievements, the criminological positivists succeeded in what would seem impossible. They separated the study of crime from the workings and theory of the state.' In short, criminology had separated crime from politics. Matza's target was not simply the biological positivism of Lombroso but also the sociological positivism of the Chicago School and the later subcultural theory. The radical criminology of the early 1970s began to shift the focus of academic criminology in part to crimes of the powerful. The excesses of the Vietnam War provided a momentum for an analysis of state crimes, particularly by criminologists in the United States. In his presidential address to the American Society of Criminology in 1989, William J. Chambliss hoped that his analysis of what he termed 'state-organized crime' would serve at the very least 'as a reminder that crime is a political phenomenon and must be analysed accordingly' (Chambliss, 1989/1994: 183). Chambliss defined 'state-organized crime' as crime carried out by officials as a matter of policy. In the words of Chambliss, by his definition it 'does not include criminal acts that benefit only individual officeholders, such as the acceptance of bribes or the illegal use of violence by the police against individuals, unless such acts violate existing criminal law and are official policy' (ibid.: 184). In his description of state-organized crime, Chambliss included state-supported piracy, narcotics smuggling, money-laundering, arms smuggling, and state-organized assassinations and murders. He did not, however, frame his discussion in the language of human rights, or even refer to human rights. Accordingly, Stanley Cohen argued that although 'questions about state crimes and human rights were placed on the criminological agenda by radicals . . . the human rights connection became lost' (1993/1996a: 490).

By the late 1980s, though, the subject re-emerged from two directions. One context was external to the discipline and lay in the growth of the international human rights movement. In Cohen's words, 'this is one way – from the outside – that criminologists as citizens who read the news, must have become aware of the subject of human rights violations and crimes of the state – not that you would know about this awareness if you only read criminological texts' (1993/1996a: 491). The other direction from which human rights re-emerged in criminology was, in Cohen's view, through the growth of victimology, in which there are many echoes of human rights – in feminist debates about female survivors of male violence, debates about children's rights, and in concerns about the victims of corporate crime.

While human rights issues have not been ignored by criminology as a discipline, criminologists only began to examine the connections between state crime, politics and human rights from the early 1990s. The issue of human rights inherently involves the state either as a guarantor – or protector – of the rights of its own citizens, or alternatively as the violator of the rights of its own citizens, or the citizens of other countries. However, some major directions have been taken. Eugene McLaughlin (2001) examines the issue of violent political crime committed by and against the state. He cites Max Weber's defining characterization of the state (1958/1970: 77) as 'a human community that successfully claims the monopoly of the legitimate use of physical force within a given territory'. The state's monopoly on the legitimate use of force is problematic in a number of ways:

- State agencies such as the military or police can legitimately use force where it is defined as being in the public interest and is sanctioned by the state. This covers wars, anti-terrorist campaigns and public order situations. State officials can legitimately kill, injure, intimidate and torture people.
- The definition of what is legitimate violence is highly contested and ideologically constructed. This can be seen in the distinctions drawn in the media and by governments to describe politically motivated violence which can be very similar in form and consequences but judged in very different ways. For instance, those condemned as 'terrorists' by some are honoured as 'freedom fighters' by others and it is now widely recognized that normative and moral considerations shape definitions and judgements. In turn, the passing of time and social change can moderate or sharpen these influential ways of thinking about these actions.

Terrorism – a useful concept?

Indeed, terrorism is not a new problem. During the 1880s, for example, Russian anti-Tsar anarchists frequently resorted to the use of political assassinations. In the post-World War Two period, tactics and actions defined as terrorism have been an integral part of political conflicts between those pursuing goals of independence from those perceived as colonialist or occupying powers (see for example the histories of Algeria, Northern Ireland, Palestine). From the 1960s, European far-left and far-right groups such as the Red Brigades, Baader Meinhoff, other nationalist groups such as ETA, the IRA and the ANC and, more recently, KLA, Chechen separatists and religious fundamentalists such as Al-Qaeda have all used terror, violence and intimidation in their attempts to achieve political and religious ends. While previously individual and small groups mainly relied on stories, songs and political writings to convey their message and to force concessions from authorities, they can now take advantage of the technological advances and increasing intensity and speed of global interconnections to get their message across – for example, 'atrocity' videos in Beirut, live broadcast of killings such as webcast beheadings in Iraq and recorded video or audio messages from leaders such as Osama bin Laden after 9/11.

According to Giddens (2005), in a globalized world there are several key differences between 'old' forms of terrorism and 'new' forms of terrorism.

'Old' terrorism (e.g. ETA, the IRA):

- tight local organization
- local political objectives
- relatively low levels of violence
- relative restraint regarding tactics
- threat to specific authorities (e.g. specific government).

'New' terrorism (e.g. Al-Qaeda):

- loose global network
- located in failed or failing states (e.g. Afghanistan)
- high levels of violence
- less restraint regarding tactics
- threat to strategic interests of the West and to the notion of cosmopolitan society
- use of high-tech communication to coordinate its actions and promote its cause.

But what exactly does terrorism mean? Brian Jenkins (2000) suggests that 'terrorism' refers to 'the use or threat of violence to create an atmosphere of fear and alarm and thus bring about a political result'. Eugene McLaughlin (2006) suggests that 'terrorism' is 'an essentially pre-meditated political act . . . [the intention of which is] to influence . . . policy by creating an atmosphere of fear or threat, generally for a political, religious or ideological cause'. Notwithstanding its popular usage in political discourse and media coverage, there is no internationally agreed legal definition of terrorism. To McLaughlin (2006: 434), there are too many variations for terrorism to be a meaningful term.

> There is a strong argument that we should not [use the terms 'terrorism' and 'terrorist']. Both . . . are polemical and a pathologizing device which makes rational discussion of the causes of political conflict impossible. . . . [It] is more fruitful to recognize that there is a continuum of politically motivated and enacted violence.

Others such as Honderich (2002) argue that we should keep the term but use it more carefully. In particular, we should signal the fact that not all politically inspired acts of anti-state violence are illegitimate and that terrorism is a feature of most modern conflicts.

State responses to terror

In response to the problem of terrorism, states have brought in special legislation and emergency powers to deal with the policing of terrorism. In the UK (e.g. in the Northern Ireland conflict), United States and Australia, state responses to terror have involved increases in broad policing powers and tougher immigration and asylum laws and procedures. Do they work? Some commentators have suggested that anti-terrorism legislation dependent upon restrictions on civil liberties can have devastating effects in alienating and politicizing communities, fostering hostility, and prolonging the conflict. States have also been known to resort to highly contentious counter-terrorism measures with limited criminal justice safeguards, such as coercive inter-rogation of suspects, detention of suspects for long periods without trial, pre-emptive bombing of terrorist bases, covert tracking and surveillance of suspects, and assassination of terrorist targets and suspects. In what Lucia Zedner (2000) has termed the rise of a 'security society', the 'breaking down of constitutional barriers between police and intelligence agencies such as MI5', the normalization of security arrangements at theatres, cinemas and shopping malls, the general use of 'high-tech' surveillance equipment, identification checks and uniformed security guards, are all justified as necessary to 'the pursuit of security'. How are we to make sense of such developments?

Torture

One particularly controversial issue in the current security debate relates to the use of torture by the state. In principle, the war against terrorism is justified as an exercise in defending the human rights of peace-loving and law-abiding citizens and the values and security of democratic societies around the world. But is torture ever justified? Writing in the latter half of the eighteenth century, Cesare Beccaria noted that

> The torture of a criminal while his trial is being put together is a cruelty accepted by most nations, whether to compel him to confess a crime, to exploit the contradictions he runs into, to uncover his accomplices, to carry out some mysterious and incomprehensible metaphysical purging of his infamy (or, lastly, to expose other crimes of which he is guilty but with which he has not been charged).
>
> (quoted in Bellamy, 1995: 39)

In the twentieth century, the overt use of torture was universally condemned. Article 5 of the Universal Declaration of Human Rights states that 'No one shall be subjected to torture or to cruel, inhuman or degrading treatment or punishment.' The condemnation of torture is echoed also in Article 7 of the International Covenant on Civil and Political Rights.

Despite the universal condemnation of torture, however, it was notoriously used in the latter half of the twentieth century as an instrument of state terror to intimidate and silence political opposition in Chile, Uruguay, Argentina and a number of other countries. (The chapter 'Torture' by Darren J. O'Byrne in his book *Human Rights: An Introduction* (2003) provides a disturbing catalogue of such use of torture.) In the twenty-first century, torture continues to be inflicted upon victims around the world. Perhaps because it is such an abhorrent subject, few criminologists have engaged with some fundamental conceptual and ethical questions about torture (though see Chapter 15). However, such questions are not simply a matter for internal academic debate, as they shed light on real dilemmas for contemporary criminal justice practice. Torture, to use the words of R. G. Frey, is 'the deliberate infliction of violence, and, through violence, severe mental and/or physical suffering upon individuals' (1992: 1252). However, a fundamental conceptual question to consider about this definition – and one that Frey raises – is precisely what counts as torture? Does it always have to include physical suffering? Can torture involve mental suffering alone? If it can solely be mental suffering, then where is the line to be drawn between mental distress that counts as torture and distress that doesn't? The 'good cop, bad cop' routine is well known from fictional representations of interrogation scenes on television: it is a form of mental intimidation, so would it qualify as torture, too?

An important ethical question about torture is whether there are ever any circumstances in which the moral evil of torture might be justifiably inflicted so that good may come. An absolutist position on this question would be that torture can never, ever be justified: the pain inflicted makes it wrong in any circumstances. But a utilitarian consequentialist approach to the question would not rule out the use of torture altogether. A case in Germany that came to trial in 2003, for example, generated considerable public debate. In September 2002, police in Frankfurt arrested the kidnapper of an 11-year-old boy when he went to collect the ransom he had demanded. After hours of questioning, however, the kidnapper failed to reveal the whereabouts of the boy, who, unbeknown to the police, had been murdered by the kidnapper before his arrest. Fearing that the victim was in imminent mortal danger if he were not found, the deputy police chief of Frankfurt ordered police officers to threaten to torture the kidnapper to attain the necessary information. Upon being threatened, the kidnapper told police the whereabouts of the boy, who was subsequently found dead. With media coverage ahead of the trial, the case aroused intense debate about whether the threat to resort to torture was justified, even though it is unlawful according to the German criminal code and the German Constitution, and contravenes international human rights provisions. Some commentators believed that the threat of torture was understandable given the circumstances. (See also Chapter 15 on punishment and Chapter 17 on policing.)

Crimes of war

While the actions of terrorists are condemned because they use terror for political ends and target innocent civilians, similar terror tactics are used by governments, particularly in war. In fact, a major feature of warfare in the twentieth century was the targeting and terrorizing of civilians as a legitimate military strategy, especially with the development of air warfare and saturation bombing. This happened during the Second World War with the destruction of Dresden and the dropping of atomic bombs on Hiroshima and Nagasaki. Of course, one moral defence of those actions is that they brought about the end of a war that had seen the Nazis and Japanese commit the most appalling crimes against humanity.

It is important that a criminology of war has emerged as another direction in the field, which has helped the incorporation of human rights concerns and crimes of the state. In 1998, Ruth Jamieson argued that war is an area consistently ignored in conventional criminology but that there are at least three reasons why it should become a central area of concern:

- As an empirical area of study, war offers a dramatic example of mass violence and victimization in the extreme.
- Acts and violations in war are carried out through state action which in many instances should be more properly understood as state crime.
- War and states of emergency usher in massive increases in social regulation, punishment, new surveillance techniques and a corresponding derogation of civil rights.

Some notable studies have been undertaken in this field of work. Kelman and Hamilton in their book *Crimes of Obedience* (1989) examined the My Lai massacre during the Vietnam War in May 1968 when a platoon of US soldiers massacred some 400 civilians. From this case and other sanctioned massacres they identify some conditions that enable crimes of obedience to occur. Zygmunt Bauman in his book *Modernity and the Holocaust* (1989) proposed that the genocidal extermination of the Holocaust was a logical extension of modern social organization: a product of modernity, not a return to some form of pre-Enlightenment barbarism. The conditions for the Holocaust are precisely those that have helped to create industrial society, and include such things as the division of labour, modern bureaucracy, rationality, science, and so forth. The central part of his explanation of the Holocaust is the social production of moral indifference in modern societies. This indifference was created by the routinization and dehumanization of the victims by ideological definition. Bureaucratization was essential in this process, as the elimination of unwanted people was considered to be an administrative task. Stanley Cohen's *States of Denial* (2001) provides an analysis of personal and political ways in which troubling realities are evaded and how organized atrocities – such as genocide, torture and political crimes – are denied by perpetrators and bystanders.

BOX 21.2 The abuse of prisoners of war: the case of Abu Ghraib prison

In May 2003 four US Army soldiers were charged under military regulations with detainee abuse at the Abu Ghraib prison, also known as the Baghdad Correctional facility, in Iraq. However, it was not until a year later in April 2004 that the record of physical and sexual abuse at Abu Ghraib came to public attention via a series of news reports. As evidence mounted, the number of those charged with involvement grew, resulting in seventeen soldiers and officers being removed from duty and seven soldiers being charged and eventually court martialled and sentenced to prison terms. To many around the world, one of the most shocking aspects of this degradation of prisoners was that their jailers had taken numerous photographs to record acts of **humiliation** and torture. It is likely that the full extent of these events – including deaths and rape of prisoners – has not yet been made publicly available and that much of the photographic record has also not been released. The United States has, of course, signed up to the Geneva Convention of 1949, which was explicitly framed to protect the rights and conditions in captivity of prisoners of war. Article 13 of the Convention is reprinted below:

Plate 21.1 The scandal surrounding Abu Ghraib military prison near Baghdad, Iraq, involved evidence of acts of torture and abuse committed by US military personnel against Iraqi prisoners during 2004.

Article 13

Prisoners of war must at all times be humanely treated. Any unlawful act or omission by the Detaining Power causing death or seriously endangering the health of a prisoner of war in its custody is prohibited, and will be regarded as a serious breach of the present Convention.

In particular, no prisoner of war may be subjected to physical mutilation or to medical or scientific experiments of any kind which are not justified by the medical, dental or hospital treatment of the prisoner concerned and carried out in his interest.

Likewise, prisoners of war must at all times be protected, particularly against acts of violence or intimidation and against insults and public curiosity.

Measures of reprisal against prisoners of war are prohibited.

Capital punishment

So far, we have considered state-sanctioned or state-sponsored actions against those considered as 'terrorists', political criminals, or non-citizens. Another area of controversy relates to the use of the death penalty as a form of state-sanctioned punishment within the formal criminal justice system. According to Amnesty International, in late 2007 the death penalty had been abolished by around half the countries in the world but had by no means disappeared (see Box 21.3).

Of those countries retaining the death penalty, the People's Republic of China accounts for the vast majority of executions. Records for executions in some states may be inaccurate for various reasons, but Amnesty International estimates that in 2006 China executed at least 1,010 individuals, with the added comment that this number is 'only the tip of the iceberg'. In the

BOX 21.3 Capital punishment: abolitionist and retentionist countries

Two-thirds of the countries in the world have now abolished the death penalty in law or practice.

Information compiled by Amnesty International shows that:

- 90 countries and territories have *abolished the death penalty for all crimes*;
- 11 countries have *abolished the death penalty for all but exceptional crimes* such as wartime crimes;
- 29 countries can be considered *abolitionist in practice*: they retain the death penalty in law but have not carried out any executions for the past ten years or more and are believed to have a policy or established practice of not carrying out executions;
- a total of 130 countries have abolished the death penalty in law or practice;
- 67 other countries and territories *retain* and use the death penalty, but the number of countries which actually execute prisoners in any one year is much smaller.

Source: Amnesty International, 2007
http://web.amnesty.org/pages/deathpenalty-facts-eng

same year 'Iran executed 177 people, Pakistan 82 and Iraq and Sudan each at least 65. There were 53 executions in 12 states in the USA.'

Moral objection to capital punishment rests on the seemingly incontrovertible proposition that the death penalty violates the basic and universal right to life, and, in the words of Amnesty International, is 'the ultimate cruel, inhuman and degrading punishment'. But is an offender's right to life forfeited when they unlawfully take a life themselves, and hence is capital punishment justified? Some moral arguments suggest that it is. One major argument is that the death penalty served on convicted murderers functions as a deterrent against potential acts of murder. This argument is concerned with utilitarian, or consequentialist, justice: in other words, the example made of the few will serve the greater good by deterring potential offenders who might be inclined to commit murder. There are, however, a number of arguments that severely weaken the deterrence argument:

- To serve as a real deterrent, the threat of punishment must be real. In some countries that retain the death penalty, however, the odds of a convicted murderer serving life imprisonment instead of losing their life are strongly in the offender's favour.
- The principle of deterrence works on the assumption that the potential for committing murder involves a means–end calculation, with potential offenders rationally weighing the odds of escaping detection against the possibility of being caught and a death sentence imposed. The offender makes a 'risk assessment', if you like: the greater the penalty, the greater the risk, the stronger the potential deterrent – in theory. However, O'Byrne (2003: 218) points out that most killings are crimes of passion. Others are committed when the

offender is under the influence of alcohol or another drug and others are suffering from a mental illness when they commit their crime. None of these circumstances involves a careful calculation of the risk involved.

- Other penalties, such as life imprisonment, may conceivably serve as a greater deterrent than the death penalty. Beccaria, for instance, argued that 'It is not the intensity, but the extent of a punishment which makes the greatest impression on the human soul. For our sensibility is more easily and lastingly moved by minute but repeated impressions than by a sharp but fleeting shock' (Bellamy, 1995: 67). Illuminating an inherent paradox in the deterrent effect of capital punishment, Beccaria further argued that 'if it is important that men often see the power of the law, executions ought not to be too infrequent: they therefore require there to be frequent crimes; so that, if this punishment is to be effective, it is necessary that it not make the impression that it should make. That is, it must be both useful and useless at the same time' (Bellamy, 1995: 68–9).

These arguments against the deterrent effect of capital punishment are essentially empirical ones that can be settled by comparing the murder rate in countries that retain the death penalty with the murder rate in those that have abolished capital punishment. O'Byrne (2003: 219) presents such a calculation, citing evidence that some studies have shown a decline in homicide after the abolition of the death penalty, and some an increase in the murder rate after the introduction of capital punishment. The deterrent effect, therefore, is not invariably borne out in practice and, on the basis of in his international review, Hood (2002: 230) observes that 'it is not prudent to accept the hypothesis that capital punishment deters murder to a marginally greater extent than does the threat and application of the supposedly lesser punishment of life imprisonment'.

There is perhaps a stronger moral argument for the use of the death penalty rooted in retributive justice (Reiman, 1988). By deliberately causing the death of another, the murderer incurs a moral debt: the loss of his or her own life is earned as a just desert. By taking another person's life, the offender has treated their victim as having lesser worth than they afford to themselves, as presumably they would not desire that their own life be taken in the same way. Capital punishment for those who commit murder restores an equilibrium. The wrongdoer experiences suffering to the same extent that they have inflicted upon another. The 'golden rule' of 'doing unto others as you would have them do unto you' is restored, as the punishment impresses upon the offender that their worth is equal to that of their victim. It also has a symbolic value by reaffirming publicly the moral commitment to the 'golden rule' as a societal value. On these grounds, Jeffrey Reiman (1988) defends capital punishment in principle. He opposes it in practice, however, as in the United States imposition of the death penalty is discriminatory. To take just one example: the odds of a black person being sentenced to death for the murder of a white victim are far higher than the corresponding odds when a white person murders a black victim (see also Chapter 7).

Conclusion

Criminology is expanding its horizons and must now embrace the serious study of global and regional problems that involve grand principles, inhuman behaviours and disputed claims about legitimacy and justice. In the past, criminology tended to take for granted the notion that the state is a fair and responsible agent acting as the protector of its citizenry and guarantor of national security. The state is the primary source of laws (hence holding power over what is defined as criminal/unacceptable) and to further the promotion and effectiveness of these laws it has a monopoly over the legitimate use of physical force. Internally, the use of force is bound by the rule of law, constitutional rights of citizens; externally, warfare is supposed to be a rule-governed activity (e.g. military targets as legitimate targets). However, when the state is revealed or perceived as itself acting in a criminal and/or illegitimate manner, then a different way of thinking about crime is required. Above all other offenders, the state is supremely positioned to conceal its criminality and violations of rights – and it is obvious that states have exercised their considerable powers of law-making and territorial control for centuries to undertake activities that would now be considered crimes of terrorism, genocide, slavery, piracy, drugs and arms sales, and so on. In a global 'economy of fear' (Bauman, 1998) and the present 'state of exception' (Agamben, 2005), terrorists, political dissidents and many other unwanted non-citizens are increasingly subject to state actions that are beyond the constraints of normative law and juridical protections. Although a human rights perspective is still underdeveloped in criminology, it offers a powerful additional prism through which to view various global forms of crime and brings into sharp relief our moral appraisals of the value, harm and the requisite punishment associated with them.

Summary

1   The issue of human rights inherently involves 'the state' either as a guarantor, or protector, of the rights of its own citizens, or alternatively as the violator of the rights of its citizens, or the citizens of other countries.
2   A focus on state crime reminds us that crime can be a political phenomenon.
3   The study of human rights and crime has been a marginal topic in academic criminology.
4   Much of the study of state crime has not been framed in the language of human rights.
5   When states attempt to guarantee the rights of their citizens, conflicting rights may collide.

Critical thinking questions

1   Can torture be proscribed absolutely?
2   Are all violations of human rights state crimes? Are there any state crimes that do not involve violations of human rights?
3   In what ways does the exceptional use of penal confinement of terrorist suspects at Guantánamo Bay detention camp challenge our conventional understanding of the purposes of imprisonment?
4   Are there any circumstances in which you think capital punishment is justified?
5   Is 'terrorism' best understood as a real phenomenon or a political label?

Further study

Bales, K. (2005) *Understanding Global Slavery*, Berkeley: University of California Press. A seminal examination of human trafficking as a modern form of slavery in the global economy.
O'Byrne, D. J. (2003) *Human Rights: An Introduction*, Harlow: Longman. An excellent introduction to human rights issues and debates.
Robertson, G. (1999) *Crimes against Humanity*, London: Penguin. A highly readable introduction to the history and philosophy of human rights and their incorporation into international law.

More information

Amnesty International
http://www.amnesty.org/
A website on the worldwide movement campaigning for internationally recognized human rights.

Death Penalty Information Centre
http://www.deathpenaltyinfo.org
This website has information on issues concerning capital punishment.

chapter 22

Criminological Futures

Key issues

- ■ This chapter poses questions about the futures of crime, control and criminology.
- ■ It reviews links between past, present and future.
- ■ The expansion of the criminological horizon is discussed.
- ■ Criminology is an exciting, ongoing but continually 'unfinished' project.

Introduction

Criminology addresses a wide range of problems, issues and challenges to society. It investigates and theorizes crime and control developments that threaten and protect the social, moral and economic orders of life that we take for granted. Most of these challenges are familiar and long-standing, but the various media (factual and fictional) and their audiences are most interested in sensational or new developments – hence the fascination with serial murderers and the success of numerous films depicting futuristic scenarios of crime, chaos and control. There is a contrast here, between the ordinary and everyday forms of crime that have a practical importance for people and that are easily grasped as local threats versus the large-scale, globally cumulative, financially significant but somehow less tangible forms of crime that are generally harder to grasp as 'our problems'. Loader and Sparks (2007: 94) make a similar point, noting that

> A concern with the implications of macrolevel developments for criminological theory and research . . . is not now (any more than at any other time) simply a licence for

preferring the novel, the fashionable, and the sweeping over the grounded, the empirical, and the local, nor for disengaging from intricate and detailed problems of policy and politics wherever we happen to encounter them.

In drawing this book to a close, we seek to reflect on the current and future state of crime and control and briefly to explore how we can take a sociological approach to the public issues and private troubles that are cast about on the changing landscape of 'criminology'.

Visions of the future?

One starting question is whether we can identify different views about the 'futures' of crime and control, as distinct from views about the 'futures' of criminology. In some respects, for example, we might reasonably predict that whatever the future nature of crime and control, different but already existing varieties of criminological theory and method will be applied and developed further. So, one 'future' of criminology could simply be 'more of the same' but with interesting and important diversifications.

On the other hand, a more dramatic vision might assume that some of the 'big changes' in crime, control and criminology referred to in earlier chapters will see further amplification, eventually resulting in 'paradigm changes' (Kuhn, 1962) in the field of study, or, at the very least, profound changes and innovations in the types and characteristics of different criminological perspectives. In some ways this may be the vision of the future we want to hear about because our fascination with the future is largely based on an assumption that it will somehow be dramatically different (whether appealingly or appallingly so).

However, the future arrives only slowly and, in reality, the idea that criminology may look a great deal different in the future than it does today may not be easily supported. This is because if we look back over the twentieth century, for all the different changes in crime (and, equally importantly, in perceptions of crime), developments in understanding have – by and large – been the products of new variations on existing criminological themes and traditions. The fact that this history is full of references to 'breaks' and 'breakthroughs', new insights and new criminologies, and so on, partly reflects criminology's amnesia (Young, 1979) about the past, as old ideas and perspectives are recycled, combined, reinvented and renamed. To be sure, much that was overlooked or required serious and overdue attention has been attended to – the development of the feminist perspective being a notable example. Similarly, debate between critical commentators and crime science adherents moves the field along, while the expansion of awareness about how criminological ideas follow through into policy and practice – sometimes with unintended consequences – provides its own lessons for a maturing subject (see e.g. Chancer and McLaughlin, 2007). Yet, the criminological kaleidoscope remains a mechanism with familiar patterns of problems, methods and theories that receive an occasional 'shake-up' to produce variations on the familiar and, every now and then, the strikingly 'new' criminological image that shapes the view of new possibilities for a new generation.

From this starting point, looking to the futures of crime, control and criminology could be a modest project that extrapolates from some current trends and considers how they may develop. This is nonetheless an important exercise, and we follow up the idea in this chapter, although readers of this book should by now feel quite well positioned to do some of this 'futurology' themselves. Our discussions of crime, control and criminology have indicated relevant dominant characteristics and trends, and so, with a little use of the criminological imagination, readers can assess for themselves whether certain kinds of crime or theory are in ascendance or decline.

Persistence of the past

As in any speculative exercise, it is worth remembering that the future is not just about 'the new' but also about the persistence of 'the old'. 'The poor are always with us', goes the saying, but so are the rich, so there are certainly persuasive reasons (based on existing evidence and theory) to assume that some current patterns of crime will simply continue as they are. At the same time, some currently insignificant areas of crime may become important in ways that we *cannot easily predict*, while others that are currently neglected will attract more attention because of social and demographic changes that we *can predict*. For example, on the one hand, in the United Kingdom (though not in the United States) early twentieth-century concerns about links between drugs and crime had largely evaporated by the end of the 1920s (Parssinen, 1983; Lee and South, 2008), and thereafter for the following decades, right into the late 1950s, there was little evidence that could have provided the basis for a prediction about the worldwide scale of the drugs and crime industry that emerged from the 1970s and 1980s. On the other hand, there are a host of previously neglected issues that have come to greater prominence in recent years as social attitudes and tolerance have changed, media and professional attention have increased, and the law has begun to catch up – issues such as child abuse, domestic violence, animal cruelty, and abuse of older people spring to mind in this context.

Take the example of victimization of older people. The growth of an ageing population in a society in which traditional family obligations of care have been eroded and the lack of state and affordable private care resources may provide the conducive conditions for the victimization of older people. But the division between the rich and the poor and the likelihood of victimization will persist here too: as more people are living longer, we can 'predict' there will be those in need of 'extra' income and resources, as savings are depleted and pensions lose value; hence an increase in the victimization of older people. At the other end of the spectrum, the households of more financially comfortable older people will have accumulated desirable household goods and may enjoy higher pension-based income than others, thereby enabling them to purchase homes in low-crime residential areas and pay for additional security.

Extension of current trends

Generally, the extension of current trends into the near future might run as follows. Left, liberal and right political perspectives tend to arrive at a consensus about future trajectories of crime even if they differ strongly about the causes and remedies. However, in terms of how policy is made and then implemented it is striking that in the United Kingdom and United States even historically familiar differences about appropriate responses to crime have faded and convergence has produced look-alike political promises, police powers and penal crises. All of this represents a trend worth watching.

There may be broad agreement that an increase in the number of those finding themselves among the socially excluded, within marginal groups in society, is likely to lead to more property crime, burglary, shoplifting, theft from the person, and similar crimes. A consumer culture, fuelled by diversity of choice, advertising and aspiration, aims to create, meet and stimulate the needs and desires of all, but it is only those with the necessary income (legal or illegal) who can be full consumers. Surrounded by the signs and symbols of consumerism, the obsessions of materialism and the fetishism of designer-label fashion, the argument that feelings of relative deprivation can provide criminal motivation is a powerful one. A culture of narcissism (Lasch, 1979) values appearances, experiences, hedonism and disposable possessions yet still leaves people feeling unfulfilled, empty, in search of more. The mountain of aspirations for people to climb just gets bigger and higher. Writers from different perspectives within criminology, from Merton's theory of adaptation to those interested in the 'seductions of crime' and a cultural criminology, have been interested in this kind of scenario.

As Sutherland (1949) suggested so many years ago, the focus of the criminal justice agencies will be upon those offenders at the bottom of the social pile rather than those in positions of advantage who are committing crimes of more economic or social seriousness. Unless the future brings radical or revolutionary social change (see Lea, 2002), this is unlikely to look much different. The crimes of the middle and managerial classes are likely to follow current trends, at least in the West – with respectable employees, professionals and employers being both victims and perpetrators of crime. As we saw in Chapter 13, the pressures of domestic and global competition, the continued erosion of the bases and virtues of trust, and the inability of late modern market capitalism to regulate corporate activity, are all factors contributing to such trends.

Drug-related crime shows little sign of abeyance, although (as discussed in Chapter 14), at least at the levels of users and small dealers, it is likely to remain unclear whether involvement in drug cultures leads to criminality or involvement in crime cultures leads to drug use and dealing. This is important for a 'future' in which both the illicit economy and the drugs trade are among the major growth industries for the two will increasingly fuel each other. Regardless of this particular debate, the profits of drug distribution will continue to stimulate significant developments in criminal organization, further diversification into legitimate commerce, and intrusion into political processes via corruption, economic influence (Castells, 1996) and the funding of military and terrorist activities. The local as well as the global dimensions of drug trafficking are complex and enormously resistant to legal controls, quasi-military interventions or development aid efforts. Criminal and legitimate enterprises blur with increasing significance (Naím, 2005; Ruggiero, 1996; Punch, 1996); global politics and financial swings can affect patterns of both legal and illegal trade and migration (Jamieson et al., 1998). The breakdown of borders is encouraging more transnational crimes, such as fraud, terrorism and extortion, directed against governments and corporations.

Armed conflicts in the Middle East, in Eastern Europe, in Africa and Asia remind us that crimes of war and violations of human rights are affecting hundreds of thousands of people on a daily basis (Chapter 21; and see Cohen, 2001). Similarly, crimes against the environment such as pollution and environmental exploitation, and resulting problems such as damage to public health and victimization of local populations, are now matters for international crime and control agendas to take seriously (Chapter 19).

In this representation of trends, we clearly seem to have moved from a world of the past where crime was generally seen as a local problem to a new landscape requiring understanding of the global contours of crime. However, we must not romanticize or produce a cosy caricature of the past. Some forms of crime have always relied on cross-border markets. There is nothing new to the international dimension of crimes of war; the cross-continental slave and then drugs trades, while legal in earlier centuries, were forerunners of today's major international crimes; the development of international travel and means of communication has a long history, always facilitating crime along the way.

We tend to assume that the past rested on more solid foundations, where the differences and continuities between localities and the nation-state were well established, and tradition was a serious social force. Yet across the West, wars and occupations, conflicts between labour and capital, the rise and decline of empires, and so on, have all meant that the securities and certainties of the past may have been more insecure and elusive than we sometimes think. The path from the past to the future may simply be one of 'continuity of change'. Nonetheless, today, globalization and glocalization, 'McDonaldization' and 'postmodernization', 'wars in the name of peace' and 'terrorism in the name of religion', may all mean that the world around us is experiencing such change at a faster pace. Does all this create new contexts and conditions for crime?

The present into the future

Criminological thinking – present and future?

Most commentators would agree that the past thirty years have seen major transformations in the nature of crime control as a result of a remarkable increase in post-war crime rates. The substantial escalation in crime has had at least three consequences for 'thinking about crime' (Carrabine, 2004).

First, it has given rise to intense debate on the left between neo-Marxist 'idealists' and social democratic 'realists', and, on the right, the return to biological positivism and folk demonism. Somewhere in between, according to current 'criminological classifications', comes the development, by officials associated with the Home Office and various academics focusing on the crime prevention agenda, of an 'administrative criminology' that has come to regard crime as a normal, if regrettable, outcome of everyday life. From a certain vantage point, all of this mix, dispute and competition makes sense in terms of how a 'postmodern' vision of the future of criminology might develop (South, 1997). The old-fashioned grand theoretical overviews that promised certainty of explanation (such as Marxism and functionalism) have been replaced by the fragmentation of narratives and a story of the collapse of deference, the embrace of difference and the disguising of difficulty.

Second, crime both in the popular imagination and in personal experience has become a central feature of public concern and cultural consumption. Moreover, certain kinds of 'hidden' crime, such as domestic violence, child sex abuse and rape, have become more visible, while forms of corporate, white-collar and state crime have periodically attracted sustained attention in ways that would have been unimaginable thirty years ago. Yet it remains the case that crimes of the powerful and those committed in the home are under-represented in recorded crime figures and, as feminist research has consistently demonstrated, violence against women is widespread and exists throughout the class structure.

The third consequence of the increase in crime is the way in which 'law and order' has become politicized since the mid-1960s. This was to prove a telling factor in the Conservative victory at the 1979 election and is now central to party politics. Through the 1980s it became clear that no political party could afford to remain silent on 'law and order' and it took Labour a substantial period of time to convince the electorate that it too could be 'tough on crime', while also being 'tough on the causes of crime'. From the 1970s, forms of government based on welfare state models of economic management and responses to social problems came under attack and were replaced by, first, New Right administrations, for example in Australia, Britain, New Zealand and the United States, and then by otherwise traditionally left-liberal governments that combined their revised philosophies with free market principles and traditional conservative values. In all this history of political realignment, the overt politicization of crime and control was, and is likely to remain, fundamentally key to vote-winner strategies and social policies. For the future, the subject of crime and its control can only become even more a matter of political significance.

Criminological futures?

While bearing in mind our earlier caution about the persistence and power of the past, it is worth considering how new 'ways of thinking' might emerge in criminology. An optimistic view might take the national and global promotion of the human rights agenda as a key starting point, albeit with realistic acknowledgement of the barriers facing this project (Cohen, 2001). Nonetheless, the gains of movements and success of some proliferating legislation concerned with human rights, civil liberties and acknowledgement of the victimization of minorities, women and children might be achievements we can project into 'one' future of responses to crime and violations. On the other hand, these developments based on rights and universalism are already matched by many other trends in the politics, practice and criminology of risk control that translate into technologies and techniques that are rather less liberal in their implications. To take one relevant vision along these lines, we can illustrate briefly how fiction is becoming reality.

In Philip Kerr's (1992) dark detective thriller *A Philosophical Investigation*, he describes a future of techno-control of criminals, of sadistic murders by a serial killer, and of life amplified by virtual reality. Kerr's novel has a nice joke about the search for the power of predictive techniques as found at the heart of positivist criminology (see Chapter 4), and in the novel, the Metropolitan Police Information Department runs the 'LOMBROSO' programme embracing: the 'philosophical' justification for acceptance of the principles of biological determinism; a computer analysis of a 'national survey of all British males' ongoing from 2010; and a clinical procedure to determine whether certain brains lack the inhibitors that prevent male aggressive behaviour. This is LOMBROSO itself – Localisation of Medullar Brain Resonations Obliging Social Orthopraxy. All marvellously impressive nonsense and yet . . . In September 2002, at a conference called 'Psychiatry and the Problem of Evil', Professor Adrian Raine of the University of California presented research arguing that 'violent and anti-social behaviour is most likely to have a neurological basis . . . triggered only when early brain impairment is combined with social factors such as breakdown in parent–child relationships'. The research identifies 'a distinctive pattern of damage to the pre-frontal cortex in murderers, suggesting the mechanisms inhibiting aggression were impaired' (Hinsliff, 2003). Elsewhere, 'computer forecasts that predict where and when crimes will happen by analysing past patterns' go beyond the already common police 'crime maps' that identify likely crime spots (Singer, 2003) and, in 2007, the leak of a draft paper from the Violent Crime Unit at the UK Home Office led some to liken the paper's proposals to the blueprint for setting up a 'Department of Precrime', a flawed crime prevention initiative featured in the film *Minority Report* (Lettice, 2007: http://www.theregister.co.uk/2007/05/23/precrime_and_soham/print.html). According to these proposals, public agencies with access to sensitive information about 'people at risk of becoming either perpetrators or victims of serious violence could be expected to alert police or other relevant authorities if they have good reason to believe that [an] act of serious violence is about to be committed'. The paper proposes two new bodies be created concerning themselves with potential criminals and with potential victims, reviewing reports from frontline agencies tasked with collecting data and undertaking full risk assessments (http://www.timesonline.co.uk/tol/news/politics/article1816772.ece).

Risk and risky populations as the future focus of control?

Kerr's LOMBROSO and the other developments described are concerned with a project that is at once both desirable and frightening. We want to prevent crime, but do we want to be able to do so by the use of a science of criminology that can predict from an early age who will, and who will not, be a good or bad citizen?

A common feature in much recent development in theories of crime, control and criminal justice is the prioritization and pursuit of earlier prediction of risk in order to enhance response. The idea of 'the present' as one of increasing precariousness and risk is worth further examination if we assume it will remain influential into the future. This is not only because of its current wide influence but also because it is now attracting some serious criticism.

The importance of the risk analysis arguments, originally associated with the idea of actuarial justice (see Chapter 7) or a 'new penology', is that this is 'in part the product of a societal accommodation to routinely high volumes of crime, as well as of the refinement of professional practices for monitoring, surveillance and aggregate management' (Sparks, 2000: 131). In other words, the causes of crime are no longer seen as important. Instead, probabilities are central for a form of actuarial justice that 'does not see a world free of crime but rather one where the best practices of damage limitation have been put in place' (Young, 1999b: 391).

It is clear that writers on risk have identified a new trend in crime control. Crime has become a risk to be calculated, by offender and potential victim, rather than a deviation from civilized conduct caused by individual pathology or faulty socialization – the hallmarks of traditional criminology. Instead, the new criminologies of everyday life see crime as an outcome of normal social interaction (Garland, 2001b). What is surprising about these new theories is the way in which policy-makers have enthusiastically taken them up and hence how the dystopian vision of Kerr's LOMBROSO programme might seem enormously attractive to those in charge of the risk-prevention agenda (for critiques of the Garland argument, see Matthews, 2002; Young, 2003).

A different future: towards a public criminology

Criminology has many problems but none is so great that it requires us to abandon the subject (Smart, 1990). Rather, renewal is one of the strengths of the field (South, 1997). The study of criminology is exciting and challenging. As Muncie *et al.* (1996: xxiv) have argued, there is and always will be an inherent tension in criminology between those who seek continually to challenge and expand the traditional boundaries of criminological discourse and those who remain content to operate within criminology's self-imposed constraints. Ultimately, the tensions and internal debates within criminology may be seen as its greatest strength rather than a signal of criminology's demise. 'Criminology will always appear to be in a process of "becoming". Its work will never seem to be complete' (ibid.).

Elsewhere (Carrabine *et al.*, 2000) we have suggested that a further development for criminology would be to pull it out of its isolation in the academy and take it closer to the public. This is the notion of a 'public criminology', working in the spaces where policy and practice meet. Thinking along similar lines, others have also been considering what a public criminology might look like, suggesting that there is genuine merit and momentum to the idea (Currie, 2007; Loader and Sparks, 2007: 93–6).

An agenda for a public criminology

We would argue that a public criminology must engage with general ignorance around crime issues, moral indifference and uncivilized intolerance. The human rights agenda and the need to revitalize and refine arguments for social justice are necessary elements of this project and provide it with opportunities. Importantly, this is a standpoint going beyond the narrow boundaries of traditional criminology and finding roots for a new perspective and political and practical action in broader arenas of public policy concern – regarding homelessness, health, public services provision, and so on, as well as recognizing the importance of differing lifestyles and new expressions of citizenship.

Let us briefly elaborate on our concerns here. Young (1999a) has argued that the contemporary nature of inequality engenders 'both chronic deprivation amongst the poor which gives rise to crime and a precarious anxiety amongst those better off which breeds intolerance and punitiveness towards the law breaker' (Young, 1999a: 8). While Young is clearly correct in pointing to the significance of intolerance and its debilitating effects on social justice and citizenship, we would observe that moral indifference is an equally troubling facet of contemporary societies. This point has been recognized by Sennett (1998: 146) in his observations on the consequences of the new capitalism:

> The system radiates indifference. It does so in terms of the outcomes of human striving, as in winner-takes-all markets, where there is little connection between risk and reward. It radiates indifference in the organization of absence of trust, where there is no reason to be needed. And it does so in the reengineering of institutions in which people are treated as disposable. Such practices obviously and brutally diminish the sense of mattering as a person, of being necessary to others.

Offenders are largely seen as 'unequal' by mainstream society. While this may occasionally be seen as requiring reform, the tendency is towards a negative evaluation of their worth and contribution (or lack of it) to society, and of their low social status ('deserved and with only themselves to blame'). They are a 'them' different to 'us' in terms of perceived inner-values and external behaviours. This powerful way of seeing offenders and crime has implications for notions of citizenship and rights and has contributed to the populist criminal justice politics that have moved the criminal justice system away from a process concerned with treatment, rehabilitation and welfare to a law-and-order machine concerned with risk-managing the rational offender and incarcerating the dangerous (Garland, 2001b). Of course, citizenship entitlements and obligations are to be properly valued. It would not be helpful to deny that crimes such as burglary, assault, rape and murder grievously offend against the rights, inviolability and lives of others. However, the aim should be to use citizenship and rights in a more inclusive way and to extend access to social capital (South, 2005).

By contrast, corporate offenders enjoy the economic and social benefits of their position with little challenge from either legal or populist quarters, while they profit from activities that damage the quality of life of others and from economic crimes that pass losses onto consumers via higher prices, workers losing pensions or jobs, and compromised health and safety programmes leading to accidents and manslaughter deaths of employees (Alvesalo and Tombs, 2002). Health harms also follow from cost-cutting – affecting production processes and transportation, creating pollution, waste disposal problems and road deaths. Such problems usually affect environmental victims who are already the least powerful and unequally resourced (Bullard, 1990).

There is a public interest agenda entailed in all of this and criminology should aspire to a stronger engagement with it.

An outline of a public criminology

Here we can only outline what such a public criminology might look like but it would explicitly seek to break boundaries and make positive connections with other arenas of social action: with agendas for improving services for people and communities; with local and national political debates that shape policy and social provision; and crucially, with means by which the disempowered can make claims for social justice and their human rights.

A public criminology would be:

- 'transparent'
- 'applied' in orientation
- evidence-based
- committed to empowerment
- committed to social justice and human rights.

More specifically, first, we recognize that although transparency is always desirable – whether in the political process, social action, or research and development initiatives – it is not always easy to achieve. Nonetheless it remains a key goal to aim for in terms of public accountability. Values and choices of the criminologist him/herself should be made explicit and communicated clearly.

Second, our meaning of 'applied' work does not mean abandoning theory, for theory will always inform political activity and debate, social action, and research and development projects. What it means is pursuing work that is applied to publicly relevant issues informed by theory and debate and conveying the details of criminological knowledge to external audiences.

Third, the idea of the use of the 'evidence base' arises from movements within health and social care services to ensure that the use of public money will be spent effectively on interventions that work. This means reviewing evidence as part of a critical exercise regarding good and bad evidence (e.g. *The Bell Curve* (Herrnstein and Murray, 1994) was not based on good evidence). Given that the political and policy successes of the Right, but also, regrettably of Labour and Democrat governments, have so frequently been based on rhetoric and the dismissal (or at best, 'convenient interpretation') of evidence (e.g. about 'what works' in penal, policing or drugs policy), this principle of holding onto and emphasizing evidence that contradicts policy is important. Furthermore, the populism of punitive and exclusionary social policy is largely legitimized by the distorted version of evidence (or its suppression or denial) presented to the public by government and sympathetic media. Popularization of critical evidence about the realities of imprisonment, policing, racism, poverty, and denial of justice, is a key goal for a public criminology (and in this respect is similar to the idea of 'Newsmaking Criminology': Barak, 2007).

Relatedly therefore, and at the heart of a public criminology, empowerment means working for the ordinary public rather than for narrow political interests, emphasizing social justice and human rights. An empowerment-oriented public criminology prioritizes the interests of the public person/s (individuals/communities) over those interest groups that disempower people, and that cause and create conditions resulting in crime, health, environmental and other social injuries and hazards (see chapters 14, 19 and 21 of the book). That there is competition and conflict within and between individuals and communities is a fact of life – the point is to help address and resolve such splits, tensions and the social damage that follows.

On this point it is worth quoting Currie (2007: 186–7) at some length for he both agrees with and expands on this line of argument, explaining the problem facing academic criminology in its current state:

> To summarize: the modern research university, and the professional disciplines which increasingly drive the university's conception of itself, often institutionally rewards work that (a) is narrowly tailored to the publication imperatives of a few journals in a given discipline, that (b) focuses on the generation of new, even if narrow, research findings, usually ones that address questions within already well-furrowed fields, as opposed to analyses of the meaning or import of those findings, and that (c) often actively penalizes work explicitly designed to broaden and deepen the audience, and hence the impact, of what we do. *Over time, the isolation this fosters begins to affect the nature of the work criminologists do in ways that can only deepen the chasm between academic criminology and the public realm*. . . .
>
> *So what is to be done about it?*
>
> I think we can attack this problem on two related levels: *getting rid of some of the negative incentives that block the social impact of criminological work, and increasing the positive opportunities to broaden that impact.* [emphasis added]

Finally, in providing an inspirational and aspirational agenda for a public criminology appropriate to late modernity, we should not dismiss or forget the inspirations and aspirations of the past. Revisiting the work of C. Wright Mills is suggestive here, reminding us of Mills's passion for making good use of 'the sociological imagination', and his advocacy of paying attention to empirical evidence while developing critical theory. Following Mills (1959), a public criminology should be committed to engagement with 'public issues *and* private troubles'. The public role of the criminologist, to paraphrase what John Scott (2005: 408) suggests in relation to the advocacy of public sociology, is 'to speak autonomously as a citizen from the standpoint of a well-grounded base of [criminological] knowledge'.

The aims of undoing social wrongs and promoting social rights in both the public and private spheres are not new, but they are particularly pertinent in the context of the trends and issues we have discussed in this book. As Zahn (1999) argued in her Presidential Address to the American Society of Criminology in 1998: 'Criminology will ultimately be judged not only by the knowledge we produce within university walls but also by how we use it in the world.'

Summary

1   This chapter has emphasized that the future for crime, control and criminology may be dramatically different but is likely to see more modest change.
2   Thinking about continuity between the past, present and future is a way of helping to think about how current crimes may mutate into crimes of the future.
3   New dimensions of crime, control and criminology have emerged around themes such as human rights and the control of risk, and there may be considerable tension between these two directions for the future.
4   Science fiction is frequently less far from science fact than we may assume.
5   Criminology is evidently a lively and 'living' subject – growing and revitalizing, with both old questions to ponder and new ones to explore.

Critical thinking questions

The 'big question' is – what do you think the future of

■   crime
■   control
■   criminology

will look like?

Further study

Barak, G. (2001) 'Crime and Crime Control in an Age of Globalization: A Theoretical Dissection', *Critical Criminology*, 10 (10): 57–72. Examines the impact of globalization on both crime and crime control at the national and global levels and draws upon a 15-nation survey of crime and crime control in developed, developing and post-traditional nation-states.

Nelken, D. (ed.) (1994b) *The Futures of Criminology*, London: Sage. Although getting a little dated as a book about 'futures', is still a very useful collection covering various directions and debates, including postmodernist and comparative approaches.

Nellis, M. (2003) 'News Media, Popular Culture and the Electronic Monitoring of Offenders in England and Wales', *Howard Journal of Criminal Justice*, 42 (1): 1–31. An article connecting a number of themes reflecting current practice in criminal justice, links to fiction and media, and to scenarios of the future.

Newburn, T. (2008) 'The Future of Policing', in T. Newburn (ed.) *The Handbook of Policing*, Cullompton: Willan. Examines the likely influences on the future of policing, e.g. demography, politics, pluralization, and outlines what possible developments may occur.

Glossary

actuarialism Probability calculations and statistical distributions to measure risk and which underpin correctional policies.

alcohol prohibition In the United States, the 'Volstead' Act (1919) prohibited the sale and production of alcohol, leading to the 'bootlegger business', i.e. the illegal production and distribution of alcohol for consumption in secret venues, providing profits for organized criminal groups. Prohibition was repealed in 1933.

anomie A condition where norms are confused or break down. There is a lack of normative regulation, which could lead to deviant behaviour. Merton produced a typology of responses to anomie.

area offence rate All recorded offences in a particular area.

area victimization rate Level of offences against a particular group in a particular area.

bifurcation Refers to the dual-edged approach to crime control whereby tougher measures are used for more serious offenders while less severe measures are used for ordinary offences.

biopiracy A term given to the practices of some companies that have asserted the right of ownership over genetic materials taken from living organisms.

capitalism An economic system in which the production of goods depends on private investment and the making of profit.

categorical imperative A principle of moral philosophy derived from the Enlightenment thinker Immanuel Kant, who insisted that certain duties are absolute and unconditional.

classicism The Enlightenment view of crime that stresses free will and rationality and the corresponding rationality of the justice system.

colonialism A process by which some nations acquired others as colonies and exercised economic, political and cultural influence.

community safety Policy initiatives to reduce crime through local partnerships involving the police and other community agencies.

concentric zone theory (or **zonal theory**) Holds that city centres are business districts bordered by a ring of factories, followed by residential rings with housing that becomes more expensive the further it stands from the noise and pollution of the city's centre.

constitutional theories Theories such as Lombroso's that locate the origins of criminality in a person's biological or psychological make-up.

constitutive criminology A postmodernist theoretical perspective on crime in contrast to a modernist one.

continuum of sexual violence Ranges from the everyday abuse of women in pornographic images, sexist jokes, sexual harassment and women's engagement in compliant but unwanted marital sex, through to the 'non-routine' episodes of rape, incest, battery and sex murder. (Note: this is not meant to be a continuum that simply moves along lines of severity of the act.)

control theory Holds that delinquent acts result when an individual's bond to society is weak or broken. There are four bonds: attachment, involvement, commitment and belief.

cross-cultural (or **comparative**) **criminology** The branch of criminology that compares different societies and their patterns of crime and control.

cultural criminology Uses mainly qualitative and cultural methods to study mostly urban subcultures with a focus on image, representation and style.

cultural property Movable or immovable property of great importance to the cultural heritage of every people.

dark figure A term used to refer to the hidden figure of unreported or unrecorded crime.

decarceration The process that refers to the deliberate move away from imprisonment as the central penal sanction towards the use of alternative sanctions, usually in the community.

defensible space Idea that it is possible to modify the built environment to reduce the opportunity for crime and to promote community responsibility.

denial A term that refers to feelings and the ideas attached to them that are not necessarily available to conscious awareness, but handle the dangerous and threatening aspects of our inner and outer worlds. For example, when husbands and wives fail to see the signs of their partner's infidelities, or when we do not notice the symptoms of illness in those we love. This is when denial acts as an unconscious defence mechanism to protect us from disturbing and upsetting realities.

determinism According to the positivist school, people become criminals through factors largely out of their control – be they biological, psychological or social.

deterrence Based on the idea that crime can be discouraged through the public's fear of the punishment they may receive if they break the law.

differential association Crime is basically learned in the same ways as everything else. Edwin Sutherland's theory came ultimately to be presented as nine propositions (given in the text of Chapter 5).

discourses Bodies of ideas and language, often backed up by institutions.

dispersal policy Introduced in the wake of a series of prison escapes in Britain in the 1960s, so that maximum security prisoners are spread around a few high-security prisons.

ecology of crime Idea that crime is linked to the (urban) environment in predictable ways.

ecosystem The system composed of the interaction of all living organisms and their natural environment.

'effects' studies Studies that seek to establish whether the media cause crime through representations of violence.

emotion A mental state involving how a person feels rather than thinks.

Enlightenment thinking Thought that emerged during the eighteenth century in the West and that championed rationality, science and progress, alongside the importance of the individual and the tolerance of different beliefs.

epistemological Relating to the theory of knowledge.

ethics A set of principles guiding research practice, especially where human participants are involved.

ethnography A research approach in which the researcher participates – overtly or covertly – for a lengthy period of time in the daily lives of those being studied and listens, observes, asks questions, and collects whatever data are available.

evaluation research Research aiming to assess the impacts of a policy intervention.

evidence-based policy Policy clearly shaped by research evidence.

experimental criminology Research which aims to test out theories in the criminal justice field and make policy recommendations based on 'hard' evidence of what works.

feminist criminology A criminology that puts women at the centre of the analysis.

forensic science Scientific techniques to investigate crime and criminality.

free will According to the classical school, people possess reason. This means that they can calculate the course of action that is in their self-interest. This in turn gives them a degree of freedom.

functionalist perspective A theory that looks at the ways in which societies become integrated as their various parts perform various functions.

gatekeepers Individuals or agencies who can aid or inhibit a researcher's access to a particular research field.

gender-aware criminology A criminology that puts gender at the centre of the analysis.

genres One of the ways in which differences between narratives can be defined through identifying the conventions that other texts in the same grouping share.

geo-data personal, local or global geographical data often involving a combination of data from different sources such as digital maps and databases.

globalization of crime The increasing interconnectedness of crime across societies.

green crimes Crimes against the environment.

green criminology A reappraisal of more traditional notions of crimes, offences and injurious behaviours and an examination of the role that societies (including corporations and governments) play in generating environmental degradation.

harm reduction As an alternative to insistence on abstaining from drug use, this is an approach to working with users to minimize the possibility of serious harms such as AIDS or overdose.

hierarchy of victimization A concept that captures the unequal status that victims experience in the crime discourse and in their treatment by criminal justice agencies. Those at the top are regarded as innocent and deserving of help and sympathy, those at the bottom less so.

human rights Rights that belong to all people.

humiliation The experience of a loss of respect or self-esteem.

industrialization Mass production of manufactured goods and a means of organizing workers, employers and finance.

instrumental laws Laws whose aim is practical: to bring about some specific desired effect such as the stopping of rape.

just deserts A justification for punishment which insists that offenders should be punished only as severely as they deserve. It was a reaction against the unfair excesses of rehabilitation and the 'get tough' drive from conservatives during the 1970s.

labelling theory Highlights social reaction and suggests that crime may be heightened by criminal sanctions.

late modernity One of many concepts used to characterize a new emerging social order after modernity and capitalism.

legitimacy In the context of prisons, is the process whereby institutional power gains a moral grounding through prisoners consenting to the authority of staff and regimes.

less eligibility A penal doctrine which maintains that offenders should endure harsher institutional regimes than the poorest free citizens.

lynching A form of extrajudicial punishment involving public torture, revived in the Southern United States as a response to the perceived erosion of white male domination in the nineteenth century. The lynchings were explicitly violent and included burning, castration and whipping as well as hanging. They were deliberately racialized and the lynch victim was often sought out as retribution for the alleged rape of a white woman by an African-American man.

McDonaldization The principles of the fast food industry become increasingly applied to all of social life.

mapping Processes by which spaces are defined and represented.

marginalization A state in which people live on the edge of society and outside the mainstream with little stake in society overall.

mediatization Refers to the process whereby the rapid expansion of the media has undermined distinctions between image and reality.

Megan's law Named after Megan Kanka, a 7-year-old girl from New Jersey who was sexually assaulted and killed by a convicted sex offender living in the same street.

mixed methods A new approach to social research which seeks to combine qualitative and quantitative methods.

money laundering Concealing the origins of money gained illegally by moving it through a series of banking transfers to 'clean' it.

moral panic The heightened awareness of certain problems relating to crime at key moments.

negotiated justice The construction of cases, negotiations (e.g. between the defence and prosecution) and social interaction involved in the routine production of justice.

neutralization, techniques of A series of strategies through which the individual's 'bond' to society is weakened, hence making that individual more likely to commit crime.

night-time economy Production and consumption of night-time recreational services.

'normalization' Although not everyone is now a drug user, nevertheless (the argument runs) it is now non-acquaintance with drugs or drug users that has become the deviation from the norm. The drugs in question are usually those associated with leisure cultures, such as cannabis, Ecstasy, amphetamines or cocaine. Others reject the idea: particularly for the majority of young people, persisting prohibitions, peer-group resistance, parental attachment and preference for alternative activities remain central to their lives. Both arguments appear to have some validity.

occupational culture The values, norms, perspectives and informal rules that can inform the conduct of those engaged in a particular occupation (in the context of this book, the police). It has many variations and can change according to particular situations and the interactional processes of each encounter.

output The means by which the findings of a research project are disseminated and circulated.

paradigm A general view of how the world works.

participant observation A qualitative research method in which the researcher observes and interacts with people, often in everyday settings.

partisan One-sided; adhering to a particular cause.

pathologization The linking of criminality, or other behaviours, to physical or bodily attributes.

patriarchies Systems of male dominance that serve the interests of men.

police A state-organised institution with specific powers and a mandate to prevent and investigate crime or disorder.

police accountability The institutional arrangements made to ensure that the police do the job required of them.

policing A set of activities aimed at maintaining security and the social order through surveillance and the threat of sanctioning. It can be carried out by a variety of people and techniques.

positivism In criminology, 'positivism' highlights (a) scientific methods in the study of crime; (b) the importance of criminal types; and (c) theories of cause or aetiology.

postmodernism Grand or absolute truths are challenged, and in their place we find partial and limited truths: a much less certain and more provisional view of the world is in the making.

prediction studies Criminological research aiming to forecast the future conduct of persons under certain conditions.

primary and secondary deviance The distinction between original and effective causes of deviance: primary deviation arises from many sources and is minor and insignificant; secondary deviation is pivotal because stigma and punishment make it so.

primary and secondary victimization Primary victimization refers to the direct impact of crime on the victims while secondary victimization refers to additional negative impact resulting from the way others (especially criminal justice agencies) respond to them and the crime.

procedural justice Formal adherence to legal rules and safeguards throughout the criminal justice process and the impartial application of neutral criteria in criminal justice decision-making.

process of attrition The process of filtering of cases at different stages of the criminal justice process.

Prohibition *See* **alcohol prohibition**.

projection A psychoanalytical concept describing one of the many unconscious defensive mechanisms by which we protect ourselves from the troubling contents of our inner worlds. It is the process by which we impute something that is actually within oneself on to some other person or object. Projection protects against danger by investing another person or object with the qualities we feel we do not have. It is also the principal psychological mechanism involved in such phenomena as racism, sexism and homophobia.

property crime Stealing and dishonestly obtaining or damaging another's property, which includes both tangible goods and intangible property.

public criminology Draws on human rights, social justice and public policy agenda to raise public awareness of crime issues and to argue against indifference, intolerance and inequality; and to provide opportunities for political and practical action in broad arenas of public policy concern.

qualitative research A form of investigation in which researchers gather data about people's beliefs, impressions and understandings.

quantitative research A form of investigation which seeks to quantify and measure social trends.

reductivist Refers to justifications of punishment that regard the prevention of future crimes as the moral basis on which to base systems of punishment.

rehabilitation Based on the idea that punishment can reduce crime if it takes a form that will improve the individual's character so that they are less likely to reoffend in the future. It tends to view criminal behaviour not as freely willed action but as a symptom of some kind of causal factor, whether this be economic, social or personal.

relative deprivation A perceived disadvantage arising from a specific comparison.

repeat victimization Occurs when the same location, person, household, business or vehicle suffers more than one crime event over a specified period of time.

research design A research plan which sets out key questions to be investigated, methods to be used, timeframe, possible problems and how the proposed work will relate to other relevant studies and related fields.

respect Deference, esteem and regard.

retributivist Justifications of punishment that insist that only the crimes of the past should be punished.

rights Claims supported by some justification.

risk society Beck's idea that modern industrial societies create many new risks – on a global scale and largely manufactured through modern technologies – that were unknown in earlier days. Examples include nuclear war and environmental pollution.

secondary deviance *See* **primary and secondary deviance**

secondary victimization *See* **primary and secondary victimization**

self-esteem A positive opinion about oneself.

self-report studies Studies of crime and other social issues which use interviews or question-naires to gather personal experiences of offending and/or victimization.

sexual script Sexuality is seen as not simply biological, but also connected to social meanings. Scripts help define the who, what, where, when and why of sexual conduct.

shame A painful emotion arising from an awareness of inadequacy, guilt or dishonour.

social construct The ways in which people shape reality.

social crime A term used by social historians to refer to the criminalization of 'everyday' practices, especially those connected to work, customary rights and the economy.

Social Darwinism The social application of Darwinian evolutionary theory.

social psychology Analyses the relationships between individuals and society, examining how individuals relate to each other and to the networks in which they operate.

social solidarity A key element of Durkheim's sociology, it refers to the sources of integration that preserve social stability and promote moral consensus in the face of rapid economic change and political upheaval.

space Locations and places where social life is lived and imagined.

splitting A psychoanalytical concept describing one of the defence mechanisms with which we deal with the inner and external worlds. It is a way of dealing with anxiety by splitting the threat into two, 'good' and 'bad', elements.

subcultures Groups with a distinct image and set of beliefs that seem to set them apart from mainstream culture.

substantive justice Just and effective outcomes of criminal justice decision-making that take into account social inequalities and their impact on different social groups.

survey Systematic data collection about the same variables or characteristics from a number of respondents or cases.

symbolic laws Laws that act to highlight (symbolize) key issues. They may serve as a litmus test for many moral panics and discourses that tap into a wide range of social anxieties.

temperance The commitment to abstinence from alcoholic drink, associated in particular with early twentieth-century social and religious movements.

text Implies not simply a novel or the written word in general but that all cultural objects generate meaning, which can equally be through images or sounds as well as the written word.

transcarceration The movement of offenders between different institutional sites, state agencies and correctional programmes, so that the network of social control is expanded rather than reduced.

transgression The act of overstepping boundaries or limits established by rules, laws, principles, custom, convention or tradition.

urban flight Movement out of inner cities by middle- and working-class groups – a movement partly driven by beliefs about crime.

urbanization The creation of large-scale urban societies linked to industrialization, migration and population growth.

victimology An area of study that is concerned with the victim of crime. Often described as a subdiscipline of criminology.

working rules Rules that those following a particular occupation – in this case, that of police officer – internalize so that they become the effective principles that guide their decisions and actions.

Bibliography

Abbott, C. (2008) *An Uncertain Future: Law Enforcement, National Security and Climate Change*, Oxford: Oxford Research Group.

Abercrombie, N. (1996) *Television and Society*, Cambridge: Polity.

Abraham, J. (1995) *Science, Politics and the Pharmaceutical Industry: Controversy and Bias in Drug Regulation*, New York: UCL/St Martin's Press.

Acheson, D. (1998) *Health Inequalities*, London: Department of Health.

Adam, B., Beck, U. and Van Loon, J. (eds) (2000) *The Risk Society and Beyond*, London: Sage.

Adam, B. D., Duyvendak, J. W. and Krouwel, A. (eds) (1999) *The Global Emergence of Gay and Lesbian Politics*, Philadelphia, PA: Temple University Press.

Adler, F. (1975) *Sisters in Crime: The Rise of the New Female Criminal*, New York: McGraw-Hill.

Adler, P. A. and Adler, P. (1998) 'Forward: Moving Backward', in J. Ferrell and M. Hamm (eds) *Ethnography at the Edge: Crime, Deviance and Field Research*, Boston, MA: Northeastern University Press.

Agamben, G. (1998) *Homo Sacer: Sovereign Power and Bare Life*, Standford, CA: Standford University Press.

Agamben, G. (2005) *State of Exception*, trans. Kevin Attell, Chicago, IL: University of Chicago Press.

Ahmed, S. (2004) *The Cultural Politics of Emotion*, Edinburgh: Edinburgh University Press.

Albrecht, H-J. (2000) 'Foreigners, Migration, Immigration and the Development of Criminal Justice in Europe', in P. Green and A. Rutherford (eds) *Criminal Policy in Transition*, Portland: Hart Publishing.

Albrow, M. (1990) *The Global Age*, Cambridge: Polity.

Alcohol Concern (2000) *Britain's Ruin*, London: Alcohol Concern.

Alcohol Concern (2001) www.alcoholconcern.org.uk/

All Party Group on Alcohol Misuse (1995) *Alcohol and Crime: Breaking the Link*, London: Alcohol Concern.

Allan, S. (1999) *News Culture*, Buckingham: Open University Press.

Allan, S. (2006) *Online News: Journalism and the Internet*, Berkshire: Open University Press.

Allen, B. (1996) *Rape Warfare: The Hidden Genocide in Bosnia-Herzegovina and Croatia*, Minneapolis: University of Minnesota Press.

Allen, H. (1987) *Justice Unbalanced*, Milton Keynes: Open University Press.

Altman, D. (2001) *Global Sex*, Chicago, IL: University of Chicago Press.

Alubo, S. O. (1994) 'Death for Sale: A Case Study of Drug Poisoning and Deaths in Nigeria', *Social Science and Medicine*, 38 (1): 97–103.

Alvesalo, A. and Tombs, S. (2002) 'Working for Criminalization of Economic Offending: Contradictions for Critical Criminology?', *Critical Criminology*, 11 (1): 21–40.

Amir, M. (1971) *Patterns of Forcible Rape*, Chicago, IL: University of Chicago Press.

Amnesty International (2001) *Crimes of Hate: Conspiracies of Silence*, London: Amnesty International.

Anderson, E. (1994) 'The Code of Streets', *Atlantic Monthly*, 5: 80–94.

Anderson, E. (1999) *Code of the Streets: Decency, Violence and the Moral Life of the Inner City*, New York: W. W. Norton.

Anderson, N. (1923) *The Hobo: The Sociology of the Homeless Man*, Chicago, IL: University of Chicago Press.

Anderson, R., Brown, J. and Campbell, E. (1993) *Aspects of Sex Discrimination within the Police Service in England and Wales*, London: Home Office Police Research Group.

Anderson, S., Kinsey, R., Loader, I. and Smith, C. (1994) *Cautionary Tales: Young People, Crime and Policing in Edinburgh*, Aldershot: Avebury.

Archer, J. (1990) *By a Flash and a Scare: Incendiarism, Animal Maiming and Poaching in East Anglia 1815–1870*, Oxford: Clarendon.

Arnot, M. and Usborne, C. (eds) (1999a) *Gender and Crime in Modern Europe*, London: UCL Press.

Arnot, M. and Usborne, C. (1999b) '"Why Gender and Crime?" Aspects of an International Debate', in M. Arnot and C. Usborne (eds) *Gender and Crime in Modern Europe*, London: UCL Press.

Arrigo, B. (1997) 'Review of Stuart Henry and Dragan Milovanovic's Constitutive Criminology', *Theoretical Criminology*, 3: 392–6.

Ashworth, A. (1986) 'Punishment and Compensation: Victims, Offenders and the State', *Oxford Journal of Legal Studies*, 6: 86–122.

Ashworth, A. (1993) 'Victim Impact Statements and Sentencing', *Criminal Law Review*, pp. 498–509.

Ashworth, A. (1998) *The Criminal Process*, 2nd edn, Oxford: Oxford University Press.

Ashworth, A. (2003) 'Is Restorative Justice the Way Forward for Criminal Justice?', in E. McLaughlin, R. Fergusson, G. Hughes and L. Westmarland (eds) *Restorative Justice: Critical Issues*, London: Sage.

Ashworth, A. (2004) 'Social Control and "Anti-Social Behaviour": The Subversion of Human Rights?', *Law Quarterly Review*, 120: 263–91.

Atton, C. (2003) 'Organization and Production in Alternative Media', in S. Cottle (ed.) *Media Organization and Production*, London: Sage.

Audit Commission (1993) *Helping with Enquiries: Tackling Crime Effectively*, London: HMSO.

Audit Commission (1996) *Streetwise: Effective Police Patrol*, London: HMSO.

Auld, J. (1973) 'Cannabis: The Changing Patterns of Use', *New Society*, September: 568–70.

Auld, J., Dorn, N. and South, N. (1986) 'Irregular Work, Irregular Pleasures: Heroin in the 1980s', in R. Matthews and J. Young (eds) *Confronting Crime*, London: Sage.

Ayers, E. (1984) *Vengeance and Justice: Crime and Punishment in the Nineteenth-century American South*, New York: Oxford University Press.

Back, L. (1996) *New Ethnicities and Urban Culture: Racisms and Multiculture in Young Lives*, London: UCL Press.

Bagaric, M. and Clarke, J. (2005) 'Not Enough Official Torture in the World? The Circumstances in which Torture is Morally Justifiable', *University of San Francisco Law Review*, 39.

Baird, V. (2001) *The No-Nonsense Guide to Sexual Diversity*, London: New Internationalist/Verso.

Baldwin, J. and Bottoms, A. E. (1976) *The Urban Criminal*, London: Tavistock.

Baldwin, J. and McConville, M. (1977) *Negotiated Justice*, London: Martin Robertson.

Bales, K. (1999) *Disposable People: New Slavery in the Global Economy*, Berkeley: University of California Press.

Bales, K. (2005) *Understanding Global Slavery*, Berkeley: University of California Press.

Ballinger, A. (2000) *Dead Woman Walking: Executed Women in England and Wales, 1900–1955*, Aldershot: Ashgate/Dartmouth.

Banton, M. (1964) *The Policeman in the Community*, London: Tavistock.

Barak, G. (ed.) (1994) *Media, Process, and the Social Construction of Crime: Studies in Newsmaking Criminology*, New York: Garland.

Barak, G. (2001) 'Crime and Crime Control in an Age of Globalization: A Theoretical Dissection', *Critical Criminology*, 10 (10): 57–72.

Barak, G. (2007) 'Doing Newsmaking Criminology from within the Academy', *Theoretical Criminology*, 11 (2): 191–207.

Barbalet, J. (1998) *Emotion, Social Theory and Social Structure: A Macrosociological Approach*, Cambridge: Cambridge University Press.

Barbalet, J. (2002) 'Moral Indignation, Class Inequality and Justice: An Exploration and

Revision of Ranulf', *Theoretical Criminology*, 6 (3): 279–97.

Barclay, G. and Tavares, C. (2002) *International Comparisons of Criminal Justice Statistics 2000*, Home Office Statistical Bulletin 05/02, London: Home Office.

Barker, M. and Petley, J. (eds) (1997) *Ill Effects: The Media/Violence Debate*, London: Routledge.

Barstow, A. L. (2000) *War's Dirty Secret: Rape, Prostitution, and Other Crimes Against Women*, Cleveland, OH: Pilgrim Press.

Barthes, R. (1975) *The Pleasure of the Text* (originally published in French, 1973), New York: Hill and Wang.

Barton, A. (2005) *Fragile Moralities and Dangerous Sexualities: Two Centuries of Semi-penal Institutionalisation for Women*, Aldershot: Ashgate.

Barton, B. F. and Barton, M. S. (1993) 'Modes of Power in Technical and Professional Visuals', *Journal of Business and Technical Communication*, 7 (1): 138–62.

Bauman, Z. (1989) *Modernity and the Holocaust*, Cambridge: Polity.

Bauman, Z. (1992) *Intimations of Postmodernity*, London: Routledge.

Bauman, Z. (1995) *Life in Fragments: Essays in Postmodern Morality*, Oxford: Blackwell.

Bauman, Z. (1998) *Globalization: The Human Consequences*, Cambridge: Polity.

Bauman, Z. (2006) *Liquid Fear*, Cambridge: Polity.

Baumgartner, F., De Boef, S. and Boydstun, A. (2008) *The Decline of the Death Penalty and the Discovery of Innocence*, Cambridge: Cambridge University Press.

Bayley, D. H. (1994) *Police for the Future*, New York: Oxford University Press.

Baylis, J. and Smith, S. (eds) (1997) *The Globalization of World Politics*, Oxford: Oxford University Press.

Bazemore, G. and Taylor-Griffiths, C. (2003) 'Conferences, Circles, Boards, and Mediations: The "New Wave" of Community Justice Decisionmaking', in E. McLaughlin, R. Fergusson, G. Hughes and L. Westmarland (eds) *Restorative Justice: Critical Issues*, London: Sage.

Bean, P. (2002) *Drugs and Crime*, Cullompton: Willan.

Bean, P. and Nemitz, T. (2004) *Drug Treatment: What Works?*, London: Routledge.

Beattie, J. (1975) 'The Criminality of Women in Eighteenth-Century England', *Journal of Social History*, 8: 80–116.

Beattie, J. (1986) *Crime and the Courts in England 1660–1800*, Oxford: Clarendon Press.

Beck, U. (1992) *Risk Society: Towards a New Modernity*, London: Sage.

Beck, U. (1995) *Ecological Politics in an Age of Risk*, Cambridge: Polity.

Beck, U. (2000) *World Risk Society*, Cambridge: Polity.

Becker, H. S. (1963) *Outsiders: Studies in the Sociology of Deviance*, New York: Free Press.

Becker, H. S. (1967) 'Whose Side Are We On?', *Social Problems*, 14: 239–47.

Behlmer, G. K. (1982) *Child Abuse and Moral Reform in England 1870–1908*, Stanford, CA: Stanford University Press.

Beirne, P. (1993) *Inventing Criminology: Essays on the Rise of 'Homo Criminalis'*, Albany: State University of New York Press.

Beirne, P. and South, N. (eds) (2007) *Issues in Green Criminology*, Cullompton: Willan.

Bellamy, R. (ed.) (1995) *Beccaria: On Crimes and Punishments and Other Writings*, Cambridge: Cambridge University Press.

Bennett, T. (1990) 'Knowledge, Power, Ideology: Detective Fiction', in T. Bennett (ed.) *Popular Fiction: Technology, Ideology, Production, Reading*, London: Routledge.

Bennett, T., Holloway, K. and Williams, T. (2001) *Drug Use and Offending*, Findings 148, London: Home Office.

Bentham, J. (1789/1970) *An Introduction to the Principles of Morals and Legislation*, ed. J. H. Burns and H. L. A. Hart, London: Athlone.

Benton, T. (1984) *The Rise and Fall of Structural Marxism: Althusser and His Influence*, Basingstoke: Macmillan.

Berger, P. (1963) *Invitation to Sociology: A Humanistic Perspective*, Garden City, NY: Doubleday.

Berridge, V. (1984) 'Drugs and Social Policy: The Establishment of Drug Control in Britain, 1900–1930', *British Journal of Addiction*, 79: 1.

Berridge, V. (1999) *Opium and the People*, revised edn, London: Free Association Books.

Best, J. (1990) *Threatened Children: Rhetoric and Concern about Child Victims*, Chicago, IL: University of Chicago Press.

Best, J. (2001) *Damned Lies and Statistics*, Berkeley, CA: University of California Press.

Biggs, S., Phillipson, C. and Kingston, P. (1995) *Elder Abuse in Perspective*, Buckingham: Open University Press.

Bishop, R. and Robinson, L. (1998) *Night Market: Sexual Cultures and the Thai Economic Miracle*, London: Routledge.

Bittner, E. (1967) 'The Police on Skid Row: A Study in Peacekeeping', *American Sociological Review*, 32: 699–715.

Bittner, E. (1974) 'Florence Nightingale in Pursuit of Willie Sutton: A Theory of the Police', in H. Jacob (ed.) *The Potential for Reform of Criminal Justice*, Beverly Hills, CA: Sage.

Blagg, H. (1997) 'A Just Measure of Shame: Aboriginal Youth and Conferencing in Australia', *British Journal of Criminology*, 37 (4): 481–501.

Blok, A. (1972) 'Social Banditry Reconsidered', *Comparative Studies in Society and History*, 14: 495–505; reprinted in A. Blok, *Honour and Violence*, Cambridge: Polity, 2001.

Blomley, N. and Sommers, J. (1999) 'Mapping Urban Space: Governmentality and Cartographic Struggles in Inner City Vancouver', in R. Smandych (ed.) *Governable Places: Readings on Governmentality and Crime Control*, Aldershot: Ashgate.

Blum, J., Levi, M., Naylor, R. and Williams, P. (1998) *Financial Havens, Banking Secrecy and Money Laundering*, New York: United Nations Office for Drug Control and Crime Prevention.

Booth, M. (2001) *The Dragon Syndicates: The Global Phenomenon of the Triad*, New York: Carroll and Graf.

Borger, J. (2001) 'U.S. Lets Fight against Smog Disappear into Thin Air', *Guardian*, 9 August: 12.

Boritch, H. and Hagan, J. (1990) 'A Century of Crime in Toronto: Gender, Class, and Patterns of Social Control, 1859 to 1955', *Criminology*, 28 (4): 567–600.

Borrill, J. and Stevens, D. (1993) 'Understanding Human Violence: The Implications of Social Structure, Gender, Social Perception and Alcohol', *Criminal Behaviour and Mental Health*, 3: 129–41.

Bosworth, M. (1999) *Engendering Resistance: Agency and Power in Women's Prisons*, Aldershot: Dartmouth.

Bosworth, M. (2000) 'Confining Femininity: A History of Gender, Power and Imprisonment', *Theoretical Criminology*, 4 (3): 265–84.

Bosworth, M. and Flavin, J. (eds) (2007) *Race, Gender and Punishment: From Colonialism to the War on Terror*, New Brunswick, NJ: Rutgers University Press.

Bosworth, M., Bowling, B. and Lee, M. (2008) 'Globalization, Ethnicity and Racism: An Introduction', *Theoretical Criminology*, 12 (3): 263–73.

Bottoms, A. (1977) 'Reflections on the Renaissance of Dangerousness', *Howard Journal of Criminal Justice*, 16: 70–96.

Bottoms, A. (1983) 'Neglected Features of Contemporary Penal Systems', in D. Garland and P. Young (eds) *The Power to Punish*, London: Heinemann.

Bottoms, A. (1987) 'Limiting Prison Use: Experience in England and Wales', *Howard Journal of Criminal Justice*, 26: 177–202.

Bottoms, A. (1995) 'The Philosophy and Politics of Punishment and Sentencing', in C. Clarkson and R. Morgan (eds) *The Politics of Sentencing Reform*, Oxford: Clarendon Press.

Bottoms, A. E. (2007) 'Place, Space, Crime and Disorder', in M. Maguire, R. Morgan and R. Reiner (eds) *Oxford Handbook of Criminology*, 4th edn, Oxford: Oxford University Press.

Bottoms, A. E. and McClean, J. D. (1976) *Defendants in the Criminal Process*, London: Routledge and Kegan Paul.

Bottoms, A. E. and Wiles, P. (2002) 'Environmental Criminology', in M. Maguire, R. Morgan and R. Reiner (eds) *The Oxford Handbook of Criminology*, 3rd edn, Oxford: Oxford University Press.

Bourdieu, P. (1984) *Distinction: A Social Critique of the Judgement of Taste*, London: Routledge.

Bourgois, P. (1995) *In Search of Respect*, Cambridge: Cambridge University Press.

Bourke, J. (2007) *Rape: A History from 1860 to the Present Day*, London: Virago.

Bowling, B. (1998) *Violent Racism: Victimization, Policing and Social Context*, Oxford: Clarendon Press.

Bowling, B. (1999) 'The Rise and Fall of New York Murder', *British Journal of Criminology*, 39 (4): 531–54.

Bowling, B. and Phillips, C. (2002) *Racism, Crime and Justice*, Harlow: Longman.

Bowling, B. and Ross, J. (2008) 'The Serious Organised Crime Agency: Should We Be Afraid?', *Criminal Law Review*, pp. 1019–34.

Box, S. (1983) *Power, Crime and Mystification*, London: Routledge.

Box, S. and Hale, C. (1984) 'Liberation/ Emancipation, Economic Marginalization or Less Chivalry', Criminology, 22: 473–97.

Box, S., Hale, C. and Andrews, G. (1988) 'Explaining Fear of Crime', *British Journal of Criminology*, 28:340–56.

Boyd, S., Chunn, D. and Menzies, R. (eds) (2002) *Toxic Criminology: Environment, Law and the State in Canada*, Halifax: Fernwood.

Boyle, K., Hadden, T. and Hillyard, P. (1975) *Law and State: The Case of Northern Ireland*, London: Martin Robertson.

Bozovic, M. (ed.) (1995) *The Panopticon Writings of Jeremy Bentham*, London Verso.

Braithwaite, J. (1984) *Corporate Crime in the Pharmaceutical Industry*, London: Routledge.

Braithwaite, J. (1989) *Crime, Shame and Reintegration*, Cambridge: Cambridge University Press.

Braithwaite, J. (2001) 'Crime in a Convict Republic', *Modern Law Review*, 64 (1): 11–50.

Braithwaite, J. (2002) *Restorative Justice and Responsive Regulation*, Oxford: Oxford University Press.

Braithwaite, J. (2003) 'What's Wrong with the Sociology of Punishment', *Theoretical Criminology*, 7 (1): 5–28.

Brajuha, M. and Hallowell, L. (1986) 'Legal Intrusion and the Politics of Fieldwork: The Impact of the Brajuha Case', *Urban Life*, 14: 454–78.

Brantingham, P. J. and Brantingham, P. L. (1991) *Environmental Criminology*, revised edn, Prospect Heights, IL: Waveland.

Brayley, N. (2001) 'Coping with the Effects of Traumatic Stress', *PCW Review*, 4: 24–5.

Bright, M. (2002) 'Fury over Delay to "Corporate Killing" Law', *Observer*, 21 July: 6.

Bright, M. (2003) 'Youth Hit Hardest by Wave of New Laws', *Observer*, 13 April: 9.

Bristow, E. J. (1977) *Vice and Vigilance: Purity Movements in Britain since 1750*, Totowa, NJ: Rowman and Littlefield.

British Institute for Brain-Injured Children (2005) *Ain't Misbehavin: Young People with Learning and Communication Difficulties and Anti-Social Behaviour*. A report prepared by BIBIC. Campaign update. www.bibic.org.uk.

Brogden, M. and Nijhar, P. (2000) *Crime, Abuse and the Elderly*, Cullompton: Willan.

Brogden, M., Jefferson, T. and Walklate, S. (1988) *Introducing Policework*, London: Unwin Hyman.

Bromley, R. D. F. and Nelson, A. L. (2002) 'Alcohol-Related Crime and Disorder across Urban Space and Time: Evidence from a British City', *Geoforum*, 33 (2): 239–54.

Broome Report (1985) *Working Party on Drugs Related Crime*, London: Association of Chief Police Officers.

Brown, C. (1984) *Black and White in Britain*, The Third PSI Survey, London: Policy Studies Institute.

Brown, J. (1996) 'Police Research: Some Critical Issues', in F. Leishman, B. Loveday and S. Savage (eds) *Core Issues in Policing*, Harlow: Longman.

Brown, J. and Heidensohn, F. (2000) *Gender and Policing: Comparative Perspectives*, Basingstoke: Macmillan.

Brown, L. R. et al. (eds) (2004) *The State of the World: 2004. A Worldwatch Institute Report on Progress toward a Sustainable Society*, London: Earthscan.

Brown, S. (1994) *Whose Challenge? Youth, Crime and Everyday Life in Middlesbrough*, published report to Middlesbrough City Challenge Partnership, Middlesbrough: Middlesbrough City Challenge.

Brown, S. (1998) *Understanding Youth and Crime: Listening to Youth?*, Buckingham: Open University Press.

Brown, S. (2003) *Crime and Law in Media Culture*, Buckingham: Open University Press.

Brownlee, I. (1998) *Community Punishment: A Critical Introduction*, Harlow: Longman.

Brownmiller, S. (1975) *Against Our Will: Men, Women and Rape*, New York: Simon and Schuster.

Brundson, C. (1998) 'Structure of Anxiety: Recent British Television Crime Fiction', *Screen*, 39 (3): 223–43.

Bucke, T. (1997) *Ethnicity and Contacts with the Police: Latest Findings from the British Crime Survey*, Home Office Research Findings 59, London: Home Office.

Budd, T. (1999) *Violence at Work: Findings from the British Crime Survey*, London: Home Office.

Budd, T. and Mattinson, J. (2000) *The Extent and Nature of Stalking: Findings from the 1998 British Crime Survey*, Home Office Research Study 210, London: Home Office.

Bullard, R. (1990) *Dumping in Dixie: Race, Class and Environmental Quality*, Boulder, CO: Westview Press.

Bulmer, M. (1984) *The Chicago School of Sociology: Institutionalization, Diversity, and the Rise of Sociological Research*, Chicago, IL: University of Chicago Press.

Burgess, A. (1962) *A Clockwork Orange*, London: Heinemann.

Burke, M. E. (1993) *Coming Out of the Blue*, London: Cassell.

Burke, R. H. (ed.) (1998) *Zero Tolerance Policing*, Leicester: Perpetuity Press.

Burke, R. H. (2001) *An Introduction to Criminological Theory*, Cullompton: Willan.

Burt, C. (1925) *The Young Delinquent*, London: University of London Press.

Bushway, S. and Weisburd, D. (2005) *Quantitative Methods in Criminology*, Aldershot: Ashgate.

Button, M. (2002) *Private Policing*, Cullompton: Willan.

Byrne, P. J. (1993) *Criminal Law and Colonial Subject: New South Wales, 1810–1830*, Cambridge: Cambridge University Press

Cain, M. (1973) *Society and the Policeman's Role*, London: Routledge and Kegan Paul.

Cain, M. (ed.) (1989) *Growing Up Good: Policing the Behaviour of Girls in Europe*, London: Sage.

Calder, A. (1991) *The Myth of the Blitz*, London: Cape.

Campbell, A. (1981) *Girl Delinquents*, Oxford: Basil Blackwell.

Campbell, A. (1984) *The Girls in the Gang: A Report from New York City*, Oxford: Basil Blackwell.

Campbell, A. (2007) 'Global Disasters Rocket by 60% in Just a Decade', *London Metro*, 13 December: 15.

Campbell, D. (1991) *That Was Business, This Is Personal*, London: Mandarin.

Campbell, D. (1994) *The Underworld*, London: BBC Books.

Caputi, J. (1988) *The Age of Sex Crime*, London: Women's Press.

Carlen, P. (1976) *Magistrates' Justice*, London: Martin Robertson.

Carlen, P. (1983) *Women's Imprisonment: A Study in Social Control*, London: Routledge and Kegan Paul.

Carlen, P. (1988) *Women, Crime and Poverty*, Buckingham: Open University Press.

Carlen, P. (1990) *Alternatives to Women's Imprisonment*, Buckingham: Open University Press.

Carlen, P. (1996) *Jigsaw: A Political Criminology of Youth Homelessness*, Buckingham: Open University Press.

Carlen, P. (1998) *Sledgehammer: Women's Imprisonment at the Millennium*, Basingstoke: Macmillan.

Carlen, P. (2002) 'Carceral Clawback: The Case of Women's Imprisonment in Canada', *Punishment and Society*, 4 (1): 115–21.

Carlen, P. and Worrall, A. (eds) (1987) *Gender, Crime, and Justice*, Milton Keynes: Open University Press.

Carrabine, E. (2004) *Power, Discourse and Resistance: A Genealogy of the Strangeways Prison Riot*, Aldershot: Dartmouth.

Carrabine, E. (2005) 'Prison Riots, Social Order and the Problem of Legitimacy', *British Journal of Criminology*, 45 (6): 896–913.

Carrabine, E. (2006) 'Punishment, Rights and Justice', in L. Morris (ed.) *Rights: Sociological Perspectives*, London: Routledge.

Carrabine, E. (2008) *Crime, Culture and the Media*, Cambridge: Polity.

Carrabine, E., Lee, M. and South, N. (2000) 'Social Wrongs and Human Rights in Late Modern Britain: Social Exclusion, Crime Control and Prospects for a Public Criminology', *Social Justice*, 27 (2): 193–211.

Carrabine, E., Cox, P., Lee, M. and South, N. (2002) *Crime in Modern Britain*, Oxford: Oxford University Press.

Carson, R. (1962) *Silent Spring*, Boston, MA: Houghton Mifflin.

Carter, F. and Turnock, D. (1993) *Environmental Problems in Eastern Europe*, London: Routledge.

Cashmore, E. and McLaughlin, E. (1991) *Out of Order? Policing Black People*, London: Routledge.

Castells, M. (1996) *The Rise of Network Society*, Oxford: Blackwell.

Castells, M. (1998) *End of Millennium*, Oxford: Blackwell.

Cavadino, M. and Dignan, J. (2002) *The Penal System: An Introduction*, 3rd edn, London: Sage.

Cavadino, M. and Dignan, J. (2005) *Penal Systems: A Comparative Approach*, London: Sage.

Cavadino, M. and Dignan, J. (2007) *The Penal System: An Introduction*, 4th edn, London: Sage.

Cavender, G. and Deutsch, S. (2007) 'CSI and Moral Authority: The Police and Science', *Crime, Media, Culture*, 3 (1): 67–81.

Centre for Contemporary Cultural Studies (1980) *Women Take Issue*, London: Hutchinson.

Centre for Contemporary Cultural Studies (1982) *The Empire Strikes Back*, London: Hutchinson.

Cere, R. (2003) 'Digital Counter-cultures and the Nature of Electronic Social and Political Movements', in Y. Jewkes (ed.) *Dot.cons: Crime, Deviance and Identity on the Internet*, Cullompton: Willan.

Chambliss, W. (1976) 'The State and Criminal Law', in W. Chambliss and M. Mankoff (eds) *Whose Law, What Order?*, New York: Wiley.

Chambliss, W. J. (1989/1994) 'State Organized Crime', in N. Passas (ed.) *Organized Crime*, London: Dartmouth.

Champion, D. J. (2005) *Research Methods for Criminal Justice and Criminology*, 3rd edn, Upper Saddle River, NJ: Prentice Hall.

Chan, J. (1997) *Changing Police Culture: Policing in a Multicultural Society*, Cambridge: Cambridge University Press.

Chan, J. (2005) 'Globalisation, Reflexivity and the Practice of Criminology', in J. Sheptycki and A. Wardak (eds) *Transnational and Comparative Criminology*, London: Glasshouse.

Chancer, L and McLaughlin, E (2007) 'Public Criminologies: Diverse Perspectives on Academia and Policy', *Theoretical Criminology*, 11 (2): 155–73.

Chandola, T. (2001) 'The Fear of Crime and Area Differences in Health', *Health and Place*, 7 (2): 105–16.

Chatterjee, B. (2001) 'Last of the Rainmacs: Thinking about Pornography in Cyberspace', in D. Wall (ed.) *Crime and the Internet*, London: Routledge.

Chatterton, P. and Hollands, R. (2003) *Urban Nightscapes: Youth Cultures, Pleasure Spaces and Corporate Power*, London: Routledge.

Chesterton, A. (1928) *Women of the Underworld*, London: Stanley Paul.

Chivite-Matthews, N. and Maggs, P. (2002) *Crime, Policing and Justice: The Experience of Older People*, Home Office Statistical Bulletin 8/02, London: Home Office.

Choo, C. (2001) *Mission Girls: Aboriginal Women on Catholic Missions in the Kimberley, Western Australia, 1900–1950*, Nedlands: University of Western Australia Press.

Christie, N. (1977) 'Conflicts as Property', *British Journal of Criminology*, 17 (1): 1–15.

Christie, N. (1986) 'The Ideal Victim', in E. A. Fattah (ed.) *From Crime Policy to Victim Policy*, Basingstoke: Macmillan.

Christie, N. (2000) *Crime Control as Industry*, 2nd edn, London: Routledge.

Cicourel, A. (1968) *The Social Organization of Juvenile Justice*, New York: John Wiley.

Clancy, A., Hough, M., Aust, R. and Kershaw, C. (2001) *Crime, Policing and Justice: The Experience of Ethnic Minorities*, Findings from the 2000 British Crime Survey, Home Office Research Study 223, London: Home Office.

Clapson, M. (1998) *Invincible Green Suburbs, Brave New Towns: Social Change and Urban Dispersal in Post-War England*, Manchester: Manchester University Press.

Clapson, M. (2003) *Suburban Century: Social Change and Urban Growth in England and the United States*, Oxford: Berg.

Clark, A. (1987) *Women's Silence, Men's Violence: Sexual Assault in England 1770–1845*, London: Pandora.

Clark, L. and Lewis, D. (1977) *Rape: The Price of Coercive Sexuality*, Toronto: Women's Press.

Clarke, J., Hall, S., Jefferson, T. and Roberts, B. (1976) 'Subcultures, Cultures and Class', in S. Hall and T. Jefferson (eds) *Resistance through Rituals: Youth Subcultures in Post-war Britain*, London: Routledge.

Clarke, R. V. and Brown, R. (2003) 'International Trafficking in Stolen Vehicles', *Crime and Justice: A Review of Research*, 30: 197–227.

Clarke, R. V. and Hough, M. (1984) *Crime and Police Effectiveness*, London: Home Office.

Clemmer, D. (1958) *The Prison Community*, New York: Rinehart.

Clifford, M. (ed.) (1998) *Environmental Crime: Enforcement, Policy and Social Responsibility*, Gaithersburg, MD: Aspen.

Cloward, R. and Ohlin, E. L. (1960) *Delinquency and Opportunity: A Theory of Delinquent Gangs*, New York: Free Press.

Cohen, A. K. (1955) *Delinquent Boys: The Culture of the Gang*, Glencoe, IL: Free Press.

Cohen, J. (2002) *Understanding Drugs and the Law*, London: Drugscope.

Cohen, P. (1972) 'Subcultural Conflict and Working

Class Community', *Working Papers in Cultural Studies*, 2: 5–52.

Cohen, P. (1979) 'Policing the Working Class City', in B. Fine, R. Kinsey, J. Lea, S. Picciotto and J. Young (eds) *Capitalism and the Rule of Law*, London: Hutchinson.

Cohen, R. and Kennedy, P. (2000) *Global Sociology*, Basingstoke: Macmillan.

Cohen, S. (ed.) (1971) *Images of Deviance*, Harmondsworth: Penguin.

Cohen, S. (1972/2002) *Folk Devils and Moral Panics: The Creation of the Mods and Rockers*, London: MacGibbon and Kee.

Cohen, S. (1973a) 'Mods and Rockers: The Inventory as Manufactured News', in S. Cohen and J. Young (eds) *The Manufacture of News*, London: Constable.

Cohen, S. (1973b) 'The Failures of Criminology', *The Listener*, 8 November: 622–5.

Cohen, S. (1979a) 'Guilt, Justice and Tolerance: Some Old Concepts for a New Criminology', in D. Downes and P. Rock (eds) *Deviant Interpretations*, Oxford: Martin Robertson.

Cohen, S. (1979b) 'The Punitive City: Notes on the Dispersal of Social Control', *Contemporary Crises*, 3 (4): 341–63.

Cohen, S. (1980) 'Symbols of Trouble: Introduction to the New Edition', in *Folk Devils and Moral Panics*, 2nd edn, London: MacGibbon and Kee.

Cohen, S. (1984) 'The Deeper Structures of the Law, or "Beware the Rulers Bearing Justice"', *Contemporary Crises*, 8: 83–93.

Cohen, S. (1985) *Visions of Social Control: Crime, Punishment and Classification*, Cambridge: Polity.

Cohen, S. (1993) 'Human Rights and Crimes of the State: The Culture of Denial', *Australian and New Zealand Journal of Criminology*, 26 (1): 87–115.

Cohen, S. (1996a) 'Human Rights and Crimes of the State', in J. Muncie, E. McLaughlin and M. Langan (eds) *Criminological Perspectives: A Reader*, London: Sage.

Cohen, S. (1996b) 'Crime and Politics: Spot the Difference', *British Journal of Sociology*, 47 (1): 1–21.

Cohen, S. (1997) 'Intellectual Scepticsm and Political Commitment', in P. Walton and J. Young (eds) *The New Criminology Revisted*, Basingstoke: Macmillan.

Cohen, S. (2001) *States of Denial: Knowing about Atrocities and Suffering*, Cambridge: Polity.

Cohen, S. and Taylor, L. (1972/1981) *Psychological Survival: The Experience of Long-Term Imprisonment*, Harmondsworth: Penguin.

Cohen, S. and Young, J. (eds) (1973) *The Manufacture of News*, London: Constable.

Cohen, Sherrill. (1992) *The Evolution of Women's Asylums since 1500: From Refuges for Ex-prostitutes to Shelters for Battered Women*, Oxford: Oxford University Press.

Coleman, C. and Moynihan, J. (1996) *Understanding Crime Data: Haunted by the Dark Figure*, Buckingham: Open University Press.

Coleman, R. and Sim, J. (2000) '"You'll Never Walk Alone": CCTV Surveillance, Order and Neo-liberal Rule in Liverpool City Centre', *British Journal of Sociology*, 51 (4): 623–39.

Collard, A. with Contrucci, J. (1988) *Rape of the Wild: Man's Violence against Animals and the Earth*, London: Women's Press.

Collier, R. (1998) *Masculinities, Crime and Criminology: Men, Heterosexuality and the Criminal(ised) Other*, London: Sage.

Collison, M. (1995) *Police, Drugs and Community*, London: Free Association Books.

Collison, M. (1996) 'In Search of the High Life: Drugs, Crime, Masculinity and Consumption', *British Journal of Criminology*, 36 (3): 428–44.

Commission for Racial Equality (2003) *The Murder of Zahid Mubarek: A Formal Investigation by the Commission for Racial Equality into HM Prison Service of England and Wales, Part 1*, London: CRE.

Conklin, J. (1994) *Art Crime*, London: Praeger.

Conrad, P. and Schneider, W. (1992) *Deviance and Medicalization*, St Louis: Mosby.

Coomber, R. and South, N. (2004) *Drug Use and Cultural Contexts 'Beyond the West'*, London: Free Association Books.

Coomber, R. and Turnbull, P. (2007) 'Arenas of Drug Transactions: Adolescent Cannabis Transactions in England – Social Supply', *Journal of Drug Issues*, Fall.

Corbett, C. (2003) *Car Crime*, Cullompton: Willan.

Cornish, D. and Clarke, R. (eds) (1986) *The Reasoning Criminal*, New York: Springer-Verlag.

Cote, S. (ed.) (2002) *Criminological Theories: Bridging the Past to the Future*, Thousand Oaks, CA: Sage.

Cottle, S. (ed.) (2003) *Media Organization and Production*, London: Sage.

Cowie, J., Cowie, V. and Slater, E. (1968) *Delinquency in Girls*, London: Heinemann.

Cox, P. (2002) 'Race, Delinquency and Difference in Twentieth Century Britain', in P. Cox and H. Shore (eds) *Becoming Delinquent: British and European Youth, 1650–1950*, Aldershot: Ashgate.

Cox, P. (2003) *Gender, Justice and Welfare: Bad Girls in Britain, 1900–1950*, Basingstoke: Palgrave.

Cox, P. and Shore, H. (eds) (2002) *Becoming Delinquent: British and European Youth, 1650–1950*, Aldershot: Ashgate.

Coy, M., Horvath, M. and Kelly, L. (2007) 'It's Just Like Going to the Supermarket: Men Buying Sex in East London', *Report for Safe Exit*, London: CWASU.

Craine, S. (1997) 'The "Black Magic Roundabout": Cyclical Transitions, Social Exclusion and Alternative Careers', in R. MacDonald (ed.) *Youth, the 'Underclass' and Social Exclusion*, London: Routledge.

Crank, J. (2004) *Understanding Police Culture*, Cincinnati, OH: Anderson and Co.

Crawford, A. (2002) *Crime and Insecurity: The Governance of Safety in Europe*, Cullompton: Willan.

Crawford, A., Jones, T., Woodhouse, T. and Young, J. (1990) *Second Islington Crime Survey*, London: Middlesex Polytechnic.

Cressey, D. R. (1969) *Theft of the Nation*, New York: Harper and Row.

Cressey, P. G. (1932) *The Taxi-Dance Hall*, Chicago, IL: University of Chicago Press.

Creswell, J. W. (2003) *Research Design: Qualitative, Quantitative, and Mixed Methods*, 2nd edn, London: Sage.

Crewe, B. (2007) 'The Sociology of Imprisonment', in Y. Jewkes (ed.) *Handbook on Prisons*, Cullompton: Willan.

Critcher, C. (2003) *Moral Panics and the Media*, Buckingham: Open University Press.

Croall, H. (1992) *White Collar Crime*, Buckingham: Open University Press.

Croall, H. (1996) 'Crime: Understanding More and Condemning Less?', *Reviewing Sociology*, 10 (3).

Croall, H. (1998) 'Business, Crime and the Community', *International Journal of Risk, Security and Crime Prevention*, 3 (4): 281–92.

Croall, H. (1998) *Crime and Society in Britain*, London: Longman.

Croall, H. (2001) *Understanding White Collar Crime*, Buckingham: Open University Press.

Croall, H. (2007) 'Food Crime', in P. Beirne and N. South (eds) *Issues in Green Criminology*, Cullompton: Willan.

Cromwell, P. F. (ed.) (2003) *In Their Own Words: Criminals on Crime*, 3rd edn, Los Angeles, CA: Roxbury.

Crow, I. (2001) *The Treatment and Rehabilitation of Offenders*, London: Sage.

Crowther, C. (2000) *Policing Urban Poverty*, Basingstoke: Macmillan.

Cullen, F. T. and Agnew, R. (2003) *Criminological Theory: Past to Present (Essential Readings)*, 2nd edn, Los Angeles, CA: Roxbury Park.

Cumming, E., Cumming, I. and Edell, L. (1965) 'The Policeman as Philosopher, Guide and Friend', *Social Problems*, 12: 276–86.

Cunneen, C. and White, R. (2006) 'Australia: Control, Containment or Empowerment?', in J. Muncie and B. Goldson (eds) *Comparative Youth Justice*, London: Sage.

Curran, J. and Seaton, J. (1994) *Power without Responsibility: The Press and Broadcasting in Britain*, London: Routledge.

Currie, E. (1996) *Is America Really Winning the War on Crime and Should Britain Follow Its Example?*, London: NACRO.

Currie, E. (2007) 'Against Marginality: Arguments for a Public Criminology', *Theoretical Criminology*, 11 (2): 175–90.

D'Cruze, S. (1998) *Crimes of Outrage: Sex, Violence and Victorian Working Women*, London: UCL Press.

D'Cruze, S. (ed.) (2000) *Everyday Violence in Britain, 1850–1950: Gender and Class*, Harlow: Longman.

D'Cruze, S., Walklate, S. and Pegg, S. (2006) *Murder: Social and Historical Approaches to Understanding Murder and Murderers*, Cullompton: Willan.

Daly, K. (1989) 'Criminal Justice Ideologies and Practices in Different Voices: Some Feminist Questions about Justice', *International Journal of the Sociology of Law*, 17: 1–18.

Daly, K. (1997) 'Different Ways of Conceptualizing Sex/Gender in Feminist Theory and Their Implications for Criminology', *Theoretical Criminology*, 1 (1): 25–51.

Daly, K. (2002) 'Restorative Justice: The Real Story', *Punishment and Society*, 4 (1): 55–79.

Daly, K. and Bordt, R. L. (1995) 'Sex Effects and Sentencing: An Analysis of the Statistical Literature', *Justice Quarterly*, 12 (1): 141–75.

Daly, K. and Chesney-Lind, M. (1988) 'Feminism and Criminology', *Justice Quarterly*, 5 (4): 498–538.

Daly, M. (2007) 'Plant Warfare', *Druglink*, March/April: 6–9.

Darbyshire, P. (1991) 'The Lamp That Shows That Freedom Lives: Is It Worth the Candle?', *Criminal Law Review*, 740.

Davies, A. (1999) '"These Viragoes Are No Less Cruel Than the Lads": Young Women, Gangs and Violence in Late Victorian Manchester and Salford', *British Journal of Criminology*, 39: 72–89.

Davies, A. (2000) 'Youth Gangs, Gender and Violence, 1870–1900', in S. D'Cruze (ed.) *Everyday Violence in Britain, 1850–1950: Gender and Class*, Harlow: Longman.

Davies, M., Croall, H. and Tyrer, J. (2005) *Criminal Justice: An Introduction to the Criminal Justice System in England and Wales*, 3rd edn, Harlow: Longman.

Davies, P., Francis, P. and Jupp, V. (eds) (2003) *Victimisation: Theory, Research and Policy*, Basingstoke: Palgrave Macmillan.

Davis, J. (1989) 'From Rookeries to Communities: Race, Poverty and Policing in London, 1850–1985', *History Workshop*, 27: 66–85.

Davis, L. (1983) *Factual Fictions: The Origins of the English Novel*, New York: Columbia University Press.

Davis, M. (1992) *City of Quartz: Excavating the Future in Los Angeles*, London: Verso.

Davis, M. (1993) 'Dead West: Ecocide in Marlboro Country', *New Left Review*, 200: 49–73.

Davis, M. (1994) *Beyond Blade Runner: Urban Control – The Ecology of Fear*, Open Magazine Pamphlet series, New York: New Press.

Davis, M. (1998) *Ecology of Fear: Los Angeles and the Imagination of Disaster*, New York: Metropolitan Books, Henry Holt (1999, Vintage Books).

Davis, P., Francis, P. and Jupp, V. (2000) *Victimization: Theory, Research and Policy*, Basingstoke: London: Macmillan.

Day, D. (1991) *The Eco-wars*, London: Paladin.

De Giorgi, A. (2006) *Re-thinking the Political Economy of Punishment: Perspectives on Post-Fordism and Penal Politics*, Aldershot: Ashgate.

de Haan, W. (1990) *The Politics of Redress: Crime, Punishment and Penal Abolition*, London: Sage.

de Haan, W. and Loader, I. (2002) 'On the Emotions of Crime, Punishment and Social Control', *Theoretical Criminology*, 6 (3): 243–53.

Deehan, A. (1999) *Alcohol and Crime: Taking Stock*, Policing and Crime Reduction Unit, London: Home Office.

Delgado, R. and Stefancic, J. (1997) *Must We Defend Nazis?* New York: New York University Press.

Dell, S. (1971) *Silence in Court*, Occasional Papers on Social Administration 42, London: Bell.

Dennis, N. (1993) *Rising Crime and the Dismembered Family*, Choice in Welfare Series 13, London: IEA.

Dershowitz, A. (2002) *Why Terrorism Works: Understanding the Threat, Responding to the Challenge*, New Haven, CT: Yale University Press.

Di Filipo, J. (2000) 'Pornography on the Web', in D. Gauntlett (ed.) *Web.studies: Rewiring Media Studies for the Digital Age*, London: Arnold.

Dingwall, G. (2005) *Alcohol and Crime*, Cullompton: Willan.

Ditton, J. (1977) *Part-Time Crime: An Ethnography of Fiddling and Pilferage*, Basingstoke: Macmillan.

Ditton, J., Bannister, J., Gilchrist, E. and Farrall, S. (1999) 'Afraid or Angry? Recalibrating the "Fear" of Crime', *International Review of Victimology*, 6: 83–99.

Dobash, R. E. and Dobash, R. P. (1992) *Women, Violence and Social Change*, London: Routledge.

Dobash, R. E., Dobash, R. P. and Noaks, L. (eds) (1995) *Gender and Crime*, Cardiff: University of Wales Press.

Dobash, R. P., Dobash, R. E. and Gutteridge, S. (1986) *The Imprisonment of Women*, Oxford: Blackwell.

Dobson, A. (1990) *Green Political Thought*, London: Unwin Hyman.

Doggett, M. (1992) *Marriage, Wife-Beating and the Law in Victorian England*, London: Weidenfeld and Nicolson.

Dorling, D. (2005) 'Prime Suspect: Murder in Britain', in P. Hillyard, C. Pantazis, S. Tombs, D. Gordon and D. Dorling (eds) *Criminal*

Obsessions: Why Harm Matters More than Crime, London: Crime and Society Foundation.

Dorn, N. and South, N. (eds) (1987) *A Land Fit for Heroin?*, Basingstoke: Macmillan.

Dorn, N. and South, N. (1990) 'Drug Markets and Law Enforcement', *British Journal of Criminology*, 30 (2): 171–88.

Dorn, N., Levi, M. and King, L. (2005) *Literature Review on Upper Level Drug Trafficking*, Online Report 22, London: Home Office.

Dorn, N., Murji, K. and South, N. (1992) *Traffickers: Drug Markets and Law Enforcement*, London: Routledge.

Douglas, J. and Rasmussen, P. (1977) *The Nude Beach*, Beverly Hills, CA: Sage.

Douglas, M. (1966) *Purity and Danger*, Harmondsworth: Penguin.

Doward, J. (2007) 'Drugs Strategy Debate "Is a Sham"', *Observer*, 21 October: 26.

Doward, J. (2007a) 'Prisoners to Be Put in Cargo', *Observer*, 18 March: 18.

Doward, J. (2007b) 'New Prison Row over Shared Cells', *Observer*, 27 May: 19.

Doward, J. (2007c) 'Outcry over "Routine" Use of Restraints on Child Prisoners', *Observer*, 18 February: 13.

Doward, J. (2007d) 'Children "At Risk" from Jail Restraint', *Observer*, 8 July: 6.

Doward, J. (2008) 'UN Rejects British Denial on Rendition', *Observer*, 2 March: 3.

Dowie, M. (1979) 'The Corporate Crime of the Century', *Mother Jones*, November.

Downes, D. (1988) 'The Sociology of Crime and Social Control in Britain, 1960–1987', in P. Rock (ed.) special issue, *British Journal of Criminology*, 28 (2): 175–87.

Downes, D. and Rock, P. (1979) *Deviant Interpretations: Problems in Criminology*, Oxford: Clarendon Press.

Downes, D. and Rock, P. (1998) *Understanding Deviance: A Guide to the Sociology of Crime and Rule Breaking*, 3rd edn (4th edn, 2003), Oxford: Oxford University Press.

Downes, D., Rock, P., Chinkin, C. and Gearty, C. (eds) (2007) *Crime, Social Control and Human Rights: From Moral Panics to States of Denial, Essays in Honour of Stanley Cohen*, Cullompton: Willan.

Du Bois, W. E. B. (1901/2002) 'The Spawn of Slavery: The Convict–Lease System in the South', reprinted in S. Gabbidon, H. T. Greene and V. D. Young (eds) (2001) *African American Classics in Criminology and Criminal Justice*, Thousand Oaks, CA: Sage.

Du Rees, H. (2001) 'Can Criminal Law Protect the Environment?', *Journal of Scandinavian Studies*, 2: 109–26.

Duff, P. and Hutton, N. (eds) (1999) *Criminal Justice in Scotland*, Aldershot: Ashgate.

Duff, R. (1996) 'Penal Communications: Recent Work in the Philosophy of Punishment', in M. Tonry (ed.) *Crime and Justice: A Review of Research*, 20: 1–97.

Duff, R. and Garland, D. (1994) 'Introduction: Thinking about Punishment', in R. Duff and D. Garland (eds) *A Reader on Punishment*, Oxford: Oxford University Press.

Dunbar, I. and Langdon, A. (1998) *Tough Justice: Sentencing and Penal Policies in the 1990s*, London: Blackstone.

Dunhill, C. (1989) 'Women, Racist Attacks and the Response from Anti-racist Groups', in C. Dunhill (ed.) *The Boys in Blue: Women's Challenge to the Police*, London: Virago.

Durkheim, É. (1893/1960) *The Division of Labor in Modern Society*, Glencoe, Ill.: Free Press.

Durkheim, É. (1895/1988) *The Rules of Sociological Method*, London: Routledge.

Durkheim, É. (1901/1984) 'Two Laws of Penal Evolution', in S. Lukes and A. Scull (eds) *Durkheim and the Law*, Oxford: Basil Blackwell.

Dworkin, A. (1981) *Pornography: Men Possessing Women*, London: Women's Press.

Dworkin, A. (1987) *Intercourse*, London: Arrow Books.

Dworkin, R. (1978) *Taking Rights Seriously*, London: Duckworth.

Eales, J. (1998) *Women in Early Modern England, 1500–1700*, London: UCL Press.

Eaton, M. (1986) *Justice for Women?* Buckingham: Open University Press.

Eck, J. and Maguire, E. (2000) 'Have Changes in Policing Reduced Violent Crime? An Assessment of the Evidence', in A. Blumstein and J. Wallman (eds) *The Crime Drop in America*, Cambridge: Cambridge University Press.

Edgar, K., O'Donnell, I. and Martin, C. (2003) *Prison Violence: The Dynamics of Conflict, Fear and Power*, Cullompton: Willan.

Edmunds, M., Hough, M. and Urquia, M. (1996)

Tackling Local Drug Markets, Crime Detection and Prevention Series Paper 80, London: Home Office.

Edwards, S. (1984) *Women on Trial*, Manchester: Manchester University Press.

Edwards, S. (1989) *Policing Domestic Violence*, London: Sage.

Edwards, S. (1990) 'Violence against Women, Feminism and the Law', in L. Gelsthorpe and A. Morris (eds) *Feminist Perspectives in Criminology*, Milton Keynes: Open University Press.

Edwards, S., Edwards, T. and Fields, C. (eds) (1996) *Environmental Crime and Criminality: Theoretical and Practical Issues*, New York: Garland.

Eisenman, S. (2007) *The Abu Ghraib Effect*, Chicago, IL: University of Chicago Press.

Eisner, M. (2003) 'Long-term Historical Trends in Violent Crime', *Crime and Justice: A Review of Research*, 30: 83–142.

Elias, N. (1939/1978) *The Civilising Process*, trans Edward Jephcott, Oxford: Blackwell.

Emsley, C. (1983) *Policing and Its Context 1750–1870*, Basingstoke: Macmillan.

Emsley, C. (1996) *The English Police: A Political and Social History*, 2nd edn, Harlow: Longman.

Emsley, C. (2002) 'The History of Crime and Crime Control Institutions', in M. Maguire, R. Morgan and R. Reiner (eds) *The Oxford Handbook of Criminology*, 3rd edn, Oxford: Oxford University Press.

Emsley, C. (2005) *Crime and Society in England 1750–1900*, 3rd edn, London: Longman.

Emsley, C. and Knafla, L. A. (eds) (1996) *Crime and Histories of Crime: Studies in the Historiography of Crime and Criminal Justice in Modern History*, Westport, CT and London: Greenwood Press.

Engels, F. (1845/1958) *The Condition of the Working Class in England*, Oxford: Basil Blackwell.

Eribon, D. (1992) *Michel Foucault*, London: Faber and Faber.

Ericson, R. (2007) *Crime in an Insecure World*, Cambridge: Polity.

Ericson, R. and Haggerty, K. (1997) *Policing the Risk Society*, Oxford: Clarendon Press.

Ericson, R., Baranek, P. and Chan, J. (1991) *Representing Order*, Milton Keynes: Open University Press.

Ettore, E. (1992) *Women and Substance Use*, Basingstoke: Macmillan.

European Committee for the Prevention of Torture (1991) *Report to the United Kingdom Government on the Visit to the United Kingdom Carried Out by the CPT from 29 July 1990 to 10 August 1990*, Strasbourg: Council of Europe.

Evans, D. J., Fyfe, N. R and Herbert, D.T. (eds) (1992) *Crime, Policing and Place: Essays in Environmental Criminology*, London: Routledge.

Farnham, F. and James, D. (2001) '"Dangerousness" and Dangerous Law', *The Lancet*, 358: 1926.

Farrall, S. and Gadd, D. (2004) 'Research Note: The Frequency of the Fear of Crime', *British Journal of Criminology*, 44: 127–32.

Farrington, D. P. (1997) 'Human Developments and Criminal Careers', in M. Maguire, R. Morgan and R. Reiner (eds) *The Oxford Handbook of Criminology*, 2nd edn, Oxford: Oxford University Press.

Farrington, D. P. (2002) 'Developmental Criminology and Risk-Focused Prevention', in M. Maguire, R. Morgan and R. Reiner (eds) *The Oxford Handbook of Criminology*, 3rd edn, Oxford: Oxford University Press.

Farrington, D. and Morris, A. (1983) 'Sex, Sentencing and Reconviction', *British Journal of Criminology*, 23 (3): 229–48.

Fattah, E. A. (1986) 'On Some Visible and Hidden Dangers of Victim Movements', in E. A. Fattah (ed.) *From Crime Policy to Victim Policy*, Basingstoke: Macmillan.

Feeley, M. (1994) 'The Decline of Women in the Criminal Process: A Comparative History', *Criminal Justice History*, 15: 235–74.

Feeley, M. and Simon, J. (1992) 'The New Penology: Notes on the Emerging Strategy of Corrections and Its Implications', *Criminology*, 30 (4): 449–74.

Feeley, M. and Simon, J. (1994) 'Actuarial Justice: The Emerging New Criminal Law', in D. Nelken (ed.) *The Futures of Criminology*, London: Sage.

Feeley, M. and Simon, J. (2007) '*Folk Devils and Moral Panics: An Appreciation from North America*', in D. Downes, P. Rock, C. Chinkin and C. Gearty (eds) *Crime, Social Control and Human Rights: From Moral Panics to States of Denial, Essays in Honour of Stanley Cohen*, Cullompton: Willan.

Felson, M. (1998) *Crime and Everyday Life*, Thousand Oaks, CA: Pine Forge.

Fenwick, M. and Hayward, K. J. (2000) 'Youth Crime Excitement and Consumer Culture: The Reconstruction of Aetiology in Contemporary Criminology', in J. Pickford (ed.) *Youth Justice: Theory and Practice*, London: Cavendish.

Ferrell, J. (1992) 'Making Sense of Crime: Review Essay on Jack Katz's *Seductions of Crime*', *Social Justice*, 19 (3): 111–23.

Ferrell, J. (1998) 'Criminological Verstehen: Inside the Immediacy of Crime', in J. Ferrell and M. Hamm (eds) *Ethnography at the Edge: Crime, Deviance and Field Research*, Boston, MA: Northeastern University Press.

Ferrell, J. (1999) 'Cultural Criminology', *Annual Review of Sociology*, 25: 395–418.

Ferrell, J. (2004) 'Boredom, Crime and Criminology', *Theoretical Criminology*, 8 (3): 287–302.

Ferrell, J. (2006) *Empire of Scrounge*, New York: New York University Press.

Ferrell, J. and Hamm, M. (eds) (1998) *Ethnography at the Edge: Crime, Deviance and Field Research*, Boston, MA: Northeastern University Press.

Ferrell, J. and Sanders, C. R. (eds) (1995) *Cultural Criminology*, Boston, MA: Northeastern University Press.

Ferrell, J., Hayward, K. and Young, J. (2008) *Cultural Criminology: An Invitation*, London: Sage.

Ferrell, J., Hayward, K., Morrison, W. and Presdee, M. (eds) (2004) *Cultural Criminology Unleashed*, London: Glasshouse Press.

Fielder, L. (1982) *What was Literature?: Class Culture and Mass Society*, New York: Simon and Schuster.

Findlay, M. (1999) *The Globalisation of Crime*, Cambridge: Cambridge University Press.

Findlay, M. and Duff, P. (eds) (1988) *The Jury under Attack*, London: Butterworths.

Fine, R. (1985) *Democracy and the Rule of Law*, London: Pluto.

Finney, A. (2006) *Domestic Violence, Sexual Assault and Stalking: Findings from the 2004/05 British Crime Survey*. Home Office Online Report 12/06. London: Home Office. http://www.home office.gov.uk/rds/pdfs06/rdsolr1206.pdf

Fishbein, D. (2000) *Biological Perspectives on Criminology*, Belmont, CA: Wadsworth.

Fiske, J. (1992) 'Popularity and the Politics of Information', in P. Dahlgren and C. Sparks (eds) *Journalism and Popular Culture*, London: Sage.

Fiske, J. (1998) 'Surveilling the City: Whiteness, the Black Man and Democratic Totalitarianism', *Theory, Culture and Society*, 15 (2): 67–88.

Fitzgerald, M. (1993) *Ethnic Minorities and the Criminal Justice System*, Royal Commission on Criminal Justice, Research Study 20, London: HMSO.

Fitzgerald, M. and Hale, C. (1996) *Ethnic Minorities, Victimization and Racial Harassment: Findings from the 1988 and 1992 British Crime Surveys*, London: Home Office.

Fitzgerald, M. and Sim, J. (1979) *British Prisons*, Oxford: Basil Blackwell.

Flew, A. (1981) *The Politics of Procrustes*, London: Temple Smith.

Fogel, D. (1975) *We Are the Living Proof: The Justice Model for Corrections*, Cincinnati, Ohio: Anderson.

Foldy, M. S. (1997) *The Trials of Oscar Wilde: Deviance, Morality and Late Victorian Society*, New Haven, CT: Yale University Press.

Ford, T. (2008) 'Jails Full as Inmates Reach Record Number', *The Times*, 9 February: www.times online.co.uk/tol/news/politics/article333803 7.ece?print=yes&randum=1208806844550 (accessed 21 April 2008).

Forrester, D., Chatterton, M. and Pease, K. (1988) *The Kirkholt Burglary Prevention Project*, Rochdale, Crime Prevention Unit Paper 13, London: Home Office.

Foster, J. (1989) 'Two Stations: An Ethnographic Study of Policing in the Inner City', in D. Downes (ed.) *Crime and the City*, Basingstoke: Macmillan.

Foster, J. (1990) *Villains: Crime and Community in the Inner City*, London: Routledge.

Foster, J. and Hope, T. (1993) *Housing, Community and Crime: The Impact of the Priority Estates Project*, Home Office Research Study 131, London: HMSO.

Foucault, M. (1975/1980) 'Prison Talk', in *Power/Knowledge: Selected Interviews and Other Writings*, Brighton: Harvester Press.

Foucault, M. (1977) *Discipline and Punish: The Birth of the Prison*, Harmondsworth: Penguin.

Foucault, M. (1978) *The History of Sexuality*, vol. 1, trans. R. Hurley, London: Allen Lane.

Fox, V. (1973) *Violence behind Bars: An Explosive Report on Prison Riots in the United States*, Westport, CT: Greenwood Press.

Fraser, F. (1994) *Mad Frank*, London: Little, Brown.

Frazier, E. F. (1949) *Crime and Delinquency: The Negro in the United States*, New York: Macmillan.

Freeman, N. (1996–7) 'That Was Business – This Is Personal: Professions of Violence in English Cinema from *Brighton Rock* to the Krays', *Close-Up: The Electronic Journal of British Cinema*, 1, Winter, www.shu.ac.uk/ services/lc/closeup

Freud, S. (1958) 'The Uncanny', in *On Creativity and the Unconscious: Papers on the Psychology of Art, Literature, Love, Religion*, New York: Harper and Row.

Frey, R. G. (1992) 'Torture', in L. C. Becker and C. B. Becker (eds) *Encyclopedia of Ethics*, Chicago, IL: St James Press.

Friman, H. R. and Andreas, P. (1999) *The Illicit Global Economy and State Power*, Oxford: Rowman and Littlefield.

Fyfe, N. (ed.) (1998) *Images of the Street: Planning, Identity and Control in Public Space*, London: Routledge.

Fyfe, N. (2004) 'Zero Tolerance, Maximum Surveillance? Deviance, Difference and Crime Control in the Late Modern City' in L. Lees (ed.) *The Emancipatory City?: Paradoxes and Possibilities*, London: Sage.

Gabbidon, S., Greene, H. T. and Young, V. D. (eds) (2001) *African American Classics in Criminology and Criminal Justice*, Thousand Oaks, CA: Sage.

Gabor, T. (1994) *Everybody Does It*, Toronto: University of Toronto Press.

Gadd, D. and Jefferson, T. (2007) *Psychosocial Criminology: An Introduction*, London: Sage.

Gagnon, J. (1977) *Human Sexuality in Today's World*, New York: Foresman.

Gagnon, J. H. and Simon, W. (1973/2005) *Sexual Conduct: The Social Sources of Human Sexuality*, New Jersey: Transaction Publishers.

Galeotti, M. (ed.) (2003) *Russian and Post-Soviet Organised Crime*, Dartmouth: Ashgate.

Galliher, J. F. (1995) 'Chicago's Two Worlds of Deviance Research: Whose Side Are They On?', in G. A. Fine (ed.) *A Second Chicago School? The Development of a Postwar American Sociology*, Chicago, IL: University of Chicago Press.

Gallo, E. and Ruggiero, V. (1991) 'The "Immaterial" Prison: Custody as the Manufacture of Handicaps', *International Journal of the Sociology of Law*, 19 (3): 273–91.

Garafalo, J. (1979) 'Victimisation and the Fear of Crime', *Journal of Research in Crime and Delinquency*, 16: 80–97.

Garfinkel, H. (1956a) 'Conditions of Successful Degradation Ceremonies', *American Journal of Sociology*, 61: 420–4.

Garfinkel, H. (1956b) 'The Trial as a Degradation Ceremony', *American Journal of Sociology*, 66.

Garland, D. (1985) *Punishment and Welfare*, Aldershot: Gower.

Garland, D. (1990) *Punishment and Modern Society: A Study in Social Theory*, Oxford: Clarendon Press.

Garland, D. (1991) 'Sociological Perspectives on Punishment', in M. Tonry (ed.) *Crime and Justice: A Review of Research*, 14: 115–65.

Garland, D. (1996) 'The Limits of the Sovereign State: Strategies of Crime Control in Contemporary Society', *British Journal of Criminology*, 36 (4): 445–71.

Garland, D. (1997) '"Governmentality" and the Problem of Crime', *Theoretical Criminology*, 1 (2): 173–214.

Garland, D. (2000) 'The Culture of High Crime Societies: Some Preconditions of Recent "Law and Order" Policies', *British Journal of Criminology*, 40 (3): 445–71.

Garland, D. (2001a) 'Introduction: The Meaning of Mass Imprisonment', *Punishment and Society*, 3 (2): 5–7.

Garland, D. (2001b) *The Culture of Control: Crime and Social Order in Contemporary Society*, Oxford: Clarendon Press.

Garland, D. (2002) 'Of Crime and Criminals: The Development of Criminology in Britain', in M. Maguire, R. Morgan and R. Reiner (eds) *The Oxford Handbook of Criminology*, 3rd edn, Oxford: Oxford University Press.

Garland, D. (2005) 'Capital Punishment and American Culture', *Punishment and Society*, 7 (4): 347–76.

Garland, D. (2007) 'Death, Denial, Discourse: On the Forms and Functions of American Capital Punishment', in D. Downes, P. Rock, C. Chinkin and C. Gearty (eds) *Crime, Social Control and Human Rights: From Moral Panics to States of Denial, Essays in Honour of Stanley Cohen*, Cullompton: Willan.

Garland, D. and Sparks, R. (2000) 'Criminology, Social Theory and the Challenge of Our Times', *British Journal of Criminology*, 40 (2): 189–204.

Garner, R. (2001) *Environmental Politics*, 2nd edn, London: Prentice Hall.

Gatrell, V. A. C. (1990) 'Crime, Authority and the Policeman State', in F. M. L. Thompson (ed.) *Cambridge Social History of Britain, 1750–1950*, vol. 3, Cambridge: Cambridge University Press.

Gatrell, V. A. C. (1994) *The Hanging Tree: Execution and the English People, 1770–1868*, Oxford: Oxford University Press.

Gatrell, V. A. C. (2006) *City of Laughter: Sex and Satire in Eighteenth-Century London*, London: Atlantic.

Gatrell, V. A. C., Lenman, B. and Parker, G. (eds) (1980) *Crime and the Law: The Social History of Crime in Western Europe since 1500*, London: Europa.

Gauntlett, D. (2000) *Web.Studies: Rewiring Media Studies for the Digital Age*, London: Arnold.

Gay, P. (1973) *The Enlightenment: An Interpretation*, London: Wildwood House.

Geis, G. and Dimento, J. (1995) 'Should We Prosecute Corporations and/or Individuals?', in F. Pearce and L. Snider (eds) *Corporate Crime*, Toronto: University of Toronto Press.

Gelsthorpe, L. (1989) *Sexism and the Female Offender*, Aldershot: Gower.

Gelsthorpe, L. and Morris, A. (2002) 'Restorative Justice: The Last Vestiges of Welfare', in J. Muncie, G. Hughes and E. McLaughlin (eds) *Youth Justice: Critical Readings*, London: Sage.

Genders, E. and Player, E. (1987) 'Women in Prison: The Treatment, the Control and the Experience', in P. Carlen and A. Worrall (eds) *Gender, Crime and Justice*, Milton Keynes: Open University Press.

Genders, E. and Player, E. (1989) *Race Relations in Prison*, Oxford: Clarendon Press.

Gever, M. (2005) 'The Spectacle of Crime, Digitized: CSI: Crime Scene Investigation and Social Anatomy', *European Journal of Cultural Studies*, 8 (4): 445–63.

Giddens, A. (1972) *Émile Durkheim: Selected Writings*, Cambridge: Cambridge University Press.

Giddens, A. (1990) *The Consequences of Modernity*, Cambridge: Polity.

Giddens, A. (1991) *Modernity and Self-Identity*, Cambridge: Polity.

Giddens, A. (1999) *Runaway World: How Globalisation Is Reshaping Our Lives*, London. Profile Books.

Giddens, A. (2005) 'Scaring People May Be the Only Way to Avoid the Risks of New Style Terrorism', *New Statesman*, 18 (840): 29–31.

Gilchrist, E., Bannister, J., Ditton, J. and Farrall, S. (1998) 'Women and the "Fear of Crime": Challenging the Accepted Stereotype', *British Journal of Criminology*, 38 (2): 283–98.

Gill, A. (2006) 'Patriarchal Violence in the Name of "Honour"', *International Journal of Criminal Justice Sciences*, 1 (1): 1–12.

Gilligan, C. (1982) *In a Different Voice*, Cambridge, MA: Harvard University Press.

Gilmore, R. (2007) *Golden Gulag: Prisons, Surplus, and Opposition in Globalizing California*, Berkeley, CA: University of California Press.

Girling, E., Loader, I. and Sparks, R. (2000) *Crime and Social Change in Middle England: Questions of Order in an English Town*, London: Routledge.

Gladfelder, H. (2001) *Criminality and Narrative in Eighteenth-Century England: Beyond the Law*, Baltimore: Johns Hopkins University Press.

Gobert, J. and Punch, M. (2003) *Rethinking Corporate Crime*, London: Butterworths.

Godfrey, B.S., Emsley, C. and Dunstall, G. (eds) (2003a) *Comparative Histories of Crime*, Cullompton: Willan.

Godfrey, B.S., Emsley, C. and Dunstall, G. (2003b) 'Introduction: Do You Have Plane-Spotters in New Zealand? Issues in Comparative Crime History at the Turn of Modernity', in G. S. Godfrey, C. Emsley and G. Dunstall (eds) *Comparative Histories of Crime*, Cullompton: Willan.

Goffman, E. (1959) *The Presentation of Self in Everyday Life*, Garden City, NY: Doubleday.

Goffman, E. (1961) *Asylums: Essays on the Social Situation of Mental Patients and Other Inmates*, Harmondsworth: Penguin.

Goffman, E. (1963) *Stigma: Notes on the Management of Spoiled Identity*, Harmondsworth: Penguin.

Goldson, B. (2000) *The New Youth Justice*, Lyme Regis: Russell House.

Goldson, B. (2006) 'Penal Custody: Intolerance, Irrationality and Indifference', in B. Goldson and J. Muncie (eds) *Youth Crime and Justice*, London: Sage.

Goldson, B. and Muncie, J. (eds) (2006) *Youth Crime and Justice*, London: Sage.

Goodey, J. (1997) 'Boys Don't Cry: Masculinities, Fear of Crime and Fearlessness', *British Journal of Criminology*, 47 (3): 401–18.

Goodey, J. (2000) 'Non-EU Citizens' Experiences of Offending and Victimization: The Case for Comparative European Research', *European Journal of Crime, Criminal Law and Criminal Justice*, 8 (1): 13–34.

Goodey, J. (2005) *Victims and Victimology: Research, Policy and Practice*, Harlow: Longman.

Goodman, E. and Moed, A. (2007) 'Community in Mashups: The Case of Personal Geodata', www.mashups.net (accessed 5 January 2008).

Gordon, P. (1983) *White Law: Racism in the Police, Courts and Prisons*, London: Pluto.

Gordon, P. (1990) *Racial Violence and Harassment*, 2nd edn, London: Runnymede Trust.

Goring, C. (1913/1972) *The English Convict: A Statistical Study*, London: HMSO.

Gottfredson, M. (1984) *Victims of Crime: The Dimensions of Risk*, Home Office Research Study 81, London: HMSO.

Gottfredson, M. R. and Hirschi, T. (1990) *A General Theory of Crime*, Stanford, CA: Stanford University Press.

Gottschalk, M. (2006) *The Prison and the Gallows: The Politics of Mass Incarceration in America*, Cambridge: Cambridge University Press.

Gould, S. J. (1996) *The Mismeasure of Man*, 2nd edn, New York: W. W. Norton.

Gouldner, A. (1968/1973) 'The Sociologist as Partisan: Sociology and the Welfare State', in *For Sociology*, London: Allen Lane.

Gouldner, A. (1973) *For Sociology: Renewal and Critique in Sociology Today*, London: Allen Lane.

Graham, K. and Wells, S. (2003) '"Somebody's Gonna Get Their Head Kicked In Tonight!": Aggression among Young Males in Bars – a Question of Values?', *British Journal of Criminology*, 43 (3): 546–66.

Graham, S. (2006) 'Surveillance, Urbanization and the US "Revolution" in Military Affairs', in D. Lyon (ed.) *Theorizing Surveillance: The Panopticon and Beyond*, Cullompton: Willan.

Gramsci, A. (1971) *Selections from Prison Notebooks*, London: Lawrence and Wishart.

Green, G., Smith, R. and South, N. (2005) 'Court-based Psychiatric Assessment: A Case for an Integrated and Diversionary Public Health Role', *Journal of Forensic Psychiatry and Psychology*, 16 (3): 577–91.

Greenberg, D. and Stender, F. (1972) 'The Prison as a Lawless Agency', *Buffalo Law Review*, 21: 799–839.

Greenberg, K. (ed.) (2006) *The Torture Debate in America*, Cambridge: Cambridge University Press.

Greene, J. A. (1999) 'Zero Tolerance: A Case Study of Police Policies and Practices in New York', *Crime and Delinquency*, 45 (2): 171–87.

Greenwood, P., Chaiken, J. and Petersilia, J. (1977) *The Criminal Investigation Process*, Lexington, MA: D. C. Heath.

Greer, C. (2008) *Crime and Media: A Reader*, London: Routledge.

Greer, S. (1994) 'Miscarriages of Justice Reconsidered', *Modern Law Review*, 57: 58.

Gregory, D. and Urry, J. (eds) (1985) *Social Relations and Spatial Structures*, London: Macmillan.

Gregory, J. and Lees, S. (1999) *Policing Sexual Assault*, London: Routledge.

Griffin, S. (1971) 'Rape: The All American Crime', *Ramparts*, September: 26–35.

Griffiths, P. (1996) *Youth and Authority: Formative Experiences in England, 1560–1640*, Oxford: Clarendon Press.

Griffiths, P. (2002) 'Juvenile Delinquency in Time', in P. Cox and H. Shore (eds) *Becoming Delinquent: British and European Youth, 1650–1950*, Aldershot: Ashgate.

Gros, J.-G. (2003) 'Trouble in Paradise: Crime and Collapsed States in the Age of Globalisation', *British Journal of Criminology*, 43 (1): 63–80.

Gusfield, J. (1981) *The Culture of Public Problems: Drinking–Driving and the Symbolic Order*, Chicago, IL: University of Chicago Press.

Guttenplan, D. D. (2000) 'The Holocaust on Trial', *Atlantic Monthly*, 285 (2): 45–66.

Habermas, J. (1987) *The Philosophical Discourse of Modernity*, Cambridge: Polity.

Hagan, J., Rymond-Richmond, W. and Parker, P. (2005) 'The Criminology of Genocide: The Death and Rape of Darfur', *Criminology*, 43 (3): 525–61.

Haggerty, K. and Ericson, R. (eds) (2006) *The New Politics of Surveillance and Visibility*, Toronto: University of Toronto Press.

Haines, K. and O'Mahony, D. (2006) 'Restorative Approaches, Young People and Youth Justice', in B. Goldson and J. Muncie (eds) *Youth Crime and Justice*, London: Sage.

Hale, C. (1992) *Fear of Crime: A Review of the Literature*, Canterbury: University of Kent.

Hale, C. (1996) 'Fear of Crime: A Review of the Literature', *International Review of Victimology*, 4: 79–150.

Halford, A. (1993) *No Way up the Greasy Pole*, London: Constable.

Hall, S. and Jefferson, T. (eds) (1976) *Resistance through Rituals: Youth Subcultures in Post-war Britain*, London: Routledge.

Hall, S. and Jefferson, T. (2006) 'Once More Around Resistance through Rituals', in S. Hall and T. Jefferson, *Resistance through Rituals: Youth Subcultures in Post-war Britain*, 2nd edn, London: Routledge.

Hall, S., Critcher, C., Jefferson, T., Clarke, J. and Roberts, B. (1978) *Policing the Crisis: Mugging, the State and Law and Order*, London: Macmillan.

Hamilton, P. (1996) 'The Enlightenment and the Birth of Social Science', in S. Hall, D. Held, D. Hubert and K. Thompson (eds) *Modernity: An Introduction to Modern Societies*, Oxford: Blackwell.

Hammersley, M. (2001) 'Which Side Was Becker On? Questioning Political and Epistemological Radicalism', *Qualitative Research*, 1 (1): 91–110.

Hammersley, R., Forsyth, A., Morrison, V. and Davis, J. (1989) 'The Relationship between Crime and Opioid Use', *British Journal of Criminology*, 84: 1029–44.

Hanmer, J. and Saunders, S. (1984) *Well Founded Fear*, London: Hutchinson.

Hanmer, J., Radford, J. and Stanko, E. (1989) *Women, Policing and Male Violence: International Perspectives*, London: Routledge.

Harcourt, B. (2001) *Illusion of Order*, London: Harvard University Press.

Harding, C., Hines, B., Ireland, B. and Rawlings, P. (1985) *Imprisonment in England and Wales: A Concise History*, London: Croom Helm.

Harland, D. (1985) 'Legal Aspects of the Export of Hazardous Products', *Journal of Consumer Policy*, 8 (3): 209–38.

Harrison, P. and Pearce, F. (2000) *AAAS Atlas of Population and Environment*, Berkeley: University of California Press.

Hartless, J., Ditton, J., Nair, G. and Phillips, S. (1995) 'More Sinned against Than Sinning: A Study of Young Teenagers' Experience of Crime', *British Journal of Criminology*, 35 (1): 114–33.

Hauck, M. (2007) 'Non-compliance in Small-scale Fisheries: A Threat to Security?', in P. Beirne and N. South (eds) *Issues in Green Criminology*, Cullompton: Willan.

Hay, D. (1975) 'Property, Authority, and the Criminal Law' in D. Hay, P. Linebaugh and E. P. Thompson (eds) *Albion's Fatal Tree: Crime and Society in Eighteenth-century England*, Harmondsworth: Penguin.

Hay, D., Linebaugh, P. and Thompson, E. P. (eds) (1975) *Albion's Fatal Tree: Crime and Society in Eighteenth-century England*, London: Allen Lane.

Hayes, P. (2001) 'Driving Up Treatment Standards: Interview', *Access*, 4 (Drugs Prevention Advisory Service newsletter).

Hayward, K. (2002) 'The Vilification and Pleasures of Youthful Transgression', in J. Muncie, G. Hughes and E. McLaughlin (eds) *Youth Justice: Critical Readings*, London: Sage.

Hayward, K. (2004) *City Limits: Crime, Consumer Culture and the Urban Experience*, London: Glasshouse Press.

Hayward, K. and Yar, M. (2006) 'The "Chav" Phenomenon: Consumption, Media and the Construction of a New Underclass', *Crime, Media, Culture*, 2 (1): 9–28.

Hebdige, D. (1988) *Hiding in the Light*, London: Comedia.

Hedderman, C. (2004), 'Why Are More Women Being Sentenced to Custody?', in G. McIvor (ed.) *Women Who Offend*, London: Jessica Kingsley.

Hedderman, C. and Hough, M. (1994) *Does the Criminal Justice System Treat Men and Women Differently?* Home Office Research Findings 10, London: Home Office.

Hedderman, C. and Moxon, D. (1992) *Magistrates' Court or Crown Court? Mode of Trial Decisions and Sentencing*, Home Office Research Study 125, London: HMSO.

Heidensohn, F. (1968) 'The Deviance of Women: A Critique and an Enquiry', *British Journal of Sociology*, 19: 160–75.

Heidensohn, F. (1987) 'Women and Crime: Questions of Criminology', in P. Carlen and A. Worrall (eds) *Gender, Crime and Justice*, Buckingham: Open University Press.

Heidensohn, F. (1996) *Women and Crime*, 2nd edn, London: Macmillan.

Heidensohn, F. (ed.) (2006) *Gender and Justice – New Concepts and Approaches*, Cullompton: Willan.

Held, D., McGrew, A. G., Goldblatt, D. and Perraton, J. (1999) *Global Transformations: Politics, Economics and Culture*, Cambridge: Polity.

Hendrick, H. (1990) 'Constructions and Reconstructions of British Childhood: An Interpretative Survey 1800 to the Present', in A. James and A. Prout (eds) *Constructing and Reconstructing Childhood*, London: Falmer.

Henry, S. and Milovanovic, D. (1996) *Constitutive Criminology: Beyond Postmodernism*, London: Sage.

Her Majesty's Inspectorate of Constabulary (1999) *Police Integrity: Securing and Maintaining Public Confidence*, London: Home Office.

Herbert, S. and Brown, E. (2006) 'Conceptions of Space and Crime in the Punitive Neoliberal City', *Antipode*, 38 (4): 755–77.

Herman, E. and Chomsky, N. (1988) *Manufacturing Consent: The Political Economy of the Mass Media*, New York: Pantheon.

Hermes, J. (2000) 'Of Irritation, Texts and Men: Feminist Audience Studies and Cultural Citizenship', *International Journal of Cultural Studies*, 3 (3): 351–67.

Herrnstein, R. and Murray, C. (1994) *The Bell Curve: Intelligence and Class Structure in American Life*, New York: Free Press.

Hershatter, G. (1997) *Dangerous Pleasures: Prostitution and Modernity in Twentieth-Century Shanghai*, Berkeley: University of California Press.

Hesketh, W. (2003) 'Medico-crime: Time for a Police–Health Professions Protocol?', *Police Journal*, 76: 121–31.

Higgins, P. (1996) *Heterosexual Dictatorship: Male Homosexuality in Postwar Britain*, London: Fourth Estate.

Hill, A. (2002) '"No One Leaves This Place with Her Sanity Intact"', *Observer*, 1 December: 10–11.

Hill, P. (2003) *The Japanese Mafia: Yakuza, Law and the State*, Oxford: Oxford University Press.

Hillyard, P., Pantazis, C., Tombs, S. and Gordon, D. (2004) *Beyond Criminology: Taking Harm Seriously*, London: Pluto.

Hindelang, M. J., Gottfredson, M. R. and Garofalo, J. (1978) *Victims of Personal Crime: An Empirical Foundation for a Theory of Personal Victimization*, Cambridge, MA: Ballinger.

Hinsliff, G. (2003) 'Diet of Fish "Can Prevent" Teen Violence', *Observer*, 14 September.

Hirschfield, A., Brown, P. and Todd, P. (1995) 'GIS and the Analysis of Spatially Referenced Crime Data: Experiences in Merseyside UK', *International Journal of Geographical Information Systems*, 9 (2): 191–210.

Hirschi, T. (1969) *Causes of Delinquency*, Berkeley, CA: University of California Press.

Hirst, P. (1975) 'Marx and Engels on Law, Crime and Morality', in I. Taylor, P. Walton and J. Young (eds) *Critical Criminology*, London: Routledge and Kegan Paul.

Hobbs, D. (1988) *Doing the Business: Entrepreneurship, the Working Class and Detectives in the East End of London*, Oxford: Clarendon Press.

Hobbs, D. (1991) 'Business as a Master Metaphor', in R. Burrows (ed.) *Deciphering the Enterprise Culture*, London: Routledge.

Hobbs, D. (1994) 'Professional and Organized Crime in Britain', in M. Maguire, R. Morgan and R. Reiner (eds) *The Oxford Handbook of Criminology*, Oxford: Oxford University Press.

Hobbs, D. (1995) *Bad Business: Professional Crime in Modern Britain*, Oxford: Oxford University Press.

Hobbs, D. (1997) 'Criminal Collaboration: Youth Gangs, Subcultures, Professional Criminals and Organized Crime', in M. Maguire, R. Morgan and R. Reiner (eds) *The Oxford Handbook of Criminology*, 2nd edn, Oxford: Oxford University Press.

Hobbs, D. (1998) 'Going Down the Glocal: The Local Context of Organised Crime', *Howard Journal of Criminal Justice*, 37 (4): 407–22.

Hobbs, D. (2001) 'The Firm: Organizational Logic and Criminal Culture on a Shifting Terrain', *British Journal of Criminology*, 41 (4): 549–60.

Hobbs, D., Lister, S., Hadfield, P., Winlow, S. and Hall, S. (2000) 'Receiving Shadows: Governance and Liminality in the Night-time Economy', *British Journal of Sociology*, 51 (4): 701–17.

Hobbs, D., Hadfield, P., Lister, S. and Winlow, S. (2002) '"Door Lore": The Art and Economics of Intimidation', *British Journal of Criminology*, 42: 352–70.

Hobbs, D., Hadfield, P., Lister, S. and Winlow, S. (2003) *Bouncers: Violence and Governance in the Night-time Economy*, Oxford: Oxford University Press.

Hobsbawm, E. (1972) *Bandits*, Harmondsworth: Penguin.

Hobsbawm, E. and Rudé, G. (1969) *Captain Swing*, London: Lawrence and Wishart.

Hochschild, A. (1983) *The Managed Heart: Commercialization of Human Feeling*, Berkeley: University of California Press.

Hodge, N. (2003) 'Manslaughter Business Placed on Hold', *Tribune*, 10 January, 67 (1): 3.

Hofrichter, R. (1993) *Toxic Struggles: The Theory and Practice of Environmental Justice*, Philadelphia: New Society.

Holdaway, S. (1983) *Inside the British Police*, Oxford: Basil Blackwell.

Holdaway, S. (1996) *The Racialisation of British Policing*, Basingstoke: Macmillan.

Holdaway, S. and Barron, A. M. (1997) *Resigners: The Experience of Black and Asian Police Officers*, Basingstoke: Macmillan.

Holdaway, S. and Rock, P. (eds) (1998) *Thinking About Criminology*, London: UCL Press.

Hollin, C. (1999) 'Treatment Programmes for Offenders: Meta-analysis, "What Works", and Beyond', *International Journal of Psychiatry and Law*, 22: 361–72.

Hollway, W. and Jefferson, T. (1997) 'The Risk Society in an Age of Anxiety: Situating Fear of Crime', *British Journal of Sociology*, 48 (2): 255–66.

Hollway, W. and Jefferson, T. (2000) 'The Role of Anxiety in Fear of Crime', in T. Hope and R. Sparks (eds) *Crime, Risk and Insecurity*, London: Routledge.

Holmes, S. T. and Holmes, R. M. (2008) *Sex Crimes: Patterns and Behavior*, 3rd edn, Thousand Oaks, CA: Sage.

Home Office (1966) *Committee of an Enquiry into Prison Escapes and Security* (Mountbatten Report), Cmnd 3175, London: HMSO.

Home Office (1997) *Criminal Statistics for England and Wales 1996*, Cm 3764, London: Home Office.

Home Office (1998) *Crime and Disorder Act 1998. Racially Aggravated Offences*, http://www.home office. gov.uk/cdact/racagoff.htm

Home Office (1999) *Digest 4: Information on the Criminal Justice System*, Research, Development and Statistics Directorate, London: Home Office.

Home Office (2000a) *A Guide to the Criminal Justice System in England and Wales*, London: Home Office, www.homeoffice.gov.uk

Home Office (2000b) *Statistics on Race and the Criminal Justice System*, Research, Development and Statistics Directorate, London: Home Office.

Home Office (2001) *Prison Statistics England and Wales 2000*, Cmnd. 5250, London: HMSO.

Home Office (2002a) *Criminal Statistics England and Wales 2001*, Cm 5696, London: Home Office, www.archive.official-documents.co.uk

Home Office (2002b) *Prison Population Brief, England and Wales: June 2002*, London: HMSO.

Home Office (2002c) *Statistics on Race and the Criminal Justice System: A Home Office Publication under Section 95 of the Criminal Justice Act 1991*, London: Home Office.

Home Office (2005a) *Crime in England and Wales 2003/4, Supplementary Volume 1: Homicide and Gun Crime*, London: Home Office.

Home Office (2005b) *Crime against retail and manufacturing premises: findings from the 2002 Commercial Victimisation Survey* (http://www.crimereduction.homeoffice.gov.uk/business/business42.htm).

Home Office (2005c) *Race and the Criminal Justice System: An Overview to the Complete Statistics, 2003–2004*, London: Home Office.

Home Office (2007a) Home Office Statistical Bulletin: Crime in England and Wales, 2006–7: http://www.homeoffice.gov.uk/rds/pdfs07/hosb1107.pdf

Home Office (2007b) Organised crime: revenues, economic and social costs, and criminal assets available for seizure, Online Report 14/07, London: Home Office.

Honderich, T. (2002) *After the Terror*, Edinburgh: Edinburgh University Press.

Hood, R. (1992) *Race and Sentencing*, Oxford: Oxford University Press.

Hood, R. (2002) *The Death Penalty: A Worldwide Perspective*, 3rd edn, Oxford: Oxford University Press.

Hope, T. (1985) *Implementing Crime Prevention Measures*, Home Office Research Study 86, London: HMSO.

Hope, T. (2001) 'Crime Victimisation and Inequality in Risk Society', in R. Matthews and J. Pitts (eds) *Crime, Disorder and Community Safety*, London: Routledge.

Hough, M. and Mayhew, P. (1983) *The British Crime*

Survey, Home Office Research Study 76, London: HMSO.

Howe, A. (1994) *Punish and Critique: Towards a Feminist Analysis of Penality*, London: Routledge.

Howe, A. (2001) 'Deprivation and Violence in the Community: A Perspective from a UK Accident and Emergency Department', *Injury*, 32 (5): 349–51.

Hudson, B. (1987) *Justice through Punishment*, Basingstoke: Macmillan.

Hudson, B. (1989) 'Discrimination and Disparity: The Influence of Race on Sentencing', *New Community*, 16 (1): 23–34.

Hudson, B. (1993) *Penal Policy and Social Justice*, Basingstoke: Macmillan.

Hudson, B. (1996) *Understanding Justice*, London: Sage.

Hudson, B. (2003) *Understanding Justice*, 2nd edn, London: Sage.

Hudson, B. (2005) 'The Culture of Control: Choosing the Future', in M. Matravers (ed.) *Managing Modernity: Politics and the Culture of Control*, London: Routledge.

Hughes, G. (2002) 'Crime and Disorder Reduction Partnerships: The Future of Community Safety?', in G. Hughes, E. McLaughlin and J. Muncie (eds) *Crime Prevention and Community Safety: New Directions*, London: Sage.

Hughes, G. (2007) *The Politics of Crime and Community*, Basingstoke: Palgrave.

Hughes, G. and Follett, M. (2006) 'Community Safety, Youth and the "Anti-Social"', in B. Goldson and J. Muncie (eds) *Youth Crime and Justice*, London: Sage.

Human Rights Watch (2002) *Hopes Betrayed: Trafficking of Women and Girls to Post-Conflict Bosnia and Herzegovina for Forces Prostitution*, New York: Human Rights Watch (www.hrw.org).

Hunt, A. (1998) 'The Great Masturbation Panic and the Discourse of Moral Regulation in Nineteenth and Early Twentieth Century Britain', *Journal of the History of Sexuality*, 8 (4): 575–615.

Hutter, B. (1986) 'An Inspector Calls: The Importance of Proactive Enforcement in the Regulatory Context', *British Journal of Criminology*, 26 (2).

Hutton, W. (1995) *The State We're In*, London: Jonathan Cape.

Huxley, A. (1994) *Brave New World*, London: Flamingo.

Ianni, E. R. and Ianni, R. (1983) 'Street Cops and Management Cops: The Two Cultures of Policing', in M. Punch (ed.) *Control in the Police Organization*, Cambridge, Mass.: MIT Press.

Iganski, P. (2001) 'Hate Crimes Hurt More', *American Behavioral Scientist*, 45 (4): 626–38.

Iganski, P. (2006) 'Free to Speak, Free to Hate?', in L. Morris (ed.) *Rights: Sociological Perspectives*, London: Routledge.

Iganski, P. (2008) *'Hate Crime' and the City*, Bristol: Policy Press

Ignatieff, M. (1978) *A Just Measure of Pain: The Penitentiary in the Industrial Revolution 1750–1850*, London: Macmillan.

Ignatieff, M. (1994) *Blood and Belonging: Journeys into the New Nationalism*, London: Vintage.

Inciardi, J. (1977) 'In Search of the Class Cannon: A Field Study of Professional Pickpockets', in R. S. Weppner (ed.) *Street Ethnography: Selected Studies of Crime and Drug Use in Natural Settings*, Beverly Hills, CA: Sage.

Inciardi, J. (1999) *The Drug Legalization Debate*, 2nd edn, Thousand Oaks, CA: Sage.

Innes, J. and Styles, J. (1993) 'The Crime Wave: Recent Writing on Crime and Justice in Eighteenth-Century England', in A. Wilson (ed.) *Rethinking Social History: English Society 1570–1920 and its Interpretation*, Manchester: Manchester University Press.

Institute for Jewish Policy Research (2000) *Combating Holocaust Denial through Law in the United Kingdom*, London: Institute for Jewish Policy Research.

International Federation of Red Cross and Red Crescent Societies (IFRC) (2003) *Disasters Report*, Geneva: IFRC.

Irwin, J. (1990) *The Jail: Managing the Underclass in American Society*, Berkeley: University of California Press.

Ishay, M. (ed.) (1997) *The Human Rights Reader*, London: Routledge.

Jackson, L. (2000) *Child Sexual Abuse in Victorian England*, London: Routledge.

Jackson, L. A. (2006) *Women Police: Gender, Welfare and Surveillance in the Twentieth Century*, Manchester: Manchester University Press.

Jackson, S. and Scott, S. (1996) *Feminism and Sexuality: A Reader*, Edinburgh: Edinburgh University Press.

Jacobson, J. (1999) *Policing Drug Hot-Spots*, Home Office Police Research Series 109, London: Home Office.

Jacoby, J. (2002) 'Punish Crime, Not Thought Crime', in P. Iganski (ed.) *The Hate Debate*, London: Profile.

Jaggar, A. (1989) 'Love and Knowledge: Emotion in Feminist Epistemology', in S. Bordo and A. Jaggar (eds) *Gender/Body/Knowledge: Feminist Reconstructions of Being and Knowing*, New York: Rutgers University Press.

Jamieson, R. (1998) 'Towards a Criminology of War in Europe', in V. Ruggiero, N. South and I. Taylor (eds) *The New European Criminology: Crime and Social Order in Europe*, London: Routledge.

Jamieson, R., South, N. and Taylor, I. (1998) 'Economic Liberalization and Cross-border Crime: The North American Free Trade Area and Canada's Border with the USA', *International Journal of the Sociology of Law*, 26 (2): 245–72 and 26 (3): 285–319.

Janowitz, M. (ed.) (1996) *W. I. Thomas on Social Organization and Social Personality*, Chicago, IL: University of Chicago Press.

Jefferson, T. (1990) *The Case against Paramilitary Policing*, Milton Keynes: Open University Press.

Jefferson, T. (2002a) 'For a Psychosocial Criminology', in K. Carrington and R. Hogg (eds) *Critical Criminology: Issues, Debates, Challenges*, Cullompton: Willan.

Jefferson, T. (2002b) 'Masculinities and Crime', in M. Maguire, R. Morgan and R. Reiner (eds) *The Oxford Handbook of Criminology*, 3rd edn, Oxford: Oxford University Press.

Jefferson, T. and Grimshaw, R. (1984) *Controlling the Constable: Police Accountability in England and Wales*, London: Muller/Cobden Trust.

Jefferson, T. and Walker, M. (1992) 'Ethnic Minorities in the Criminal Justice System', *Criminal Law Review*, 81: 83–95.

Jefferson, T. and Walker, M. (1993) 'Attitudes to the Police of Ethnic Minorities in a Provincial City', *British Journal of Criminology*, 33 (2): 251–66.

Jeffery-Poulter, S. (1991) *Peers, Queers, and Commons: The Struggle for Gay Law Reform from 1950 to the Present*, London: Routledge.

Jenkins, B. (2000) 'Terrorism', in E. Borgatta and R. Montgomery (eds) *Encyclopedia of Sociology*, New York: Macmillan.

Jenkins, P. (1998) *Moral Panic: Changing Concepts of the Child Molester in Modern America*, New Haven, CT: Yale University Press.

Jenkins, P. (2001) *Beyond Tolerance: Child Pornography on the Internet*, New York: New York University Press.

Jesilow, P., Pontell, H. and Geis, G. (1985) 'Medical Criminals: Physicians and White-Collar Offences', *Justice Quarterly*, 2 (2): 149–65.

Jewkes, Y. (1999) *Moral Panics in a Risk Society: A Critical Evaluation*, Crime, Order and Policing Occasional Paper Series 15, Scarman Centre, Leicester: University of Leicester.

Jewkes, Y. (ed.) (2003a) *Dot.cons: Crime, Deviance and Identity on the Internet*, Cullompton: Willan.

Jewkes, Y. (2003b) 'Policing the Net: Crime, Regulation and Surveillance in Cyberspace', in Y. Jewkes (ed.) *Dot.cons: Crime, Deviance and Identity on the Internet*, Cullompton: Willan.

Jewkes, Y. (2004) *Media and Crime*, London: Sage.

Jewkes, Y. (ed.) (2007a) *Crime Online*, Cullompton: Willan.

Jewkes, Y. (ed.) (2007b) *Handbook on Prisons*, Cullompton: Willan.

Jewkes, Y. and Andrews, C. (2005) 'Policing the Filth: The Problems of Investigating Online Child Pornography in England and Wales', *Policing and Society*, 15 (1): 42–62.

Johnston, L. (2000) *Policing Britain: Risk, Security and Governance*, Harlow: Longman.

Jones, T. and Newburn, T. (1996) *Policing and Disaffected Communities: A Review of the Literature*, London: Policy Studies Institute.

Jones, T. and Newburn, T. (2002) 'The Transformation of Policing', *British Journal of Criminology*, 42 (1): 129–46.

Jones, T., Maclean, B. and Young, J. (1986) *The Islington Crime Survey*, Aldershot: Gower.

Jowit, J. (2007) 'Amazon Tribe Hits Back at Green "Colonialism"', *Observer*, 14 October: 43.

Jupp, V., Davies, P. and Francis, P. (1999) 'The Features of Invisible Crimes', in P. Davies, P. Francis and V. Jupp (eds) *Invisible Crimes: Their Victims and Their Regulation*, Basingstoke: Macmillan.

Jupp, V., Davies, P. and Francis, P. (eds) (2000) *Doing Criminological Research*, London: Sage.

Justice (1989) *Justice, Sentencing: A Way Ahead*, London: Justice.

Karmen, A. (1990) *Crime Victims: An Introduction to Victimology*, Pacific Grove, CA: Brooks Cole.

Karstedt, S. (2002) 'Emotions and Criminal Justice', *Theoretical Criminology*, 6 (3): 299–317.

Karstedt, S. and Farrall, S. (2007) 'Law-abiding Majority? The Everyday Crimes of the Middle Classes', *Crime and Society Briefing 3*, London: Centre for Crime and Justice Studies (free download at: http://www.crimeandjustice. org.uk/opus45/middle-class-crime-2007.pdf)

Karstedt, S., Levi, M. and Godfrey, B. (eds) (2006) 'Markets, Risk and "White Collar" Crimes: Moral Economies from Victorian Times to Enron', *British Journal of Criminology*, special issue, 46 (6).

Katz, J. (1988) *Seductions of Crime: Moral and Sensual Attractions of Doing Evil*, New York: Basic Books.

Keane, J. (1996) *Reflections on Violence*, London: Verso.

Kearon, A. and Leach, R. (2000) 'Invasion of the "Bodysnatchers": Burglary Reconsidered', *Theoretical Criminology*, 4 (4): 451–72.

Kearon, T. and Godfrey, B. (2007) 'Setting the Scene: A Question of History', in S. Walklate (ed.) *Handbook of Victims and Victimology*, Cullompton: Willan.

Keith, M. (1993) *Race, Riots and Policing: Law and Disorder in a Multi-racist Society*, London: UCL Press.

Kelly, D. (1990) 'Victim Participation in the Criminal Justice System', in A. J. Lurigio, W. G. Skoken and R. C. Davis (eds) *Victims of Crime: Problems, Policies and Programs*, Newbury Park, CA: Sage.

Kelly, L. (1988) *Surviving Sexual Violence*, Cambridge: Polity Press.

Kelly, L. (2005) *Fertile Fields: Trafficking in Persons in Central Asia*, Vienna: IOM.

Kelly, L., Lovett, J. and Regan, L. (2005) *A Gap or a Chasm? Attrition in Reported Rape Cases*, Home Office Research Study 293, London: Home Office.

Kelman, H. C. and Hamilton, V. L. (1989) *Crimes of Obedience*, New Haven, CT: Yale University Press.

Kempadoo, K. and Doezema, J. (1998) *Global Sex Workers: Rights, Resistance and Redefinition*, London: Routledge.

Kemper, T. (1978) *A Social Interactional Theory of Emotions*, New York: John Wiley.

Kemper, T. (1987) 'How Many Emotions Are There? Wedding the Social and Automatic Components', *American Journal of Sociology*, 93: 263–89.

Kennedy, H. (2004) *Just Law*, London: Chatto and Windus.

Kerr, P. (1992) *A Philosophical Investigation*, London: Arrow.

Kershaw, C., Budd, T., Kinshott, G., Mattinson, J., Mayhew, P. and Myhill, A. (2000) *The 2000 British Crime Survey*, London: Home Office.

Kersten, J. (1993) 'Street Youths, *Bosozoku* and *Yakuza*: Subculture Formation and Social Reactions in Japan', *Crime and Delinquency*, 39 (3): 277–95.

Kesteren, J. N. van, Mayhew, P. and Nieuwbeerta, P. (2000) *Criminal Victimisation in Seventeen Industrialised Countries: Key-findings from the 2000 International Crime Victims Survey*, The Hague: Ministry of Justice.

Kidd-Hewitt, D. (1995) 'Crime and the Media: A Criminological Perspective', in D. Kidd-Hewitt and R. Osborne (eds) *Crime and the Media: The Post-modern Spectacle*, London: Pluto.

Kiley, S. (2007) 'How Rare Shellfish Fuel Drug Mania', *Observer*, 23 September: 41.

King, C. (2003) 'A Case to Answer?', *Care and Health*, 42, 13–26 August: 10–11.

King, P. (1999) 'Locating Histories of Crime: A Bibliographical Study', *British Journal of Criminology*, 39 (1): 161–74.

King, R. (2007) 'Imprisonment: Some International Comparisons and the Need to Revisit Panopticisim', in Y. Jewkes (ed.) *Handbook on Prisons*, Cullompton: Willan.

King, R. D. and Wincup, E. (eds) (2007) *Doing Research on Crime and Justice*, 2nd edn, Oxford: Oxford University Press.

Kinsey, R. (1984) *Merseyside Crime Survey*, Edinburgh: Centre for Criminology, University of Edinburgh.

Kivisto, P. (1998) *Key Ideas in Sociology*, London: Sage/Pine Forge Press.

Klein, N. (2000) *No Logo*, London: Flamingo.

Klockars, C. (1975) *The Professional Fence*, London: Tavistock.

Knafla, L. A. (2003) 'Introduction', in L. A. Knafla

(ed.) *Violent Crime in North America*, London/Westport, CT: Praeger.

Knepper, P. (2007) *Criminology and Social Policy*, London: Sage.

Kohn, M. (1992) *Dope Girls: The Birth of the British Drug Underground*, London: Lawrence and Wishart.

Kretsmer, D. (2007) 'The Torture Debate: Israel and Beyond', in D. Downes, P. Rock, C. Chinkin and C. Gearty (eds) *Crime, Social Control and Human Rights: From Moral Panics to States of Denial, Essays in Honour of Stanley Cohen*, Cullompton: Willan.

Kuhn, T. S. (1962) *The Structure of Scientific Revolutions*, Chicago, IL: University of Chicago Press.

Lacey, N. (1988) *State Punishment: Political Principles and Community Values*, London: Routledge.

Lacey, N. (2000) *Narrative and Genre: Key Concepts in Media Studies*, Basingstoke: Macmillan.

Lancet, The (1999) 'Alcohol and Violence', *The Lancet*, 336, 17 November: 1223–4.

Landesco, J. (1929) *Organized Crime in Chicago*, Chicago: Illinois Association for Criminal Justice.

Langbein, J. (1983) 'Albion's Fatal Flaws', *Past and Present*, 98: 96–120.

Langfield, M. (2004) 'Voluntarism, Salvation, and Rescue: British Juvenile Migration to Australia and Canada, 1890–1939', *Journal of Imperial and Commonwealth History*, 32 (2): 86–114.

Lasch, C. (1979) *The Culture of Narcissism*, New York: Norton.

Lauer, J. (2005) 'Driven to Extremes: Fear of Crime and the Rise of the Sport Utility Vehicle in the United States', *Crime, Media, Culture*, 1 (2): 149–68.

Lawrence, F. M. (1999) *Punishing Hate: Bias Crimes under American Law*, Cambridge, MA: Harvard University Press.

Lazarus, L. (2004) *Contrasting Prisoners' Rights: A Comparative Examination of Germany and England*, Oxford: Oxford University Press.

Lea, J. (1999) 'Social Crime Revisited', *Theoretical Criminology*, 3: 307–26.

Lea, J. (2000) 'The Macpherson Report and the Question of Institutional Racism', *Howard Journal of Criminal Justice*, 39 (2): 219–37.

Lea, J. (2002) *Crime and Modernity*, London: Sage.

Lea, J. and Young, J. (1984) *What Is To Be Done about Law and Order?*, London: Pluto.

Lee, J. A. (1981) 'Some Structural Aspects of Police Deviance in Relations with Minority Groups', in C. Shearing (ed.) *Organizational Police Deviance*, Toronto: Butterworths.

Lee, M. (1998) *Youth, Crime and Police Work*, Basingstoke: Macmillan.

Lee, M. (2001) 'The Genesis of "Fear of Crime"', *Theoretical Criminology*, 5 (4): 467–85.

Lee, M. (2007a) 'Women's Imprisonment as a Mechanism of Migration Control in Hong Kong', *British Journal of Criminology*, 47 (6): 847–60.

Lee, M. (ed.) (2007b) *Human Trafficking*, Cullompton: Willan.

Lee, M. and South, N. (2003) 'Policing and Drugs', in T. Newburn (ed.) *The Handbook of Policing*, Cullompton: Willan.

Lee, M. and South, N. (2008) 'Policing and Drugs', in T. Newburn (ed.) *The Handbook of Policing*, 2nd edn, Cullompton: Willan.

Lees, S. (1996a) 'Unreasonable Doubt: The Outcomes of Rape Trials', in M. Hester, L. Kelly and J. Radford (eds) *Women, Violence and Male Power*, Buckingham: Open University Press.

Lees, S. (1996b) *Carnal Knowledge: Rape on Trial*, London: Penguin.

Legambiente, G. (2003) *The Illegal Trafficking in Hazardous Waste in Italy and Spain*, Rome: European Commission.

Leishman, F. and Mason, P. (2004) *Policing and the Media: Facts, Fictions and Factions*, Cullompton: Willan.

Lemert, E. (1951) *Social Pathology*, New York: McGraw-Hill.

Lemert, E. (1958) 'The Behavior of the Systematic Check Forger', *Social Problems*, 6: 141–9.

Lemert, E. (1967) *Human Deviance, Social Problems and Social Control*, Englewood Cliffs, NJ: Prentice Hall.

Leo, R. A. (1995) 'Trial and Tribulation: Courts, Ethnography, and the Need for Evidentiary Privilege for Academic Researchers', *American Sociologist*, 26: 113–34.

Leonard, E. B. (1982) *Women, Crime and Society*, New York: Longman.

Levi, M. (1981) *The Phantom Capitalists*, Aldershot: Gower.

Levi, M. (1993) *The Investigation, Prosecution and Trial of Serious Fraud*, Research Paper Report 14,

London: Royal Commission on Criminal Justice.

Levi, M. and Pithouse, A. (1992) 'The Victims of Fraud', in D. Downes (ed.) *Unravelling Criminal Justice*, Basingstoke: Macmillan.

Levi, M. and van Duyne, P. (2005) *Drugs and Money*, London: Routledge.

Levin, J. and McDevitt, J. (2002) *Hate Crimes Revisited: America's War on Those Who Are Different*, Boulder, CO: Westview Press.

Lewis, R. (1989) 'European Markets in Cocaine', *Contemporary Crises*, 13: 35–52.

Liazos, A. (1972) 'The Poverty of the Sociology of Deviance: Nuts, Sluts and Perverts', *Social Problems*, 20: 103–20.

Linebaugh, P. (1976) 'Karl Marx, the Theft of Wood and Working Class Composition', *Crime and Social Justice*, 6: 5–16.

Linebaugh, P. (1991) *The London Hanged: Crime and Civil Society in the Eighteenth Century*, London: Allen Lane/Penguin.

Lipstadt, D. (1994) *Denying the Holocaust: The Growing Assault on Truth and Memory*, New York: Plume.

Lister, R. et al. (eds) (1996) *Charles Murray and the Underclass: The Developing Debate*, London: IEA Health and Welfare Unit in association with the *Sunday Times*.

Livingstone, S. (1996) 'On the Continuing Problem of Media Effects', in J. Curran and M. Gurevitch (eds) *Mass Media and Society*, London: Arnold.

Loader, I. (1996) *Youth, Policing and Democracy*, Basingstoke: Macmillan.

Loader, I. (2000) 'Plural Policing and Democratic Governance', *Social and Legal Studies*, 9: 323–45.

Loader, I. and Sparks, R. (2007) 'Contemporary Landscapes of Crime', in M. Maguire, R. Morgan and R. Reiner (eds) *The Oxford Handbook of Criminology*, 4th edn, Oxford: Oxford University Press.

Loader, I. and Walker, N. (2007) *Civilizing Security*, Cambridge: Cambridge University Press.

Loffreda, B. (2000) *Losing Matt Shepard: Life and Politics in the Aftermath of Anti-gay Murder*, New York: Columbia University Press.

Lofland, J. (1966) *Doomsday Cult*, Englewood Cliffs, NJ: Prentice Hall.

Lombroso, C. (1876) *L'uomo delinquente*, Turin: Fratelli Bocca.

Lombroso, C. (1911/1968) *Crime: Its Causes and Remedies*, Montclair, NJ: Patterson Smith.

Lombroso-Ferrero, G. (1911) *Criminal Man: According to the Classification of Cesare Lombroso*, New York: Putnam; repr. Montclair, NJ: Paterson Smith, 1972.

Loseke, D. (2003a) 'We Hold These Truths to Be Self Evident: Problems in Pondering the Pedophile Priest Problem: Symposium on Paedophile Priests', *Sexualities*, 6, February: 6–14.

Loseke, D. (2003b) *Thinking about Social Problems: An Introduction to Constructionist Perspectives*, 2nd edn, New York: Aldine de Gruyter.

Low, D. (1982) *Thieves' Kitchen: The Regency Underworld*, London: Dent.

Lowman, J., Menzies, R. and Palys, T. (eds) (1987) *Transcarceration: Essays in the Sociology of Social Control*, Aldershot: Gower.

Lupton, D. and Tulloch, J. (1999) 'Theorizing Fear of Crime: Beyond the Rational/Irrational Opposition', *British Journal of Sociology*, 50 (3): 507–23.

Lupton, R., Wilson, A., May, T., Warburton, H. and Turnbull, P. (2002) *A Rock and a Hard Place: Drug Markets in Deprived Neighbourhoods*, Home Office Research Study 240, London: Home Office.

Lurigio, A. J., Skogan, W. G. and Davis, R. C. (eds) (1990) *Victims of Crime: Problems, Policies and Programs*, Newbury Park, CA: Sage.

Lury, K. (2005) *Interpreting Television*, London: Hodder Arnold.

Lustgarten, L. (1986) *The Governance of Police*, London: Sweet and Maxwell.

Lynch, M. J. (1990) 'The Greening of Criminology: A Perspective on the 1990s', *Critical Criminologist*, 2 (3): 1–4, 11–12.

Lyng, S. (1990) 'Edgework: A Social Psychological Analysis of Voluntary Risk Taking', *American Journal of Sociology*, 95 (4): 851–86.

Lyng, S. (2004) 'Crime, Edgework and Corporeal Transaction', *Theoretical Criminology*, 8 (3): 359–75.

Lyng, S. and Snow, D. (1986) 'Vocabularies of Motive and High Risk Behavior: The Case of Skydiving', in E. J. Lawler (ed.) *Advances in Group Processes*, Greenwich, CT: JAI.

Lyon, D. (2001) *Surveillance Society: Monitoring Everyday Life*, Buckingham: Open University Press.

Lyon, D. (2003) *Surveillance after September 11*, Cambridge: Polity.

Lyon, D. (ed.) (2006) *Theorizing Surveillance: The Panopticon and Beyond*, Cullompton: Willan.

Mac an Ghaill, M. (1994) *The Making of Men*, Buckingham: Open University Press.

Mcalinden, A-M. (2006) 'Managing Risk: From Regulation to the Reintegration of Sexual Offenders', *Criminology and Criminal Justice*, 6 (2): 197–218.

McAllister, W. (2000) *Drug Diplomacy in the Twentieth Century*, London: Routledge.

McAra, L. (2005) 'Modelling Penal Transformation', *Punishment and Society*, 7 (3): 277–302.

McBarnet, D. (1981) *Conviction: Law, the State and the Construction of Justice*, London: Macmillan.

McCabe, A. and Raine, J. (1997) *Framing the Debate: The Impact of Crime on Public Health*, Birmingham: Public Health Alliance.

McConville, M. and Wilson, G. (2002) *The Handbook of the Criminal Justice Process*, Oxford: Oxford University Press.

McConville, M., Sanders, A. and Leng, R. (1991) *The Case for the Prosecution*, London: Routledge.

McConville, S. (1998) 'The Victorian Prison: England, 1865–1965', in N. Morris and D. Rothman (eds) *The Oxford History of the Prison: The Practice of Punishment in Western Society*, Oxford: Oxford University Press.

McCracken, S. (1998) *Pulp: Reading Popular Fiction*, Manchester: Manchester University Press.

McDermott, K. and King, R. (1988) 'Mind Games: Where the Action Is in Prisons', *British Journal of Criminology*, 28 (3): 357–77.

MacDonald, R. and Marsh, J. (2002) 'Crossing the Rubicon: Youth Transitions, Poverty, Drugs and Social Exclusion', *International Journal of Drug Policy*, 13: 27–38.

McGuire, J. (ed.) (1995) *What Works: Reducing Re-offending*, Chichester: Wiley.

McIntosh, M. (1975) *The Organisation of Crime*, London: Macmillan.

McIntosh, M. (1978) 'Who Needs Prostitutes?', in C. Smart (ed.) *Women, Sexuality and Social Control*, London: Routledge.

Mack, J. (1964) 'Full-Time Miscreants, Delinquent Neighbourhoods and Criminal Networks', *British Journal of Sociology*, 15: 38–53.

MacKinnon, C. A. (1987) *Feminism Unmodified: Discourses on Life and Law*, Cambridge, MA: Harvard University Press.

MacKinnon, C. A. (1998) 'Rape, Genocide, and Women's Human Rights', in S. G. French, W. Teays and L. M. Purdy (eds) *Violence Against Women: Philosophical Perspectives*, Ithaca, NY and London: Cornell University Press.

McLaren, A. (1997) *The Trials of Masculinity*, Chicago, IL: University of Chicago Press.

McLaughlin, E. (1994) *Community, Policing and Accountability*, Aldershot: Avebury.

McLaughlin, E. (2001) 'Political Violence, Terrorism and States of Fear', in J. Muncie and E. McLaughlin (eds) *The Problem of Crime*, 2nd edn, London: Sage/Open University.

McLaughlin, E. (2006) 'Terrorism', in E. McLaughlin and J. Muncie (eds) *Sage Dictionary of Criminology*, 2nd edn, London: Sage.

McLaughlin, E. (2007) *The New Policing*, London: Sage.

McLaughlin, E. and Murji, K. (1997) 'The Future Lasts a Long Time: Public Policework and the Managerialist Paradox', in P. Francis, P. Davies and V. Jupp (eds) *Policing Futures: The Police, Law Enforcement and the Twenty-First Century*, Basingstoke: Macmillan.

McLaughlin, E. and Muncie, J. (1999) 'Walled Cities: Surveillance, Regulation and Segregation', in S. Pile, C. Brook and G. Mooney (eds) *Unruly Cities*, London: Routledge.

McLaughlin, E. and Muncie, J. (2000) 'The Criminal Justice System: New Labour's New Partnerships', in J. Clarke, S. Gewirtz and E. McLaughlin (eds) *New Managerialism, New Welfare?*, London: Sage.

McLaughlin, E., Fergusson, R., Hughes, G. and Westmarland, L. (2003) *Restorative Justice: Critical Issues*, London: Sage.

McLeod, E. (1982) *Women Working: Prostitution Now*, London: Croom Helm.

McMurran, M. and Hollin, C. (1989) 'Drinking and Delinquency', *British Journal of Criminology*, 29 (4): 386–93.

McNaughton, J. (2003) 'Maddening Thing Is That Record Firms Could Have Done It', *Observer*, Business Section, 4 May: 6.

McNay, L. (1994) *Foucault: A Critical Introduction*, Cambridge: Polity.

Macpherson, Sir W. (1999) *The Stephen Lawrence Inquiry: Report of an Inquiry by Sir William Macpherson of Cluny*, Cm 4262, London: The Stationery Office.

McRobbie, A. (1994) *Postmodernism and Popular Culture*, London: Routledge.

McRobbie, A. (2005) *The Uses of Cultural Studies*, London: Sage.

McRobbie, A. (2006) 'Vulnerability, Violence and (Cosmopolitan) Ethics: Butler's *Precarious Life*', British Journal of Sociology, 57 (1): 69–86.

McRobbie, A. (2008) *The Aftermath of Feminism: Gender, Culture and Social Change*, London: Sage.

McRobbie, A. and Thornton, S. (1995) 'Rethinking Moral Panics for Multi-mediated Social Worlds', British Journal of Sociology, 46 (4): 559–74.

McVeigh, D. (2003) 'Rogue Advisors Profit from Asylum Misery', Tribune, 67 (3)2: 5.

Maguire, M. (1982) *Burglary in a Dwelling*, London: Heinemann.

Maguire, M. (1997) 'Crime Statistics, Patterns, and Trends: Changing Perceptions and their Implications', in M. Maguire, R. Morgan and R. Reiner (eds) *The Oxford Handbook of Criminology*, 2nd edn, Oxford: Clarendon Press.

Maguire, M. and Corbett, C. (1987) *The Effects of Crime and the Work of Victim Support Schemes*, Aldershot: Gower.

Maguire, M. and Corbett, C. (1991) *A Study of the Police Complaints System*, London: Home Office.

Maguire, M., Morgan, R. and Reiner, R. (2002) *The Oxford Handbook of Criminology*, 3rd edn (4th edn, 2007), Oxford: Oxford University Press.

Maher, L. and Dixon, D. (1999) 'Policing and Public Health', British Journal of Criminology, 39 (4): 488–512.

Mahood, L. (1995) *Policing Gender: Class and Family Britain, 1800–1945*, London: UCL Press.

Man, L.-H., Best, D., Marshall, J., Godfrey, C. and Budd, T. (2002) *Dealing with Alcohol Related Detainees in the Custody Suite*, Home Office Findings 178, London: Home Office.

Manning, P. (1979) 'The Social Control of Police Work', in S. Holdaway (ed.) *The British Police*, London: Edward Arnold.

Manning, P. K. (2000) 'Policing New Social Spaces', in J. Sheptycki (ed.) *Issues in Transnational Policing*, London: Routledge.

Mars, G. (1982) *Cheats at Work: An Anthropology of Workplace Crime*, London: George Allen and Unwin.

Mars, G. (2006) 'Changes in Occupational Deviance: Scams, Fiddles and Sabotage in the 21st Century', Crime, Law and Social Change, 12: 285–96.

Martin, C. (1996) 'The Impact of Equal Opportunities Policies on the Day-to-Day Experiences of Women Police Constables', British Journal of Criminology, 36 (4): 510–28.

Martin, T. and Romero, A. (1992) *Multinational Crime*, London: Sage.

Martinson, R. (1974) 'What Works? Questions and Answers about Prison Reform', The Public Interest, 35: 22–54.

Marx, K. (1843/1971) *Critique of Hegel's 'Philosophy of Right'*, Cambridge: Cambridge University Press.

Marx, K. and Engels, F. (1845/1975) *Collected Works*, vol. 4: 248–9, Moscow: Progress Publishers; London: Lawrence and Wishart.

Mason, P. (2006) 'Turn on, Tune in, Slop out', in P. Mason (ed.) *Captured by the Media: Prison Discourse in Popular Culture*, Collumpton: Willan.

Mathiesen, T. (1965) *The Defences of the Weak*, London: Tavistock.

Mathiesen, T. (1974) *The Politics of Abolition*, London: Martin Robertson.

Matravers, M. (2000) *Justice and Punishment: The Rationale of Coercion*, Oxford: Oxford University Press.

Matravers, M. (ed.) (2005) *Managing Modernity: Politics and the Culture of Control*, London: Routledge.

Matrix Knowledge Group (2007) *The Illicit Drug Trade in the United Kingdom*, London: Home Office Online Report 20/07.

Matthews, M. (2002) 'Crime Control in Late Modernity: A Review Essay', Theoretical Criminology, 6 (2): 217–27.

Matthews, R. (1989) *Privatizing Criminal Justice*, London: Sage.

Matthews, R. (1999) *Doing Time: An Introduction to the Sociology of Imprisonment*, Basingstoke: Macmillan.

Matthews, R. (2002) *Armed Robbery*, Cullompton: Willan.

Matza, D. (1964) *Delinquency and Drift*, New York: Wiley.

Matza, D. (1969) *Becoming Deviant*, Englewood Cliffs, NJ: Prentice Hall.

Mauer, M. (1997) *Intended and Unintended Consequences: State Racial Disparities in Imprisonment*, Washington, DC: The Sentencing Project.

Mauer, M. (2001) 'The Causes and Consequences of Prison Growth in the United States', *Punishment and Society*, 3 (2): 9–20.

Maung, N. A. (1995) *Young People, Victimisation and the Police*, Home Office Research Study 140, London: Home Office.

Mawby, R. (ed.) (1999) *Policing across the World: Issues for the Twenty-first Century*, London: UCL Press.

Mawby, R. (2001) *Burglary*, Cullompton: Willan.

Mawby, R. and Walklate, S. (1994) *Critical Victimology*, London: Sage.

Maxfield, M. G. and Babbie, E. (2007) *Research Methods for Criminal Justice and Criminology*, 5th edn, Belmont, CA: Wadsworth.

May, T. (1991) *Probation: Politics, Policy and Practice*, Milton Keynes: Open University Press.

Mayhew, P. and Van Dijk, J. J. M. (1997) *Criminal Victimisation in Eleven Industrialised Countries: Key Findings from the 1996 International Crime Victims Survey*, The Hague: Ministry of Justice, WODC.

Mead, G. H. (1918) 'The Psychology of Punitive Justice', *American Journal of Sociology*, 23: 577–602.

Mead, G. H. (1934) *Mind, Self and Society*, Chicago, IL: University of Chicago Press.

Melossi, D. and Pavarini, M. (1978) *The Prison and the Factory: The Origins of the Penitentiary System*, Basingstoke: Macmillan.

Mendelsohn, B. (1956) 'Une nouvelle branche de la science bio-psycho-sociale: victimologie', *Revue Internationale de Criminologie et de Police Technique*, pp. 10–31.

Mendelson, S. (2005) *Barracks and Brothels – Peacekeepers and Human Trafficking in the Balkans*, Washington, DC: Centre for Strategic and International Studies Press.

Merton, R. K. (1938) 'Social Structure and Anomie', *American Sociological Review*, 3: 672–82.

Messerschmidt, J. W. (1993) *Masculinities and Crime: Critique and Reconceptualization of Theory*, Lanham, MD: Rowman and Littlefield.

Messerschmidt, J. W. (1997) *Crime as Structured Action*, London: Sage.

Messerschmidt, J. W. (2000) *Nine Lives: Adolescence Masculinities, the Body and Violence*, Boulder, CO: Westview.

Messerschmidt, J. W. (2007) '"We Must Protect Our Southern Women": On Whiteness, Masculinities and Lynching', in M. Bosworth and J. Flavin (eds) *Race, Gender and Punishment: From Colonialism to the War on Terror*, New Brunswick, NJ: Rutgers University Press.

Meyers, M. (1997) *News Coverage of Violence against Women: Engendering Blame*, London: Sage.

Michalowski, R. and Kramer, R. (1987) 'The Space between Laws: The Problem of Corporate Crime in a Transnational Context', *Social Problems*, 34 (1): 34–53.

Miers, D. (1992) 'The Responsibilities and the Rights of Victims of Crime', *Modern Law Review*, 55: 482.

Miers, S. (2003) *Slavery in the Twentieth Century. The Evolution of a Global Problem*, Walnut Creek, CA: Alta Mira Press.

Miller, A. (1962) 'The Bored and the Violent', *Harper's*, 25, November, reprinted in P. O'Malley and S. Mugford (1994) 'Crime, Excitement, and Modernity', in G. Barak (ed.) *Varieties of Criminology: Readings from a Dynamic Discipline*, Westport, CT: Praeger.

Miller, D. and Kitzinger, J. (1998) 'AIDS, the Policy Process and Moral Panics', in D. Miller, J. Kitzinger, K. Williams and P. Beharrell (eds) *The Circuit of Mass Communication*, London: Sage.

Miller, E. (1986) *Street Women*, Philadelphia: Temple.

Millie, A., Jacobson, J. and Hough, M. (2005) 'Understanding the Growth in the Prison Population in England and Wales', in C. Elmsley (ed.) *The Persistent Prison: Problems, Images and Alternatives*, London: Francis Boutle.

Millington, G. (2005) 'Meaning, Materials and Melancholia: Understanding the Palace Hotel', *Social and Cultural Geography*, 6 (4): 531–49.

Mills, C.W. (1959) *The Sociological Imagination*, New York: Oxford University Press.

Ministry of Justice (2007) *Judicial and Court Statistics 2006*, London: Ministry of Justice.

Mirrlees-Black, C. (1999) *Domestic Violence: Findings from a New British Crime Survey Self-Completion Questionnaire*, Home Office Research Study 191, London: Home Office.

Mirrlees-Black, C. and Ross, A. (1995) *Crimes against Retail and Manufacturing Premises: Findings from the 1994 Commercial Victimization Survey*, Home Office Research Study 146, London: Home Office.

Mirrlees-Black, C., Budd, T., Partridge, S. and Mayhew, P. (1998) *The 1998 British Crime Survey*, Home Office Statistical Bulletin 19/96, London: Home Office.

Modood, T. and Berthoud, R. (1997) *Ethnic Minorities in Britain: Diversity and Disadvantage*, London: Policy Studies Institute.

Mollen Commission (1994) *Report of the Commission to Investigate Allegations of Police Corruption and the Anticorruption Procedures of the Police Department*, New York: Mollen Commission.

Mooney, J. (1993) *The North London Domestic Violence Survey*, London: Middlesex University.

Moretti, F. (1990) 'Clues', in T. Bennett (ed.) *Popular Fiction: Technology, Ideology, Production, Reading*, London: Routledge.

Morgan, P. (1978) *Delinquent Fantasies*, London: Temple Smith.

Morgan, R. (2000) 'The Utilitarian Justification of Torture: Denial, Desert and Disinformation', *Punishment and Society*, 2 (2): 181–96.

Morgan, R. (2002) 'Imprisonment: A Brief History, the Contemporary Scene, and Likely Prospects', in M. Maguire, R. Morgan and R. Reiner (eds) *The Oxford Handbook of Criminology*, 3rd edn, Oxford: Oxford University Press.

Morgan, R. (2007) 'Children and Young Persons', in Y. Jewkes (ed.) *Handbook on Prisons*, Cullompton: Willan.

Morgan, R. and Liebling, A. (2007) 'Imprisonment: An Expanding Scene', in M. Maguire, R. Morgan and R. Reiner (eds) *The Oxford Handbook of Criminology*, 4th edn, Oxford: Oxford University Press.

Morgan, R. and Newburn, T. (1997) *The Future of Policing*, Oxford: Clarendon Press.

Morgan, R. and Sanders, A. (1999) *The Uses of Victim Statements*, Home Office RDS Occasional Paper, London: Home Office.

Morgan, R. and Russell, N. (2000) *The Judiciary in the Magistrates' Courts*, Home Office RDS Occasional Paper 66, London: Home Office.

Morris, L. (1994) *The Dangerous Classes: The Underclass and Citizenship*, London: Routledge.

Morris, L. (ed.) (2006) *Rights: Sociological Perspectives*, London: Routledge.

Morton, J. (1992) *Gangland*, London: Little, Brown.

Moses, E. R. (1947) 'Differentials in Crime Rates between Negroes and Whites Based on Comparisons of Four Socio-economically Equated Areas', *American Sociological Review*, 12: 411–20.

Muncie, J. (1999) *Youth and Crime: A Critical Introduction*, London: Sage.

Muncie, J. (2001) 'The Construction and Deconstruction of Crime', in J. Muncie and E. McLaughlin (eds) *The Problem of Crime*, 2nd edn, London: Sage/Open University.

Muncie, J. (2004) *Youth and Crime: A Critical Introduction*, 2nd edn, London: Sage.

Muncie, J., McLaughlin, E. and Langan, M. (eds) (1996) *Criminological Perspectives: A Reader* (2nd edn, 2003), London: Sage/Open University.

Murdock, G. (1997) 'Reservoirs of Dogma: An Archaeology of Popular Anxieties', in M. Barker and J. Petley (eds) *Ill Effects: The Media/Violence Debate*, London: Routledge.

Murphy, J. G. (1994) 'Marxism and Retribution', in R. Duff and D. Garland (eds) *A Reader on Punishment*, Oxford: Oxford University Press.

Murray, A. (1998) 'Debt-bondage and Trafficking: Don't Believe the Hype', in K. Kempadoo and J. Doezema (eds) *Global Sex Workers*, London: Routledge.

Murray, C. (1997) *Does Prison Work?* London: Institute for Economic Affairs.

Murray, C. et al. (1990) *The Emerging British Underclass*, London: IEA Health and Welfare Unit.

NACRO (2001) 'Children, Health and Crime', *Impact: International Journal of Health Equality*, 1: 13–15.

NACRO (2001–2) 'Women Offenders', *Safer Society*, 11: 27–8.

NACRO (2002) 'Drug Misuse Is a Health Issue, Say Police Chiefs', *Safer Society*, 13: 14.

Nadelman, E. (1990) 'Global Prohibition Regimes: The Evolution of Norms in International Society', *International Organization*, 44 (4): 479–526.

Naffine, N. (1990) *Law and the Sexes*, London: Allen and Unwin.

Naffine, N. (1995) *Gender, Crime and Feminism*, Aldershot: Dartmouth.

Naffine, N. (1997) *Feminism and Criminology*, Cambridge: Polity.

Naím, M (2005) *Illicit: How Smugglers, Traffickers, and Copycats are Hijacking the Global Economy*, New York: Doubleday.

Namrouqa, H. (2007) 'Experts Focus on Water Management, Conflict Resolution', *The Jordan Times*, 23 October: 3.

National Board for Crime Prevention (1994) *Wise after the Event: Tackling Repeat Victimisation*, London: Home Office.

Naudé, C. M .B., Prinsloo, J. H. and Ladikos, A. (2006) *Experiences of Crime in Thirteen African Countries: Results from the International Crime Victim Survey*, Turin: UNICRI-UNODC.

Naughton, M. (2007) *Rethinking Miscarriages of Justice: Beyond the Tip of the Iceberg*, Basingstoke: Macmillan.

Neale, J. (2004) 'Measuring the Health of Scottish Drug Users', *Health and Social Care in the Community*, 12 (3): 202–11.

Nelken, D. (1989) 'Discipline and Punish: Some Notes on the Margin', *Howard Journal of Criminal Justice*, 28 (4): 245–54.

Nelken, D. (1994a) 'White Collar Crime', in M. Maguire, R. Morgan and R. Reiner (eds) *The Oxford Handbook of Criminology*, Oxford: Oxford University Press.

Nelken, D. (ed.) (1994b) *The Futures of Criminology*, London: Sage.

Nellis, M. (2003) 'News Media, Popular Culture and the Electronic Monitoring of Offenders in England and Wales', *Howard Journal of Criminal Justice*, 42 (1): 1–31.

Newburn, T. (1999) *Understanding and Preventing Police Corruption: Lessons from the Literature*, Home Office Police Research Studies 110, London: Home Office.

Newburn, T. (2002a) 'Young People, Crime, and Youth Justice', in M. Maguire, R. Morgan and R. Reiner (eds) *The Oxford Handbook of Criminology*, 3rd edn, Oxford: Oxford University Press.

Newburn, T. (2002b) 'Community Safety and Policing: Some Implications of the Crime and Disorder Act 1998', in G. Hughes, E. McLaughlin and J. Muncie (eds) *Crime Prevention and Community Safety: New Directions*, London: Sage.

Newburn, T. (ed.) (2003/2008) *Handbook of Policing*, Cullompton: Willan.

Newburn, T. (ed.) (2005) *Policing: Key Readings*, Cullompton: Willan.

Newburn, T. and Stanko, E. (eds) (1994) *Just Boys Doing Business?*, London: Routledge.

Newman, G. (ed.) (1999) *Global Report on Crime and Justice*, New York: Oxford University Press.

Newman, O. (1972) *Defensible Space*, New York: Macmillan.

Newman, O. (1996) *Creating Defensible Space*, New York: Rutgers and US Department of Housing and Urban Development.

Nicholas, S. and Walker, A. (2004) *Crime in England and Wales 2002/2003: Supplementary Volume 2: Crime, Disorder and the Criminal Justice System – Public Attitudes and Perceptions*, London: Home Office.

Nicholas, S., Povey, D., Walker, A. and Kershaw, C. (2005) *Crime in England and Wales 2004/2005*, Home Office Statistical Bulletin 11/05, London: Home Office.

Nicholas, S., Kershaw, C. and Walker, A. (2007) *Crime in England and Wales 2006/7*, 4th edn, London: Home Office.

Nietzsche, F. (1887/1996) *On the Genealogy of Morals*, Oxford: Oxford University Press.

Nightingale, C. (1993) *On the Edge*, New York: Basic Books.

Noaks, L. and Wincup, E. (2004) *Criminological Research: Understanding Qualitative Methods*, London: Sage.

Norris, C., Fielding, N., Kemp, C. and Fielding, J. (1992) 'Black and Blue: An Analysis of the Influence of Race on Being Stopped by the Police', *British Journal of Sociology*, 43: 207–24.

O'Byrne, D. J. (2003) *Human Rights: An Introduction*, Harlow: Longman.

O'Connell, R., Price, J. and Barrow, C. (2004) *Cyber Stalking, Abusive Cyber Sex and Online Grooming: A Programme for Teenagers*, Preston: Cyberspace Research Unit.

O'Donnell, I. and Milner, C. (2007) *Child Pornography: Crime, Computers and Society*, Cullompton: Willan.

O'Donovan, K. (1993) 'Law's Knowledge: The Judge, the Expert, the Battered Woman, and Her Syndrome', *Journal of Law and Society*, 20 (4): 427–37.

O'Hear, M. (2004) 'Sentencing the Green Collar

Offender: Punishment, Culpability and Environmental Crime', *Journal of Criminal Law and Criminology*, 95 (1): 133–276.

O'Mahony, D. and Quinn, K. (1999) 'Fear of Crime and Locale: The Impact of Community Related Factors upon Fear of Crime', *International Review of Victimology*, 6: 231–51.

O'Malley, P. (1992) 'Risk, Power and Crime Prevention', *Economy and Society*, 21 (3): 242–75.

O'Malley, P. (1999) 'Volatile and Contradictory Punishment', *Theoretical Criminology*, 3 (2): 175–96.

O'Malley, P. and Mugford, S. (1994) 'Crime, Excitement and Modernity', in G. Barak (ed.) *Varieties of Criminology: Readings from a Dynamic Discipline*, Westport, CT: Praeger.

O'Toole, L. (1998) *Pornocopia: Porn, Sex, Technology and Desire*, London: Serpent's Tail.

Oberwittler, D. (2005) 'Social Exclusion and Youth Crime in Europe – The Spatial Dimension', Plenary Presentation at the Fifth Annual Conference of the European Society of Criminology, Krakow, Poland.

Ogg, J. and Munn-Giddings, C. (1993) 'Researching Elder Abuse', *Ageing and Society*, 13: 389–413.

Ogletree, C. and Sarat, A. (eds) (2006) *From Lynch Mobs to the Killing State: Race and the Death Penalty in America*, New York: NYU Press.

Orwell, G. (1933) *Down and Out in London and Paris*, London: Victor Gollancz.

Osborne, R. (1995) 'Crime and the Media: From Media Studies to Post-modernism', in D. Kidd-Hewitt and R. Osborne (eds) *Crime and the Media: The Post-modern Spectacle*, London: Pluto.

Ost, S. (2004) 'Getting to Grips with Sexual Grooming? The New Offence under the Sexual Offences Act 2003', *Journal of Social Welfare and Family Law*, 26 (2): 147–59.

Owers, A. (2003) 'BIHR Human Rights Lecture: Prison Inspection and the Protection of Human Rights' www.homeoffice.gov.uk/docs2/bihr lecture.html (accessed 19 September 2004), reprinted in *European Human Rights Law Review*, 2004, No. 2.

Paehlke, R. (1995) 'Environmental Harm and Corporate Crime', in F. Pearce and L. Snyder (eds) *Corporate Crime: Contemporary Debates*, Toronto: University of Toronto Press.

Pain, R. (1991) 'Space, Sexual Violence and Social Control: Integrating Geographical and Feminist Analyses of Women's Fear of Crime', *Progress in Human Geography*, 15 (4): 415–31.

Pain, R. and Smith, S. J. (2008) *Fear: Critical Geopolitics and Everyday Life*, Aldershot: Ashgate.

Painter, K. and Farrington, D. (1998) 'Marital Violence in Great Britain and Its Relationship to Marital and Non-marital Rape', *International Review of Victimology*, 5: 257–76.

Pantazis, C. (1999) 'The Criminalization of Female Poverty', in S. Watson and L. Doyal (eds) *Engendering Social Policy*, Buckingham: Open University Press.

Pantazis, C. (2000) 'Tackling Inequalities in Crime and Social Harm', in C. Pantazis and D. Gordon (eds) *Tackling Inequalities: Where are We Now and What Can be Done?*, Bristol: Policy Press.

Paoli, L. (2003) *Mafia Brotherhoods: Organized Crime, Italian Style*, Oxford: Oxford University Press.

Park, C. (2001) 'The Three Faces of Retail Theft', *New Zealand Security*, February/March (available online: www.ecoliving.co.nz/nzsecurity/mag (accessed 20 December 2001)).

Park, E., Burgess, E. W. and McKenzie, R. D. (1925) *The City*, Chicago, IL: University of Chicago Press.

Parker, H. J. (1974) *View from the Boys: A Sociology of Down-Town Adolescents*, Newton Abbot: David and Charles.

Parker, H., Sumner, M. and Jarvis, G. (1989) *Unmasking the Magistrates: The 'Custody or Not' Decision in Sentencing Young Offenders*, Milton Keynes: Open University Press.

Parker, H., Aldridge, J. and Measham, F. (1998) *Illegal Leisure: The Normalization of Adolescent Recreational Drug Use*, London: Routledge.

Parmentier, R. (1999) 'Greenpeace and the Dumping of Waste at Sea: A Case of Non-State Actors' Intervention in International Affairs', *International Negotiation: A Journal of Theory and Practice*, 4 (3): 435–57.

Parsons, T. (1960) *Structure and Process in Modern Society*, New York: Free Press.

Parssinen, T. (1983) *Secret Passions, Secret Remedies: Narcotic Drugs in British Society, 1820–1930*, Manchester: Manchester University Press.

Pascoe, P. (1990) *Relations of Rescue: The Search for Female*

Moral Authority in the American West, 1874–1939, New York: Oxford University Press.

Pashukanis, E. B. (1924/1978) *Law and Marxism: A General Theory*, London: Ink Links.

Passas, N. (1995) '"I Cheat, Therefore I Exist?" The BCCI Scandal in Context', in N. Passas (ed.) *Organized Crime*, Aldershot: Dartmouth.

Patrick, J. (1973) *A Glasgow Gang Observed*, London: Eyre Methuen.

Pearce, F. (1976) *Crimes of the Powerful*, London: Pluto.

Pearce, F. and Tombs, S. (1998) *Toxic Capitalism: Corporate Crime and the Chemical Industry*, Aldershot: Ashgate.

Pearson, G. (1983) *Hooligan: A History of Respectable Fears*, London: Macmillan.

Pearson, G. (1987) 'Social Deprivation, Unemployment and Patterns of Heroin Use', in N. Dorn and N. South (eds) *A Land Fit for Heroin? Drug Policies, Prevention and Practice*, Basingstoke: Macmillan.

Pearson, G. (1992) 'The Role of Culture in the Drug Question', in G. Edwards, M. Lader and C. Drummond (eds) *The Nature of Alcohol and Drug Related Problems*, Oxford: Oxford University Press.

Pearson, J. (1973) *The Profession of Violence*, London: Panther.

Pease, K. (1998) *Repeat Victimisation: Taking Stock*, Crime Detection and Prevention Paper 90, London: Home Office.

Peay, J. (2007) 'Detain – Restrain – Control: Sliding Scale or Slippery Slope?', in D. Downes, P. Rock, C. Chinkin and C. Gearty (eds) *Crime, Social Control and Human Rights: From Moral Panics to States of Denial, Essays in Honour of Stanley Cohen*, Cullompton: Willan.

Percy, A. (1998) *Ethnicity and Victimization: Findings from the 1996 British Crime Survey*, Home Office Statistical Bulletin 6/98, London: Home Office.

Petchesky, R. P. (2000) 'Sexual Rights: Inventing a Concept, Mapping an International Practice', in R. Parker, R. M. Barbosa and P. Aggleton (eds) *Framing the Sexual Subject: The Politics of Gender, Sexuality and Power*, Berkeley: University of California Press.

Petrow, S. (1994) *Policing Morals: The Metropolitan Police and the Home Office 1870–1994*, Oxford: Clarendon Press.

Philips, D. (1983) '"A Just Measure of Crime, Authority, Hunters and Blue Locusts": The "Revisionist" Social History of Crime and the Law in Britain, 1780–1850', in S. Cohen and A. Scull (eds) *Social Control and the State: Historical and Comparative Essays*, Oxford: Basil Blackwell.

Phillips, C. and Bowling, B. (2007) 'Ethnicities, Racism, Crime, and Criminal Justice', in M. Maguire, R. Morgan and R. Reiner (eds) *The Oxford Handbook of Criminology*, 4th edn, Oxford: Oxford University Press.

Phillips, C. and Brown, D. (1998) *Entry into the Criminal Justice System: A Survey of Police Arrests and Their Outcomes*, Home Office Research Study 185, London: Home Office.

Phillips, M. (2001) *America's Social Revolution*, London: Civitas.

Phillips, M. (2002) 'Hate Crime: The Orwellian Response to Prejudice', in P. Iganski (ed.) *The Hate Debate: Should Hate be Punished as a Crime?*, London: Profile.

Phillips, T. (2005) *Knock-Off: The Deadly Trade in Counterfeit Goods*, London: Kogan Page.

Phillips, T. (2006) 'Counterfeiting Becomes a Really Big Business', *Manufacturing and Technology News*, at: http://www.manufacturingnews.com/news/editorials/phillips.html

Pick, D. (1989) *Faces of Degeneration: A European Disorder, c.1848–c.1918*, Cambridge: Cambridge University Press.

Pinder, D. (2003) 'Mapping Worlds: Cartography and the Politics of Representation', in A. Blunt, P. Gruffudd, J. May, M. Ogborn and D. Pinder (eds) *Cultural Geography in Practice*, London: Arnold.

Piquero, A. R., Farrington, D. P. and Blumstein, A. (2007) *Key Issues in Criminal Career Research: New Analyses of the Cambridge Study in Delinquent Development*, Cambridge: Cambridge University Press.

Pitts, J. (2003) *The New Politics of Youth Crime: Discipline or Solidarity*, 2nd edn, Lyme Regis: Russell House.

Player, E. (1989) 'Women and Crime in the Inner City', in D. Downes (ed.) *Crime in the City*, Basingstoke: Macmillan.

Player, E. (2005) 'The Reduction of Women's Imprisonment in England and Wales: Will the Reform of Short Prison Sentences Help?', *Punishment and Society*, 7 (4): 419–39.

Plummer, K. (1979) 'Misunderstanding Labelling Perspectives', in D. Downes and P. Rock (eds) *Deviant Interpretations*, London: Martin Robertson.

Plummer, K. (1995) *Telling Sexual Stories*, London: Routledge.

Plummer, K. (ed.) (1997) *The Chicago School: Critical Assessments*, London: Routledge.

Plummer, K. (ed.) (2002) *Sexualities: Critical Concepts in Sociology*, London: Routledge.

Plummer, K. (2003) *Intimate Citizenship: Private Decisions and Public Dialogue*, Seattle, WA: University of Washington Press.

Policy Studies Institute (1983) *Police and People in London*, 4 vols, London: Policy Studies Institute.

Polsky, N. (1967) *Hustlers, Beats and Others*, Chicago, IL: Aldine.

Powell, L. (2008) 'Cancer Drugs at Risk as Plant Species Die Off', *Observer*, 20 January: 12.

Pratt, J. (2007) *Penal Populism*, London: Routledge.

Presdee, M. (2000) *Cultural Criminology and the Carnival of Crime*, London: Routledge.

Presdee, M. (2004) 'The Story of Crime: Biography and the Excavation of Transgression', in J. Ferrell, K. Hayward, W. Morrison and M. Presdee (eds) *Cultural Criminology Unleashed*, London: Glasshouse Press.

Prime, J., White, S., Liriano, S. and Patel, K. (2001) *Criminal Careers of Those Born between 1953 and 1978, England and Wales*, Home Office Statistical Bulletin 4/01, London: Home Office.

Prison Reform Trust (2006) *Bromley Briefings: Prison Factfile November 2006*, London: Prison Reform Trust.

Prison Service (2001) *Prison Service: Annual Report and Accounts, April 2000 to March 2001*, HC 29, London: Prison Service.

Prison Service (2005) *Annual Report and Accounts, 2004–2005*, HC 193, London: Prison Service.

Prison Service (2008) 'Female Prisoners': www.hmprisonservice.gov.uk/adviceand support/prison_life/femaleprisoners/ (accessed 20 February 2008).

Pudney, S. (2002) *The Road to Ruin? Sequences of Initiation into Drug Use and Offending by Young People in Britain*, Home Office Research Studies 253, London: Home Office.

Pugh, R. (1968) *Imprisonment in Medieval England*, Cambridge: Cambridge University Press.

Punch, M. (1985) *Conduct Unbecoming*, London: Tavistock.

Punch, M. (1996) *Dirty Business: Exploring Corporate Misconduct*, London: Sage.

Punch, M. (1999) 'Tackling Business Crime Within Companies', *Security Journal*, 12 (2): 39–52.

Punch, M. (2000) 'Suite Violence: Why Managers Murder and Corporations Kill', *Crime, Law and Social Change*, 33: 243–80.

Punch, M. (2003) 'Rotten Orchards: "Pestilence", Police Misconduct and System Failure', *Policing and Society*, 13 (2): 171–96.

Punch, M. (2007) *Zero Tolerance Policing*, Bristol: Policy Press.

Punch, M. and Naylor, T. (1973) 'The Police: A Social Service', *New Society*, 24: 358–61.

Quinney, R. (1970) *The Social Reality of Crime*, Boston, MA: Little, Brown.

Radford, J. (1987) 'Policing Male Violence – Policing Women', in J. Hanmer and M. Maynard (eds) *Women, Violence and Social Control*, Basingstoke: Macmillan.

Radzinowicz, L. and King, J. (1979) *The Growth of Crime: The International Experience*, Harmondsworth: Penguin.

Rafter, N. H. (1997) *Creating Born Criminals*, Chicago: University of Illinois Press.

Raistrick, D., Hodgson, R. and Ritson, B. (eds) (1999) *Tackling Alcohol Together*, London: Free Association Books.

Rawlings, P. (1992) *Drunks, Whores and Idle Apprentices: Criminal Biographies of the Eighteenth Century*, London: Routledge.

Rawlings, P. (1995) 'The Idea of Policing: A History', *Policing and Society*, 5: 129–49.

Rawlings, P. (1999) *Crime and Power: A History of Criminal Justice, 1688–1998*, Harlow: Longman.

Rawlings, P. (2002) *Policing: A Short History*, Cullompton: Willan.

Rawlinson, P. (1998) 'Russian Organised Crime: Moving Beyond Ideology', in V. Ruggiero, N. South and I. Taylor (eds) *The New European Criminology*, London: Routledge.

Rawls, J. (1972) *A Theory of Justice*, Oxford: Oxford University Press.

Ray, L., Smith, D. and Wastell, L. (2003) 'Understanding Racist Violence', in E. A. Stanko (ed.) *The Meanings of Violence*, London: Routledge.

Raynor, P. (2007) 'Community Penalties: Probation, "What Works", and Offender Management', in M. Maguire, R. Morgan and R. Reiner (eds) *Oxford Handbook of Criminology*, 4th edn, Oxford: Oxford University Press.

Raynor, P. and Vanstone, M. (2002) *Understanding Community Penalties*, Buckingham: Open University Press.

Reiman, J. (1979) *The Rich Get Richer and the Poor Get Prison: Ideology, Class and Criminal Justice*, New York: Wiley.

Reiman, J. (1988) 'The Justice of the Death Penalty in an Unjust World', in K. Haas and J. A. Inciardi (eds) *Challenging Capital Punishment: Legal and Social Science Approaches*, Newbury Park, CA: Sage.

Reiman, J. (2001) *The Rich Get Richer and the Poor Get Prison*, 6th edn (7th edn, 2005), Boston, MA: Allyn and Bacon.

Reiman, J. and Leighton, P. (2003) 'Getting Tough on Corporate Crime? Enron and a Year of Corporate Financial Scandals' (supplement to Reiman, 2001).

Reiner, R (1992) 'Police Research in the United Kingdom: A Critical Review', in N. Morris and M. Tonry (eds) *Modern Policing*, Chicago, IL: University of Chicago Press.

Reiner, R. (1993) 'Race, Crime and Justice: Models of Interpretation', in L. Gelsthorpe (ed.) *Minority Ethnic Groups in the Criminal Justice System*, Cambridge: Institute of Criminology, University of Cambridge.

Reiner, R. (2000) *The Politics of the Police*, 3rd edn, Oxford: Oxford University Press.

Reiner, R. (2002) 'Media Made Criminality: The Representation of Crime in the Mass Media', in M. Maguire, R. Morgan and R. Reiner (eds) *The Oxford Handbook of Criminology*, 3rd edn, Oxford: Oxford University Press.

Reiner, R. (2007a) 'Success or Statistics? New Labour and Crime Control', *Criminal Justice Matters*, 67: 4–5.

Reiner, R. (2007b) 'Political Economy, Crime, and Criminal Justice', in M. Maguire, R. Morgan and R. Reiner (eds) *The Oxford Handbook of Criminology*, 4th edn, Oxford: Oxford University Press.

Reiner, R. and Spencer, S. (eds) (1993) *Accountable Policing: Effectiveness, Empowerment and Equity*, London: Institute for Public Policy Research.

Reiner, R., Livingstone, S. and Allen, J. (2001) 'Casino Culture: Media and Crime in a Winner–Loser Society', in K. Stenson and R. Sullivan (eds) *Crime, Risk and Justice: The Politics of Crime Control in Liberal Democracies*, Cullompton: Willan.

Retzinger, S. and Scheff, T. (1996) 'Strategy for Community Conferences: Emotions and Social Bonds', in B. Galaway and J. Hudson (eds) *Restorative Justice: International Perspectives*, Monsey, NY: Criminal Justice Press.

Reuter, P. (1984) *Disorganised Crime*, Cambridge, MA: MIT Press.

Reuter, P., MacCoun, R. J. and Murphy, P. (1990) *Money from Crime: A Study of the Economics of Drug Dealing in Washington, DC*, Santa Monica, CA: Rand.

Reynolds, L. (1974) 'Rape as Social Control', *Catalyst*, 8: 62–88.

Ridley, A. and Dunford, L. (1994) 'Corporate Liability for Manslaughter: Reform and the Art of the Possible', *International Journal of the Sociology of Law*, 22: 309–28.

Ringdal, N. J. (2003) *Love for Sale: A World History of Prostitution*, trans. Richard Daly, New York: Grove/Atlantic.

Ringius, L. (2001) *Radioactive Waste Disposal at Sea*, Cambridge, MA: MIT Press.

Ritzer, G. (2002) *The McDonaldization Reader*, London: Sage.

Robb, G. (1992) *White Collar Crime in Modern England: Financial Fraud and Business Morality 1845–1929*, Cambridge: Cambridge University Press.

Roberts, B. (2002) 'On Not Becoming Delinquent: Raising Adolescent Boys in the Dutch Republic, 1600–1750', in P. Cox. and H. Shore (eds) *Becoming Delinquent: British and European Youth, 1650–1950*, Aldershot: Ashgate.

Roberts, M. (2003) *Drugs and Crime: From Warfare to Welfare*, London: NACRO.

Robertson, G. (1993) *Freedom, the Individual and the Law*, London: Penguin.

Robertson, G. (1999) *Crimes against Humanity*, London: Penguin.

Robertson, R. (1992) *Globalization*, London: Sage.

Robinson, F., Keithley, J., Robinson, S. and Childs, S. (1998) *Exploring the Impacts of Crime on Health and Health Services: A Feasibility Study*, Durham: Sociology and Social Policy, University of Durham.

Rock, P. (1996) *Reconstructing a Woman's Prison: The Holloway Redevelopment Project*, Oxford: Clarendon Press.

Rock, P. (1998) *After Homicide*, Oxford: Clarendon Press.

Rock, P. (2002) 'Sociological Theories of Crime', in M. Maguire, R. Morgan and R. Reiner (eds) *The Oxford Handbook of Criminology*, 3rd edn, Oxford: Oxford University Press.

Roebuck, J. and Windham, G. (1983) 'Professional Theft', in G. P. Waldo (ed.) *Criminal Careers*, Beverly Hills, CA: Sage.

Rojek, C. (2003) *Stuart Hall*, Cambridge: Polity.

Rolles, S. (2007) 'Field of Dreams', *Druglink*, March/April: 5.

Roper, L. (1994) *Oedipus and the Devil: Witchcraft, Sexuality and Religion in Early Modern Europe*, London: Routledge.

Rose, N. (1996) 'The Death of the Social? Re-figuring the Territory of Government', *Economy and Society*, 25 (3): 327–56.

Rothman, D. (1971) *The Discovery of the Asylum*, Boston, MA: Little, Brown.

Rothman, D. (1980) *Conscience and Convenience: The Asylum and Its Alternatives in Progressive America*, Boston, MA: Little, Brown.

Rothman, M., Entzel, P. and Dunlop, B. (eds) (2000) *Elders, Crime and the Criminal Justice System*, New York: Springer-Verlag.

Rowell, A. (1996) *Green Backlash: Global Subversion of the Environment Movement*, London: Routledge.

Rowntree Foundation (1995) *Income and Wealth: Report of the Joseph Rowntree Foundation Inquiry Group*, York: Joseph Rowntree Foundation.

Royal College of Psychiatrists (1986) *Alcohol: Our Favourite Drug*, London: Tavistock.

Royal Commission on Criminal Justice (RCCJ) (1993) Report, Cm 2263, London: HMSO.

Royal Society of Arts Commission on Illegal Drugs, Communities and Public Policy (2007) *Drugs: Facing Facts*, London: Royal Society of Arts.

Rozenberg, J. (1993) 'Miscarriages of Justice', in E. Stockdale and S. Casale (eds) *Criminal Justice under Stress*, London: Blackstone.

Ruback, R.B. and Thompson, M. P. (2001) *Social and Psychological Consequences of Violent Victimisation*, Thousand Oaks, CA: Sage.

Rubin, G. (1984) 'Thinking Sex', in C. S. Vance (ed.) *Pleasure and Danger*, London. Routledge.

Rudé, G. (1964) *The Crowd in History*, New York: Wiley.

Ruff, J. R. (2001) *Violence in Early Modern Europe 1500–1800*, Cambridge: Cambridge University Press.

Ruggiero, V. (1996) *Organized and Corporate Crime in Europe: Offers That Can't Be Refused*, Aldershot: Dartmouth.

Ruggiero, V. (2000) 'Transnational Crime: Official and Alternative Fears', *International Journal of the Sociology of Law*, 28: 187–99.

Ruggiero, V. and South, N. (1995) *Eurodrugs: Drug Use, Markets and Trafficking in Europe*, London: UCL Press.

Runciman Report (2000) *Report of the Independent Inquiry into the Misuse of Drugs Act 1971*, London: Police Foundation.

Rusche, G. and Kirchheimer, O. (1939/1968) *Punishment and Social Structure*, New York: Russell and Russell.

Russo, L. (2000) 'Date Rape: A Hidden Crime', Australian Institute for Criminology, *Trends in Crime and Criminal Justice*, 157: 1–6.

Ryan, M. and Ward, T. (1992) 'From Positivism to Postmodernism: Some Theoretical and Strategic Reflections on the Evolution of the Penal Lobby in Britain', *International Journal of the Sociology of Law*, 20 (4): 321–35.

Sampson, R. J. and Raudenbush, S. W. (2004) 'Seeing Disorder: Neighborhood Stigma and the Social Construction of "Broken Windows"', *Social Psychology Quarterly*, 67 (4): 319–42.

Samson, C. (2003) *A Way of Life that Does Not Exist: Canada and the Extinguishment of the Innu*, London: Verso.

Samuel, R. (1981) *East End Underworld: Chapters in the Life of Arthur Harding*, London: Routledge.

Sandberg, S. (2008) 'Street Capital: Ethnicity and Violence on the Streets of Oslo', *Theoretical Criminology*, 12 (2): 153–71.

Sanders, A. and Young, R. (2002) 'From Suspect to Trial', in M. Maguire, R. Morgan and R. Reiner (eds) *The Oxford Handbook of Criminology*, 3rd edn, Oxford: Oxford University Press.

Sanders, A. and Young, R. (2007) *Criminal Justice*, 3rd edn, Oxford: Oxford University Press.

Savage, S., Charman, S. and Cope, S. (2000) *Policing and the Power of Persuasion: The Changing Role* of the *Association of Chief Police Officers*, London: Blackstone.

Scarce, R. (1994) '(No) Trial (But) Tribulations: When Courts and Ethnography Conflict', *Journal of Contemporary Ethnography*, 23: 123–49.

Scarce, R. (1995) 'Scholarly Ethics and Courtroom Antics: Where Researchers Stand in the Eyes of the Law', *American Sociologist*, 26: 87–112.

Scarman, Lord (1981) *The Scarman Report: Report of an Inquiry*, London: HMSO.

Scarpitti, A. and Block, A. (1987) 'America's Toxic Waste Racket', in T. S. Bynum (ed.) *Organized Crime in America: Concepts and Controversies*, New York: Criminal Justice Publishers.

Schechter, H. (2005) *Savage Pastimes: A Cultural History of Violent Entertainment*, New York: St Martin's Press.

Scheff, T. J. (1966) *Being Mentally Ill*, London: Weidenfeld and Nicolson.

Scheff, T. J. (1979) *Catharsis in Healing, Ritual, and Drama*, Berkeley: University of California Press.

Scheff, T. J., Retzinger, S. M. and Ryan, M. T. (1989) 'Crime, Violence, and Self-Esteem: Review and Proposals', in A. Mecca, N. J. Smelser and J. Vasconcellos (eds) *The Social Importance of Self-Esteem*, Berkeley: University of California Press.

Scheper-Hughes, N. and Wacquant, L. (eds) (2002) *Commodifying Bodies*, London: Sage.

Schlesinger, P. and Tumber, H. (1994) *Reporting Crime: The Media Politics of Criminal Justice*, Oxford: Clarendon Press.

Schlesinger, P., Dobash, R., Dobash, R. and Weaver, K. (1992) *Women Watching Violence*, London: British Film Institute.

Schone, J. (2001) 'The Short Life and Painful Death of Prisoners' Rights', *Howard Journal of Criminal Justice*, 40 (1): 70–82.

Schubart, R. (1995) 'From Desire to Deconstruction: Horror Films and Audience Reactions', in D. Kidd-Hewitt and R. Osborne (eds) *Crime and the Media: The Post-modern Spectacle*, London: Pluto.

Schulenberg, J. L. (2007) 'Analysing Police Decision-making: Assessing the Application of a Mixed-Method/Mixed-Model Research Design', *International Journal of Social Research Methodology*, 10 (2): 99–119.

Schulz, D. M. (1995) *From Social Worker to Crimefighter: Women in United States Municipal Policing*, London/Westport, CT: Praeger.

Schur, E. (1965) *Crimes without Victims: Deviant Behavior and Public Policy*, Englewood Cliffs, NJ: Prentice Hall.

Schwendinger, H. J. and Schwendinger, J. (1970/1975) 'Guardians of Order or Defenders of Human Rights?', in I. Taylor, P. Walton and J. Young (eds) *Critical Criminology*, London: Routledge and Kegan Paul.

Scott, D. (2008) *Penology*, London: Sage.

Scott, J. (1996) *Stratification and Power: Structures of Class, Status and Command*, Cambridge: Polity.

Scott, J. (2005) 'Who Will Speak, and Who Will Listen? Comments on Burawoy and Public Sociology', *British Journal of Sociology*, 56 (3): 405–9.

Scott, M. (1968) *The Racing Game*, Chicago, IL: Aldine.

Scott, W. R. (2001) *Institutions and Organizations*, 2nd edn, London: Sage.

Scraton, P. (1990) 'Scientific Knowledge or Masculine Discourses? Challenging Patriarchy in Criminology', in L. Gelsthorpe and A. Morris (eds) *Feminist Perspectives in Criminology*, Milton Keynes: Open University Press.

Scraton, P. (1999) 'Policing with Contempt: The Degrading of Truth and Denial of Justice in the Aftermath of the Hillsborough Disaster', *Journal of Law and Society*, 26 (3): 273–97.

Scraton, P. and Moore, L. (2004) *The Hurt Inside: The Imprisonment of Women and Girls in Northern Ireland*, Northern Ireland: Northern Ireland Human Rights Commission.

Scull, A. (1977) *Decarceration: Community Treatment and the Deviant – A Radical View*, Englewood Cliffs, NJ: Prentice Hall.

Seddon, T. (2002) 'Five Myths about Drugs and Crime', *Safer Society*, 14, Autumn.

Sennett, R. (1998) *The Corrosion of Character: The Personal Consequences of Work in the New Capitalism*, New York: W. W. Norton.

Shapland, J. (1986) 'Victim Assistance and the Criminal Justice System', in E. A. Fattah (ed.) *From Crime Policy to Victim Policy*, Basingstoke: Macmillan.

Shapland, J. and Hobbs, D. (1989) 'Policing on the Ground', in R. Morgan and D. Smith (eds) *Coming to Terms with Policing*, London: Routledge.

Shapland, J., Willmore, J. and Duff, P. (1985) *Victims in the Criminal Justice System*, Aldershot: Gower.

Sharpe, J. A. (1999) *Crime in Early Modern England, 1550–1750*, 2nd edn, London: Longman.

Sharpe, J. A. (2001) *Witchcraft in Early Modern England*, Harlow: Longman.

Shaw, C. (1930) *The Jack Roller*, Chicago, IL: University of Chicago Press.

Shaw, C. R. and McKay, H. D. (1942) *Juvenile Delinquency and Urban Areas*, Chicago, IL: University of Chicago Press.

Shearing, C. and Stenning, P. (1987) '"Say Cheese!" The Disney Order That Is Not So Mickey Mouse', in C. Shearing and P. Stenning (eds) *Private Policing*, Newbury Park, CA: Sage.

Shelley, L. (1999) 'Transnational Organized Crime: The New Authoritarianism', in H. Friman and P. Andreas (eds) *Illicit Global Economy and State Power*, Lanham, MD: Rowman and Littlefield.

Shepherd, J. (1990) 'Violent Crime in Bristol: An Accident and Emergency Department Perspective', *British Journal of Criminology*, 30: 289–305.

Shepherd, J. and Farrington, D. (1993) 'Assault as a Public Health Problem', *Journal of the Royal Society of Medicine*, 86: 89–92.

Shepherd, J. and Lisles, C. (1998) 'Towards Multi-agency Violence Prevention and Victim Support', *British Journal of Criminology*, 3: 351–70.

Sheptycki, J. (1995) 'Transnational Policing and the Makings of a Postmodern State', *British Journal of Criminology*, 35 (4): 613–35.

Sheptycki, J. (1998) 'The Global Cops Cometh: Reflections on Transnationalization, Knowledge Work and Policing Subculture', *British Journal of Sociology*, 49 (1): 57–74.

Sherman, L. (1974) *Police Corruption*, New York: Anchor.

Sherman, L. W. (1995) 'Hot Spots of Crime and Criminal Careers of Places', in J. Eck and D. Weisburd (eds) *Crime and Place*, New York: Criminal Justice Press.

Sherman, L. W. (2005) 'The Use and Usefulness of Criminology, 1751–2005: Enlightened Justice and its Failures', *Annals of the American Academy of Political and Social Science*, 600: 115–35.

Shilling, C. (2002) 'The Two Traditions in the Sociology of Emotions', in J. Barbalet (ed.) *Emotions and Sociology*, Oxford: Blackwell.

Shiner, M. and Newburn, T. (1999) 'Taking Tea with Noel: The Place and Meaning of Drug Use in Everyday Life', in N. South (ed.) *Drugs, Cultures, Controls and Everyday Life*, London: Sage.

Shore, H. (1999) *Artful Dodgers: Youth and Crime in Early Nineteenth Century London*, Woodbridge: Boydell Press.

Shover, N. (1991) 'Burglary', in M. Tonry (ed.) *Crime and Justice: A Review of Research*, vol. 14, Chicago, IL: University of Chicago Press.

Shover, N. (1996) *Great Pretenders: Pursuits and Games of Persistent Thieves*, Boulder, CO: Westview Press.

Showalter, E. (1990) *Sexual Anarchy: Gender and Culture at the Fin de Siècle*, London. Bloomsbury.

Sibley, D. (1995) *Geographies of Exclusion: Society and Difference in the West*, London: Routledge.

Sikka, P. (2008) 'Heart of Darkness', 9 January, at: http://commentisfree.guardian.co.uk/prem_sikka_/2008/01/heart_of_darkness.html.

Silverman, E. (1999) *NYPD Battles Crime: Innovative Strategies in Policing*, Boston, MA: Northeastern University Press.

Silverman, J. and Wilson, D. (2002) *Innocence Betrayed: Paedophilia, the Media and Society*, Cambridge: Polity.

Sim, J. (1990) *Medical Power in Prisons*, Buckingham: Open University Press.

Sim, J., Scraton, P. and Gordon, P. (1987) 'Introduction: Crime, the State and Critical Analysis', in P. Scraton (ed.) *Law, Order and the Authoritarian State*, Milton Keynes: Open University Press.

Simmons, J. et al. (2002) *Crime in England and Wales 2001/2*, Home Office Statistical Bulletin 7/02, London: Home Office.

Simmons, J. and Dodd, T. (2003) *Crime in England and Wales 2002/2003*, London: Home Office.

Simon, J. (2007) *Governing through Crime: How the War on Crime Transformed American Democracy and Created a Culture of Fear*, New York: Oxford University Press.

Sims, L. and Myhill, A. (2001) *Policing and the Public: Findings from the 2000 British Crime Survey*, Home Office Research Findings 136, London: Home Office.

Singer, E. (2003) '"And Here Is the Local Crime Forecast . . ."', *New Scientist*, 16 August, 179 (2408): 13.

Skolnick, J. (1966) *Justice without Trial*, London: Wiley.

Skolnick, J. and Bayley, D. (1986) *The New Blue Line*, New York: Free Press.

Skrobankek, S., Boonpakdee, N. and Jatateero, C. (1997) *The Traffic in Women: Human Realities of the International Sex Trade*, London: Zed Books.

Slapper, G. and Tombs, S. (1999) *Corporate Crime*, Harlow: Longman.

Smandych, R. (ed.) (1999) *Governable Places: Readings on Governmentality and Crime Control*, Aldershot: Ashgate.

Smart, C. (1976) *Women, Crime and Criminology: A Feminist Critique*, London: Routledge and Kegan Paul.

Smart, C. (1979) 'The New Female Criminal: Reality or Myth?', *British Journal of Criminology*, 19: 50–9.

Smart, C. (1989) *Feminism and the Power of the Law*, London: Routledge.

Smart, C. (1990) 'Feminist Approaches to Criminology, or Postmodern Woman Meets Atavistic Man', in L. Gelsthorpe and A. Morris (eds) *Feminist Perspectives in Criminology*, Buckingham: Open University Press.

Smart, C. (1995) *Law, Crime and Sexuality: Essays in Feminism*, London: Sage.

Smelser, N. (1962) *Theory of Collective Behavior*, New York: Free Press.

Smith, D. (1994) *The Sleep of Reason: The James Bulger Case*, London: Century.

Smith, D. (2005) 'Probation and Social Work', *British Journal of Social Work*, 35: 621–37.

Snider, L. (2000) 'The Sociology of Corporate Crime: An Obituary (or Whose Knowledge Claims Have Legs?)', *Theoretical Criminology*, 4 (2): 169–206.

Snodgrass, J. (1982) *The Jack-Roller at Seventy*, Lexington, MA: D. C. Heath.

Snyder, L. (1991) 'The Regulatory Dance: Understanding Reform Processes in Corporate Crime', *International Journal of the Sociology of Law*, 19: 209–36.

SOCA (2006/7) *The United Kingdom Threat Assessment of Serious Organised Crime*, London: Serious Organised Crime Agency. http://www.soca.gov.uk/assessPublications/downloads/threat_assess_unclass_250706.pdf

Sollund, R (2008) *Global Harms Ecological Crime and Speciesism*, New York: Nova.

Soloway, I. and Walters, J. (1977) 'Workin' the Corner: The Ethics and Legality of Ethnographic Fieldwork among Active Heroin Addicts', in R. S. Weppner (ed.) *Street Ethnography: Selected Studies of Crime and Drug Use in Natural Settings*, Beverly Hills, CA: Sage.

South, N. (1988) *Policing for Profit*, London: Sage.

South, N. (ed.) (1995) *Drugs, Crime and Criminal Justice*, 2 vols, Aldershot: Dartmouth.

South, N. (1997) 'Late-Modern Criminology: "Late" as in "Dead" or "Modern" as in "New"?', in D. Owen (ed.) *Sociology after Postmodernism*, London and Thousand Oaks, CA: Sage.

South, N. (1998a) 'Corporate and State Crimes against the Environment: Foundations for a Green Perspective in European Criminology', in V. Ruggiero, N. South and I. Taylor (eds) *The New European Criminology*, London and New York: Routledge.

South, N. (1998b) 'A Green Field for Criminology? A Proposal for a Perspective', *Theoretical Criminology*, 2 (2): 211–34.

South, N. (ed.) (1999a) *Youth Crime, Deviance and Delinquency*, 2 vols, Aldershot: Dartmouth.

South, N. (ed.) (1999b) *Drugs: Cultures, Controls and Everyday Life*, London: Sage.

South, N. (2002) 'Drugs, Alcohol and Crime', in M. Maguire, R. Morgan and R. Reiner (eds) *The Oxford Handbook of Criminology*, 3rd edn, Oxford: Oxford University Press.

South, N. (2004) 'Managing Work, Hedonism and "the Borderline" between the Legal and Illegal Markets: Two Case Studies of Recreational Heavy Drug Users', *Addiction Research and Theory*, 12 (6): 525–38.

South, N. (2005) 'Inequalities, Crime and Citizenship', in M. Romero and E. Margolis (eds) *The Blackwell Companion on Social Inequalities*, Malden, MA: Blackwell.

South, N. (2007) 'The "Corporate Colonisation of Nature": Bio-Prospecting, Bio-Piracy and the Development of Green Criminology', in P. Beirne and N. South (eds) *Toward a Green Criminology: Confronting Harms Against Humanity, Animals and Nature*, Cullompton: Willan.

South, N. and Beirne, P. (1998) in 'For a Green Criminology', special issue of *Theoretical Criminology*, 2 (2).

South, N. and Beirne, P. (eds) (2006) *Green Criminology*, Aldershot: Dartmouth.

South, N. and Weiss, R. (eds) (1998) *Comparing Prison Systems: Toward a Comparative and International Penology*, Reading: Gordon and Breach.

Southwell, D. (2002) *Dirty Cash: Organised Crime in the 21st Century*, London: Virgin.

Spalek, B. (2001) 'Regulation, White Collar Crime and the Bank of Credit and Commerce International', *Howard Journal of Criminal Justice*, 40 (2): 166–79.

Spalek, B. (2007) 'Knowledgeable Consumers?: Corporate Fraud and Its Devastating Impacts', Briefing 4, London: Centre for Crime and Justice Studies. Available to download free at: http://www.crimeandjustice.org.uk/opus309/KC_Final_version_200807.pdf

Sparks, R. (1992) *Television and the Drama of Crime: Moral Tales and the Place of Crime in Public Life*, Milton Keynes: Open University Press.

Sparks, R. (1993) 'Inspector Morse: "The Last Enemy"', in G. Brandt (ed.) *British Television Drama in the 1980s*, Cambridge: Cambridge University Press.

Sparks, R. (2000) 'Perspectives on Risk and Penal Politics', in T. Hope and R. Sparks (eds) *Crime, Risk and Insecurity*, London: Routledge.

Sparks, R. (2002) 'Prisons, Punishment and Penality', in E. McLaughlin and J. Muncie (eds) *Controlling Crime*, 2nd edn, London: Sage.

Sparks, R., Bottoms, A. and Hay, W. (1996) *Prisons and the Problem of Order*, Oxford: Clarendon Press.

Spelman, E. (1989) 'Anger and Insubordination', in A. Garry and M. Pearsall (eds) *Women, Knowledge, and Reality: Explorations in Feminist Philosophy*, Boston, MA: Unwin Hyman.

Spierenburg, P. (1984) *The Spectacle of Suffering: Executions and the Evolution of Repression*, Cambridge: Cambridge University Press.

Spierenburg, P. (ed.) (1998a) *Men and Violence: Gender, Honor, and Rituals in Modern Europe and America*, Ohio: Ohio State University Press.

Spierenburg, P. (1998b) 'The Body and the State: Early Modern Europe', in N. Morris and D. Rothman (eds) *The Oxford History of the Prison:* *The Practice of Punishment in Western Society*, Oxford: Oxford University Press.

Spierenburg, P. (2005) 'Origins of the Prison', in C. Elmsley (ed.) *The Persistent Prison: Problems, Images and Alternatives*, London: Francis Boutle.

Spitzer, S. (1987) 'Security and Control in Capitalist Societies: The Fetishism of Security and the Secret Thereof', in J. Lowman, R. J. Menzies and T. S. Palys (eds) *Transcarceration: Essays in the Sociology of Social Control*, Aldershot: Gower.

Springhall, J. (1998) *Youth, Popular Culture and Moral Panics: Penny Gaffs to Gangsta-Rap, 1830–1996*, Basingstoke: Macmillan.

Squires, G. and Hartman, C. (2006) *There Is No Such Thing as a Natural Disaster: Race, Class and Katrina*, London: Routledge.

Stanko, B. (1987) 'Typical Violence, Normal Precaution: Men, Women, and Interpersonal Violence in England, Wales and the USA', in J. Hanmer and M. Maynard (eds) *Women, Violence and Social Control*, Basingstoke: Macmillan.

Stanko, B. (1988) 'Fear of Crime and the Myth of the Safe Home: A Feminist Critique of Criminology', in K. Yllo and M. Bograd (eds) *Feminist Perspectives on Wife Abuse*, London: Sage.

Stanko, B. (1997) 'Safety Talk: Conceptualising Women's Risk Assessment as a "Technology of the Soul"', *Theoretical Criminology*, 1 (4): 479–99.

Stanko, E. (1990) *Everyday Violence*, London: Pandora.

Stanko, E. (1994) *Perspectives on Violence*, London: Quartet.

Stanko, E., Marian, L., Crisp, D., Manning, R., Smith, J. and Cowan, S. (1998) *Taking Stock*, Uxbridge, Middlesex: Brunel University.

Stein, A. (2001) *Strangers in Our Midst*, Boston, MA: Beacon.

Stelfox, P. (1998) 'Policing Lower Levels of Organised Crime in England and Wales', *Howard Journal of Criminal Justice*, 37 (4): 393–406.

Stern, V. (1993) *Bricks of Shame*, London: Penguin.

Stevenson, D. (2003) *Cities and Urban Culture*, Buckingham: Open University Press.

Stevenson, N. (1999) *The Transformation of the Media: Globalisation, Morality and Ethics*, Harlow: Longman.

Steward, K. (2006) 'Gender Decisions in Remand Decision-Making', in F. Heidensohn (ed.) *Gender and Justice*, Cullompton: Willan.

Stimson, G. (1995) 'Aids and Injecting Drug Use in the United Kingdom, 1987–1993: The Policy

Response and the Prevention of the Epidemic', *Social Science and Medicine*, 41 (5): 699–716.

Stoler, A. L. (2002) *Carnal Knowledge and Imperial Power: Race and the Intimate in Colonial Rule*, Berkeley: University of California Press.

Stones, R. (1996) *Sociological Reasoning*, Basingstoke: Macmillan.

Storch, R. (1975) 'The Plague of Blue Locusts: Police Reform and Popular Resistance in Northern England 1840–57', *International Review of Social History*, 20: 61–90.

Storch, R. (1976) 'The Policeman as Domestic Missionary', *Journal of Social History*, 9 (4): 481–509.

Strang, J. and Stimson, G. (eds) (1991) *AIDS and Drug Misuse*, London: Routledge.

Strang, J. and Gossop, M. (eds) (2004) *Heroin Addiction and the British System: Volume I, Origins and Evolution*, London: Routledge.

Strang, J. and Gossop, M. (2005) *Heroin Addiction and the British System: Volume II, Treatment and Other Responses*, London: Routledge.

Strang, J., Wilks, M., Wells, B. and Marshall, J. (1998) 'Missed Problems and Missed Opportunities for Addicted Doctors', Editorial, *British Medical Journal*, 7 (129): 316.

Streatfeild, D. (2002) *Cocaine: A Definitive History*, London: Virgin Books.

Strongman, K. (2003) *The Psychology of Emotion: From Everyday Life to Theory*, Chichester: Wiley.

Sumner, C. (1976) 'Marxism and Deviancy Theory', in P. Wiles (ed.) *Sociology of Crime and Delinquency in Britain*, vol. 2, London: Martin Robertson.

Sumner, C. (1994) *The Sociology of Deviance: An Obituary*, Buckingham: Open University Press.

Surette, R. (1998) *Media, Crime and Criminal Justice: Images and Realities*, Belmont, CA: Wadsworth.

Sutherland, E. (1937) *The Professional Thief*, Chicago, IL: University of Chicago Press.

Sutherland, E. (1949) *White Collar Crime*, New York: Holt, Rinehart and Winston.

Sutherland, E. (1950) 'The Diffusion of Sexual Psychopath Laws', *American Journal of Sociology*, 56: 142–8.

Sutherland, E. (1956) *The Sutherland Papers*, ed. A. K. Cohen, A. R. Lindesmith and K. Schlussler, Bloomington: Indiana University Press.

Republished as Sutherland, E. (1973) *On Analyzing Crime*, ed. K. Schlussler, Chicago, IL: University of Chicago Press.

Sutherland, E. with Locke, H. J. (1936) *Twenty Thousand Homeless Men*, Philadelphia: J. B. Lippincott.

Sutton, M. (1998) *Handling Stolen Goods and Theft*, Home Office Research Study 178, London: Home Office.

Sutton, R. and Farrall, S. (2005) 'Gender, Socially Desirable Responding and the Fear of Crime: Are Women Really More Anxious about Crime?', *British Journal of Criminology*, 45 (2): 212–24.

Sykes, G. (1958) *The Society of Captives*, Princeton, NJ: Princeton University Press.

Sykes, G. M. and Matza, D. (1957) 'Techniques of Neutralization: A Theory of Delinquency', *American Sociological Review*, 22: 664–70.

Szasz, A. (1986) 'Corporations, Organised Crime and the Disposal of Hazardous Waste: An Examination of the Making of a Criminogenic Regulatory Structure', *Criminology*, 24 (1): 1–27.

Szasz, A. (1994) *EcoPopulism: Toxic Waste and the Movement for Environmental Justice*, Minneapolis: University of Minnesota Press.

Tame, C. (1991) 'Freedom, Responsibility and Justice: The Criminology of the "New Right"', in K. Stenson and D. Cowell (eds) *The Politics of Crime Control*, London: Sage.

Tannenbaum, F. (1938) *Crime and the Community*, New York: McGraw-Hill.

Tappan, P. (1947) 'Who Is the Criminal?', *American Sociological Review*, 12: 96–102.

Tappan, P. (1954) 'The Legal Rights of Prisoners', *The Annals*, 293: 99–111.

Taylor, I. (1996) 'Fear of Crime, Urban Fortunes and Suburban Social Movements: Some Reflections on Manchester', *Sociology*, 30 (2): 317–37.

Taylor, I. (1997) 'Crime, Anxiety, and Locality: Responding to the Condition of England at the End of the Century', *Theoretical Criminology*, 1 (1): 53–76.

Taylor, I. (1999) *Crime in Context: A Critical Criminology of Market Societies*, Cambridge: Polity.

Taylor, I. and Taylor, L. (eds) (1973) *Politics and Deviance*, Harmondsworth: Penguin.

Taylor, I. and Jamieson, R. (1997) '"Proper Little Mesters": Nostalgia and Protest in De-industrialised Sheffield', in S. Westwood and J. Williams (eds) *Imagining Cities: Scripts, Signs, Memory*, London: Routledge.

Taylor, I. and Jamieson, R. (1998) 'Fear of Crime and Fear of Falling: English Anxieties Approaching the Millennium', *Arch. European Journal of Sociology*, 39 (1): 149–75.

Taylor, I., Walton, P. and Young, J. (1973) *The New Criminology: For a Social Theory of Deviance*, London: Routledge and Kegan Paul.

Taylor, J. (2004) *Crime against Retail and Manufacturing Premises: Findings from the 2002 Commercial Victimisation Survey*, Home Office Research Findings No. 259, London: Home Office.

Taylor, L. (1973) *Deviance and Society*, London: Joseph.

Taylor, P. (1999) *Hackers: Crime in the Digital Sublime*, London: Routledge.

Taylor, P. (2000) 'Hackers – Cyberpunks or Microserfs?', in D. Thomas, and B. D. Loader (eds) *Cybercrime: Law Enforcement, Security and Surveillance in the Information Age*, London: Routledge.

Taylor, P. (2003) 'Maestros or Misogynists? Gender and the Social Construction of Hacking', in Y. Jewkes (ed.) *Dot.cons: Crime, Deviance and Identity on the Internet*, Cullompton: Willan.

Temko, N. (2006) 'Jail Racism Rife, Says Inquiry', *Observer*, 11 June: 5.

Thomas, D. and Loader, B. D. (eds) (2000) *Cybercrime: Law Enforcement, Security and Surveillance in the Information Age*, London: Routledge.

Thomas, T. (2000) *Sex Crime: Sex Offending and Society*, Cullompton: Willan.

Thomas, T. (2004) 'When Public Protection Becomes Punishment? The UK Use of Civil Measures to Contain the Sex Offender', *European Journal on Criminal Policy and Research*, 10 (4): 337–51.

Thomas, W. I. (1923) *The Unadjusted Girl*, Boston, MA: Little, Brown.

Thompson, E. P. (1963) *The Making of the English Working Class*, London: Victor Gollancz.

Thompson, E. P. (1975) *Whigs and Hunters: The Origin of the Black Act*, London: Allen Lane.

Thompson, E. P. (1991) *Customs in Common*, London: Merlin Press.

Thompson, J. (1995) *The Media and Modernity*, Cambridge: Polity.

Thompson, K. (1998) *Moral Panics*, London: Routledge.

Thrasher, F. (1927) *The Gang*, Chicago, IL: University of Chicago Press.

Tikoff, V. (2002) 'Before the Reformatory: A Correctional Orphanage in Ancien Régime Seville', in P. Cox and H. Shore (eds) *Becoming Delinquent: British and European Youth, 1650–1950*, Aldershot: Ashgate.

Tithecott, R. (1997) *Of Men and Monsters: Jeffrey Dahmer and the Construction of the Serial Killer*, Madison: University of Wisconsin Press.

Tombs, S. (2000) 'Official Statistics and Hidden Crime: Researching Safety Crimes', in V. Jupp, P. Davies and P. Francis (eds) *Doing Criminological Research*, London: Sage.

Tombs, S. and Whyte, D. (eds) (2003) *Unmasking the Crimes of the Powerful: Scrutinizing States and Corporations*, New York: Peter Lang.

Tomsen, S. (1997) 'A Top Night: Social Protest, Masculinity and the Culture of Drinking Violence', *British Journal of Criminology*, 37 (1): 90–102.

Tonry, M. (2004) *Punishment and Politics: Evidence and Emulation in the Making of English Crime Control Policy*, Cullompton: Willan.

Travis, A. (2007) 'From Foreign Fields to UK Streets – The Anatomy of an £8bn Industry', *Guardian*, 21 November.

Tremblay, M. (1986) 'Designing Crime: The Short Life Expectancy and the Workings of a Recent Wave of Credit Card Bank Frauds', *British Journal of Criminology*, 26: 234–53.

Trend, D. (2007) *The Myth of Media Violence: A Critical Introduction*, Oxford: Blackwell.

Tuan, Y. (1979) *Landscapes of Fear*, New York: Pantheon Books.

Turner, B. (1996) *The Body and Society*, 2nd edn, London: Sage.

Turner, J. and Stets, J. (2005) *The Sociology of Emotions*, Cambridge: Cambridge University Press.

Turton, J. (2007) *Child Abuse, Gender and Society*, London: Routledge.

Uglow, S. (2002) *Criminal Justice*, London: Sweet and Maxwell.

Ungar, S. (2001) 'Moral Panic versus the Risk Society: The Implications of the Changing Sites of Social Anxiety', *British Journal of Sociology*, 52 (2): 271–91.

United Nations Centre for International Crime Prevention (UNCICP) (2000) *Assessing Transnational Organised Crime: Results of a Pilot Survey of 40 Selected Organised Criminal Groups in 16 Countries*, Vienna: UNCICP.

United Nations Educational, Scientific and Cultural Organization (UNESCO) (1997) *Preventing the Illicit Traffic in Cultural Property. A Resource Handbook for the Implementation of the 1970 UNESCO Convention*, Paris: UNESCO.

United Nations Office on Drugs and Crime (UNODC) (2007) *Annual Report*, Vienna: UNODC.

US Federal Bureau of Investigation (1999) *Hate Crime Data Collection Guidelines*, Washington, DC: Federal Bureau of Investigation, US Department of Justice.

Useem, B. and Kimball, P. (1989) *States of Siege: U.S. Prison Riots, 1971–1986*, Oxford: Oxford University Press.

Valier, C. (2002a) *Theories of Crime and Punishment*, Harlow: Pearson.

Valier, C. (2002b) 'Punishment, Border Crossings and the Powers of Horror', *Theoretical Criminology*, 6 (3): 319–37.

Valverde, M. (1996) 'Social Facicity and the Law: A Social Expert's Eyewitness Account of the Law', *Social and Legal Studies*, 5 (2): 201–18.

van den Haag, E. (1975) *Punishing Criminals: Concerning a Very Old and Painful Question*, New York: Basic Books.

van den Haag, E. (1985) *Deterring Potential Criminals*, London: Social Affairs Unit.

Van Dijk, J. J. M. (1985) 'Regaining a Sense of Community and Order', in European Committee on Crime Problems, *Research on Crime Victims*, Strasbourg: Council of Europe, 145–64.

Van Duyne, P. (1993) 'Organised Crime and Business Crime Enterprises in the Netherlands', *Crime, Law and Social Change*, 19: 103–42.

van Zyl Smit, D. (2007) 'Prisoners' Rights', in Y. Jewkes (ed.) *Handbook on Prisons*, Cullompton: Willan.

Vann, I. B. and Garson, G. D. (2001) 'Crime Mapping and Its Extension to Social Science Analysis', *Social Science Computer Review*, 19 (4): 471–9.

Vanstone, M. (2007) *Supervising Offenders in the Community: A History of Probation Theory and Practice*, Aldershot: Ashgate.

Vass, A. (1986) *AIDS: A Plague in Us*, Cambridge: Venus Academica.

Venkatesh, S. (2008) *Gang Leader for a Day: A Rogue Sociologist Takes to the Streets*, London: Penguin.

Vine, I. (1997) 'The Dangerous Psycho-logic of Media "Effects"', in M. Barker and J. Petley (eds) *Ill Effects: The Media/Violence Debate*, London: Routledge.

Virdee, S. (1997) 'Racial Harassment', in T. Modood and R. Berthoud (eds) *Ethnic Minorities in Britain*, London: Policy Studies Institute.

Vogel, D. (1986) *National Styles of Regulation: Environmental Policy in Great Britain and the United States*, Ithaca, NY: Cornell University Press.

Vold, G. B. (1958) *Theoretical Criminology*, Oxford: Oxford University Press.

von Hentig, H. (1948) *The Criminal and His Victim*, New Haven, CT: Yale University Press.

von Hirsch, A. (1976) *Doing Justice: The Choice of Punishments*, New York: Hill and Wang.

von Hirsch, A. (1985) *Past or Future Crimes: Deservedness and Dangerousness in the Sentencing of Criminals*, Manchester: Manchester University Press.

Wachholz, S. (2007) '"At Risk": Climate Change and its Bearing on Women's Vulnerability to Male Violence', in P. Beirne and N. South (eds) *Toward a Green Criminology: Confronting Harms Against Humanity, Animals and Nature*, Cullompton: Willan.

Wacquant, L. (2001) 'Deadly Symbiosis: When Prison and Ghetto Meet and Merge', *Punishment and Society*, 3 (1): 95–134.

Waddington, P. A. J. (1996) 'Public Order Policing: Citizenship and Moral Ambiguity', in F. Leishman, B. Loveday and S. Savage (eds) *Core Issues in Policing*, Harlow: Longman.

Walker, C. and Starmer, K. (1999) *Miscarriages of Justice: A Review of Justice in Error*, London: Blackstone.

Walker, G. (2003) *Crime, Gender and Social Order in Early Modern England*, Cambridge: Cambridge University Press.

Walker, N. (1991) *Why Punish?*, Oxford: Oxford University Press.

Walklate, S. (1995) *Gender and Crime: An Introduction*, London: Prentice Hall.

Walklate, S. (1998) 'Excavating the Fear of Crime:

Fear, Anxiety or Trust?', *Theoretical Criminology*, 2 (4): 403–18.

Walklate, S. (2001) *Gender, Crime and Criminal Justice* (2nd edn, 2004), Cullompton: Willan.

Walklate, S. (2007a) *Imagining the Victim of Crime*, Berkshire: Open University Press.

Walklate, S. (ed.) (2007b) *Handbook of Victims and Victimology*, Cullompton: Willan.

Walkowitz, J. (1984) 'Male Vice and Female Virtue: Feminism and the Politics of Prostitution in Nineteenth Century Britain', in A. Snitow, C. Stansell and S. Thompson (eds) *Power and Desire: The Politics of Sexuality*, London: Virago.

Walkowitz, J. R. (1992) *City of Dreadful Delight: Narratives of Sexual Danger in Late Victorian London*, London: Virago.

Wall, D. (2001) 'Cybercrimes on the Internet', in D. Wall (ed.) *Crime and the Internet*, London: Routledge.

Wall, D. (2007) *Cybercrime: The Transformation of Crime in the Information Age*, Cambridge: Polity.

Walmsley, R. (2003) *World Prison Population List*, 4th edn, London: The Stationery Office.

Walmsley, R. (2006) *World Prison Population List*, 7th edn, London: International Centre for Prison Studies.

Walters, R. (2007) 'Crime, Regulation and Radioactive Waste', in P. Bierne and N. South (eds) *Toward a Green Criminology: Confronting Harms Against Humanity, Animals and Nature*, Cullompton: Willan.

Walton, P. and Young, J. (1997) *The New Criminology Revisited*, Basingstoke: Macmillan.

Walzer, M. (1986) 'The Politics of Michel Foucault', in D. Couzens Hoy (ed.) *Foucault: A Critical Reader*, Oxford: Basil Blackwell.

Watney, S. (1997) *Policing Desire: Pornography, AIDS and the Media*, 3rd edn, London: Cassell.

Watt, P. (1998) 'Going Out of Town: Youth, Race and Place in the South East of England', *Environment & Planning D: Society and Space*, 16 (6): 687–703.

Weatherburn, D. and Lind, B. (2001) *Delinquent-Prone Communities*, Cambridge: Cambridge University Press.

Weber, M. (1958/1970) *From Max Weber: Essays in Sociology*, trans. and ed. H. J. H. Gerth and C. W. Mills, London: Routledge and Kegan Paul.

Webster, C. (1994) *The Keighley Crime Survey*, Bradford and Ilkley Community College.

Week, The (2007) 'The Cannabis Boom', *The Week*, 19 May: 13.

Weinberger, B. (1981) 'The Police and the Public in Mid 19th Century Warwickshire', in V. Bailey (ed.) *Policing and Punishment in 19th Century Britain*, London: Croom Helm.

Weisburd, D., Waring, E. and Chayel, E. (2001) *White Collar Crime and Criminal Careers*, Cambridge: Cambridge University Press.

Weiss, R. P. (ed.) (1999) *Social History of Crime, Policing and Punishment*, Aldershot: Ashgate.

Welch, M. (2007) 'The Re-emergence of Torture in Political Culture: Tracking Its Discourse and Genealogy', in *Capítulo Criminológico*, 3 (4). http://www.serbi.luz.edu.ve/scielo.php?script=sci_arttext&pid=S0798–959820070120 (accessed 23 April 2008).

Wells, C. (1993) *Corporations and Criminal Responsibility*, Oxford: Clarendon Press.

Western, B. (2006) *Punishment and Inequality in America*, New York: Russell Sage Foundation.

White, K. (1993) *The First Sexual Revolution*, New York: New York Press.

White, R. (ed.) (2005) 'Green/Environmental Criminology', special issue, *Current Issues in Criminal Justice*, 16 (3).

White, R. and Sutton, A. (1995) 'Crime Prevention, Urban Space and Social Exclusion', *Journal of Sociology*, 31 (1): 82–99.

Whitehead, P. and Statham, R. (2006) *The History of Probation: Politics, Power and Cultural Change*, Kent: Shaw and Sons.

Wiener, M. J. (1998) 'The Victorian Criminalization of Men', in P. Spierenburg (ed.) *Men and Violence: Gender, Honor, and Rituals in Modern Europe and America*, Ohio: Ohio State University Press.

Wiesner, M. E. (ed.) (2007) *Witchcraft in Early Modern Europe*, Boston, MA: Houghton Mifflin.

Wikström, P.-O. and Sampson, R. J. (2003) 'Social Mechanisms on Crime and Pathways into Criminality', in B. B. Lahey, T. E. Moffitt and A. Caspi (eds) *Causes of Conduct Disorder and Juvenile Delinquency*, New York: Conduct Press.

Wilkins, L. T. (1964) *Social Deviance: Social Policy, Action and Research*, London: Tavistock.

Wilkins, L. T. (1967) *Social Policy, Action and Research*, London: Tavistock.

Williams, C. (1996) 'Environmental Victims: An Introduction', in C. Williams (ed.) *Environmental Victims*, special issue of *Social Justice*, 23 (4): 1–6.

Williams, S. (2001) *Emotion and Social Theory*, London: Sage.

Willis, P. (1977) *Learning to Labour: How Working Class Kids Get Working Class Jobs*, London: Saxon House.

Wilson, D., Sharp, C. and Patterson, A. (2006) *Young People and Crime: Findings from the 2005 Offending, Crime and Justice Survey*, Home Office Statistical Bulletin 17/06, London: Home Office.

Wilson, J. Q. (1975) *Thinking about Crime*, New York: Basic Books.

Wilson, J. Q. and Kelling, G. (1982) 'Broken Windows', *Atlantic Monthly*, March: 29–37.

Winlow, S. (2001) *Badfellas: Crime, Tradition and New Masculinities*, Oxford: Berg.

Winlow, S. and Hall, S. (2006) *Violent Night: Urban Leisure and Contemporary Culture*, Oxford: Berg.

Wiseman, J. P. (1970) *Stations of the Lost*, Englewood Cliffs, NJ: Prentice Hall.

Witte, R. (1996) *Racist Violence and the State*, Harlow: Longman.

Wolch, J. and Dear, M. (eds) (1989) *The Power of Geography: How Territory Shapes Social Life*, Boston, MA: Unwin Hyman.

Wolfgang, M. (1958) *Patterns in Criminal Homicide*, Philadelphia: University of Pennsylvania Press.

Wolfgang, M. (1960) 'Cesare Lombroso', in M. Hermann (ed.) *Pioneers in Criminology*, London: Stevens.

Wollstein, J. (1967) *The Case Against Victimless Crimes*, Silver Springs, MD: Society for Individual Liberty.

Woolf, H. and Tumim, S. (1991) *Prison Disturbances April 1990*, Cm 1456, London: HMSO.

Worrall, A. (1990) *Offending Women: Female Lawbreakers and the Criminal Justice System*, London: Routledge.

Worrall, A. (1997) *Punishment in the Community: The Future of Criminal Justice*, Harlow: Addison Wesley Longman.

Worrall, A. and Hoy, C. (2005) *Punishment in the Community: Managing Offenders, Making Choices*, 2nd edn, Cullompton: Willan.

Wright, A (2006) *Organised Crime*, Cullompton: Willan.

Wright, M. (1991) *Justice for Victims and Offenders*, Buckingham: Open University Press.

Yablonsky, L. (1965) 'Experiences with the Criminal Community', in A. Gouldner and S. M. Miller (eds) *Applied Sociology*, New York: Free Press.

Young, A. (1996) *Imagining Crime: Textual Outlaws and Criminal Conversations*, London: Sage.

Young, J. (1971) *The Drugtakers*, London: Paladin.

Young, J. (1973) 'The Myth of the Drug Taker in the Mass Media', in S. Cohen and J. Young (eds) *The Manufacture of News*, London: Constable.

Young, J. (1974) 'Mass Media, Drugs and Deviance', in P. Rock and M. Mackintosh (eds) *Deviance and Social Control*, London: Tavistock.

Young, J. (1975) 'Working Class Criminology', in I. Taylor, P. Walton and J. Young (eds) *Critical Criminology*, London: Routledge.

Young, J. (1979) 'Left Idealism, Reformism and Beyond: From New Criminology to Marxism', in B. Fine, R. Kinsey, J. Lea, S. Picciotto and J. Young (eds) *Capitalism and the Rule of Law*, London: Hutchinson.

Young, J. (1986) 'The Failure of Criminology: The Need for a Radical Realism', in J. Young and R. Matthews (eds) *Confronting Crime*, London: Sage.

Young, J. (1987) 'The Tasks Facing a Realist Criminology', *Contemporary Crises*, 11: 337–56.

Young, J. (1992) 'The Rising Demand for Law and Order and Our Maginot Lines of Defence against Crime', in N. Abercrombie and A. Warde (eds) *Social Change in Contemporary Britain*, Cambridge: Polity.

Young, J. (1997) 'Left Realist Criminology: Radical in Its Analysis, Realist in Its Policy', in M. Maguire, R. Morgan and R. Reiner (eds) *The Oxford Handbook of Criminology*, 2nd edn, Oxford: Clarendon Press.

Young, J. (1999a) *The Exclusive Society: Social Exclusion, Crime and Difference in Late Modernity*, London: Sage.

Young, J. (1999b) 'Cannibalism and Bulimia: Patterns of Social Control in Late Modernity', *Theoretical Criminology*, 3 (4): 387–407.

Young, J. (2002) 'Searching for a New Criminology of Everyday Life: A Review of the Culture of Control by David Garland', *British Journal of Criminology*, 42: 228–43.

Young, J. (2004) 'Voodoo Criminology and the Numbers Game', in J. Ferrell, K. Hayward, W. Morrison and M. Presdee (eds) *Cultural Criminology Unleashed*, London: Glasshouse Press.

Young, J. (2007a) *The Vertigo of Late Modernity*, London: Sage.

Young, J. (2007b) 'Slipping Away – Moral Panics Each Side of "the Golden Age"', in D. Downes, P. Rock, C. Chinkin and C. Gearty (eds) *Crime, Social Control and Human Rights: From Moral Panics to States of Denial, Essays in Honour of Stanley Cohen*, Cullompton: Willan.

Young, V. D. and Greene, H. T. (2002) 'Pedagogical Reconstruction: Incorporating African American Perspectives into the Curriculum', in S. Gabbidon, H. T. Greene and V. D. Young (eds) *African American Classics in Criminology and Criminal Justice*, Thousand Oaks, CA: Sage.

Zahn, M. A. (1999) 'Thoughts on the Future of Criminology', *Criminology*, 37: 1–16.

Zander, M. and Henderson, P. (1993) *Crown Court Study, Royal Commission on Criminal Justice Research Study 19*, London: HMSO.

Zedner, L. (1991a) 'Women, Crime, and Penal Responses: A Historical Account', in M. Tonry (ed.) *Crime and Justice: A Review of Research*, 14: 307–62.

Zedner, L. (1991b) *Women, Crime and Custody in Victorian England*, Oxford: Clarendon.

Zedner, L. (1995) 'Wayward Sisters: The Prison for Women', in N. Morris and D. Rothman (eds) *The Oxford History of the Prison*, Oxford: Oxford University Press.

Zedner, L. (2000) 'The Pursuit of Security', in T. Hope and R. Sparks (eds) *Crime, Risk and Insecurity*, London: Routledge.

Zedner, L. (2005) 'Securing Liberty in the Face of Terror: Reflections from Criminal Justice', *Journal of Law and Society*, 32 (4): 507–33.

Zedner, L. (2007a) 'Pre-crime and Post-criminology?', *Theoretical Criminology*, 11: 261–81.

Zedner, L. (2007b) 'Seeking Security by Eroding Rights: The Side-stepping of Due Process', in B. Goold and L. Lazarus (eds) *Security and Human Rights*, Oxford: Hart.

Zehr, H. (1990) *Changing Lenses*, Scottdale, PA: Herald Press.

Zellick, G. (1974) 'Prisoners' Rights in England', *University of Toronto Law Review*, 24: 334–9.

Zhang, S. and Chin, K.-L. (2003) 'The Declining Significance of Triad Societies in Transnational Illegal Activities', *British Journal of Criminology*, 43 (3): 469–88.

Zimring, F. and Hawkins, E. (1995) *Incapacitation: Penal Confinement and the Restraint of Crime*, Oxford: Oxford University Press.

Žižek, S. (2002) 'Are We in a War? Do We Have an Enemy?', *London Review of Books*, 23 May: http://www.lrb.co.uk/v24/n10/print/zize01.html (accessed 14 March 2008).

Zola, I. (1972) 'Medicine as an Institution of Social Control', *Sociological Review*, 20: 487–504.

Zurcher, L. A., Jr and Kirkpatrick, R.G. (1976) *Citizens for Decency: Antipornography Crusades as Status Defense*, Austin: University of Texas Press.

Webliography

2 Histories of Crime

National Archives
http://www.nationalarchives.gov.uk/

Old Bailey (the Central Criminal Court in England)
http://www.oldbaileyonline.org/proceedings/publishinghistory.html

3 Researching Crime

Statistics Canada
http://www.statcan.ca/start.html
Produces national statistics on the population, resources, economy, society and culture of Canada.

Federal Bureau of Investigation
http://www.fbi.gov/homepage.htm
The FBI is the principal investigative arm of the United States Department of Justice.

FBI: Hate Crime Data Collection Guidelines
http://www.fbi.gov/ucr/hatecrime.pdf
FBI: National Incident-Based Reporting System on Hate Crimes

Australian Bureau of Statistics
http://www.abs.gov.au/
The Australian Bureau of Statistics is Australia's official statistical organization.

The Home Office
http://www.homeoffice.gov.uk/
The Home Office is the government department responsible for internal affairs in England and Wales.

The Scottish Executive
http://www.scotland.gov.uk
The Scottish Executive is the devolved government for Scotland. It is responsible for most of the issues of day-to-day concern to the people of Scotland, including health, education, justice, rural affairs, and transport.

UK Data Archive at the University of Essex
http://www.data-archive.ac.uk/
The UKDA provides resource discovery and support for secondary use of quantitative and qualitative data in research.

The Question Bank
http://qb.soc.surrey.ac.uk/
Questions from the British Crime Survey can be read online at the Question Bank, University of Surrey.

Dmoz Open Directory Project
http://www.dmoz.org/Society/Issues/Crime_and_Justice/Prisons/Organizations/
This section of this large web directory lists some of the many voluntary organizations working in the criminal justice field.

United Nations Office on Drugs and Crime
http://www.unodc.org/unodc/index.html

United Nations Interregional Crime and Justice Research Institute
http://www.unicri.it/

EC Europa – Justice and Home Affairs
http://ec.europa.eu/justice_home/fsj/crime/fsj_crime_intro_en.htm

Association of Southeast Asian Nations
http://www.aseansec.org/

4 The Enlightenment and Early Traditions

Crimetheory.Com
www.crimetheory.com
A website that provides a brief introduction to a number of theories and theorists.

5 Early Sociologies of Crime

Émile Durkheim Archive
http://durkheim.itgo.com/anomie.html
A comprehensive Website on Durkheim's life and works.

University of Chicago: Department of Sociology
http://sociology.uchicago.edu/overview/history/html
Gives a brief history of the original Chicago School theorists.

The Chicago School of Pragmatism
http://www.pragmatism.org/genealogy/Chicago.htm
Provides a brief history of the foundation of the Chicago School of Pragmatism and its members.

Society for Human Ecology (SHE).
http://www.societyforhumanecology.org/
This is an international interdisciplinary professional society that promotes the use of an ecological perspective in both research and application.

Chicago Area Project
http://www.chicagoareaproject.org/
Continues to operate today.

6 Radicalizing Traditions

Howard S. Becker Homepage
http://home.earthlink.net/~hsbecker/
A comprehensive site with a selection of published papers and links.

Allyn & Bacon Publishers
http://www.ablongman.com/signup
Jeffrey Reiman's book: *The Rich Get Richer and the Poor Get Prison: Ideology, Class, and Criminal Justice*, 7th edn.

7 Crime, Social Theory and Social Change

New Internationalist
http://www.newint.org
This monthly magazine contains a wealth of global information.

Centre for International Crime Prevention
http://www.uncjin.org/CIP/cicp.html

United Nations Crime and Justice Information Network

http://www.uncjin.org

Provides links and information on the United Nations organizations combating crime on an international level including the following link:

United Nations Office on Drugs and Crime

http://www.odccp.org/crime_cicp_sitemap.html

The United Nations Office on Drugs and Crime (UNODC) is a global leader in the fight against illicit drugs and international crime.

United Nations Interregional Crime and Justice Research Institute: LMS bibliographic Database

http://www.unicri.it/bibliographic_database.htm

The Library Collection includes some 6,000 authors, as well as more than 300 series and 600 publishers. Documents are classified according to the LMS bibliographic field structure and subjects that are described according to the UNCRI Thesaurus: http://www.unicri.it/unicri_thesaurus.htm

United Nations Interregional Crime and Justice Research Institute: World Directory of Criminal Resources

World Directory of Criminological Resources

www.unicri.it/html/world_directory_of_criminology.htm

This site contains more than 470 institutes covering some 70 countries. A number of countries, in particular developing ones, which do not have criminological institutes, have nevertheless requested that some of their bodies' services be included in the Directory.

http://www.culturalcriminology.org.

A website produced by criminologists based at the University of Kent, UK, that provides a resource for students interested in this growing area of criminology.

http://www.governing throughcrime.blogspot.com

Jonathan Simon's blog that interprets current events through his own distinctive criminological analysis.

http://www.deathpenaltyinfo.org

A useful website for data on the death penalty in America.

8 Crime, place and space

Home Office Statistical Bulletin: Crime in England and Wales, 2006–7

http://www.homeoffice.gov.uk/rds/pdfs07/hosb1107.pdf

Chicago Crime Map

http://www.chicagocrime.org/

ACORN
http://www.caci.co.uk/acorn/default.asp

9 Victims and Victimization

Criminal Justice System Online: 'Victims Virtual Walkthrough'
http://www.cjsonline.gov.uk/victim/walkthrough/index.html
An interactive virtual tour that provides information about the British criminal justice process as it relates to victims of crime.

UNICRI website on ICVS
http://www.unicri.it/wwd/analysis/icvs/
Provides information on various international crime victimization surveys.

Human Rights Watch
www.hrw.org

United Nations Declaration of Basic Principles of Justice for Victims of Crime and Abuse of Power (1985)
http://www.unhchr.ch/htm1/menu3/b/h comp49.htm
One of the landmark documents demonstrating the global significance of victims.

10 Crime and Property

The Home Office: Research Development Statistics – Publications
http://www.homeoffice.gov.uk/rds/bcs.html
The National British Crime Survey provides up-to-date annual information on different types of crime, including property crime, which may or may not be reported to and recorded by the police. Full reports and summaries of BCS findings and many other research studies funded by the Home Office can be found here.

International Crime Victimization Surveys
http://www.unicri.it/icvs/
Information, publications and statistics on international crime victimization surveys are available at this site.

11 Crime, Sexuality and Gender

Office of Public Sector Information
http://www.opsi.gov.uk/acts/acts2003/ukpga_20030042_en_2#pt1-pb1-l1g1
For information on the 2003 Sexual Offence Act.

National Organisation for the Treatment of Abusers

www.nota.co.uk

NOTA is a growing group comprising practitioners, managers and policy-makers for the public, private and voluntary sectors. As a result, NOTA brings a wide variety of perspectives to interventions with sexual aggressors.

Child and Woman Abuse Unit

http://www.cwasu.org/

The Child and Woman Abuse Unit is based at London Metropolitan University and has a national and international reputation for its research, training and consultancy work. The unit exists to develop feminist research methodologies, theory and practice, especially in relation to connections between forms of sexualized violence.

The Fawcett Society

http://www.fawcettsociety.org.uk/

Date rape drugs and other date rape resources

http://news.bbc.co.uk/2/hi/uk_news/6518397.stm

12 Crime, the Emotions and Social Psychology

American Psychological Association: 'Hate Crimes Today: An Age-Old Foe in Modern Dress'

http://www.apa.org/pubinfo/hate/homepage.html

A question-and-answer site shedding some clarification on the hate crime debate.

Hate Crime.org

http://www.hatecrime.org/

Information and links to related news articles concerning current events, political choices, and victims and further information.

National Gay and Lesbian Task Force: information on hate crime laws

http://www.nglft.org/issues/issue.cfm?issueID=12

NGLTF is the national progressive organization working for the civil rights of gay, lesbian, bisexual and transgender people.

Crime reduction

http://www.crimereduction.homeoffice.gov.uk/toolkits/fc00.htm

A typical Home Office site offering advice and information on how to tackle fear and disorder in the community.

13 Organizational and Professional Forms of Crime

Web of Justice
http://www.co.pinellas.fl.us/bcc/juscoord/eorganized.htm
This site provides numerous links to other websites concerned with crime, corruption and power.

United Nations
http://www.unodc.org/unodc/organized_crime.html
This site on organized crime provides a source about global developments in crime and control and links to national sites.

Nathanson Centre
http://www.yorku.ca/nathanson/search.htm
This site provides a searchable bibliographic database to help locate other relevant studies.

Criminal Justice Resources
http://www.lib.msu.edu/harris23/crimjust/orgcrime.htm
This site provides links to other sites both official – such as the FBI and the Royal Canadian Mounted Police – and unofficial – such as journalist and community sites concerned with various forms of crime.

Association for Accountancy and Business Affairs
http://www.aabaglobal.org/

Paul's Justice Page
http://www.paulsjusticepage.com/
This site provides useful links and material concerning corporate crime and crimes of the powerful.

14 Drugs, Alcohol, Health and Crime

Drugscope
http://www.drugscope.org.uk/
An invaluable site with access to an online encyclopaedia about drugs and to Drugscope's library.

Alcohol Concern
http://www.alcoholconcern.org.uk/
This site provides links to many other useful sites.

15 Thinking about Punishment

The Home Office: Publications: A Guide to the Criminal Justice System in England and Wales
http://www.homeoffice.gov.uk/rds/cjspub1.html
Publication available online, on the criminal justice process in England and Wales.

Criminal Justice System
http://www.cjsonline.org/home.html
This is another site that has useful information on the criminal justice process in England and Wales.

Crown Office and Procurator Fiscal Service
http://www.crownoffice.gov.uk/
This site has information on the Scottish criminal justice system plus a selection of other links for reference.

Criminal Justice System Northern Ireland
http://www.cjsni.gov.uk/
A site on the criminal justice process in Northern Ireland.

Proceedings of the Old Bailey
http://www.oldbaileyonline.org/
A fully searchable online edition of the largest body of texts detailing the lives of non-elite people ever published, containing accounts of over 100,000 criminal trials held at London's central criminal court.

Restorative Justice Online
www.restorativejustice.org
Excellent resource providing access to thousands of publications on restorative justice.

16 The Criminal Justice Process

Home Office
http://www.homeoffice.gov.uk

Ministry of Justice
http://www.justice.gov.uk

Crown Prosecution Service
http://www.cps.gov.uk

World Factbook of Criminal Systems

http://www.ojp.gov/bjs/abstract/wfcj.htm

This factbook provides narrative descriptions of the criminal justice systems of 45 countries around the world.

Criminal Justice System

http://www.cjsonline.org

This is another site that has useful information on the criminal justice process in England and Wales.

Crown Office and Procurator Fiscal Service

http://www.crownoffice.gov.uk/

This site has information on the Scottish criminal justice system plus a selection of other links for reference.

Criminal Justice System Northern Ireland

http://www.cjsni.gov.uk/

A site on the criminal justice process in Northern Ireland.

Proceedings of the Old Bailey

http://www.oldbaileyonline.org/

A fully searchable online edition of the largest body of texts detailing the lives on non-elite people ever published, containing accounts of over 100,000 criminal trials held at London's central criminal court.

17 Police and Policing

UK Police Service

http://www.homeoffice.gov.uk/police/

This site provides links to official police forces – both regional and non-regional – and related organizations.

Police Complaints Authority

http://www.pca.gov.uk/

The PCA is an independent body set up by the government to oversee public complaints against police officers in England and Wales, plus the National Crime Squad, National Criminal Intelligence Service, British Transport, Ministry of Defence, Port of Liverpool, Port of Tilbury, Royal Parks and UKAEA police.

Association of Police Authorities

http://www.apa.police.uk/apa/

The national voice for police authorities in England, Wales and Northern Ireland. Includes publications and links to other useful sites.

State Watch

http://www.statewatch.org/

State Watch is a non-profit-making voluntary group founded in 1991. This site provides useful police policy documentation and investigative case studies in Europe.

18 Prisons and Imprisonment

The Home Office

http://www.homeoffice.gov.uk

Provides access to a wide range of information on the CJS generally.

The Home Office: Publications

http://www.homeoffice.gov.uk/rds/pubsintro1.html

Provides access to a wide range of publications.

HM Prison Service

http://www.hmprisonservice.gov.uk/

Contains news, reports, statistics and prison rules for prisons in England and Wales.

Scottish Prison Service

http://www.sps.gov.uk

Contains news, reports, statistics and prison rules for prisons in Scotland.

Prison and Probation Ombudsman

http://www.ppo.gov.uk/

The Prisons and Probation Ombudsman provides access to annual reports and publications.

Report of Her Majesty's Chief Inspector of Prisons

http://www.homeoffice.gov.uk/justice/prisons/index.html

A link to a report by the Inspector of Prisons can be found here along with further information on the Inspectorate.

Howard League for Penal Reform

http://www.howardleague.org/

Information, links and publications on penal reform.

National Association for the Care and Rehabilitation of the Offender (NACRO)

http://www.nacro.org.uk/

This site has information on penal reform and lists relevant publication.

Prison Reform Trust

http://www.prisonreformtrust.org.uk/

Information on the Prison Reform Trust, which aims at creating a just, humane and effective penal system.

Youth Justice Board for England and Wales

www.youth-justice-board.gov.uk.

Contains information on policies, news, press releases and details of youth offending teams.

The Guardian: Prisons

http://www.guardian.co.uk/prisons

The *Guardian*'s coverage of prison issues is an excellent resource.

The Observer: Special Reports

http://www.observer.guardian.co.uk/crimedebate

This offers further critical commentary on prison issues.

The Zahid Mubarek Inquiry

www.zahidmubarekinquiry.org.uk

This site is a link to the final report.

19 Green Criminology

One of many mappings of the environmental crisis can be found in the *AAAS Atlas of Population and Environment* (Berkeley: University of California Press, 2000) edited by Paul Harrison and Fred Pearce. Probably the prime resource for up-to-date information and discussion on ecosystems and the environment is the World Resources Institute. It produces a major annual volume (e.g. *World Resources 2000–1, People and Ecosystems – The Fraying Web of Life*. Elsevier Science), and its website is http://www.wri.org/wri/

The online environmental community

http://www.envirolink.org/

A major resource for websites connected to the environment.

Europe and Environmental Crime

http://europa.eu.int.comm/environment/crime/

The pages of the European online site that deals with the environment and crime.

Earthscan

http://www.earthscan.co.uk/

Provides resources and books giving information about the state of the environment.

Friends of the Earth

http://www.foe.org/

Major activist website.

Greenpeace

http://www.greenpeace.org/international_en/

Major activist website.

20 Crime and the Media

Independent Media Centre
www.indymedia.org
Daily articles produced by a collective of independent media organizations and journalists.

Media Studies.Com
http://www.newmediastudies.com
A website for the study of new media, with articles, reviews, guides and other resources.

'Media Panics' podcast
http://britac.studyserve.com/home/lecture.asp?ContentContainerID=124
A discussiion on 'Moral Panics: Then and Now' by Stan Cohen, Stuart Hall and David Garland at the British Academy in March 2007.

21 Terrorism, State Crime and Human Rights

Amnesty International
http://www.amnesty.org/
A website on the worldwide movement campaigning for internationally recognized human rights.

Death Penalty Information Centre
http://www.deathpenaltyinfo.org
This website has information on issues concerning capital punishment.

Index